Easy to use

Whether you know exactly in which town you want to stay or have only an idea of the area you wish to visit, it couldn't be easier to find accommodation to suit you in *Where to Stay*.

Turn to the Information section beginning on page 381 for lots of useful information and advice on making a booking, as well as events and location maps. It's all there to make finding your accommodation easy and put your mind at rest - and make sure you've nothing to think about but planning what to visit when you arrive!

For this reason, we've included a comprehensive town index and full colour location maps to help you locate your accommodation easily. We've also listed establishment entries in alphabetical order by location, region by region. In fact, you'll find all the information you need is listed in an easy-to-follow format.

a SIGN OF OF QUALITY

The English Tourist Board's National Quality Grading and Classification Scheme will help you find the accommodation that really suits you. Whatever the size of the establishment, the Scheme provides you with the kind of detailed, reliable information you need about facilities, comfort and service.

Classification of facilities

An establishment's assessment under the Scheme will usually consist of two parts: the first, using the Crown symbol, classifies the range of services and facilities provided for guests; the second, from De Luxe to Approved, indicates the overall quality standard of these services and facilities.

The range of services and facilities provided is classified under one of six bands: from **Listed** (clean and comfortable accommodation, but limited range of services and facilities) to **Five Crown** (providing a full range of services and facilities). Please note that a higher number of Crowns does not necessarily imply that the quality on offer is superior to that available at an establishment with fewer Crowns.

Quality grading

A separate quality grading indicates the overall standard of services and facilities. Graded establishments are awarded one of the following quality gradings:

DE LUXE
(excellent overall standard)

HIGHLY COMMENDED
(very good overall standard)

COMMENDED
(good overall standard)

APPROVED
(acceptable overall standard)

Before awarding a quality grading, Tourist Board inspectors check in as a guest, only identifying themselves after paying the bill. They assess the warmth of the welcome and level of care and service they receive, as well as the standard and state of the decor, furnishings and fittings. Their overall assessment takes the nature and size of the

establishments into account; you will therefore find that all types of accommodation have been able to achieve a Highly Commended or De Luxe quality grading.

If no quality grade appears alongside the Crown classification, it means that the proprietor has applied for but was still awaiting inspection at the time of going to press.

WHERE TO STAY ENGLAND 98

CONTENTS

Upfront

Places to Stay

Information Pages

Town Index and Location Maps

Key to Symbols

Front cover:
Peartree Cottage, Wilmcote, Stratford-upon-Avon

Back cover: (from top)
Meadowland, Bath, Bath & North East Somerset
The Courtyard, Corbridge, Northumberland
Holmfield, Kendal, Cumbria

Welcome to THE GUIDE

If you're looking for accommodation look no further than* Where to Stay. *It offers a selection of establishments throughout England. You'll also find ideas about what to do while you're away, plus a wealth of useful information and maps. Have a great trip!

Sure signs of where to stay

Many different types of accommodation are described in this guide, though they all have one thing in common. Each entry has been inspected (or applied for inspection) under the ETB's official National Quality Grading and Classification Scheme.

The Scheme is your assurance of facilities and service: Crowns show you the range of facilities provided to guests; Quality Gradings indicate the overall standard of welcome, service and accommodation.

To find out more, turn to page 4.

Range of facilities

Listed and then **One to Five Crown** tell you the range of facilities provided. The more Crowns, the wider the range. Below is an indication of some of the facilities you can expect under each classification.

Listed Clean and comfortable accommodation, but limited range of facilities and services.

There will be additional facilities, including washbasin and chair in your bedroom, and you will have the use of a telephone.

There will be a colour TV in your bedroom or in a lounge and you can enjoy morning tea/coffee in your room. At least some of the bedrooms will have private bath (or shower) and WC.

At least half of the bedrooms will have private bath (or shower) en-suite. You will also be able to order a hot evening meal.

Your bedroom will have a colour TV, radio and telephone; 90% of bedrooms will have private bath and/or shower and WC en-suite. There will be lounge service until midnight and evening meals can be ordered up to 2030 hours.

Every bedroom will have private bath, fixed shower and WC en-suite. The restaurant will be open for breakfast, lunch and dinner (or you can take meals in your room from breakfast until midnight) and you will benefit from an all-night lounge service. A night porter will also be on duty.

Lodge accommodation

The Lodge classification covers purpose-built bedroom accommodation that you will find along major roads and motorways. The range of facilities is indicated by **One** to **Three Moon** symbols. A separate quality grading indicates the overall standard of these facilities.

Your bedroom will have at least a washbasin and radio or colour TV. Tea/coffee may be from a vending machine in a public area.

Your room will have colour TV, tea/coffee-making facilities and en-suite bath or shower with WC.

You will find colour TV and radio, tea/coffee-making facilities and comfortable seating in your bedroom and there will be a bath, shower and WC en-suite. The reception will be staffed throughout the night.

Accessible Scheme

If you have difficulty walking or are a wheelchair user, it is important to be able to identify those establishments that will be able to cater for your requirements. If you book accommodation displaying an Accessible symbol, there's no longer any guesswork involved. Establishments can be awarded one of these categories of accessibility:

Category 1 accessible to all wheelchair users including those travelling independently

Category 2 accessible to a wheelchair user with assistance

Category 3 accessible to a wheelchair user able to walk short distances and up at least three steps.

See page 10 for a full list of establishments in this guide who have an Accessible symbol.

FINDING YOUR IDEAL ACCOMMODATION

Whatever your requirements, your preferences or your price range, Where to Stay will lead you straight to a selection of fine accommodation in England. From prices, quality and facilities on offer, you can see what's available at a glance.

Regional sections

The guide is divided into ten regional sections. See the map on page 12. Each section contains an alphabetical listing of the region's cities, towns and villages with their accommodation establishments.

At the beginning of each section is a brief description of the area and a selection of interesting places to visit which may persuade you to stay a little longer - an illustrative map shows where they can be found.

Town index and location maps

The town index on page 407 and the colour location maps at the back of the guide show all the places featuring accommodation in this guide.

If the place you plan to visit is included in the town index, turn to the page number given for accommodation.

If, however, it is not included in the town index - or you just have a general idea of the area in which you wish to stay - use the colour location maps. You will find accommodation in all the places printed in black. Then simply refer back to the town index for the relevant page.

Service and facilities

Each accommodation listing contains detailed information to help you decide if it is right for you. This information has been provided by the proprietors themselves, and our aim has been to ensure that it is as objective and factual as possible.

Below the establishment name you will find the Crown classification, Listed or One to Five Crown, which indicates the range of services and facilities provided. The quality grading, De Luxe, Highly Commended, Commended or Approved tells you the overall standard of services and facilities. Detailed information on classification and gradings can be found on page 382.

At-a-glance symbols at the end of each entry give you additional information on services and facilities - a key to symbols can be found on the back cover flap. Keep this open to refer to as you read.

Accessibility

If you are a wheelchair user or have difficulty walking, look for the Accessible symbol. You will find a full list of entries participating in the National Accessible Scheme on page 10.

Check for changes

Please remember that changes may occur after the guide is printed. When you have found a suitable place to stay we advise you to contact the establishment to check availability, and also to confirm prices and any specific facilities which may be important to you. The coupons at the back of the guide will help you with your enquiries.

Then make your booking and, if you have time, confirm it in writing.

Further information

You may find it useful to read the information pages at the back of this guide (see page 381), particularly the section on cancellations.

Town Name ▶

KNUTSFORD

Map reference ▶

Cheshire
Map Ref 4 A2

Town description ▶

Derives its name from Canute, King of the Danes, said to have forded the local stream. Ancient and colourful May Day celebrations. Nearby is the Georgian mansion of Tatton Park. Tourist Information Centre ☎ (01565) 632611 or 632210

Establishment name ▶

Picklings Lodge

National Crown classification and quality grading ▶

COMMENDED

Address, telephone and fax numbers ▶

Longtown Road, Pickmere,
Nr Knutsford, WA16 0YZ
☎ (01565) 989

Establishment description ▶

17th C former lodge with extensive landscaped gardens, private woodland and lake. In the heart of the Cheshire countryside yet only 5 minutes from the M6 motorway. Home-grown produce.

National wheelchair access category ▶

Wheelchair access category 2

Accommodation, price guide and facilities ▶

Bedrooms: 2 single, 1 double
Bathrooms: 5 private

Bed & breakfast per night:	£min	£max
Single	27.00	35.00
Double	54.00	70.00

Half board per person:	£min	£max
Daily	37.00	45.00

Lunch available
Evening meal 1800 (last orders 2130)
Parking for 18
Cards accepted: Access, Visa

At-a-glance symbols - see flap on back cover ▶

a LOOK AT SOME OF THE BEST

The award of a DE LUXE quality grade recognises an establishment's excellent overall standard of things such as a warm welcome, general atmosphere and ambience, efficiency of service, as well as the quality of facilities and standard of fittings.

The inspector's overall assessment takes the nature and size of an establishment into account; you will therefore find all types of accommodation can achieve a DE LUXE quality grading.

This page features those establishments in *Where to Stay* that have achieved the highest quality grade of DE LUXE. Use the Town Index at the back of the guide to find page numbers for their fully detailed entries.

Holly Lodge, Bath, Bath & North East Somerset

Broadview Gardens, Crewkerne, Somerset

The Courtyard, Corbridge, Northumberland

Holly Lodge, Bath, Bath & North East Somerset

Holmfield, Kendal, Cumbria

Meadowland, Bath, Bath & North East Somerset

Middle Ord Manor House, Berwick-upon-Tweed, Northumberland

Tavern House, Tetbury, Gloucestershire

Tree Tops, Berwick-upon-Tweed, Northumberland

Tavern House, Tetbury, Gloucestershire

Treetops, Berwick-upon-Tweed, Northumberland

Use your i's

When it comes to your next England break, the first stage of your journey could be closer than you think. You've probably got a Tourist Information Centre nearby which is there to serve the local community - as well as visitors.

So make us your first stop. We'll be happy to help you, wherever you're heading.

Many Tourist Information Centres can provide you with maps and guides, helping you plan well in advance. And sometimes it's even possible for us to book your accommodation, too.

A visit to your nearest Information Centre can pay off in other ways as well. We can point you in the right direction when it comes to finding out about all the special events which are happening in the local region.

In fact, we can give you details of places to visit within easy reach... and perhaps tempt you to plan a day trip or weekend away.

Across the country, there are more than 550 Tourist Information Centres so you're never far away. You'll find the address of your nearest Tourist Information Centre in your local Phone Book, or call Freepages on 0800 192 192.

Tourist Information *i*

NATIONAL ACCESSIBLE SCHEME

Throughout Britain, the Tourist Boards are inspecting all types of places to stay, on holiday or business, that provide accessible accommodation for wheelchair users and others who may have difficulty walking.

The Tourist Boards recognise three categories of accessibility:

Category 1
Accessible to all wheelchair users including those travelling independently.

Category 2
Accessible to a wheelchair user with assistance.

Category 3
Accessible to a wheelchair user able to walk short distances and up at least three steps.

If you have additional needs or special requirements of any kind, we strongly recommend that you make sure these can be met by your chosen establishment before you confirm your booking.

The criteria the Tourist Boards have adopted do not necessarily conform to British Standards or to Building Regulations. They reflect what the Boards understand to be acceptable to meet the practical needs of wheelchair users.

The following establishments listed in this *Where to Stay* guide had been inspected and given an access category at the time of going to press. Use the Town Index at the back of the guide to find page numbers for their full entries.

Category 1

DULVERTON, SOMERSET
- Scatterbrook Farm

FARNHAM, SURREY
- High Wray

LUDLOW, SHROPSHIRE
- Corndene

SALISBURY, WILTSHIRE
- Websters

SHEFFIELD, SOUTH YORKSHIRE
- University of Sheffield

WELLS, SOMERSET
- Burcott Mill

Category 2

ERLESTOKE, WILTSHIRE
- Longwater

GARBOLDISHAM, NORFOLK
- Ingleneuk Lodge

PENRITH, CUMBRIA
- Newton Rigg College

Category 3

AMBLESIDE, CUMBRIA
- Rowanfield Country Guesthouse
ARUNDEL, WEST SUSSEX
- Mill Lane House
ASHBURTON, DEVON
- New Cott Farm
BAKEWELL, DERBYSHIRE
- Tannery House
CHESTERFIELD, DERBYSHIRE
- Abbeydale Hotel
DEVIZES, WILTSHIRE
- Pinecroft
EARLS COLNE, ESSEX
- Riverside Motel
ELLERBY, NORTH YORKSHIRE
- Ellerby Hotel
FROME, SOMERSET
- Fourwinds Guest House
HENLEY-ON-THAMES, OXFORDSHIRE
- Holmwood
HENSTRIDGE, SOMERSET
- Fountain Inn Motel
HERSTMONCEUX, EAST SUSSEX
- Conquerors
HILLINGTON, NORFOLK
- Ffolkes Arms Hotel
INGLETON, NORTH YORKSHIRE
- Riverside Lodge
LENHAM, KENT
- The Dog & Bear Hotel
LINCOLN, LINCOLNSHIRE
- Damon's Motel
LITTLE PRESTON, NORTHAMPTONSHIRE
- Bee Close House
LYMINGTON, HAMPSHIRE
- Our Bench
MANCHESTER, GREATER MANCHESTER
- YHA Manchester
NAILSWORTH, GLOUCESTERSHIRE
- Apple Orchard House
NORTHALLERTON, NORTH YORKSHIRE
- Lovesome Hill Farm
OKEHAMPTON, DEVON
- Week Farm
RICHMOND, NORTH YORKSHIRE
- Mount Pleasant Farm
SANDBACH, CHESHIRE
- Canal Centre and Village Store
SARRE, KENT
- Crown Inn (The Famous Cherry Brandy House)
STRATFORD-UPON-AVON, WARWICKSHIRE
- Church Farm
SWAFFHAM, NORFOLK
- Glebe Bungalow
THIRSK, NORTH YORKSHIRE
- Doxford House
WESTOW, NORTH YORKSHIRE
- Blacksmiths Arms Inn
WHITLEY BAY, TYNE & WEAR
- York House Hotel
WINCHESTER, HAMPSHIRE
- Shawlands
YORK, NORTH YORKSHIRE
- Heworth Court Hotel

The National Accessible Scheme forms part of the Tourism for All Campaign that is being promoted by all National and Regional Tourist Boards. Additional help and guidance on finding suitable holiday accommodation for those with special needs can be obtained from:
Holiday Care Service
2nd Floor, Imperial Buildings,
Victoria Road,
Horley, Surrey RH6 7PZ
Tel: (01293) 774535
Fax: (01293) 784647
Minicom: (01293) 776943

MAP AND KEY TO REGIONAL SECTIONS

This* Where to Stay *guide is divided into 10 regional sections as shown on the map below. To identify each regional section and its page number, please refer to the key opposite. The index lists the counties of England and indicates under which regional section you will find them.

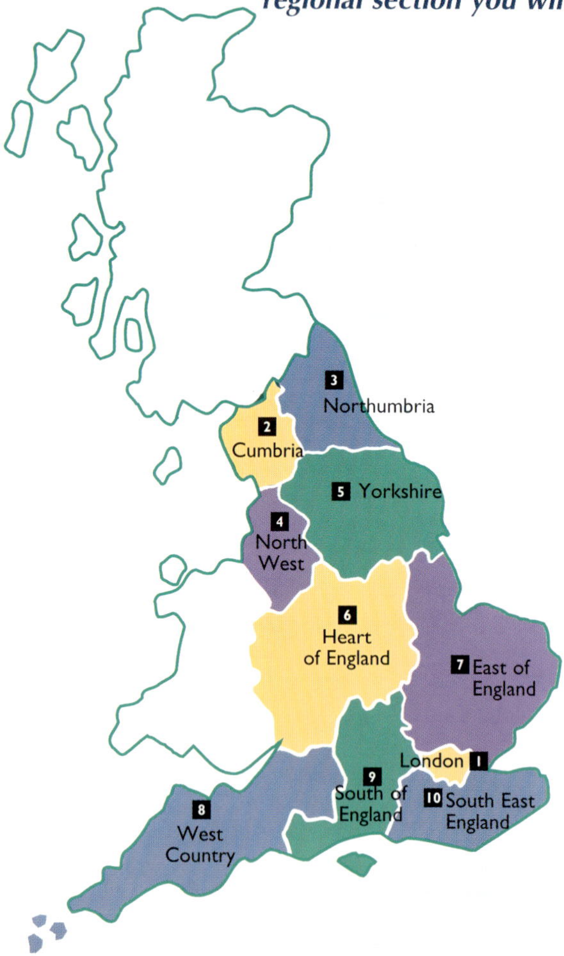

Colour location maps showing all the cities, towns and villages with accommodation listed in this guide, and an index to the place names, can be found at the back of the guide.

As you are probably aware, the boundaries and names of a number of counties in England were recently changed as the result of local government reorganisation. The main county changes have been reflected in *Where to Stay*, particularly in the county index opposite, the regional section maps, in the colour location maps at the back and in the town descriptions.**

If you want to find out more about what there is to see and do in a particular area, contact the appropriate Regional Tourist Board. Details are given both at the beginning and end of each regional section.

KEY TO MAP

COUNTY INDEX

** This is how you will find the following county changes have been reflected in *Where to Stay*:
Avon is replaced by Bath & North East Somerset, City of Bristol, North Somerset and South Gloucestershire
Cleveland is replaced by Tees Valley
Humberside is replaced by East Riding of Yorkshire and North Lincolnshire

Although there have been changes to the unitary authority boundaries in the following areas, you will see that the familiar regional names have been retained for: Greater Manchester, Merseyside, South Yorkshire, Tyne & Wear, West Midlands and West Yorkshire

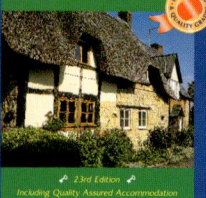

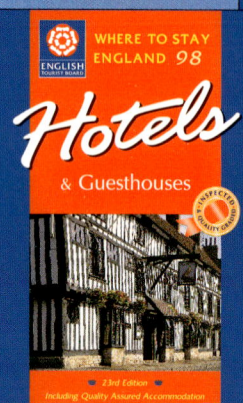

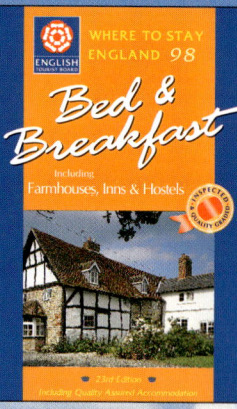

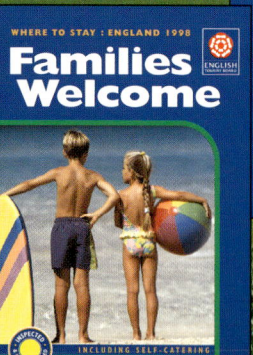

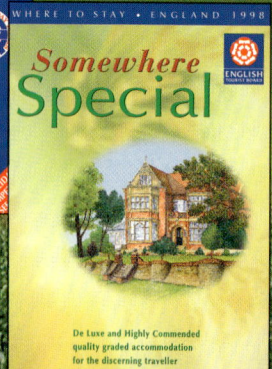

WHERE TO STAY IN ENGLAND

Published by: English Tourist Board, Thames Tower, Black's Road, Hammersmith, London W6 9EL.
ISBN 0 86143 202 9
Managing Editor: Jane Collinson
Technical Manager: Marita Sen
Compilation & Production: Guide Associates, Croydon
Design and illustrations: Jackson Lowe Marketing, Lewes, East Sussex
Colour Photography: Mike Williams (front cover)
Cartography: Colin Earl
Typesetting: Reed Technologies and Information Services, London and Jackson Lowe Marketing, Lewes
Printing and Binding: Bemrose Security Printing, Derby
Advertisement Sales: Madison Bell Ltd, 3 St. Peter's Street, Islington Green, London N1 8JD. (0171) 359 7737.

Important:
The information contained in this guide has been published in good faith on the basis of information submitted to the English Tourist Board by the proprietors of the premises listed, who have paid for their entries to appear. The English Tourist Board cannot guarantee the accuracy of the information in this guide and accepts no responsibility for any error or misrepresentation. All liability for loss, disappointment, negligence or other damage caused by reliance on the information contained in this guide, or in the event of bankruptcy, or liquidation, or cessation of trade of any company, individual or firm mentioned, is hereby excluded. Please check carefully all prices and other details before confirming a reservation.

The English Tourist Board
The Board is a statutory body created by the Development of Tourism Act 1969 to develop and market England's tourism. Its main objectives are to provide a welcome for people visiting England; to encourage people living in England to take their holidays there; and to encourage the provision and improvement of tourist amenities and facilities in England. The Board has a statutory duty to advise the Government on tourism matters relating to England and, with Government approval and support, administers the national classification and grading schemes for tourist accommodation in England.

LONDON

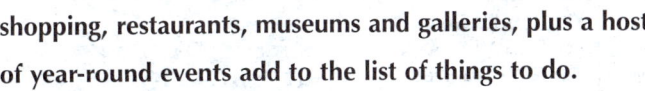

Welcome to a voyage of discovery. In a truly great city like London, contrasts, interest and enjoyment are endless. There's the glitter of theatre land, West End shopping, the historic Tower of London and St. Katharine's Dock. Excellent shopping, restaurants, museums and galleries, plus a host of year-round events add to the list of things to do.

For a feel of the open air stroll on Hampstead Heath, or in one of the great parks. Try surprising Little Venice, with its pretty canals, colourful boats and towpath walk past the rich and famous, or perhaps one of London's many lively street markets.

London has so many distinctly different areas, each with its own special atmosphere to fit your mood and interests.

Greater London, comprising the 32 London Boroughs

FOR MORE INFORMATION CONTACT:
London Tourist Board
6th floor, Glen House, Stag Place, London SW1E 5LT

Where to Go in London – see pages 18-20
Where to Stay in London – see pages 24-33

LONDON

Where to Go and What to See

You will find hundreds of interesting places to visit during your stay in London, just some of which are listed in these pages. Contact any Tourist Information Centre in the region for more ideas on days out in London.

■ Bank of England Museum
Bartholomew Lane,
London EC2R 8AH
Tel: (0171) 601 5545/5491
Museum illustrating the history of the Bank since 1694. Displays include gold bars, banknotes, modern dealing desk and interactive video systems.

■ British Library Exhibition Galleries
Great Russell Street,
London WC1B 3DG
Tel: (0171) 412 7000
Manuscript Saloon, Grenville Library and King's Library - displaying the Magna Carta, Gutenberg Bible, Shakespeare and illuminated manuscripts.

■ British Museum
Great Russell Street,
London WC1B 3DG
Tel: (0171) 636 1555
One of the great museums of the world, showing the works of man from all over the world from prehistoric times to the present day.

■ Cabinet War Rooms
Clive Steps,
King Charles Street,
London SW1A 2AQ
Tel: (0171 903 6961
The underground headquarters used by Winston Churchill and the British Government during World War II. Includes Cabinet Room, Transatlantic Telephone Room and Map Room.

■ Chislehurst Caves
Old Hill,
Chislehurst,
Kent BR7 5NB
Tel: (0181) 467 3264
Over 20 miles of caves, parts of which date from 6000 BC. Features include the Druid's Altar, Roman well, haunted pool and World War II exhibition.

■ Design Museum
Shad Thames,
London SE1 2YD
Tel: (0171) 403 6933
A study collection showing the development of design in mass production. Review of new products, graphics gallery and temporary exhibitions.

■ Hampton Court Palace
Hampton Court,
Surrey KT8 9AU
Tel: (0181) 781 9500
Oldest Tudor palace in England with many attractions including Tudor kitchens, tennis courts, maze, state apartments and King's apartment.

HMS Belfast
Morgan's Lane, Tooley Street,
London SE1 2JH
Tel: (0171) 407 6434
World War II cruiser weighing 11,500 tonnes, now a floating naval museum with seven decks to explore. Many naval exhibits also on show.

Imperial War Museum
Lambeth Road,
London SE1 6HZ
Tel: (0171) 416 5000
The story of 20thC war from Flanders to Bosnia. Features include the Blitz Experience, Operation Jericho and the Trench Experience.

Kensington Palace State Apartments
Kensington Gardens,
London W8 4PX
Tel: (0171) 937 9561
Furniture and ceiling paintings from Stuart-Hanoverian periods, rooms from the Victorian era and works of art from the Royal Collection. Also Royal Ceremonial Dress Collection.

London Aquarium
County Hall,
Riverside Building,
London SE1 7PB
Tel: (0171) 967 8000
Visitors are submerged into a stunning display of hundreds of varieties of fish and sealife from around the world.

London Brass Rubbing Centre
St Martin-in-the-Fields Church,
Trafalgar Square,
London WC2N 4JJ
Tel: (0171) 930 9306
Knights, unicorns and kings are traditional brass rubbings for visitors to buy or make themselves. Also unusual Celtic designs and historical gifts.

London Dungeon
28-34 Tooley Street,
London SE1 2SZ
Tel: (0171) 403 0606
The world's first medieval horror museum. Now featuring two major shows, 'The Jack the Ripper Experience' and 'The Theatre of the Guillotine'.

London Planetarium
Marylebone Road,
London NW1 5LR
Tel: (0171) 935 6861
Completely refurbished, visitors can now experience a virtual reality trip through space and wander through interactive Space Zones before the show.

London Toy and Model Museum
21-23 Craven Hill, Bayswater,
London W2 3EN
Tel: (0171) 706 800
Over 20 themed galleries housing toys from trains to dolls and working models. Ride-on carousel and steam train in the garden.

London Zoo
Regent's Park,
London NW1 4RY
Tel: (0171) 722 3333
One of the world's most famous zoos with over 8,000 animals including rhinos, venomous snakes, penguins and piranhas. Programme of events, Moonlight World and Children's Zoo.

Madame Tussaud's
Marylebone Road,
London NW1 5LR
Tel: (0171) 935 6861
World-famous collection of wax figures in themed settings which include The Garden Party, 200 Years, Superstars, The Grand Hall, The Chamber of Horrors and The Spirit of London.

Museum of Mankind
6 Burlington Gardens,
London W1X 2EX
Tel: (0171) 437 2224
Ethnography department of the British Museum housing collections from Africa, Australia, the Pacific Islands, North and South America.

National Gallery
Trafalgar Square,
London WC2N 5DN
Tel: (0171) 747 2885
Gallery displaying Western painting from 1260-1920. Includes work by Botticelli, Leonardo da Vinci, Rembrandt, Gainsborough, Turner, Renoir, Cezanne and Van Gogh.

National Portrait Gallery
St. Martin's Place
London WC2H 0HE
Tel: (0171) 306 0055
Permanent collection of portraits of famous men and women from the Middle Ages to the present day.

National Maritime Museum
Romney Road, Greenwich,
London SE10 9NF
Tel: (0181) 858 4422/
(0181) 312 6565
Britain's maritime heritage illustrated through artefacts, models, paintings, navigation instruments, archives and photographs. Regular exhibitions and a children's gallery.

Natural History Museum
Cromwell Road,
London SW7 5BD
Tel: (0171) 938 9123
Home of the wonders of the natural world, one of the most popular museums in the world and one of London's finest landmarks.

Old Royal Observatory
Greenwich Park,
London SE10 9NF
Tel: (0181) 858 4422/
(0181) 312 6565
Museum of time and space and site of the Greenwich Meridian. Working telescopes and planetarium, timeball, Wren's Octagon Room and intricate clocks and computer simulations.

Rock Circus
London Pavilion, Piccadilly Circus,
London W1V 9LA
Tel: (0171) 734 7203/8025
Amazing combination of stereo sound through personal headsets, audio-animatronic (moving) and Madame Tussaud's wax figures of over 50 rock stars.

Royal Mews
Buckingham Palace,
London SW1A 1AA
Tel: (0171) 839 1377/
(0171) 799 2331
See the Queen's carriage horses, carriages and harness used on State occasions including the Coronation Coach built 1761.

Science Museum
Exhibition Road,
London SW7 2DD
Tel: (0171) 938 8000/8080
Over 200,000 exhibits covering almost every imaginable sector of science, technology, industry and medicine.

Thames Barrier Visitors' Centre
Unity Way, London SE18 5NJ
Tel: (0181) 305 4188
Exhibition with 10-minute video, a working scale model and a multimedia show. Also riverside walkways, children's play area and buffet.

Theatre Museum
Russell Street,
London WC2E 7PA
Tel: (0171) 836 7891
Five galleries illustrating the history of performance in the United Kingdom. The collection includes displays on theatre, ballet, dance, musical stage, rock and pop music.

Tower Bridge Experience
Tower Bridge, London SE1 2UP
Tel: (0171) 403 3761
Exhibition explaining the history of the bridge and how it operates. Original steam-powered engines on view. Panoramic views from fully-glazed walkways. Gift shop.

Tower of London
Tower Hill,
London EC3N 4AB
Tel: (0171) 709 0765
Home of the 'Beefeaters' and ravens, the building spans 900 years of British history. On display are the nation's Crown Jewels, regalia and armoury robes.

FIND OUT MORE
A free information pack about holidays and attractions in London is available on written request from:
London Tourist Board and Convention Bureau,
6th floor, Glen House,
Stag Place, London SW1E 5LT.

Tourist Information

Tourist and leisure information can be obtained from Tourist Information Centres throughout England. Details of centres and other information services in Greater London are given below. The symbol 🛏 means that an accommodation booking service is provided.

Tourist Information Centres

Points of arrival

Victoria Station, Forecourt, SW1 🛏
Easter-October, daily 0800-1900. November-Easter, reduced opening hours.

Liverpool Street Underground Station, EC2 🛏
Monday-Friday 0800-1800. Saturday-Sunday 0845-17.30.

Heathrow Terminals 1, 2, 3 Underground Station Concourse (Heathrow Airport) 🛏
Daily 0800-1800.

Heathrow Terminal 3 Arrivals Concourse 🛏
0600-2300.

Waterloo International Arrivals Hall 🛏
0830-2230.

The above information centres provide a London and Britain tourist information service, offer a hotel accommodation booking service, stock free and saleable publications on Britain and London and sell theatre tickets, tourist tickets for bus and underground and tickets for sightseeing tours.

Inner London

British Travel Centre 🛏
12 Regent Street, Piccadilly Circus, SW1Y 4PQ
Monday-Friday 0900-1830. Saturday-Sunday 1000-1600 (0900-1700 Saturdays May-September).

Canary Wharf Tourist Information Centre
Ground Floor, Cabot Place West, London E14
Tel: (0171) 512 9800
Monday-Friday 0900-1800. Saturday, Sunday & Bank Holiday Monday 1000-1700.

Greenwich Tourist Information Centre 🛏
46 Greenwich Church Street, SE10 9BL.
Tel: (0181) 858 6376
April-September, daily 1015-1645. October-March, reduced opening hours.

Hackney Museum and Tourist Information Centre
Central Hall, Mare Street, E8
Tel: (0181) 985 9055
Tuesday-Friday 1000-1700. Closed 1230-1330. Saturday 1330-1700.

Islington Tourist Information Centre 🛏
44 Duncan Street, N1 8BW
Tel: (0171) 278 8787
Monday 1400-1600. Tuesday-Saturday 1000-1700. Closed Saturday 1330-1430.

Lewisham Tourist Information Centre
Lewisham Library, 199-201 Lewisham High Street, SE13 6LG
Tel: (0181) 297 8317
Monday 1000-1700. Tuesday-Friday 0900-1700

Southwark Tourist Information Centre 🛏
Unit 4, Lower Level, Cotton's Centre, Middle Yard
SE1 2QJ
Tel: (0171) 403 8299
Monday-Friday 1000-1700. Saturday-Sunday 1100-1700. (Reduced winter opening).

Tower Hamlets Tourist Information Centre
107a Commercial Street, E1 6BG
Tel: (0181) 375 2549
Monday-Friday 0930-1630.

Outer London

Bexley Tourist Information Centre
Central Library, Townley Road, Bexleyheath DA6 7HJ
Tel: (0181) 303 9052
Monday, Tuesday, Thursday 0930-2000. Wednesday & Friday 0930-1730. Saturday 0930-1700.

Also at Hall Place Visitor Centre
Bourne Road, Bexley
Tel: (01322) 558676
June-September, daily 1130-1630.

Croydon Tourist Information Centre 🛏
Katharine Street, Croydon CR9 1ET
Tel: (0181) 253 1009
Monday-Wednesday & Friday 0900-1800. Thursday 0930-1800. Saturday 0900-1700.

Foots Cray Tourist Information Centre
Tesco Store Car Park, Edgington Way, Sidcup DA14 5AH
Summer only, Monday-Saturday 0900-1700. Sunday 1000-1600.

Harrow Tourist Information Centre
Civic Centre, Station Road, Harrow HA1 2XF
Tel: (0181) 424 1103
Monday-Friday 0900-1700.

Hillingdon Tourist Information Centre
Central Library, 14 High Street, Uxbridge UB8 1HD
Tel: (01895) 250706
Monday, Tuesday & Thursday 0930-2000. Friday & Wednesday 0930-1730. Saturday 0930-1600.

Hounslow Tourist Information Centre
24 The Treaty Centre, Hounslow High Street, Hounslow TW3 1ES
Tel: (0181) 572 8279
Monday, Wednesday, Friday & Saturday 0930-1730.
Tuesday, Thursday 0930-2000.

Kingston Tourist Information Centre
The Market House, The Market Place, Kingston upon Thames KT1 1JS.
Tel: (0181) 547 5592
Monday-Friday 1000-1700.
Saturday 0900-1600.

Redbridge Tourist Information Centre
Town Hall, High Road, Ilford, Essex IG1 1DD
Tel: (0181) 478 3020
Monday-Friday 0830-1700.

Richmond Tourist Information Centre
Old Town Hall, Whittaker Avenue, Richmond upon Thames TW9 1TP
Tel: (0181) 940 9125
Monday-Friday 1000-1800.
Saturday 1000-1700. May-October, also Sunday 1015-1615.

Twickenham Tourist Information Centre
The Atrium, Civic Centre, York Street, Twickenham TW1 3BZ
Tel: (0181) 891 7272
Monday-Thursday 0900-1715.
Friday 0900-1700.

Visitorcall

The London Tourist Board and Convention Bureau's 'Phone Guide to London' operates 24 hours a day. To access a full range of information call 0839 123456. To access specific lines dial 0839 123 followed by:

What's on this week - 400
What's on next 3 months - 401
Sunday in London - 407
Rock and pop concerts - 422
Popular attractions - 480
Where to take children - 424
Museums - 429
Palaces (including Buckingham Palace) - 481
Current exhibitions - 403
Changing the Guard - 411
Popular West End shows - 416
London dining - 485
Calls cost 49p per minute at all times (as at April 97).
To order a Visitorcall card please call (0171) 971 0026.
Information for callers using push-button telephones: (0171) 971 0027.

Artsline

London's information and advice service for disabled people on arts and entertainment.
Call (0171) 388 2227.

Hotel Accommodation Service

The London Tourist Board and Convention Bureau helps visitors to find and book accommodation at a wide range of prices in hotels and guesthouses, including budget accommodation, throughout the Greater London area.

Reservations are made with hotels which are members of LTB, denoted in this guide with the symbol by their name. Reservations can be made by credit card holders via the telephone accommodation reservations service on (0171) 932 2020 by simply giving the reservation clerk your card details (Mastercard, Visa or Switch) and room requirements. LTB takes an administrative booking fee. The service operates Monday-Friday 0930-1730.

Reservations on arrival are handled at the Tourist Information Centres operated by LTB at Victoria Station, Heathrow Underground, Liverpool Street Station, Waterloo International and Heathrow Terminal 3. Go to any of them on the day when you need accommodation. A communication charge and a refundable deposit are payable when making a reservation.

Which part of London?

The majority of tourist accommodation is situated in the central parts of London and is therefore very convenient for most of the city's attractions and night life.

However, there are many hotels in outer London which provide other advantages, such as easier parking. In the 'Where to Stay' pages which follow, you will find accommodation listed under INNER LONDON (covering the E1 to W14 London Postal Area) and OUTER LONDON (covering the remainder of Greater London). Colour maps 6 and 7 at the back of the guide show place names and London Postal Area codes and will help you to locate accommodation in your chosen area of London.

LONDON INDEX

If you are looking for accommodation in a particular establishment in London and you know its name, this index will give you the page number of the full entry in the guide.

WHERE TO STAY (LONDON)

Accommodation entries in this section are listed under **Inner London** (covering the postcode areas E1 to W14) and **Outer London** (covering the remainder of Greater London) - please refer to the colour location maps 6 and 7 at the back of this guide.

If you want to look up a particular establishment, use the index on the previous page which will give you the page number.

At-a-glance symbols at the end of each accommodation entry give useful information about services and facilities. A key to symbols can be found inside the back cover flap. Keep this open for easy reference.

INNER LONDON

Colour maps 6 & 7 at the back of the guide show place names and London Postal Area Codes and will help you locate accommodation in your chosen area of London

LONDON E10

Sleeping Beauty Motel

APPROVED

543 Lea Bridge Road, Leyton, London E10 7EB
☎ (0181) 556 8080
Fax (0181) 556 8080

All rooms en-suite with bath and shower, satellite TV, direct-dial telephone, hairdryer, hospitality tray, trouser press, mini fridge, safe. Ironing facilities, 24-hour reception, lift, free car park, bar.

Bedrooms: 16 double, 61 twin, 4 triple
Bathrooms: 80 en-suite

Bed & breakfast per night:	£min	£max
Single	40.00	50.00
Double	45.00	60.00

Parking for 74
Cards accepted: Amex, Diners, Mastercard, Visa, Switch/Delta
3

LONDON N1

Kandara Guest House

Listed APPROVED

68 Ockendon Road, London N1 3NW
☎ (0171) 226 5721 & 226 3379

Small family-run guesthouse near the Angel, Islington. Free street parking and good public transport to West End and City.

Bedrooms: 4 single, 2 double, 2 twin, 2 triple
Bathrooms: 3 public

Bed & breakfast per night:	£min	£max
Single	27.00	30.00
Double	38.00	40.00

Cards accepted: Mastercard, Visa
UL OAP SP T

LONDON N7

Five Kings Guest House

APPROVED

59 Anson Road, Tufnell Park, London N7 0AR
☎ (0171) 607 3996 & 607 6466

Privately-run guesthouse in a quiet residential area. 15 minutes to central London. Unrestricted parking in road.

Bedrooms: 6 single, 3 double, 3 twin, 2 triple, 2 family rooms
Bathrooms: 9 en-suite, 3 public, 2 private showers

Bed & breakfast per night:	£min	£max
Single	20.00	28.00
Double	30.00	38.00

Cards accepted: Mastercard, Visa
3 UL TV SP T

LONDON N13

71 Berkshire Gardens

Listed APPROVED

Palmers Green, London N13 6AA
☎ (0181) 888 5573

Two-storey house with garden, 5 minutes' bus ride from Wood Green Piccadilly line underground station. Car parking available.

Bedrooms: 1 single, 1 twin
Bathrooms: 1 public

Bed & breakfast per night:	£min	£max
Single	15.00	18.00
Double	30.00	34.00

Evening meal 1800 (last orders 2000)
Parking for 1
10 UL S TV

LONDON N22

Pane Residence

Listed APPROVED

154 Boundary Road, Wood Green, London N22 6AE
☎ (0181) 889 3735

In a pleasant location 6 minutes' walk from Turnpike Lane underground station and near Alexandra Palace. Kitchen facilities available.

Bedrooms: 1 single, 2 twin
Bathrooms: 1 public

Bed & breakfast per night:	£min	£max
Single	17.00	19.50
Double	25.00	29.00

Parking for 2
1 UL

LONDON NW4

Rilux House

1 Lodge Road, London NW4 4DD
(0181) 203 0933
Fax (0181) 203 6446
High standard, all private facilities, kitchenette and garden. Quiet. Close to underground, buses, M1, 20 minutes West End. Convenient for Wembley, easy route to Heathrow, direct trains to Gatwick and Luton airports. Close to Middlesex University.
Bedrooms: 1 twin
Bathrooms: 1 en-suite

Bed & breakfast per night:	£min	£max
Single	30.00	35.00
Double	50.00	60.00

Half board per person:	£min	£max
Daily	38.00	42.00

Parking for 1

LONDON NW6

Cavendish Guest House

APPROVED
24 Cavendish Road, London NW6 7XP
(0181) 451 3249
In a quiet residential street, 5 minutes' walk from Kilburn underground station, 15 minutes' travelling time to the West End. Easy access to Wembley Stadium, Heathrow, Gatwick. 10 minutes from M1.
Bedrooms: 4 single, 1 double, 1 twin, 2 triple
Bathrooms: 2 en-suite, 2 public

Bed & breakfast per night:	£min	£max
Single	26.00	28.00
Double	40.00	46.00

Parking for 4

LONDON NW10

30 All Souls Avenue

Listed
Willesden, London NW10 6AR
(0181) 965 6051
Fax (0181) 965 6051
Family-run house, 20 minutes from Baker Street.
Bedrooms: 1 single, 2 twin
Bathrooms: 2 public

Bed & breakfast per night:	£min	£max
Single	15.00	18.00
Double	28.00	34.00

8

J and T Guest House

Listed COMMENDED
98 Park Avenue North, Willesden Green, London NW10 1JY
(0181) 452 4085
Fax (0181) 450 2503
Small guesthouse in north west London close to underground. Easy access to Wembley Stadium complex. 5 minutes from M1.
Bedrooms: 1 single, 1 double, 3 twin, 1 triple
Bathrooms: 6 en-suite

Bed & breakfast per night:	£min	£max
Single	30.00	35.00
Double	42.00	54.00

Parking for 2
Cards accepted: Mastercard, Visa, Switch/Delta

LONDON SE3

3 Kelsall Close

Listed APPROVED
Blackheath, London SE3 0JJ
(0181) 488 8261
In a quiet close, about 2 miles from the historic heart of Greenwich and only 25 minutes by train from central London.
Bedrooms: 1 single, 1 twin
Bathrooms: 1 en-suite, 1 public

Bed & breakfast per night:	£min	£max
Single	21.00	24.00
Double	42.00	48.00

Half board per person:	£min	£max
Daily	28.00	31.00
Weekly	147.00	168.00

Parking for 1

LONDON SE4

British Family Home Stay

Listed
2 Crofton Gate Way, Crofton Park, London SE4 2DL
(0181) 694 0011
Reach us via Crofton Park or Honor Oak train station, or underground to Brixton, then P4 bus. 20 minutes from London Victoria. Convenient for Greenwich (Millennium 2000) and Thames Barrier.
Bedrooms: 2 twin
Bathrooms: 1 public

Bed & breakfast per night:	£min	£max
Single	10.00	10.00
Double	20.00	20.00

Evening meal from 1800
Parking for 3

LONDON SE6

41 Minard Road

Listed COMMENDED
Catford, London SE6 1NP
(0181) 697 2596
English home in quiet residential area off A205 South Circular Road. 10 minutes' walk to Hither Green station for 20-minute journey to central London.
Bedrooms: 1 single, 2 twin
Bathrooms: 1 public

Bed & breakfast per night:	£min	£max
Single	18.00	18.00
Double	36.00	36.00

Half board per person:	£min	£max
Daily	24.50	24.50
Weekly	171.50	171.50

Evening meal 1700 (last orders 2000)

LONDON SE12

Kingsland House

Listed APPROVED
45 Southbrook Road, Lee, London SE12 8LJ
(0181) 318 4788
Detached house in conservation area, close to Blackheath and Greenwich and with easy access to City and West End. Off A205 South Circular Road and 8 minutes' walk from Lee station. Homely atmosphere.
Bedrooms: 3 twin
Bathrooms: 2 public

Bed & breakfast per night:	£min	£max
Single	25.00	27.00
Double	48.00	50.00

Please mention this guide when making your booking.

For further information on accommodation establishments use the coupons at the back of this guide.

LONDON SE22

Bedknobs

Listed COMMENDED

58 Glengarry Road, East Dulwich, London SE22 8QD
☎ (0181) 299 2004
Fax (0181) 693 5611

Carefully restored Victorian family-run house offering many home comforts, excellent service and a warm welcome. Past winner of BTA London B&B Award.

Bedrooms: 1 double, 2 twin
Bathrooms: 2 public

Bed & breakfast per night:	£min	£max
Single	25.00	40.00
Double	45.00	60.00

Cards accepted: Mastercard, Visa, Switch/Delta

LONDON SW1

Brindle House Hotel

Listed APPROVED

1 Warwick Place North, London SW1V 1QW
☎ (0171) 828 0057
Fax (0171) 931 8805

Small and quiet (off main road) bed and breakfast ideally located for Victoria bus, train and underground stations. Good atmosphere.

Bedrooms: 4 single, 4 double, 3 twin, 2 triple
Bathrooms: 2 public, 5 private showers

Bed & breakfast per night:	£min	£max
Single	30.00	32.00
Double	40.00	46.00

Cards accepted: Amex, Diners, Mastercard, Visa

Carlton Hotel

Listed APPROVED

90 Belgrave Road, Victoria, London SW1V 2BJ
☎ (0171) 976 6634 & 932 0913
Fax (0171) 821 8020

Small, friendly bed and breakfast near Victoria station and within walking distance of famous landmarks such as Buckingham Palace, Trafalgar Square and Piccadilly Circus.

Bedrooms: 4 single, 5 double, 2 twin, 6 triple
Bathrooms: 11 en-suite, 1 public, 1 private shower

Bed & breakfast per night:	£min	£max
Single	35.00	39.00
Double	45.00	49.00

Cards accepted: Amex, Mastercard, Visa, Switch/Delta

You are advised to confirm your booking in writing.

Caswell Hotel

Listed APPROVED

25 Gloucester Street, London SW1V 2DB
☎ (0171) 834 6345

Pleasant, family-run hotel, near Victoria coach and rail stations, yet in a quiet location.

Bedrooms: 1 single, 6 double, 6 twin, 3 triple, 2 family rooms
Bathrooms: 7 en-suite, 5 public

Bed & breakfast per night:	£min	£max
Single	30.00	55.00
Double	42.00	70.00

Cards accepted: Mastercard, Visa, Switch/Delta

Chester House

Listed

134 Ebury Street, London SW1W 9QQ
☎ (0171) 730 3632
Fax (0171) 824 8446

Small, friendly bed and breakfast close to Sloane Square and 10 minutes' walk from Harrods. Convenient for public transport.

Bedrooms: 3 single, 2 double, 5 twin, 2 triple
Bathrooms: 6 en-suite, 2 public

Bed & breakfast per night:	£min	£max
Single	35.00	50.00
Double	55.00	62.00

Cards accepted: Amex, Diners, Mastercard, Visa

Colliers Hotel

Listed

97 Warwick Way, London SW1V 1QL
☎ (0171) 834 6931 & 828 0210
Fax (0171) 834 8439

Modern-style family hotel with spacious rooms. Very clean, budget priced, centrally located. Ideal for easy connections to London's major tourist spots.

Bedrooms: 4 single, 7 double, 5 twin, 1 triple, 1 family room
Bathrooms: 2 en-suite, 3 public, 3 private showers

Bed & breakfast per night:	£min	£max
Single	26.00	32.00
Double	36.00	40.00

Cards accepted: Amex, Diners, Mastercard, Visa

Easton Hotel

Listed

36-40 Belgrave Road, Victoria, London SW1V 1RG
☎ (0171) 834 5938
Fax (0171) 976 6560

Bed and breakfast hotel close to Victoria station with good rail, underground and coach connections.

Bedrooms: 16 single, 18 double, 11 twin, 7 triple, 2 family rooms
Bathrooms: 11 en-suite, 10 public

Bed & breakfast per night:	£min	£max
Single	28.00	38.00
Double	38.00	48.00

Cards accepted: Amex, Diners, Mastercard, Visa

Elizabeth Hotel

COMMENDED

37 Eccleston Square, Victoria, London SW1V 1PB
☎ (0171) 828 6812

Friendly, quiet hotel overlooking magnificent gardens of stately residential square (circa 1835), close to Belgravia yet within 5 minutes' walk of Victoria. Free colour brochure.

Bedrooms: 6 single, 5 double, 4 twin, 16 triple, 7 family rooms
Bathrooms: 35 en-suite, 2 public

Bed & breakfast per night:	£min	£max
Single	40.00	55.00
Double	62.00	80.00

Ad See display advertisement on page 27

Georgian House Hotel

APPROVED

35 St George's Drive, London
SW1V 4DG
☎ (0171) 834 1438
Fax (0171) 976 6085

Traditional B&B in a quiet residential area of City of Westminster, within walking distance of Victoria station, shopping areas and important sights. Student rooms.

Bedrooms: 8 single, 13 double, 2 twin, 6 triple, 5 family rooms
Bathrooms: 29 en-suite, 1 public

Bed & breakfast per night:	£min	£max
Single	19.00	39.00
Double	32.00	55.00

Cards accepted: Mastercard, Visa, Switch/Delta

Huttons Hotel

Listed APPROVED

55 Belgrave Road, London
SW1V 2BB
☎ (0171) 834 3726
Fax (0171) 834 3389

5 minutes' walk from Victoria and Pimlico, easy access to central London.

Bedrooms: 5 single, 11 double, 27 twin, 8 triple, 2 family rooms
Bathrooms: 26 en-suite, 10 public

Bed & breakfast per night:	£min	£max
Single	40.00	43.00
Double	51.00	51.00

Cards accepted: Amex, Diners, Mastercard, Visa

Oxford House Hotel

Listed APPROVED

92 Cambridge Street, Victoria, London SW1V 4QG
☎ (0171) 834 6467
Fax (0171) 834 0225

Small family-run bed and breakfast hotel within walking distance of Westminster.

Bedrooms: 2 single, 5 double, 4 twin, 5 triple, 1 family room
Bathrooms: 4 public

Bed & breakfast per night:	£min	£max
Single	32.00	34.00
Double	42.00	44.00

Cards accepted: Mastercard, Visa

Windermere Hotel

COMMENDED

142-144 Warwick Way, Victoria, London SW1V 4JE
☎ (0171) 834 5163 & 834 5480
Fax (0171) 630 8831
Email: 100773.1171
@compuserve.com

BTA Trophy winner. Small, friendly hotel with well-equipped bedrooms and a cosy lounge. English breakfast and dinner are served in the elegant licensed restaurant.

Bedrooms: 3 single, 11 double, 5 twin, 1 triple, 3 family rooms
Bathrooms: 19 en-suite, 2 public

Bed & breakfast per night:	£min	£max
Single	49.00	67.00
Double	59.00	92.00

Half board per person:	£min	£max
Daily	40.00	56.50

Evening meal 1800 (last orders 2130)
Cards accepted: Amex, Mastercard, Visa, Switch/Delta

LONDON SW3

Blair House Hotel

APPROVED

34 Draycott Place, London
SW3 2SA
☎ (0171) 581 2323 & 225 0771
Fax (0171) 823 7752

Homely hotel in a quiet, elegant street, close to Harrods and museums.

Bedrooms: 1 single, 4 double, 6 twin
Bathrooms: 11 en-suite, 1 public

Bed & breakfast per night:	£min	£max
Single	70.00	85.00
Double	90.00	115.00

Cards accepted: Amex, Diners, Mastercard, Visa, Switch/Delta

LONDON SW5

Beaver Hotel

APPROVED

57-59 Philbeach Gardens, London
SW5 9ED
☎ (0171) 373 4553
Fax (0171) 373 4555

In a quiet, tree-lined crescent of late Victorian terraced houses, close to Earl's Court Exhibition Centre and 10 minutes from the West End.

Bedrooms: 17 single, 6 double, 10 twin, 4 triple
Bathrooms: 24 en-suite, 5 public

Bed & breakfast per night:	£min	£max
Single	30.00	50.00
Double		70.00

Parking for 23
Cards accepted: Amex, Diners, Mastercard, Visa

Please check prices and other details at the time of booking.

LONDON SW5

Continued

Kensington Court Hotel

APPROVED

33 Nevern Place, Earl's Court, London SW5 9NP
☎ (0171) 370 5151
Fax (0171) 370 3499

Purpose-built hotel with private car park. Centrally situated for both the underground and exhibition centres. All rooms with en-suite facilities.

Bedrooms: 10 single, 5 double, 5 twin, 10 triple, 5 family rooms
Bathrooms: 35 en-suite

Bed & breakfast per night:	£min	£max
Single	59.00	59.00
Double	70.00	75.00

Evening meal 1900 (last orders 2100)
Parking for 10
Cards accepted: Amex, Mastercard, Visa, Switch/Delta

Please check prices and other details at the time of booking.

Merlyn Court Hotel

2 Barkston Gardens, London SW5 0EN
☎ (0171) 370 1640
Fax (0171) 370 4986

Well-established, family-run, good value hotel in quiet Edwardian square, close to Earl's Court and Olympia. Direct underground link to Heathrow, the West End and rail stations. Car park nearby.

Bedrooms: 4 single, 4 double, 4 twin, 2 triple, 3 family rooms
Bathrooms: 11 en-suite, 6 public, 1 private shower

Bed & breakfast per night:	£min	£max
Single	28.00	50.00
Double	45.00	60.00

Cards accepted: Mastercard, Visa, Switch/Delta

Swiss House Hotel

Listed COMMENDED

171 Old Brompton Road, London SW5 0AN
☎ (0171) 373 2769 & 373 9383
Fax (0171) 373 4983
Email: recep@swiss-hh.demon.co.uk

High quality budget priced hotel, conveniently situated near London museums, shopping/exhibition centres. Gloucester Road underground station is within easy walking distance. Winner of BTA award for best value B&B in London.

Bedrooms: 5 single, 5 double, 2 twin, 4 triple
Bathrooms: 15 en-suite, 1 public, 1 private shower

Bed & breakfast per night:	£min	£max
Single	42.00	59.00
Double	75.00	75.00

Cards accepted: Amex, Diners, Mastercard, Visa, Switch/Delta

Windsor House

Listed APPROVED

12 Penywern Road, London
SW5 9ST
☎ (0171) 373 9087
Fax (0171) 385 2417

Budget-priced bed and breakfast establishment in Earl's Court. Easily reached from airports and motorway. The West End is minutes away by underground. NCP parking.
Bedrooms: 2 single, 4 double, 4 twin, 1 triple, 7 family rooms
Bathrooms: 10 en-suite, 6 public, 7 private showers

Bed & breakfast per night:	£min	£max
Single	26.00	40.00
Double	34.00	50.00

Ad See display advertisement on page 28

York House Hotel

APPROVED

27-28 Philbeach Gardens, London
SW5 9EA
☎ (0171) 373 7519 & 373 7579
Fax (0171) 370 4641
Conveniently located close to Earl's Court and Olympia exhibition centres and the West End. Underground direct to Heathrow Airport.
Bedrooms: 16 single, 3 double, 3 twin, 2 triple, 3 family rooms
Bathrooms: 1 en-suite, 6 public

Bed & breakfast per night:	£min	£max
Single	29.00	
Double	47.00	

Cards accepted: Amex, Diners, Mastercard, Visa

LONDON SW7

Five Sumner Place Hotel

Listed HIGHLY COMMENDED

5 Sumner Place, South Kensington, London SW7 3EE
☎ (0171) 584 7586
Fax (0171) 823 9962
Email: no.5@dial.pipex.com
Recent winner of Best Small Hotel in London Award. Situated in South Kensington, the most fashionable area. This family-owned and run hotel offers first-class service and personal attention.
Bedrooms: 3 single, 5 double, 5 twin
Bathrooms: 13 en-suite, 1 public

Bed & breakfast per night:	£min	£max
Single	81.00	95.00
Double	105.00	135.00

Cards accepted: Amex, Mastercard, Visa

LONDON SW14

The Plough Inn

APPROVED

42 Christchurch Road, East Sheen, London SW14 7AF
☎ (0181) 876 7833 & 876 4533
Fax (0181) 392 8801

Delightful old pub, part 16th C, next to Richmond Park. En-suite accommodation, traditional ales, home-cooked food.
Bedrooms: 3 double, 3 twin, 1 triple
Bathrooms: 6 en-suite, 1 private

Bed & breakfast per night:	£min	£max
Single	55.00	60.00
Double	70.00	75.00

Half board per person:	£min	£max
Daily	62.00	70.00

Lunch available
Evening meal 1930 (last orders 2130)
Parking for 4
Cards accepted: Amex, Mastercard, Visa

LONDON SW19

Compton Guest House

Listed

65 Compton Road, Wimbledon, London SW19 7QA
☎ (0181) 947 4488 & 879 3245
Fax (0181) 947 4488
Family-run guesthouse in pleasant, peaceful area, 5 minutes from Wimbledon station (British Rail and District Line). Easy access to the West End, central London, M1, M2, M3, M4 and M25. Quality rooms, with excellent service. About 12 minutes' walk to Wimbledon tennis courts.
Bedrooms: 2 single, 1 double, 2 twin, 1 triple, 2 family rooms
Bathrooms: 2 public

Bed & breakfast per night:	£min	£max
Single	35.00	40.00
Double	48.00	66.00

Parking for 2

LONDON W1

Lincoln House Hotel

COMMENDED

33 Gloucester Place, London
W1H 3PD
☎ (0171) 486 7630
Fax (0171) 486 0166
Georgian hotel of distinctive character. En-suite rooms with all modern comforts. Superb location, competitively priced, in the heart of London's West End.
Bedrooms: 6 single, 8 double, 4 twin, 3 triple, 1 family room
Bathrooms: 20 en-suite, 2 private, 2 public

Bed & breakfast per night:	£min	£max
Single	59.00	69.00
Double	75.00	89.00

Cards accepted: Amex, Diners, Mastercard, Visa, Switch/Delta

Wyndham Hotel

Listed

30 Wyndham Street, London
W1H 1DD
☎ (0171) 723 7204 & 723 9400
Fax (0171) 723 7204
Small family-run B&B in a Georgian terrace, around the corner from Baker Street and a short walk from Oxford Street.
Bedrooms: 5 single, 4 double, 2 twin
Bathrooms: 1 public, 9 private showers

Bed & breakfast per night:	£min	£max
Single	34.00	36.00
Double	44.00	46.00

TOWN INDEX

This can be found at the back of the guide. If you know where you want to stay, the index will give you the page number listing all accommodation in your chosen town, city or village.

LONDON W2

Abbey Court Hotel

Listed

174 Sussex Gardens, London
W2 1TP
☎ (0171) 402 0704
Fax (0171) 262 2055

Central London hotel, reasonable prices. Within walking distance of Lancaster Gate, Paddington station and Hyde Park. Easy access to tourist attractions and shopping. Car parking at modest charge.

Bedrooms: 14 single, 24 double, 7 twin, 10 triple, 2 family rooms
Bathrooms: 57 en-suite

Bed & breakfast per night:	£min	£max
Single	29.00	39.00
Double	39.00	58.00

Parking for 20
Cards accepted: Amex, Mastercard, Visa, Switch/Delta

Ad See display advertisement on page 31

Beverley House Hotel

COMMENDED

142 Sussex Gardens, London
W2 1UB
☎ (0171) 723 3380
Fax (0171) 262 0324

Refurbished bed and breakfast hotel, serving traditional English breakfast and offering high standards at low prices. Close to Paddington station, Hyde Park and museums.

Bedrooms: 6 single, 5 double, 6 twin, 6 triple
Bathrooms: 23 en-suite

Bed & breakfast per night:	£min	£max
Single	40.00	55.00
Double	49.00	73.00

Evening meal 1800 (last orders 2200)
Parking for 2
Cards accepted: Amex, Diners, Mastercard, Visa

Information on accommodation listed in this guide has been supplied by the proprietors. As changes may occur you are advised to check details at the time of booking.

Hyde Park Rooms Hotel

Listed

137 Sussex Gardens, Hyde Park, London W2 2RX
☎ (0171) 723 0225 & 723 0965

Small centrally located private hotel with personal service. Clean, comfortable and friendly. Within walking distance of Hyde Park and Kensington Gardens. Car parking available.

Bedrooms: 5 single, 6 double, 2 twin, 1 triple
Bathrooms: 7 en-suite, 2 private, 2 public

Bed & breakfast per night:	£min	£max
Single	26.00	38.00
Double	38.00	50.00

Parking for 3
Cards accepted: Amex, Diners, Mastercard, Visa, Switch/Delta

Kings Arms Hotel

APPROVED

254 Edgware Road, Paddington, London W2 1DS
☎ (0171) 262 8441
Fax (0171) 258 0556
Email: kingsarmshotel@compuserve.com

Victorian public house/hotel conveniently located for London's West End shopping and theatres.

Bedrooms: 2 single, 2 double, 7 twin, 2 triple
Bathrooms: 8 en-suite, 2 public

Bed & breakfast per night:	£min	£max
Single	29.00	39.00
Double	49.00	59.00

Half board per person:	£min	£max
Daily	34.50	44.50
Weekly	207.00	267.00

Lunch available
Evening meal 1700 (last orders 2200)
Cards accepted: Amex, Mastercard, Visa, Switch/Delta

Manor Court Hotel

Listed

7 Clanricarde Gardens, London
W2 4JJ
☎ (0171) 727 5407 & 729 3361
Fax (0171) 229 2875

Family-run bed and breakfast hotel within walking distance of Hyde Park and Kensington Gardens. Near Notting Hill Gate underground and Airbus stop. All rooms have colour TV and telephone.

Bedrooms: 5 single, 5 double, 4 twin, 5 triple, 1 family room
Bathrooms: 6 en-suite, 3 private, 4 public, 7 private showers

Bed & breakfast per night:	£min	£max
Single	25.00	30.00
Double	45.00	55.00

Cards accepted: Amex, Diners, Mastercard, Visa

Nayland Hotel

COMMENDED

132-134 Sussex Gardens, London
W2 1UB
☎ (0171) 723 4615
Fax (0171) 402 3292

Centrally located, close to many amenities and within walking distance of Hyde Park and Oxford Street. Quality you can afford.

Bedrooms: 11 single, 8 double, 17 twin, 5 triple
Bathrooms: 41 en-suite

Bed & breakfast per night:	£min	£max
Single	46.00	62.00
Double	52.00	78.00

Evening meal 1800 (last orders 2100)
Parking for 5
Cards accepted: Amex, Diners, Mastercard, Visa

Prince William Hotel

Listed APPROVED

42-44 Gloucester Terrace, London
W2 3DA
☎ (0171) 724 7414
Fax (0171) 706 2411

Central location in Paddington, close to Hyde Park and Oxford Street. Clean, comfortable accommodation, residents' lounge, restaurant and bar. Secretarial and fax services.

Bedrooms: 23 single, 7 double, 11 twin, 2 triple
Bathrooms: 34 private, 2 public, 6 private showers

Bed & breakfast per night:	£min	£max
Single	39.00	55.00
Double	55.00	75.00

Evening meal 1730 (last orders 2230)
Cards accepted: Amex, Diners, Mastercard, Visa, Switch/Delta

ACCOMMODATION

Central London

Budget Prices

WESTPOINT HOTEL

170 Sussex Gardens, Hyde Park, London W2 1PT.
Tel: (0171) 402 0281 (Reservations) Fax: (0171) 224 9114.

All rooms with private shower & toilet, radio/intercom & colour TV. Lift to all floors.

This hotel has long been a popular choice amongst tourists because of its central location, being near to Hyde Park and only 2 minutes from Paddington and Lancaster Gate tube stations. The West End's tourist attractions, including theatres, museums and Oxford Street stores, are within easy reach. Individuals, families and groups are all welcome.

● CAR PARK BY ARRANGEMENT ● DIRECT A2 BUS FROM HEATHROW ●

RATES: ***Low Season***
Singles from £28 per person.
Doubles from £24 per person.
Family rooms from £18 per person.

High Season
Singles from £36 per person.
Doubles from £26 per person.
Family rooms from £22 per person.

ABBEY COURT HOTEL

174 Sussex Gardens, Hyde Park, London W2 1TP.
Tel: (0171) 402 0704 Fax: (0171) 262 2055.

Open all year. Radio Intercom in every room. Children welcome. All rooms with private shower, toilet and colour TV. Lift to all floors.

● CAR PARKING BY ARRANGEMENT ● A2 BUS FROM HEATHROW ●

Central London hotel in a pleasant avenue near Hyde Park and within 2 minutes' walking distance of Paddington main line and tube station and Lancaster Gate tube station. The tourist attractions of the West End including theatres, museums and Oxford Street are within easy reach. Individuals, families, school parties and groups are all welcome and group tours can be arranged.

TERMS per person:
Low Season: Single from £30, double from £24 p.p., family rooms from £19 p.p.
High Season: Single from £38, double from £28 p.p., family rooms from £23 p.p.

SASS HOUSE HOTEL

11 Craven Terrace, Hyde Park, London W2 3QD.
Tel: (0171) 262 2325 Fax: (0171) 262 0889

★ Centrally located – within easy reach of London's most famous tourist attractions.
★ Nearest underground Paddington and Lancaster Gate. ★ Served by a network of bus routes.
★ Colour television lounge. ★ Centrally heated. ★ Radio and intercom in all rooms.
★ All rooms with showers/toilets. ★ Parking facilities by arrangement.
★ A2 bus from Heathrow.

TERMS per person:
Low Season: Singles from £24, doubles from £22 p.p., family rooms from £18 p.p.
High Season: Singles from £34, doubles from £25 p.p., family rooms from £22 p.p.

Rhodes House Hotel

COMMENDED

195 Sussex Gardens, London W2 2RJ
☎ (0171) 262 5617 & 262 0537
Fax (0171) 723 4054

Rooms with private facilities and satellite TV, telephone, refrigerator, hairdryer and tea/coffee-making facilities. Friendly atmosphere. Families especially welcome. Excellent transport for sightseeing and shopping. www.rhodeshotel.co.uk
Bedrooms: 3 single, 3 double, 4 twin, 4 triple, 4 family rooms
Bathrooms: 15 en-suite, 1 public

Bed & breakfast per night:	£min	£max
Single	40.00	60.00
Double	60.00	80.00

Cards accepted: Mastercard, Visa

Rose Court Hotel

APPROVED

1-3 Talbot Square, London W2 1TR
☎ (0171) 723 5128 & 723 8671
Fax (0171) 723 1855
Privately-run Victorian town house in a quiet garden square. Close to Paddington and the West End.
Bedrooms: 7 single, 11 double, 16 twin, 5 triple, 3 family rooms
Bathrooms: 41 en-suite, 1 public

Bed & breakfast per night:	£min	£max
Single	40.00	56.00
Double	48.00	70.00

Half board per person:	£min	£max
Daily	50.00	64.00
Weekly	325.00	380.00

Lunch available
Evening meal 1800 (last orders 2100)
Cards accepted: Amex, Diners, Mastercard, Visa, Switch/Delta

Ruddimans Hotel

Listed APPROVED

160-162 Sussex Gardens, London W2 1UD
☎ (0171) 723 1026 & 723 6715
Fax (0171) 262 2983
Comfortable hotel close to West End and London's attractions, offering generous English breakfast and good service at reasonable prices. Car park.
Bedrooms: 8 single, 13 double, 6 twin, 11 triple, 3 family rooms
Bathrooms: 33 en-suite, 2 public

Bed & breakfast per night:	£min	£max
Single	26.00	36.00
Double	42.00	50.00

Parking for 4
Cards accepted: Amex, Mastercard, Visa, Switch/Delta

Sass House Hotel

Listed APPROVED

10-11 Craven Terrace, London W2 3QD
☎ (0171) 262 2325
Fax (0171) 262 0889
Budget accommodation, convenient for central London, Hyde Park and West End. Paddington and Lancaster Gate underground stations nearby. Easy access to tourist attractions.
Bedrooms: 8 double, 7 twin, 8 triple
Bathrooms: 23 en-suite, 1 public

Bed & breakfast per night:	£min	£max
Single	26.00	36.00
Double	35.00	54.00

Cards accepted: Amex, Mastercard, Visa, Switch/Delta

Ad See display advertisement on page 31

Westpoint Hotel

Listed

170-172 Sussex Gardens, London W2 1TP
☎ (0171) 402 0281
Fax (0171) 224 9114
Inexpensive accommodation in central London. Close to Paddington and Lancaster Gate underground stations. Easy access to tourist attractions, shopping and Hyde Park.
Bedrooms: 12 single, 15 double, 16 twin, 14 triple, 6 family rooms
Bathrooms: 31 en-suite, 10 public, 9 private showers

Bed & breakfast per night:	£min	£max
Single	28.00	38.00
Double	38.00	56.00

Parking for 15
Cards accepted: Amex, Mastercard, Visa, Switch/Delta

Ad See display advertisement on page 31

LONDON W5

Corfton Guest House

APPROVED

42 Corfton Road, Ealing, London W5 2HT
☎ (0181) 998 1120
Close to Ealing Broadway station, in a quiet residential area of considerable character.
Bedrooms: 3 single, 3 double, 1 twin, 2 triple
Bathrooms: 5 en-suite, 2 public

Bed & breakfast per night:	£min	£max
Single	17.00	37.00
Double	25.00	37.00

Parking for 6

Grange Lodge Hotel

APPROVED

48-50 Grange Road, Ealing, London W5 5BX
☎ (0181) 567 1049
Fax (0181) 579 5350
Quiet, comfortable hotel within a few hundred yards of the underground station. Midway between central London and Heathrow.
Bedrooms: 8 single, 2 double, 2 twin, 2 triple
Bathrooms: 9 en-suite, 2 public

Bed & breakfast per night:	£min	£max
Single	35.00	40.00
Double	47.00	52.00

Parking for 8
Cards accepted: Diners, Mastercard, Visa, Switch/Delta

LONDON W8

Clearlake Hotel

Listed APPROVED

18-19 Prince of Wales Terrace, Kensington, London W8 5PQ
☎ (0171) 937 3274
Fax (0171) 376 0604
Comfortable rooms in a hotel in a quiet cul-de-sac, with view of Hyde Park. Self-catering apartments also available. Close to shops and transport.
Bedrooms: 1 single, 5 double, 6 triple, 4 family rooms
Bathrooms: 16 en-suite

Bed & breakfast per night:	£min	£max
Single	40.00	50.00
Double	50.00	75.00

Cards accepted: Amex, Diners, Mastercard, Visa

OUTER LONDON

Colour maps 6 & 7 at the back of the guide show place names and London Postal Area Codes and will help you locate accommodation in your chosen area of London

CROYDON

Tourist Information Centre ☎ (0181) 253 1009

Iverna

Listed

1 Annandale Road, Addiscombe, Croydon CR0 7HP
☎ (0181) 654 8639
Large house in quiet road, close to East Croydon station: London Victoria 15 minutes away. One smoking area available.
Bedrooms: 3 single, 1 twin
Bathrooms: 1 public

Bed & breakfast per night:	£min	£max
Single	22.00	25.00
Double	40.00	44.00

Evening meal 1800 (last orders 2100)
Parking for 2

ISLEWORTH

Regency Bed and Breakfast

Number Nine Regency Mews, Isleworth, Middlesex TW7 7LX
☎ (0181) 894 9190
Regency-style terraced cottage. M3 and Heathrow Airport nearby. Close to several famous attractions. Resident proprietor.
Bedrooms: 1 single, 2 double
Bathrooms: 3 private

Bed & breakfast per night:	£min	£max
Single	27.00	33.00
Double	48.00	58.00

Parking for 3
Cards accepted: Amex, Mastercard, Visa

WEMBLEY

Elm Hotel

APPROVED

1-7 Elm Road, Wembley, Middlesex HA9 7JA
☎ (0181) 902 1764
Fax (0181) 903 8365
Ten minutes' walk (1200 yards) from Wembley Stadium and Conference Centre. 150 yards from Wembley Central underground and mainline station.
Bedrooms: 5 single, 8 double, 8 twin, 3 triple, 2 family rooms
Suites available
Bathrooms: 26 en-suite

Bed & breakfast per night:	£min	£max
Single	35.00	45.00
Double	47.00	57.00

Parking for 7
Cards accepted: Mastercard, Visa, Switch/Delta
30

USE YOUR i's

There are more than 550 Tourist Information Centres throughout England offering friendly help with accommodation and holiday ideas as well as suggestions of places to visit and things to do. You'll find TIC addresses in the local Phone Book or simply call Freepages on 0800 192 192.

AT-A-GLANCE SYMBOLS

Symbols at the end of each accommodation entry give useful information about services and facilities. A key to symbols can be found inside the back cover flap.

Keep this open for easy reference.

USE YOUR i's

There are more than 550 Tourist Information Centres throughout England offering friendly help with accommodation and holiday ideas as well as suggestions of places to visit and things to do. There may well be a centre in your home town which can help you before you set out. You'll find addresses in the local Phone Book or simply call Freepages 0800 192 192.

CHECK THE MAPS

The colour maps at the back of this guide show all the cities, towns and villages for which you will find accommodation entries.

Refer to the town index to find the page on which it is listed.

ENQUIRY COUPONS

To help you obtain further information about advertisers and accommodation featured in this guide you will find enquiry coupons at the back. Send these directly to the establishments in which you are interested. Remember to complete both sides of the coupon.

CUMBRIA

Cumbria's glorious lakeland is surely the jewel in the crown of England's scenic heritage. Its vistas of shining water, majestic mountains and forests inspire artists, writers and all lovers of beauty.

The area is a paradise for walkers and climbers, while the less energetic can marvel at the views from the comfort of a steam train or one of the picturesque lake steamers.

Beyond the lakes are villages and working farms, as well as museums devoted to topics ranging from the worlds of Wordsworth and Beatrix Potter, to Roman life and the region's shipbuilding past. Today, Cumbria's coastal fringe of long, sandy beaches is a favourite with families.

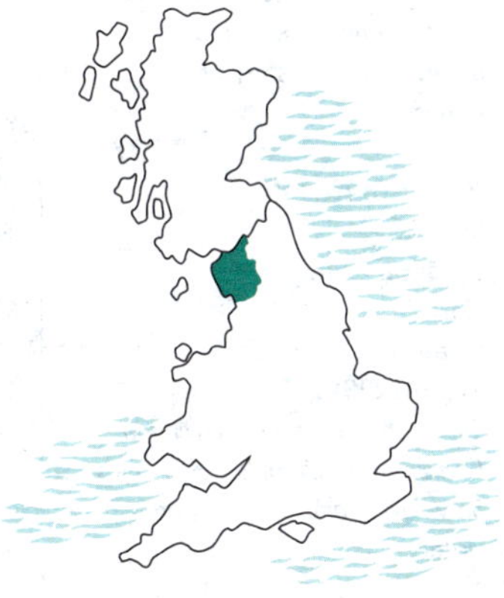

The county of Cumbria

FOR MORE INFORMATION CONTACT:

Cumbria Tourist Board
Ashleigh, Holly Road, Windermere,
Cumbria LA23 2AQ
Tel: (015394) 44444 **Fax:** (015394) 44041

Where to Go in Cumbria – see pages 36-39
Where to Stay in Cumbria – see pages 40-58

CUMBRIA

Where to Go and What to See

You will find hundreds of interesting places to visit during your stay in Cumbria, just some of which are listed in these pages. The number against each name will help you locate it on the map (page 39). Contact any Tourist Information Centre in the region for more ideas on days out in Cumbria.

1 Birdoswald Roman Fort
Gilsland, Carlisle,
Cumbria CA6 7DD
Tel: (016977) 47602/47604
Remains of a Roman fort on one of the best parts of Hadrian's Wall with excellent views of the Irthing Gorge. The visitor centre brings to life the story of Birdoswald.

2 Linton Tweeds
Shaddon Mills,
Shaddon Gate,
Carlisle,
Cumbria CA2 5TZ
Tel: (01228) 27569
Shows the history of weaving in Carlisle up to Linton's day. Hands-on weaving and other activities for visitors.

3 Tullie House Museum and Art Gallery
Castle Street, Carlisle,
Cumbria CA3 8TP
Tel: (01228) 34781
Major tourist complex featuring a museum, art gallery, education facility, lecture theatre, shops, herb garden, restaurant and terrace bars.

4 Four Seasons Farm Experience
Sceugh Mire,
Southwaite, Carlisle,
Cumbria CA4 0LS
Tel: (016974) 73753
An open farm where you can meet the animals, bottle feed the lambs in spring and make your own bread and butter.

5 South Tynedale Railway
Railway Station, Alston,
Cumbria CA9 3JB
Tel: (01434) 381696
A 2ft gauge railway along part of the route of the former Alston to Haltwhistle branch line through South Tynedale. Preserved British and overseas steam and diesel engines.

6 Hutton-in-the-Forest
Skelton, Penrith,
Cumbria CA11 9TH
Tel: (017684) 84449
A 13thC pele tower with later additions. Tapestries, armour, furniture, paintings, china. Formal gardens, ornamental lake, dovecote, woods with specimen trees and nature walk.

7 Senhouse Roman Museum
The Battery,
Sea Brows, Maryport,
Cumbria CA15 6JD
Tel: (01900) 816168
Once the headquarters of Hadrian's Coastal Defence system. UK's largest group of Roman altar stones and inscriptions. Roman military equipment, stunning sculpture.

8 **Jennings Brothers plc**
The Castle Brewery,
Cockermouth,
Cumbria CA13 9NE
Tel: (01900) 823214
Guided tours of Jennings - a traditional brewery producing distinctive local beers. Gift and souvenir shop.

9 **Lakeland Sheep and Wool Centre**
Egremont Road, Cockermouth,
Cumbria CA13 OQX
Tel: (01900) 822673
An all weather attraction with live sheep shows and working dog demonstrations. Includes large screen and other tourism exhibitions on the area, a wool shop and cafe/restaurant.

10 **Whinlatter Forest Park and Visitor Centre**
Braithwaite, Keswick,
Cumbria CA12 5TW
Tel: (017687) 78469
Forestry interpretative exhibition with audiovisual presentations. Working model of forest operations. Lecture theatre, walks, trails, orienteering, shop and cafe.

11 **Threlkeld Quarry and Mining Museum**
Threlkeld, Keswick,
Cumbria CA12 4TT
Tel: (017687) 79747
Unique collection of mining and quarrying artefacts, memorabilia and minerals including earth-moving machines, quarry and mining tubs.

12 **The Beacon**
West Strand, Whitehaven,
Cumbria CA28 7LY
Tel: (01946) 592302
Discover the industrial, maritime and social history of Whitehaven and surrounding area. Includes meteorology office weather gallery with satellite linked equipment.

13 **Sellafield Visitor Centre**
Sellafield, Seascale,
Cumbria CA20 1PG
Tel: (019467) 27027
Exhibition of nuclear power and the nuclear industry.

14 **Dove Cottage and Wordsworth Museum**
Town End,
Grasmere, Ambleside,
Cumbria LA22 9SH
Tel: (015394) 35544/35003
Wordsworth's home from 1799-1808. Poet's possessions, museum with manuscripts, farmhouse reconstruction, paintings and drawings. Special events throughout the year.

15 **Rydal Mount**
Ambleside,
Cumbria LA22 9LU
Tel: (015394) 33002
William Wordsworth's home for 37 years. Family portraits, furniture, first editions and personal possessions. Garden landscaped by the poet, 9thC Norse mound, magnificent views.

16 **Muncaster Castle, Gardens and Owl Centre**
Ravenglass,
Cumbria CA18 1RQ
Tel: (01229) 717614/717203
A 14thC pele tower with 15thC and 19thC additions. Gardens contain an exceptional collection of rhododendrons and azaleas. Extensive collection of owls.

17 **Ravenglass and Eskdale Railway**
Ravenglass,
Cumbria CA18 1SW
Tel: (01229) 717171
England's oldest narrow-gauge railway runs for 7 miles through glorious scenery to the foot of England's highest hills. Most trains are steam hauled.

18 **Steam Yacht Gondola**
Pier Cottage, Coniston,
Cumbria LA21 8AJ
Tel: (015394) 41288
Victorian steam-powered vessel, now National Trust owned, cruises Coniston Water. Completely renovated with wonderful saloon.

19 Amazónia
Glebe Road,
Bowness-on-Windermere,
Windermere,
Cumbria LA23 3HE
Tel: (015394) 48002
Large display of exotic reptiles and insects from around the world including pythons, crocodiles and tarantula spiders! Visitors are able to handle certain animals.

20 The World of Beatrix Potter
The Old Laundry, Crag Brow,
Bowness-on-Windermere,
Windermere,
Cumbria LA23 3BX
Tel: (015394) 88444
The life and works of Beatrix Potter presented on a 9-screen video wall. Film on her life, and 3-dimensional recreations of some of the scenes from her popular tales.

21 Sizergh Castle
Kendal,
Cumbria LA8 8AE
Tel: (015395) 60070
Strickland family home for 750 years, now National Trust owned. 14thC pele tower, 15thC great hall, 16thC wings. Stuart connections. Rock garden, rose garden, daffodils.

22 Ullswater Navigation and Transit Co
13 Maude Street, Kendal,
Cumbria LA9 4QD
Tel: (01539) 721626/
(017684) 82229
One or two hour cruises on beautiful Ullswater, or combine a walk with a return boat ride.

23 Graythwaite Hall Gardens
Newby Bridge, Ulverston,
Cumbria LA12 8BA
Tel: (015395) 31248
Rhododendrons, azaleas and flowering shrubs. Laid out by T Mawson 1888-1890.

24 Lakeland Wildlife Oasis
Hale, Milnthorpe,
Cumbria LA7 7BW
Tel: (015395) 63027
A wildlife exhibition where living animals and 'hands-on' displays illustrate evolution in the animal kingdom. Gift shop.

25 Lakeside and Haverthwaite Railway
Haverthwaite Station,
Ulverston,
Cumbria LA12 8AL
Tel: (015395) 31594
Standard gauge steam railway operating a daily seasonal service through the beautiful Leven valley. Steam and diesel locomotives on display.

26 Holker Hall and Gardens
Cark in Cartmel,
Cumbria LA11 7PL
Tel: (015395) 58328
Victorian new wing, formal and woodland garden, deer park, motor museum, adventure playground and gift shop. Exhibitions include Timeless Toys and Teddies.

27 South Lakes Wild Animal Park
Crossgates,
Dalton-in-Furness,
Cumbria LA15 8JR
Tel: (01229) 466086
Wild animal park in over 14 acres with more than 120 species from around the world. Large water fowl ponds, cafe, miniature railway.

28 The Dock Museum
North Road,
Barrow-in-Furness,
Cumbria LA14 2PW
Tel: (01229) 870871
Presents the story of steel shipbuilding for which Barrow is famous. Interactive displays, nautical adventure playground.

FIND OUT MORE

Further information about holidays and attractions in Cumbria is available from:
Cumbria Tourist Board,
Ashleigh,
Holly Road,
Windermere,
Cumbria LA23 2AQ.
Tel: (015394) 44444

These publications are available from the Cumbria Tourist Board:

- **Cumbria The Lake District Touring Map** - including tourist information and touring caravan and camping parks £3.95.
- **Days Out in Cumbria** - Over 200 ideas for a great day out £1.25.
- **Short Walks** - Good for Families - route descriptions, maps and information for 14 walks in lesser known areas of Cumbria 95p.
- **Wordsworth's Lake District** - folded map showing major Wordsworthian sites plus biographical details 60p. Japanese language version £1. Laminated poster £1.

WHERE TO STAY (CUMBRIA)

Accommodation entries in this region are listed in alphabetical order of place name, and then in alphabetical order of establishment.

Map references refer to the colour location maps at the back of this guide. The first number indicates the map to use; the letter and number which follow refer to the grid reference on the map.

At-a-glance symbols at the end of each accommodation entry give useful information about services and facilities. A key to symbols can be found inside the back cover flap. Keep this open for easy reference.

AMBLESIDE

Cumbria
Map ref 5A3

Market town situated at the head of Lake Windermere and surrounded by fells. The historic town centre is now a conservation area and the country around Ambleside is rich in historic and literary associations. Good centre for touring, walking and climbing.
Tourist Information Centre
☎ *(015394) 32582*

Broadview

Listed COMMENDED

Low Fold, Lake Road, Ambleside LA22 0DN
☎ (015394) 32431
Spacious, comfortable Victorian guesthouse with some en-suite rooms and superb views. Easy walk to village and lake.
Bedrooms: 3 double, 1 twin, 1 triple, 1 family room
Bathrooms: 2 en-suite, 2 public

Bed & breakfast per night:	£min	£max
Single	20.00	22.00
Double	35.00	44.00

Open February–November
UL S

Glenside

COMMENDED

Old Lake Road, Ambleside LA22 0DP
☎ (015394) 32635
17th C farm cottage, comfortable bedrooms with original oak beams, TV lounge. Between town and lake, ideal centre for walking. Private parking.
Bedrooms: 2 double, 1 twin
Bathrooms: 2 public

Bed & breakfast per night:	£min	£max
Single	15.00	16.00
Double	30.00	32.00

Parking for 3
Open February–November
5 UL TV OAP T

Greenbank

HIGHLY COMMENDED

Skelwith Bridge, Ambleside LA22 9NW
☎ (015394) 33236
Set in a beautiful rural location just 3 miles from Ambleside. Glorious views from delightfully furnished, cosy rooms. Home-made bread and cakes a speciality.
Bedrooms: 2 double, 1 twin
Bathrooms: 3 en-suite, 1 public

Bed & breakfast per night:	£min	£max
Single	24.00	26.00
Double	38.00	42.00

Parking for 6
8 UL S SP

High Wray Farm

Listed COMMENDED

High Wray, Ambleside LA22 0JE
☎ (015394) 32280

173-acre livestock farm. Charming 17th C old world farmhouse, once owned by Beatrix Potter, with oak beams and log fire. In quiet location, ideal centre for touring or walking. Panoramic views and lake shore walks close by.
Bedrooms: 2 double, 1 twin
Bathrooms: 1 en-suite, 1 public

Bed & breakfast per night:	£min	£max
Single	17.00	18.00
Double	34.00	36.00

Parking for 7
UL S TV SP

Hillsdale

APPROVED

Church Street, Ambleside LA22 0BT
☎ (015394) 33174
Family-run hotel in centre of village. Generous English/vegetarian breakfast. Good value for money. Ideal base for walks, eating out, etc.
Bedrooms: 1 single, 6 double, 1 twin
Bathrooms: 1 en-suite, 1 public, 4 private showers

Bed & breakfast per night:	£min	£max
Double	30.00	40.00

UL S

Laurel Villa

HIGHLY COMMENDED

Lake Road, Ambleside LA22 0DB
☎ (015394) 33240
Detached Victorian house, visited by Beatrix Potter. En-suite bedrooms overlooking the fells. Within easy reach of Lake Windermere and the village. Private car park.
Bedrooms: 7 double, 1 twin
Bathrooms: 8 en-suite

Bed & breakfast per night:	£min	£max
Single	50.00	50.00
Double	60.00	80.00

Half board per person:	£min	£max
Daily	50.00	100.00

Evening meal 1900 (last orders 1700)
Parking for 10
Cards accepted: Amex, Mastercard, Visa

Lyndhurst Hotel

COMMENDED

Wansfell Road, Ambleside
LA22 0EG
☎ (015394) 32421

Small, attractive Lakeland hotel with private car park. Quietly situated for town and lake. Pretty rooms, delicious food - a delightful experience.

Bedrooms: 5 double, 1 twin
Bathrooms: 6 en-suite

Bed & breakfast per night:	£min	£max
Single	25.00	30.00
Double	39.00	50.00

Half board per person:	£min	£max
Daily	33.00	39.00
Weekly	225.00	250.00

Evening meal 1830 (last orders 1830)
Parking for 9

Mill Cottage

Listed APPROVED

Rydal Road, Ambleside LA22 9AN
☎ (015394) 34830

Grade II listed restaurant and guesthouse in riverside location adjacent to the famous Bridge House.

Bedrooms: 4 double, 1 twin, 1 family room
Bathrooms: 5 en-suite, 1 private shower

Bed & breakfast per night:	£min	£max
Single	18.00	20.00
Double	38.00	40.00

Half board per person:	£min	£max
Daily	48.00	50.00

Lunch available
Evening meal 1830 (last orders 2100)

The Old Vicarage

COMMENDED

Vicarage Road, Ambleside
LA22 9DH
☎ (015394) 33364
Fax (015394) 34734

Quietly situated in own grounds in heart of village. Car park, quality en-suite accommodation, friendly service. Family-run. Pets welcome.

Bedrooms: 7 double, 1 twin, 1 triple, 1 family room
Bathrooms: 10 en-suite

Bed & breakfast per night:	£min	£max
Double	46.00	

Parking for 12
Cards accepted: Mastercard, Visa, Switch/Delta

20

Riverside Lodge Country House

COMMENDED

Rothay Bridge, Ambleside
LA22 0EH
☎ (015394) 34208
Fax (015374) 31884

Georgian country house of character with 2 acres of grounds through which the River Rothay flows. 500 yards from the centre of Ambleside.

Bedrooms: 1 single, 2 double, 1 twin, 1 triple
Bathrooms: 3 en-suite, 2 private

Bed & breakfast per night:	£min	£max
Double	48.00	60.00

Parking for 20
Cards accepted: Mastercard, Visa

11

For further information on accommodation establishments use the coupons at the back of this guide.

Rowanfield Country Guesthouse

HIGHLY COMMENDED

Kirkstone Road, Ambleside
LA22 9ET
☎ (015394) 33686
Fax (015394) 31569

Idyllic setting, panoramic lake and mountain views. Laura Ashley style decor. Scrumptious food created by proprietor/chef. Superior room available at supplement.

Wheelchair access category 3
Bedrooms: 5 double, 1 twin, 1 triple
Bathrooms: 7 en-suite

Bed & breakfast per night:	£min	£max
Double	54.00	60.00

Half board per person:	£min	£max
Daily	44.00	47.00
Weekly	267.00	286.00

Evening meal 1900 (last orders 1900)
Parking for 8
Open March–December
Cards accepted: Mastercard, Visa, Switch/Delta

5

Scandale Brow

HIGHLY COMMENDED

Rydal Road, Ambleside LA22 9PL
☎ (015394) 34528
Fax (015394) 34528

Traditional Lakeland-stone house set in secluded grounds commanding southerly views of the Rothay Valley and surrounding fells. 10 minutes' walk from the centre of Ambleside.

Bedrooms: 2 double, 1 twin
Suites available
Bathrooms: 3 en-suite

Bed & breakfast per night:	£min	£max
Double	38.00	52.00

Parking for 6

10

APPLEBY-IN-WESTMORLAND

Cumbria
Map ref 5B3

Former county town of Westmorland, at the foot of the Pennines in the Eden Valley. The castle was rebuilt in the 17th C, except for its Norman keep, ditches and ramparts. It now houses a Rare Breeds Survival Trust Centre. Good centre for exploring the Eden Valley.
Tourist Information Centre
☎ (017683) 51177

Asby Grange Farm

COMMENDED

Great Asby,
Appleby-in-Westmorland CA16 6HF
☎ (017683) 52881
300-acre mixed farm. 18th C farmhouse in beautiful and peaceful countryside, 5 miles south of Appleby. Ideal for touring Lakes and Yorkshire Dales. Convenient for M6.
Bedrooms: 2 double
Bathrooms: 1 public

Bed & breakfast per night:	£min	£max
Double	28.00	30.00

Parking for 4
Open April–October

Bongate House

COMMENDED

Appleby-in-Westmorland
CA16 6UE
☎ (017683) 51245
Family-run Georgian guesthouse on the outskirts of a small market town. Large garden. Relaxed friendly atmosphere, good home cooking.
Bedrooms: 1 single, 3 double, 2 twin, 1 triple, 1 family room
Bathrooms: 5 en-suite, 1 public

Bed & breakfast per night:	£min	£max
Single	17.50	17.50
Double	35.00	40.00

Half board per person:	£min	£max
Daily	26.50	29.00
Weekly	170.00	190.00

Evening meal 1900 (last orders 1800)
Parking for 10

Bridge End Farm

HIGHLY COMMENDED

Kirkby Thore, Penrith CA10 1UZ
☎ (017683) 61362
450-acre arable & dairy farm. Relax in 18th C farmhouse in Eden Valley. Spacious rooms overlooking Pennine Hills, alongside River Eden. Delicious home-made breakfast and dinners.
Bedrooms: 2 double, 1 twin
Bathrooms: 2 en-suite, 1 private, 1 public

Bed & breakfast per night:	£min	£max
Single	21.00	25.00
Double	40.00	42.00

Half board per person:	£min	£max
Daily	30.00	31.00
Weekly	203.00	210.00

Evening meal 1800 (last orders 1930)
Parking for 3

Dufton Hall Farm

APPROVED

Dufton, Appleby-in-Westmorland
CA16 6DD
☎ (017683) 51573
60-acre mixed farm. Spacious 18th C farmhouse offering en-suite, well-appointed rooms. Ideal walking area. Village pub close by.
Bedrooms: 2 double, 1 twin
Bathrooms: 2 en-suite, 1 private

Bed & breakfast per night:	£min	£max
Single	20.00	
Double	32.00	

Parking for 3
Open April–October

BASSENTHWAITE

Cumbria
Map ref 5A2

Standing in an idyllic setting, nestled at the foot of Skiddaw and Ullock Pike, this village is just a mile from Bassenthwaite Lake, the one true "lake" in the Lake District. The area is visited by many varieties of migrating birds.

Kiln Hill Barn

COMMENDED

Bassenthwaite, Keswick CA12 4RG
☎ (017687) 76454
Family rooms with en-suite facilities, log fires and central heating. Meals served in the Barn dining room, adjacent to the farmhouse.
Bedrooms: 2 single, 4 double, 1 twin
Bathrooms: 5 en-suite, 1 public

Bed & breakfast per night:	£min	£max
Single	19.50	19.50
Double	39.00	39.00

Half board per person:	£min	£max
Daily	28.50	28.50
Weekly	185.00	185.00

Evening meal 1830 (last orders 1900)
Parking for 15
Open January–November

BORROWDALE

Cumbria
Map ref 5A3

Stretching south of Derwentwater to Seathwaite in the heart of the Lake District, the valley is walled by high fellsides. It can justly claim to be the most scenically impressive valley in the Lake District. Excellent centre for walking and climbing.

Yew Craggs

Listed COMMENDED

Rosthwaite, Keswick CA12 5XB
☎ (017687) 77260
Beside Rosthwaite Bridge in the centre of the Borrowdale Valley. Good for walking, superb views in all directions.
Bedrooms: 3 double, 2 triple
Bathrooms: 1 public

Bed & breakfast per night:	£min	£max
Double	30.00	38.00

Parking for 6
Open March–November

BROUGHTON-IN-FURNESS

Cumbria
Map ref 5A3

Old market village whose historic charter to hold fairs is still proclaimed every year on the first day of August in the market square. Good centre for touring the pretty Duddon Valley.

Broom Hill

HIGHLY COMMENDED

New Street, Broughton-in-Furness
LA20 6JD
☎ (01229) 716358 & 0860 724719
Fax (01229) 716358
Manor house with large secluded gardens and fine views. All usual facilities.
Bedrooms: 3 double
Bathrooms: 2 en-suite, 1 private

Bed & breakfast per night:	£min	£max
Single	18.00	22.00
Double	36.00	44.00

Parking for 7
Open March–October

CALDBECK

Cumbria
Map ref 5A2

Quaint limestone village lying on the northern fringe of the Lake District National Park. John Peel, the famous huntsman who is immortalised in song, is buried in the churchyard. The fells surrounding Caldbeck were once heavily mined, being rich in lead, copper and barytes.

The Briars

Listed COMMENDED

Caldbeck, Wigton CA7 8DS
☎ (016974) 78633
140-acre mixed farm. In the lovely village of Caldbeck overlooking Caldbeck Fells. Ideal for touring the Lakes and Scottish Borders. On Cumbria Way route.
Bedrooms: 1 single, 1 double, 1 twin
Bathrooms: 1 en-suite, 1 private, 2 public

Bed & breakfast per night:	£min	£max
Single	18.50	19.50
Double	37.00	39.00

Parking for 3
Open March–October

Swaledale Watch

HIGHLY COMMENDED

Whelpo, Caldbeck, Wigton CA7 8HQ
☎ (016974) 78409
300-acre mixed farm. Enjoy great comfort, fine food, beautiful surroundings and peaceful countryside on this working farm, central for touring or walking the rolling northern fells.
Bedrooms: 2 double, 2 triple
Bathrooms: 4 en-suite

Bed & breakfast per night:	£min	£max
Single	18.00	21.00
Double	34.00	40.00

Half board per person:	£min	£max
Daily	28.50	31.50
Weekly	199.50	220.50

Evening meal 1900 (last orders 1400)
Parking for 10

CARLISLE

Cumbria
Map ref 5A2

Cumbria's only city is rich in history. Attractions include the small red sandstone cathedral and 900-year-old castle with magnificent view from the keep. Award-winning Tullie House Museum and Art Gallery brings 2,000 years of Border history dramatically to life. Excellent centre for shopping.
Tourist Information Centre ☎ (01228) 512444

Beech Croft

COMMENDED

Aglionby, Carlisle CA4 8AQ
☎ (01228) 513762
Spacious, modern, detached house in a delightful rural setting. 1 mile on the A69 from M6 junction 43. High quality accommodation in a friendly family atmosphere.
Bedrooms: 1 single, 1 double, 1 twin
Bathrooms: 1 en-suite, 2 private

Bed & breakfast per night:	£min	£max
Single	20.00	20.00
Double	38.00	42.00

Parking for 4

Corner House Hotel and Bar

APPROVED

4 Grey Street, Off London Road, Carlisle CA1 2JP
☎ (01228) 33239
Fax (01228) 46628
Refurbished family-run hotel and bar. Short/long stay. All rooms en-suite. Four poster/family rooms available. Sky TV in lounge, games room, pool/darts. Easy access city attractions, bus, trains, golf, racing. M6 junctions 42/43.
Bedrooms: 3 single, 4 double, 2 twin, 1 triple
Bathrooms: 10 en-suite, 1 public

Bed & breakfast per night:	£min	£max
Single	25.00	30.00
Double	40.00	45.00

Half board per person:	£min	£max
Daily	33.00	38.00
Weekly	196.00	224.00

Lunch available
Evening meal 1730 (last orders 2030)
Cards accepted: Mastercard, Visa, Switch/Delta

The Gill Farm

COMMENDED

Blackford, Carlisle CA6 4EL
☎ (01228) 575326
124-acre arable & livestock farm. Ideal halfway stopping place or a good base for touring Cumbria's beauty spots. In peaceful countryside, 3 miles from M6 junction 44. From Carlisle go north to Blackford, fork right at sign for Longpark, Cliff and Scaleby, after 100 yards turn right, half a mile turn left, Gill Farm on left up this road.
Bedrooms: 1 double, 1 twin, 1 triple
Bathrooms: 2 public

Bed & breakfast per night:	£min	£max
Single	17.50	19.50
Double	33.00	35.00

Parking for 6

Metal Bridge House

COMMENDED

Metal Bridge, Rockcliffe, Carlisle CA6 4HG
☎ (0122874) 695

Just off A74 (Metal Bridge) 4 miles north of M6 junction 44 (Carlisle), large detached house adjacent to restaurant/bar. Country setting, comfortable and spacious rooms, friendly welcome.
Bedrooms: 1 double, 2 twin
Bathrooms: 1 public

Bed & breakfast per night:	£min	£max
Single	18.00	20.00
Double	28.00	32.00

Parking for 5

New Pallyards

COMMENDED

Hethersgill, Carlisle CA6 6HZ
☎ (01228) 577 308
Fax (01228) 577 308
65-acre mixed farm. Warmth and hospitality await you in this 18th C modernised farmhouse. Country setting, easily accessible from M6, A7, M74. En-suite rooms. National award winner.
Bedrooms: 1 double, 1 twin, 1 triple
Bathrooms: 3 en-suite, 1 public

Bed & breakfast per night:	£min	£max
Single	18.00	26.00

Continued ▶

CARLISLE

Continued

Half board per person:	£min	£max
Daily	28.00	35.00
Weekly	145.00	180.00

Evening meal 1900 (last orders 1930)
Parking for 7
Cards accepted: Mastercard, Visa

CONISTON

Cumbria
Map ref 5A3

The 803m fell Coniston Old Man dominates the skyline to the east of this village at the northern end of Coniston Water. Arthur Ransome set his "Swallows and Amazons" stories here. Coniston's most famous resident was John Ruskin, whose home, Brantwood, is open to the public. Good centre for walking.

Arrowfield Country Guest House

HIGHLY COMMENDED

Little Arrow, Coniston LA21 8AU
☎ (015394) 41741
Elegant Lakeland house in rural setting, offering quality accommodation. Immediate access to fells. Superb breakfasts, including home-made bread and preserves.
Bedrooms: 1 single, 3 double, 1 twin
Bathrooms: 5 en-suite, 1 public

Bed & breakfast per night:	£min	£max
Single	21.00	24.00
Double	42.00	48.00

Parking for 6
Open February–November

WELCOME HOST

This is a nationally recognised customer care programme which aims to promote the highest standards of service and a warm welcome. Establishments who are taking part in this initiative are indicated by the symbol.

Brigg House

HIGHLY COMMENDED

Torver, Coniston LA21 8AY
☎ (015394) 41592
Country house in beautiful setting at the foot of Coniston Old Man. All rooms en-suite. Varied breakfast menu. Non-smoking.
Bedrooms: 2 double, 1 twin
Bathrooms: 3 en-suite, 1 public

Bed & breakfast per night:	£min	£max
Double	40.00	42.00

Parking for 4
Open March–November
8

Church House Inn

COMMENDED

Torver, Coniston LA21 8AZ
☎ (015394) 41282
Delightful unspoilt 14th C inn in the beautiful Torver Valley. Bar food, restaurant, beer garden and large car park.
Bedrooms: 4 double, 1 twin, 1 triple
Bathrooms: 4 en-suite, 2 private, 1 public

Bed & breakfast per night:	£min	£max
Single	21.00	25.00
Double	45.00	

Half board per person:	£min	£max
Daily	31.00	
Weekly	210.00	

Lunch available
Evening meal 1815 (last orders 2130)
Parking for 60
Cards accepted: Amex, Diners, Mastercard, Visa, Switch/Delta
30

Crook Farm

Listed COMMENDED

Torver, Coniston LA21 8BP
☎ (015394) 41453
Farmhouse beautifully decorated and furnished to the highest standards. See your breakfast being cooked in the cosy Aga-warmed kitchen.
Bedrooms: 2 double, 1 triple
Bathrooms: 1 public

Bed & breakfast per night:	£min	£max
Single	17.00	17.00
Double	34.00	34.00

Parking for 6

Lakeland House

APPROVED

Tilberthwaite Avenue, Coniston LA21 8ED
☎ (015394) 41303
Friendly, family-run guesthouse in village location within easy reach of Lakes and fells. Also, daytime tea rooms and evening restaurant.
Bedrooms: 2 single, 2 double, 1 twin, 2 triple
Bathrooms: 3 en-suite, 2 public

Bed & breakfast per night:	£min	£max
Single	17.00	20.00
Double	32.00	46.00

Lunch available
Evening meal 1900 (last orders 2130)
Parking for 2
Cards accepted: Mastercard, Visa

Thwaite Cottage

COMMENDED

Waterhead, Coniston LA21 8AJ
☎ (015394) 41367
Beautiful 17th C cottage with oak beams and log fires, in secluded wooded garden near lake and village. Country club membership included.
Bedrooms: 2 double, 1 twin
Bathrooms: 1 en-suite, 2 private

Bed & breakfast per night:	£min	£max
Double	40.00	44.00

Parking for 3

Townson Ground

COMMENDED

East of Lake Road, Coniston LA21 8AA
☎ (015394) 41272

Fascinating 400-year-old farmhouse providing quality accommodation between Coniston and Hawkshead. Log fires. Private lake access.
Bedrooms: 1 single, 2 double, 2 triple
Bathrooms: 4 en-suite, 1 private, 1 public

Bed & breakfast per night:	£min	£max
Single	20.00	25.00
Double	40.00	52.00

Parking for 10
Cards accepted: Mastercard, Visa
3

CROSTHWAITE

Cumbria
Map ref 5A3

Small village in the picturesque Lyth Valley off the A5074. St Kentigern's church is home to a memorial to the poet Robert Southey. The valley itself is famous for its Damson plums.

The Punch Bowl Inn

COMMENDED

Crosthwaite, Kendal LA8 8HR
☎ (015395) 68237
Fax (015395) 68875

Coaching inn with bar food, choice of oak-beamed rooms, log fires. 3 bedrooms with private facilities and 4-poster beds. Adjacent to Crosthwaite Church in the Lyth Valley. 5 miles from Windermere and Kendal.

Bedrooms: 3 double
Bathrooms: 3 en-suite

Bed & breakfast per night:	£min	£max
Single	35.00	35.00
Double	50.00	50.00

Lunch available
Evening meal 1800 (last orders 2100)
Parking for 25
Cards accepted: Mastercard, Visa, Switch/Delta

DENT

Cumbria
Map ref 5B3

Very picturesque village with narrow cobbled streets, lying within the boundaries of the Yorkshire Dales National Park.

The Old Vicarage

HIGHLY COMMENDED

Flintergill, Dent, Sedbergh LA10 5QR
☎ (01539) 625366

The house is a Victorian vicarage with large well proportioned rooms, sympathetically modernised. Village centre site, good for walking and cycling.

Bedrooms: 1 double, 1 twin, 1 triple
Bathrooms: 2 en-suite, 1 public

Bed & breakfast per night:	£min	£max
Single	16.00	18.00
Double	28.00	36.00

Parking for 4
Open March–October

Sun Inn

Listed COMMENDED

Main Street, Dent, Sedbergh LA10 5QL
☎ (01539) 625208

17th C inn with original beams, in an outstanding conservation area. Reputation for good value bar meals and serves beer from the local Dent Brewery.

Bedrooms: 2 double, 1 twin, 1 triple
Bathrooms: 1 public

Bed & breakfast per night:	£min	£max
Single	18.00	18.00
Double	36.00	36.00

Lunch available
Evening meal 1830 (last orders 2030)
Parking for 20
Cards accepted: Mastercard, Visa, Switch/Delta

ESKDALE

Cumbria
Map ref 5A3

Several minor roads lead to the west end of this beautiful valley, or it can be approached via the east over the Hardknott Pass, the Lake District's steepest pass. Scafell Pike and Bow Fell lie to the north and a miniature railway links the Eskdale Valley with Ravenglass on the coast.

Woolpack Inn

APPROVED

Boot, Eskdale CA19 1TH
☎ (01946) 723230
Fax (01946) 723230

Comfortable hotel serving real ale and home-cooked food, set in beautiful scenery at the head of the Eskdale Valley.

Bedrooms: 3 double, 4 twin, 1 family room
Bathrooms: 1 public, 4 private showers

Bed & breakfast per night:	£min	£max
Single	19.50	27.00
Double	39.00	54.00

Lunch available
Evening meal 1800 (last orders 2100)
Parking for 40
Cards accepted: Mastercard, Visa

GARRIGILL

Cumbria
Map ref 5B2

Old lead-mining village high in the Pennines. Nearby attractions include the 50-foot Ash Hill Force waterfall and the heritage centre at Killhope which details the history of lead mining in the area.

Ivy Farmhouse

Listed COMMENDED

Garrigill, Alston CA9 3DU
☎ (01434) 382501
Fax (01434) 382501
Email: 100125,2716 @compuserve.com

Historic village farmhouse high in North Pennines. Located on the Pennine Way and Coast to Coast Cycleway. Ideal for birdwatching, walking, cycling.

Bedrooms: 1 double, 2 twin
Bathrooms: 2 en-suite, 1 public

Bed & breakfast per night:	£min	£max
Single	15.00	20.00
Double	30.00	40.00

Half board per person:	£min	£max
Daily	25.00	30.00
Weekly	160.00	195.00

Evening meal 1800 (last orders 1900)
Parking for 10

For further information on accommodation establishments use the coupons at the back of this guide.

Information on accommodation listed in this guide has been supplied by the proprietors. As changes may occur you are advised to check details at the time of booking.

GRASMERE

Cumbria
Map ref 5A3

Described by William Wordsworth as "the loveliest spot that man hath ever found", this village, famous for its gingerbread, is in a beautiful setting overlooked by Helm Grag. Wordsworth lived at Dove Cottage. The cottage and museum are open to the public.

Beck Allans

Listed HIGHLY COMMENDED

College Street, Grasmere LA22 9SZ
☎ (015394) 35563
Fax (015394) 35563

Lakeland guesthouse hidden in the delightful well timbered grounds of Beck Allans Holiday Apartments. Centre of village, adjacent River Rothay, super views. Accommodation also includes 2-bedroom family suite. Aga-cooked breakfasts, Sky movies, swimming pool, jacuzzi.

Bedrooms: 5 double
Bathrooms: 5 en-suite

Bed & breakfast per night:	£min	£max
Single	21.50	26.00
Double	43.00	52.00

Parking for 15
Open January–November
Cards accepted: Mastercard, Visa, Switch/Delta

Craigside House

COMMENDED

Grasmere, Ambleside LA22 9SG
☎ (015394) 35292

Delightfully furnished Victorian house on the edge of the village near Dove Cottage. In a large, peaceful garden overlooking the lake and hills.

Bedrooms: 2 double, 1 twin
Bathrooms: 3 en-suite

Bed & breakfast per night:	£min	£max
Single	30.00	55.00
Double	60.00	64.00

Parking for 6

The symbols in each entry give information about services and facilities. A key to these symbols appears at the back of this guide.

Dunmail House

COMMENDED

Keswick Road, Grasmere, Ambleside LA22 9RE
☎ (015394) 35256

Traditional stone house in lovely grounds, with friendly family atmosphere and beautiful views from all rooms.

Bedrooms: 1 single, 1 double, 1 twin, 1 triple
Bathrooms: 2 en-suite, 1 public

Bed & breakfast per night:	£min	£max
Single	18.50	33.50
Double	35.00	47.00

Parking for 6

Redmayne

HIGHLY COMMENDED

Grasmere LA22 9QY
☎ (015394) 35635

Superb elevated private situation. Magnificent panoramic views. Comfortable, beautifully appointed en-suite rooms with colour TV, tea/coffee facilities. Non-smoking. Private parking.

Bedrooms: 2 double
Bathrooms: 2 en-suite

Bed & breakfast per night:	£min	£max
Double	38.00	50.00

Parking for 2
Open February–November

Travellers Rest

COMMENDED

Grasmere, Ambleside LA22 9RR
☎ (015394) 35604

Charming 16th C inn nestling in the heart of Lakeland and with superb views. Cumbrian hospitality includes good food, real ales, open fires and comfortable accommodation.

Bedrooms: 5 double, 3 twin
Bathrooms: 4 en-suite, 2 public

Bed & breakfast per night:	£min	£max
Single	18.95	29.95
Double	39.90	59.90

Half board per person:	£min	£max
Weekly	132.65	279.30

Lunch available
Evening meal 1900 (last orders 2130)
Parking for 45
Cards accepted: Mastercard, Visa, Switch/Delta

Woodland Crag Guest House

HIGHLY COMMENDED

Howe Head Lane, Grasmere, Ambleside LA22 9SG
☎ (015394) 35351

Charming Victorian Lakeland-stone house with lake and fell views. Beautiful walks radiate from here. Peacefully situated in landscaped grounds on edge of village. No smoking, please.

Bedrooms: 2 single, 2 double, 1 twin
Bathrooms: 3 en-suite, 1 public

Bed & breakfast per night:	£min	£max
Single	24.00	26.00
Double	52.00	56.00

Parking for 5

GRAYRIGG

Cumbria
Map ref 5B3

Village on the A685 north of Kendal. Important in the development of the Quaker church.

Grayrigg Hall Farm

Listed COMMENDED

Grayrigg, Kendal LA8 9BU
☎ (01539) 824689

1400-acre mixed farm. 18th C working farm in beautiful open countryside. Easy access to Lakes and dales. Good home cooking and a friendly welcome.

Bedrooms: 1 double, 1 triple
Bathrooms: 1 public

Bed & breakfast per night:	£min	£max
Single	15.00	16.00
Double	30.00	32.00

Half board per person:	£min	£max
Daily	22.00	23.00

Evening meal 2000 (last orders 2100)
Parking for 2
Open March–October

HAWKSHEAD

Cumbria
Map ref 5A3

Lying near Esthwaite Water, this village has great charm and character. Its small squares are linked by flagged or cobbled alleys and the main square is dominated by the market house, or Shambles, where the butchers had their stalls in days gone by.

The Drunken Duck Inn

HIGHLY COMMENDED

Barngates, Ambleside LA22 0NG
☎ (015394) 36347
Fax (015394) 36781

An old-fashioned inn amidst magnificent scenery. Oak-beamed bars, cosy log fires and charming bedrooms. Good food and beers.
Bedrooms: 8 double, 1 twin
Bathrooms: 9 en-suite

Bed & breakfast per night:	£min	£max
Single	42.50	55.00
Double	65.00	85.00

Lunch available
Evening meal 1830 (last orders 2100)
Parking for 60
Cards accepted: Amex, Mastercard, Visa, Switch/Delta

All accommodation in this guide has been graded, or is awaiting a grading, by a trained Tourist Board inspector.

The Sun Inn

COMMENDED

Hawkshead, Ambleside LA22 0NT
☎ (015394) 36352
Fax (015394) 36674
16th C inn with original beams. A family-run business with friendly atmosphere, good food and wine. Very good value for money, families welcome.
Bedrooms: 6 double, 2 twin
Bathrooms: 8 en-suite

Bed & breakfast per night:	£min	£max
Single	35.00	45.00
Double	56.00	65.00

Lunch available
Evening meal 1800 (last orders 2130)
Parking for 8
Cards accepted: Amex, Mastercard, Visa, Switch/Delta

KENDAL

Cumbria
Map ref 5B3

The "Auld Grey Town" lies in the valley of the River Kent with a backcloth of limestone fells. Situated just outside the Lake District National Park, it is a good centre for touring the Lakes and surrounding country. Ruined castle, reputed birthplace of Catherine Parr.
Tourist Information Centre ☎ (01539) 725758

Garnett House Farm

COMMENDED

Burneside, Kendal LA9 5SF
☎ (01539) 724542
270-acre mixed farm. 15th C farmhouse set in lovely countryside 10 minutes from Windermere. Some en-suite rooms. Oak panelling, 4 ft thick walls. 3-night breaks November-March.
Bedrooms: 1 double, 1 twin, 1 triple, 2 family rooms
Bathrooms: 5 en-suite, 2 public

Bed & breakfast per night:	£min	£max
Double	32.00	40.00

Half board per person:	£min	£max
Daily	25.00	29.00

Evening meal 1830 (last orders 1730)
Parking for 6

Gateside Farm

Listed COMMENDED

Windermere Road, Kendal LA9 5SE
☎ (01539) 722036

300-acre dairy & livestock farm. Traditional Lakeland farm easily accessible from the motorway and on the main tourist route through Lakeland. One night and short stays are welcome.
Bedrooms: 3 double, 1 twin, 1 family room
Bathrooms: 2 private, 2 public

Bed & breakfast per night:	£min	£max
Single	18.00	22.00
Double	34.00	40.00

Half board per person:	£min	£max
Daily	24.00	28.00

Evening meal (last orders 1700)
Parking for 7

Holmfield

Listed DE LUXE

41 Kendal Green, Kendal LA9 5PP
☎ (01539) 720790
Fax (01539) 720790
Superb location. Elegant Edwardian house in large gardens. Panoramic views, swimming pool, croquet. Spacious bathrooms, lovely bedrooms, including four-poster. No smoking.
Bedrooms: 2 double, 1 twin
Bathrooms: 1 private, 2 public

Bed & breakfast per night:	£min	£max
Single	25.00	30.00
Double	40.00	46.00

Parking for 7

The map references refer to the colour maps towards the end of the guide. The first figure is the map number; the letter and figure which follow indicate the grid reference on the map.

KENDAL

Continued

Newalls Farmhouse

COMMENDED

Skelsmergh, Kendal LA9 6NU
☎ (01539) 723202

500-acre dairy farm. Tastefully modernised farmhouse, with visitors' own private entrance into a large garden. Pubs and restaurants within 2 miles. Warm welcome assured.

Bedrooms: 2 double
Bathrooms: 1 en-suite, 1 private

Bed & breakfast per night:	£min	£max
Single	18.00	
Double	32.00	

Parking for 2
Open April–October
3

Sonata

Listed COMMENDED

19 Burneside Road, Kendal LA9 4RL
☎ (01539) 732290

Three-storey house within easy walking distance of town centre. Located off Windermere Road, Kendal.

Bedrooms: 1 single, 2 double, 1 twin, 1 triple
Bathrooms: 2 en-suite, 2 private, 1 public

Bed & breakfast per night:	£min	£max
Single	16.50	19.00
Double	33.00	38.00

Half board per person:	£min	£max
Daily	24.00	27.50
Weekly	150.00	180.00

Lunch available
Evening meal 1830 (last orders 2000)
Cards accepted: Mastercard, Visa
SP

7 Thorny Hills

COMMENDED

Kendal LA9 7AL
☎ (01539) 720207

Beautiful, unspoilt Georgian town house. Peaceful, pretty location close to town centre. Good home cooking. Self-catering available. Non-smokers only, please.

Bedrooms: 2 double, 1 twin
Bathrooms: 3 private

Bed & breakfast per night:	£min	£max
Single	22.00	22.00
Double	38.00	38.00

Half board per person:	£min	£max
Daily	47.00	47.00

Evening meal from 1800
Parking for 3
Open January–November

KESWICK

Cumbria
Map ref 5A3

Beautifully positioned town beside Derwentwater and below the mountains of Skiddaw and Blencathra. Excellent base for walking, climbing, watersports and touring. Motor-launches operate on Derwentwater and motor boats, rowing boats and canoes can be hired.

Tourist Information Centre
☎ (017687) 72645

Acorn House Hotel

HIGHLY COMMENDED

Ambleside Road, Keswick CA12 4DL
☎ (017687) 72553
Fax (017687) 75332

Elegant Georgian house set in colourful garden. All bedrooms tastefully furnished, some four-poster beds. Cleanliness guaranteed. Close to town centre. Good off-street parking.

Bedrooms: 6 double, 1 twin, 3 triple
Bathrooms: 9 en-suite, 1 private

Bed & breakfast per night:	£min	£max
Single	27.50	40.00
Double	50.00	60.00

Parking for 10
Open February–November
Cards accepted: Mastercard, Visa
6

Anworth House

Listed COMMENDED

27 Eskin Street, Keswick CA12 4DQ
☎ (017687) 72923

Small, friendly, guesthouse. All rooms en-suite. In quiet situation, yet close to town centre, leisure pool, parks and lake.

Bedrooms: 1 single, 2 double, 2 triple
Bathrooms: 5 en-suite

Bed & breakfast per night:	£min	£max
Single	21.00	21.00
Double	40.00	50.00

SP

Badgers Wood

Listed COMMENDED

30 Stanger Street, Keswick CA12 5JU
☎ (017687) 72621

Spacious, comfortable Victorian house. All bedrooms have mountain views, most have own toilet. Quiet, elevated location, close to town centre.

Bedrooms: 1 single, 3 double, 2 triple
Bathrooms: 2 en-suite, 1 public

Bed & breakfast per night:	£min	£max
Single	16.50	16.50
Double	33.00	40.00

Open February–June, August–November
5

Beckside

COMMENDED

5 Wordsworth Street, Keswick CA12 4HU
☎ (017687) 73093

Friendly guesthouse offering clean, tastefully decorated en-suite accommodation. Excellent breakfasts and optional evening meal. Close to all amenities.

Bedrooms: 3 double, 1 twin
Bathrooms: 4 en-suite

Bed & breakfast per night:	£min	£max
Single	15.00	18.50
Double	30.00	37.00

Half board per person:	£min	£max
Daily	25.00	29.50
Weekly	175.00	190.00

Evening meal 1800 (last orders 1300)
SP

Birkrigg Farm

Listed APPROVED

Newlands, Keswick CA12 5TS
☎ (017687) 78278

250-acre mixed farm. Pleasantly and peacefully located in the lovely Newlands Valley, amongst beautiful mountain scenery. 5 miles from Keswick, between Braithwaite and Buttermere.

Bedrooms: 1 single, 2 double, 1 twin, 1 triple, 1 family room
Bathrooms: 2 public

Bed & breakfast per night:	£min	£max
Single	15.00	17.00
Double	30.00	34.00

Parking for 6
Open March–November
SP

Kings Head Hotel

APPROVED

Thirlspot, Keswick CA12 4TN
☎ (017687) 72393
Fax (017687) 72309

Situated at the foot of Helvellyn on the main A591, approximately 5 miles south of Keswick. This 17th C former coaching inn is family-run and offers a wide range of real ales and wines, with good food and comfortable accommodation.

Bedrooms: 3 single, 8 double, 3 twin, 2 triple, 1 family room
Bathrooms: 17 en-suite, 1 public

Bed & breakfast per night:	£min	£max
Single	19.95	32.95
Double	39.90	65.90

Half board per person:	£min	£max
Daily	39.95	45.95
Weekly	239.70	275.70

Lunch available
Evening meal 1800 (last orders 2130)
Parking for 60
Cards accepted: Mastercard, Visa, Switch/Delta

Littletown Farm

COMMENDED

Newlands, Keswick CA12 5TU
☎ (017687) 78353

150-acre mixed farm. In the beautiful, unspoilt Newlands Valley. En-suite bedrooms. Comfortable residents' lounge, dining room and cosy bar. Traditional 4-course dinner 6 nights a week.

Bedrooms: 1 single, 4 double, 2 twin, 1 triple, 1 family room
Bathrooms: 6 en-suite, 1 public

Bed & breakfast per night:	£min	£max
Single	24.00	30.00
Double	48.00	56.00

Half board per person:	£min	£max
Daily	36.00	40.00
Weekly	220.00	250.00

Evening meal from 1900
Parking for 10
Open March–December
Cards accepted: Mastercard, Visa

Lonnin Garth Country Guesthouse

COMMENDED

Portinscale, Keswick CA12 5RS
☎ (017687) 74095

Country house set in own grounds overlooking the northern fells, with lovely views. A friendly base for walking, touring and relaxing.

Bedrooms: 3 double, 2 twin
Bathrooms: 5 en-suite

Bed & breakfast per night:	£min	£max
Double	41.00	44.00

Parking for 6

Lynwood House

COMMENDED

35 Helvellyn Street, Keswick
CA12 4EP
☎ (017687) 72398

Non-smoking, Victorian, licensed guesthouse, 5 minutes from town centre. Comfortable lounge, colour TV in each room, own key. Genuine home cooking.

Bedrooms: 1 single, 2 double, 1 triple
Suite available
Bathrooms: 1 en-suite, 1 public

Bed & breakfast per night:	£min	£max
Single	15.00	15.50
Double	30.00	38.00

Half board per person:	£min	£max
Daily	24.50	28.50
Weekly	162.00	189.00

Evening meal 1830 (last orders 1930)

Please mention this guide when making your booking.

Ravensworth Hotel

HIGHLY COMMENDED

29 Station Street, Keswick
CA12 5HH
☎ (017687) 72476

Non-smoking family-run licensed hotel, decorated to a high standard of comfort, situated close to Keswick's amenities. An ideal Lake District base.

Bedrooms: 7 double, 1 twin
Bathrooms: 7 en-suite, 1 private

Bed & breakfast per night:	£min	£max
Double	32.00	50.00

Parking for 5
Open February–November and Christmas
Cards accepted: Mastercard, Visa

Richmond House

APPROVED

37-39 Eskin Street, Keswick
CA12 4DG
☎ (017687) 73965

Family-run guesthouse, home-from-home, easy walking distance to town centre and lake. Vegetarians catered for. Non-smokers only, please.

Bedrooms: 3 single, 4 double, 1 twin, 1 triple
Bathrooms: 8 en-suite, 1 public

Bed & breakfast per night:	£min	£max
Single	15.00	22.00
Double	36.00	40.00

Half board per person:	£min	£max
Daily	24.50	31.00
Weekly	165.00	190.00

Evening meal 1900 (last orders 1700)
Cards accepted: Amex, Mastercard, Visa

Swan Hotel and Country Inn

APPROVED

Thornthwaite, Keswick CA12 5SQ
☎ (01768) 78256

Set amidst magnificent Lakeland scenery, in a quiet, elevated position overlooking Skiddaw and the Derwent Valley.

Bedrooms: 5 double, 4 twin, 2 triple, 1 family room
Bathrooms: 12 en-suite, 2 public

Bed & breakfast per night:	£min	£max
Single	20.00	
Double	25.00	

Continued ▶

KESWICK

Continued

Half board per person:	£min	£max
Daily	40.00	
Weekly	270.00	

Lunch available
Evening meal (last orders 2200)
Parking for 30
Open February–December
Cards accepted: Mastercard, Visa

Watendlath Guest House

Listed COMMENDED

15 Acorn Street, Keswick
CA12 4EA
☎ (017687) 74165

Within easy walking distance of the lake, hills and town centre. We offer a warm and friendly welcome and traditional English breakfast.

Bedrooms: 4 double, 1 twin
Bathrooms: 2 en-suite, 1 public

Bed & breakfast per night:	£min	£max
Double	30.00	38.00

Open February–December

Whitehouse Guest House

COMMENDED

15 Ambleside Road, Keswick
CA12 4DL
☎ (017687) 73176

Fully refurbished, small, friendly guesthouse 5 minutes' walk from the town centre. Colour TV, electric blankets, tea/coffee. Most rooms with en-suite facilities.

Bedrooms: 4 double
Bathrooms: 3 private, 1 public, 1 private shower

Bed & breakfast per night:	£min	£max
Double	32.00	38.00

Parking for 3
Open March–October

You are advised to confirm your booking in writing.

For ideas on places to visit refer to the introduction at the beginning of this section.

KIRKBY LONSDALE

Cumbria
Map ref 5B3

Charming old town of narrow streets and Georgian buildings, set in the superb scenery of the Lune Valley. The Devil's Bridge over the River Lune is probably 13th C.
Tourist Information Centre
☎ (015242) 71437

Fowlstone

Listed COMMENDED

Lupton, Carnforth, Lancashire
LA6 2PP
☎ (015395) 67238
Fax (015395) 67238

250-acre mixed farm. Large farmhouse c 1665, originally an old coaching inn. Five minutes from junction 36 on M6 towards Kirkby Lonsdale on A65.

Bedrooms: 1 double, 2 twin
Bathrooms: 1 public

Bed & breakfast per night:	£min	£max
Single	17.50	22.00
Double	35.00	44.00

Parking for 12

KIRKBY-IN-FURNESS

Cumbria
Map ref 5A3

Commercial Inn

APPROVED

Askew Gate Brow,
Kirkby-in-Furness LA17 7TE
☎ (01229) 889039

En-suite accommodation with own entrance, adjoining 200-year-old licensed freehouse. Situated south of the Lake District, 12 miles from Coniston, 20 miles from Windermere.

Bedrooms: 2 double
Bathrooms: 2 en-suite

Bed & breakfast per night:	£min	£max
Single	23.50	25.00
Double	35.00	40.00

Evening meal 1800 (last orders 2000)
Parking for 8

Half board prices are given per person, but in some cases these may be based on double/twin occupancy.

LAMPLUGH

Cumbria
Map ref 5A3

Near the A5086 between Cockermouth and Cleator Moor, Lamplugh is a scattered village famous for its "Lamplugh Pudding". Ideal touring base for the western Lake District.

Briscoe Close Farm

Listed COMMENDED

Scalesmoor, Lamplugh, Workington
CA14 4TZ
☎ (01946) 861633

Bungalow close to family-run farm. Near Loweswater and Ennerdale, half a mile from A5086. Home cooking using produce grown on farm.

Bedrooms: 1 double, 1 triple
Bathrooms: 1 public

Bed & breakfast per night:	£min	£max
Single	16.00	17.00
Double	32.00	34.00

Half board per person:	£min	£max
Daily	24.00	25.00
Weekly	150.00	150.00

Evening meal from 1900
Parking for 2

LANGDALE

Cumbria
Map ref 5A3

The two Langdale valleys (Great Langdale and Little Langdale) lie in the heart of beautiful mountain scenery. The craggy Langdale Pikes are almost 2500 ft high. An ideal walking and climbing area and base for touring.

Britannia Inn

COMMENDED

Elterwater, Ambleside LA22 9HP
☎ (015394) 37210
Fax (015394) 37311

A 400-year-old traditional Lake District inn on a village green in the beautiful Langdale Valley. Cosy bars with log fires, home-cooked food and real ales. Very well-appointed accommodation.

Bedrooms: 1 single, 9 double, 3 twin

Bathrooms: 9 en-suite, 1 private, 1 public

Bed & breakfast per night:	£min	£max
Single	19.00	24.00
Double	38.00	62.00

Lunch available
Evening meal 1830 (last orders 2130)
Parking for 7
Cards accepted: Amex, Mastercard, Visa, Switch/Delta

LAZONBY

Cumbria
Map ref 5B2

Busy, working village of stone cottages, set beside the River Eden amid sweeping pastoral landscape. Good fishing available.

Banktop House

COMMENDED

Lazonby, Penrith CA10 1AQ
☎ (01768) 898268
Fax (017668) 898851

Listed house in garden and cobbled courtyard setting. Ideal for Eden Valley walks and attractions, central Ullswater, Pennines and Scottish borders.

Bedrooms: 1 double, 1 twin
Bathrooms: 1 en-suite, 1 private

Bed & breakfast per night:	£min	£max
Single	20.00	25.00
Double	32.00	38.00

Parking for 3
Open March–October

LONGTOWN

Cumbria
Map ref 5A2

Perfect base from which to explore the magnificent Borderlands, lying adjacent to the site of the Battle of Solway Moss fought in 1542 between the English and the Scots. Handsome bridge and England's largest sheep market.
Tourist Information Centre ☎ (01228) 791876

Briar Lea House

Listed COMMENDED

Brampton Road, Longtown, Carlisle CA6 5TN
☎ (01228) 791538
Fax (01228) 791538

Substantial country house in 1.75 acres, with pool. Easy access M6, A74, A7. Carlisle, North Lakes and Scotland await.

Bedrooms: 1 double, 1 family room
Bathrooms: 2 en-suite

Bed & breakfast per night:	£min	£max
Single	19.50	21.50
Double	39.00	43.00

Parking for 14

Craigburn

COMMENDED

Penton, Longtown, Carlisle CA6 5QP
☎ (01228) 577214
Fax (01228) 577214

250-acre mixed farm. One of the best farmhouses for delicious food. Beautiful bedrooms, some four-poster beds. Easily accessible from M6, A7 and M74.

Bedrooms: 4 double, 3 twin, 1 triple
Bathrooms: 8 en-suite

Bed & breakfast per night:	£min	£max
Single	26.00	28.00
Double	42.00	44.00

Half board per person:	£min	£max
Daily	38.00	40.00
Weekly	194.00	208.00

Evening meal 1800 (last orders 1400)
Parking for 20
Cards accepted: Mastercard, Visa

LOWESWATER

Cumbria
Map ref 5A3

Scattered village lying between Loweswater, one of the smaller lakes, and Crummock Water. Mountains surround this quiet valley of three lakes, giving some marvellous views.

Brook Farm

COMMENDED

Thackthwaite, Loweswater, Cockermouth CA13 0RP
☎ (01900) 85606
Fax (01900) 85606

300-acre hill farm. In quiet surroundings and a good walking area, 5 miles from Cockermouth. Carrying sheep and suckler cows.

Bedrooms: 1 double, 1 triple
Bathrooms: 1 public

Bed & breakfast per night:	£min	£max
Single	18.00	20.00
Double	36.00	40.00

Half board per person:	£min	£max
Daily	26.00	28.00
Weekly	175.00	

Evening meal from 1900
Parking for 3
Open May–October

Kirkstile Inn

Listed COMMENDED

Loweswater, Cockermouth CA13 0RU
☎ (0190085) 219

16th C inn near an oak-fringed beck running between Loweswater and Crummock Water lakes, surrounded by fells.

Bedrooms: 5 double, 2 twin, 3 triple
Bathrooms: 8 private, 2 public

Bed & breakfast per night:	£min	£max
Double	45.00	60.00

Lunch available
Evening meal 1830 (last orders 2100)
Parking for 40
Cards accepted: Mastercard, Visa

ORTON

Cumbria
Map ref 5B3

Small, attractive village with the background of Orton Scar, it has some old buildings and a spacious green. George Whitehead, the itinerant Quaker preacher, was born here in 1636.

Vicarage

Listed COMMENDED

Orton, Penrith CA10 3RQ
☎ (015396) 24873
Fax (015396) 24873

Warm, comfortable accommodation in a working vicarage overlooking rooftops and fells. Ideal for walkers visiting the Lakes and Yorkshire Dales. M6 junction 38.

Bedrooms: 1 double, 2 twin
Bathrooms: 1 public

Bed & breakfast per night:	£min	£max
Double		34.00

Continued ▶

ORTON
Continued

Half board per person:	£min	£max
Daily		27.00

Evening meal 1900 (last orders 2100)
Parking for 2

PENRITH

Cumbria
Map ref 5B2

Ancient and historic market town, the northern gateway to the Lake District. Penrith Castle was built as a defence against the Scots. Its ruins, open to the public, stand in the public park. High above the town is the Penrith Beacon, made famous by William Wordsworth.
Tourist Information Centre ☎ (01768) 867466

Glendale

Listed COMMENDED

4 Portland Place, Penrith
CA11 7QN
☎ (01768) 862579
Victorian town house overlooking pleasant gardens. Spacious family rooms. Children and pets welcome. Special diets catered for on request.
Bedrooms: 1 single, 1 double, 3 triple
Bathrooms: 1 public

Bed & breakfast per night:	£min	£max
Single	17.00	20.00
Double	30.00	34.00

Parking for 1

Hornby Hall Country House Hotel

Listed HIGHLY COMMENDED

Hornby Hall, Brougham, Penrith
CA10 2AR
☎ (01768) 891114
Fax (01768) 891114

16th C farmhouse with original dining hall. Fishing on Eamont available. Easy reach of Lakes and Yorkshire Dales. Home-cooked local produce.
Bedrooms: 1 single, 2 double, 4 twin
Bathrooms: 2 en-suite, 3 public

Bed & breakfast per night:	£min	£max
Single	22.50	27.50
Double	50.00	65.00

Half board per person:	£min	£max
Daily	35.00	45.00

Evening meal 1900 (last orders 2100)
Parking for 10
Cards accepted: Mastercard, Visa

Newton Rigg College

Listed APPROVED

Penrith CA11 0AH
☎ (01768) 863791
Fax (01768) 867249
Email: resmll@newtonrigg.ac.uk
College in beautiful setting with standard and en-suite accommodation. Bar, dining room, shop, sporting facilities. Self-catering also available.
Wheelchair access category 2
Bedrooms: 8 single, 4 twin
Bathrooms: 12 en-suite

Bed & breakfast per night:	£min	£max
Single	15.00	20.00
Double	28.00	36.00

Half board per person:	£min	£max
Daily	22.00	27.00
Weekly	130.00	160.00

Lunch available
Evening meal 1800 (last orders 1930)
Parking for 300
Open June–August and Christmas

Old Victoria Hotel

APPROVED

46 Castlegate, Penrith CA11 7HY
☎ (01768) 862467
Fax (01768) 890438
Family-run hotel with public bar. Bar lunches and evening meals with home-cooked specialities. Your hosts are Roy and Christine Bacon.
Bedrooms: 1 single, 4 double, 2 twin
Bathrooms: 2 en-suite, 1 public, 5 private showers

Bed & breakfast per night:	£min	£max
Single	25.00	30.00
Double	44.00	50.00

Half board per person:	£min	£max
Daily	30.00	35.00

Lunch available
Evening meal 1900 (last orders 2030)
Parking for 12

ST BEES

Cumbria
Map ref 5A3

Small seaside village with fine Norman church and a public school founded in the 16th C. Dramatic red sandstone cliffs make up impressive St Bees Head, parts of which are RSPB reserves and home to puffins and black guillemot. Start or finishing point of Wainwright's Coast to Coast Walk.

Stonehouse Farm

Listed APPROVED

Main Street, Next to Railway Station, St Bees CA27 0DE
☎ (01946) 822 224
50-acre livestock farm. Modernised Georgian listed farmhouse, conveniently and attractively situated next to station, shops and hotels. Start of Coast-to-Coast Walk. Golf-course, long-stay car park.
Bedrooms: 3 double, 2 twin, 1 family room
Bathrooms: 1 en-suite, 2 public

Bed & breakfast per night:	£min	£max
Single	19.00	21.00
Double	32.00	38.00

Parking for 8

SCOTBY

Cumbria
Map ref 5A2

Oakleigh Bed and Breakfast

Listed COMMENDED

10 Broomfallen Road, Scotby, Carlisle CA4 8DB
☎ (01228) 513993
Detached Victorian house with 1 acre of garden, situated in quiet village.
Bedrooms: 1 double, 1 twin
Bathrooms: 1 en-suite, 1 public

Bed & breakfast per night:	£min	£max
Single	22.00	34.00
Double	26.00	45.00

Evening meal 1900 (last orders 2000)
Parking for 3

SEDBERGH

Cumbria
Map ref 5B3

This busy market town set below the Howgill Fells is an excellent centre for walkers and touring the Dales and Howgills. The noted boys' school was founded in 1525.

The Moss House

COMMENDED

Garsdale Road, Sedbergh LA10 5JL
☎ (015396) 20940

Large Georgian house set in half an acre of lovely garden. Quarter-of-a-mile outside Sedbergh on Hawes to Garsdale road.
Bedrooms: 2 double, 1 twin
Bathrooms: 1 private, 2 public

Bed & breakfast per night:	£min	£max
Single	25.00	
Double	37.00	44.00

Half board per person:	£min	£max
Daily	28.50	35.00
Weekly	199.50	245.00

Evening meal 1800 (last orders 2000)
Parking for 6
Open March–November

STAVELEY

Cumbria
Map ref 5A3

Large village built in slate, set between Kendal and Windermere at the entrance to the lovely Kentmere Valley.

Stock Bridge Farm

Listed COMMENDED

Kendal Road, Staveley, Kendal LA8 9LP
☎ (01539) 821580
20-acre mixed farm. Comfortable, well-appointed 17th C farmhouse on edge of bypassed village midway between Kendal and Windermere on A591. Central heating. English breakfast. Friendly, personal attention.
Bedrooms: 1 single, 4 double, 1 triple
Bathrooms: 1 public

Bed & breakfast per night:	£min	£max
Single	15.00	16.00
Double	30.00	32.00

Parking for 6
Open March–October

TEBAY

Cumbria
Map ref 5B3

Village lying amongst high fells at the north end of the Lune Gorge.

Primrose Cottage

Listed COMMENDED

Orton Road, Tebay, Penrith CA10 3TL
☎ (015396) 24791
Approximately 50 yards from M6, junction 38. Overnight stops/short breaks, excellent facilities. Close to Lakes and Yorkshire Dales.
Bedrooms: 2 double, 1 twin
Bathrooms: 1 private, 1 public

Bed & breakfast per night:	£min	£max
Single	18.00	25.00
Double	35.00	42.00

Half board per person:	£min	£max
Daily	27.50	31.50

Lunch available
Parking for 6

THRELKELD

Cumbria
Map ref 5A3

This village is a centre for climbing the Saddleback range of mountains, which tower high above it.

Scales Farm Country Guesthouse

HIGHLY COMMENDED

Scales, Threlkeld, Keswick CA12 4SY
☎ (017687) 79660
Fax (017687) 79660

Tastefully modernised 17th C farmhouse by Blencathra, convenient for Keswick and M6. Well appointed en-suite bedrooms and snug guest lounge with wood burning stove. Warm friendly welcome by proprietors. Private parking.
Bedrooms: 3 double, 1 twin, 1 family room
Bathrooms: 5 en-suite

Bed & breakfast per night:	£min	£max
Single	26.00	28.00
Double	43.00	45.00

Parking for 6

TROUTBECK

Cumbria
Map ref 5A2

On the Penrith to Keswick road, Troutbeck was the site of a series of Roman camps. The village now hosts a busy weekly sheep market.

Lane Head Farm Guest House

COMMENDED

Troutbeck, Penrith CA11 0SY
☎ (017687) 79220
Charming 17th C former farmhouse in quiet location, 4 miles from Ullswater lake. Good home cooking, table licence. Log fire, some en-suite and four-poster rooms.
Bedrooms: 1 single, 5 double, 2 twin, 1 family room
Bathrooms: 5 en-suite, 1 public

Bed & breakfast per night:	£min	£max
Single	18.00	25.00
Double	36.00	50.00

Half board per person:	£min	£max
Daily	27.00	34.00
Weekly	189.00	238.00

Evening meal 1700 (last orders 1900)
Parking for 10
Open April–December

Please check prices and other details at the time of booking.

The National Grading and Classification Scheme is explained at the back of this guide.

TROUTBECK

Cumbria
Map ref 5A3

Most of the houses in this picturesque village are 17th C, some retain their spinning galleries and oak-mullioned windows. At the south end of the village is Townend, owned by the National Trust and open to the public, an excellently preserved example of a yeoman farmer's or statesman's house.

High Fold Farm

COMMENDED

Troutbeck, Windermere LA23 1PG
☎ (015394) 32200
Unbeatable views over the Troutbeck Valley. Well furnished, comfortable accommodation of a high standard. Excellent breakfasts.
Bedrooms: 2 double, 3 triple
Bathrooms: 3 en-suite, 1 public

Bed & breakfast per night:	£min	£max
Single	17.00	22.00
Double	34.00	44.00

Parking for 10
Cards accepted: Visa

ULLSWATER

Cumbria
Map ref 5A3

This beautiful lake, which is over 7 miles long, runs from Glenridding to Pooley Bridge. Lofty peaks ranging around the lake make an impressive background. A steamer service operates along the lake between Pooley Bridge, Howtown and Glenridding in the summer.

Bank House Farm

HIGHLY COMMENDED

Matterdale End, Penrith CA11 0LF
☎ (017684) 82040 & 0831 236076
Fax (017684) 82040
Elevated former farmhouse set in 12 acres. Large garden offering peace and tranquillity in a fellside location. Extensive views of the Ullswater fells. Laura Ashley/Liberty furnishings and Aga-cooked breakfast.
Bedrooms: 3 double, 1 twin
Bathrooms: 4 en-suite

Bed & breakfast per night:	£min	£max
Double	50.00	52.00

Parking for 4

Bridge End Farm

COMMENDED

Hutton, Hutton John, Penrith CA11 0LZ
☎ (017684) 83273
14-acre mixed farm. Warmest hospitality in 17th C farmhouse, situated in own grounds with gardens to river. Lakeland fell views. 5 miles west of M6, half a mile A66, 3 miles Ullswater.
Bedrooms: 2 double, 1 twin, 1 triple
Bathrooms: 3 en-suite, 1 private

Bed & breakfast per night:	£min	£max
Double	32.00	36.00

Half board per person:	£min	£max
Daily	23.00	26.00
Weekly	155.00	160.00

Evening meal 1830 (last orders 1700)
Parking for 6
Open April–October

Elm House

COMMENDED

Pooley Bridge, Penrith CA10 2NH
☎ (017684) 86334
Fax (017684) 86334
Pleasant country house set in unspoilt village. Ideal base for visiting Lakes. A warm and friendly stay assured.
Bedrooms: 4 double, 1 twin
Bathrooms: 2 private, 1 public

Bed & breakfast per night:	£min	£max
Single	20.00	22.00
Double	32.00	40.00

Parking for 5

Land Ends

COMMENDED

Watermillock, Ullswater, Penrith CA11 0NB
☎ (017684) 86438
Fax (017684) 86959
Converted farmhouse in 7 acres of gardens and natural woodland, with 2 large ponds teeming with wildlife. Peaceful, idyllic location 1 mile from Ullswater.
Bedrooms: 3 single, 4 double, 2 twin
Bathrooms: 9 en-suite

Bed & breakfast per night:	£min	£max
Single	28.00	30.00
Double	52.00	56.00

Parking for 15

Netherdene Guest House

COMMENDED

Troutbeck, Penrith CA11 0SJ
☎ (017684) 83475
Traditional country house in its own quiet grounds, with extensive mountain views, offering comfortable well-appointed rooms and personal attention. Ideal base for touring Lakeland.
Bedrooms: 1 single, 2 double, 1 twin, 1 triple
Bathrooms: 5 en-suite

Bed & breakfast per night:	£min	£max
Single	20.00	24.00
Double	35.00	40.00

Half board per person:	£min	£max
Daily	27.00	30.00
Weekly	165.00	180.00

Evening meal 1830 (last orders 1600)
Parking for 6

Tymparon Hall

COMMENDED

Newbiggin, Stainton, Penrith CA11 0HS
☎ (017684) 83236

150-acre livestock farm. Delightful 18th C manor house with colourful summer garden in excellent location. Lake Ullswater a 10-minute drive.
Bedrooms: 1 single, 2 double, 1 twin
Bathrooms: 3 en-suite, 1 public

Bed & breakfast per night:	£min	£max
Single	18.00	32.00
Double	36.00	42.00

Half board per person:	£min	£max
Daily	30.00	34.00
Weekly	210.00	230.00

Evening meal 1830 (last orders 1430)
Open April–October

The symbol after an establishment name indicates that it is a Regional Tourist Board member.

White Lion Inn

COMMENDED

Patterdale, Penrith CA11 0NW
☎ (017684) 82214

Old world country inn with friendly atmosphere, on Lake Ullswater near Helvellyn. An ideal centre for walking, fishing and sailing. Traditional beer.

Bedrooms: 2 single, 2 double, 3 twin
Bathrooms: 5 en-suite, 2 private

Bed & breakfast per night:	£min	£max
Single	25.00	25.00
Double	50.00	50.00

Lunch available
Evening meal 1830 (last orders 2145)
Parking for 50
Cards accepted: Mastercard, Visa, Switch/Delta

UNDERBARROW

Cumbria
Map ref 5A3

At the foot of limestone escarpment Scout Scar, Underbarrow is close to the National Trust's Brigsteer Woods, west of Kendal. A quiet, spread-out village, overlooking the Lyth Valley.

Tranthwaite Hall

COMMENDED

Underbarrow, Kendal LA8 8HG
☎ (015395) 68285

260-acre dairy/sheep farm. Magnificent 11th C farmhouse, with oak beams and doors, offering immaculate en-suite accommodation. Ideal location for touring Lakeland.

Bedrooms: 1 double, 1 triple
Bathrooms: 1 en-suite, 1 private

Bed & breakfast per night:	£min	£max
Single	22.00	25.00
Double	38.00	43.00

Parking for 3

WALTON

Cumbria
Map ref 5B2

Lovely little village with sandstone church, just north of Brampton at the western end of Hadrian's Wall.

Town Head Farm

Listed COMMENDED

Walton, Brampton CA8 2DJ
☎ (016977) 2730

100-acre mixed farm. Enjoy comfort and hospitality on this working farm. The cosy farmhouse offers scenic views and overlooks the village green, which has a play area. Hadrian's Wall nearby.

Bedrooms: 1 double, 1 triple
Bathrooms: 1 public

Bed & breakfast per night:	£min	£max
Single	15.00	16.00
Double	28.00	30.00

Parking for 4

WASDALE

Cumbria
Map ref 5A3

A very dramatic valley with England's deepest lake, Wastwater, highest mountain, Scafell Pike, and smallest church. The eastern shore of Wastwater is dominated by the 1,500 ft screes dropping steeply into the lake. A good centre for walking and climbing.

Church Stile Farm House

COMMENDED

Church Stile, Nether Wasdale, Wasdale, Seascale CA20 1ET
☎ (019467) 26028

495-acre hill farm. Traditional Cumbrian farmhouse in the pretty village of Nether Wasdale. Superb views, walks, climbing and a warm welcome.

Bedrooms: 1 single, 1 double, 1 triple
Bathrooms: 2 en-suite, 1 private

Bed & breakfast per night:	£min	£max
Single	18.00	19.00
Double	40.00	42.00

Half board per person:	£min	£max
Daily	32.00	33.00
Weekly	230.00	240.00

Evening meal 1830 (last orders 2000)
Parking for 2
Open January–November

WINDERMERE

Cumbria
Map ref 5A3

Once a tiny hamlet before the introduction of the railway in 1847, now adjoins Bowness which is on the lakeside. Centre for sailing and boating. A good way to see the lake is a trip on a passenger steamer. Steamboat Museum has a fine collection of old boats.
Tourist Information Centre
☎ (015394) 46499

Aaron Slack

COMMENDED

48 Ellerthwaite Road, Windermere LA23 2BS
☎ (015394) 44649
Email: s.townsend @aaronslack.demon.co.uk

Small, friendly guesthouse for non-smokers in a quiet part of Windermere, close to all amenities and concentrating on personal service.

Bedrooms: 2 double, 1 twin
Bathrooms: 2 en-suite, 1 private

Bed & breakfast per night:	£min	£max
Single	17.00	22.00
Double	32.00	42.00

Cards accepted: Amex, Mastercard, Visa

12

Beckmead House

COMMENDED

5 Park Avenue, Windermere LA23 2AR
☎ (015394) 42757

Delightful stone-built Victorian house with reputation for high standards, comfort and friendliness. Delicious breakfasts. Convenient for lake, shops, restaurants and golf-course.

Bedrooms: 1 single, 2 double, 1 twin, 1 family room
Bathrooms: 2 private, 1 public, 2 private showers

Bed & breakfast per night:	£min	£max
Single	16.00	18.00
Double	32.00	42.00

Establishments should be open throughout the year, unless otherwise stated.

WINDERMERE

Continued

Beckside Cottage

Listed COMMENDED

4 Park Road, Windermere
LA23 2AW
☎ (015394) 42069 & 88105

Comfortable cottage. En-suite bedrooms with full central heating, colour TV, tea/coffee and clock/radio. Full English breakfast served. Ideally situated, close to Windermere village.

Bedrooms: 1 single, 2 double, 1 triple
Bathrooms: 4 en-suite

Bed & breakfast per night:	£min	£max
Single	15.00	19.00
Double	30.00	38.00

Parking for 3

Braemount House Hotel

HIGHLY COMMENDED

Sunny Bank Road, Windermere
LA23 2EN
☎ (015394) 45967
Fax (015394) 45967

Charming, detached Victorian house in quiet, central location. Relaxed, friendly atmosphere, large garden, excellent breakfast, genuine cheerful welcome. What more could you need?

Bedrooms: 3 double, 1 twin, 1 family room
Bathrooms: 5 en-suite

Bed & breakfast per night:	£min	£max
Single	35.00	
Double	40.00	70.00

Half board per person:	£min	£max
Daily	35.00	50.00
Weekly	225.00	330.00

Evening meal 1900 (last orders 2030)
Parking for 6
Cards accepted: Mastercard, Visa

College House

COMMENDED

15 College Road, Windermere
LA23 1BU
☎ (015394) 45767
Email: clghse@ad.com

Warm, comfortable, Victorian family house. En-suite rooms with gorgeous mountain views. Nice garden. Quiet location. Close to village centre. Private parking. Non-smoking.

Bedrooms: 2 double, 1 twin
Bathrooms: 2 en-suite, 1 private

Bed & breakfast per night:	£min	£max
Double	32.00	50.00

Parking for 3

The Common Farm

COMMENDED

Windermere LA23 1JQ
☎ (015394) 43433

200-acre dairy farm. Picturesque and homely 17th C farmhouse in peaceful surroundings, less than 1 mile from Windermere village.

Bedrooms: 1 double, 1 family room
Bathrooms: 1 public

Bed & breakfast per night:	£min	£max
Double	30.00	34.00

Parking for 4
Open March–November

Crookleigh

COMMENDED

15 Woodland Road, Windermere
LA23 2AE
☎ (015394) 48480 & (041053) 8061 (Mobile)
Fax (015394) 48480

Comfortable, tastefully furnished accommodation. Home-baked rolls, free range eggs, local produce and generous hospitality trays. Excellent value for money.

Bedrooms: 1 double, 1 twin, 1 triple
Suites available
Bathrooms: 1 en-suite, 2 private

Bed & breakfast per night:	£min	£max
Single	17.50	25.00
Double	30.00	45.00

Fairfield Country House Hotel

COMMENDED

Brantfell Road,
Bowness-on-Windermere,
Windermere LA23 3AE
☎ (015394) 46565
Fax (015394) 46565
Email: ray&barb@fairfield.dial.lakesnet.co.uk

Small, friendly 200-year-old country house with half an acre of peaceful secluded gardens. 2 minutes' walk from Lake Windermere and village. Private car park, leisure facilities.

Bedrooms: 1 single, 5 double, 1 twin, 1 triple, 1 family room
Bathrooms: 8 en-suite, 1 private, 1 public

Bed & breakfast per night:	£min	£max
Single	23.00	30.00
Double	46.00	60.00

Half board per person:	£min	£max
Daily	42.50	49.50
Weekly	291.50	321.50

Evening meal 1900 (last orders 1900)
Parking for 14
Cards accepted: Mastercard, Visa

Hazel Bank

COMMENDED

Hazel Street, Windermere
LA23 1EL
☎ (015394) 45486

Beautiful detached Victorian house, containing many original features. Log fire, mature walled garden, en-suite rooms, private parking.

Bedrooms: 3 double
Bathrooms: 3 en-suite

Bed & breakfast per night:	£min	£max
Double	38.00	56.00

Parking for 5

Holly Lodge

COMMENDED

6 College Road, Windermere
LA23 1BX
☎ (015394) 43873
Fax (015394) 43873

Traditional Lakeland stone guesthouse, built in 1854. In a quiet area off the main road, close to the village centre, buses, railway station and all amenities.

Bedrooms: 1 single, 5 double, 2 twin, 3 triple
Bathrooms: 6 en-suite, 2 public

Bed & breakfast per night:	£min	£max
Single	18.00	21.00
Double	36.00	42.00

Half board per person:	£min	£max
Daily	29.00	32.00

Evening meal from 1830
Parking for 7

Invergarry

Listed COMMENDED

3 Thornbarrow Road,
Bowness-on-Windermere,
Windermere LA23 2EW
☎ (015394) 44561

Warm and friendly non-smoking accommodation, ideally located midway between Windermere and Bowness. Lovely en-suite rooms with colour TV, tea/coffee-making facilities. Hearty breakfasts. Parking.

Bedrooms: 1 double, 1 twin, 1 triple
Bathrooms: 3 en-suite

Bed & breakfast per night:	£min	£max
Single	16.00	20.00
Double	35.00	45.00

Lunch available
Parking for 4

Ivy Bank

COMMENDED

Holly Road, Windermere LA23 2AF
☎ (015394) 42601

Attractively furnished Victorian family home on quiet street, 2 minutes' walk from village facilities. Large choice for breakfast, homely atmosphere.

Bedrooms: 4 double, 1 twin, 1 family room
Bathrooms: 3 en-suite, 1 public

Bed & breakfast per night:	£min	£max
Single	14.00	25.00
Double	28.00	40.00

Parking for 8
Cards accepted: Mastercard, Visa, Switch/Delta

WELCOME HOST

This is a nationally recognised customer care programme which aims to promote the highest standards of service and a warm welcome. Establishments who are taking part in this initiative are indicated by the symbol.

Laurel Cottage

COMMENDED

St Martin's Square,
Bowness-on-Windermere,
Windermere LA23 3EF
☎ (015394) 45594
Fax (015394) 45594

Charming early 17th C cottage with front garden, situated in centre of Bowness. Superb selection of restaurants within one minute's stroll.

Bedrooms: 2 single, 10 double, 1 twin, 2 triple
Bathrooms: 10 en-suite, 2 public

Bed & breakfast per night:	£min	£max
Single	21.00	25.00
Double	34.00	60.00

Parking for 8

Lingmoor

7 High Street, Windermere
LA23 1AF
☎ (015394) 44947

Friendly, clean, comfortable, homely accommodation, family-run, close to train station, buses, shops and Tourist Information Centre. Good full English breakfast guaranteed.

Bedrooms: 1 single, 3 double, 2 twin, 1 family room
Bathrooms: 3 en-suite, 1 public

Bed & breakfast per night:	£min	£max
Single	12.00	20.00
Double	25.00	45.00

Half board per person:	£min	£max
Daily	20.00	30.00
Weekly	140.00	200.00

Lingwood

COMMENDED

Birkett Hill,
Bowness-on-Windermere,
Windermere LA23 3EZ
☎ (015394) 44680

A warm welcome awaits you at this family-run guesthouse. En-suite rooms. Ideal for walking and lake use. Special rates for 3-day breaks.

Bedrooms: 3 double, 1 twin, 1 family room
Bathrooms: 3 en-suite, 2 private, 1 public

Bed & breakfast per night:	£min	£max
Single	18.00	25.00

Parking for 6

Oldfield House

COMMENDED

Oldfield Road, Windermere
LA23 2BY
☎ (015394) 88445
Fax (015394) 43250

Friendly, informal atmosphere within a traditionally-built Lakeland residence. Quiet central location, free use of swimming and leisure club.

Bedrooms: 2 single, 4 double, 1 triple, 1 family room
Bathrooms: 8 en-suite, 1 public

Bed & breakfast per night:	£min	£max
Single	20.00	32.50
Double	38.00	60.00

Parking for 7
Open February–December
Cards accepted: Amex, Mastercard, Visa, Switch/Delta

The Poplars

COMMENDED

Lake Road, Windermere LA23 2EQ
☎ (015394) 42325 & 46690
Fax (015394) 42325

Small family-run guesthouse on the main lake road, offering en-suite accommodation coupled with fine cuisine and homely atmosphere. Golf and fishing can be arranged.

Bedrooms: 1 single, 3 double, 2 twin, 1 triple
Bathrooms: 6 en-suite, 1 private, 1 public

Bed & breakfast per night:	£min	£max
Single	20.00	22.50
Double	40.00	45.00

Half board per person:	£min	£max
Daily	32.00	34.50
Weekly	210.00	224.00

Evening meal 1800 (last orders 1800)
Parking for 7
Open February–December

Please mention this guide when making your booking.

WINDERMERE

Continued

Rayrigg Villa Guest House

COMMENDED

Ellerthwaite Square, Windermere LA23 1DP
☎ (015394) 88342

Traditional detached family-run Lakeland guesthouse, built in 1873. Ideally situated in heart of Windermere village. Upgraded by new owners during 1997.

Bedrooms: 4 double, 1 twin, 1 triple, 1 family room
Bathrooms: 4 en-suite, 1 private, 1 public

Bed & breakfast per night:	£min	£max
Single	16.00	25.00
Double	32.00	50.00

Parking for 7

St John's Lodge

COMMENDED

Lake Road, Windermere LA23 2EQ
☎ (015394) 43078

Small private hotel midway between Windermere and the lake, managed by the chef/proprietor and convenient for all amenities and services. Facilities of local sports and leisure club available to guests.

Bedrooms: 1 single, 9 double, 2 twin, 2 triple
Bathrooms: 12 en-suite, 2 private

Bed & breakfast per night:	£min	£max
Single	20.00	28.00
Double	38.00	52.00

Half board per person:	£min	£max
Daily	32.50	38.50
Weekly	210.00	250.00

Evening meal 1900 (last orders 1800)
Parking for 11
Open February–October
Cards accepted: Mastercard, Visa

Please check prices and other details at the time of booking.

Upper Oakmere

Listed COMMENDED

3 Upper Oak Street, Windermere LA23 2LB
☎ (015394) 45649

Ideal location, 100 yards from main High Street. Friendly atmosphere, home cooking. Single people/party bookings. Open all year. Pets welcome.

Bedrooms: 3 double, 1 triple, 1 family room
Bathrooms: 2 en-suite, 1 public

Bed & breakfast per night:	£min	£max
Single	12.00	14.00
Double	22.00	32.00

Lunch available
Evening meal 1730 (last orders 1830)
Parking for 2

White Lodge Hotel

COMMENDED

Lake Road, Windermere LA23 2JJ
☎ (015394) 43624
Fax (015394) 47000

Victorian family-owned hotel with good home cooking, only a short walk from Bowness Bay. All bedrooms have private bathroom, colour TV and tea-making facilities, some with lake views and four-posters.

Bedrooms: 3 single, 6 double, 2 twin, 1 triple
Bathrooms: 12 en-suite

Bed & breakfast per night:	£min	£max
Single	24.00	31.00
Double	48.00	60.00

Half board per person:	£min	£max
Daily	34.00	42.00
Weekly	240.00	265.00

Lunch available
Evening meal 1900 (last orders 2000)
Parking for 20
Open March–November
Cards accepted: Mastercard, Visa

National gradings and classifications were correct at the time of going to press but are subject to change. Please check at the time of booking.

Woodlands

HIGHLY COMMENDED

New Road, Windermere LA23 2EE
☎ (015394) 43915 & (0468) 596142
Fax (015394) 48558

Family-run hotel in a convenient location. Renowned for its high standard of cleanliness and comfort. Ample car parking.

Bedrooms: 2 single, 10 double, 1 twin, 1 family room
Bathrooms: 14 en-suite

Bed & breakfast per night:	£min	£max
Single	22.00	40.00
Double	44.00	80.00

Half board per person:	£min	£max
Daily	35.50	53.50
Weekly	248.50	

Evening meal from 1900
Parking for 14
Cards accepted: Mastercard, Visa, Switch/Delta

WORKINGTON

Cumbria
Map ref 5A2

A deep-water port on the west Cumbrian coast. There are the ruins of the 14th C Workington Hall, where Mary Queen of Scots stayed in 1568.

Morven Guest House

APPROVED

Siddick Road, Siddick, Workington CA14 1LE
☎ (01900) 602118 & 602002
Fax (01900) 602118

Detached house north-west of town. Ideal base for western Lakes and coast. Start of coast to coast cycleway. Car park, cycle storage.

Bedrooms: 2 single, 1 double, 3 twin
Bathrooms: 5 en-suite, 1 private

Bed & breakfast per night:	£min	£max
Single	25.00	32.00
Double	40.00	46.00

Half board per person:	£min	£max
Daily	36.00	42.00

Lunch available
Evening meal 1800 (last orders 1600)
Parking for 20

NORTHUMBRIA

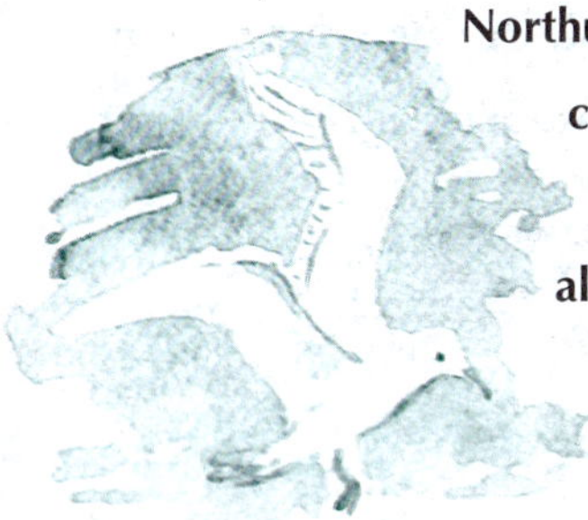

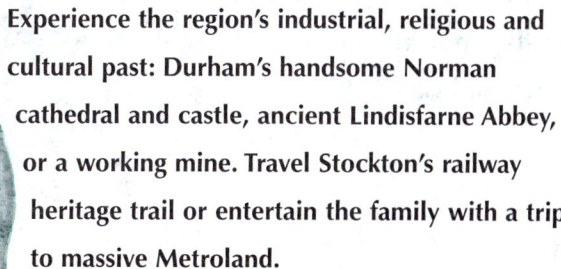

Northumbria is an area of breathtaking contrasts. Here you can discover magnificent forests, the seals of the Farne Islands, seaside resorts and charming villages dotted along golden beaches. Or simply take in the stunning scenery of the Durham Dales, the Pennines and Hadrian's Wall.

Experience the region's industrial, religious and cultural past: Durham's handsome Norman cathedral and castle, ancient Lindisfarne Abbey, or a working mine. Travel Stockton's railway heritage trail or entertain the family with a trip to massive Metroland.

Revel in sophisticated, big-city pleasures too, with exciting attractions, shopping and great night life!

The counties of Durham, Northumberland, Tees Valley and Tyne & Wear

FOR MORE INFORMATION CONTACT:
Northumbria Tourist Board
Aykley Heads, Durham DH1 5UX
Tel: (0191) 375 3000 **Fax:** (0191) 386 0899
Internet http://www.ntb.org.uk

Where to Go in Northumbria – see pages 60-63
Where to Stay in Northumbria – see pages 64-77

Northumbria

Where to Go and What to See

You will find hundreds of interesting places to visit during your stay in Northumbria, just some of which are listed in these pages. The number against each name will help you locate it on the map (page 63). Contact any Tourist Information Centre in the region for more ideas on days out in Northumbria.

1 Lindisfarne Castle
Holy Island
Berwick-upon-Tweed TD15 2SH
Tel: (01289) 389244
Fort converted into a private home in 1903 for Edward Hudson by the architect Sir Edwin Lutyens.

2 Farne Islands
Seahouses off
Northumberland Coast,
Northumberland
Tel: (01665) 720651
Bird reserve holding around 55,000 pairs of breeding birds of 21 species. Also home to a large colony of grey seals.

3 Bamburgh Castle
Bamburgh,
Northumberland NE69 7DF
Tel: (01668) 214515
Magnificent coastal castle completely restored in 1900. Collections of china, porcelain, furniture, paintings, arms and armour.

4 Alnwick Castle
Alnwick,
Northumberland NE66 1NQ
Tel: (01665) 510777
Largest inhabited castle in England after Windsor Castle. Home of the Percys, Dukes of Northumberland since 1309.

5 Kielder Water
Leaplish Waterside Park,
Kielder,
Hexham,
Northumberland NE48 1BX
Tel: (01434) 250312
Largest man-made lake in Western Europe. Water sports, fishing, log cabins, cycle hire, crazy golf, restaurant, sauna, solarium and pool.

6 Whitehouse Farm Centre
North White House Farm,
Stannington, Morpeth,
Northumberland NE61 6AW
Tel: (01670) 789998/789571
A great day out in the country. Learn how a farm works and see guinea pigs, rabbits, chicks, ducks and exotic animals.

7 Belsay Hall, Castle and Gardens
Belsay,
Newcastle upon Tyne NE20 0DX
Tel: (01661) 881636
House of the Middleton family for 600 years in 30 acres of landscaped gardens and winter garden. 14thC castle, ruined 17thC manor house and neo-classical hall.

8 **Sea Life Centre**
Grand Parade,
Long Sands,
Tynemouth,
North Shields,
Tyne and Wear NE30 4JF
Tel: (0191) 257 6100/258 1031
More than 30 hi-tech displays provide encounters with dozens of sea creatures. Journey beneath the North Sea and discover thousands of amazing creatures.

9 **South Shields Museum**
Ocean Road,
South Shields,
Tyne and Wear NE33 2AU
Tel: (0191) 456 8740
Visit the fascinating reconstruction of William Black Street where famous novelist Catherine Cookson grew up. Discover how the area's natural environment and history were shaped.

10 **Souter Point Lighthouse**
Coast Road,
Whitburn,
South Shields,
Tyne and Wear SR6 7NH
Tel: (0191) 529 3161
The lighthouse and associated buildings were constructed in 1871 and contained the most advanced lighthouse technology of its day. See the engine room, battery room and light tower.

11 **Castle Keep**
Saint Nicholas Street,
Castle Garth,
Newcastle upon Tyne NE1 1RQ
Tel: (0191) 232 7938
Built 1168-1178. One of the finest surviving examples of a Norman keep in the country. Panoramic views of the city from the roof. Small museum within keep.

12 **Laing Art Gallery**
Higham Place,
Newcastle upon Tyne NE1 8AG
Tel: (0191) 232 7734/6989
Paintings and watercolours, including works by Northumbrian born artist John Martin. Award-winning interactive displays 'Art on Tyneside' and 'Children's Gallery'. Cafe and shop.

13 **Newcastle Discovery Museum**
Blandford House,
Blandford Square,
Newcastle upon Tyne NE1 4JA
Tel: (0191) 232 6789.
A wide variety of experiences for all the family to enjoy. Visit the Science Factory, Great City, Fashion Works, maritime history and Pioneers Gallery.

14 **Hadrian's Wall**
Hexham,
Northumberland NE46 4EP
Tel: (01434) 681379
Fort built for 500 cavalrymen. Remains include five gateways, barrack blocks, commandant's house and headquarters. Finest Roman military bath-house in Britain.

15 **Cherryburn: Thomas Bewick Birthplace Museum**
Cherryburn,
Station Bank,
Mickley ,
Stocksfield,
Northumberland NE43 7DB
Tel: (01661) 843276
Birthplace cottage (1700) and farmyard. Printing house using original printing blocks. Introductory exhibition of the life, work and countryside from 1753 to 1828.

16 **Metroland**
MetroCentre,
Gateshead,
Tyne and Wear NE11 9YZ
Tel: (0191) 493 2048
Europe's only indoor theme park within a large shopping complex. Roller coaster, dodgems, swinging chairs, pirate ship plus live entertainment daily.

17 The Wildfowl and Wetlands Trust
District 15,
Washington,
Tyne and Wear NE38 8LE
Tel: (0191) 416 5454/416 5801
Collection of 1,250 wildfowl of 108 varieties. Viewing gallery, picnic areas, hides and winter wild bird feeding station. Flamingos, wild grey heron. Food available.

18 Beamish
The North of England
Open Air Museum,
Beamish,
County Durham DH9 ORG
Tel: (01207) 231811
Visit a town, colliery village, farm and railway station recreated to show life in the North of England early this century. Pockerley Manor illustrates life in the early 1800s.

19 Durham Castle
Palace Green,
Durham DH1 3RW
Tel: (0191) 374 3863/3800
Castle founded in 1072, Norman chapel dating from 1080. Kitchens and great hall dated 1499 and 1284 respectively. Fine example of motte and bailey castle.

20 Durham Cathedral
The College,
Durham DH1 3EH
Tel: (0191) 386 4266
Widely considered to be the finest example of Norman church architecture in England. Has the tombs of St Cuthbert and The Venerable Bede.

22 High Force Waterfall
Forest-in-Teesdale,
Middleton-in-Teesdale,
County Durham DL12
Tel: (01833) 640209
High Force is the most majestic of the waterfalls on the River Tees. The falls are only a short walk from a bus stop, car park and picnic area.

23 Otter Trust
North Pennines Reserve,
Vale House Farm,
Bowes,
Barnard Castle,
County Durham DL12 9RH
Tel: (01833) 628457
A branch of the famous Otter Trust. See Asian and British otters, red and fallow deer and several rare breeds of farm animals in this 230-acre wildlife reserve.

24 Killhope Leadmining Centre
Cowshill, St John's Chapel,
Bishop Auckland,
County Durham DL13 1AR
Tel: (01388) 537505
Britain's most complete lead mining site. Includes crushing mill with 34ft water wheel, reconstruction of Victorian machinery and miners' accommodation.

25 Hartlepool Historic Quay
Maritime Avenue, Hartlepool,
Cleveland TS24 0XZ
Tel: (01429) 860006/860077
An exciting reconstruction of a seaport of the 1800s with buildings and lively quayside authentically reconstructed.

26 Saltburn Smugglers Heritage Centre
Ship Inn, Saltburn-by-the-Sea,
Cleveland TS12 1HF
Tel: (01287) 625252/622422
Experience the authentic sights, sounds and smells of Saltburn's smuggling heritage. Listen to tales of John Andrew, 'King of the Smugglers'.

27 Gisborough Priory
Church Street, Guisborough,
Cleveland TS14 6HG
Tel: (01287) 633801/
(01642) 444000
Remains of a priory founded by Robert de Brus in 1119AD in the grounds of Gisborough Hall. Main arch and window of east wall virtually intact.

28 Preston Hall Museum
Yarm Road,
Stockton-on-Tees,
Cleveland TS18 3RH
Tel: (01642) 781184/791424
A Georgian country house set in a park which is a museum of Victoriana. Return to a bygone age, stroll along a high street and explore 100 acres of parkland overlooking the Tees.

FIND OUT MORE

Further information about holidays and attractions in Northumbria is available from:

Northumbria Tourist Board,
Aykley Heads,
Durham DH1 5UX.
Tel: (0191) 375 3000
Internet - http://www.ntb.org.uk

The following publications are available free from the Northumbria Tourist Board:

- **Northumbria 1998** - information on the region, including hotels, self-catering and caravan and camping parks
- **North of England Bed & Breakfast Map** - value for money bed and breakfast accommodation in Northumbria and Cumbria
- **Going Places** - information on what to do, where to go, what to see and where to eat throughout the region
- **Educational Opportunities** - guide to group accommodation and attractions
- **Selected North Country Inns** - accommodation in traditional Inns in Northumbria and Cumbria
- **Stay on a Farm** - farm holidays in Northumbria
- **Freedom** - caravan/camping guide to the North of England

WHERE TO STAY (NORTHUMBRIA)

Accommodation entries in this region are listed in alphabetical order of place name, and then in alphabetical order of establishment.

Map references refer to the colour location maps at the back of this guide. The first number indicates the map to use; the letter and number which follow refer to the grid reference on the map.

At-a-glance symbols at the end of each accommodation entry give useful information about services and facilities. A key to symbols can be found inside the back cover flap. Keep this open for easy reference.

ALNMOUTH

Northumberland
Map ref 5C1

Quiet village with pleasant old buildings, at the mouth of the River Aln where extensive dunes and sands stretch along Alnmouth Bay. 18th C granaries, some converted to dwellings, still stand.

High Buston Hall

HIGHLY COMMENDED

High Buston, Alnmouth, Alnwick NE66 3QH
☎ (01665) 830341
Fax (01665) 830341

Elegant listed Georgian house with commanding coastal views. Comfortable and stylish with traditional furnishings. Relaxed atmosphere, warm hospitality and peaceful village setting.

Bedrooms: 3 double
Bathrooms: 2 en-suite, 1 private

Bed & breakfast per night:	£min	£max
Single	25.00	40.00
Double	50.00	60.00

Half board per person:	£min	£max
Daily	50.00	65.00

Evening meal (last orders 1900)
Parking for 9
Open January–November
12

A key to symbols can be found inside the back cover flap.

ALNWICK

Northumberland
Map ref 5C1

Ancient and historic market town, entered through the Hotspur Tower, an original gate in the town walls. The medieval castle, the second biggest in England and still the seat of the Dukes of Northumberland, was restored from ruin in the 18th C.

Tourist Information Centre ☎ (01665) 510665

Hawkhill Farmhouse

COMMENDED

Lesbury, Alnwick NE66 3PG
☎ (01665) 830380
Fax (01665) 830380

Spacious farmhouse with spectacular views over Aln Valley and the coast. Two miles from Alnwick and Alnmouth. Secluded off-road parking. Large grounds.

Bedrooms: 1 double, 2 twin
Bathrooms: 3 en-suite

Bed & breakfast per night:	£min	£max
Single	25.00	30.00
Double	40.00	45.00

Parking for 10
Open April–October

For further information on accommodation establishments use the coupons at the back of this guide.

BAMBURGH

Northumberland
Map ref 5C1

Village with a spectacular red sandstone castle standing 150 ft above the sea. On the village green the magnificent Norman church stands opposite a museum containing mementoes of the heroine Grace Darling.

Mizen Head Hotel

COMMENDED

Lucker Road, Bamburgh NE69 7BS
☎ (01668) 214254

Privately-owned, fully licensed hotel in own grounds, with accent on good food and service. Convenient for beaches, castle and golf. 2 minutes' walk from village centre.

Bedrooms: 2 single, 5 double, 4 twin, 4 family rooms
Bathrooms: 11 en-suite, 2 public

Bed & breakfast per night:	£min	£max
Single	22.50	45.00
Double	45.00	79.00

Half board per person:	£min	£max
Daily	34.00	58.00
Weekly	231.00	325.00

Lunch available
Evening meal 1830 (last orders 2000)
Parking for 30
Cards accepted: Mastercard, Visa
30

BARNARD CASTLE

Durham
Map ref 5B3

High over the Tees, a thriving market town with a busy market square. Bernard Baliol's 12th C castle (now ruins) stands nearby. The Bowes Museum, housed in a grand 19th C French chateau, holds fine paintings and furniture. Nearby are some magnificent buildings.
Tourist Information Centre ☎ (01833) 690909 or 630272

Browns Antiques

Listed COMMENDED

34 The Bank, Barnard Castle, County Durham DL12 8PN
☎ (01833) 637891 & 0802 915935
Fax (01833) 637891

The guest suite is on the first floor behind the antique shop and dates from 1540. It has original beams and fireplace and an adjoining sitting room with fridge, TV and own bathroom. Furnished with antiques.

Bedrooms: 1 twin
Bathrooms: 1 private

Bed & breakfast per night:	£min	£max
Single	30.00	35.00
Double	35.00	40.00

Open March–May, July–November

East Mellwaters Farm

COMMENDED

Bowes, Barnard Castle, County Durham DL12 9RH
☎ (01833) 628269
Fax (01833) 628269

350-acre livestock farm. Half a mile off the A66, 2 miles west of Bowes. 17th C farm in attractive setting. Riverside walks, fishing. Comfortable rooms, open log fires, wonderful food, licensed.

Bedrooms: 1 single, 3 double, 1 twin
Bathrooms: 5 en-suite

Bed & breakfast per night:	£min	£max
Single	18.00	20.00
Double	36.00	40.00

Half board per person:	£min	£max
Daily	28.00	30.00
Weekly	180.00	200.00

Lunch available
Evening meal 1730 (last orders 1900)
Parking for 12
Cards accepted: Mastercard, Visa

15

George & Dragon Inn

Listed APPROVED

Boldron, Barnard Castle, County Durham DL12 9RF
☎ (01833) 638215

Attractive inn in beautiful Teesdale, offering comfortable accommodation and friendly hospitality.

Bedrooms: 1 double, 1 twin
Bathrooms: 1 public

Bed & breakfast per night:	£min	£max
Single	15.50	16.00
Double	31.00	32.00

Half board per person:	£min	£max
Daily	20.50	21.00
Weekly	140.00	140.00

Lunch available
Evening meal 1900 (last orders 1730)
Parking for 20

Old Well Inn

COMMENDED

21 The Bank, Barnard Castle, County Durham DL12 8PH
☎ (01833) 690130
Fax (01833) 690140

Historic inn and popular restaurant, tastefully decorated, with spacious en-suite bedrooms. Home-cooked food and real ales. North Pennines Area of Outstanding Natural Beauty.

Bedrooms: 1 single, 2 double, 2 twin, 2 triple
Bathrooms: 7 en-suite

Bed & breakfast per night:	£min	£max
Single	35.00	37.00
Double	46.00	49.00

Lunch available
Evening meal 1900 (last orders 2130)
Cards accepted: Amex, Mastercard, Visa, Switch/Delta

WELCOME HOST

This is a nationally recognised customer care programme which aims to promote the highest standards of service and a warm welcome. Establishments who are taking part in this initiative are indicated by the symbol.

BELLINGHAM

Northumberland
Map ref 5B2

Set in the beautiful valley of the North Tyne close to the Kielder Forest, Kielder Water and lonely moorland below the Cheviots. The church has an ancient stone wagon roof fortified in the 18th C with buttresses.
Tourist Information Centre ☎ (01434) 220616

Lyndale Guest House

HIGHLY COMMENDED

Off The Square, Bellingham, Hexham NE48 2AW
☎ (01434) 220361
Fax (01434) 220361

Enjoy a remarkable welcome break. Relax in our walled garden. Sun lounge with panoramic views. Excellent dinners, good breakfasts. Good base for walking, Hadrian's Wall, Pennine Way, Kielder Water, National Trust houses.
http:/wwws-h-systems.co.uk/

Bedrooms: 2 double, 1 twin
Bathrooms: 2 en-suite, 1 private, 1 public

Bed & breakfast per night:	£min	£max
Single	22.50	25.00
Double	45.00	50.00

Half board per person:	£min	£max
Daily	35.00	37.50
Weekly	235.00	252.00

Evening meal 1800 (last orders 1900)
Parking for 6

BERWICK-UPON-TWEED

Northumberland
Map ref 5B1

Guarding the mouth of the Tweed, England's northernmost town with the best 16th C city walls in Europe. The handsome Guildhall and barracks date from the 18th C. Three bridges cross to Tweedmouth, the oldest built in 1634.
Tourist Information Centre ☎ (01289) 330733

Ladythorne House

Listed COMMENDED

Cheswick, Berwick-upon-Tweed TD15 2RW
☎ (01289) 387382

Continued ▶

BERWICK-UPON-TWEED

Continued

Grade II listed building, dated 1721, set in farmland. Only 15 minutes' walk from the beaches.
Bedrooms: 1 single, 1 double, 2 twin, 2 triple
Bathrooms: 3 public

Bed & breakfast per night:	£min	£max
Single	13.00	15.00
Double	26.00	30.00

Parking for 8

Middle Ord Manor House

DE LUXE

Middle Ord Farm,
Berwick-upon-Tweed TD15 2XQ
☎ (01289) 306323
Fax (01289) 308423

550-acre mixed farm. Experience the quality and warmth of hospitality in this award-winning elegant Georgian farmhouse. Relax in spacious en-suite rooms (four-poster if desired). Central for touring Borders, coast and Holy Island. 3 miles west of Berwick off A698.
Bedrooms: 2 double, 1 twin
Bathrooms: 3 en-suite, 1 public

Bed & breakfast per night:	£min	£max
Single	36.00	
Double	52.00	

Parking for 6
Open April–October

Tree Tops

DE LUXE

The Village Green, East Ord,
Berwick-upon-Tweed TD15 2NS
☎ (01289) 330679
ETB England for Excellence award-winner 1995. Bed and Breakfast of the year. Spacious, elegant single-storey guesthouse. One acre garden, croquet lawn, peaceful village, Berwick 2 miles. Beautiful en-suite bedrooms, residents' lounge. Non-smokers only.
Bedrooms: 1 double, 1 twin
Bathrooms: 2 en-suite

Bed & breakfast per night:	£min	£max
Double	46.00	56.00

Evening meal 1900 (last orders 1600)
Parking for 4
Open April–October

West Sunnyside House

COMMENDED

Tweedmouth, Berwick-upon-Tweed TD15 2QH
☎ (01289) 305387
Old farmhouse on the outskirts of Tweedmouth, convenient for beach and walks. Next to sports centre and handy for golf and fishing.
Bedrooms: 1 twin, 1 triple
Bathrooms: 1 public

Bed & breakfast per night:	£min	£max
Double	30.00	34.00

Parking for 4

BISHOP AUCKLAND

Durham
Map ref 5C2

Busy market town on the bank of the River Wear. The Bishop's Palace, a castellated Norman manor house altered in the 18th C, stands in beautiful gardens. Entered from the market square by a handsome 18th C gatehouse, the park is a peaceful retreat of trees and streams.
Tourist Information Centre ☎ (01388) 604922 or 602610

Albion Cottage Guest House

COMMENDED

Albion Terrace, Bishop Auckland, County Durham DL14 6EL
☎ (01388) 602217
Detached early Victorian house with front and rear gardens, close to the shops, station and national bus routes.
Bedrooms: 2 single, 1 double, 1 twin
Bathrooms: 2 public

Bed & breakfast per night:	£min	£max
Single	16.00	16.00
Double	30.00	30.00

Parking for 10

For ideas on places to visit refer to the introduction at the beginning of this section.

Five Gables

COMMENDED

Binchester, Bishop Auckland, County Durham DL14 8AT
☎ (01388) 608204
300 yards from A688 between Bishop Auckland and Spennymoor. Victorian house with views over countryside and Weardale. 15 minutes from Durham City, and within easy reach of all popular tourist attractions in the North of England.
Bedrooms: 1 single, 1 double, 1 triple
Bathrooms: 2 en-suite, 1 private

Bed & breakfast per night:	£min	£max
Single	20.00	22.50
Double	35.00	37.50

Evening meal 1800 (last orders 2100)
Parking for 3

CASTLESIDE

Durham
Map ref 5B2

Village on the edge of the North Pennines on the A68, one of the main routes from England to Scotland.

Castleneuk Guest House

APPROVED

18-20 Front Street, Castleside, Consett, County Durham DH8 9AR
☎ (01207) 506634
On A68 within easy reach of Durham City, Hadrian's Wall, Beamish Museum and MetroCentre. Excellent village amenities. Evening meals must be pre-booked.
Bedrooms: 1 double, 2 twin, 1 triple
Suites available
Bathrooms: 4 en-suite

Bed & breakfast per night:	£min	£max
Single	18.00	20.00
Double	36.00	36.00

Half board per person:	£min	£max
Daily	26.00	30.00
Weekly	168.00	182.00

Lunch available
Evening meal 1800 (last orders 1950)
Parking for 5

CHESTER-LE-STREET

Durham
Map ref 5C2

Originally a Roman military site, town with modern commerce and light industry on the River Wear. The ancient church replaced a wooden sanctuary which sheltered the remains of St Cuthbert for 113 years. The Anker's house beside the church is now a museum. Home of Durham County Cricket Club.

Waldridge Fell House

HIGHLY COMMENDED

Waldridge Lane, Waldridge, Chester-Le-Street, County Durham DH2 3RY
☎ (0191) 389 1908

Former village chapel, stone-built in 1868. Panoramic views and country walks. Children half price. One and a half miles from cricket ground.

Bedrooms: 3 triple, 2 family rooms
Bathrooms: 1 en-suite, 1 public, 1 private shower

Bed & breakfast per night:	£min	£max
Single	23.00	32.00
Double	38.00	42.00

Parking for 8

CONSETT

Durham
Map ref 5B2

Former steel town on the edge of rolling moors. Modern development includes the shopping centre and a handsome Roman Catholic church, designed by a local architect. To the west, the Derwent Reservoir provides water sports and pleasant walks.

Bee Cottage Farm

HIGHLY COMMENDED

Castleside, Consett, County Durham DH8 9HW
☎ (01207) 508224

46-acre livestock farm. 1.5 miles west of the A68, between Castleside and Tow Law. Unspoilt views. Ideally located for Beamish Museum and Durham. No smoking. Tea-room open 1-6 pm.

Bedrooms: 1 single, 3 double, 2 twin, 1 triple, 2 family rooms
Suites available
Bathrooms: 1 en-suite, 2 private, 5 public

Bed & breakfast per night:	£min	£max
Single	25.00	
Double	44.00	

Half board per person:	£min	£max
Daily	38.50	

Lunch available
Evening meal 1930 (last orders 2000)
Parking for 20

CORBRIDGE

Northumberland
Map ref 5B2

Small town on the River Tyne. Close by are extensive remains of the Roman military town Corstopitum, with a museum housing important discoveries from excavations. The town itself is attractive with shady trees, a 17th C bridge and interesting old buildings, notably a 14th C vicarage.

Clive House

HIGHLY COMMENDED

Appletree Lane, Corbridge NE45 5DN
☎ (01434) 632617

Old village school (1840) converted to dwelling house; tasteful decor throughout, exposed beams, gallery, and a log fire in breakfast room. Good eating places nearby.

Bedrooms: 2 double, 1 twin
Bathrooms: 3 en-suite

Bed & breakfast per night:	£min	£max
Single	25.00	30.00
Double	40.00	44.00

Parking for 3

15

Please mention this guide when making your booking.

For ideas on places to visit refer to the introduction at the beginning of this section.

The Courtyard

DE LUXE

Mount Pleasant, Sandhoe, Corbridge NE45 4LX
☎ (01434) 606850
Fax (01434) 606632

A warm, friendly welcome greets visitors to this lovingly restored and beautifully furnished country house, dating from 1730. Surrounded by open countryside, with panoramic views over the beautiful Tyne Valley.

Bedrooms: 1 double, 1 twin, 1 triple
Bathrooms: 3 en-suite

Bed & breakfast per night:	£min	£max
Single	40.00	
Double	50.00	

Parking for 6

Dilston Mill

Listed COMMENDED

Corbridge NE45 5QZ
☎ (01434) 633493
Fax (01434) 633513

Somewhere special. Historic former watermill, on the banks of Devils Water. Overlooked by Dilston Castle ruins. Comfort, warm welcome, beautiful setting, excellent breakfasts. Close to amenities.

Bedrooms: 1 double, 1 twin, 1 triple
Bathrooms: 3 private

Bed & breakfast per night:	£min	£max
Single	25.00	30.00
Double	46.00	50.00

Parking for 3

WELCOME HOST

This is a nationally recognised customer care programme which aims to promote the highest standards of service and a warm welcome. Establishments who are taking part in this initiative are indicated by the symbol.

CORBRIDGE

Continued

Fellcroft

HIGHLY COMMENDED

Station Road, Corbridge NE45 5AY
☎ (01434) 632384

Well-appointed stone-built Edwardian house with full private facilities and colour TV in both bedrooms. Quiet road in country setting, half a mile south of market square. Excellent choice of eating places nearby. Non-smokers only, please. 10 per cent reduction for weekly half board stays.

Bedrooms: 2 twin
Bathrooms: 1 en-suite, 1 private

Bed & breakfast per night:	£min	£max
Single	17.50	20.50
Double	30.00	33.00

Half board per person:	£min	£max
Daily	23.50	25.00
Weekly	125.00	

Parking for 3

Fox & Hounds Hotel

COMMENDED

Stagshaw Bank, Corbridge
NE45 5QW
☎ (01434) 633024
Fax (01434) 633024

400-year-old coaching inn with a 70-seat conservatory restaurant. Owners operate and live on premises.

Bedrooms: 1 single, 3 double, 3 twin, 1 triple
Bathrooms: 8 en-suite

Bed & breakfast per night:	£min	£max
Single	30.00	30.00
Double	40.00	40.00

Lunch available
Evening meal 1800 (last orders 2100)
Parking for 50

Establishments should be open throughout the year, unless otherwise stated.

COTHERSTONE

Durham
Map ref 5B3

Village with remains of Norman castle, 3 miles north-west of Barnard Castle. Home of Cotherstone cheese.

Glendale

HIGHLY COMMENDED

Cotherstone, Barnard Castle, County Durham DL12 9UH
☎ (01833) 650384

Dormer bungalow with beautiful gardens and large pond, in quiet, rural surroundings. Take Briscoe road from Cotherstone for 200 yards.

Bedrooms: 3 double
Bathrooms: 3 en-suite, 1 public

Bed & breakfast per night:	£min	£max
Single	18.00	22.00
Double	32.00	32.00

Parking for 4

CRASTER

Northumberland
Map ref 5C1

Small fishing village with a fine northward view of Dunstanburgh Castle. Fishing cobles in the tiny harbour, stone cottages at the water's edge and a kippering shed where Craster's famous delicacy is produced give the village its unspoilt charm.

Cottage Inn

COMMENDED

Dunstan Village, Craster, Alnwick NE66 3SZ
☎ (01665) 576658
Fax (01665) 576788

Family-run inn half a mile from the sea. All rooms are ground floor and have garden view. Noted for food. Special breaks available.

Bedrooms: 2 double, 8 twin
Bathrooms: 10 en-suite

Bed & breakfast per night:	£min	£max
Single	35.00	
Double	63.00	

Half board per person:	£min	£max
Daily	45.00	
Weekly	280.00	

Lunch available
Evening meal 1800 (last orders 2130)
Parking for 30
Cards accepted: Mastercard, Visa, Switch/Delta

DALTON

Tyne and Wear
Map ref 5B2

Hazel Cottage

HIGHLY COMMENDED

Eachwick, Dalton, Newcastle upon Tyne, Northumberland NE18 0BE
☎ (01661) 852415

Very comfortable stone farmhouse, good home cooking. Easy access Roman Wall, airport, Newcastle, MetroCentre. Ideal for Northumbria.

Bedrooms: 1 double, 1 twin
Bathrooms: 2 en-suite

Bed & breakfast per night:	£min	£max
Single	25.00	25.00
Double	40.00	40.00

Half board per person:	£min	£max
Daily	35.00	35.00
Weekly	220.00	220.00

Evening meal 1900 (last orders 1830)
Parking for 4

DURHAM

Durham
Map ref 5C2

Ancient city with its Norman castle and cathedral, now a World Heritage site, set on a bluff high over the Wear. A market and university town and regional centre, spreading beyond the market-place on both banks of the river.
Tourist Information Centre ☎ (0191) 384 3720

The Anchorage

COMMENDED

25 Langley Road, Newton Hall, Durham DH1 5LR
☎ (0191) 386 2323
Fax (0191) 384 1842
Email: 101711.3535@compuserve.com

Large detached family home, 1 mile

north of city, convenient for commercial, countryside, tourist areas. 1 double bed, 1 bed-settee. Spacious accommodation, en-suite bath/shower. Non-smoking.
Bedrooms: 1 double
Bathrooms: 1 en-suite

Bed & breakfast per night:	£min	£max
Single	20.00	20.00
Double	40.00	40.00

Parking for 2

The Avenue Inn

Listed APPROVED

Avenue Street, High Shincliffe, Durham DH1 2PT
☎ (0191) 386 5954
Village pub and restaurant serving home-cooked food and real ales.
Bedrooms: 3 single, 2 twin, 3 triple
Suites available
Bathrooms: 2 public, 3 private showers

Bed & breakfast per night:	£min	£max
Single	17.50	17.50
Double	35.00	35.00

Lunch available
Evening meal 1900 (last orders 2100)
Parking for 10

Bay Horse Inn

COMMENDED

Brandon Village, Durham DH7 8ST
☎ (0191) 378 0498
Ten stone-built chalets 3 miles from Durham city centre. All have shower, toilet, TV, tea and coffee facilities and telephone. Ample car parking.
Bedrooms: 3 double, 6 twin, 1 family room
Bathrooms: 10 en-suite

Bed & breakfast per night:	£min	£max
Single	31.00	31.00
Double	40.00	40.00

Lunch available
Evening meal 1900 (last orders 2200)
Parking for 25
Cards accepted: Mastercard, Visa

Castledene

Listed COMMENDED

37 Nevilledale Terrace, Durham DH1 4QG
☎ (0191) 384 8386
Fax (0191) 384 8386
Edwardian end-of-terrace house half a mile west of the market place. Within walking distance of the riverside, cathedral and castle.
Bedrooms: 2 twin
Bathrooms: 1 public

Bed & breakfast per night:	£min	£max
Single	20.00	25.00
Double		38.00

Parking for 6

Collingwood College Cumbrian Wing

COMMENDED

South Road, Durham, County Durham DH1 3LT
☎ (0191) 374 4500
Fax (0191) 374 4595
Durham's newest college, situated in woodland near the city centre. En-suite rooms coupled with unrivalled cuisine. Perfect for conferences and holidaymakers alike.
Bedrooms: 197 single, 16 twin
Bathrooms: 213 en-suite

Bed & breakfast per night:	£min	£max
Single	26.50	27.00
Double	45.00	47.00

Half board per person:	£min	£max
Daily	33.25	35.00
Weekly	210.00	230.00

Lunch available
Evening meal 1800 (last orders 1900)
Parking for 130
Open January, March–April, July–September, December
Cards accepted: Mastercard, Visa, Switch/Delta

Elmgarth

COMMENDED

Mainsforth, Ferryhill, County Durham DL17 9AA
☎ (01740) 652676
300-year-old cottage in quiet village and conservation area. Local walks, nature reserve. Ideal centre for dales, coast and city. A1M, exit 60. Brochure available.
Bedrooms: 1 double, 1 triple
Bathrooms: 1 en-suite, 1 private

Bed & breakfast per night:	£min	£max
Single	18.00	20.00
Double	32.00	36.00

Parking for 3

Trevelyan College

APPROVED

Elvet Hill Road, Durham DH1 3LN
☎ (0191) 374 3765 & 374 3768
Fax (0191) 374 3789
Email: john.wright@dur.ac.uk
Set in parkland within easy walking distance of Durham City. Comfortable Cloister Bar, TV lounges, ample parking. Standard and en-suite rooms available.
Bedrooms: 253 single, 8 double, 27 twin
Bathrooms: 58 en-suite, 47 public

Bed & breakfast per night:	£min	£max
Single	18.00	27.50
Double	32.40	49.50

Half board per person:	£min	£max
Daily	26.30	55.80
Weekly	165.00	225.00

Lunch available
Evening meal 1800 (last orders 1930)
Parking for 100
Open January, March–April, June–September, December

EGGLESTON

Durham
Map ref 5B3

Small village between Barnard Castle and Middleton-in-Teesdale on the edge of the moors. Once a smelting centre for the North Pennines lead industry but no trace of it remains today.

Moorcock Inn

APPROVED

Hill Top, Gordon Bank, Eggleston, Barnard Castle, County Durham DL12 0AU
☎ (01833) 650395
Fax (01833) 650052
Country inn of character, with modern amenities and spectacular views from all rooms, popular with both tourists and locals.
Bedrooms: 1 single, 3 double, 1 twin, 1 triple
Bathrooms: 2 en-suite, 3 public

Bed & breakfast per night:	£min	£max
Single	20.00	25.00
Double	32.00	37.00

Lunch available
Evening meal 1900 (last orders 2100)
Parking for 50

HALTWHISTLE

Northumberland
Map ref 5B2

Small market town with interesting 12th C church, old inns and blacksmith's smithy. North of the town are several important sites and interpretation centres of Hadrian's Wall. Ideal centre for archaeology, outdoor activity or touring holidays.
Tourist Information Centre ☎ (01434) 322002

Ashcroft

HIGHLY COMMENDED
Lantys Lonnen, Haltwhistle
NE49 0DA
☎ (01434) 320213
Large, stone-built, early 19th C residence, south facing, with mature terraced gardens. Well placed for exploring the Roman Wall and Northumberland.
Bedrooms: 2 single, 2 double, 1 twin, 1 triple, 2 family rooms
Bathrooms: 6 en-suite, 2 public

Bed & breakfast per night:	£min	£max
Single	18.00	25.00
Double	40.00	45.00

Parking for 14

Broomshaw Hill Farm

HIGHLY COMMENDED
Willia Road, Haltwhistle NE49 9NP
☎ (01434) 320866 & 0378 240048
Fax (01434) 320866
5-acre livestock farm. Attractive, modernised 18th C stone-built farmhouse. Set in beautiful wooded valley, close to Hadrian's Wall and all major Roman sites.
Bedrooms: 2 double, 1 twin
Bathrooms: 2 en-suite, 1 private

Bed & breakfast per night:	£min	£max
Single	20.00	25.00
Double	38.00	40.00

Parking for 8
Open February–October

COLOUR MAPS

Colour maps at the back of this guide pinpoint all places in which you will find accommodation listed.

Hall Meadows

COMMENDED
Main Street, Haltwhistle NE49 0AZ
☎ (01434) 321021
Built in 1888, a large family house with pleasant garden in the centre of town. Ideally placed for Hadrian's Wall.
Bedrooms: 1 single, 1 double, 1 twin
Bathrooms: 1 public

Bed & breakfast per night:	£min	£max
Single	16.00	16.00
Double	32.00	32.00

Parking for 3

Oaky Knowe Farm

Listed COMMENDED
Haltwhistle NE49 0NB
☎ (01434) 320648
300-acre livestock farm. Overlooking the Tyne Valley, within walking distance of Haltwhistle and the Roman Wall, this comfortable farmhouse offers friendly family holidays.
Bedrooms: 1 twin, 2 triple
Bathrooms: 1 public

Bed & breakfast per night:	£min	£max
Single	18.00	20.00
Double	30.00	36.00

Half board per person:	£min	£max
Daily	23.00	28.00
Weekly	160.00	190.00

Evening meal 1700 (last orders 1530)
Parking for 8

HAMSTERLEY FOREST

Durham

See under Barnard Castle, Bishop Auckland

HAYDON BRIDGE

Northumberland
Map ref 5B2

Small town on the banks of the South Tyne with an ancient church, built of stone from sites along the Roman Wall just north. Ideally situated for exploring Hadrian's Wall and the Border country.

Hadrian Lodge

APPROVED
Hindshield Moss, North Road, Haydon Bridge, Hexham NE47 6NF
☎ (01434) 688688
Fax (01434) 684867
Conversion of single-storey hunting/fishing lodge. In 18 acres with trout lake, near Housesteads Roman Fort and Hadrian's Wall. Cosy residents' bar, tea-room/lounge. Brochure available.
Bedrooms: 1 single, 1 double, 1 twin, 1 triple, 1 family room
Bathrooms: 3 en-suite, 3 public

Bed & breakfast per night:	£min	£max
Single	15.00	18.00
Double	28.00	36.00

Half board per person:	£min	£max
Daily	18.00	23.00
Weekly	95.00	119.00

Parking for 25
Cards accepted: Mastercard, Visa
20

HEIGHINGTON

Durham
Map ref 5C3

Village 2 miles south-west of Newton Aycliffe. Built around a large green giving fine views of the Tees Valley.

Eldon House

HIGHLY COMMENDED
East Green, Heighington, Darlington, County Durham DL5 6PP
☎ (01325) 312270
17th C manor house with large garden overlooking the village green. Large, comfortable, well-appointed rooms. Ample parking. Tennis court. Coal/wood fire in sitting room.
Bedrooms: 3 twin
Bathrooms: 1 en-suite, 2 private

Bed & breakfast per night:	£min	£max
Single	30.00	35.00
Double	45.00	50.00

Parking for 6

WELCOME HOST

This is a nationally recognised customer care programme which aims to promote the highest standards of service and a warm welcome. Establishments who are taking part in this initiative are indicated by the symbol.

HEXHAM

Northumberland
Map ref 5B2

Old coaching and market town near Hadrian's Wall. Since pre-Norman times a weekly market has been held in the centre with its market-place and abbey park, and the richly-furnished 12th C abbey church has a superb Anglo- Saxon crypt.
Tourist Information Centre ☎ (01434) 605225

Anick Grange

COMMENDED

Hexham NE46 4LP
☎ (01434) 603807
363-acre mixed farm. 17th C farmhouse, 1 mile from Hexham. Superb open views. Comfortable, informal and with a warm welcome.
Bedrooms: 1 single, 1 twin, 1 triple
Bathrooms: 1 en-suite, 1 public

Bed & breakfast per night:	£min	£max
Single	16.00	18.00
Double	32.00	34.00

Parking for 4
Open April–September

Dene House

HIGHLY COMMENDED

Juniper, Hexham NE46 1SJ
☎ (01434) 673413

Stone farmhouse with beamed ceilings, log fires and flowers everywhere. Very quietly situated in 9 acres of farmland, 4 miles south of Hexham.
Bedrooms: 1 single, 1 double, 1 twin
Bathrooms: 1 en-suite, 1 private, 1 public

Bed & breakfast per night:	£min	£max
Single	18.00	20.00
Double	36.00	40.00

Parking for 3

Map references apply to the colour maps at the back of this guide.

Kitty Frisk House

HIGHLY COMMENDED

Corbridge Road, Hexham
NE46 1UN
☎ (01434) 601533
Fax (01434) 601533

Large, detached elegant Edwardian house set in mature woodland. Comfortable, spacious bedrooms with en-suite and private facilities.
Bedrooms: 1 double, 2 twin
Bathrooms: 2 en-suite, 1 private

Bed & breakfast per night:	£min	£max
Single	22.50	30.00
Double	45.00	50.00

Parking for 6

Peth Head Cottage

HIGHLY COMMENDED

Juniper Village, Steel, Hexham
NE47 0LA
☎ (01434) 673286
Fax (01434) 673038

Rose-covered stone cottage in quiet hamlet. Charming bedrooms and attractive lounge for guests. Picturesque rural location, ideal for walking, cycling and touring holidays.
Bedrooms: 1 single, 1 double, 1 twin
Bathrooms: 3 en-suite

Bed & breakfast per night:	£min	£max
Single	18.00	18.00
Double	36.00	36.00

Parking for 5

All accommodation in this guide has been graded, or is awaiting a grading, by a trained Tourist Board inspector.

Rose and Crown Inn

HIGHLY COMMENDED

Main Street, Slaley, Hexham
NE47 0AA
☎ (01434) 673263
Fax (01434) 673305
Warm, friendly, family-run business with good wholesome home cooking and a la carte restaurant. All bedrooms en-suite in this 200-year-old listed village freehouse in Slaley.
Bedrooms: 1 single, 2 twin
Bathrooms: 3 en-suite

Bed & breakfast per night:	£min	£max
Single	20.00	27.50
Double	40.00	50.00

Half board per person:	£min	£max
Daily	30.00	37.50

Lunch available
Evening meal 1830 (last orders 2200)
Parking for 32
Cards accepted: Amex, Mastercard, Visa, Switch/Delta

Rye Hill Farm

COMMENDED

Slaley, Hexham NE47 0AH
☎ (01434) 673259
Fax (01434) 673608
Email: enquiries
@consultcourage.co.uk

30-acre livestock farm. Warm and comfortable barn conversion, 5 miles south of Hexham, where you can enjoy the peace of rural life. Noted for the food and the friendly atmosphere.
Bedrooms: 2 double, 2 twin, 2 family rooms
Bathrooms: 6 en-suite

Bed & breakfast per night:	£min	£max
Single	24.00	24.00
Double	40.00	40.00

Half board per person:	£min	£max
Daily	32.00	36.00
Weekly	210.00	235.00

Evening meal 1930 (last orders 1700)
Parking for 6
Cards accepted: Visa

HEXHAM

Continued

Thistlerigg Farm

COMMENDED

High Warden, Hexham NE46 4SR
☎ (01434) 602041
630-acre mixed farm. Farmhouse built in 1908. Scenic views, within walking distance of a Roman hill fort and close to Northumberland National Park.
Bedrooms: 2 double, 1 twin
Bathrooms: 1 public

Bed & breakfast per night:	£min	£max
Single	15.00	16.00
Double	30.00	32.00

Parking for 3
Open April–October

HOLY ISLAND

Northumberland
Map ref 5B1

Still an idyllic retreat, tiny island and fishing village and cradle of northern Christianity. It is approached from the mainland at low water by a causeway. The clifftop castle (National Trust) was restored by Sir Edwin Lutyens.

Britannia

Holy Island, Berwick-upon-Tweed TD15 2RX
☎ (01289) 389218
Comfortable, friendly bed and breakfast in centre of Holy Island. Tea-making facilities in all rooms. TV lounge. En-suite available.
Bedrooms: 1 double, 1 twin, 1 triple
Bathrooms: 1 en-suite, 1 public

Bed & breakfast per night:	£min	£max
Single		17.00
Double		34.00

Parking for 4
Open March–October

The map references refer to the colour maps towards the end of the guide. The first figure is the map number; the letter and figure which follow indicate the grid reference on the map.

North View

HIGHLY COMMENDED

Marygate, Holy Island, Berwick-upon-Tweed TD15 2SD
☎ (01289) 389222
400-year-old listed building on historic and beautiful island. Ideally situated for visiting many of Northumberland's tourist attractions.
Bedrooms: 2 double, 1 twin
Bathrooms: 3 en-suite

Bed & breakfast per night:	£min	£max
Single	25.00	32.00
Double		50.00

Half board per person:	£min	£max
Daily	35.00	45.00

Lunch available
Evening meal 1900 (last orders 2100)
Parking for 6
Cards accepted: Mastercard, Visa

KIELDER FOREST

Northumberland

See under Bellingham, Kielder Water, West Woodburn

KIELDER WATER

Northumberland
Map ref 5B2

A magnificent man-made lake, the largest in Northern Europe, with over 27 miles of shoreline. On the edge of the Northumberland National Park and near the Scottish border, Kielder can be explored by car, on foot or by ferry.

The Pheasant Inn (by Kielder Water)

COMMENDED

Stannersburn, Falstone, Hexham NE48 1DD
☎ (01434) 240382

Historic inn with beamed ceilings and open fires. Home cooking. Fishing, riding and all water sports nearby. Close to Kielder Water, Hadrian's Wall and the Scottish border.
Bedrooms: 4 double, 3 twin, 1 family room
Bathrooms: 8 en-suite

Bed & breakfast per night:	£min	£max
Single	22.00	35.00
Double	44.00	56.00

Half board per person:	£min	£max
Daily	39.00	46.00

Lunch available
Evening meal 1900 (last orders 2100)
Parking for 30
Cards accepted: Mastercard, Visa, Switch/Delta

Ridge End Farm

COMMENDED

Falstone, Hexham NE48 1DE
☎ (01434) 240395
150-acre hill farm. 16th C Grade II listed Bastle house, 5ft thick walls, former home to Border Reivers. Surrounded by breathtaking North Tyne scenery.
Bedrooms: 1 twin, 1 triple
Bathrooms: 2 en-suite

Bed & breakfast per night:	£min	£max
Single	25.00	25.00
Double	36.00	36.00

Parking for 100

LESBURY

Northumberland
Map ref 5C1

Village 1 mile north-west of Alnmouth near the Northumberland coast.

Dukes Ryde

HIGHLY COMMENDED

Longhoughton Road, Lesbury, Alnwick NE66 3AT
☎ (01665) 830855
Delightful and imposing early 20th C house set in secluded gardens, on the outskirts of Lesbury village, near beaches and golf-courses.
Bedrooms: 1 double, 2 twin
Bathrooms: 2 en-suite, 1 private

Bed & breakfast per night:	£min	£max
Single	25.00	
Double	45.00	

Parking for 6

You are advised to confirm your booking in writing.

LOWICK

Northumberland
Map ref 5B1

Inland from Holy Island and near the A1, Lowick has a long, wide main street with a few shops and inns and is in agricultural land between the foothills of the Cheviots and the coast.

Black Bull Inn

COMMENDED

Main Street, Lowick,
Berwick-upon-Tweed TD15 2UA
☎ (01289) 388228

Originally built in 1645, the inn has seen many changes, including a separate dining room in 1988, and en-suite bedrooms in 1994. Informality and comfort are the aims.

Bedrooms: 1 double, 2 twin
Bathrooms: 3 en-suite

Bed & breakfast per night:	£min	£max
Single		26.00
Double		52.00

Lunch available
Evening meal 1830 (last orders 2100)
Parking for 40
Cards accepted: Mastercard, Visa, Switch/Delta

The symbols in each entry give information about services and facilities. A key to these symbols appears at the back of this guide.

National gradings and classifications were correct at the time of going to press but are subject to change. Please check at the time of booking.

MIDDLESBROUGH

Tees Valley
Map ref 5C3

Boom-town of the mid 19th C, today's Teesside industrial and conference town has a modern shopping complex and predominantly modern buildings. An engineering miracle of the early 20th C is the Transporter Bridge which replaced an old ferry.
Tourist Information Centre ☎ (01642) 243425 or 264330

Maltby Farm

APPROVED

Maltby, Middlesbrough, Cleveland TS8 0BP
☎ (01642) 590121

187-acre mixed farm. Traditional Yorkshire farmhouse, over 200 years old, looking south on to the Cleveland Hills.

Bedrooms: 1 single, 1 twin, 1 triple
Bathrooms: 1 public

Bed & breakfast per night:	£min	£max
Single	16.00	17.00
Double	32.00	34.00

Half board per person:	£min	£max
Daily	23.00	24.00
Weekly	135.00	140.00

Evening meal 1800 (last orders 2000)
Parking for 6

MIDDLETON-IN-TEESDALE

Durham
Map ref 5B3

Small stone town of hillside terraces overlooking the river, developed by the London Lead Company in the 18th C. Five miles up-river is the spectacular 70-ft waterfall, High Force.

Bluebell House

APPROVED

Market Place, Middleton-in-Teesdale, Barnard Castle, County Durham DL12 0QG
☎ (01833) 640584

Quiet, comfortable rooms at the rear of the house, all with private shower and WC and tea/coffee facilities. Guest TV lounge. Reduced double/twin rates for longer stays.

Bedrooms: 2 double, 1 twin
Bathrooms: 2 en-suite, 1 private

Bed & breakfast per night:	£min	£max
Single	21.00	
Double	33.00	

Parking for 3

NEWCASTLE UPON TYNE

Tyne and Wear
Map ref 5C2

Commercial and cultural centre of the North East, with a large indoor shopping centre, Quayside market, museums and theatres which offer an annual 6 week season by the Royal Shakespeare Company. Norman castle keep, medieval alleys, old Guildhall.
Tourist Information Centre ☎ (0191) 261 0610 or 230 0030 or 261 0691

Grosvenor Hotel

APPROVED

Grosvenor Road, Jesmond, Newcastle upon Tyne NE2 2RR
☎ (0191) 281 0543
Fax (0191) 281 9217

Friendly hotel in quiet residential suburb, offering a wide range of facilities. Close to city centre.

Bedrooms: 17 single, 8 double, 9 twin, 7 triple
Bathrooms: 33 en-suite, 5 public

Bed & breakfast per night:	£min	£max
Single	25.00	45.00
Double	40.00	60.00

Half board per person:	£min	£max
Daily	35.00	60.00
Weekly	210.00	360.00

Lunch available
Evening meal 1830 (last orders 2100)
Parking for 30
Cards accepted: Amex, Diners, Mastercard, Visa, Switch/Delta
120

You are advised to confirm your booking in writing.

The National Grading and Classification Scheme is explained at the back of this guide.

NORHAM

Northumberland
Map ref 5B1

Border village on the salmon-rich Tweed, dominated by its dramatic castle ruin. Near Castle Street is the church, like the castle destroyed after the Battle of Flodden, but rebuilt. Norham Station Railway Museum is just outside the town.

Dromore House

Listed COMMENDED

12 Pedwell Way, Norham, Berwick-upon-Tweed TD15 2LD
☎ (01289) 382313

Guesthouse in a small village on the River Tweed, between the Cheviot and Lammermuir Hills. Quiet beaches are within easy reach.

Bedrooms: 1 double, 1 twin, 1 triple
Bathrooms: 2 private, 1 public

Bed & breakfast per night:	£min	£max
Single	16.00	19.00
Double	32.00	38.00

Half board per person:	£min	£max
Daily	24.00	27.00
Weekly	168.00	189.00

Evening meal 1700 (last orders 1900)
Parking for 3

OTTERBURN

Northumberland
Map ref 5B1

Small village set at the meeting of the River Rede with Otter Burn, the site of the Battle of Otterburn in 1388. A peaceful tradition continues in the sale of Otterburn tweeds in this beautiful region, which is ideal for exploring the Border country and the Cheviots.

Low Byrness

COMMENDED

Otterburn, Newcastle upon Tyne NE19 1TF
☎ (01830) 520648
Fax (01830) 520648
Email: 105510.3340 @compuserve.com

One-hundred-and-fifty-year-old country cottage retaining many original features. Situated on the A68 with views overlooking the Pennine Way and Kielder Forest.

Bedrooms: 1 double, 1 triple
Bathrooms: 2 en-suite

Bed & breakfast per night:	£min	£max
Single	18.00	22.00
Double	36.00	40.00

Half board per person:	£min	£max
Daily	26.00	

Evening meal 1800 (last orders 2000)
Parking for 4

PIERCEBRIDGE

Durham
Map ref 5C3

Small village of whitewashed cottages around a green, with a graceful bridge over the River Tees. This is the site of a Roman fort built to defend Dere Street.

The Bridge House

Listed COMMENDED

Piercebridge, Darlington, County Durham DL2 3SG
☎ (01325) 374727

18th C Grade II listed cottage with gardens, bordering the River Tees. Spacious, comfortable accommodation, with antiques, oak beams and log fires. Convenient for the Durham and Yorkshire Dales.

Bedrooms: 1 double, 2 twin
Bathrooms: 1 en-suite, 1 public

Bed & breakfast per night:	£min	£max
Single	20.00	22.00
Double	36.00	38.50

Parking for 3

REDCAR

Tees Valley
Map ref 5C3

Lively holiday resort near Teesside with broad sandy beaches, a fine racecourse, a large indoor funfair at Coatham and other seaside amusements. Britain's oldest existing lifeboat can be seen at the Zetland Museum.

Willow House

APPROVED

8 Newcomen Terrace, Redcar, Cleveland TS10 1AT
☎ (01642) 485330

Large, terraced property overlooking the sea and close to the town centre. Warm, friendly atmosphere and home cooking.

Bedrooms: 1 single, 2 triple, 3 family rooms
Bathrooms: 3 public

Bed & breakfast per night:	£min	£max
Single	14.00	16.00
Double	25.00	27.00

Half board per person:	£min	£max
Daily	19.50	22.00
Weekly	136.50	154.00

Evening meal 1700 (last orders 1900)

ROTHBURY

Northumberland
Map ref 5B1

Old market town on the River Coquet near the Simonside Hills. It makes an ideal centre for walking and fishing or for exploring this beautiful area from the coast to the Cheviots. Cragside House and Gardens (National Trust) are open to the public.

Silverton House

Listed HIGHLY COMMENDED

Silverton Lane, Rothbury, Morpeth NE65 7RJ
☎ (01669) 621395

Imaginative and comfortable conversion from an old workhouse, on the outskirts of Rothbury in lovely countryside.

Bedrooms: 1 double, 1 twin
Bathrooms: 1 en-suite, 1 private

Bed & breakfast per night:	£min	£max
Single	25.00	36.00
Double	33.00	36.00

Thropton Demesne Farmhouse

HIGHLY COMMENDED

Thropton, Rothbury, Morpeth NE65 7LT
☎ (01669) 620196
Fax (01669) 620196

24-acre mixed farm. Traditional farmhouse peacefully situated in the picturesque Coquet Valley. Spectacular views. Ideally placed for fishing, golf and walking. Home-made bread. Non-smoking house.

Bedrooms: 1 double, 2 twin
Bathrooms: 2 en-suite, 1 private

Bed & breakfast per night:	£min	£max
Single	30.00	42.00
Double	40.00	42.00

Parking for 6

RYTON

Tyne and Wear
Map ref 5C2

On a wooded site above the Tyne, Ryton has a 12th C church with a Jacobean screen and good 19th C oak carving. Small pit working, notable for the spectacular 1826 Stargate Explosion, ceased in 1967. Easy access to the A1, Hadrian's Wall and rural Northumbria.

Barmoor Old Manse

Listed APPROVED

The Old Manse, Barmoor, Ryton
NE40 3BD
☎ (0191) 413 2438

Large stone Victorian house, built as manse for Congregational church in 1862. Delightful garden. Near MetroCentre, Roman Wall and Beamish Museum.

Bedrooms: 1 double, 2 twin
Bathrooms: 1 public

Bed & breakfast per night:	£min	£max
Single	16.00	
Double	32.00	

Parking for 2

SEAHOUSES

Northumberland
Map ref 5C1

Small modern resort developed around a 19th C herring port. Just offshore, and reached by boat from here, are the rocky Farne Islands (National Trust) where there is an important bird reserve. The bird observatory occupies a medieval pele tower.

'Leeholme'

Listed COMMENDED

93 Main Street, Seahouses
NE68 7TS
☎ (01665) 720230

A warm welcome awaits you at this small homely bed and breakfast. 5 minutes' walk to Seahouses harbour and shops. Hearty breakfast assured.

Bedrooms: 1 double, 1 twin
Bathrooms: 1 public

Bed & breakfast per night:	£min	£max
Single	18.00	
Double	30.00	

Parking for 2
Open March–October

SPENNYMOOR

Durham
Map ref 5C2

Booming coal and iron town from the 18th C until early in the present century when traditional industry gave way to lighter manufacturing and trading estates were built. On the moors south of the town there are fine views of the Wear Valley.

Idsley House

HIGHLY COMMENDED

4 Green Lane, Spennymoor, County Durham DL16 6HD
☎ (01388) 814237

Detached Victorian residence in quiet area at junction of A167/A688, opposite council offices. Just 8 minutes south of Durham City. Tastefully furnished, spacious bedrooms, safe parking on premises.

Bedrooms: 1 single, 1 double, 2 twin, 1 triple
Bathrooms: 4 en-suite, 1 private, 1 public

Bed & breakfast per night:	£min	£max
Single	20.00	20.00
Double	40.00	40.00

Parking for 8
Cards accepted: Amex, Mastercard, Visa, Switch/Delta

The symbol after an establishment name indicates that it is a Regional Tourist Board member.

For farm holidays and accommodation suitable for young people and organised groups, please refer to the special sections at the back of this guide.

STAINDROP

Durham
Map ref 5B3

Village 5 miles north-east of Barnard Castle, not far from Raby Castle, one of the most impressive castles in the north of England.

Fawn Lea

COMMENDED

10 Winston Road, Staindrop, Darlington, County Durham
DL2 3NN
☎ (01833) 660356

Cosy and comfortable accommodation. All rooms en-suite and with colour TV and tea/coffee facilities. Double rooms are on ground floor.

Bedrooms: 2 double, 1 twin
Bathrooms: 3 en-suite

Bed & breakfast per night:	£min	£max
Single	24.00	24.00
Double	36.00	36.00

Parking for 6

Gazebo House

HIGHLY COMMENDED

4 North Green, Staindrop, Darlington, County Durham
DL2 3JN
☎ (01833) 660222
Fax (01833) 660222

18th C house with listed gazebo (illustrated) in garden. Adjacent Raby Park and Castle. Ideal base for Lake District and Yorkshire Dales.

Bedrooms: 1 double, 1 twin
Bathrooms: 1 en-suite, 1 private

Bed & breakfast per night:	£min	£max
Single	20.00	22.00
Double	40.00	42.00

Half board per person:	£min	£max
Daily	37.00	39.00

Evening meal 1900 (last orders 2200)

THROPTON

Northumberland
Map ref 5B1

Pretty village in Coquetdale with an ancient but well-preserved castle house at the west end of the village. Cragside (National Trust) is 2 miles to the east.

Farm Cottage

HIGHLY COMMENDED

Thropton, Morpeth NE65 7NA
☎ (01669) 620831
150-year-old stone-built cottage in centre of village. In the Coquet Valley, well situated for Northumbria's beauty spots.
Bedrooms: 1 double, 1 twin
Bathrooms: 1 en-suite, 1 private

Bed & breakfast per night:	£min	£max
Single	26.00	35.00
Double	36.00	40.00

Parking for 3

WARKWORTH

Northumberland
Map ref 5C1

A pretty village overlooked by its medieval castle. A 14th C fortified bridge across the wooded Coquet gives a superb view of 18th C terraces climbing to the castle. Upstream is a curious 14th C Hermitage and in the market square is the Norman church of St Lawrence.

Beck 'N' Call

HIGHLY COMMENDED

Birling West Cottage, Warkworth, Morpeth NE65 0XS
☎ (01665) 711653
Country cottage set in half an acre of terraced gardens with stream. First cottage on the right entering Warkworth from Alnwick.
Bedrooms: 2 double, 1 triple
Bathrooms: 1 en-suite, 1 private, 1 public

Bed & breakfast per night:	£min	£max
Single	17.00	19.00
Double	34.00	38.00

Parking for 4

Bide A While

Listed COMMENDED

4 Beal Croft, Warkworth, Morpeth NE65 0XL
☎ (01665) 711753
Bungalow on small executive housing estate of 8 dwellings.
Bedrooms: 1 double, 1 family room
Bathrooms: 1 en-suite, 1 public

Bed & breakfast per night:	£min	£max
Single	17.50	19.50
Double	31.00	35.00

Parking for 3

North Cottage

HIGHLY COMMENDED

Birling, Warkworth, Morpeth NE65 0XS
☎ (01665) 711263

Attractive cottage, with ground floor, en-suite non-smoking rooms. Extensive gardens, with patio where visitors are welcome to relax. Off-street parking.
Bedrooms: 1 single, 2 double, 1 twin
Bathrooms: 3 en-suite, 1 public

Bed & breakfast per night:	£min	£max
Single	19.00	19.50
Double	38.00	39.00

Parking for 8

Roxbro House

APPROVED

5 Castle Terrace, Warkworth, Morpeth NE65 0UP
☎ (01665) 711416
Small family guesthouse overlooked by historic Warkworth Castle. Half a mile from sandy beach, in a designated Area of Outstanding Natural Beauty.
Bedrooms: 1 double, 1 twin, 1 family room
Bathrooms: 1 public, 3 private showers

Bed & breakfast per night:	£min	£max
Single	18.00	20.00
Double	35.00	37.00

Parking for 3

WEST WOODBURN

Northumberland
Map ref 5B2

Small hamlet on the River Rede in rolling moorland country.

Bay Horse Inn

COMMENDED

West Woodburn, Hexham NE48 2RX
☎ (01434) 270218
Fax (01434) 270118
18th C coaching inn beside River Rede. On A68 between Corbridge and Otterburn and near Bellingham.
Bedrooms: 2 double, 2 twin, 1 family room
Bathrooms: 5 en-suite, 1 public

Bed & breakfast per night:	£min	£max
Single	20.00	27.00
Double	36.00	42.00

Lunch available
Evening meal 1900 (last orders 2100)
Parking for 25
Cards accepted: Mastercard, Visa, Switch/Delta

Plevna House

HIGHLY COMMENDED

West Woodburn, Hexham NE48 2RA
☎ (01434) 270369
Traditional, stone-built house and walled garden. All comforts and amenities. Ideally placed for Scottish Borders, Roman Wall, Kielder, Wallington and Cragside.
Bedrooms: 2 double
Bathrooms: 2 en-suite

Bed & breakfast per night:	£min	£max
Single	20.00	23.00
Double	32.00	36.00

Half board per person:	£min	£max
Daily	26.00	28.00
Weekly	180.00	190.00

Evening meal 1800 (last orders 2030)
Parking for 4
Open March–October

For ideas on places to visit refer to the introduction at the beginning of this section.

WHITLEY BAY

Tyne and Wear
Map ref 5C2

Traditional seaside resort with long beaches of sand and rock and many pools to explore. St Mary's lighthouse is open to the public.
Tourist Information Centre ☎ (0191) 200 8535

York House Hotel

COMMENDED

30 Park Parade, Whitley Bay
NE26 1DX
☎ (0191) 252 8313
Fax (0191) 251 3953

Ideally located for exploring historic Northumbria or visiting the excellent shopping facilities at Newcastle and MetroCentre. High standard en-suite accommodation and imaginative menu choice. No charge for children when sharing. Ground floor bedrooms suitable for disabled. Secure car parking.

Wheelchair access category 3
Bedrooms: 4 single, 8 double, 2 twin
Bathrooms: 13 en-suite, 1 private shower

Bed & breakfast per night:	£min	£max
Single	25.00	35.00
Double	40.00	50.00

Half board per person:	£min	£max
Daily	35.00	45.00
Weekly	220.00	285.00

Lunch available
Evening meal 1800 (last orders 1930)
Parking for 3
Cards accepted: Amex, Mastercard, Visa, Switch/Delta

WYLAM

Northumberland
Map ref 5B2

Well-kept village on the River Tyne, famous as the birthplace of the railway pioneer, George Stephenson. The cottage in which he was born is open to the public, and the Wylam Railway Museum also commemorates William Hedley and Timothy Hackworth.

Wormald House

HIGHLY COMMENDED

Main Street, Wylam NE41 8DN
☎ (01661) 852529 & 852552

Pleasant country home located near centre of Wylam, George Stephenson's birthplace. House stands on site of Timothy Hackworth's birthplace (Stephenson's contemporary).

Bedrooms: 1 double, 1 twin
Bathrooms: 2 en-suite

Bed & breakfast per night:	£min	£max
Single	17.50	19.00
Double	35.00	38.00

Parking for 4
Cards accepted: Visa

AT-A-GLANCE SYMBOLS

Symbols at the end of each accommodation entry give useful information about services and facilities. A key to symbols can be found inside the back cover flap.

Keep this open for easy reference.

USE YOUR *i*'s

There are more than 550 Tourist Information Centres throughout England offering friendly help with accommodation and holiday ideas as well as suggestions of places to visit and things to do. There may well be a centre in your home town which can help you before you set out. You'll find addresses in the local Phone Book or simply call Freepages 0800 192 192.

COUNTRY CODE

Always follow the Country Code

- Enjoy the countryside and respect its life and work
- Guard against all risk of fire
- Fasten all gates
- Keep your dogs under close control
- Keep to public paths across farmland
- Use gates and stiles to cross fences, hedges and walls
- Leave livestock, crops and machinery alone
- Take your litter home
- Help to keep all water clean
- Protect wildlife, plants and trees
- Take special care on country roads
- Make no unnecessary noise

NORTH WEST

The North West is an all-round holiday destination. Choose from the glittering excitement of resorts like Blackpool and Morecambe, or the beautiful, untamed countryside of Derbyshire and the West Pennine Moors - perfect for serious walkers and cyclists.

Explore the grand old city of Chester, with its medieval walls, or the colourful heritage of Merseyside, from Liverpool's old docks to Beatlemania. In Greater Manchester visit stately homes or a Victorian sewer. Further afield, find bargains in Lancashire's mill shops and markets.

Why not time your visit to take in one of the region's 450 annual festivals, from the popular transport and tram event to an annual oyster festival?

The counties of Cheshire, Derbyshire High Peak, Greater Manchester, Lancashire and Merseyside

FOR MORE INFORMATION CONTACT:

North West Tourist Board
Swan House, Swan Meadow Road,
Wigan Pier, Wigan WN3 5BB
Tel: (01942) 821222 **Fax:** (01942) 820002

Where to Go in the North West –
see pages 80-83
Where to Stay in the North West –
see pages 84-92

North West

Where to Go and What to See

You will find hundreds of interesting places to visit during your stay in the North West, just some of which are listed in these pages. The number against each name will help you locate it on the map (page 83). Contact any Tourist Information Centre in the region for more ideas on days out in the North West.

1 Frontierland Western Theme Park
Marine Road West,
Morecambe,
Lancashire LA4 4DG
Tel: (01524) 410024/(01524) 833434
Over 40 thrilling rides and attractions, including the Texas Tornado, Polo Tower, Perculator and Stampede roller coaster. The indoor Fun House complex features live shows in summer.

2 Lancaster Castle
Shire Hall,
Castle Parade,
Lancaster,
Lancashire LA1 1YJ
Tel: (01524) 64998
The hall houses a coat of arms collection, crown court, grand jury room, 'drop room', dungeons and 'Jane Scott's chair'. External tour of castle walls.

3 Blackpool Pleasure Beach
Ocean Boulevard,
Blackpool,
Lancashire FY4 1EZ
Tel: (01253) 341033
Europe's greatest amusement park offers over 145 rides and attractions, including the Space Invader, Big Dipper and the Revolution.

4 Blackpool Sea Life Centre
The Promenade,
Blackpool,
Lancashire FY1 5AA
Tel: (01253) 22445
Tropical sharks up to 8ft in length, housed in a 100,000 gallon water display, with underwater walkway. Also see the Blue Ringed Octopus.

5 Camelot Theme Park and Rare Breeds Farm
Park Hall Road,
Charnock Richard,
Chorley,
Lancashire PR7 5LP
Tel: (01257) 453044/452100
The magical kingdom of Camelot is a world of thrills, fantastic entertainment and family fun, with over 100 rides and attractions, plus medieval entertainment.

6 Wildfowl and Wetland Centre
Martin Mere,
Burscough,
Ormskirk,
Lancashire L40 0TA
Tel: (01704) 895181
45 acres of gardens with over 1,600 ducks, geese and swans.

7 East Lancashire Railway
Bolton Street Station,
Bury,
Lancashire BL9 OEY
Tel: (0161) 764 7790
Eight miles of preserved railway, operated principally by steam. Traction Transport Museum close by.

8 Rufford Old Hall
Rufford,
Ormskirk,
Lancashire L40 ISG
Tel: (01704) 821254
One of the finest 16thC buildings in Lancashire with a magnificent Great Hall, particularly noted for its immense moveable screen.

9 Wigan Pier
Wallgate, Wigan,
Greater Manchester WN3 4EU
Tel: (01942) 323666
Opened by the Queen in 1986. The pier concentrates on life in Wigan in the 1900s. Facilities include a shop, cafe and picnic area.

10 Granada Studios Tour
Water Street,
Greater Manchester M60 9EA
Tel: (0161) 832 9090
Europe's only major television theme park providing a unique insight into the fascinating world behind the television screen.

11 Manchester United Football Club
Museum and Tour Centre,
Old Trafford,
Greater Manchester M16 0RA
Tel: (0161) 877 4002
The official museum and tour of Old Trafford offers every fan a unique insight into the Club.

12 Museum of Science and Industry in Manchester
Liverpool Road,
Castlefield,
Manchester M3 4FP
Tel: (0161) 832 2244/
(0161) 833 0027
The museum is based in the world's oldest passenger railway station with galleries that amaze, amuse and entertain.

13 The Beatles Story
Britannia Vaults,
Albert Dock,
Liverpool,
Merseyside L3 4AA
Tel: (0151) 709 1963
Liverpool's award-winning number one visitor attraction, with a replica of the original Cavern Club.

14 Croxteth Hall and Country Park
Off Muirhead Avenue East,
Liverpool,
Merseyside L12 OHB
Tel: (0151) 228 5311
A 500-acre country park and hall, furnished rooms and walled garden. Farm with rare breeds, miniature railway, gift shop, picnic area, riding centre and adventure playground.

15 Merseyside Maritime Museum
Albert Dock,
Liverpool,
Merseyside L3 4AA
Tel: (0151) 207 0001
Set in the heart of Liverpool's historic waterfront. The museum holds craft demonstrations, working displays and permanent galleries.

16 Tate Gallery
Albert Dock,
Liverpool,
Merseyside L3 4BB
Tel: (0151) 709 3223
The Tate Gallery at Liverpool exhibits the National Collection of modern art.

17 Knowsley Safari Park
Prescot,
Merseyside L34 4AN
Tel: (0151) 430 9009
On a 5-mile drive through the game reserves set in 400 acres of parkland, see lions, tigers, elephants and rhinos. Large picnic areas and children's amusement park.

18 Dunham Massey Hall and Park

Altrincham,
Cheshire WA14 4SJ
Tel: (0161) 941 1025

An 18thC mansion in a 250-acre wooded deer park. Over 30 rooms open to the public. Collections of furniture, paintings and silver. Restaurant and shop.

19 Lyme Park

Disley,
Stockport,
Cheshire SK12 2NX
Tel: (01663) 762023

A National Trust country estate set in 1,377 acres of moorland, woodland and park. This magnificent house has 17 acres of historic gardens.

20 Quarry Bank Mill

Styal,
Wilmslow,
Cheshire SK9 4LA
Tel: (01625) 527468

A Georgian water-powered cotton spinning mill with four floors of displays and demonstrations plus 284 acres of surrounding parkland.

21 CATALYST: The Museum of the Chemical Industry

Gossage Building,
Mersey Road,
Widnes,
Cheshire WA8 0DF
Tel: (0151) 420 1121

Catalyst offers a unique, award-winning formula of interactive exhibits and historical displays. Hands-on exploration will allow you to discover the chemical industry.

22 Cheshire Oaks Designer Outlet Village

Kinsey Road,
Ellesmere Port,
South Wirral L65 9JJ
Tel: (0151) 357 3633

Over 60 individual stores selling famous branded goods.

23 Tatton Park

Knutsford,
Cheshire WA16 6QN
Tel: (01565) 654822/750250

A historic mansion with a 50-acre garden, traditional working farm, medieval manor house and 2,000-acre deer park. A sailing and outdoor centre and adventure playground.

24 Macclesfield Silk Museum

The Heritage Centre,
Roe Street,
Macclesfield,
Cheshire SK11 6UT
Tel: (01625) 613210

Information centre with a town history exhibition and silk museum. The heritage centre was originally built as a Sunday school for the child labourers.

25 Gawsworth Hall

Gawsworth,
Macclesfield,
Cheshire SK11 9RN
Tel: (01260) 223456

A Tudor half-timbered manor house with tilting ground featuring pictures, sculpture, furniture and an open air theatre.

26 Jodrell Bank Science Centre Planetarium and Arboretum,

Lower Withington,
Macclesfield,
Cheshire SK11 9DL
Tel: (01477) 571339

Exhibition and interactive exhibits on astronomy, space, satellites, energy and the environment. Planetarium and the world famous Lovell telescope. Plus a 35-acre arboretum.

27 Chester Zoo

Upton-by-Chester,
Chester,
Cheshire CH2 1LH
Tel: (01244) 380280

A penguin pool with underwater views, tropical house and spectacular displays of spring and summer bedding plants. Chimpanzee house with outdoor enclosure.

28 Beeston Castle

Beeston,
Tarporley,
Cheshire CW6 9TX
Tel: (01829) 260464

A ruined 13thC castle situated on top of the Peckforton Hills with views of the surrounding countryside. Exhibitions featuring the castle's history.

29 Stapeley Water Gardens

London Road,
Stapeley,
Nantwich,
Cheshire CW5 7LH
Tel: (01270) 623868

Large water garden centre filled with display lakes, pools and fountains. Trees and shrubs, pot plants, gifts, garden sundries and pets. Thousands of items on display.

FIND OUT MORE

Further information about holidays and attractions in the North West is available from:

North West Tourist Board,
Swan House,
Swan Meadow Road,
Wigan Pier, Wigan WN3 5BB.
Tel: (01942) 821222

These publications are available free from the North West Tourist Board:

- **North West Welcome Guide**
- **England's North West**

Discovery Map

- **Group Travel Guide**
- **Bed & Breakfast Map**
- **Caravan and Camping Parks Guide**

WHERE TO STAY (NORTH WEST)

Accommodation entries in this region are listed in alphabetical order of place name, and then in alphabetical order of establishment.

Map references refer to the colour location maps at the back of this guide. The first number indicates the map to use; the letter and number which follow refer to the grid reference on the map.

At-a-glance symbols at the end of each accommodation entry give useful information about services and facilities. A key to symbols can be found inside the back cover flap. Keep this open for easy reference.

ACTON BRIDGE

Cheshire
Map ref 4A2

Village with old farmsteads and cottages on a picturesque section of the River Weaver. Riverside walks pass the great Dutton Viaduct on the former Grand Junction Railway and shipping locks on the Weaver Navigation Canal.

Ash House Farm

Listed COMMENDED

Chapel Lane, Acton Bridge, Northwich CW8 3QS
☎ (01606) 852717

200-acre mixed farm. Georgian farmhouse in a quiet, rural location. Within easy access of M6, M56 motorways and many National Trust properties. Ideal for country walks.

Bedrooms: 1 twin, 1 family room
Bathrooms: 1 public, 1 private shower

Bed & breakfast per night:	£min	£max
Single	18.00	20.00
Double	36.00	36.00

Parking for 3

ASHLEY

Greater Manchester
Map ref 4A2

Birtles Farm

HIGHLY COMMENDED

Ashley, Altrincham, Cheshire WA14 3QH
☎ (0161) 928 0458

170-acre mixed farm. Set in peaceful countryside neighbouring Tatton Park yet close to motorway network and Manchester Airport.

Bedrooms: 1 twin, 1 triple
Suites available
Bathrooms: 2 public

Bed & breakfast per night:	£min	£max
Single	17.00	
Double	34.00	

Half board per person:	£min	£max
Daily	23.00	
Weekly	161.00	

Evening meal 1800 (last orders 1930)
Parking for 10

BACUP

Lancashire
Map ref 4B1

Best preserved cotton town in Britain, surrounded by stretches of moorland and close to the South Yorkshire border. The Natural History Society Museum has collections of 19th C relics, geology and natural history.

Irwell Inn

Listed APPROVED

71 Burnley Road, Bacup OL13 8DB
☎ (01706) 873346

Warm and friendly public house, with bed and breakfast accommodation.

Bedrooms: 2 single, 1 double, 1 twin, 1 triple, 1 family room
Bathrooms: 3 en-suite, 2 public

Bed & breakfast per night:	£min	£max
Single	15.00	18.00
Double	30.00	36.00

Half board per person:	£min	£max
Daily	20.00	22.00
Weekly	120.00	132.00

Lunch available
Evening meal (last orders 2200)
Cards accepted: Mastercard, Visa, Switch/Delta

Pasture Bottom Farm

APPROVED

Bacup OL13 9UZ
☎ (01706) 873790

100-acre beef farm. Farmhouse accommodation in a quiet rural area. Magnificient country views. Centrally located for M66, Pennines and Yorkshire Moors.

Bedrooms: 2 twin
Bathrooms: 1 public

Bed & breakfast per night:	£min	£max
Single	14.00	14.00
Double	28.00	28.00

Half board per person:	£min	£max
Daily	21.00	21.00
Weekly	147.00	147.00

Evening meal 1900 (last orders 1900)
Parking for 3

Please mention this guide when making your booking.

BLACKPOOL

Lancashire
Map ref 4A1

Britain's largest fun resort, with Blackpool Pleasure Beach, 3 piers and the famous Tower. Host to the spectacular autumn illuminations - "the greatest free show on earth".
Tourist Information Centre ☎ (01253) 21623

The Ashbeian Guest House

COMMENDED

49 High Street, Blackpool FY1 2BN
☎ (01253) 26301; changing to (01253) 626301
Just 5 bedrooms, all en-suite. Good public parking. Splendid menus. Terrific value. Just off seafront. A very easy walk to everywhere in the town.
Bedrooms: 1 single, 2 double, 1 triple, 1 family room
Bathrooms: 5 en-suite

Bed & breakfast per night:	£min	£max
Single	16.00	21.00
Double	32.00	42.00

Half board per person:	£min	£max
Daily	23.00	28.00
Weekly	116.00	181.00

Evening meal from 1700
Cards accepted: Mastercard, Visa

Sunray

COMMENDED

42 Knowle Avenue, Blackpool FY2 9TQ
☎ (01253) 351937
Fax (01253) 593307
Modern semi in quiet residential part of north Blackpool. Friendly personal service and care. 1.75 miles north of Tower along promenade. Turn right at Uncle Tom's Cabin. Sunray is about 300 yards on left.
Bedrooms: 3 single, 2 double, 2 twin, 2 triple
Bathrooms: 9 en-suite, 1 public

Bed & breakfast per night:	£min	£max
Single	26.00	29.00
Double	52.00	58.00

Half board per person:	£min	£max
Daily	38.00	41.00
Weekly	228.00	246.00

Evening meal 1750 (last orders 1500)
Parking for 6
Cards accepted: Amex, Mastercard, Visa

BOLTON-LE-SANDS

Lancashire
Map ref 5A3

Originally a fishing village, on the main A6 trunk road with the picturesque Lancaster Canal running around the village. Ideal touring base.

Blue Anchor Hotel

APPROVED

68 Main Road, Bolton-le-Sands, Carnforth LA5 8DN
☎ (01524) 823241 & 824745
Fax (01524) 824745
Friendly village inn, off main A6 road. Ideally positioned between City of Lancaster and the Lake District.
Bedrooms: 3 double, 1 twin
Bathrooms: 4 en-suite

Bed & breakfast per night:	£min	£max
Single	20.00	22.00
Double	35.00	40.00

Half board per person:	£min	£max
Daily	25.00	27.50
Weekly	140.00	157.50

Lunch available
Evening meal 1800 (last orders 2100)
Parking for 4
Cards accepted: Mastercard, Visa

CARNFORTH

Lancashire
Map ref 5B3

Carnforth station was the setting for the film "Brief Encounter". Nearby are Borwick Hall, an Elizabethan manor house, and Leighton Hall which has good paintings and Gillow furniture and is open to the public.

Longlands Hotel

Tewitfield, Carnforth LA6 1JH
☎ (01524) 781256
Fax (01524) 69393
Old world coaching inn, on the A6070 half a mile from M6 exit 35. Convenient for the Lakes and Yorkshire Dales.
Bedrooms: 2 double, 4 twin
Bathrooms: 3 en-suite, 3 private, 2 public

Bed & breakfast per night:	£min	£max
Single	20.00	22.50
Double	40.00	45.00

Half board per person:	£min	£max
Daily	22.95	39.30
Weekly	160.00	275.00

Lunch available
Evening meal 1800 (last orders 2100)
Parking for 175
Cards accepted: Mastercard, Visa, Switch/Delta

CHESTER

Cheshire
Map ref 4A2

Roman and medieval walled city rich in treasures. Black and white buildings are a hallmark, including "The Rows" - two-tier shopping galleries. 900-year-old cathedral and the famous Chester Zoo.
Tourist Information Centre ☎ (01244) 317962 or 351609 or 322220

Cheyney Lodge Hotel

COMMENDED

77-79 Cheyney Road, Chester CH1 4BS
☎ (01244) 381925
Small, friendly hotel of unusual design, featuring indoor garden and fish pond. 10 minutes' walk from city centre and on main bus route. Personally supervised with emphasis on good food.
Bedrooms: 1 single, 4 double, 2 twin, 1 triple
Bathrooms: 8 en-suite

Bed & breakfast per night:	£min	£max
Single	24.00	24.00
Double	39.00	44.00

Half board per person:	£min	£max
Daily	28.95	31.95
Weekly	202.65	223.65

Lunch available
Evening meal 1800 (last orders 2000)
Parking for 12
Cards accepted: Mastercard, Visa

You are advised to confirm your booking in writing.

CHESTER

Continued

Curzon Hotel

COMMENDED

52-54 Hough Green, Chester
CH4 8JQ
☎ (01244) 678581
Fax (01244) 680866

A warm welcome awaits in this privately owned large Victorian house with beautiful gardens. Close to racecourse, River Dee and golf. Fine cuisine prepared by chef-proprietor Markus Imfeld.

Bedrooms: 1 single, 7 double, 1 twin, 4 triple, 3 family rooms
Bathrooms: 16 en-suite

Bed & breakfast per night:	£min	£max
Single	40.00	50.00
Double	50.00	70.00

Half board per person:	£min	£max
Daily	40.00	50.00
Weekly	245.00	315.00

Evening meal 1900 (last orders 2100)
Parking for 60
Cards accepted: Mastercard, Visa, Switch/Delta

Grove House

HIGHLY COMMENDED

Holme Street, Tarvin, Chester
CH3 8EQ
☎ (01829) 740893
Fax (01829) 741769

Warm welcome in relaxing environment. Spacious, comfortable rooms, attractive garden. Ample parking. Within easy reach of Chester (4 miles) and major North West and North Wales tourist attractions. NWTB Place to Stay Award 1996 and 1997.

Bedrooms: 1 single, 1 double, 1 twin
Bathrooms: 1 en-suite, 1 public

Bed & breakfast per night:	£min	£max
Single	23.00	38.00
Double	48.00	56.00

Parking for 8

Mitchells of Chester

HIGHLY COMMENDED

Green Gables House, 28 Hough Green, Chester CH4 8JQ
☎ (01244) 679004
Fax (01244) 679004

Tastefully restored, elegant Victorian residence, with steeply pitched slated roofs, a sweeping staircase, antique furniture in tall rooms with moulded cornices. Compact landscaped gardens. Close to city centre.

Bedrooms: 1 single, 1 double, 1 twin, 1 family room
Bathrooms: 4 en-suite, 1 public

Bed & breakfast per night:	£min	£max
Single	25.00	28.00
Double	40.00	40.00

Parking for 5

Tickeridge House

Listed COMMENDED

Whitchurch Road, Milton Green, Chester CH3 9DS
☎ (01829) 770443

Chester 5 miles, off A41 at Milton Green. Worth looking for and certainly worth staying. Beautifully appointed house with all rooms on ground floor. Very warm welcome. Succulent full English breakfast. Look forward to meeting you, all facilities for your comfort.

Bedrooms: 2 double, 1 family room
Bathrooms: 1 en-suite, 1 public

Bed & breakfast per night:	£min	£max
Single	16.50	20.00
Double	35.00	40.00

Parking for 6

Please check prices and other details at the time of booking.

A key to symbols can be found inside the back cover flap.

CHORLEY

Lancashire
Map ref 4A1

Set between the Pennine moors and the Lancashire Plain, Chorley has been an important town since medieval times, with its "Flat-Iron" and covered markets. The rich heritage includes Astley Hall and Park, Hoghton Tower, Rivington Country Park and the Leeds-Liverpool Canal.

Parr Hall Farm

Listed COMMENDED

Parr Lane, Eccleston, Chorley
PR7 5SL
☎ (01257) 451917
Fax (01257) 451917

15-acre mixed farm. 18th C listed farmhouse, tastefully restored. Oak beams, open views. Village location within walking distance of good pubs and restaurants. Easy access to Lakes and Yorkshire Dales.

Bedrooms: 4 double, 1 twin
Bathrooms: 4 en-suite, 1 private

Bed & breakfast per night:	£min	£max
Single	25.00	30.00
Double	35.00	45.00

Parking for 20
Cards accepted: Mastercard, Visa

CLITHEROE

Lancashire
Map ref 4A1

Ancient market town with an 800-year-old castle keep and a wide range of award-winning shops. Good base for touring Ribble Valley, Trough of Bowland and Pennine moorland. Country market on Tuesdays and Saturdays.
Tourist Information Centre ☎ (01200) 425566

Brooklands

Listed COMMENDED

9 Pendle Road, Clitheroe BB7 1JQ
☎ (01200) 422797

Comfortable, detached Victorian home in Ribble Valley. 5 minutes' walk town/train. Ideal base for Lakes, dales, West Coast and motorways. Brochure available.

Bedrooms: 1 double, 2 twin
Suite available
Bathrooms: 1 en-suite, 2 public

Bed & breakfast per night:	£min	£max
Single	16.00	18.50
Double	32.00	38.00

Parking for 5

Mitton Hall Lodgings

APPROVED

Mitton Road, Mitton, Clitheroe
BB7 9PQ
☎ (01254) 826544
Fax (01254) 826386

16th C listed hall in Ribble Valley. Restaurant, pizzeria, tavern, lodgings. Two miles Whalley Abbey, 3 miles Clitheroe Castle, close Trough of Bowland. Eleven miles junction 31 of M6, 7 miles M65.

Bedrooms: 2 single, 6 double, 5 twin, 1 triple
Bathrooms: 14 en-suite

Bed & breakfast per night:	£min	£max
Single	41.50	51.50
Double	47.00	57.00

Lunch available
Evening meal 1830 (last orders 2230)
Parking for 150
Cards accepted: Amex, Mastercard, Visa, Switch/Delta

50

Rakefoot Farm

Listed COMMENDED

Chaigley, Clitheroe BB7 3LY
☎ (01995) 61332 & (0589) 279063

100-acre dairy farm. Traditional B & B (with optional evening meal) in farmhouse in beautiful Forest of Bowland. 5 miles from Clitheroe, 3 miles from Chipping, 8 miles M6 junction 31A. Panoramic views, home cooking and a warm welcome await. Self-catering available in stone barn conversion.

Bedrooms: 2 double, 1 twin
Bathrooms: 1 en-suite, 1 public

Bed & breakfast per night:	£min	£max
Single	15.00	19.00
Double	27.00	35.00

Half board per person:	£min	£max
Daily	25.00	27.50
Weekly	150.00	175.00

Evening meal 1700 (last orders 1900)
Parking for 6

COLNE

Lancashire
Map ref 4B1

Old market town with mixed industries bordering the moorland Bronte country. Nearby are the ruins of Wycoller House, featured in Charlotte Bronte's "Jane Eyre" as Ferndean Manor.

Middle Beardshaw Head Farm

Listed APPROVED

Burnley Road, Trawden, Colne
BB8 8PP
☎ (01282) 865257

15-acre dairy farm. 17th-18th C Lancashire longhouse with oak beams, panelling, log fires. Panoramic views with pools, woods and stream. Half mile from Trawden. Caravan and camping site on farm, with bathroom, hot shower and electricity.

Bedrooms: 2 single, 1 family room
Bathrooms: 1 en-suite, 2 public

Bed & breakfast per night:	£min	£max
Single	17.50	20.00
Double	35.00	40.00

Half board per person:	£min	£max
Daily	25.50	28.00
Weekly	175.00	

Evening meal 1900 (last orders 2030)
Parking for 10

Reedymoor Farm

Listed HIGHLY COMMENDED

Reedymoor Lane, Foulridge, Colne
BB8 7LJ
☎ (01282) 865074

A 16th C house by the side of Lake Burwain. Extensive gardens and large parking area.

Bedrooms: 1 single, 1 twin, 1 triple
Suite available
Bathrooms: 1 en-suite, 2 public

Bed & breakfast per night:	£min	£max
Single	18.00	25.00
Double	40.00	60.00

Half board per person:	£min	£max
Daily	32.00	40.00
Weekly	200.00	250.00

Evening meal 1830 (last orders 2000)
Parking for 10

Wickets

HIGHLY COMMENDED

118 Keighley Road, Colne BB8 0PJ
☎ (01282) 862002

Edwardian town house. Comfortable, attractive bedrooms. Friendly and helpful hosts. Close to open countryside. Non-smokers only, please.

Bedrooms: 1 single, 1 double
Bathrooms: 1 private, 1 public

Bed & breakfast per night:	£min	£max
Single	17.00	17.00
Double	34.00	38.00

Parking for 1
Open March–December

11

CREWE

Cheshire
Map ref 4A2

Famous for its railway junction, this small market town is at the heart of the beautiful south Cheshire countryside and well located for visiting local attractions. Original home of the Rolls Royce motor car.

The Hand and Trumpet Inn

COMMENDED

Main Road, Wrinehill, Crewe
CW3 9BJ
☎ (01270) 820048
Fax (01270) 820087

Comfortable rural inn, convenient for Crewe and the Potteries. Set in landscaped gardens. 10 minutes from M6, junction 16.

Bedrooms: 4 double, 2 twin
Bathrooms: 6 en-suite

Bed & breakfast per night:	£min	£max
Single	28.00	
Double	38.00	

Lunch available
Evening meal 1900 (last orders 2200)
Parking for 70
Cards accepted: Mastercard, Visa

60

Information on accommodation listed in this guide has been supplied by the proprietors. As changes may occur you are advised to check details at the time of booking.

GARSTANG

Lancashire
Map ref 4A1

Picturesque country market town. The gateway to the fells, it stands on the Lancaster Canal and is a popular cruising centre. Close by are the remains of Greenhalgh Castle (no public access) and the Bleasdale Circle. Discovery Centre shows history of Over Wyre and Bowland fringe areas.
Tourist Information Centre ☎ (01995) 602125

Ashdene

APPROVED

Parkside Lane, Nateby, Garstang, Preston PR3 0JA
☎ (01995) 602676
Family-run bed and breakfast. All rooms en-suite and with colour TV. 5 miles junctions 32/33 of M6, 20 minutes Blackpool, 30 minutes Lake District.
Bedrooms: 1 double, 2 twin
Bathrooms: 3 en-suite, 1 public

Bed & breakfast per night:	£min	£max
Single	20.00	20.00
Double	34.00	34.00

Parking for 6

Guy's Thatched Hamlet

COMMENDED

Canalside, St Michael's Road, Bilsborrow, Garstang, Preston PR3 0RS
☎ (01995) 640849 & 640010
Fax (01995) 640141

Friendly, family-run thatched canalside tavern, restaurant, pizzeria, lodgings, craft shops, cricket ground with thatched pavilion and crown green bowling. Conference centre. Off junction 32 of M6, then 3 miles north on A6 to Garstang.
Bedrooms: 28 double, 20 twin, 5 family rooms
Bathrooms: 53 en-suite

Bed & breakfast per night:	£min	£max
Single	41.50	55.00
Double	47.50	60.50

Half board per person:	£min	£max
Daily	35.75	42.25

Lunch available
Evening meal 1800 (last orders 2330)
Parking for 300
Cards accepted: Amex, Mastercard, Visa, Switch/Delta

GREAT ECCLESTON

Lancashire
Map ref 4A1

Cartford Hotel

APPROVED

Cartford Lane, Little Eccleston, Preston PR3 0YP
☎ (01995) 670166
Fax (01995) 671785
Country riverside pub and coaching inn, with 1.5 miles of fishing rights. Within easy reach of Blackpool and the Lake District.
Bedrooms: 1 single, 4 double, 1 twin
Bathrooms: 6 en-suite

Bed & breakfast per night:	£min	£max
Single	32.50	36.50
Double	44.50	48.50

Lunch available
Evening meal 1900 (last orders 2130)
Parking for 100
Cards accepted: Mastercard, Visa

HYDE

Greater Manchester
Map ref 4B2

Needhams Farm

COMMENDED

Uplands Road, Werneth Low, Gee Cross, Hyde, Cheshire SK14 3AQ
☎ (0161) 368 4610
Fax (0161) 367 9106
30-acre beef farm. 500-year-old farmhouse with exposed beams in all rooms and an open fire in bar/dining room. Excellent views. Well placed for Manchester city and the airport.
Bedrooms: 1 single, 4 double, 1 twin, 1 triple
Bathrooms: 5 en-suite, 1 public

Bed & breakfast per night:	£min	£max
Single	19.00	20.00
Double	30.00	32.00

Evening meal 1900 (last orders 2130)
Parking for 12
Cards accepted: Mastercard, Visa

KNUTSFORD

Cheshire
Map ref 4A2

Delightful town with many buildings of architectural and historic interest. The setting of Elizabeth Gaskell's "Cranford". Annual May Day celebration and decorative "sanding" of the pavements are unique to the town. Popular Heritage Centre.
Tourist Information Centre ☎ (01565) 632611 or 632210

Laburnum Cottage Guest House

HIGHLY COMMENDED

Knutsford Road, Mobberley, Knutsford WA16 7PU
☎ (01565) 872464
Fax (01565) 872464
Small country house in Cheshire countryside on B5085 close to Tatton Park, 6 miles from Manchester Airport, 4 miles from M6 exit 19 and 4 miles from M56. Taxi service to airport. Non-smokers only, please. Winner of NWTB Place to Stay '93/'94/'95 Guesthouse Award and Cheshire Tourist Board B&B of the Year '93/'94.
Bedrooms: 1 single, 1 double, 1 twin
Bathrooms: 3 en-suite, 1 public

Bed & breakfast per night:	£min	£max
Single	30.00	39.00
Double	42.00	50.00

Parking for 12

LIVERPOOL

Merseyside
Map ref 4A2

Vibrant city which became prominent in the 18th C as a result of its sugar, spice and tobacco trade with the Americas. Today the historic waterfront is a major attraction. Home to the Beatles, the Grand National and two 20th C cathedrals, as well as many museums and galleries.
Tourist Information Centre ☎ (0151) 709 3631 or 708 8854

Anna's

COMMENDED

65 Dudlow Lane, Calderstones, Liverpool L18 2EY
☎ (0151) 722 3708
Fax (0151) 722 8699
Large family house with friendly atmosphere, in select residential area close to all amenities. Direct transport routes to city centre. 1 mile from end of M62 motorway.

Bedrooms: 1 double, 3 twin
Bathrooms: 1 public

Bed & breakfast per night:	£min	£max
Single	18.00	22.00
Double	33.00	35.00

Parking for 6

LYDGATE

Greater Manchester
Map ref 4B1

Higher Quick Farm

Listed HIGHLY COMMENDED

Stockport Road, Saddleworth, Oldham OL4 4JJ
☎ (01457) 872424

45-acre beef farm. Comfortable Grade II listed farmhouse, with oak-beams and magnificent views from all rooms. Good centre for walking or touring. Easy journey to Manchester and M62. Close to Uppermill centre. Centrally heated, non-smoking.

Bedrooms: 2 double, 1 twin
Bathrooms: 1 en-suite, 1 public

Bed & breakfast per night:	£min	£max
Single	20.00	20.00
Double	35.00	35.00

Parking for 4

MACCLESFIELD

Cheshire
Map ref 4B2

Cobbled streets and quaint old buildings stand side by side with modern shops and three markets. Centuries of association with the silk industry; museums feature working exhibits and social history. Stunning views of the Peak District National Park.
Tourist Information Centre ☎ (01625) 504114 or 504115

Sandpit Farm

COMMENDED

Messuage Lane, Marton, Macclesfield SK11 9HS
☎ (01260) 224254

110-acre arable farm. Comfortable, oak-beamed house. Twin and double rooms are en-suite. Convenient for stately homes and National Trust properties. Easy access to Peak District, Chester and Manchester Airport. 4 miles north of Congleton, 1 mile west of A34.

Bedrooms: 1 double, 2 twin
Bathrooms: 2 en-suite, 1 public

Bed & breakfast per night:	£min	£max
Single	17.00	20.00
Double	34.00	40.00

Parking for 4

MALPAS

Cheshire
Map ref 4A2

Millhey Farm

APPROVED

Barton, Malpas SY14 7HY
☎ (01829) 782431

140-acre mixed farm. Typical, lovely Cheshire black and white part-timbered farmhouse in conservation area, 9 miles from Chester, close to Welsh Border country. On A534, just off A41.

Bedrooms: 1 single, 1 triple, 1 family room
Bathrooms: 2 en-suite, 1 public

Bed & breakfast per night:	£min	£max
Single	16.00	16.00
Double	32.00	32.00

Parking for 2

MANCHESTER

Greater Manchester
Map ref 4B1

The Gateway to the North, offering one of Britain's largest selections of arts venues and theatre productions, a wide range of chain stores and specialist shops, a legendary, lively nightlife, spectacular architecture and a plethora of eating and drinking places.
Tourist Information Centre ☎ (0161) 234 3157 or 234 3158 or 436 3344

Anbermar

COMMENDED

32 Gibwood Road, Northenden, Manchester M22 4BS
☎ (0161) 998 2375

A warm welcome awaits you in this very comfortable privately owned house, 4 miles from Manchester Airport and city centre. Spacious room with all facilities, private bathroom.

Bedrooms: 1 twin
Bathrooms: 1 private

Bed & breakfast per night:	£min	£max
Single	20.00	
Double	40.00	

Parking for 2

MANCHESTER AIRPORT

See under Ashley, Hyde, Knutsford, Manchester, Stockport, Styal, Wilmslow

NANTWICH

Cheshire
Map ref 4A2

Old market town on the River Weaver made prosperous in Roman times by salt springs. Fire destroyed the town in 1583 and many buildings were rebuilt in Elizabethan style. Churche's Mansion (open to the public) survived the fire.
Tourist Information Centre ☎ (01270) 610983

Lea Farm

COMMENDED

Wrinehill Road, Wybunbury, Nantwich CW5 7NS
☎ (01270) 841429

160-acre dairy farm. Charming farmhouse in beautiful gardens where peacocks roam. Comfortable lounge, pool/snooker, fishing pool. Ideal surroundings.

Bedrooms: 1 double, 1 twin, 1 triple
Bathrooms: 2 en-suite, 1 public

Bed & breakfast per night:	£min	£max
Single	17.00	25.00
Double	30.00	34.00

Half board per person:	£min	£max
Daily	26.00	34.00
Weekly	170.00	220.00

Evening meal 1800 (last orders 1900)
Parking for 22

For ideas on places to visit refer to the introduction at the beginning of this section.

For further information on accommodation establishments use the coupons at the back of this guide.

NANTWICH

Continued

The Limes

HIGHLY COMMENDED

157 Wistaston Road, Willaston, Nantwich CW5 6QS
☎ (01270) 669112 & 0976 655762

Contact Anne and Malcolm Croughan to stay in this lovely home. Set in half-acre garden, close to Bridgemere and Stapeley garden centres, Chester and North Wales.
Bedrooms: 2 double, 1 twin
Bathrooms: 2 en-suite, 1 private

Bed & breakfast per night:	£min	£max
Single	23.00	25.00
Double	34.00	36.00

Parking for 9

Oakland House

HIGHLY COMMENDED

252 Newcastle Road (A500), Blakelow, Shavington, Nantwich CW5 7ET
☎ (01270) 567134 & (0589) 683418
Fax (01270) 651752
Friendly welcome, home comforts, rural views. Superior accommodation at reasonable rates. On A500 (A52) 5 miles from M6 junction 16. Within easy reach of Nantwich, Chester, Stapeley Water Gardens and Bridgemere Garden World. Recent winner of North-west Place to Stay, B&B category.
Bedrooms: 3 double, 2 twin
Bathrooms: 5 en-suite

Bed & breakfast per night:	£min	£max
Single	26.00	30.00
Double	32.00	38.00

Parking for 10
Cards accepted: Visa

All accommodation in this guide has been graded, or is awaiting a grading, by a trained Tourist Board inspector.

Stapeley Manor

HIGHLY COMMENDED

Stapeley Water Gardens, London Road, Stapeley, Nantwich CW5 7JL
☎ (01270) 611792
Fax (01270) 624919
Edwardian mock-Tudor manor, next door to Stapeley Water Gardens. Super-king, four-poster bedroom with large circular bath and leaded-glass bay window seat.
Bedrooms: 4 double
Bathrooms: 2 en-suite, 2 private, 1 public

Bed & breakfast per night:	£min	£max
Single	20.00	
Double		50.00

Parking for 10
Cards accepted: Mastercard, Visa

NORTHWICH

Cheshire
Map ref 4A2

An important salt-producing town since Roman times, Northwich has been replanned with a modern shopping centre and a number of black and white buildings. Unique Anderton boat-lift on northern outskirts of town.

Manor Farm

HIGHLY COMMENDED

Cliff Road, Acton Bridge, Northwich CW8 3QP
☎ (01606) 853181
Fax (01606) 853181
100-acre livestock farm. Secluded Georgian-style farmhouse and traditional buildings, set in 100 acres of grassland with river frontage in the Weaver Valley.
Bedrooms: 1 single, 2 twin
Bathrooms: 1 en-suite, 2 private

Bed & breakfast per night:	£min	£max
Single	20.00	24.00
Double	40.00	48.00

Parking for 14

COLOUR MAPS

Colour maps at the back of this guide pinpoint all places in which you will find accommodation listed.

Springfield Guest House

COMMENDED

Chester Road, Delamere, Oakmere, Northwich CW8 2HB
☎ (01606) 882538
Family guesthouse erected in 1863. On A556 close to Delamere Forest, midway between Chester and M6 junction 19. Manchester Airport 25 minutes' drive.
Bedrooms: 4 single, 1 twin, 1 family room
Bathrooms: 2 en-suite, 1 public

Bed & breakfast per night:	£min	£max
Single	19.00	25.00
Double	35.00	45.00

Parking for 12

OLDHAM

Greater Manchester
Map ref 4B1

The magnificent mill buildings which made Oldham one of the world's leading cotton-spinning towns still dominate the landscape. Ideally situated on the edge of the Peak District, it is now a centre of culture, sport and shopping. Art gallery has fine collections.
Tourist Information Centre ☎ (0161) 627 1024

Boothstead Farm

Listed COMMENDED

Rochdale Road, Denshaw, Oldham OL3 5UE
☎ (01457) 878622
200-acre livestock farm. 18th C farmhouse on fringe of Saddleworth (A640) between junctions 21 and 22 of M62 motorway.
Bedrooms: 1 double, 1 twin
Bathrooms: 1 public

Bed & breakfast per night:	£min	£max
Single	18.00	20.00
Double	34.00	36.00

Parking for 4

The map references refer to the colour maps towards the end of the guide. The first figure is the map number; the letter and figure which follow indicate the grid reference on the map.

Globe Farm Guest House

COMMENDED

Huddersfield Road, Standedge, Delph, Oldham OL3 5LU
☎ (01457) 873040
Fax (01457) 873040
18-acre mixed farm. Quarter of a mile from the Pennine Way and high walking country. En-suite bed and breakfast accommodation, 18-bed bunkhouse (self-catering or with meals) and small campsite.
Bedrooms: 3 single, 2 double, 3 twin, 1 family room
Bathrooms: 9 en-suite

Bed & breakfast per night:	£min	£max
Single	20.00	
Double	35.00	

Half board per person:	£min	£max
Daily	27.00	
Weekly	110.00	

Evening meal 1830 (last orders 1900)
Parking for 30
Cards accepted: Mastercard, Visa

RIBBLE VALLEY

See under Clitheroe

ST MICHAEL'S ON WYRE

Lancashire
Map ref 4A1

Village near Blackpool with interesting 13th C church of St Michael containing medieval stained glass window depicting sheep shearing, and clock tower bell made in 1548.

Compton House

COMMENDED

Garstang Road, St Michael's on Wyre, Preston PR3 0TE
☎ (01995) 679378
Fax (01995) 679378
Well-furnished country house in own grounds in a picturesque village, near M6 and 40 minutes from Lake District. Fishing in the Wyre. "Best-Kept Guesthouse" award 1995 and 1996.
Bedrooms: 1 single, 1 double, 1 twin
Bathrooms: 2 en-suite, 1 private

Bed & breakfast per night:	£min	£max
Single	20.00	20.00
Double	40.00	40.00

Parking for 6

SANDBACH

Cheshire
Map ref 4A2

Small Cheshire town, originally important for salt production. Contains narrow, winding streets, timbered houses and a cobbled market-place. Town square has 2 Anglo-Saxon crosses to commemorate the conversion to Christianity of the King of Mercia's son.

Canal Centre and Village Store

Listed COMMENDED

Hassall Green, Sandbach CW11 4YB
☎ (01270) 762266

The house and shop, built circa 1777 at the side of Lock 57 on the Trent and Mersey Canal, have served canal users for over 200 years. Off A533 near Sandbach and junction 17 on M6 - signposted. Gift shop, tearooms, store and licensed restaurant (Tues-Sat from 7pm).
Wheelchair access category 3
Bedrooms: 1 single, 3 double, 2 twin
Bathrooms: 2 en-suite, 1 private, 1 public

Bed & breakfast per night:	£min	£max
Single	18.00	22.00
Double	36.00	44.00

Lunch available
Evening meal 1900 (last orders 2130)
Parking for 7
Cards accepted: Mastercard, Visa, Switch/Delta

Establishments should be open throughout the year, unless otherwise stated.

Half board prices are given per person, but in some cases these may be based on double/twin occupancy.

Moss Cottage Farm

HIGHLY COMMENDED

Hassall Road, Winterley, Sandbach CW11 4RU
☎ (01270) 583018
Beamed farmhouse in quiet location just off A534, with lovely walks, fishing and golf. All rooms have TV, tea-making facilities and hand basins. Evening meals by arrangement.
Bedrooms: 1 single, 1 double, 1 twin
Bathrooms: 1 en-suite, 2 public

Bed & breakfast per night:	£min	£max
Single	18.00	20.00
Double	36.00	40.00

Evening meal 1700 (last orders 2000)
Parking for 10

SINGLETON

Lancashire
Map ref 4A1

Ancient parish dating from 1175, mentioned in Domesday Book. Chapel and day school dating back to 1865. Mainly rural area to the north of St Anne's.

Old Castle Farm

Listed APPROVED

Garstang Road, Singleton, Blackpool FY6 8ND
☎ (01253) 883839
Take junction 3 off M55, follow Fleetwood sign to first traffic lights. Turn right, travel 200 yards on A586 to bungalow on the right.
Bedrooms: 1 twin, 1 triple, 1 family room
Bathrooms: 1 public

Bed & breakfast per night:	£min	£max
Single	17.00	
Double	34.00	

Parking for 20
Open April–October

Please mention this guide when making your booking.

The National Grading and Classification Scheme is explained at the back of this guide.

SOUTHPORT

Merseyside
Map ref 4A1

Delightful Victorian resort noted for gardens, sandy beaches and 6 golf-courses, particularly Royal Birkdale. Attractions include the Atkinson Art Gallery, Southport Railway Centre, Pleasureland and the annual Southport Flower Show. Excellent shopping, particularly in Lord Street's elegant boulevard.
Tourist Information Centre ☎ (01704) 533333

Sandy Brook Farm

COMMENDED

52 Wyke Cop Road, Scarisbrick, Southport PR8 5LR
☎ (01704) 880337

27-acre arable farm. Comfortable accommodation in converted farm buildings in rural area of Scarisbrick, offering a friendly welcome. 3.5 miles from seaside town of Southport. Special facilities for disabled guests. Silver award-winner NWTB "Place to Stay".

Bedrooms: 1 single, 1 double, 2 twin, 1 triple, 1 family room
Bathrooms: 6 en-suite

Bed & breakfast per night:	£min	£max
Single	19.00	19.00
Double	33.00	33.00

Parking for 9

STOCKPORT

Greater Manchester
Map ref 4B2

Once an important cotton-spinning and manufacturing centre, Stockport has an impressive railway viaduct, a shopping precinct built over the River Mersey and a new leisure complex. Lyme Hall and Vernon Park Museum nearby.
Tourist Information Centre ☎ (0161) 474 3320 or 474 3321

Shire Cottage Farmhouse

COMMENDED

Benches Lane, Marple Bridge, Stockport, Cheshire SK6 5RY
☎ (01457) 866536

180-acre mixed farm. Opposite Woodheys Restaurant off the A626 Stockport to Glossop road, close to the Peak District, Buxton, Derwent Dams and Kinder Scout. 20 minutes from the airport, 16 miles from Manchester. Swimming, horse riding, fishing and boating nearby. Peaceful location.

Bedrooms: 1 single, 1 double, 1 twin, 1 family room
Bathrooms: 2 en-suite, 1 public

Bed & breakfast per night:	£min	£max
Single	19.00	24.00
Double	36.00	40.00

Parking for 7

STYAL

Cheshire
Map ref 4B2

Willow Cottage

HIGHLY COMMENDED

56 Hollin Lane, Styal, Wilmslow SK9 4JH
☎ (01625) 523630

Comfortable modern dormer bungalow set in rural surroundings yet convenient for motorways, airport, restaurants and Styal Country Park and Mill. Free transport to and from airport.

Bedrooms: 1 single, 1 twin
Bathrooms: 1 public

Bed & breakfast per night:	£min	£max
Single	19.00	20.00
Double	35.00	40.00

Parking for 6
Cards accepted: Mastercard, Visa

TARPORLEY

Cheshire
Map ref 4A2

Old town with gabled houses and medieval church of St Helen containing monuments to the Done family, a historic name in this area. Spectacular ruins of 13th C Beeston Castle nearby.

Foresters Arms

COMMENDED

92 High Street, Tarporley CW6 0AX
☎ (01829) 733151
Fax (01829) 730020

Country public house, on the edge of the village of Tarporley, offering a homely and friendly service. Weekly rates negotiable.

Bedrooms: 1 double, 2 twin
Bathrooms: 1 en-suite, 2 public, 1 private shower

Bed & breakfast per night:	£min	£max
Single	20.50	26.50
Double	32.00	45.00

Half board per person:	£min	£max
Daily	26.00	45.00

Lunch available
Evening meal 1730 (last orders 2030)
Parking for 30
Cards accepted: Mastercard, Visa

WILMSLOW

Cheshire
Map ref 4B2

Nestling in the valleys of the Rivers Bollin and Dane, Wilmslow retains an intimate village atmosphere. Easy-to-reach attractions include Quarry Bank Mill at Styal. Lindow Man was discovered on a nearby common. Romany's Caravan sits in a memorial garden.

Marigold House

COMMENDED

132 Knutsford Road, Wilmslow SK9 6JH
☎ (01625) 584414 & 0378 509565

18th C period house with oak beams, flagged floors and antique furnishings. Log fires in winter. Private sitting room and dining room.

Bedrooms: 2 twin
Bathrooms: 2 en-suite

Bed & breakfast per night:	£min	£max
Single	25.00	25.00
Double	35.00	35.00

Parking for 4

For ideas on places to visit refer to the introduction at the beginning of this section.

WELCOME HOST

This is a nationally recognised customer care programme which aims to promote the highest standards of service and a warm welcome. Establishments who are taking part in this initiative are indicated by the symbol.

YORKSHIRE

The wide open spaces of Yorkshire and North East Lincolnshire promise a stunning variety of holiday experiences. The breathtaking landscape offers everything from the serenity of the Wolds and the Dales, to picturesque Herriot country, Brontë country, and the dramatic North Yorkshire moors.

Ancient York is a fine touring base and has fascinating Roman and Viking remains. There are pretty coastal spots, too, including the family resort of Cleethorpes, and the colourful port of Whitby at the heart of Captain Cook country.

There's excellent shopping and night life in the region's big towns, while Grimsby has the National Fishing Heritage Centre and hosts an annual seafood festival.

The counties of East Riding of Yorkshire, North East Lincolnshire, North Lincolnshire, North Yorkshire, South Yorkshire and West Yorkshire

FOR MORE INFORMATION CONTACT:
Yorkshire Tourist Board
312 Tadcaster Road, York YO2 2HF
Tel: (01904) 707961 or 707070 (24 hour brochure line)
Fax: (01904) 701414

Where to Go in Yorkshire – see pages 94-97
Where to Stay in Yorkshire – see pages 98-121

YORKSHIRE

Where to Go and What to See

You will find hundreds of interesting places to visit during your stay in Yorkshire, just some of which are listed in these pages. The number against each name will help you locate it on the map (page 97). Contact any Tourist Information Centre in the region for more ideas on days out in Yorkshire.

1 Music in Miniature Exhibition
Albion Road,
Robin Hood's Bay, Whitby,
North Yorkshire YO22 4SH
Tel: (01947) 880512
Exhibition of 50 one-twelfth scale dioramic models set in illuminated recesses - depicting man's love of music from stone age to space age.

2 The Honey Farm
Racecourse Road,
East Ayton, Scarborough,
North Yorkshire YO13 9HT
Tel: (01723) 864001
Working honey farm with an extensive exhibition of live honey bees. Guided tour with a description of the life and history of bees. Farm shop. Cafe.

3 Scarborough Millennium
Harbourside, Scarborough,
North Yorkshire YO11 1PG
Tel: (01723) 501000
A time travel experience unlike any other. An epic adventure through 1,000 years from 966 to 1966.

4 North Yorkshire Moors Railway
Pickering Station, Pickering,
North Yorkshire YO18 7AJ
Tel: (01751) 472508
Operates the route between Grosmont and Pickering, through some of the most magnificent scenery of the North York Moors National Park.

5 Castle Howard
Coneysthorpe,
York YO6 7DA
Tel: (01653) 648444
Set in 1,000 acres of magnificent parkland with nature walks, scenic lake and stunning rose gardens. Attractions include important furniture and works of art.

6 Island Heritage Pott Hall Farm
Healey, Ripon,
North Yorkshire HG4 4LT
Tel: (01765) 689651
A working dales farm producing natural, undyed woollen products from its own flock of rare breed, primitive sheep. See lambing, shearing, spinning. Shop.

7 Fountains Abbey and Studley Royal
Ripon,
North Yorkshire HG4 3DY
Tel: (01765) 608888
Largest monastic ruin in Britain, founded by Cistercian monks in 1132. Landscape garden laid out 1720-40 with lake, formal watergarden and temples. Deer park.

8 **White Scar Caves**
Ingleton, Carnforth,
Lancashire LA6 3AW
Tel: (01524) 241244
Britain's longest show cave, underground waterfalls and streams, massive ice-age cavern, floodlighting.

9 **Yorkshire Dales Falconry and Conservation Centre**
Crows Nest,
Giggleswick, Settle,
North Yorkshire LA2 8AS
Tel: (01729) 825164/822832
Falconry centre with many species of birds of prey from around the world including vultures, eagles, hawks, falcons and owls. Free flying displays, lecture room and aviaries.

10 **Skipton Castle**
Skipton,
North Yorkshire BD23 1AQ
Tel: (01756) 792442
One of the most complete and well-preserved medieval castles in England. Explore massive round towers and see beautiful Conduit Court with its famous yew.

11 **Jorvik Viking Centre**
Coppergate,
York YO1 1NT
Tel: (01904) 643211/613711
Travel back in time in a timecar to a recreation of Viking York. See excavated remains of Viking houses and a display of objects found.

12 **National Railway Museum**
Leeman Road,
York YO2 4XJ
Tel: (01904) 621261
Experience nearly 200 years of technical and social history on the railways and see how they shaped the world.

13 **York Castle Museum**
The Eye of York,
York YO1 1RY
Tel: (01904) 653611
England's most popular museum of everyday life including reconstructed streets and period rooms, Edwardian park, costume and jewellery, arms and armour, craft workshops.

14 **Harewood House**
Harewood, Leeds LS17 9LQ
Tel: (0113) 288 6331
18thC Carr/Adam house, Capability Brown landscape, fine Sevres and Chinese porcelain, English and Italian paintings, Chippendale furniture. Exotic bird garden.

15 **National Museum of Photography, Film & Television**
Pictureville, Bradford,
West Yorkshire BD1 1NQ
Tel: (01274) 727488
Museum housing the largest cinema screen (Imax) in Britain, 64 x 52 ft. Fly on a magic carpet, operate a TV camera, or become a newsreader for a day.

16 **Transperience**
Transperience Way,
Low Moor, Bradford,
West Yorkshire
BD12 7HQ
Tel: (01274) 690909
With historic vehicle rides and state of the art interactive technology, travel on a unique journey through the past, present and future of transport.

17 **Royal Armouries Museum**
Leeds LS10 1LT
Tel: (0113) 220 1900
See the thrill of jousting tournaments and the terror of the battlefield recaptured. The museum includes one of the world's finest collections of arms and armour.

18 **Tetley's Brewery Wharf**
The Waterfront, Leeds LS1 1QG
Tel: (0113) 242 0666/243 1888
A unique development which brings to life the story through the ages of probably the greatest British traditions - the pub.

19 Hull & East Riding Museum
33 High Street, Hull
Tel: (01482) 613902/613925
The museum explores the story of Hull and the East Riding area, covering geology and archaeology. Also features the Hasholme Boat - over 3,000 years old.

20 National Fishing Heritage Centre
Alexandra Dock,
Grimsby,
North East Lincolnshire
DN31 1UZ
Tel: (01472) 323345
Spectacular 1950s steam trawler experience. See, hear, smell and touch a series of recreated environments. Museum displays, shop, aquarium and historic fishing vessels.

21 Cleethorpes Coast Light Railway
Kingsway Station, Cleethorpes,
North East Lincolnshire
DN35 0AG
Tel: (01472) 604657/602118
A delightful scenic railway journey from Kingsway Station with panoramic views of the Humber Estuary.

22 Pleasure Island Family Theme Park
Kings Road, Cleethorpes,
North East Lincolnshire
DN35 0PL
Tel: (01472) 211511
The East coast's biggest fun day out, with over 50 rides and attractions, many undercover. Shows from around the world.

23 Barnsley Metrodome Leisure Complex
Queens Road, Barnsley,
South Yorkshire S71 1AN
Tel: (01226) 730060
One of the North's largest leisure facilities with five pools, dry sports and leisure complex.

24 Yorkshire Sculpture Park
West Bretton, Wakefield,
West Yorkshire WF4 4LG
Tel: (01924) 830302
International open-air gallery with changing exhibitions of contemporary sculpture, set in 260 acres of beautiful 18thC landscaped grounds.

25 Eureka! The Museum for Children
Discovery Road, Halifax,
West Yorkshire HX1 2NE
Tel: (01422) 330069/
(01426) 983191
First museum of its kind designed especially for children up to the age of 12. There are over 400 hands-on exhibits to touch, listen to, feel and smell as well as look.

26 Kirklees Light Railway
Railway Station,
Park Mill Way, Clayton,
West Huddersfield HD8 9XJ
Tel: (01484) 865727
A 15-inch gauge steam railway with original Lancashire and Yorkshire station. Steam and diesel locomotives and enclosed carriages. Shop and cafe. Children's play area.

27 National Coal Mining Museum for England
Caphouse Collier, New Road,
Overton, Wakefield,
West Yorkshire WF4 4RH
Tel: (01924) 848806
Award-winning museum of the English coalfields, including guided underground tour in authentic old workings, surface displays, working steam winder.

28 Heeley City Farm
Richards Road,
Sheffield S2 3DT
Tel: (0114) 258 0482
Four-acre farm with horses, cows, goats, pigs, sheep, ducks, chickens, turkeys, bees, rabbits, herb gardens, organic gardens, wild flowers. Cafe. Garden centre.

29 Rother Valley Country Park
Mansfield Road, Wales Bar,
Sheffield S31 8PE
Tel: (0114) 247 1452
Watersports centre, visitor and craft centres, nature reserve, special events, shop, cafe and walks.

FIND OUT MORE

Further information about holidays and attractions in the Yorkshire region is available from

Yorkshire Tourist Board,
312 Tadcaster Road,
York YO2 2HF.
Tel: (01904) 707961 or 707070
(24 hour brochure line)

These publications are available free from the Yorkshire Tourist Board:

- **Yorkshire Holidays and Short Breaks** - information on the region, including hotels, self-catering, caravan and camping parks
- **Yorkshire - a Great Day Out** - the official guide of what to do, where to go, what to see, where to eat and how to get there, the list goes on!
- **Bed & Breakfast Touring Map** - forming part of a 'family' of maps covering England, this guide provides information on bed and breakfast establishments in the Yorkshire region
- **What's on** - listing of events. Published three times a year

WHERE TO STAY (YORKSHIRE)

Accommodation entries in this region are listed in alphabetical order of place name, and then in alphabetical order of establishment.

Map references refer to the colour location maps at the back of this guide. The first number indicates the map to use; the letter and number which follow refer to the grid reference on the map.

At-a-glance symbols at the end of each accommodation entry give useful information about services and facilities. A key to symbols can be found inside the back cover flap. Keep this open for easy reference.

AMPLEFORTH

North Yorkshire
Map ref 5C3

Stone-built village in Hambleton Hills. Famous for its abbey and college, a Benedictine public school, founded in 1802, of which Cardinal Hume was once abbot.

Carr House Farm

COMMENDED

Shallowdale, Ampleforth, York YO6 4ED
(01347) 868526

375-acre mixed farm. "Good food, welcome, walking" in peaceful "Herriot/Heartbeat" countryside. Romantic en-suite four-poster bedrooms. Just 30 minutes from York. Has been featured in the "Sunday Observer".

Bedrooms: 3 double
Bathrooms: 3 en-suite

Bed & breakfast per night:	£min	£max
Single	15.00	
Double	30.00	

Half board per person:	£min	£max
Daily	25.00	

Evening meal 1800 (last orders 1800)
Parking for 3

A key to symbols can be found inside the back cover flap.

ARKENGARTHDALE

North Yorkshire
Map ref 5B3

Picturesque Yorkshire dale, once an important and prosperous lead-mining valley developed by Charles Bathurst in the 18th C.

Croft House

HIGHLY COMMENDED

Arkengarthdale, Richmond DL11 6EN
(01748) 884051
Fax (01748) 884051

Stone-built traditional Yorkshire Dales house set in its own grounds. Superb views. Ample private parking. Warm welcome.

Bedrooms: 1 double, 1 twin
Bathrooms: 1 en-suite, 1 private

Bed & breakfast per night:	£min	£max
Double	37.00	40.00

Parking for 10
Cards accepted: Mastercard, Visa

The Ghyll

COMMENDED

Arkle Town, Richmond DL11 6EU
(01748) 884353
Fax (01748) 884015

Set in wonderful countryside with spectacular views of Arkengarthdale. All bedrooms have en-suite facilities and colour TV. Ideal for walking and touring.

Bedrooms: 2 double, 1 twin
Bathrooms: 3 en-suite

Bed & breakfast per night:	£min	£max
Single	18.00	18.00
Double	36.00	36.00

Parking for 10
Open January–November
Cards accepted: Mastercard, Visa, Switch/Delta

ASKRIGG

North Yorkshire
Map ref 5B3

The name of this dales village means "ash tree ridge". It is centred on a steep main street of high, narrow 3-storey houses and thrived on cotton and later wool in 18th C. Once famous for its clock making.

Home Farm

Listed HIGHLY COMMENDED

Stalling Busk, Askrigg, Leyburn DL8 3DH
(01969) 650360

65-acre mixed farm. Licensed 17th C dales farmhouse with log fires, beams, beautiful Victorian and antique furnishings, brass bedsteads and patchwork quilts. Traditional cooking and home-made bread.

Bedrooms: 3 double
Bathrooms: 2 public

Bed & breakfast per night:	£min	£max
Double		35.00

Half board per person:	£min	£max
Daily		27.50

Evening meal 1930 (last orders 1800)
Parking for 4

Thornsgill Guest House

HIGHLY COMMENDED

Moor Road, Askrigg, Leyburn
DL8 3HH
☎ (01969) 650617

Spacious family house in the Yorkshire Dales National Park. En-suite bedrooms. Wholesome Yorkshire food. Relaxed, friendly atmosphere. Licensed.

Bedrooms: 2 double, 1 twin
Bathrooms: 2 en-suite, 1 private

Bed & breakfast per night:	£min	£max
Double	43.00	43.00

Half board per person:	£min	£max
Daily	35.00	35.00

Evening meal from 1830
Parking for 3

10

BEVERLEY

East Riding of Yorkshire
Map ref 4C1

Beverley's most famous landmark is its beautiful medieval Minster with Percy family tomb. Many attractive squares and streets, notably Wednesday and Saturday Market and North Bar Gateway. Famous racecourse.
Tourist Information Centre ☎ (01482) 867430

Eastgate Guest House

COMMENDED

7 Eastgate, Beverley, East Riding of Yorkshire HU17 0DR
☎ (01482) 868464
Fax (01482) 871899

Family-run Victorian guesthouse, established and run by the same proprietor for 29 years. Close to the town centre, Beverley Minster, Museum of Army Transport and railway station.

Bedrooms: 6 single, 3 double, 3 twin, 3 triple, 3 family rooms
Bathrooms: 7 en-suite, 3 public

Bed & breakfast per night:	£min	£max
Single	19.50	30.00
Double	32.00	44.00

COLOUR MAPS

Colour maps at the back of this guide pinpoint all places in which you will find accommodation listed.

BOLTON PERCY

North Yorkshire
Map ref 4C1

Secluded village of limestone with red-brick buildings. Exceptional 15th C parish church contains medieval stained glass and monuments to Fairfaxes. 15th C half-timbered gatehouse with carved timber-work.

Glebe Farm

HIGHLY COMMENDED

Bolton Percy, York YO5 7AL
☎ (01904) 744228

225-acre mixed farm. Excellent accommodation in self-contained en-suite annexe on family-run farm. Conservatory, garden, ample parking.

Bedrooms: 1 double
Bathrooms: 1 en-suite

Bed & breakfast per night:	£min	£max
Double	35.00	45.00

Parking for 2

BRADFORD

West Yorkshire
Map ref 4B1

City founded on wool, with fine Victorian and modern buildings. Attractions include the cathedral, city hall, Cartwright Hall, Lister Park, Moorside Mills Industrial Museum and National Museum of Photography, Film and Television.
Tourist Information Centre ☎ (01274) 753678

Carlton House Guest House

Listed APPROVED

Thornton Road, Thornton, Bradford
BD13 3QE
☎ (01274) 833397

Detached, Victorian house in open countryside between the Bronte villages of Thornton and Haworth.

Bedrooms: 1 single, 1 double, 2 triple
Bathrooms: 4 en-suite

Bed & breakfast per night:	£min	£max
Single	20.00	
Double	35.00	

Parking for 6

For ideas on places to visit refer to the introduction at the beginning of this section.

Ivy Guest House

Listed APPROVED

3 Melbourne Place, Bradford
BD5 0HZ
☎ (01274) 727060 & (0421) 509207
Fax (01274) 306347
Email: 101524-3725@compuserve.com

Large, detached, listed house built of Yorkshire stone. Car park and gardens. Close to city centre, National Museum of Photography, Film and Television and Alhambra Theatre.

Bedrooms: 3 single, 2 double, 4 twin, 1 triple
Bathrooms: 3 public

Bed & breakfast per night:	£min	£max
Single	18.00	18.00
Double	30.00	30.00

Lunch available
Evening meal 1800 (last orders 2000)
Parking for 15
Cards accepted: Amex, Diners, Mastercard, Visa, Switch/Delta

BRIGG

North Lincolnshire
Map ref 4C1

Small town at an ancient crossing of the River Ancholme.
Tourist Information Centre ☎ (01652) 657053

Holcombe Guest House

COMMENDED

34 Victoria Road, Barnetby, North Lincolnshire DN38 6JR
☎ 0850 764002

Pleasant, homely accommodation in centre of Barnetby village. 5 minutes from M180 and railway station, 3 miles from Humberside Airport, 10 minutes from Brigg, 15-30 minutes from Grimsby, Scunthorpe and Hull.

Bedrooms: 3 single, 3 twin, 2 triple
Bathrooms: 4 en-suite, 2 public, 1 private shower

Bed & breakfast per night:	£min	£max
Single	17.50	22.50
Double	30.00	35.00

Half board per person:	£min	£max
Daily	22.50	27.50

Evening meal 1900 (last orders 2000)
Parking for 4
Cards accepted: Mastercard, Visa

CLAPHAM

North Yorkshire
Map ref 5B3

Neat village of grey-stone houses and whitewashed cottages; a pot-holing centre. Upstream are Ingleborough Cave and Gaping Gill with its huge underground chamber. National Park Centre.

Flying Horseshoe Hotel

COMMENDED

Clapham Station, Clapham, Lancaster LA2 8ES
☎ (015242) 51229
Fax (015242) 51229

Family-run Georgian coaching house with real fires, real ales and real food. In superb surroundings, close to Lakes and West Coast, with free trout and salmon fishing and health club membership. Bargain breaks available all year.

Bedrooms: 3 double, 1 twin
Bathrooms: 4 en-suite

Bed & breakfast per night:	£min	£max
Single	20.00	30.00
Double	30.00	40.00

Lunch available
Evening meal 1800 (last orders 2100)
Parking for 50
Cards accepted: Mastercard, Visa

COTTINGHAM

East Riding of Yorkshire
Map ref 4C1

The Bungalow

Listed COMMENDED

Dunswell Road, Cottingham, East Riding of Yorkshire HU16 4JF
☎ (01482) 843278

5-acre market garden. Five-bedroomed bungalow, on the outskirts of Cottingham in a very pleasant area. Close to Beverley, York, the Humber Bridge and 6 miles to North Sea ferries.

Bedrooms: 1 single, 2 double
Bathrooms: 1 public

Bed & breakfast per night:	£min	£max
Single	15.00	
Double	30.00	

Parking for 10

CROPTON

North Yorkshire
Map ref 5C3

Moorland village at the top of a high ridge with stone houses, some of cruck construction, a Victorian church and the remains of a 12th C moated castle. Cropton Forest nearby.

Burr Bank Cottage

HIGHLY COMMENDED

Cropton, Pickering YO18 8HL
☎ (01751) 417777
Fax (01751) 417789

Stone cottage in 50 acres with wonderful views. Peaceful, well-appointed accommodation, a warm welcome and home cooking.

Bedrooms: 1 single, 1 double, 1 twin
Bathrooms: 3 en-suite

Bed & breakfast per night:	£min	£max
Single	21.00	21.00
Double	42.00	42.00

Half board per person:	£min	£max
Daily	33.00	33.00
Weekly	210.00	210.00

Evening meal 1900 (last orders 1900)
Parking for 10

DRIFFIELD

East Riding of Yorkshire
Map ref 4C1

Lively market town on edge of Wolds with fine Early English church, All Saints. Popular with anglers for its trout streams which flow into the River Hull. Its 18th C canal is lined with barges and houseboats.

The White Horse Inn

COMMENDED

Main Street, Hutton Cranswick, Driffield, East Riding of Yorkshire YO25 9QN
☎ (01377) 270383
Fax (01377) 270383

Set beside the village green and pond. A unique combination of village inn/hotel, restaurant, cabaret and function venue.

Bedrooms: 2 single, 3 double, 1 twin, 2 family rooms
Bathrooms: 8 en-suite

Bed & breakfast per night:	£min	£max
Single	25.00	29.50
Double	35.00	45.00

Half board per person:	£min	£max
Daily	30.00	
Weekly	180.00	

Lunch available
Evening meal 1730 (last orders 2100)
Parking for 100
Cards accepted: Amex, Mastercard, Visa, Switch/Delta

EASINGWOLD

North Yorkshire
Map ref 5C3

Market town of charm and character with a cobbled square and many fine Georgian buildings.

Old Farmhouse Country Hotel & Restaurant

COMMENDED

Raskelf, York YO6 3LF
☎ (01347) 821971

Former farmhouse converted to a comfortable country hotel, offering home cooking, open fires and a warm, friendly welcome. In Herriot country, 3 miles from Easingwold and 15 miles from York.

Bedrooms: 1 single, 7 double, 1 twin, 1 triple
Bathrooms: 10 en-suite

Bed & breakfast per night:	£min	£max
Single	32.00	35.00
Double	56.00	60.00

Half board per person:	£min	£max
Daily	41.00	43.00
Weekly	273.00	287.00

Evening meal 1930 (last orders 2030)
Parking for 10

WELCOME HOST

This is a nationally recognised customer care programme which aims to promote the highest standards of service and a warm welcome. Establishments who are taking part in this initiative are indicated by the symbol.

The Old Vicarage

COMMENDED

Market Place, Easingwold, York YO6 3AL
☎ (01347) 821015
Fax (01347) 823465
Delightful 18th C country house with extensive lawned gardens and croquet lawn. In centre of market town, 12 miles north of York, and ideal as a touring centre for North Yorkshire.
Bedrooms: 3 double, 2 twin, 1 family room
Bathrooms: 6 en-suite

Bed & breakfast per night:	£min	£max
Double	45.00	58.00

Parking for 5
Open February–November

ELLERBY

North Yorkshire
Map ref 5C3

Hamlet 3 miles south of Staithes.

Ellerby Hotel

COMMENDED

Ellerby, Saltburn-by-the-Sea, Cleveland TS13 5LP
☎ (01947) 840342
Fax (01947) 841221

Residential country inn within the North York Moors National Park, 9 miles north of Whitby, 1 mile inland from Runswick Bay.
Wheelchair access category 3
Bedrooms: 5 double, 4 triple
Bathrooms: 9 en-suite

Bed & breakfast per night:	£min	£max
Single	35.00	37.00
Double	54.00	58.00

Lunch available
Evening meal 1900 (last orders 2200)
Parking for 60
Cards accepted: Mastercard, Visa, Switch/Delta
40

Please mention this guide when making your booking.

FIRBECK

South Yorkshire
Map ref 4C2

Near the romantic setting of the 12th C ruins of Roche Abbey, the grounds of which were laid out in the 18th C by Capability Brown.

Black Lion Inn

COMMENDED

New Road, Firbeck, Worksop, Nottinghamshire S81 8JY
☎ (01709) 812575
Fax (01709) 790496
Old world country inn on the Yorkshire/Lancashire border. Fine range of beers and food, excellent accommodation.
Bedrooms: 1 double, 1 twin
Bathrooms: 2 en-suite

Bed & breakfast per night:	£min	£max
Single	50.00	60.00
Double	55.00	70.00

Lunch available
Evening meal 1800 (last orders 2130)
Parking for 40
Cards accepted: Mastercard, Visa, Switch/Delta
80

FLAXTON

North Yorkshire
Map ref 5C3

Attractive village with broad greens, just west of the A64 York to Malton highway.

Grange Farm

APPROVED

Oak Busk Lane, Flaxton, York YO6 7RL
☎ (01904) 468219
130-acre arable & livestock farm. South-facing, modernised farmhouse in its own gardens. 8 miles from York, off the A64 York to Scarborough road, through Flaxton village and right down Oak Busk Lane. After half a mile turn right to farm.
Bedrooms: 2 double, 1 twin
Bathrooms: 1 en-suite, 1 public

Bed & breakfast per night:	£min	£max
Single	15.00	17.00
Double	30.00	34.00

Parking for 10

GARFORTH

West Yorkshire
Map ref 4B1

Town 7 miles east of Leeds, between Temple Newsam Estate and Lotherton Hall.

Myrtle House

Listed APPROVED

31 Wakefield Road, Garforth, Leeds LS25 1AN
☎ (0113) 286 6445
Spacious Victorian terraced house between M62 and A1. All rooms have tea and coffee making facilities, TV, vanity basins and central heating.
Bedrooms: 1 single, 1 double, 2 twin, 2 triple
Bathrooms: 3 public

Bed & breakfast per night:	£min	£max
Single	16.00	18.00
Double	32.00	36.00

GIGGLESWICK

North Yorkshire
Map ref 5B3

Picturesque Pennine village of period stone cottages with ancient market cross, stocks and tithe barn. Parish church is dedicated to St Alkeda, an Anglo-Saxon saint. During restoration work the tomb of a 15th C knight with his horse was discovered.

Black Horse Hotel

Listed COMMENDED

Church Street, Giggleswick, Settle BD24 0BJ
☎ (01729) 822506
16th C coaching inn, adjacent to Yorkshire Dales and near Lake District. Ideal for touring, walking, caving. En-suite accommodation, excellent food.
Bedrooms: 2 double, 1 twin
Bathrooms: 3 en-suite

Bed & breakfast per night:	£min	£max
Single	25.00	
Double	44.00	

Lunch available
Evening meal 1900 (last orders 2100)
Parking for 20
Cards accepted: Diners, Mastercard, Visa

GIGGLESWICK

Continued

Ottawa

COMMENDED

Station Road, Giggleswick, Settle
BD24 0AE
☎ (01729) 822757

A warm welcome is extended with a homely atmosphere in this quiet location, 1 mile from town centre. No smoking, please.

Bedrooms: 1 double, 1 twin
Bathrooms: 1 en-suite, 1 private

Bed & breakfast per night:	£min	£max
Double	38.00	42.00

Parking for 2

GILLAMOOR

North Yorkshire
Map ref 5C3

Village much admired by photographers for its views of Farndale, including "Surprise View" from the churchyard.

Royal Oak Inn

COMMENDED

Gillamoor, York YO6 6HX
☎ (01751) 431414

Old country inn on the edge of the North York Moors. Tastefully renovated, with plenty of character and charm. Open log fires.

Bedrooms: 5 double, 1 twin
Bathrooms: 6 en-suite

Bed & breakfast per night:	£min	£max
Single	25.00	38.00
Double	40.00	54.00

Lunch available
Evening meal 1900 (last orders 2100)
Parking for 9
Cards accepted: Mastercard, Visa
10

TOWN INDEX

This can be found at the back of the guide. If you know where you want to stay, the index will give you the page number listing all accommodation in your chosen town, city or village.

GOLDSBOROUGH

North Yorkshire
Map ref 4B2

Charming village with pub and historic church, 10 minutes' drive from Harrogate.

Goldsborough House Barn Flat

COMMENDED

Goldsborough House, Goldsborough, Knaresborough
HG5 8PS
☎ (01423) 860300
Fax (01423) 860301

Charming flat converted from old barn. Large sitting room with kitchen area, balcony, private garden. Bed and breakfast or self-catering by arrangement. Well situated for Harrogate and York.

Bedrooms: 2 twin
Bathrooms: 1 public

Bed & breakfast per night:	£min	£max
Single	20.00	20.00
Double	36.00	36.00

Parking for 6

GRASSINGTON

North Yorkshire
Map ref 5B3

Tourists visit this former lead-mining village to see its "smiddy", antique and craft shops and Upper Wharfedale Museum of country trades. Popular with fishermen and walkers. Numerous prehistoric sites. Grassington Feast in October. National Park Centre.

Clarendon Hotel

COMMENDED

Hebden, Grassington, Skipton
BD23 5DE
☎ (01756) 752446

Yorkshire Dales village inn serving good food and ales. Personal supervision at all times. Steaks and fish dishes are specialities. Seven nights for the price of six.

Bedrooms: 2 double, 1 twin
Bathrooms: 3 en-suite

Bed & breakfast per night:	£min	£max
Single	30.00	
Double	40.00	50.00

Lunch available
Evening meal 1900 (last orders 2100)
Parking for 30
12

Craiglands

COMMENDED

1 Brooklyn, Threshfield, Skipton
BD23 5ER
☎ (01756) 752093

Welcoming guesthouse offering comfortable accommodation, just 10 minutes' walk from Grassington centre. Ideal as a dales touring base and for walking.

Bedrooms: 1 single, 2 double, 1 twin
Bathrooms: 3 en-suite, 1 private

Bed & breakfast per night:	£min	£max
Single	19.00	22.00
Double	40.00	48.00

Parking for 3
Cards accepted: Mastercard, Visa

Franor House

COMMENDED

3 Wharfeside Avenue, Threshfield, Skipton BD23 5BS
☎ (01756) 752115

Large semi-detached house in quiet surroundings. Take B6265 from Skipton, turning right for Grassington. Wharfeside Avenue is half a mile - first turning on left.

Bedrooms: 1 single, 1 double, 1 twin
Bathrooms: 2 en-suite, 1 private

Bed & breakfast per night:	£min	£max
Single	18.00	20.00
Double	36.00	40.00

Parking for 4

Grange Cottage

HIGHLY COMMENDED

Linton, Skipton BD23 5HH
☎ (01756) 752527

Stone-built cottage with open fires and warm hospitality. In a quiet backwater of a picture postcard village, perfect for hiking and car touring in the dales.

Bedrooms: 1 double, 1 twin
Bathrooms: 1 public, 1 private shower

Bed & breakfast per night:	£min	£max
Single	18.00	20.00
Double	36.00	40.00

Parking for 4
Open March–October

Please mention this guide when making your booking.

GUNNERSIDE

North Yorkshire
Map ref 5B3

Taking its name from the Viking chieftain "Gunner", the village has a humpbacked bridge known as "Ivelet Bridge" spanning the river which is said to be haunted by a headless dog.

Oxnop Hall

COMMENDED

Low Oxnop, Gunnerside, Richmond DL11 6JJ
☎ (01748) 886253

1000-acre hill farm. Traditional farmhouse in the heart of Swaledale, featuring oak beams and mullion windows. All rooms have private facilities. Entirely non-smoking.

Bedrooms: 1 single, 3 double, 1 twin, 1 family room
Bathrooms: 5 en-suite, 1 private

Bed & breakfast per night:	£min	£max
Single	23.00	23.00
Double	46.00	46.00

Half board per person:	£min	£max
Daily	37.00	37.00
Weekly	222.00	222.00

Evening meal 1630 (last orders 1630)
Parking for 8
Open March–October

HALIFAX

West Yorkshire
Map ref 4B1

Founded on the cloth trade, and famous for its building society, textiles, carpets and toffee. Most notable landmark is Piece Hall where wool merchants traded, now restored to house shops, museums and art gallery. Home also to Eureka! The Museum for Children.
Tourist Information Centre ☎ (01422) 368725

Beech Court

Listed COMMENDED

40 Prescott Street, Halifax HX1 2QW
☎ (01422) 366004

Late Victorian residence, just off the town centre. Well furnished and decorated, with emphasis on high standards and good service.

Bedrooms: 1 single, 1 twin, 1 triple
Bathrooms: 2 public

Bed & breakfast per night:	£min	£max
Single	10.00	
Double	34.00	

Parking for 3

Claytons

COMMENDED

146 Pye Nest Road, Halifax HX2 7HS
☎ (01422) 835053

Detached dormer bungalow with gardens and ample parking. Spacious comfortable rooms with pleasant views. Non-smoking.

Bedrooms: 1 double, 1 triple
Bathrooms: 1 public

Bed & breakfast per night:	£min	£max
Single	20.00	25.00
Double	36.00	36.00

Parking for 4

The Elms

COMMENDED

Keighley Road, Illingworth, Halifax HX2 8HT
☎ (01422) 244430

Victorian residence with gardens and original ornate ceilings, within 3 miles of Halifax. Traditional Yorkshire family welcome. Sorry, no late night keys.

Bedrooms: 2 single, 1 double, 1 triple
Bathrooms: 1 en-suite, 1 private, 1 public

Bed & breakfast per night:	£min	£max
Single	20.00	21.00
Double	38.00	40.00

Half board per person:	£min	£max
Daily	29.00	30.00

Evening meal 1800 (last orders 2000)
Parking for 14

Establishments should be open throughout the year, unless otherwise stated.

For further information on accommodation establishments use the coupons at the back of this guide.

HARROGATE

North Yorkshire
Map ref 4B1

A major conference, exhibition and shopping centre, renowned for its spa heritage and award winning floral displays, spacious parks and gardens. Famous for antiques, toffee, fine shopping and excellent tea shops, also its Royal Pump Rooms and Baths.
Tourist Information Centre ☎ (01423) 537300

Alamah

COMMENDED

88 Kings Road, Harrogate HG1 5JX
☎ (01423) 502187
Fax (01423) 566175

Comfortable rooms, personal attention, friendly atmosphere and full English breakfast. 300 metres from town centre. Garages/parking.

Bedrooms: 2 single, 2 double, 2 twin, 1 family room
Bathrooms: 5 en-suite, 2 private showers

Bed & breakfast per night:	£min	£max
Single	24.00	27.00
Double	44.00	50.00

Evening meal 1830 (last orders 1400)
Parking for 8

Crescent Lodge

COMMENDED

20 Swan Road, Harrogate HG1 2SA
☎ (01423) 503688
Fax (01423) 503688

Elegant and well-appointed town house, welcoming a maximum of 6 guests. Quiet, yet close to all amenities. Grade II listed.

Bedrooms: 2 single, 2 twin
Bathrooms: 2 en-suite, 1 public

Bed & breakfast per night:	£min	£max
Single	23.00	
Double	46.00	50.00

Parking for 2

COLOUR MAPS

Colour maps at the back of this guide pinpoint all places in which you will find accommodation listed.

HARROGATE

Continued

Croft House

HIGHLY COMMENDED

Markington, Harrogate HG3 3TU
☎ (01765) 677782

Farmhouse-style detached house in rural location north of Harrogate. TV, tea-making. Convenient for Fountains Abbey, dales, Ripon and Harrogate. No children, no smoking.

Bedrooms: 1 double, 1 twin
Bathrooms: 1 en-suite, 1 private

Bed & breakfast per night:	£min	£max
Single	25.00	
Double	40.00	

Parking for 4

Hatton House Farm

Listed HIGHLY COMMENDED

Colber Lane, Bishop Thornton, Harrogate HG3 3JA
☎ (01423) 770315

150-acre dairy & livestock farm. Farmhouse accommodation north of Harrogate with special emphasis on well-presented, home-cooked food. Open all year round. No smoking indoors, please. Very safe parking area.

Bedrooms: 2 double, 1 twin
Bathrooms: 1 public

Bed & breakfast per night:	£min	£max
Single	20.00	25.00
Double	37.00	40.00

Evening meal 1830 (last orders 1800)
Parking for 10

Hollins House

COMMENDED

17 Hollins Road, Harrogate HG1 2JF
☎ (01423) 503646 & 0836 755549
Fax (01423) 503646

Non-smoking establishment offering quiet, clean accommodation in warm, friendly, family-run Victorian house. Excellent food. Close to shops (including antiques), leisure facilities and restaurants. Short leisure courses in painting and illustration available.

Bedrooms: 1 double, 3 twin
Bathrooms: 3 en-suite, 1 private

Bed & breakfast per night:	£min	£max
Single	24.00	28.00
Double	40.00	46.00

Open January–November
Cards accepted: Mastercard, Visa

Knabbs Ash

HIGHLY COMMENDED

Skipton Road, Felliscliffe, Harrogate HG3 2LT
☎ (01423) 771040
Fax (01423) 771515

Award-winning country house, set back off the A59 Harrogate to Skipton road, 6 miles west of Harrogate. In its own grounds, in a panoramic, tranquil setting. Ideal area for walking and exploring the Yorkshire Dales.

Bedrooms: 2 double, 1 twin
Bathrooms: 3 en-suite

Bed & breakfast per night:	£min	£max
Single	30.00	30.00
Double	42.00	42.00

Parking for 6

HAWES

North Yorkshire
Map ref 5B3

The capital of Upper Wensleydale on the famous Pennine Way, renowned for great cheeses. Popular with walkers. Dales National Park Information Centre and Folk Museum. Nearby is spectacular Hardraw Force waterfall.

Beech House

Listed COMMENDED

Burtersett Road, Hawes DL8 3NP
☎ (01969) 667486

Semi-detached stone house with drive and garage, facing on to a main road. Central heating and double glazing.

Bedrooms: 1 double, 1 twin
Bathrooms: 1 public

Bed & breakfast per night:	£min	£max
Single	15.00	16.00
Double	30.00	32.00

Parking for 7
Open March–September

Ebor Guest House

COMMENDED

Burtersett Road, Hawes DL8 3NT
☎ (01969) 667337

Small, family-run guesthouse, double-glazed and centrally-heated throughout. Walkers are particularly welcome. Centrally located for touring the dales.

Bedrooms: 2 double, 1 twin
Bathrooms: 2 en-suite, 1 public

Bed & breakfast per night:	£min	£max
Single	16.00	17.00
Double	36.00	38.00

Parking for 5

Springbank House

COMMENDED

Springbank, Townfoot, Hawes DL8 3NW
☎ (01969) 667376

Delightful Victorian house near the centre of Hawes with superb views over the surrounding fells.

Bedrooms: 2 triple
Bathrooms: 2 en-suite

Bed & breakfast per night:	£min	£max
Double	32.00	34.00

Parking for 3
Open February–October

White Hart Inn

APPROVED

Main Street, Hawes DL8 3QL
☎ (01969) 667259

17th C coaching inn with a friendly welcome, offering traditional fare. Open fires, Yorkshire ales. Central for exploring the dales.

Bedrooms: 1 single, 4 double, 2 twin
Bathrooms: 2 public

Bed & breakfast per night:	£min	£max
Single	18.50	25.00
Double	35.00	40.00

Lunch available
Evening meal 1900 (last orders 2100)
Parking for 7
Cards accepted: Amex, Mastercard, Visa

HAWNBY

North Yorkshire
Map ref 5C3

Remote and beautiful Bilsdale village near the source of the River Rye. 6 miles upstream from Helmsley.

Laskill Farm

COMMENDED

Hawnby, York YO6 5NB
☎ (01439) 798268

600-acre mixed farm. In a peaceful setting within the North York Moors National Park. Ideal location for historic stately homes and walking. Own natural spring water. Peace and tranquillity in idyllic surroundings. Every comfort assured. York only 45 minutes.
Bedrooms: 1 single, 3 double, 3 twin
Bathrooms: 4 en-suite, 1 private, 1 public, 2 private showers

Bed & breakfast per night:	£min	£max
Single	20.00	22.50
Double	43.00	50.00

Half board per person:	£min	£max
Daily	31.00	36.00
Weekly	217.00	252.00

Evening meal from 1900
Parking for 10

HAWORTH

West Yorkshire
Map ref 4B1

This Pennine town is famous as home of the Bronte family. The Parsonage is now a Bronte Museum where furniture and possessions of the family are displayed. Moors and Bronte waterfalls nearby and steam trains on the Keighley and Worth Valley Railway pass through.
Tourist Information Centre ☎ (01535) 642329

The Apothecary Guest House & Tea Rooms

APPROVED

86 Main Street, Haworth, Keighley BD22 8DA
☎ (01535) 643642
Fax (01535) 643642
At the top of Haworth Main Street opposite the famous Bronte church, 1 minute from the Parsonage and moors.
Bedrooms: 1 single, 4 double, 1 twin, 1 triple
Bathrooms: 6 en-suite, 1 private

Bed & breakfast per night:	£min	£max
Single	18.00	19.00
Double	34.00	39.00

Parking for 7
Cards accepted: Mastercard, Visa

Ashmount

COMMENDED

Mytholmes Lane, Haworth, Keighley BD22 8EZ
☎ (01535) 645726
Victorian Gothic villa with half acre of garden. Outstanding views across Haworth and the moors. 300 yards from the village centre.
Bedrooms: 3 double, 3 twin
Bathrooms: 5 en-suite, 1 private

Bed & breakfast per night:	£min	£max
Single	25.00	25.00
Double	35.00	35.00

Half board per person:	£min	£max
Daily	30.00	37.50
Weekly	168.00	262.50

Evening meal 1800 (last orders 2000)
Parking for 8
Cards accepted: Amex, Mastercard, Visa

Ebor House

APPROVED

Lees Lane, Haworth, Keighley BD22 8RA
☎ (01535) 645869
Yorkshire stone-built house of character, conveniently placed for the main tourist attractions of Haworth, including the Worth Valley Railway and Bronte Parsonage and Museum.
Bedrooms: 3 twin
Bathrooms: 1 en-suite, 1 public

Bed & breakfast per night:	£min	£max
Single	15.00	15.00
Double	32.00	35.00

Parking for 2

You are advised to confirm your booking in writing.

Hole Farm

HIGHLY COMMENDED

Dimples Lane, Haworth, Keighley BD22 8QS
☎ (01535) 644755
8-acre smallholding. 17th C farmhouse, 10 minutes' walk from Bronte Parsonage and 2 minutes' walk from the moors. Panoramic views of Haworth. Farm has pigs, peacocks, geese, cattle and horses.
Bedrooms: 2 double
Bathrooms: 2 en-suite

Bed & breakfast per night:	£min	£max
Double	38.00	40.00

Parking for 4

Old White Lion Hotel

COMMENDED

Haworth, Keighley BD22 8DU
☎ (01535) 642313
Fax (01535) 646222
Family-run, centuries old coaching inn. Candlelit restaurant using local fresh produce, cooked to order. Old world bars serving home-made bar meals and traditional ales. Special rates available all year. Confirmed prices on application.
Bedrooms: 3 single, 8 double, 1 twin, 2 triple
Bathrooms: 14 en-suite

Bed & breakfast per night:	£min	£max
Single	60.00	70.00
Double	85.00	95.00

Lunch available
Evening meal 1900 (last orders 2130)
Parking for 8
Cards accepted: Amex, Diners, Mastercard, Visa

A key to symbols can be found inside the back cover flap.

Information on accommodation listed in this guide has been supplied by the proprietors. As changes may occur you are advised to check details at the time of booking.

HEBDEN BRIDGE

West Yorkshire
Map ref 4B1

Originally a small town on packhorse route, Hebden Bridge grew into a booming mill town in 18th C with rows of "up-and-down" houses of several storeys built against hillsides. Ancient "pace-egg play" custom held on Good Friday.
Tourist Information Centre ☎ (01422) 843831

Robin Hood Inn

Listed COMMENDED

Pecket Well, Hebden Bridge
HX7 8QR
☎ (01422) 842593
Traditional inn on the edge of Calderdale and Pennine Way, Bronte country, Hardcastle Crags. Near Hebden Bridge. Real ale and home-made food.
Bedrooms: 1 double, 1 twin, 1 triple, 1 family room
Suite available
Bathrooms: 1 en-suite, 2 public

Bed & breakfast per night:	£min	£max
Single	18.50	22.50
Double	35.00	42.50

Half board per person:	£min	£max
Daily	22.50	27.50
Weekly	150.00	170.00

Lunch available
Evening meal 1700 (last orders 2130)
Parking for 28
Cards accepted: Visa, Switch/Delta

HELLIFIELD

North Yorkshire
Map ref 4B1

Dales village on the edge of the Yorkshire Dales National Park, 5 miles south-east of Settle.

Wenningber Farm

HIGHLY COMMENDED

Airton Road, Hellifield, Skipton
BD23 4JR
☎ (01729) 850856
120-acre mixed farm. Charming farmhouse, with log fire and oak beams, just 5 miles from Malham in the heart of the Yorkshire Dales.
Bedrooms: 1 double, 1 twin
Bathrooms: 1 public

Bed & breakfast per night:	£min	£max
Single	23.00	25.00
Double	37.00	40.00

Parking for 10

HELMSLEY

North Yorkshire
Map ref 5C3

Pretty town on the River Rye at the entrance to Ryedale and the North York Moors, with large square and remains of 12th C castle, several inns and All Saints' Church.

Sproxton Hall

HIGHLY COMMENDED

Sproxton, Helmsley, York YO6 5EQ
☎ (01439) 770225
Fax (01439) 771373
300-acre mixed farm. 17th C Grade II listed stone farmhouse, beamed, beautifully decorated and comfortably furnished. In a peaceful setting with panoramic views, 1.5 miles from Helmsley. Excellent base for the North York Moors, York, the coast and dales. Non-smokers only, please.
Bedrooms: 2 double, 1 twin
Bathrooms: 1 en-suite, 2 private

Bed & breakfast per night:	£min	£max
Single	27.00	33.00
Double	40.00	50.00

Parking for 10

Stilworth House

COMMENDED

1 Church Street, Helmsley, York
YO6 5AD
☎ (01439) 771072 & 770507
Comfortable relaxed atmosphere in elegant Georgian town house off the market square of Helmsley. Pretty en-suite rooms with colour TV, hairdryer, tea/coffee facilities. Private car park.
Bedrooms: 3 double, 1 twin, 1 triple
Bathrooms: 5 en-suite

Bed & breakfast per night:	£min	£max
Single	30.00	35.00
Double	40.00	50.00

Parking for 4

Please check prices and other details at the time of booking.

HOLMFIRTH

West Yorkshire
Map ref 4B1

This village has become famous as the location for the filming of the TV series "Last of the Summer Wine". It has a postcard museum and is on the edge of the Peak District National Park.
Tourist Information Centre ☎ (01484) 687603

29 Woodhead Road

COMMENDED

Holmfirth, Huddersfield HD7 1JU
☎ (01484) 683962
200-year-old family home, 5 minutes' walk from Holmfirth. Tea and coffee available at any time. Good walking area and pleasant countryside.
Bedrooms: 1 twin
Bathrooms: 1 private

Bed & breakfast per night:	£min	£max
Single	15.00	15.00
Double	30.00	30.00

Parking for 2

HORSFORTH

West Yorkshire
Map ref 4B1

Kirkstall Hall Trinity and All Saints University College

Brownberrie Lane, Horsforth, Leeds
LS18 5HD
☎ (0113) 2837100
Fax (0113) 2837200
Email: j.cressey @ tasc.ac.uk
University college offering quality single en-suite accommodation with breakfast. Rural location 6 miles north of Leeds in the small town of Horsforth. Close to Leeds/Bradford Airport, M1/M62. Ideal base for touring Yorkshire Dales.
Bedrooms: 96 single, 384 double
Bathrooms: 96 en-suite, 40 public

Bed & breakfast per night:	£min	£max
Single		23.65

Half board per person:	£min	£max
Daily		28.65

Lunch available
Evening meal 1800 (last orders 1900)
Parking for 400
Open March–April, June–September

HUDDERSFIELD

West Yorkshire
Map ref 4B1

Founded on wool and cloth, has a famous choral society. Town centre redeveloped, but several good Victorian buildings remain, including railway station, St Peter's Church, Tolson Memorial Museum, art gallery and nearby Colne Valley Museum.
Tourist Information Centre ☎ (01484) 223200

White House

APPROVED

Holthead, Slaithwaite, Huddersfield HD7 5TY
☎ (01484) 842245
Fax (01484) 842245
Lovely 18th C inn with traditional ale and comfortable en-suite accommodation. Notable cuisine in warm and friendly surroundings. In the country, only 4 miles from Huddersfield on B6107 Meltham to Marsden road.
Bedrooms: 1 single, 6 double, 1 twin
Bathrooms: 5 en-suite, 1 public

Bed & breakfast per night:	£min	£max
Single	28.00	35.00
Double	40.00	40.00

Lunch available
Evening meal 1800 (last orders 2130)
Parking for 100
Cards accepted: Amex, Diners, Mastercard, Visa, Switch/Delta

ILKLEY

West Yorkshire
Map ref 4B1

This moorland town is famous for its ballad. The 16th C manor house, now a museum, displays local prehistoric and Roman relics. Popular walk leads up Heber's Ghyll to Ilkley Moor, with the mysterious Swastika Stone and White Wells, 18th C plunge baths.
Tourist Information Centre ☎ (01943) 602319

Robert's Family Bed and Breakfast

Listed APPROVED

63 Skipton Road, Ilkley LS29 9HF
☎ (01943) 817542
Pleasant, detached house with garden. Near Yorkshire Dales and within easy reach of motorway connections, airport and other towns and cities in the region.
Bedrooms: 2 double, 1 twin
Bathrooms: 2 en-suite, 1 public

Bed & breakfast per night:	£min	£max
Single	30.00	32.00
Double	38.00	40.00

Parking for 5
Cards accepted: Visa

Summerhill Guest House

COMMENDED

24 Crossbeck Road, Ilkley LS29 9TN
☎ (01943) 607067
On the edge of Ilkley Moor with lovely views and within easy walking distance of the town.
Bedrooms: 1 single, 1 double, 3 twin
Bathrooms: 1 private, 1 public

Bed & breakfast per night:	£min	£max
Single	16.00	19.00
Double	32.00	38.00

Half board per person:	£min	£max
Daily	24.00	27.00
Weekly	210.00	217.00

Evening meal 1830 (last orders 1830)
Parking for 5

INGLETON

North Yorkshire
Map ref 5B3

Thriving tourist centre for fell-walkers, climbers and pot-holers. Popular walks up beautiful Twiss Valley to Ingleborough Summit, Whernside, White Scar Caves and waterfalls.

Ferncliffe Guest House

COMMENDED

55 Main Street, Ingleton, Carnforth, Lancashire LA6 3HJ
☎ (015242) 42405
Lovely detached Victorian house in quiet location, with a growing reputation for good food and high standard of accommodation. All rooms en-suite.
Bedrooms: 1 double, 4 twin
Bathrooms: 5 en-suite

Bed & breakfast per night:	£min	£max
Single	30.00	30.00
Double	44.00	44.00

Half board per person:	£min	£max
Daily	34.50	42.00
Weekly	218.00	275.00

Evening meal 1830 (last orders 2030)
Parking for 5
Open February–October
12

Langber Country Guest House

APPROVED

Tatterthorne Road, Ingleton, Carnforth LA6 3DT
☎ (015242) 41587
Detached country house in hilltop position with panoramic views. Good touring centre for dales, lakes and coast. Comfortable accommodation. Friendly service - everyone welcome.
Bedrooms: 1 single, 2 double, 1 twin, 2 triple, 1 family room
Bathrooms: 4 en-suite, 1 public

Bed & breakfast per night:	£min	£max
Single	16.50	22.00
Double	32.00	42.00

Half board per person:	£min	£max
Daily	22.50	32.00
Weekly	138.00	170.00

Evening meal 1830 (last orders 1700)
Parking for 6

New Butts Farm

Listed APPROVED

High Bentham, Lancaster LA2 7AN
☎ (015242) 41238
16-acre mixed farm. Attractive stone-built farmhouse in an area of outstanding beauty. Good home cooking, open fires and a warm welcome.
Bedrooms: 2 double, 1 twin, 2 triple
Bathrooms: 3 en-suite, 1 public

Bed & breakfast per night:	£min	£max
Single	15.50	
Double	31.00	

Half board per person:	£min	£max
Daily	26.00	
Weekly	180.00	

Evening meal from 1900
Parking for 6

All accommodation in this guide has been graded, or is awaiting a grading, by a trained Tourist Board inspector.

INGLETON

Continued

Riverside Lodge

COMMENDED

24 Main Street, Ingleton, Carnforth, Lancashire LA6 3HJ
☎ (015242) 41359

Victorian house with conservatory, set in the Yorkshire Dales. Pets welcome. Sauna, games room, river fishing, pleasant gardens.

Wheelchair access category 3
Bedrooms: 5 double, 3 twin
Bathrooms: 8 en-suite

Bed & breakfast per night:	£min	£max
Single	20.00	22.00
Double	40.00	44.00

Parking for 8
Cards accepted: Mastercard, Visa

KIRKLINGTON

North Yorkshire
Map ref 5C3

Attractive village situated between Masham and Thirsk.

Upsland Farm

HIGHLY COMMENDED

Kirklington, Bedale DL8 2PA
☎ (01845) 567709

45-acre mixed farm. Surrounded by remains of ancient moat, recently rebuilt using original materials. Spacious accommodation. All bedrooms en-suite. Ideally situated for moors and dales.

Bedrooms: 2 double, 1 twin
Bathrooms: 3 en-suite

Bed & breakfast per night:	£min	£max
Single	20.00	20.00
Double	40.00	40.00

Half board per person:	£min	£max
Daily	29.50	29.50
Weekly	185.00	185.00

Evening meal 1900 (last orders 2000)
Parking for 6

Half board prices are given per person, but in some cases these may be based on double/twin occupancy.

KNARESBOROUGH

North Yorkshire
Map ref 4B1

Picturesque market town on the River Nidd, famous for its 11th C castle ruins, overlooking town and river gorge. Attractions include oldest chemist's shop in country, prophetess Mother Shipton's cave, Dropping Well and Court House Museum. Boating on river.

Yorkshire Lass

APPROVED

High Bridge, Harrogate Road, Knaresborough HG5 8DA
☎ (01423) 862962
Fax (01423) 869091

Detached inn on main Harrogate/York road, with attractive bedrooms overlooking River Nidd. Real ales, wines, large selection of whiskies. Specialising in traditional Yorkshire dishes. Special seasonal rates available.

Bedrooms: 1 single, 2 double, 2 twin, 1 triple
Bathrooms: 6 en-suite

Bed & breakfast per night:	£min	£max
Single	30.00	39.50
Double	40.00	55.00

Half board per person:	£min	£max
Daily	37.50	45.00
Weekly	262.50	

Lunch available
Evening meal 1700 (last orders 2200)
Parking for 34
Cards accepted: Amex, Mastercard, Visa, Switch/Delta

SP T

LEEDS/BRADFORD AIRPORT

See under Bradford, Otley

LEYBURN

North Yorkshire
Map ref 5B3

Attractive dales market town where Mary Queen of Scots was reputedly captured after her escape from Bolton Castle. Fine views over Wensleydale from nearby.
Tourist Information Centre ☎ (01969) 623069 or 622773

Hayloft Suite

HIGHLY COMMENDED

Foal Barn, Spennithorne, Leyburn DL8 5PR
☎ (01969) 622580

200-year-old barn. Private suite exclusive to 1 party. Beams, log fire. Warm welcome, peace and comfort. Garden courtyard.

Bedrooms: 1 double, 1 twin
Bathrooms: 2 private

Bed & breakfast per night:	£min	£max
Single	24.50	24.50
Double	49.00	49.00

Parking for 1

Park Gate House

HIGHLY COMMENDED

Constable Burton, Leyburn DL8 5RG
☎ (01677) 450466

18th C house of character and charm, offering a high standard of comfort with a warm and welcoming atmosphere.

Bedrooms: 3 double, 1 twin
Bathrooms: 3 en-suite, 1 private

Bed & breakfast per night:	£min	£max
Double	43.00	55.00

Parking for 5

12

LONG MARSTON

North Yorkshire
Map ref 4C1

Close to the site of the Battle of Marston Moor, a decisive Civil War battle of 1644. A monument commemorates the event.

Gill House Farm

HIGHLY COMMENDED

Tockwith Road, Long Marston, York YO5 8PJ
☎ (01904) 738379 & 0850 511140

600-acre mixed farm. Peaceful period farmhouse set in glorious countryside overlooking the Vale of York. Warm welcome. Good bus route and lots of local eating places.

Bedrooms: 2 double, 1 triple, 1 family room
Bathrooms: 4 en-suite

Bed & breakfast per night:	£min	£max
Single	30.00	
Double	44.00	

Parking for 5
Open April–December
Cards accepted: Mastercard, Visa

LUND

East Riding of Yorkshire
Map ref 4C1

Village near Beverley close to the route of "The Minster Way".

Clematis House, Farmhouse Bed and Breakfast

COMMENDED

1 Eastgate, Lund, Driffield, East Riding of Yorkshire YO25 9TQ
☎ (01377) 217204
Fax (01377) 217204

389-acre arable & livestock farm. Family-run working farm in pretty, rural village. Farmhouse with character, spacious yet cosy. En-suite rooms with TV and tea/coffee making facilities. Secluded walled garden, TV lounge.

Bedrooms: 1 double, 1 twin
Bathrooms: 2 en-suite

Bed & breakfast per night:	£min	£max
Single	19.50	19.50
Double	37.00	37.00

Parking for 4

MALHAM

North Yorkshire
Map ref 5B3

Hamlet of stone cottages amid magnificent rugged limestone scenery in the Yorkshire Dales National Park. Malham Cove is a curving, sheer white cliff 240 ft high. Malham Tarn, one of Yorkshire's few natural lakes, belongs to the National Trust. National Park Centre.

Beck Hall Guest House

APPROVED

Malham, Skipton BD23 4DJ
☎ (01729) 830332

Family-run guesthouse set in a spacious riverside garden. Homely atmosphere, four-poster beds, log fires, large car park.

Bedrooms: 11 double, 3 twin
Bathrooms: 9 en-suite, 2 private, 1 public

Bed & breakfast per night:	£min	£max
Single	17.00	26.00
Double	32.00	40.00

Half board per person:	£min	£max
Daily	23.25	27.25

Lunch available
Evening meal 1900 (last orders 2000)
Parking for 30

MALTON

North Yorkshire
Map ref 5D3

Thriving farming town on the River Derwent with large livestock market. Famous for racehorse training. The local museum has Roman remains and the Eden Camp Modern History Theme Museum transports visitors back to wartime Britain. Castle Howard within easy reach.
Tourist Information Centre ☎ (01653) 600048

New Globe Inn

Listed APPROVED

Yorkersgate, Malton YO17 0AA
☎ (01653) 692395

Quaint old pub, right in the centre of town.

Bedrooms: 1 double, 2 twin
Bathrooms: 1 public

Bed & breakfast per night:	£min	£max
Single	16.00	18.00
Double	32.00	34.00

Parking for 22

MARKET WEIGHTON

East Riding of Yorkshire
Map ref 4C1

Small town on the western side of the Yorkshire Wolds. A tablet in the parish church records the death of William Bradley in 1820 at which time he was 7 ft 9 in tall and weighed 27 stone!

Arras Farmhouse

Listed APPROVED

Arras Farm, Market Weighton, York YO4 3RN
☎ (01430) 872404
Fax (01430) 872404

460-acre arable farm. Large farmhouse and grounds, peaceful and comfortable, on A1079 between Market Weighton and Beverley. 3 miles from Market Weighton at crossroads.

Bedrooms: 2 double, 1 twin
Bathrooms: 2 en-suite, 1 public

Bed & breakfast per night:	£min	£max
Single	19.00	21.00
Double	34.00	38.00

Parking for 5

MASHAM

North Yorkshire
Map ref 5C3

Famous market town on the River Ure, with a large market square. St Mary's Church has Norman tower and 13th C spire. Theakston's "Old Peculier" ale is brewed here.

Limetree Farm

COMMENDED

Hutts Lane, Grewelthorpe, Ripon HG4 3DA
☎ (01765) 658450

60-acre mixed farm. Small farm nature reserve. Open fires, beams, oak panelling, exposed stonework and antique furniture. Private facilities all rooms. Colour brochure.

Bedrooms: 2 double, 1 twin
Bathrooms: 2 en-suite, 1 private

Bed & breakfast per night:	£min	£max
Single	18.50	23.50
Double	37.00	

Half board per person:	£min	£max
Daily	31.00	32.00
Weekly	205.00	240.00

Evening meal 1800 (last orders 1900)
Parking for 10

Establishments should be open throughout the year, unless otherwise stated.

The symbols in each entry give information about services and facilities. A key to these symbols appears at the back of this guide.

MIDDLEHAM

North Yorkshire
Map ref 5C3

Town famous for racehorse training, with cobbled squares and houses of local stone. Norman castle, once principal residence of Warwick the Kingmaker and later Richard III. Ruins of Jervaulx Abbey nearby.

Black Swan Hotel

COMMENDED

Market Place, Middleham DL8 4NP
☎ (01969) 622221
Fax (01969) 622221
Unspoilt 17th C inn, with open fires and beamed ceilings, allied to 20th C comforts. Emphasis on food.
Bedrooms: 1 single, 4 double, 1 twin, 1 triple
Bathrooms: 7 en-suite

Bed & breakfast per night:	£min	£max
Single	27.00	32.00
Double	48.00	65.00

Half board per person:	£min	£max
Daily	33.00	42.00

Lunch available
Evening meal 1830 (last orders 2100)
Parking for 3
Cards accepted: Mastercard, Visa
30

MYTON-ON-SWALE

North Yorkshire
Map ref 5C3

Small village on the mighty River Swale.

Plump House Farm

COMMENDED

Myton-on-Swale, York YO6 2RA
☎ (01423) 360650
Fax (01423) 360650
160-acre mixed farm. A warm welcome with comfortable en-suite accommodation on a working family farm. Easy access to York and Harrogate and an ideal centre for the coast, dales and moors. Reductions for children.
Bedrooms: 1 double, 1 family room
Bathrooms: 2 en-suite

Bed & breakfast per night:	£min	£max
Single	16.00	

Half board per person:	£min	£max
Daily	22.00	

Evening meal 1800 (last orders 2000)
Parking for 4

NORTHALLERTON

North Yorkshire
Map ref 5C3

Formerly a staging post on coaching route to the North and later a railway town. Today a lively market town and administrative capital of North Yorkshire. Parish church of All Saints dates from 1200.
Tourist Information Centre ☎ (01609) 776864

Lovesome Hill Farm

COMMENDED

Lovesome Hill, Northallerton DL6 2PB
☎ (01609) 772311
165-acre mixed farm. 19th C farmhouse. Tastefully converted granary adjoins with spacious, quality en-suite rooms. Conversion won architectural award in 1995. 4 miles north of Northallerton on A167. Brochure available.
Wheelchair access category 3
Bedrooms: 1 single, 2 double, 1 triple, 1 family room
Bathrooms: 5 en-suite

Bed & breakfast per night:	£min	£max
Single	20.00	30.00
Double	38.00	50.00

Evening meal from 1900
Parking for 10
Open February–November

Porch House

HIGHLY COMMENDED

68 High Street, Northallerton DL7 8EG
☎ (01609) 779831

16th/17th C Grade II listed family house, with original beams, fireplaces and walled garden. Guests have included Charles I. Centrally positioned, ideal for discovering the Yorkshire Dales, moors and coast. Winner of White Rose Award for best B&B 1997.
Bedrooms: 1 single, 2 double, 1 twin
Bathrooms: 4 en-suite

Bed & breakfast per night:	£min	£max
Single	25.00	32.00
Double	45.00	50.00

Evening meal 1800 (last orders 1930)
Parking for 5
8

OAKWORTH

West Yorkshire
Map ref 4B1

This village lies on the route of the Keighley and Worth Valley Railway which was the location of the film "The Railway Children", and is only 1 mile north of Haworth.

Railway Cottage

Listed APPROVED

59 Station Road, Oakworth, Keighley BD22 0DZ
☎ (01535) 642693
Small guesthouse adjacent to Oakworth station on the Keighley and Worth Valley Railway. Ground floor accommodation suitable for disabled visitors.
Bedrooms: 2 single, 3 double
Bathrooms: 5 en-suite

Bed & breakfast per night:	£min	£max
Single	14.50	17.50
Double	24.00	30.00

Parking for 5

OSMOTHERLEY

North Yorkshire
Map ref 5C3

The famous "Lyke Wake Walk", across the Cleveland Hills to Ravenscar 40 miles away, starts here in this ancient village. Attached to the village cross is a large stone table used as a "pulpit" by John Wesley.

Quintana House

Listed COMMENDED

Back Lane, Osmotherley, Northallerton DL6 3BJ
☎ (01609) 883258
Detached, stone cottage near national park village centre, within 90 metres of the Cleveland Way, affording panoramic views of Black Hambleton. Non-smokers only, please.
Bedrooms: 1 double, 1 twin
Bathrooms: 1 public

Bed & breakfast per night:	£min	£max
Double	36.00	39.00

Half board per person:	£min	£max
Daily	26.00	39.00
Weekly	182.00	273.00

Evening meal 1830 (last orders 2000)
Parking for 5

OTLEY

West Yorkshire
Map ref 4B1

Charming market and small manufacturing town in Lower Wharfedale, the birthplace of Thomas Chippendale, painted by Turner. Old inns, medieval 5-arched bridge, local history museum, maypole, historic All Saints' Church. Beautiful countryside. Location for "Emmerdale Farm" and "Heartbeat".
Tourist Information Centre ☎ (0113) 247 7707

Paddock Hill

APPROVED
Norwood, Otley LS21 2QU
☎ (01943) 465977
Converted farmhouse on B6451. Open fires, lovely views; a quiet and rural setting. Convenient for "Emmerdale" and "Heartbeat" country and for the dales. Leeds 16 miles, York 28 miles.
Bedrooms: 2 single, 1 double, 1 twin
Bathrooms: 1 public, 1 private shower

Bed & breakfast per night:	£min	£max
Single	14.00	14.00
Double	32.00	36.00

Parking for 3

Scaife Hall Farm

HIGHLY COMMENDED
Blubberhouses, Otley LS21 2PL
☎ (01943) 880354
450-acre mixed farm. Picturesque rural location 7 miles north of Otley. Cosy bedrooms with en-suite facilities. Sitting room with log fires and colour TV.
Bedrooms: 2 double, 1 twin
Bathrooms: 3 en-suite

Bed & breakfast per night:	£min	£max
Single	28.00	28.00
Double	40.00	40.00

Parking for 3

PICKERING

North Yorkshire
Map ref 5D3

Market town and tourist centre on edge of North York Moors. Parish church has complete set of 15th C wall paintings depicting lives of saints. Part of 12th C castle still stands. Beck Isle Museum. The North York Moors Railway begins here.
Tourist Information Centre ☎ (01751) 473791

Eden House

COMMENDED
120 Eastgate, Pickering YO18 7DW
☎ (01751) 472289 & 476066
Fax (01751) 476066
Delightful listed cottage situated on the A170 road to the East Coast. On the outskirts of a small market town.
Bedrooms: 2 double, 1 twin
Bathrooms: 1 en-suite, 1 public

Bed & breakfast per night:	£min	£max
Single	20.00	28.00
Double	35.00	38.00

Half board per person:	£min	£max
Daily	32.50	40.00

Evening meal 1830 (last orders 2000)
Parking for 4

Heathcote House

COMMENDED
100 Eastgate, Pickering YO18 7DW
☎ (01751) 476991
Fax (01751) 476991
Early Victorian house 5 minutes from town centre. Ideal for walking and touring. All bedrooms have en-suite. Optional dinners. Relaxed, friendly atmosphere. Secluded parking. Non-smoking throughout.
Bedrooms: 3 double, 2 twin
Bathrooms: 5 en-suite, 1 public

Bed & breakfast per night:	£min	£max
Single	25.00	26.50
Double	40.00	43.00

Half board per person:	£min	£max
Daily	32.00	38.50
Weekly	210.00	242.00

Evening meal 1900 (last orders 1100)
Parking for 7
Open February–December
Cards accepted: Mastercard, Visa, Switch/Delta

RAVENSCAR

North Yorkshire
Map ref 5D3

Splendidly-positioned small coastal resort with magnificent views over Robin Hood's Bay. Its Old Peak is the end of the famous Lyke Wake Walk or "corpse way".

Smugglers Rock Country Guest House

COMMENDED
Ravenscar, Scarborough YO13 0ER
☎ (01723) 870044
Georgian country house, reputedly a former smugglers' haunt, with panoramic views over the surrounding national park and sea. Half a mile from Ravenscar village. Ideal centre for touring, walking and pony trekking.
Bedrooms: 2 single, 2 double, 2 twin, 1 triple, 1 family room
Bathrooms: 8 en-suite

Bed & breakfast per night:	£min	£max
Single	23.00	25.00
Double	42.00	48.00

Half board per person:	£min	£max
Daily	29.50	32.00
Weekly	185.00	190.00

Evening meal 1830 (last orders 1630)
Parking for 12
Open March–November

Half board prices are given per person, but in some cases these may be based on double/twin occupancy.

National gradings and classifications were correct at the time of going to press but are subject to change. Please check at the time of booking.

REDMIRE

North Yorkshire
Map ref 5B3

Peaceful and little-known dales village at east end of Wensleydale. Pale stone cottages scattered around a large green with ancient oak tree and pinfold where stray animals were penned.

Bolton Arms

COMMENDED

Redmire, Leyburn DL8 4EA
☎ (01969) 624336

An old inn - quiet and friendly atmosphere. In an unspoilt village in the heart of Wensleydale - near castles, waterfalls and market towns.
Bedrooms: 2 double, 2 twin
Bathrooms: 4 en-suite

Bed & breakfast per night:	£min	£max
Single	22.00	25.00
Double	44.00	50.00

Half board per person:	£min	£max
Daily	34.50	37.50
Weekly	241.50	262.50

Lunch available
Evening meal 1900 (last orders 2100)
Parking for 12
Cards accepted: Mastercard, Visa

RICCALL

North Yorkshire
Map ref 4C1

Historic village, for here it was Harold Hardrada sailed with his fleet of 300 ships and disembarked to march to the battlefield at Stamford Bridge. Magnificent Norman doorway in village church.

South Newlands Farm

Listed COMMENDED

Selby Road, Riccall, York YO4 6QR
☎ (01757) 248203

8-acre fruit farm. Friendly accommodation just off the main A19 Selby to York road, 3 miles north of Selby. Traditional English breakfast. Winter break weekends with evening meals.
Bedrooms: 1 double, 1 twin, 1 triple
Bathrooms: 2 en-suite, 1 public

Bed & breakfast per night:	£min	£max
Single	17.00	21.00
Double	30.00	36.00

Half board per person:	£min	£max
Daily	23.00	26.00
Weekly	150.00	170.00

Evening meal 1900 (last orders 2000)
Parking for 4

RICHMOND

North Yorkshire
Map ref 5C3

Market town on edge of Swaledale with 11th C castle, Georgian and Victorian buildings surrounding cobbled market-place. Green Howards' Museum is in the former Holy Trinity Church. Attractions include the Georgian Theatre, Richmondshire Museum and Easby Abbey.
Tourist Information Centre ☎ (01748) 850252

Carlin House

COMMENDED

6 Frenchgate, Richmond DL10 4JG
☎ (01748) 826771

Grade II listed 18th C town house at Richmond market square's lower entrance. Four-poster bed. Ideal for Yorkshire Dales.
Bedrooms: 1 single, 1 double
Bathrooms: 1 en-suite, 1 private

Bed & breakfast per night:	£min	£max
Single	18.00	22.00
Double	36.00	40.00

Greencroft

COMMENDED

Middleton Tyas, Richmond
DL10 6PE
☎ (01325) 377392
Fax (01833) 621423

Village near Scotch Corner. Lovely en-suite rooms with TV, tea/coffee. Ideal for Yorkshire Dales, York, East Coast, Durham. Good restaurants within half a mile.
Bedrooms: 1 twin, 1 family room
Bathrooms: 2 en-suite

Bed & breakfast per night:	£min	£max
Single	25.00	
Double	34.00	

Parking for 4

Holmedale

COMMENDED

Dalton, Richmond DL11 7HX
☎ (01833) 621236

Georgian house in a quiet village, midway between Richmond and Barnard Castle. Ideal for the Yorkshire and Durham dales.
Bedrooms: 1 double, 1 triple
Bathrooms: 1 public

Bed & breakfast per night:	£min	£max
Single	15.00	
Double	27.00	

Half board per person:	£min	£max
Daily	22.00	
Weekly	150.00	

Evening meal 1800 (last orders 1200)
Parking for 2

Mount Pleasant Farm

COMMENDED

Whashton, Richmond DL11 7JP
☎ (01748) 822784

40-acre mixed farm. Just the place for a special holiday or short break. Cosy en-suite cottage bedrooms in converted stables, each with own front door. Well known for our farmer's breakfast, warm welcome and personal service. Real peace and quiet in beautiful countryside.
Wheelchair access category 3
Bedrooms: 1 double, 2 triple, 1 family room
Bathrooms: 4 en-suite

Bed & breakfast per night:	£min	£max
Single	22.00	22.00
Double	40.00	40.00

Half board per person:	£min	£max
Daily	29.50	33.00

Evening meal 1830 (last orders 1200)
Parking for 6

Please mention this guide when making your booking.

St Trinians Hall

COMMENDED

Easby, Richmond DL10 7ET
☎ (01748) 826248
Grade II listed family-run country house between Richmond and Brompton-on-Swale. Peaceful situation, ample parking, gardens.
Bedrooms: 2 double, 1 twin
Bathrooms: 1 en-suite, 2 private

Bed & breakfast per night:	£min	£max
Single	25.00	
Double	38.00	

Parking for 12
Open March–November

RIPON

North Yorkshire
Map ref 5C3

Small, ancient city with impressive cathedral containing Saxon crypt which houses church treasures from all over Yorkshire. "Setting the Watch" tradition kept nightly by horn-blower in Market Square. Fountains Abbey nearby.

The Coopers

APPROVED

36 College Road, Ripon HG4 2HA
☎ (01765) 603708
Spacious, comfortable Victorian house in quiet area. En-suite facilities available. Special rates for children. Cyclists welcome (storage for bicycles). Take-away meals acceptable in rooms.
Bedrooms: 1 single, 1 twin, 1 triple
Bathrooms: 1 en-suite, 1 public

Bed & breakfast per night:	£min	£max
Single	17.00	18.00
Double	30.00	36.00

Parking for 3

Mallard Grange

HIGHLY COMMENDED

Aldfield, Ripon HG4 3BE
☎ (01765) 620242
460-acre mixed farm. Rambling 16th C farmhouse in open countryside near Fountains Abbey. Welcoming, spacious and comfortable with high quality traditionally furnished rooms. Delicious breakfast!
Bedrooms: 1 double, 1 twin
Bathrooms: 1 en-suite, 1 private

Bed & breakfast per night:	£min	£max
Double	40.00	

Parking for 2
Open March–October

Moor End Farm

COMMENDED

Knaresborough Road, Littlethorpe, Ripon HG4 3LU
☎ (01765) 677419
41-acre livestock farm. Comfortable rooms, TV lounge with log fire. Home cooking and a warm Yorkshire welcome. Non-smokers only, please. Ideal centre for Yorkshire Dales, York and Harrogate.
Bedrooms: 2 double, 1 twin
Bathrooms: 2 en-suite, 1 public

Bed & breakfast per night:	£min	£max
Double	33.00	35.00

Half board per person:	£min	£max
Daily	26.00	27.00
Weekly	175.00	180.00

Evening meal 1500 (last orders 1830)
Parking for 7

St George's Court

COMMENDED

Old Home Farm, Grantley, Ripon HG4 3EU
☎ (01765) 620618
20-acre arable farm. Set in 20 acres of beautifully secluded farmland. Comfortable rooms in renovated farm buildings. Enjoy a delicious breakfast in our listed farmhouse.
Bedrooms: 3 double, 1 twin, 1 family room
Bathrooms: 5 en-suite

Bed & breakfast per night:	£min	£max
Single	28.00	30.00
Double	40.00	45.00

Evening meal 1900 (last orders 2000)
Parking for 12
Cards accepted: Mastercard, Visa

You are advised to confirm your booking in writing.

Map references apply to the colour maps at the back of this guide.

Yew Tree Farm

COMMENDED

Main Street, Kirkby Malzeard, Ripon HG4 3SE
☎ (01765) 658474
Fax (01765) 658474

Yew Tree Farm offers accommodation in sympathetically converted farm buildings. Set in the delightful village of Kirkby Malzeard, west of Ripon. On the doorstep is James Herriot country and within striking distance is the ancient town of Ripon.
Bedrooms: 1 single, 3 double, 3 twin, 1 family room
Bathrooms: 5 en-suite, 1 public

Bed & breakfast per night:	£min	£max
Single	25.00	30.00
Double	36.00	44.00

Parking for 7
Cards accepted: Mastercard, Visa

SCACKLETON

North Yorkshire
Map ref 5C3

Church Farm

Listed HIGHLY COMMENDED

Scackleton, York YO6 4NB
☎ (01653) 628403
Fax (01653) 628403
212-acre arable & livestock farm. Farmhouse and garden with wonderful views, in the quiet hamlet of Scackleton, close to Castle Howard and York.
Bedrooms: 2 double, 1 twin
Bathrooms: 1 en-suite, 1 public

Bed & breakfast per night:	£min	£max
Single	16.00	20.00
Double	36.00	40.00

Evening meal 1800 (last orders 2000)
Parking for 6
Open March–November

The National Grading and Classification Scheme is explained at the back of this guide.

SCARBOROUGH

North Yorkshire
Map ref 5D3

Large, popular East Coast seaside resort, formerly a spa town. Beautiful gardens and two splendid sandy beaches. Castle ruins date from 1100; fine Georgian and Victorian houses. Scarborough Millennium depicts 1,000 years of town's history. Sea Life Centre.
Tourist Information Centre ☎ (01723) 373333

Killerby Cottage Farm

COMMENDED

Killerby Lane, Cayton, Scarborough YO11 3TP
☎ (01723) 581236
Fax (01723) 585465
400-acre arable farm. Character farmhouse, with stained glass craft centre. Farm also has horses. 1.5 miles from Cayton Bay, between Scarborough and Filey.
Bedrooms: 2 double, 1 twin
Bathrooms: 1 en-suite, 1 public

Bed & breakfast per night:	£min	£max
Single	18.00	25.00
Double	32.00	48.00

Parking for 10
Open January–November
Cards accepted: Mastercard, Visa

SETTLE

North Yorkshire
Map ref 5B3

Town of narrow streets and Georgian houses in an area of great limestone hills and crags. Panoramic view from Castleberg Crag which stands 300 ft above town.
Tourist Information Centre ☎ (01729) 825192

Golden Lion Hotel

APPROVED

Duke Street, Settle BD24 9DU
☎ (01729) 822203
Fax (01729) 824103

17th C coaching inn with log fire, offering simply furnished bedrooms and a reputation for excellent meals. Prime location for Yorkshire Dales and Settle-Carlisle railway.
Bedrooms: 1 single, 6 double, 5 twin, 2 triple
Bathrooms: 2 en-suite, 2 public

Bed & breakfast per night:	£min	£max
Single	23.50	30.00
Double	47.00	56.00

Lunch available
Evening meal 1800 (last orders 2200)
Parking for 9
Cards accepted: Mastercard, Visa

Husbands Barn

HIGHLY COMMENDED

Stainforth, Settle BD24 9PN
☎ (01729) 822240 & 822580
40-acre hill farm. Character barn conversion offering very high standards. En-suite rooms with TV, tea/coffee, etc. Open fire and CH. Good breakfast. "Feel at home".
Bedrooms: 2 double, 1 twin
Bathrooms: 3 en-suite

Bed & breakfast per night:	£min	£max
Single	30.00	35.00
Double	45.00	60.00

Parking for 5

Maypole Inn

COMMENDED

Maypole Green, Main Street, Long Preston, Skipton BD23 4PH
☎ (01729) 840219
Email: landlord@maypole.co.uk
17th C inn, with open fires, on the village green. Easy access to many attractive walks in the surrounding dales. 4 miles from Settle.
Bedrooms: 1 single, 2 double, 1 twin, 1 triple, 1 family room
Bathrooms: 6 en-suite

Bed & breakfast per night:	£min	£max
Single	26.00	35.00
Double	39.00	43.00

Lunch available
Evening meal 1830 (last orders 2100)
Parking for 25
Cards accepted: Amex, Diners, Mastercard, Visa

Scar Close Farm

HIGHLY COMMENDED

Feizor, Austwick, Lancaster LA2 8DF
☎ (01729) 823496
250-acre mixed farm. High standard en-suite farmhouse accommodation and food in a picturesque hamlet near Settle. A tourist centre for the dales, Lakes and seaside.
Bedrooms: 1 double, 1 twin, 1 triple, 1 family room
Bathrooms: 4 en-suite

Bed & breakfast per night:	£min	£max
Single		30.00
Double	40.00	

Half board per person:	£min	£max
Daily	30.00	
Weekly	206.50	

Evening meal 1800 (last orders 1830)
Parking for 10

SUTTON BANK

North Yorkshire
Map ref 5C3

Escarpment of the Hambleton Hills, 5 miles east of Thirsk. Spectacular views. Gliding from summit.

High House Farm

COMMENDED

Sutton Bank, Thirsk YO7 2HA
☎ (01845) 597557
113-acre mixed farm. Family-run, set in open countryside and offering magnificent views. Splendid walking country, ideal for a quiet relaxing holiday. Good food and hospitality. East Coast 1 hour, York and North York Moors half an hour.
Bedrooms: 2 triple
Bathrooms: 1 public

Bed & breakfast per night:	£min	£max
Single	25.00	
Double	40.00	

Parking for 2
Open April–October

THIRSK

North Yorkshire
Map ref 5C3

Thriving market town with cobbled square surrounded by old shops and inns and also with a local museum. St Mary's Church is probably the best example of Perpendicular work in Yorkshire.

Angel Inn

COMMENDED

Long Street, Topcliffe, Thirsk YO7 3RW
☎ (01845) 577237
Fax (01845) 578000
Well-appointed, attractive village inn,

renowned for good food and traditional ales. Ideal centre for touring York and Herriot country
Bedrooms: 2 single, 8 double, 4 twin, 1 family room
Bathrooms: 15 en-suite

Bed & breakfast per night:	£min	£max
Single	39.00	42.50
Double	55.00	60.00

Lunch available
Evening meal 1830 (last orders 2130)
Parking for 150
Cards accepted: Mastercard, Visa, Switch/Delta
2 150

Doxford House

APPROVED
Front Street, Sowerby, Thirsk YO7 1JP
☎ (01845) 523238
Handsome, Georgian house with attractive garden, overlooking greens of Sowerby. Comfortable rooms, all en-suite. Ideal centre for touring moors and dales.
Wheelchair access category 3
Bedrooms: 1 double, 1 twin, 1 triple, 1 family room
Bathrooms: 4 en-suite

Bed & breakfast per night:	£min	£max
Single	22.00	23.00
Double	34.00	36.00

Parking for 4

Lavender House

COMMENDED
27 Kirkgate, Thirsk YO7 1PL
☎ (01845) 522224
Two doors from James Herriot's Skieldale House, close to Market Square. Good touring base. Small, friendly bed and breakfast.
Bedrooms: 1 single, 2 triple
Bathrooms: 2 public

Bed & breakfast per night:	£min	£max
Single	18.00	18.00
Double	30.00	30.00

Parking for 3

The symbol after an establishment name indicates that it is a Regional Tourist Board member.

Plump Bank

COMMENDED
Felixkirk Road, Thirsk YO7 2LW
☎ (01845) 522406
From Thirsk take the A170 Scarborough road. After 1 mile turn left for Felixkirk and Boltby and house is on the left after 100 yards.
Bedrooms: 1 double, 1 twin
Bathrooms: 2 en-suite

Bed & breakfast per night:	£min	£max
Double	32.00	36.00

Parking for 9
Open June–September

Thornborough House Farm

COMMENDED
South Kilvington, Thirsk YO7 2NP
☎ (01845) 522103
Fax (01845) 522103
28-acre mixed farm. 200-year-old farmhouse in an ideal position for walking and touring in the North York Moors and Yorkshire Dales.
Bedrooms: 1 double, 1 twin, 1 triple
Bathrooms: 2 en-suite, 1 private

Bed & breakfast per night:	£min	£max
Single	15.00	19.00
Double	29.00	36.00

Half board per person:	£min	£max
Daily	25.00	29.00

Evening meal from 1830
Parking for 6
Cards accepted: Mastercard, Visa

Town Pasture Farm

COMMENDED
Boltby, Thirsk YO7 2DY
☎ (01845) 537298
180-acre mixed farm. Farmhouse with views of the Hambleton Hills, in picturesque Boltby village within the boundary of the North York Moors National Park.
Bedrooms: 1 twin, 1 triple
Bathrooms: 2 en-suite

Bed & breakfast per night:	£min	£max
Single	16.50	
Double	33.00	

Half board per person:	£min	£max
Daily	25.00	

Parking for 4

THORNTON WATLASS

North Yorkshire
Map ref 5C3

Picturesque village in Lower Wensleydale.

The Buck Inn

COMMENDED
Thornton Watlass, Ripon HG4 4AH
☎ (01677) 422461
Fax (01677) 422447
Friendly village inn overlooking the delightful cricket green in a small village, 3 miles from Bedale on the Masham road, and close to the A1. Ideal centre for exploring both the dales and North York Moors.
Bedrooms: 1 single, 3 double, 2 twin, 1 triple
Bathrooms: 5 en-suite, 1 public

Bed & breakfast per night:	£min	£max
Single	34.00	
Double	52.00	

Half board per person:	£min	£max
Daily	37.00	

Lunch available
Evening meal 1830 (last orders 2130)
Parking for 40
Cards accepted: Amex, Diners, Mastercard, Visa, Switch/Delta
70

TODMORDEN

West Yorkshire
Map ref 4B1

In beautiful scenery on the edge of the Pennines at junction of 3 sweeping valleys. Until 1888 the county boundary between Yorkshire and Lancashire cut this old cotton town in half, running through the middle of the Town Hall.
Tourist Information Centre ☎ (01706) 818181

Cherry Tree Cottage

COMMENDED
Woodhouse Road, Todmorden, Lancashire OL14 5RJ
☎ (01706) 817492
Sympathetically restored, part 17th C country cottage with modern amenities and lovely views. Emphasis on friendly atmosphere and fresh, home-cooked fare.
Bedrooms: 2 twin
Suites available
Bathrooms: 1 en-suite, 1 private

Continued ▶

TODMORDEN

Continued

Bed & breakfast per night:	£min	£max
Single	16.50	19.00
Double	33.00	38.00

Half board per person:	£min	£max
Daily	23.50	26.00
Weekly	164.00	176.00

Evening meal 1800 (last orders 1900)
Parking for 4

ULLESKELF

North Yorkshire
Map ref 4C1

Village of Danish origin alongside the River Wharfe, with small railway station on the York to Sheffield route.

Ulleskelf Arms

Listed APPROVED

Church Fenton Lane, Ulleskelf, Tadcaster LS24 9DW
☎ (01937) 832136

Village free-house offering bed and breakfast. Cask-conditioned beers and quality bar meals. Separate dining area, and beer garden. "Good Beer Guide" 1997. Ideal location for golfers, fishing, walking.

Bedrooms: 2 single, 1 double, 3 twin
Bathrooms: 1 public

Bed & breakfast per night:	£min	£max
Single	18.00	
Double	32.00	34.00

Half board per person:	£min	£max
Daily	22.00	30.00

Lunch available
Evening meal 1900 (last orders 2200)
Parking for 16
Cards accepted: Diners, Mastercard, Visa

WALSDEN

West Yorkshire
Map ref 4B1

Highstones Guest House

Listed COMMENDED

Lane Bottom, Walsden, Todmorden, Lancashire OL14 6TY
☎ (01706) 816534

Detached house set in half an acre with lovely views over open country, yet close to facilities.

Bedrooms: 1 single, 2 double
Bathrooms: 2 public

Bed & breakfast per night:	£min	£max
Single	15.00	16.00
Double	30.00	32.00

Parking for 4

WEST TANFIELD

North Yorkshire
Map ref 5C3

The Bull Inn

COMMENDED

Church Street, West Tanfield, Ripon HG4 5JQ
☎ (01423) 872627
Fax (01423) 872627

11th C inn with riverside garden and private fishing lake. Ideal centre for historic villages, stately homes and gardens and Herriot country. Half board prices are based on a minimum 2-night stay.

Bedrooms: 1 single, 2 double, 2 twin
Bathrooms: 5 en-suite

Bed & breakfast per night:	£min	£max
Single	39.50	54.50
Double	59.90	59.90

Half board per person:	£min	£max
Daily	42.50	42.50

Lunch available
Evening meal 1830 (last orders 2200)
Parking for 30
Cards accepted: Mastercard, Visa

WESTOW

North Yorkshire
Map ref 5C3

The grey walls and red roofs of Westow are on a slope of the Derwent's wooded valley. The Hall, where the Idle family had their seat, stands at a corner of the village by the wayside and the solitary church stands in fields outside.

Blacksmiths Arms Inn

COMMENDED

Westow, York YO6 7NE
☎ (01653) 618365 & 618343

Inn of character. Family-run establishment with very good facilities. All welcome.

Wheelchair access category 3
Bedrooms: 2 single, 2 double, 2 twin
Bathrooms: 6 en-suite

Bed & breakfast per night:	£min	£max
Single	21.00	23.50
Double	42.00	47.00

Lunch available
Evening meal 1900 (last orders 2130)
Parking for 12
Cards accepted: Amex, Mastercard, Visa, Switch/Delta

WOLD NEWTON

East Riding of Yorkshire
Map ref 5D3

The Wold Cottage

HIGHLY COMMENDED

Wold Newton, Driffield, East Riding of Yorkshire YO25 0HL
☎ (01262) 470696
Fax (01262) 470696

440-acre mixed farm. Georgian farmhouse in own grounds, overlooking woodlands and continuous Wold land. Come and relax and forget the pressures of everyday life. Observe the wildlife and history. Both rooms en-suite with tea/coffee-making facilities. Lambing breaks January-March.

Bedrooms: 1 double, 1 twin
Bathrooms: 2 en-suite

Bed & breakfast per night:	£min	£max
Single	24.00	
Double	38.00	

Half board per person:	£min	£max
Daily	29.00	

Evening meal from 1900
Parking for 4

The map references refer to the colour maps towards the end of the guide. The first figure is the map number; the letter and figure which follow indicate the grid reference on the map.

YORK

North Yorkshire
Map ref 4C1

Ancient walled city nearly 2000 years old containing many well-preserved medieval buildings. Its Minster has over 100 stained glass windows. Attractions include Castle Museum, National Railway Museum, Jorvik Viking Centre and York Dungeon.
Tourist Information Centre ☎ (01904) 621756 or 621757 or 620557

Aberford House Hotel

Listed APPROVED

35-36 East Mount Road, York YO2 2BD
☎ (01904) 622694
Centrally situated, privately-owned small hotel. Colour TV in all bedrooms. Brochure on request.
Bedrooms: 2 double, 2 twin, 1 family room
Bathrooms: 1 en-suite, 2 public

Bed & breakfast per night:	£min	£max
Single	20.00	25.00
Double	34.00	50.00

Parking for 7
Cards accepted: Amex, Mastercard, Visa

Arndale Hotel

HIGHLY COMMENDED

290 Tadcaster Road, York YO2 2ET
☎ (01904) 702424

Delightful Victorian house, directly overlooking racecourse. Beautiful enclosed walled gardens giving a country atmosphere within the city. Antiques, fresh flowers, four-poster beds, whirlpool baths. Enclosed gated car park.
Bedrooms: 7 double, 2 twin, 1 triple
Bathrooms: 10 en-suite

Bed & breakfast per night:	£min	£max
Single	39.00	49.00
Double	47.00	69.00

Parking for 20
Cards accepted: Mastercard, Visa

Black Bull Inn

COMMENDED

91 Main Street, Escrick, York YO4 6JP
☎ (01904) 728245
Fax (01904) 728154

Cottage-style village inn of character, beams, open fires, en-suite accommodation. Fine restaurant and lounge bar meals. Close to York by car or bus.
Bedrooms: 1 single, 6 double, 2 twin, 1 family room
Suites available
Bathrooms: 10 en-suite

Bed & breakfast per night:	£min	£max
Single	40.00	40.00
Double	50.00	56.00

Half board per person:	£min	£max
Daily	35.00	50.00
Weekly	345.00	350.00

Lunch available
Parking for 14
Cards accepted: Mastercard, Visa, Switch/Delta

Bloomsbury Hotel

COMMENDED

127 Clifton, York YO3 6BL
☎ (01904) 634031

An elegantly appointed, large Victorian town house, centrally situated, with large private car park. Recently totally refurbished. Completely non-smoking.
Bedrooms: 2 single, 3 double, 3 twin, 2 triple
Bathrooms: 10 en-suite

Bed & breakfast per night:	£min	£max
Single	35.00	65.00
Double	45.00	65.00

Parking for 8
Cards accepted: Mastercard, Visa, Switch/Delta

Bowen House

COMMENDED

4 Gladstone Street, Huntington Road, York YO3 7RF
☎ (01904) 636881
Fax (01904) 636881
Within a short walk of York Minster and city centre, this late Victorian, family-run guesthouse combines high quality facilities with old-style charm. Private car park. Traditional or vegetarian breakfasts. Non-smoking throughout.
Bedrooms: 1 single, 2 double, 1 twin, 1 family room
Bathrooms: 3 en-suite, 1 public, 1 private shower

Bed & breakfast per night:	£min	£max
Single	20.00	25.00
Double	32.00	45.00

Parking for 4
Cards accepted: Mastercard, Visa

Burton Villa

Listed COMMENDED

22 Haxby Road, York YO3 7JX
☎ (01904) 626364
Fax (01904) 626364

Noted for friendly atmosphere, good breakfasts and high standards. 7 minutes' walk from York Minster. Private parking.
Bedrooms: 1 single, 6 double, 2 twin, 1 triple, 2 family rooms
Bathrooms: 8 private, 1 public

Bed & breakfast per night:	£min	£max
Single	16.50	30.00
Double	33.00	50.00

Parking for 7
Cards accepted: Mastercard, Visa, Switch/Delta

ACCESSIBILITY

Look for the symbols which indicate accessibility for wheelchair users. These are described in detail at the front of this guide.

YORK

Continued

Cook's Guest House

COMMENDED

120 Bishopthorpe Road, York
YO2 1JX
☎ (01904) 652519

Featured on TV's "This Morning", small, friendly and comfortable guesthouse with unique decor. 10 minutes' walk to city, railway station and racecourse.

Bedrooms: 1 double, 1 triple
Bathrooms: 2 en-suite, 1 public

Bed & breakfast per night:	£min	£max
Double	32.00	40.00

Cumbria House

Listed COMMENDED

2 Vyner Street, Haxby Road, York
YO3 7HS
☎ (01904) 636817

Family-run guesthouse, 12 minutes' walk from York Minster. En-suites available. Easily located from ring road. Private car park. Brochure.

Bedrooms: 1 single, 1 double, 1 twin, 1 triple, 1 family room
Bathrooms: 2 en-suite, 2 public

Bed & breakfast per night:	£min	£max
Single	17.00	20.00
Double	32.00	40.00

Parking for 5

Curzon Lodge and Stable Cottages

HIGHLY COMMENDED

23 Tadcaster Road, Dringhouses, York YO2 2QG
☎ (01904) 703157

Delightful 17th C listed house and old stables overlooking racecourse within historic city. Country antiques, beams, fresh flowers,cottagey bedrooms all en-suite, four-posters and brass beds. Cosy and informal. Floodlit parking in grounds. Restaurants one minute's walk.

Bedrooms: 1 single, 4 double, 3 twin, 1 triple, 1 family room
Bathrooms: 10 en-suite

Bed & breakfast per night:	£min	£max
Single	30.00	42.00
Double	45.00	62.00

Parking for 16
Cards accepted: Mastercard, Visa, Switch/Delta

Fairthorne

COMMENDED

356 Strensall Road, Earswick, York
YO3 9SW
☎ (01904) 768609
Fax (01904) 768609

Detached dormer bungalow with spacious gardens. Four miles from York city centre.

Bedrooms: 1 double, 1 triple
Bathrooms: 2 en-suite

Bed & breakfast per night:	£min	£max
Single	18.00	18.00
Double	30.00	30.00

Parking for 6

Foss Bank Guest House

APPROVED

16 Huntington Road, York YO3 7RB
☎ (01904) 635548

Small Victorian family-run guesthouse, comfortable and friendly, on the north-east side of the city. 5 minutes' walk from the city wall.

Bedrooms: 2 single, 3 double, 1 twin
Bathrooms: 2 en-suite, 4 private showers

Bed & breakfast per night:	£min	£max
Single	16.00	19.00
Double	32.00	39.00

Parking for 5
Open February–December

Four Seasons Hotel

HIGHLY COMMENDED

7 St Peter's Grove, Bootham, York
YO3 6AQ
☎ (01904) 622621
Fax (01904) 620976

Delightful, high-quality Victorian hotel, in quiet tree-lined grove. Only 5 minutes' walk from city centre. All rooms en-suite. Private car park.

Bedrooms: 2 double, 1 twin, 1 triple, 1 family room
Bathrooms: 5 en-suite

Bed & breakfast per night:	£min	£max
Double	52.00	58.00

Parking for 8
Open February–December
Cards accepted: Mastercard, Visa

George Hotel

COMMENDED

6 St George's Place, Tadcaster Road, York YO2 2DR
☎ (01904) 625056
Fax (01904) 625009

Small family-run hotel in a quiet cul-de-sac near the racecourse and convenient for the city centre. Good car parking facilities.

Bedrooms: 5 double, 3 triple, 2 family rooms
Bathrooms: 10 en-suite

Bed & breakfast per night:	£min	£max
Single	20.00	30.00
Double	35.00	50.00

Evening meal 1900 (last orders 2100)
Parking for 9
Cards accepted: Amex, Diners, Mastercard, Visa

Hedley House

COMMENDED

3-4 Bootham Terrace, York
YO3 7DH
☎ (01904) 637404

Family-run hotel close to the city centre. 1 ground floor bedroom. All rooms en-suite. Home cooking, special diets catered for.

Bedrooms: 2 single, 5 double, 5 twin, 2 triple, 1 family room
Bathrooms: 15 en-suite

Bed & breakfast per night:	£min	£max
Single	20.00	34.00
Double	36.00	60.00

Half board per person:	£min	£max
Daily	30.00	40.00

Evening meal 1830 (last orders 1900)
Parking for 18
Cards accepted: Amex, Diners, Mastercard, Visa, Switch/Delta

Heworth Court Hotel

COMMENDED

76-78 Heworth Green, York YO3 7TQ
☎ (01904) 425156
Fax (01904) 415290

Privately-owned, family-run hotel close to York Minster and surrounding countryside. Special short breaks. Bar, restaurant, car park, lounge. Brochure available.

Wheelchair access category 3
Bedrooms: 5 single, 14 double, 4 triple, 2 family rooms
Bathrooms: 25 en-suite

Bed & breakfast per night:	£min	£max
Single	44.00	54.00
Double	44.00	78.00

Half board per person:	£min	£max
Daily	30.00	42.00
Weekly	175.00	245.00

Lunch available
Evening meal 1830 (last orders 2130)
Parking for 26
Cards accepted: Amex, Diners, Mastercard, Visa, Switch/Delta

Hillcrest Guest House

COMMENDED

110 Bishopthorpe Road, York YO2 1JX
☎ (01904) 653160

Elegant Victorian town house, 10 minutes' walk from city centre. Private car park. Generous breakfast selection. Special diets catered for. Bargain winter breaks (November-March).

Bedrooms: 3 single, 5 double, 2 twin, 1 triple, 2 family rooms
Bathrooms: 7 en-suite, 3 public

Bed & breakfast per night:	£min	£max
Single	15.00	20.00
Double	28.00	42.00

Half board per person:	£min	£max
Daily	24.00	29.00
Weekly	160.00	195.00

Evening meal 1800 (last orders 1500)
Parking for 8
Cards accepted: Mastercard, Visa

A key to symbols can be found inside the back cover flap.

Holly Lodge

COMMENDED

206 Fulford Road, York YO1 4DD
☎ (01904) 646005

Listed Georgian building on the A19, convenient for both the north and south and within walking distance of the city centre. Close to university, golf course and Barbican centre. Quiet rooms and private car park.

Bedrooms: 3 double, 1 twin, 1 family room
Bathrooms: 5 en-suite

Bed & breakfast per night:	£min	£max
Single	30.00	50.00
Double	40.00	60.00

Parking for 5
Cards accepted: Amex, Mastercard, Visa

Jacobean Lodge Hotel

COMMENDED

Plainville Lane, Wigginton, York YO3 8RG
☎ (01904) 762749
Fax (01904) 768403

Converted 17th C farmhouse, 4 miles north of York. Set in picturesque gardens with ample parking. Warm, friendly atmosphere and traditional cuisine.

Bedrooms: 2 single, 9 double, 1 twin, 2 triple
Bathrooms: 14 en-suite

Bed & breakfast per night:	£min	£max
Single	30.00	35.00
Double	52.00	60.00

Lunch available
Evening meal 1900 (last orders 2200)
Parking for 70
Cards accepted: Mastercard, Visa, Switch/Delta

COLOUR MAPS

Colour maps at the back of this guide pinpoint all places in which you will find accommodation listed.

Midway House Hotel

COMMENDED

145 Fulford Road, York YO1 4HG
☎ (01904) 659272
Fax (01904) 659272

Non-smoking, family-run hotel. Spacious en-suite bedrooms with four-poster and ground floor rooms available. Close to city centre and university. Private parking.

Bedrooms: 8 double, 2 twin, 2 triple
Bathrooms: 11 en-suite, 1 private, 1 public

Bed & breakfast per night:	£min	£max
Single	27.00	45.00
Double	36.00	60.00

Evening meal 1900 (last orders 1900)
Parking for 14
Cards accepted: Amex, Diners, Mastercard, Visa

Moorgarth Guest House

APPROVED

158 Fulford Road, York YO1 4DA
☎ (01904) 636768

Victorian town house with a warm, friendly atmosphere. Close to all tourist attractions and 10 minutes' walk from the city centre.

Bedrooms: 2 single, 2 double, 2 triple, 1 family room
Bathrooms: 4 en-suite, 1 public

Bed & breakfast per night:	£min	£max
Single	16.00	
Double	34.00	

Parking for 5
Open March–December
Cards accepted: Mastercard, Visa

Newton Guest House

APPROVED

Neville Street, Haxby Road, York YO3 7NP
☎ (01904) 635627

Family-run, friendly guesthouse, a few minutes' walk from city centre. Private car park. Non-smoking. Breakfast menu. Your comfort is first priority.

Bedrooms: 1 single, 2 double, 1 twin, 1 triple
Bathrooms: 4 en-suite, 1 private

Bed & breakfast per night:	£min	£max
Single	18.00	20.00
Double	32.00	40.00

Parking for 5
Cards accepted: Mastercard, Visa

YORK

Continued

Oaklands Guest House

COMMENDED

351 Strensall Road, Old Earswick, York YO3 9SW
☎ (01904) 768443
Friendly, well-furnished house, 3 miles from the city and within easy reach of the A64 and A1237.
Bedrooms: 1 double, 1 twin, 1 triple
Bathrooms: 1 en-suite, 1 public

Bed & breakfast per night:	£min	£max
Single	17.00	23.00
Double	34.00	40.00

Parking for 7

Orillia House

COMMENDED

89 The Village, Stockton-on-the-Forest, York YO3 9UP
☎ (01904) 400600 & (0402) 125903
A warm welcome awaits you in this 300-year-old house of charm and character, opposite church. Three miles north east of York.
Bedrooms: 3 double, 1 twin, 2 triple
Bathrooms: 6 en-suite

Bed & breakfast per night:	£min	£max
Single	23.00	25.00
Double	36.00	40.00

Parking for 10
Cards accepted: Mastercard, Visa

Papillon Hotel

Listed APPROVED

43 Gillygate, York YO3 7EA
☎ (01904) 636505
Small, friendly city centre guesthouse with personal attention at all times. 300 yards from York Minster. En-suite available. No smoking, please. Car parking. Phone for details.
Bedrooms: 2 single, 1 double, 2 twin, 3 triple
Bathrooms: 3 en-suite, 2 public

Bed & breakfast per night:	£min	£max
Single	20.00	25.00
Double	38.00	50.00

Parking for 7

Riverside Walk Hotel

APPROVED

9 Earlsborough Terrace, Marygate, York YO3 7BQ
☎ (01904) 620769 & 646249
Fax (01904) 646249

Licensed B&B, 450-yard riverside walk to city and 5 minutes' walk to York Minster, rail/bus stations and all main attractions. Quiet location, private car park. Bargain breaks in low season. No single-night Saturday bookings.
Bedrooms: 2 single, 6 double, 2 triple
Bathrooms: 10 en-suite

Bed & breakfast per night:	£min	£max
Single	23.00	28.00
Double	30.00	52.00

Parking for 14
Cards accepted: Mastercard, Visa, Switch/Delta

Rosedale Guest House

COMMENDED

Wetherby Road, Rufforth, York YO2 3QB
☎ (01904) 738297
Family-run guesthouse with a homely atmosphere and all facilities, in a delightful, unspoilt village 4 miles west of York on the B1224. Private parking available.
Bedrooms: 1 single, 3 double, 1 twin
Bathrooms: 1 en-suite, 2 public, 2 private showers

Bed & breakfast per night:	£min	£max
Single	17.00	18.00
Double	36.00	38.00

Parking for 5

Southlands Bed and Breakfast

HIGHLY COMMENDED

Huntington Road, Huntington, York YO3 9PX
☎ (01904) 766796
Fax (01904) 764536
Southlands stands in its own attractive gardens in the village of Huntington, only 1.8 miles from York city centre.
Bedrooms: 2 double, 1 twin
Bathrooms: 3 en-suite

Bed & breakfast per night:	£min	£max
Single	24.00	26.00
Double	32.00	39.00

Parking for 4
Cards accepted: Mastercard, Switch/Delta

Stanley Guest House

COMMENDED

Stanley Street, Haxby Road, York YO3 7NW
☎ (01904) 637111
Friendly, comfortable guesthouse, 10 minutes' walk to York Minster and city and close to many attractions. All rooms en-suite. No smoking. Warm welcome assured.
Bedrooms: 2 single, 2 double, 1 twin, 1 triple
Bathrooms: 6 en-suite

Bed & breakfast per night:	£min	£max
Single	20.00	22.50
Double	35.00	40.00

Parking for 5
Cards accepted: Amex, Mastercard, Visa

Victoria Villa

Listed APPROVED

72 Heslington Road, York YO1 5AU
☎ (01904) 631647
Victorian town house, close to city centre. Offering clean and friendly accommodation and a full English breakfast.
Bedrooms: 1 single, 2 double, 1 twin, 2 triple
Bathrooms: 2 public

Bed & breakfast per night:	£min	£max
Single	16.00	20.00
Double	28.00	36.00

Parking for 4

Warrens Guest House

COMMENDED

30 Scarcroft Road, York YO2 1NF
☎ (01904) 643139
Centrally situated guesthouse. All rooms en-suite with colour TV and tea/coffee-making facilities. Full English breakfast. Four-poster beds available, also some ground-floor bedrooms. Private car park with CCTV.
Bedrooms: 1 single, 1 double, 2 twin, 1 triple, 1 family room
Bathrooms: 5 en-suite, 1 private

Bed & breakfast per night:	£min	£max
Single	25.00	35.00
Double	38.00	45.00

Parking for 8
Open March–November

Wellgarth House

COMMENDED

Wetherby Road, Rufforth, York YO2 3QB
☎ (01904) 738592 & 738595
Fax (01904) 738595

Comfort and friendliness assured at this individual and attractive country guesthouse in the delightful village of Rufforth. Ideal touring base for York and the Yorkshire Dales.

Bedrooms: 1 single, 3 double, 2 twin, 1 triple
Bathrooms: 6 en-suite, 1 private

Bed & breakfast per night:	£min	£max
Single	18.00	25.00
Double	36.00	50.00

Parking for 10
Open February–December
Cards accepted: Mastercard, Visa

2 20

York Lodge Guest House

Listed APPROVED

61 Bootham Crescent, Bootham, York YO3 7AH
☎ (01904) 654289
Fax (01904) 430117

Family-run guesthouse, within 10 minutes' walk of city centre attractions, offering a warm, friendly and relaxing stay.

Bedrooms: 1 single, 3 double, 2 twin, 1 triple, 1 family room
Bathrooms: 4 en-suite, 2 public

Bed & breakfast per night:	£min	£max
Single	14.50	19.00
Double	30.00	40.00

Parking for 3
Cards accepted: Mastercard, Visa

COUNTRY CODE

Always follow the Country Code

Enjoy the countryside and respect its life and work · Guard against all risk of fire · Fasten all gates · Keep your dogs under close control · Keep to public paths across farmland · Use gates and stiles to cross fences, hedges and walls · Leave livestock, crops and machinery alone · Take your litter home · Help to keep all water clean · Protect wildlife, plants and trees · Take special care on country roads · Make no unnecessary noise

USE YOUR *i*'s

There are more than 550 Tourist Information Centres throughout England offering friendly help with accommodation and holiday ideas as well as suggestions of places to visit and things to do. There may well be a centre in your home town which can help you before you set out. You'll find addresses in the local Phone Book or simply call Freepages 0800 192 192.

CHECK THE MAPS

The colour maps at the back of this guide show all the cities, towns and villages for which you will find accommodation entries.

Refer to the town index to find the page on which it is listed.

ENQUIRY COUPONS

To help you obtain further information about advertisers and accommodation featured in this guide you will find enquiry coupons at the back. Send these directly to the establishments in which you are interested. Remember to complete both sides of the coupon.

HEART OF ENGLAND

The exciting diversity of the Heart of England takes in rural, industrial, social, and artistic heritage, where unspoiled landscapes and black-and-white villages contrast with mellow market towns and major cities.

The region is home to the Cotswolds, the Malverns, the beautiful Wye valley, the marches of Hereford and Shropshire, and traditional brewing and pottery centres like Stafford and Burton-on-Trent.

Try popular local delicacies like Bakewell tarts and cheeses from Leicester. Tour famous Sherwood Forest or marvel at Northampton's unforgettable hot air balloon festival. England's heart beats fast in Coventry and Birmingham, both excellent touring bases and packed with things to do and see.

The counties of Derbyshire, Gloucestershire, Hereford & Worcester, Leicestershire, Northamptonshire, Nottinghamshire, Rutland, Shropshire, Staffordshire, Warwickshire and West Midlands

FOR MORE INFORMATION CONTACT:
Heart of England Tourist Board
Lark Hill Road, Worcester WR5 2EZ
Tel: (01905) 763436 **Fax:** (01905) 763450

Where to Go in the Heart of England –
see pages 124-128
Where to Stay in the Heart of England –
see pages 129-196

HEART OF ENGLAND

Where to Go and What to See

You will find hundreds of interesting places to visit during your stay in the Heart of England, just some of which are listed in these pages. The number against each name will help you locate it on the map (page 128). Contact any Tourist Information Centre in the region for more ideas on days out in the Heart of England.

1 Chatsworth House and Garden
Bakewell,
Derbyshire DE45 1PP
Tel: (01246) 582204
Built in 1687-1707 with a collection of fine pictures, books, drawings and furniture. Garden laid out by Capability Brown with fountains, cascades, a farmyard and playground.

2 The Heights of Abraham
Matlock Bath, Matlock,
Derbyshire DE4 3PD
Tel: (01629) 582365
A cable car ride across the Derwent Valley gives access to the Alpine Centre with refreshments, superb views, woodland, prospect tower and two show caves.

3 Peak District Mining Museum
The Pavilion, Matlock Bath,
Derbyshire DE4 3NR
Tel: (01629) 583834
Exhibition on 2,500 years of lead mining with displays on geology, mines and miners, tools and engines. The climbing shafts make it suitable for children.

4 The National Tramway Museum
Crich, Matlock,
Derbyshire DE4 5DP
Tel: (01773) 852565
Over 70 trams from Britain and overseas from 1873-1957 with tram rides on a one mile route, a period street scene, depots, a power station, workshops and exhibitions.

5 Midland Railway Centre
Butterley Station, Ripley,
Derby DE5 3QZ
Tel: (01773) 747674/570140
Over 25 locomotives and over 80 items of historic rolling stock of Midland and LMS origin with a steam-hauled passenger service, museum site, country and farm park.

6 American Adventure World

Pit Lane, Ilkeston,
Derbyshire DE7 5SX
Tel: (01773) 531521

The new American Adventure World has action and entertainment for all ages. Ride the missile white-knuckle rollercoasters, rapid rides motion master and see the Sooty Show.

7 Newark Air Museum

The Airfield,
Winthorpe, Newark,
Nottinghamshire NG24 2NY
Tel: (01636) 707170

Aircraft parts and memorabilia with exhibition hall showing Anson, Prentice, Swift, Provost, Vulcan, Vampire, Meteors, Varsity and Sycamores. Book and model shop.

8 White Post Modern Farm Centre

Farnsfield, Newark,
Nottinghamshire NG22 8HL
Tel: (01623) 882977

A working farm with over 4,000 farm animals, an 8,000 egg incubator, free-range hens, lambs, lakes, picnic areas, tea gardens and an indoor countryside night walk.

9 The Canal Museum

Canal Street, Nottingham,
Tel: (0115) 959 8835

A former canal warehouse with landing areas and wharves, displays on the history of the River Trent, canal and river transport, bridges, floods and natural history.

10 Nottingham Industrial Museum

Courtyard Buildings,
Wollaton Park,
Nottingham NG8 2AE
Tel: (0115) 928 4602

An 18thC stables presenting the history of Nottingham's industries: printing, pharmacy, hosiery and lace. There is also a Victorian beam engine, a horse gin and transport.

11 The Tales of Robin Hood

30-38 Maid Marian Way,
Nottingham NG1 6GF
Tel: (0115) 9414414/9483284

Join the world's greatest medieval adventure hide-out in the Sheriff's eerie cave. Ride through the magical green wood and play the Silver Arrow game.

12 Belvoir Castle

Belvoir,
Lincolnshire NG32 1PD
Tel: (01476) 870262

The present castle is the fourth to be built on this site and dates from 1816. Art treasures include works by Poussin, Rubens, Holbein and Reynolds. Queens Royal Lancers display.

13 Alton Towers Theme Park

Alton,
Stoke-on-Trent,
Staffordshire ST10 4DB
Tel: (0990) 204060/
(01538) 703344

Theme Park with over 125 rides and attractions including Nemesis, Haunted House, Runaway Mine Train, Congo River Rapids, Log Flume and Toyland Tours.

14 Spode Museum and Visitor Centre

Spode Works, Church Street,
Stoke-on-Trent,
Staffordshire ST4 1BX
Tel: (01782) 744011

Watch the various processes in the making of bone china. Samples can be bought at the Spode Shop.

15 Wedgwood Visitor Centre

Barlaston,
Stoke-on-Trent,
Staffordshire ST12 9ES
Tel: (01782) 204141/204218

Located in the Wedgwood factory which lies within a 500-acre country estate. You can see potters and decorators at work. Museum and shop.

16 Ye Olde Pork Pie Shoppe

10 Nottingham Street,
Melton Mowbray,
Leicestershire LE13 1NW
Tel: (01664) 62341

Pork pie shop and bakery in a 17thC building. History of the shop and the Melton Mowbray pork pie industry. Traditional hand raising demonstration.

17 Rutland Water

Whitwell, Oakham,
Leicestershire LE15 8PX
Tel: (01780) 460321/
(01480) 846427

Water and land based recreational facilities. Pleasure cruiser, church museum, butterfly and aquatic centre.

18 Twycross Zoo

Twycross, Atherstone,
Warwickshire CV9 3PX
Tel: (01827) 880250/880440

Gorillas, orangutans, chimpanzees, a modern gibbon complex, elephants, lions, cheetahs, giraffes, a reptile house, pets corner and rides.

19 Drayton Manor Theme Park and Zoo

Tamworth,
Staffordshire B78 3TW
Tel: (01827) 287979

Family theme park with 250 acres of parkland and lakes. Open plan zoo. Amusement park with 50 rides. Wristbands for unlimited rides or discount tickets.

20 The Shrewsbury Quest

193 Abbey Foregate,
Shrewsbury,
Shropshire SY2 6AH
Tel: (01743) 243324/355990

12thC historical site. Visitors are invited to solve three mysteries, creating manuscripts and playing medieval garden games.

21 Ironbridge Gorge Museum
Ironbridge, Telford,
Shropshire TF8 7AW
Tel: (01925) 433522
World's first cast-iron bridge, Museum of the River Visitor Centre, Tar Tunnel, Jackfield Tile Museum, Coalport China Museum, Rosehill House, Blists Hill Museum and Museum of Iron.

22 Acton Scott Historic Working Farm
Wenlock Lodge,
Acton Scott Church, Stretton,
Shropshire SY6 6QN
Tel: (01694) 781306/781307
Living history in the Shropshire Hills - dairy farming, milking, butter making and craft demonstrations.

23 Black Country Living Museum
Tipton Road, Dudley,
West Midlands DY1 4SQ
Tel: (0121) 557 9643
Midlands open air museum with shops, chapel, canal trip into limestone cavern, underground mining experience and electric tramway. Britain's industrial past brought to life.

24 Stanford Hall and Motor Cycle Museum
Lutterworth,
Leicestershire LE17 6DH
Tel: (01788) 860250
A William and Mary house on the River Avon with family costumes, furniture, pictures, a replica 1898 flying machine, motorcycle museum, rose garden and nature trail.

25 National Sea Life Centre
The Water's Edge,
Brindleyplace,
Birmingham B1 2HL
Tel: (0121) 633 4700/643 6777
Over 55 fascinating displays. The opportunity to come face-to-face with hundreds of fascinating sea creatures from sharks to shrimps.

26 National Motorcycle Museum
Coventry Road,
Bickenhill, Solihull,
West Midlands B92 OEJ
Tel: (01675) 443311
Collection of 650 British machines from 1898-1993, housed in a new high architectural standard building.

27 Brandon Marsh Nature Centre
Brandon Lane, Coventry,
West Midlands CV3 3GW
Tel: (01203) 302912
Two-hundred acre nature reserve with lakes, marshes and woodland. Ideal place to see natural wildlife. Nature trail with disabled access. Nature centre with displays and shop.

28 Cadbury World
Linden Road, Bournville,
Birmingham,
West Midlands B30 2LD
Tel: (0121) 451 4180/4159
Story of chocolate from Aztec times to present day. Chocolate-making demonstration and children's fantasy factory.

29 Rugby School Museum
10 Little Church Street,
Rugby,
Warwickshire CV21 3AW
Tel: (01788) 574117/565871
Tells the story of the school, scene of Tom Brown's Schooldays, *and contains memorabilia of the game of rugby invented on the School Close.*

30 Holdenby House, Gardens and Falconry Centre

Holdenby,
Northampton NN6 8DJ
Tel: (01604) 770074
The remains of an Elizabethan palace and garden by Rosemary Verey with a fragrant border, falconry centre, armoury, a 17thC homestead, tearoom and shop.

31 Warwick Castle

Warwick,
Warwickshire CV34 4QU
Tel: (01926) 406600/495421
Set in 60 acres of grounds with state rooms, armoury, dungeon, torture chamber, clock tower. Exhibits include 'A Royal Weekend Party 1898' and 'Kingmaker - a preparation for battle'.

32 Shakespeare's Birthplace

Henley Street,
Stratford-upon-Avon,
Warwickshire CV37 6QW
Tel: (01789) 204016
Beginning with an evocation of the busy market town into which he was born, the exhibition covers Shakespeare's home background, school, marriage and theatre career in London.

33 Elgar's Birthplace Museum

Crown East Lane,
Lower Broadheath,
Worcester,
Worcestershire WR2 6RH
Tel: (01905) 333224
Cottage where Edward Elgar was born, housing a museum of photographs, musical scores, letters and records associated with the composer.

34 Mappa Mundi & Chained Library Exhibition

Hereford Cathedral,
5 The Cloister,
Hereford HR1 2NG
Tel: (01432) 359880
The new library of Hereford Cathedral is open to the public. See the unique Mappa Mundi, the largest and most complete map in the world, drawn in 1289.

35 Eastnor Castle

Eastnor, Ledbury,
Herefordshire HR8 1RD
Tel: (01531) 633160/632302
Medieval in appearance, the castle stands at the end of the Malvern Hills. Fine collections of armour, pictures, tapestries and Italian furniture.

36 The National Birds of Prey Centre

Newent,
Gloucestershire GL18 1JJ
Tel: (01531) 820286
Large collection of birds of prey. Flying demonstrations daily (weather permitting), with eagles, falcons, hawks, owls and vultures.

37 World of Butterflies

Jubilee Park, Symonds Yat,
West Ross-on-Wye,
Herefordshire HR9 6DA
Tel: (01600) 890471
A collection of butterflies flying freely in their natural environment inside a large tropical glass house.

FIND OUT MORE

Further information about holidays and attractions in the Heart of England is available from:

Heart of England Tourist Board,
Lark Hill Road,
Worcester WR5 2EZ.
Tel: (01905) 763436 (24 hours)

These publications are available free from the Heart of England Tourist Board:

- **Bed & Breakfast Touring Map**
- **Great Escapes - short breaks and leisure holidays for all seasons**
- **Events list**

Also available are:

Places to Visit in the Heart of England - a comprehensive guide to over 750 varied attractions and things to see, also great ideas for where to go in winter, (over £40 in discount vouchers included). *£3.99*

- **Cotswolds Map** *£2.95*
- **Cotswold/Wyndean Map** *£3.25*
- **Shropshire/Staffordshire Map** *£3.25*

Please add *60p* postage for up to 3 items, plus *25p* for each additional 3 items.

WHERE TO STAY (HEART OF ENGLAND)

Accommodation entries in this region are listed in alphabetical order by place name, and then by establishment. As West Oxfordshire and Cherwell are also promoted under Heart of England, places in the area with accommodation are listed in this section. See South of England for full West Oxfordshire and Cherwell entries.

Map references refer to the colour location maps at the back of this guide. The first number indicates the map to use; the letter and number which follow refer to the grid reference on the map.

At-a-glance symbols at the end of each accommodation entry give useful information about services and facilities. A key to symbols can be found inside the back cover flap.

ABBOTS BROMLEY

Staffordshire
Map ref 4B3

Attractive conservation village with a green, a Butter Cross and 18th C almshouses. Well-known for the ancient Horn Dance which takes place each year in September when dancers in Tudor dress bear reindeer antlers. Nearby are Shugborough Hall (National Trust) and Alton Towers.

Crown Inn

APPROVED

Market Place, Abbots Bromley, Rugeley WS15 3BS
☎ (01283) 840227
Fax (01283) 840227

Comfortable and friendly English country inn in centre of attractive village. Home-cooked food using local fresh produce, fully licensed.

Bedrooms: 1 single, 2 double, 2 twin, 1 triple
Bathrooms: 2 public

Bed & breakfast per night:	£min	£max
Single	20.00	29.00
Double	40.00	

Half board per person:	£min	£max
Daily	29.00	35.00

Lunch available
Evening meal 1800 (last orders 2100)
Parking for 30
Cards accepted: Mastercard, Visa, Switch/Delta

S 40 OAP

ALCESTER

Warwickshire
Map ref 2B1

Town has Roman origins and many old buildings around the High Street. It is close to Ragley Hall, the 18th C Palladian mansion with its magnificent baroque Great Hall.

Orchard Lawns

HIGHLY COMMENDED

Wixford, Alcester B49 6DA
☎ (01789) 772668

Charming house with character, set in delightful gardens, in small village 7 miles from Stratford-upon-Avon. Ideal touring centre.

Bedrooms: 1 single, 1 double, 1 twin
Bathrooms: 1 en-suite, 1 public

Bed & breakfast per night:	£min	£max
Single	17.00	19.00
Double	34.00	38.00

Parking for 6
Cards accepted: Mastercard, Visa

5 UL S TV

Sambourne Hall Farm

HIGHLY COMMENDED

Wike Lane, Sambourne, Redditch, Worcestershire B96 6NZ
☎ (01527) 852151

315-acre arable & livestock farm. Beautiful mid-17th C farmhouse in a peaceful village, close to local pub. Just off the A435 between Alcester and Studley and 9 miles from Stratford-upon-Avon.

Bedrooms: 1 double, 1 family room
Bathrooms: 1 en-suite, 1 private

Bed & breakfast per night:	£min	£max
Single	20.00	25.00
Double	40.00	40.00

Parking for 6

UL S TV

ALDWARK

Derbyshire
Map ref 4B2

Tithe Farm

COMMENDED

Aldwark, Grange Mill, Matlock DE4 4HX
☎ (01629) 540263

Peacefully situated, within 10 miles of Matlock, Bakewell, Ashbourne, the dales and historic houses. Extensive breakfast menu with home-made bread and preserves.

Bedrooms: 1 twin, 1 triple
Bathrooms: 1 en-suite, 1 private

Bed & breakfast per night:	£min	£max
Single	25.00	26.00
Double	40.00	42.00

Parking for 6
Open April–October

UL S TV T

Information on accommodation listed in this guide has been supplied by the proprietors. As changes may occur you are advised to check details at the time of booking.

ALTON

Staffordshire
Map ref 4B2

Alton Castle, an impressive 19th C building, dominates the village which is set in spectacular scenery. Nearby is Alton Towers, a romantic 19th C ruin with innumerable tourist attractions within one of England's largest theme parks in its 800 acres of magnificent gardens.

Bank House

APPROVED

Smithy Bank, Alton, Stoke-on-Trent ST10 4AA
☎ (01538) 702524

Central in Alton village, 1 mile from Alton Towers and close to Dovedale and Manifold Valley. 3 good inns serving meals within 200 metres. Family-run.

Bedrooms: 2 double, 1 twin, 3 family rooms
Bathrooms: 4 en-suite, 1 public

Bed & breakfast per night:	£min	£max
Single	20.00	20.00
Double	38.00	38.00

Parking for 6

Bradley Elms Farm

HIGHLY COMMENDED

Threapwood, Cheadle, Stoke-on-Trent ST10 4RA
☎ (01538) 753135

Well-appointed farm accommodation providing a comfortable and relaxing atmosphere for that well-earned break. On the edge of the Staffordshire Moorlands. 3 miles from Alton Towers, close to Potteries and Peak District National Park.

Bedrooms: 3 double, 3 twin, 2 triple, 1 family room
Bathrooms: 9 en-suite, 1 public

Bed & breakfast per night:	£min	£max
Double		45.00

Evening meal 1830 (last orders 2000)
Parking for 10

The Dale

Listed COMMENDED

Alton, Stoke-on-Trent ST10 4BG
☎ (01538) 702394

Modern detached house, set in its own grounds overlooking beautiful countryside. Five minutes' drive to Alton Towers.

Bedrooms: 2 twin
Bathrooms: 1 public

Bed & breakfast per night:	£min	£max
Single	16.00	
Double	32.00	

Parking for 6

Fields Farm

HIGHLY COMMENDED

Chapel Lane, Threapwood, Alton, Stoke-on-Trent ST10 4QZ
☎ (01538) 752721 & 0850 310381
Fax (01538) 752721

Traditional farmhouse hospitality and comfort in picturesque Churnet Valley, 10 minutes from Alton Towers. Near Peak Park and within easy reach of Potteries and many stately homes. Stabling available. Ideal for walking, cycling, riding and fishing. Dogs by arrangement. Proprietor Pat Massey.

Bedrooms: 2 double, 1 twin
Bathrooms: 2 en-suite, 1 private

Bed & breakfast per night:	£min	£max
Single	22.00	
Double	32.00	37.00

Half board per person:	£min	£max
Daily	27.00	34.00

Evening meal 1900 (last orders 2200)
Parking for 6

Hillside Farm

Listed APPROVED

Alton Road, Denstone, Uttoxeter ST14 5HG
☎ (01889) 590760

Victorian farmhouse with extensive views to the Weaver Hills and Churnet Valley. Situated 2 miles south of Alton Towers on B5032.

Bedrooms: 1 double, 2 triple, 1 family room
Bathrooms: 1 private, 1 public

Bed & breakfast per night:	£min	£max
Single	15.00	18.00
Double	28.00	32.00

Parking for 7
Open March–November

ARLINGHAM

Gloucestershire
Map ref 2B1

Small, quiet village in a horseshoe bend of the River Severn. The parish church contains medieval glass and interesting sculptures. Berkeley Castle and the Wildfowl Trust at Slimbridge are nearby and there is easy access from the M5 and A38.

Horseshoe View

Listed COMMENDED

Overton Lane, Arlingham, Gloucester GL2 7JJ
☎ (01452) 740293

Ideally situated for touring. Close to the Forest of Dean, Wildfowl Trust and the M5, with many other places of interest nearby.

Bedrooms: 1 single, 2 double
Bathrooms: 1 en-suite, 1 public

Bed & breakfast per night:	£min	£max
Single	13.50	13.50
Double	32.00	32.00

Parking for 5

ARMSCOTE

Warwickshire
Map ref 2B1

Willow Corner

COMMENDED

Armscote, Stratford-upon-Avon CV37 8DE
☎ (01608) 682391 & 0836 556639
Fax (01608) 682391

Spacious, 300-year-old, Cotswold-stone thatched cottage, nestled in a peaceful hamlet with a pub. Open fireplaces, beams throughout, all en-suite. Cottage garden.

Bedrooms: 2 double, 1 twin
Bathrooms: 3 en-suite

Bed & breakfast per night:	£min	£max
Single	30.00	40.00
Double	50.00	80.00

Parking for 3

ASCOTT-UNDER-WYCHWOOD

Oxfordshire
Map ref 2C1

The Mill

See South of England region for full entry details

ASHBOURNE

Derbyshire
Map ref 4B2

Market town on the edge of the Peak District National Park and an excellent centre for walking. Its impressive church with 212-ft spire stands in an unspoilt old street. Ashbourne is well-known for gingerbread and its Shrovetide football match.
Tourist Information Centre ☎ (01335) 343666

Bentley Brook Inn

APPROVED

Fenny Bentley, Ashbourne DE6 1LF
☎ (01335) 350278
Fax (01335) 350422

Traditional country inn with on-site brewery, in large gardens in Peak District National Park. Close to Dovedale, Alton Towers and Chatsworth.
Bedrooms: 1 single, 5 double, 3 twin
Suites available
Bathrooms: 6 en-suite, 1 private, 2 public

Bed & breakfast per night:	£min	£max
Single	31.50	37.50
Double	47.50	57.50

Half board per person:	£min	£max
Daily	38.75	43.75
Weekly	190.00	210.00

Lunch available
Evening meal 1900 (last orders 2130)
Parking for 60
Cards accepted: Amex, Diners, Mastercard, Visa, Switch/Delta

Collycroft Farm

Listed COMMENDED

Clifton, Ashbourne DE6 2GN
☎ (01335) 342187
260-acre mixed farm. A warm welcome is assured in this pleasant farmhouse. Lovely garden and excellent views across the surrounding countryside. South of Ashbourne on the A515 Lichfield road.
Bedrooms: 1 double, 1 twin, 1 triple
Bathrooms: 1 en-suite, 1 public

Bed & breakfast per night:	£min	£max
Single	18.00	20.00
Double	36.00	40.00

Parking for 8

Jinglers Inn

Listed APPROVED

Fox and Hounds, Belper Road, Bradley, Ashbourne DE6 3EN
☎ (01335) 370855
Fax (01335) 370855

Country coaching inn with 2 names, set in 18 acres. 6 letting rooms and caravan site. Clay pigeon shooting. Just outside Ashbourne on A517.
Bedrooms: 1 single, 1 double, 3 twin, 1 family room
Bathrooms: 4 en-suite, 2 private

Bed & breakfast per night:	£min	£max
Single	15.00	17.50
Double	30.00	40.00

Lunch available
Evening meal 1800 (last orders 2200)
Parking for 100

Meadow Bank

Listed HIGHLY COMMENDED

Belle Vue Road, Ashbourne DE6 1AT
☎ (01335) 346034
Private bungalow, 5 minutes' walk from the town centre with views over the open countryside. Spacious bedrooms, TV lounge, separate dining room.
Bedrooms: 1 double, 1 triple
Bathrooms: 1 public

Bed & breakfast per night:	£min	£max
Single	18.00	18.00
Double	36.00	36.00

Parking for 6
Open February–November

Mercaston Hall

COMMENDED

Mercaston, Brailsford, Ashbourne DE6 3BL
☎ (01335) 360263 & 0836 648102
55-acre mixed farm. Listed buildings in attractive, quiet countryside. Hard tennis court. Kedleston Hall (National Trust) 1 mile, Carsington Reservoir 5 minutes away.
Bedrooms: 2 double, 1 twin
Bathrooms: 2 en-suite, 1 private

Bed & breakfast per night:	£min	£max
Single	23.00	26.00
Double	36.00	40.00

Parking for 16

White Cottage

Listed COMMENDED

Wyaston, Ashbourne DE6 2DR
☎ (01335) 345503

Character cottage with country views in quiet rural village, 2 miles from Ashbourne. Ground-floor room overlooking large secluded garden. Every effort made to ensure a comfortable, peaceful and relaxed stay. TV and tea/coffee facilities. Leaflet available.
Bedrooms: 1 double
Bathrooms: 1 en-suite

Bed & breakfast per night:	£min	£max
Single	16.50	16.50
Double	33.00	33.00

Parking for 5

Please mention this guide when making your booking.

A key to symbols can be found inside the back cover flap.

ASHFORD IN THE WATER

Derbyshire
Map ref 4B2

Limestone village in attractive surroundings of the Peak District approached by 3 bridges over the River Wye. There is an annual well-dressing ceremony and the village was well-known in the 18th C for its black marble quarries.

Gritstone House

HIGHLY COMMENDED

Greaves Lane, Ashford in the Water, Bakewell DE45 1QH
☎ (01629) 813563
Fax (01629) 813563

Charming 18th C Georgian house offering friendly service and accommodation designed with comfort and style in mind. Ideal centre for exploring the Peak District's scenery and country houses, and close to an extensive range of dining-out facilities.

Bedrooms: 2 double, 1 twin
Bathrooms: 1 en-suite, 1 public

Bed & breakfast per night:	£min	£max
Double	38.00	45.00

Warlands

Listed COMMENDED

Hill Cross, Ashford in the Water, Bakewell DE45 1QL
☎ (01629) 813736

Attractive country cottage with panoramic views over the village. Lovely walks and very good eating houses. Close to the market town of Bakewell and stately homes.

Bedrooms: 1 single, 1 double
Bathrooms: 1 public

Bed & breakfast per night:	£min	£max
Single	20.00	22.00
Double	32.00	34.00

You are advised to confirm your booking in writing.

For further information on accommodation establishments use the coupons at the back of this guide.

ASHLEWORTH

Gloucestershire
Map ref 2B1

Ashleworth Court

Listed COMMENDED

Ashleworth, Gloucester GL19 4JA
☎ (01452) 700241
Fax (01452) 700411

180-acre mixed farm. 15th C manor house near River Severn. Jacobean four-poster and 2 well-appointed bathrooms. Large garden. Church and tithe barn next door, 2 pubs within walking distance.

Bedrooms: 2 double, 1 twin
Bathrooms: 2 public

Bed & breakfast per night:	£min	£max
Single	16.00	20.00
Double	32.00	40.00

Parking for 10

ASHOVER

Derbyshire
Map ref 4B2

Unspoilt village with a 13th C church.

Old School Farm

COMMENDED

Uppertown, Ashover, Chesterfield S45 0JF
☎ (01246) 590813

25-acre mixed farm. A working farm welcoming children but not pets, suitable for visitors with their own transport. In a small hamlet bordering the Peak District, ideal for Chatsworth House, Chesterfield and Matlock Bath.

Bedrooms: 1 single, 1 double, 2 family rooms
Bathrooms: 2 en-suite, 1 public

Bed & breakfast per night:	£min	£max
Single	20.00	
Double	40.00	

Half board per person:	£min	£max
Daily	28.00	
Weekly	196.00	

Evening meal 1900 (last orders 0930)
Parking for 10
Open March–November

AVON DASSETT

Warwickshire
Map ref 2C1

Village on the slopes of the Dasset Hills, with good views. The church, with its impressive tower and spire, dates from 1868 but incorporates a 14th C window with 15th C glass.

Crandon House

HIGHLY COMMENDED

Avon Dassett, Leamington Spa CV33 0AA
☎ (01295) 770652
Fax (01295) 770652

20-acre mixed farm. Farmhouse offering a high standard of accommodation with superb views over unspoilt countryside. Quiet and peaceful. Easy access to Warwick, Stratford and Cotswolds. 4 miles from junctions 11 and 12 of M40.

Bedrooms: 2 double, 3 twin
Bathrooms: 4 en-suite, 1 private

Bed & breakfast per night:	£min	£max
Single	25.00	30.00
Double	38.00	46.00

Parking for 22
Cards accepted: Mastercard, Visa
12 SP

For ideas on places to visit refer to the introduction at the beginning of this section.

The symbols in each entry give information about services and facilities. A key to these symbols appears at the back of this guide.

BAKEWELL

Derbyshire
Map ref 4B2

Pleasant market town, famous for its pudding. It is set in beautiful countryside on the River Wye and is an excellent centre for exploring the Derbyshire Dales, the Peak District National Park, Chatsworth and Haddon Hall.
Tourist Information Centre ☎ (01629) 813227

Castle Cliffe Private Hotel

COMMENDED

Monsal Head, Bakewell DE45 1NL
☎ (01629) 640258
Fax (01629) 640258
Victorian stone house overlooking beautiful Monsal Dale. Noted for its friendly atmosphere, good food and exceptional views.
Bedrooms: 1 single, 2 double, 4 twin, 2 family rooms
Bathrooms: 6 en-suite, 2 public, 3 private showers

Bed & breakfast per night:	£min	£max
Single	30.00	37.50
Double	48.00	55.00

Half board per person:	£min	£max
Daily	37.50	50.00
Weekly	235.00	270.00

Evening meal 1900 (last orders 1700)
Parking for 15
Cards accepted: Mastercard, Visa
15

Castle Inn

Listed COMMENDED

Castle Street, Bakewell DE4 1DU
☎ (01629) 812103
Delightful wayside inn, built in 16th C. Famous for its open fires and Bakewell pudding. Excellent range of traditional beers and taking pride in its home cooking.
Bedrooms: 1 double, 2 twin, 1 triple
Bathrooms: 4 en-suite

Bed & breakfast per night:	£min	£max
Double	44.00	48.00

Lunch available
Evening meal 1800 (last orders 2100)
Parking for 14
Cards accepted: Mastercard, Visa

Tannery House

HIGHLY COMMENDED

Matlock Street, Bakewell DE45 1EE
☎ (01629) 815011
Fax (01629) 815327
Central Bakewell: all bedrooms are en-suite with French windows opening on to the secluded gardens. The private dining room overlooks the swimming pool.
Wheelchair access category 3
Bedrooms: 2 double, 1 twin
Bathrooms: 3 en-suite

Bed & breakfast per night:	£min	£max
Single	27.50	27.50
Double	40.00	50.00

Evening meal 1900 (last orders 1930)
Parking for 8
Open January–November
10

BALSALL COMMON

West Midlands
Map ref 4B3

Close to Kenilworth and within easy reach of Coventry.

Blythe Paddocks

COMMENDED

Barston Lane, Balsall Common, Coventry CV7 7BT
☎ (01676) 533050
Family home standing in 5 acres. Ten minutes from Birmingham Airport and National Exhibition Centre. NAC Stoneleigh 8 miles. Countryside location.
Bedrooms: 2 single, 1 double, 1 twin
Bathrooms: 1 public

Bed & breakfast per night:	£min	£max
Single	16.00	20.00
Double	32.00	40.00

Parking for 10

Please check prices and other details at the time of booking.

All accommodation in this guide has been graded, or is awaiting a grading, by a trained Tourist Board inspector.

Camp Farm

Listed COMMENDED

Hob Lane, Balsall Common, Coventry CV7 7GX
☎ (01676) 533804
200-year-old farmhouse used as a campsite by Cromwell for the siege of Kenilworth.
Bedrooms: 1 double, 2 twin
Bathrooms: 1 public

Bed & breakfast per night:	£min	£max
Single	20.00	25.00
Double	33.00	38.00

Parking for 6

BAMFORD

Derbyshire
Map ref 4B2

Village in the Peak District near the Upper Derwent Reservoirs of Ladybower, Derwent and Howden. An excellent centre for walking.

Pioneer House

COMMENDED

Station Road, Bamford S30 2BN
☎ (01433) 650638
Comfortable, spacious rooms, all with private facilities, in Edwardian family home. Friendly atmosphere, hearty breakfasts. Central location in Peak District.
Bedrooms: 2 double, 1 twin
Bathrooms: 2 en-suite, 1 private

Bed & breakfast per night:	£min	£max
Double	30.00	40.00

Parking for 8

BAMPTON

Oxfordshire
Map ref 2C1

Cedars
See South of England region for full entry details

BANBURY

Oxfordshire
Map ref 2C1

The Lodge
Roxtones
See South of England region for full entry details

Please mention this guide when making your booking.

BARLASTON

Staffordshire
Map ref 4B2

Wedgwood Memorial College

APPROVED

Station Road, Barlaston, Stoke-on-Trent ST12 9DG
☎ (01782) 372105 & 373427
Fax (01782) 372393

Pleasant, well-appointed adult residential college with relaxed, homely ambience. In quiet village, yet close to National Trust downs and Potteries. Convenient for Peak District, Alton Towers. Good quality, home-cooked food with an imaginative repertoire of vegetarian dishes. Limited facilities for disabled.

Bedrooms: 9 single, 7 twin, 3 triple, 2 family rooms
Bathrooms: 6 en-suite, 7 public

Bed & breakfast per night:	£min	£max
Single	13.50	
Double	27.00	

Half board per person:	£min	£max
Daily	19.00	
Weekly	133.00	

Lunch available
Evening meal 1830 (last orders 1830)
Parking for 40
Cards accepted: Mastercard, Visa

BARNBY MOOR

Nottinghamshire
Map ref 4C2

Village on the former Great North Road, within easy reach of Clumber Park, Sherwood Forest and Pilgrim Father country.

White Horse Inn and Restaurant

COMMENDED

Great North Road, Barnby Moor, Retford DN22 8QS
☎ (01777) 707721

Beautifully decorated bedrooms separate from public house. Close to Robin Hood land and market town of Retford. A1 1.5 miles away. Please ask for details of reduced rates.

Bedrooms: 1 double, 2 twin
Bathrooms: 2 en-suite, 1 private

Bed & breakfast per night:	£min	£max
Single	20.00	23.00
Double	32.00	38.00

Half board per person:	£min	£max
Daily	19.95	29.00

Lunch available
Evening meal 1900 (last orders 2200)
Parking for 30
Cards accepted: Amex, Mastercard, Visa

BELPER

Derbyshire
Map ref 4B2

Pleasant old market town in the valley of the River Derwent. Attractive scenery and a wealth of industrial history.

Chevin Green Farm

COMMENDED

Chevin Road, Belper, Derby DE56 2UN
☎ (01773) 822328

38-acre mixed farm. Extended and improved 300-year-old beamed farmhouse accommodation with all bedrooms en-suite, an ideal base for exploring Derbyshire.

Bedrooms: 3 double, 2 twin, 1 family room
Bathrooms: 6 en-suite

Bed & breakfast per night:	£min	£max
Single	17.00	27.00
Double	32.00	38.00

Parking for 6

West Lodge

HIGHLY COMMENDED

Bridge Hill, Belper DE56 2BY
☎ (01773) 823596
Fax (01773) 880810

Detached, modern, stone house on the edge of the countryside with outstanding views, half a mile from the town centre and well situated for tourist attractions. Garaging available.

Bedrooms: 1 double, 1 triple
Bathrooms: 1 public

Bed & breakfast per night:	£min	£max
Single	18.00	
Double	33.00	

Parking for 5

> Establishments should be open throughout the year, unless otherwise stated.

BERKSWELL

West Midlands
Map ref 4B3

Pretty village with an unusual set of 5-holed stocks on the green. It has some fine houses, cottages, a 16th C inn and a windmill open to the public Sunday afternoons, May to end September. The Norman church is one of the finest in the area, with many interesting features.

Elmcroft Country Guesthouse

Listed HIGHLY COMMENDED

Elmcroft, Hodgetts Lane, Berkswell, Coventry CV7 7HO
☎ (01676) 535204
Fax (01676) 535204

Country guesthouse in close proximity to the National Exhibition Centre and an ideal base for all of Warwickshire's tourist attractions.

Bedrooms: 1 single, 2 double, 2 twin
Bathrooms: 5 en-suite

Bed & breakfast per night:	£min	£max
Single	25.00	
Double	45.00	

Parking for 8

BIBURY

Gloucestershire
Map ref 2B1

Village on the River Coln with stone houses and the famous 17th C Arlington Row, former weavers' cottages. Arlington Mill is now a folk museum. Trout farm and Bansley House Gardens nearby are open to the public.

Cotteswold House

HIGHLY COMMENDED

Arlington, Bibury, Cirencester GL7 5ND
☎ (01285) 740609
Fax (01285) 740609

Enjoy the relaxed friendly atmosphere of this family home. Ideally situated for touring the Cotswolds. All bedrooms en-suite with TV and tea/coffee making facilities. Guest lounge/dining room. No smoking, please. Parking.

Bedrooms: 2 double, 1 twin
Bathrooms: 3 en-suite

Bed & breakfast per night:	£min	£max
Single		25.00
Double		40.00

Parking for 4

BICESTER

Oxfordshire
Map ref 2C1

Manor Farm
See South of England region for full entry details

BIDFORD-ON-AVON

Warwickshire
Map ref 2B1

Attractive village with an ancient 8-arched bridge, riverside picnic area and a main street with some interesting 15th C houses.

Broom Hall Inn

APPROVED

Bidford Road, Broom, Alcester B50 4HE
☎ (01789) 773757

Family-owned country inn with carvery restaurant and extensive range of bar meals. Close to Stratford-upon-Avon and Cotswolds.
Bedrooms: 4 single, 4 double, 4 twin
Bathrooms: 9 en-suite, 3 private

Bed & breakfast per night:	£min	£max
Single	20.00	37.50
Double	40.00	60.00

Half board per person:	£min	£max
Daily	34.50	35.50

Lunch available
Evening meal 1900 (last orders 2200)
Parking for 80
Cards accepted: Amex, Diners, Mastercard, Visa

Half board prices are given per person, but in some cases these may be based on double/twin occupancy.

BIRDLIP

Gloucestershire
Map ref 2B1

Hamlet at the top of a very steep descent down to the Gloucester Vale with excellent viewpoint over Crickley Hill Country Park.

Beechmount

COMMENDED

Birdlip, Cirencester GL4 8JH
☎ (01452) 862262
Fax (01452) 862262
Family-run guesthouse with personal attention. Ideal centre for the Cotswolds. Choice of menu for breakfast, unrestricted access.
Bedrooms: 1 single, 2 double, 1 twin, 2 triple, 1 family room
Bathrooms: 2 en-suite, 1 public

Bed & breakfast per night:	£min	£max
Single	16.00	30.00
Double	28.00	44.00

Evening meal 1900 (last orders 1000)
Parking for 7
Cards accepted: Mastercard, Visa, Switch/Delta

BIRMINGHAM

West Midlands
Map ref 4B3

Britain's second city, whose attractions include Centenary Square and the ICC with Symphony Hall, the NEC, the City Art Gallery, Barber Institute of Fine Arts, 17th C Aston Hall, science and railway museums, Jewellery Quarter, Cadbury World, 2 cathedrals and Botanical Gardens.
Tourist Information Centre ☎ (0121) 643 2514 or 780 4321 or 693 6300

Heath Lodge Hotel

APPROVED

Coleshill Road, Marston Green, Birmingham B37 7HT
☎ (0121) 779 2218
Fax (0121) 779 2218

Licensed family-run hotel, quietly situated and less than 2 miles from the National Exhibition Centre and Birmingham Airport. Most rooms en-suite.
Bedrooms: 9 single, 3 double, 6 twin
Bathrooms: 13 en-suite, 1 public, 1 private shower

Bed & breakfast per night:	£min	£max
Single	30.00	42.00
Double	42.00	48.00

Evening meal 1830 (last orders 2030)
Parking for 24
Cards accepted: Amex, Diners, Mastercard, Visa

Lyndhurst Hotel

APPROVED

135 Kingsbury Road, Erdington, Birmingham B24 8QT
☎ (0121) 373 5695
Fax (0121) 373 5695
Within half a mile of M6 (junction 6) and within easy reach of the city and National Exhibition Centre. Comfortable bedrooms, spacious restaurant. Personal service in a quiet friendly atmosphere.
Bedrooms: 10 single, 2 double, 2 twin
Bathrooms: 13 en-suite, 1 private

Bed & breakfast per night:	£min	£max
Single	25.00	39.50
Double	39.50	52.50

Half board per person:	£min	£max
Daily	35.00	51.50

Evening meal 1800 (last orders 2000)
Parking for 12
Cards accepted: Amex, Diners, Mastercard, Visa

BIRMINGHAM AIRPORT

West Midlands

See under Balsall Common, Berkswell, Birmingham, Coventry, Hampton in Arden, Meriden, Solihull

You are advised to confirm your booking in writing.

The National Grading and Classification Scheme is explained at the back of this guide.

BISHOP'S CASTLE

Shropshire
Map ref 4A3

A 12th C Planned Town with a castle site at the top of the hill and a church at the bottom of the main street. Many interesting buildings with original timber frames hidden behind present day houses. On the Welsh border close to the Clun Forest in quiet, unspoilt countryside.

The Boars Head Hotel

COMMENDED

Church Street, Bishop's Castle
SY9 5AE
☎ (01588) 638521 & (0468) 882248
Fax (01588) 630126
Email: 101327.1457
@compuserve.com

Old world inn, with en-suite accommodation in original stables. Comfortable dining area serves wide choice of bar meals. A la carte restaurant also available.

Bedrooms: 1 double, 2 twin, 1 family room
Bathrooms: 4 en-suite

Bed & breakfast per night:	£min	£max
Single	33.00	38.00
Double	50.00	60.00

Half board per person:	£min	£max
Daily	60.00	70.00
Weekly	360.00	420.00

Lunch available
Evening meal 1830 (last orders 2130)
Parking for 20
Cards accepted: Amex, Diners, Mastercard, Visa, Switch/Delta

Old Time

APPROVED

29 High Street, Bishop's Castle
SY9 5BE
☎ (01588) 638467

Grade II listed 15th C house in town centre with shop, courtyard, garden and craft workshop. Originally a "cruck cottage".

Bedrooms: 2 double
Bathrooms: 2 en-suite

Bed & breakfast per night:	£min	£max
Single	20.00	24.00
Double	30.00	38.00

BLEDINGTON

Gloucestershire
Map ref 2B1

Village close to the Oxfordshire border, with a pleasant green and a beautiful church.

Kings Head Inn & Restaurant

COMMENDED

The Green, Bledington, Oxford
OX7 6XQ
☎ (01608) 658365
Fax (01608) 658902

15th C inn located in the heart of the Cotswolds, facing the village green. Authentic lounge bars, notable restaurant. Delightful en-suite rooms.

Bedrooms: 10 double, 2 twin
Bathrooms: 12 en-suite

Bed & breakfast per night:	£min	£max
Single	40.00	45.00
Double	60.00	75.00

Lunch available
Evening meal 1900 (last orders 2200)
Parking for 60
Cards accepted: Mastercard, Visa, Switch/Delta

BLOCKLEY

Gloucestershire
Map ref 2B1

This village's prosperity was founded in silk mills and other factories but now it is a quiet, unspoilt place. An excellent centre for exploring pretty Cotswold villages, especially Chipping Campden and Broadway.

21 Station Road

COMMENDED

Blockley, Moreton-in-Marsh
GL56 9ED
☎ (01386) 700402

Beautifully presented Cotswold-stone house on edge of delightful village. Ideal base for touring Cotswolds and Shakespeare country. Tastefully decorated, comfortable, non-smoking accommodation with full en-suite facilities. A warm welcome awaits you.

Bedrooms: 1 double, 2 twin
Bathrooms: 3 en-suite

Bed & breakfast per night:	£min	£max
Single	25.00	
Double	35.00	

Parking for 9

BLYTH

Nottinghamshire
Map ref 4C2

Village on the old Great North Road. A busy staging post in Georgian times with many examples of Georgian Gothic architecture. The remains of a Norman Benedictine priory survive as the parish church.

Priory Farm Guesthouse

APPROVED

Hodsock Priory Estate, Blyth,
Worksop S81 OTY
☎ (01909) 591515
Fax (01427) 890611
Email: gaggfarms@farmline.com

18th C farmhouse in peaceful surroundings on a private country estate. Easy access from the A1 and M1.

Bedrooms: 2 single, 1 double, 1 twin
Bathrooms: 2 en-suite, 1 public

Bed & breakfast per night:	£min	£max
Single	17.50	20.00
Double	35.00	40.00

Half board per person:	£min	£max
Daily	24.00	26.50

Evening meal 1800 (last orders 1900)
Parking for 6

BOURTON-ON-THE-HILL

Gloucestershire
Map ref 2B1

Attractive village with 18th C Bourton House and impressive 16th C tithe barn. Sezincote House is nearby, built at the beginning of the 19th C in Indian style with Repton landscaped gardens which are open to the public, as is Batsford Arboretum.

Bourton Heights

COMMENDED

Blockley Road, Bourton-on-the-Hill,
Moreton-in-Marsh GL56 9AJ
☎ (01386) 700544

Country house with a beautiful view of

surrounding fields and garden. Rooms separate from owners' accommodation.
Bedrooms: 3 double
Bathrooms: 3 en-suite

Bed & breakfast per night:	£min	£max
Double	30.00	45.00

Parking for 3

BOURTON-ON-THE-WATER

Gloucestershire
Map ref 2B1

The River Windrush flows through this famous Cotswold village which has a green, and cottages and houses of Cotswold stone. Its many attractions include a model village, Birdland, a Motor Museum and the Cotswold Perfumery.

Berkeley Guesthouse

COMMENDED
Moore Road,
Bourton-on-the-Water, Cheltenham
GL54 2AZ
☎ (01451) 810388
Fax (01451) 810388
Detached house with a homely, relaxed atmosphere, furnished to a high standard. Personal attention. Attractive gardens, sun lounge, car park. No smoking.
Bedrooms: 2 double, 1 twin
Bathrooms: 3 en-suite

Bed & breakfast per night:	£min	£max
Single	18.50	21.00
Double	35.00	39.00

Parking for 4

Farncombe

HIGHLY COMMENDED
Clapton, Bourton-on-the-Water,
Cheltenham GL54 2LG
☎ (01451) 820120 & 0378 843123
Fax (01451) 820120
Quiet comfortable accommodation with superb views of the Windrush Valley. In the hamlet of Clapton, 2.5 miles from Bourton-on-the-Water. No-smoking house.
Bedrooms: 2 double, 1 twin
Bathrooms: 1 en-suite, 2 private showers

Bed & breakfast per night:	£min	£max
Single	18.00	28.00
Double	37.00	42.00

Parking for 3

Holly House

COMMENDED
Station Road,
Bourton-on-the-Water, Cheltenham
GL54 2ER
☎ (01451) 821302

Detached Cotswold-style house only 5 minutes' walk from village centre. All rooms en-suite, guests' TV lounge and spacious conservatory for breakfasts. Ample off-road parking.
Bedrooms: 2 double, 1 twin
Bathrooms: 3 en-suite

Bed & breakfast per night:	£min	£max
Single	15.00	25.00
Double	30.00	45.00

Parking for 5

Lamb Inn

COMMENDED
Great Rissington,
Bourton-on-the-Water, Cheltenham
GL54 2LP
☎ (01451) 820388
Fax (01451) 820724
Country inn in rural setting, with home-cooked food, including steaks and local trout, served in attractive restaurant. Beer garden and real ale. Honeymoon suite also available.
Bedrooms: 13 double, 1 twin
Suite available
Bathrooms: 14 en-suite

Bed & breakfast per night:	£min	£max
Single	35.00	65.00
Double	50.00	85.00

Lunch available
Evening meal 1900 (last orders 2130)
Parking for 10
Cards accepted: Amex, Mastercard, Visa

National gradings and classifications were correct at the time of going to press but are subject to change. Please check at the time of booking.

Lansdowne House

COMMENDED
Lansdowne, Bourton-on-the-Water,
Cheltenham GL54 2AT
☎ (01451) 820812

Large period stone family house. Tastefully furnished en-suite accommodation with a combination of old and antique furniture. Tea/coffee trays, colour TVs, parking, garden.
Bedrooms: 2 double, 1 triple
Bathrooms: 3 en-suite

Bed & breakfast per night:	£min	£max
Single	28.00	32.00
Double	32.00	37.00

Parking for 4

Polly Perkins

COMMENDED
1 The Chestnuts,
Bourton-on-the-Water, Cheltenham
GL54 2AN
☎ (01451) 820244
Fax (01451) 820A558
Situated above Polly Perkins restaurant in the centre of village. The building is 300 years old and the establishment retains old world charm. 15 miles from Cheltenham off A40. Discount for guests in restaurant.
Bedrooms: 6 double, 1 twin, 1 triple
Bathrooms: 8 en-suite

Bed & breakfast per night:	£min	£max
Single	30.00	40.00
Double	37.00	47.00

Lunch available
Evening meal 1830 (last orders 2130)
Parking for 15
Cards accepted: Amex, Mastercard, Visa, Switch/Delta

For farm holidays and accommodation suitable for young people and organised groups, please refer to the special sections at the back of this guide.

BOURTON-ON-THE-WATER

Continued

The Ridge

HIGHLY COMMENDED

Whiteshoots Hill,
Bourton-on-the-Water, Cheltenham
GL54 2LE
☎ (01451) 820660

Large country house surrounded by beautiful grounds. Central for visiting many places of interest and close to all amenities. Ground floor en-suite bedrooms available.

Bedrooms: 2 double, 2 twin, 1 triple
Bathrooms: 4 en-suite, 1 private, 1 public

Bed & breakfast per night:	£min	£max
Single	25.00	30.00
Double	35.00	40.00

Parking for 12

Rooftrees Guesthouse

COMMENDED

Rissington Road,
Bourton-on-the-Water, Cheltenham
GL54 2DX
☎ (01451) 821943

Detached Cotswold-stone family house, all rooms individually decorated, 8 minutes' level walk from village centre. Home cooking with fresh local produce. 3 en-suite bedrooms: 2 rooms are on ground floor, 2 rooms have four-posters. No smoking.

Bedrooms: 3 double
Bathrooms: 3 en-suite

Bed & breakfast per night:	£min	£max
Double	38.00	42.00

Half board per person:	£min	£max
Daily	31.00	33.00
Weekly	200.00	210.00

Evening meal 1830 (last orders 1200)
Parking for 8
Cards accepted: Mastercard, Visa, Switch/Delta

ACCESSIBILITY

Look for the symbols which indicate accessibility for wheelchair users. These are described in detail at the front of this guide.

BRACKLEY

Northamptonshire
Map ref 2C1

Historic market town of mellow stone, with many fine buildings lining the wide High Street and Market Place. Sulgrave Manor (George Washington's ancestral home) and Silverstone Circuit are nearby.
Tourist Information Centre ☎ (01280) 700111

The Red Lion

Listed COMMENDED

39 The Green, Evenley, Brackley
NN13 5SH
☎ (01280) 703469

Grade II listed cricketing inn on the green, dating back to the early 1800s. Log fires and home-cooked food.

Bedrooms: 1 twin
Suite available
Bathrooms: 1 en-suite

Bed & breakfast per night:	£min	£max
Single	35.00	35.00
Double	55.00	55.00

Lunch available
Evening meal 1900 (last orders 2200)
Parking for 20
Cards accepted: Mastercard, Visa, Switch/Delta

Walltree House Farm

COMMENDED

Steane, Brackley NN13 5NS
☎ (01295) 811235 & 0860 913399
Fax (01295) 811147

200-acre arable farm. En-suite individual ground floor rooms in courtyard adjacent to Victorian farmhouse. Gardens and woods to relax in. Near major historic sites, shopping and sporting attractions, including Silverstone. M40 junctions 10/11. Perfect base for touring 4 counties.

Bedrooms: 2 double, 3 twin, 1 triple, 2 family rooms
Bathrooms: 6 en-suite, 2 private

Bed & breakfast per night:	£min	£max
Single	30.00	40.00
Double	40.00	50.00

Half board per person:	£min	£max
Daily	35.00	45.00

Evening meal 1900 (last orders 1900)
Parking for 10
Cards accepted: Mastercard, Visa

BRAILES

Warwickshire
Map ref 2C1

Agdon Farm

Listed APPROVED

Brailes, Banbury, Oxfordshire
OX15 5JJ
☎ (01608) 685226 & 0850 847786

520-acre mixed farm. Old Cotswold-stone farmhouse in a "Designated Area of Outstanding Natural Beauty". We keep sheep, horses, cats and dogs. Well situated for touring the Cotswolds, Oxford, Warwick and Stratford-upon-Avon.

Bedrooms: 2 double, 1 twin
Bathrooms: 1 public

Bed & breakfast per night:	£min	£max
Single	20.00	
Double	35.00	

Half board per person:	£min	£max
Daily	26.50	
Weekly	160.00	

Evening meal 1800 (last orders 2100)
Parking for 8

BREDENBURY

Hereford and Worcester
Map ref 2A1

Redhill Farm

Listed APPROVED

Bredenbury, Bromyard,
Herefordshire HR7 4SY
☎ (01885) 483255 & 483535
Fax (01885) 483535

86-acre mixed & livestock farm. 17th C farmhouse in peaceful, unspoilt countryside with panoramic views. Central for Malvern, Hereford, Worcester, Ledbury and Ludlow. Children and pets welcome. A home-from-home on the A44 road. Horses and gallop on farm.

Bedrooms: 1 double, 1 twin, 1 triple
Bathrooms: 1 public

Bed & breakfast per night:	£min	£max
Single	18.00	20.00
Double	30.00	32.00

Evening meal 1900 (last orders 2100)
Parking for 11

BRIDGNORTH

Shropshire
Map ref 4A3

Red sandstone riverside town in 2 parts - High and Low - linked by a cliff railway. Much of interest including a ruined Norman keep, half-timbered 16th C houses, Midland Motor Museum and Severn Valley Railway.
Tourist Information Centre ☎ (01746) 763358

The Albynes

HIGHLY COMMENDED

Nordley, Bridgnorth WV16 4SX
☎ (01746) 762261

263-acre arable and mixed farm. Large country house, peacefully set in parkland with spectacular views of Shropshire countryside. On B4373 - Bridgnorth 3 miles, Ironbridge 4 miles.
Bedrooms: 1 double, 2 twin
Bathrooms: 2 en-suite, 1 private

Bed & breakfast per night:	£min	£max
Single	20.00	24.00
Double	40.00	42.00

Parking for 8

Aldenham Weir

COMMENDED

Muckley Cross, Bridgnorth WV16 4RR
☎ (01746) 714352
Superb country house, set in 11.5 acres, with working mill race, weir and trout stream for fishing. All rooms en-suite. Close to Ironbridge Gorge Museum. Quietly located off the A458, central between Much Wenlock and Bridgnorth.
Bedrooms: 3 double, 2 twin, 1 triple
Bathrooms: 6 en-suite

Bed & breakfast per night:	£min	£max
Single	28.00	28.00
Double	40.00	40.00

Parking for 7

Church House

Aston Eyre, Bridgnorth WV16 6XD
☎ (01746) 714248
Fax (01746) 714248
You are invited to a peaceful holiday in this oak-beamed cottage on a 6-acre smallholding. Overlooking Shropshire's rolling hills, it nestles behind a Norman church. Evening meals by arrangement.
Bedrooms: 1 double, 1 twin
Bathrooms: 1 en-suite, 1 private

Bed & breakfast per night:	£min	£max
Double		37.00

Evening meal 1800 (last orders 2000)
Parking for 4
Open April–October

Middleton Lodge

HIGHLY COMMENDED

Middleton Priors, Bridgnorth WV16 6UR
☎ (01746) 712228
Fax (01746) 712675
Imposing stone building in its own grounds, in a quiet hamlet in the Shropshire hills, 6 miles from Bridgnorth. Non-smokers only, please.
Bedrooms: 2 double, 1 twin
Bathrooms: 2 en-suite, 1 private

Bed & breakfast per night:	£min	£max
Single	30.00	35.00
Double	45.00	55.00

Parking for 4
12

Oldfield Cottage

COMMENDED

Oldfield, Bridgnorth WV16 6AQ
☎ (01746) 789257
Peaceful 17th C cottage in idyllic surroundings. En-suite rooms in converted stable give freedom and privacy. Ideal for exploring Shropshire.
Bedrooms: 2 twin
Bathrooms: 2 en-suite

Bed & breakfast per night:	£min	£max
Double	38.00	40.00

Evening meal (last orders 1500)
Parking for 2

The symbol after an establishment name indicates that it is a Regional Tourist Board member.

BROADWAY

Hereford and Worcester
Map ref 2B1

Beautiful Cotswold village called the "Show village of England", with 16th C stone houses and cottages. Near the village is Broadway Tower with magnificent views over 12 counties and a country park with nature trails and adventure playground.

Broadway Court

Listed HIGHLY COMMENDED

89-93 High Street, Broadway, Worcestershire WR12 7AL
☎ (01386) 852237
Fax (01386) 852237
Grade II listed barn conversion overlooking secluded, walled cottage garden with country views. Delightful and spacious en-suite bedrooms, beautiful panelled dining room. Two minutes' walk to village centre.
Bedrooms: 3 double, 1 twin
Bathrooms: 4 en-suite

Bed & breakfast per night:	£min	£max
Single	25.00	35.00
Double	50.00	50.00

Parking for 10

Crown and Trumpet Inn

APPROVED

Church Street, Broadway, Worcestershire WR12 7AE
☎ (01386) 853202
Fax (01386) 853874
Traditional English inn with log fires and oak beams, quietly located just off the village green. Home-cooked local and seasonal English food.
Bedrooms: 4 double, 1 twin
Bathrooms: 5 en-suite

Bed & breakfast per night:	£min	£max
Double	40.00	60.00

Lunch available
Evening meal 1830 (last orders 2130)
Parking for 6
Cards accepted: Diners, Mastercard, Visa, Switch/Delta

COLOUR MAPS

Colour maps at the back of this guide pinpoint all places in which you will find accommodation listed.

BROADWAY

Continued

Eastbank

Station Drive, Broadway, Worcestershire WR12 7DF
☎ (01386) 852659
Quiet location, half a mile from village. All rooms fully en-suite (bath/shower), with colour TV and beverage facilities. Homely atmosphere. Free brochure.
Bedrooms: 2 double, 2 twin, 2 triple
Bathrooms: 6 en-suite

Bed & breakfast per night:	£min	£max
Single	20.00	40.00
Double	40.00	55.00

Parking for 6

Leasow House

HIGHLY COMMENDED
Laverton Meadow, Broadway, Worcestershire WR12 7NA
☎ (01386) 584526
Fax (01386) 584596
Email: bmeeking@compuserve.com

17th C Cotswold-stone farmhouse tranquilly set in open countryside close to Broadway village.
Bedrooms: 3 double, 2 twin, 2 triple
Bathrooms: 7 en-suite

Bed & breakfast per night:	£min	£max
Double	53.00	62.00

Parking for 10
Cards accepted: Amex, Mastercard, Visa

Millhay Cottage

Listed COMMENDED
Bury End, Broadway, Worcestershire WR12 7JS
☎ (01386) 858241
House set in a superb garden off the Snowshill Road and adjacent to Cotswold Way. Accommodation is a self-contained suite (2 bedrooms, bathroom, wc): maximum 4 persons.
Bedrooms: 1 family room
Bathrooms: 1 private

Bed & breakfast per night:	£min	£max
Single	22.00	24.00
Double	40.00	44.00

Parking for 12
Open January, March–December

Olive Branch Guest House

COMMENDED
78 High Street, Broadway, Worcestershire WR12 7AJ
☎ (01386) 853440
Fax (01386) 853440
Email: mark@olivebr.u-net.com
16th C house with modern amenities close to centre of village. Traditional English breakfast served. Reduced rates for 3 nights or more.
Bedrooms: 2 single, 3 double, 2 twin, 1 triple
Suite available
Bathrooms: 6 en-suite, 1 public

Bed & breakfast per night:	£min	£max
Single	19.00	19.50
Double	40.00	56.00

Parking for 8
Cards accepted: Amex

Shenberrow Hill

Listed HIGHLY COMMENDED
Stanton, Broadway, Worcestershire WR12 7NE
☎ (01386) 584468
9-acre farm with horses. Attractive country house, quietly situated in beautiful unspoilt Cotswold village. Heated swimming pool. Friendly, helpful service. Inn nearby.
Bedrooms: 2 double, 2 twin
Bathrooms: 2 private, 2 public

Bed & breakfast per night:	£min	£max
Single	25.00	25.00
Double	39.00	45.00

Evening meal 1800 (last orders 2000)
Parking for 6

Southwold Guest House

COMMENDED
Station Road, Broadway, Worcestershire WR12 7DE
☎ (01386) 853681 & (0589) 950833
Fax (01386) 854610

Warm welcome, friendly service, good cooking at this large Edwardian house, only 4 minutes' walk from village centre. Reductions for 2 or more nights; bargain winter breaks.
Bedrooms: 1 single, 4 double, 2 twin, 1 family room
Suite available
Bathrooms: 6 en-suite, 2 public

Bed & breakfast per night:	£min	£max
Single	17.00	20.00
Double	34.00	44.00

Parking for 8
Cards accepted: Amex, Mastercard, Visa, Switch/Delta

Tudor Cottage

HIGHLY COMMENDED
High Street, Broadway, Worcestershire WR12 7DT
☎ (01386) 852674
Classic 17th C Cotswold-stone Grade II house in centre of the village. All bedrooms en-suite. Off-street parking.
Bedrooms: 2 double, 1 twin
Bathrooms: 3 en-suite

Bed & breakfast per night:	£min	£max
Single	30.00	40.00
Double	45.00	60.00

Parking for 4

White Acres Guesthouse

HIGHLY COMMENDED
Station Road, Broadway, Worcestershire WR12 7DE
☎ (01386) 852320
Spacious Victorian house with en-suite bedrooms, 3 with four-poster beds. Off-road parking. 4 minutes' walk from village centre. Reductions for 3 or more nights. Bargain winter breaks.
Bedrooms: 5 double, 1 twin
Bathrooms: 6 en-suite

Bed & breakfast per night:	£min	£max
Double	38.00	42.00

Parking for 8
Open March–October

The map references refer to the colour maps towards the end of the guide. The first figure is the map number; the letter and figure which follow indicate the grid reference on the map.

BROMSGROVE

Hereford and Worcester
Map ref 4B3

This market town near the Lickey Hills has an interesting museum and craft centre and 14th C church with fine tombs and a Carillon tower. The Avoncroft Museum of Buildings is nearby where many old buildings have been re-assembled, having been saved from destruction.
Tourist Information Centre ☎ (01527) 831809

The Durrance

COMMENDED

Berry Lane, Upton Warren, Bromsgrove, Worcestershire B61 9EL
☎ (01562) 777533
Fax (01562) 777533

Victorian farmhouse in picturesque rural setting. Large, comfortably furnished en-suite rooms. Central to NEC, the Cotswolds, Severn Valley Railway. 5 miles junction 5, M5; 7 miles junction 1 M42.
Bedrooms: 3 twin
Bathrooms: 3 en-suite

Bed & breakfast per night:	£min	£max
Single	20.00	25.00
Double	36.00	45.00

Evening meal 1900 (last orders 2000)
Parking for 20

The Grahams

Listed COMMENDED

95 Old Station Road, Bromsgrove, Worcestershire B60 2AF
☎ (01527) 874463
Modern house in quiet, pleasant location close to the A38, 3 miles from the M5 and 1.5 miles from the M42. Within easy reach of National Exhibition Centre, Worcester and Stratford. Car parking, TV lounge, tea/coffee facilities.
Bedrooms: 2 single, 1 twin
Bathrooms: 1 public

Bed & breakfast per night:	£min	£max
Single	16.00	16.00
Double	32.00	32.00

Half board per person:	£min	£max
Daily	22.00	22.00
Weekly	132.00	132.00

Evening meal 1800 (last orders 0900)
Parking for 2

BROMYARD

Hereford and Worcester
Map ref 2B1

Market town on the River Frome surrounded by orchards, with black and white houses and a Norman church. Nearby at Lower Brockhampton is a 14th C half-timbered moated manor house owned by the National Trust. Heritage Centre.
Tourist Information Centre ☎ (01684) 862175

Park House

APPROVED

28 Sherford Street, Bromyard, Herefordshire HR7 4DL
☎ (01885) 482294
Close to town centre, restaurant and shops, and a desirable location for touring. Ample parking.
Bedrooms: 1 single, 1 double, 1 twin, 2 triple
Bathrooms: 3 en-suite, 1 public

Bed & breakfast per night:	£min	£max
Single	16.00	20.00
Double	30.00	34.00

Parking for 6

Wyndhurst

Listed APPROVED

Avenbury, Bromyard, Herefordshire HR7 4JR
☎ (01885) 490700
5-acre smallholding. Nearly self sufficient smallholding supplying own organic vegetables. Situated on the B4214 2 miles north of Bishops Frome. Children welcome by prior arrangement.
Bedrooms: 1 single, 1 double, 1 twin
Bathrooms: 1 public

Bed & breakfast per night:	£min	£max
Single	16.00	
Double	32.00	

Half board per person:	£min	£max
Daily	26.00	
Weekly	156.00	

Evening meal 1900 (last orders 1700)
Parking for 1
Open May–September

BROUGHTON ASTLEY

Leicestershire
Map ref 4C3

First mentioned in the Domesday Book when it was three separate villages, Broctone, Sutone and Torp.

The Old Farm House

Listed COMMENDED

Old Mill Road, Broughton Astley, Leicester LE9 6PQ
☎ (01455) 282254
Recently converted Georgian farmhouse overlooking fields. Quietly situated behind the church, near village centre. Near junctions 20/21 of M1, junction 1 of M69. French spoken. Evening meal with prior notice. No smoking, please.
Bedrooms: 1 single, 1 twin, 1 triple
Bathrooms: 2 public

Bed & breakfast per night:	£min	£max
Single	17.00	19.00

Half board per person:	£min	£max
Daily	22.00	27.00

Evening meal from 1830
Parking for 4

BRUNTINGTHORPE

Leicestershire
Map ref 4C3

Knaptoft House Farm

HIGHLY COMMENDED

Bruntingthorpe Road, Shearsby, Lutterworth LE17 6PR
☎ (0116) 247 8388
Fax (0116) 247 8388
145-acre mixed farm. Very quiet, warm, comfortable, beautifully appointed family home surrounded by farmland. Family historians welcome - many records on premises and only 4 miles from County Records Office. A14 junction 1, M1 junction 20, M6 junction 1, A5199 Shearsby 1 mile. Ample parking. JCB card also accepted.
Bedrooms: 2 double, 1 twin
Bathrooms: 2 en-suite, 1 public

Bed & breakfast per night:	£min	£max
Single	24.00	
Double	37.00	42.00

Continued ▶

BRUNTINGTHORPE

Continued

Parking for 5
Cards accepted: Mastercard, Visa, Switch/Delta

BUCKNELL

Shropshire
Map ref 4A3

Village by the River Redlake with thatched black and white cottages, a Norman church and the remains of an Iron Age fort on a nearby hill. It is a designated Area of Outstanding Natural Beauty.

The Hall

COMMENDED

Bucknell SY7 0AA
☎ (01547) 530249
Fax (01547) 530249
200-acre mixed farm. Georgian farmhouse in the picturesque village of Bucknell, with a peaceful and relaxed atmosphere.
Bedrooms: 2 double, 1 twin
Bathrooms: 1 en-suite, 1 public

Bed & breakfast per night:	£min	£max
Single	17.00	19.00
Double	34.00	38.00

Half board per person:	£min	£max
Daily	27.00	29.00
Weekly	185.00	185.00

Evening meal 1800 (last orders 1200)
Parking for 4
Open March–November

BURFORD

Oxfordshire
Map ref 2B1

Bee Cottage
The Bird in Hand
Hillborough House
Romany Inn
St Winnow
See South of England region for full entry details

For further information on accommodation establishments use the coupons at the back of this guide.

BURTON UPON TRENT

Staffordshire
Map ref 4B3

An important brewing town with the Bass Museum of Brewing, where the Bass shire horses are stabled. There are 3 bridges with views over the river and some interesting public buildings including the 18th C St Modwen's Church.
Tourist Information Centre ☎ (01283) 516609 or 508589

New Inn Farm

Listed APPROVED

Needwood, Burton upon Trent DE13 9PB
☎ (01283) 575435 & 0831 099621
122-acre mixed & dairy farm. In the heart of Needwood Forest on the main B5234 Newborough to Burton upon Trent road. B5017 goes right past the farmhouse gate. Central for Uttoxeter, Lichfield, Derby and Burton upon Trent.
Bedrooms: 1 single, 1 double, 1 triple
Bathrooms: 1 public

Bed & breakfast per night:	£min	£max
Single	15.00	
Double	30.00	

Parking for 6

BURTON DASSETT

Warwickshire
Map ref 2C1

The church tower looks out over the site of the Battle of Edgehill and it is said that Cromwell himself climbed the tower to watch the fighting. Nearby is a 16th C beacon tower from which news of the battle was sent.

The White House Bed and Breakfast

Listed COMMENDED

Burton Dassett, Leamington Spa CV33 0AB
☎ (01295) 770143 & 0374 790391
Fax (01295) 250815
Large country house situated at the top of the Burton Dassett Hills, enjoying superb views over the Warwickshire and Oxfordshire countryside. Evening meal on request.
Bedrooms: 2 double, 1 twin
Bathrooms: 1 public

Bed & breakfast per night:	£min	£max
Single	17.00	20.00
Double	34.00	40.00

Half board per person:	£min	£max
Daily	32.00	35.00
Weekly	195.00	220.00

Parking for 6

BUTTERTON

Staffordshire
Map ref 4B2

Village close to Thor's Cave, Hartington and the beautiful scenery of Dovedale.

Butterton Moor House

HIGHLY COMMENDED

Parsons Lane, Butterton, Leek ST13 7PD
☎ (01538) 304506
Fax (01538) 304506

Beautiful 17th C Peak District farmhouse with beams, antiques. Superb facilities, all en-suite. Indoor swimming pool, snooker room.
Bedrooms: 2 double, 1 twin
Bathrooms: 3 en-suite, 1 public

Bed & breakfast per night:	£min	£max
Single	20.00	25.00
Double	35.00	50.00

Evening meal 1830 (last orders 1930)
Parking for 12

BUXTON

Derbyshire
Map ref 4B2

The highest market town in England and one of the oldest spas, with an elegant Crescent, Poole's Cavern, Opera House and attractive Pavilion Gardens. An excellent centre for exploring the Peak District.
Tourist Information Centre ☎ (01298) 25106

Barn House

COMMENDED

Litton Mill, Buxton SK17 8SW
☎ (01298) 872751
Fax (01298) 872751
Converted barn dating back to the late 18th C within the Peak District

National Park. Beautiful views, good walking and adjacent to the River Wye.
Bedrooms: 1 double, 1 twin
Bathrooms: 2 en-suite

Bed & breakfast per night:	£min	£max
Single	18.00	20.00
Double	36.00	40.00

Parking for 6

Devonshire Arms

COMMENDED

Peak Forest, Buxton SK17 8EJ
☎ (01298) 23875 & 0831 707325
A warm and friendly welcome awaits you at this 17th C former coaching inn. Set in a village location in the heart of the Peak District and close to attractions. All rooms recently refurbished to a high standard, offering en-suite facilities, tea/coffee and colour TV.
Bedrooms: 1 double, 1 twin, 1 triple
Bathrooms: 3 en-suite

Bed & breakfast per night:	£min	£max
Single	27.50	27.50
Double	37.00	37.00

Lunch available
Evening meal 1830 (last orders 2145)
Parking for 40
Cards accepted: Mastercard, Visa

Fairhaven

Listed APPROVED

1 Dale Terrace, Buxton SK17 6LU
☎ (01298) 24481
Fax (01298) 24481
Within easy reach of the Opera House, Pavilion Gardens, 2 golf courses and the many and varied attractions of Derbyshire's Peak District.
Bedrooms: 1 single, 1 double, 1 twin, 2 triple, 1 family room
Bathrooms: 1 public

Bed & breakfast per night:	£min	£max
Single	17.00	
Double	30.00	

Half board per person:	£min	£max
Daily	25.00	
Weekly	168.00	

Evening meal 1800 (last orders 1600)
Cards accepted: Amex, Mastercard, Visa

Please check prices and other details at the time of booking.

Hawthorn Farm Guesthouse

COMMENDED

Fairfield Road, Buxton SK17 7ED
☎ (01298) 23230
A 400-year-old former farmhouse which has been in the family for 10 generations. Full English breakfast. En-suite rooms available. Tea/coffee facilities, colour TV.
Bedrooms: 4 single, 2 double, 2 twin, 4 triple
Bathrooms: 5 en-suite, 2 public

Bed & breakfast per night:	£min	£max
Single	21.00	22.00
Double	42.00	48.00

Parking for 15
Open April–October

Lynstone Guesthouse

3 Grange Road, Buxton SK17 6NH
☎ (01298) 77043
A spacious homely house. Home cooking, traditional and vegetarian. Ideal base for touring and walking. Children welcome, cleanliness assured. Off-street parking. No smoking and no pets, please.
Bedrooms: 1 triple, 1 family room
Bathrooms: 1 private, 2 public

Bed & breakfast per night:	£min	£max
Double	32.00	33.00

Parking for 3
Open March–December

Pedlicote Farm

Listed HIGHLY COMMENDED

Peak Forest, Buxton SK17 8EG
☎ (01298) 22241
1681 oak-beamed farmhouse conversion in the Peak Park, full of character, with a charming atmosphere and magnificent views.
Bedrooms: 1 double, 2 twin
Bathrooms: 2 public

Bed & breakfast per night:	£min	£max
Single	18.00	20.00
Double	28.00	30.00

Half board per person:	£min	£max
Daily	25.00	27.00
Weekly	175.00	175.00

Lunch available
Evening meal 1830 (last orders 2030)
Parking for 9

The Victorian Guesthouse

COMMENDED

5 Wye Grove, Off Macclesfield Road, Buxton SK17 9AJ
☎ (01298) 78759
Tasteful en-suite rooms. Delightful conservatory with local guide books. Delicious breakfasts, diets catered for. Old fashioned hospitality. Quiet cul-de-sac in a central residential area. Non-smoking. Parking.
Bedrooms: 2 double, 1 triple
Bathrooms: 3 en-suite

Bed & breakfast per night:	£min	£max
Double	37.00	

Evening meal 1800 (last orders 1600)
Parking for 4

CALVER

Derbyshire
Map ref 4B2

Attractive Peak District village beside the River Derwent.

Hydrangea Cottage

Listed HIGHLY COMMENDED

Hall Fold, Main Street, Calver, Sheffield S30 1XR
☎ (01433) 630760
Fax (01433) 631123
Traditional stone-built house in a quiet location. Rooms furnished with antiques and with views across to Curbar Edge. Only 5 minutes from Chatsworth House.
Bedrooms: 1 double
Bathrooms: 1 private

Bed & breakfast per night:	£min	£max
Single	35.00	
Double	50.00	

Parking for 2

WELCOME HOST

This is a nationally recognised customer care programme which aims to promote the highest standards of service and a warm welcome. Establishments who are taking part in this initiative are indicated by the symbol.

CASTLETON

Derbyshire
Map ref 4B2

Large village in a spectacular Peak District setting with ruined Peveril Castle and 4 great show caverns, where the Blue John stone and lead were mined. One cavern offers a mile-long underground boat journey.

Bargate Cottage

COMMENDED

Bargate, Pindale Road, Castleton, Sheffield S30 2WG
☎ (01433) 620201
Fax (01433) 621739

Unspoilt, renovated 17th C cottage adjacent to Peveril Castle in the centre of the village. An ideal base for relaxing, walking or touring. Many recreational facilities available locally. Non-smokers only, please, and sorry, no pets.

Bedrooms: 2 double, 1 twin
Bathrooms: 2 en-suite, 1 private

Bed & breakfast per night:	£min	£max
Single	37.00	
Double	43.00	47.00

Half board per person:	£min	£max
Daily	32.00	

Evening meal from 1830
Parking for 6

Ye Olde Cheshire Cheese Inn

Listed COMMENDED

How Lane, Castleton, Sheffield S30 2WJ
☎ (01433) 620330 & 0836 369636

17th C inn in the heart of the Peak District. En-suite rooms. Restaurant with 30 home-made dishes, including roast wild boar, pheasant, game pie. Two beamed lounge bars with real ale - no pool tables or machines! Family-run.

Bedrooms: 2 single, 6 double, 1 twin
Bathrooms: 2 en-suite, 7 private

Bed & breakfast per night:	£min	£max
Single	25.00	25.00
Double	45.00	60.00

Lunch available
Evening meal 1800 (last orders 2100)
Parking for 65
Cards accepted: Mastercard, Visa

CHARLBURY

Oxfordshire
Map ref 2C1

Banbury Hill Farm
See South of England region for full entry details

CHEADLE

Staffordshire
Map ref 4B2

Caverswall Castle

HIGHLY COMMENDED

Caverswall ST11 9EA
☎ (01782) 393239
Fax (01782) 394590

Grade I listed medieval and Jacobean castle with panelled en-suite bedrooms, billiard room, swimming pool (seasonal) and extensive grounds. Once home to Wedgwood family. Near Potteries, Peak District and Alton Towers.

Bedrooms: 3 double
Bathrooms: 3 en-suite

Bed & breakfast per night:	£min	£max
Double	65.00	

Parking for 18
Open February–November

CHELMARSH

Shropshire
Map ref 4A3

An unspoilt village near the River Severn, with old timbered cottages and an imposing 14th C church.

Bulls Head Inn

COMMENDED

Chelmarsh, Bridgnorth WV16 6BA
☎ (01746) 861469
Fax (01746) 862646

17th C village inn with warm, friendly atmosphere. All bedrooms en-suite. Ground floor bedrooms suitable for people with disabilities. Jacuzzi. Magnificent views.

Bedrooms: 1 single, 6 double, 2 twin, 3 triple
Bathrooms: 12 en-suite

Bed & breakfast per night:	£min	£max
Single	25.00	28.00
Double	36.00	43.00

Half board per person:	£min	£max
Daily	35.00	38.00
Weekly	245.00	266.00

Lunch available
Evening meal 1900 (last orders 2130)
Parking for 50
Cards accepted: Mastercard, Visa, Switch/Delta

CHELTENHAM

Gloucestershire
Map ref 2B1

Cheltenham was developed as a spa town in the 18th C and has some beautiful Regency architecture, in particular the Pittville Pump Room. It holds international music and literature festivals and is also famous for its race meetings and cricket.
Tourist Information Centre ☎ (01242) 522878

Elmington Bed and Breakfast

Listed HIGHLY COMMENDED

44 Leckhampton Road, Cheltenham GL53 0BB
☎ (01242) 573357
Fax (01242) 263201

Attractive Victorian mid-terrace house on 4 levels, in wide tree-lined road leading to town centre.

Bedrooms: 1 single, 1 double, 1 twin
Bathrooms: 1 en-suite, 1 public

Bed & breakfast per night:	£min	£max
Single	18.00	25.00
Double	40.00	50.00

Ham Hill Farm

HIGHLY COMMENDED

Whittington, Cheltenham GL54 4EZ
☎ (01242) 584415 & (0585) 094223
Fax (01242) 222535

160-acre mixed farm. Farmhouse, built in 1983 to a high standard, with good views of the Cotswolds. 2 miles from Cheltenham, on the Cotswold Way.

Bedrooms: 3 double, 2 twin, 1 family room
Bathrooms: 6 en-suite, 1 public

Bed & breakfast per night:	£min	£max
Single	23.50	23.50
Double	40.00	44.00

Parking for 7

Hamilton House

COMMENDED

65 Bath Road, Cheltenham
GL53 7LH
☎ (01242) 527772

Extremely central terraced town house within easy walking distance of all Cheltenham's facilities.

Bedrooms: 2 single, 1 double, 1 twin, 2 triple
Bathrooms: 3 en-suite, 1 public

Bed & breakfast per night:	£min	£max
Single	18.00	25.00
Double	40.00	50.00

Lonsdale House

COMMENDED

Montpellier Drive, Cheltenham
GL50 1TX
☎ (01242) 232379
Fax (01242) 232379

Regency house situated 5 minutes' walk from the town hall, Promenade, shopping centre, parks and theatre. Easy access to all main routes.

Bedrooms: 4 single, 2 double, 1 twin, 2 triple, 1 family room
Bathrooms: 3 en-suite, 1 private, 3 public

Bed & breakfast per night:	£min	£max
Single	19.00	30.00
Double	38.00	44.00

Parking for 6
Cards accepted: Mastercard, Visa, Switch/Delta

St. Michaels

COMMENDED

4 Montpellier Drive, Cheltenham
GL50 1TX
☎ (01242) 513587
Fax (01242) 513587

Elegant Edwardian guesthouse offering delightful non-smoking accommodation with parking, five minutes' walk from town centre. Excellent breakfast menu and a warm welcome.

Bedrooms: 2 double, 1 twin, 2 triple
Bathrooms: 3 en-suite, 1 public

Bed & breakfast per night:	£min	£max
Single	25.00	35.00
Double	36.00	48.00

Parking for 3
Cards accepted: Mastercard, Visa

The Wynyards

HIGHLY COMMENDED

Butts Lane, Woodmancote,
Cheltenham GL52 4QH
☎ (01242) 673876

Secluded old Cotswold-stone house in elevated position with panoramic views. Set in open countryside on outskirts of small village, 4 miles from Cheltenham.

Bedrooms: 1 double, 2 twin
Bathrooms: 2 private, 1 public

Bed & breakfast per night:	£min	£max
Single	20.00	20.00
Double	36.00	36.00

Parking for 6

CHERINGTON

Warwickshire
Map ref 2C1

Cherington Arms

APPROVED

Cherington, Shipston-on-Stour
CV36 5HS
☎ (01608) 686233

Village pub with bar, lounge and restaurant. Bar snacks and a la carte meals served lunchtime and evenings, 7 days a week. Large secluded garden.

Bedrooms: 2 double
Bathrooms: 1 public

Bed & breakfast per night:	£min	£max
Single	20.00	
Double	30.00	

Lunch available
Evening meal 1900 (last orders 2130)
Parking for 30

All accommodation in this guide has been graded, or is awaiting a grading, by a trained Tourist Board inspector.

CHESTERFIELD

Derbyshire
Map ref 4B2

Famous for the twisted spire of its parish church, Chesterfield has some fine modern buildings and excellent shopping facilities, including a large, traditional open-air market. Hardwick Hall and Bolsover Castle are nearby.
Tourist Information Centre ☎ (01246) 345777

Abbeydale Hotel

COMMENDED

Cross Street, Chesterfield S40 4TD
☎ (01246) 277849
Fax (01246) 558223

Resident proprietors. Quiet location within walking distance of town centre, close to Peak District and Chatsworth. Short breaks available.

Wheelchair access category 3
Bedrooms: 3 single, 7 double, 1 twin, 1 triple
Bathrooms: 12 en-suite

Bed & breakfast per night:	£min	£max
Single	42.00	47.00
Double	60.00	60.00

Lunch available
Evening meal 1900 (last orders 2030)
Parking for 12
Cards accepted: Amex, Diners, Mastercard, Visa

15

CHIPPING CAMPDEN

Gloucestershire
Map ref 2B1

Outstanding Cotswold wool town with many old stone gabled houses, a splendid church and 17th C almshouses. Nearby are Kiftsgate Court Gardens and Hidcote Manor Gardens (National Trust).

Manor Farm

COMMENDED

Weston Subedge, Chipping
Campden GL55 6QH
☎ (01386) 840390 & (0589) 108812

600-acre mixed farm. Traditional 17th C farmhouse, an excellent base for touring the Cotswolds, Shakespeare country and Hidcote Gardens. Warm, friendly atmosphere. Walled garden. All rooms en-suite with tea/coffee making facilities, TV/radio. 1.5 miles from Chipping Campden.

Bedrooms: 2 double, 1 twin

Continued ▶

CHIPPING CAMPDEN

Continued

Bathrooms: 3 en-suite

Bed & breakfast per night:	£min	£max
Single	30.00	30.00
Double	40.00	40.00

Parking for 8

Nineveh Farm

COMMENDED

Campden Road, Mickleton, Chipping Campden GL55 6PS
☎ (01386) 438921 & 438923

27-acre livestock & horses farm. 18th C farmhouse with Virginia creeper, beams and flagstones. Working farm with homely accommodation and log fires. Ideal for Cotswolds, Stratford, Warwick Castle and Chipping Campden with its famous High Street.
Bedrooms: 2 double, 1 twin
Bathrooms: 2 en-suite, 1 private

Bed & breakfast per night:	£min	£max
Single	28.00	35.00
Double	38.00	50.00

Parking for 7

Orchard Hill House

HIGHLY COMMENDED

Broad Campden, Chipping Campden GL55 6UU
☎ (01386) 841473
Fax (01386) 841030

17th C Cotswold-stone restored farmhouse. Breakfast in flagstoned dining room with inglenook fireplace around 10ft elm farmhouse table.
Bedrooms: 2 double, 1 twin, 1 triple
Bathrooms: 3 en-suite, 1 private

Bed & breakfast per night:	£min	£max
Single	40.00	50.00
Double	45.00	57.00

Parking for 6

Sparlings

COMMENDED

Leysbourne, High Street, Chipping Campden GL55 6HL
☎ (01386) 840505

Fully centrally heated, comfortable, attractive 18th C Cotswold house in Chipping Campden High Street. Walled garden. Easy parking. Children over 6 welcome.
Bedrooms: 1 double, 1 twin
Bathrooms: 1 en-suite, 1 private

Bed & breakfast per night:	£min	£max
Single	26.50	28.00
Double	45.00	49.50

Weston Park Farm

COMMENDED

Dovers Hill, Chipping Campden GL55 6UW
☎ (01386) 840835
20-acre mixed farm. Self-contained wing of secluded, magnificently situated farmhouse, 1 mile from Chipping Campden, adjacent to National Trust land.
Bedrooms: 1 triple
Bathrooms: 1 private

Bed & breakfast per night:	£min	£max
Double	45.00	45.00

Parking for 10

CHIPPING NORTON

Oxfordshire
Map ref 2C1

Oak House

See South of England region for full entry details

Map references apply to the colour maps at the back of this guide.

CHURCH STRETTON

Shropshire
Map ref 4A3

Church Stretton lies under the eastern slope of the Longmynd surrounded by hills. It is ideal for walkers, with marvellous views, golf and gliding. Wenlock Edge is not far away.

Acton Scott Farm

COMMENDED

Acton Scott, Church Stretton SY6 6QN
☎ (01694) 781260
320-acre mixed farm. Conveniently situated 17th C farmhouse of character with comfortable rooms and log fires. Beautiful countryside, good walking area.
http://www.webscape.co.uk/farmaccom/england/south-shropshire
Bedrooms: 1 double, 1 twin, 1 family room
Bathrooms: 2 en-suite, 1 public

Bed & breakfast per night:	£min	£max
Single	15.00	
Double	30.00	

Parking for 6
Open March–October

Berry's

COMMENDED

17 High Street, Church Stretton SY6 6BU
☎ (01694) 724452
Fax (01694) 724460
One of Stretton's historic houses (Grade II), convenient for all amenities in the old town Square, yet only a stroll from National Trust land. This unusual house offers interest, comfort and the best breakfast, including vegetarian.*
Bedrooms: 1 double, 1 twin
Bathrooms: 2 private

Bed & breakfast per night:	£min	£max
Double	36.00	40.00

The Elms

Listed COMMENDED

Little Stretton, Church Stretton SY6 6RD
☎ (01694) 723084
Victorian country house in spacious grounds, decorated and furnished in Victorian style.
Bedrooms: 2 double, 1 twin
Bathrooms: 2 public

Bed & breakfast per night:	£min	£max
Single	19.00	
Double	33.00	

Parking for 3

Gilberries Cottage

COMMENDED

Wall-under-Heywood, Church Stretton SY6 7HZ
☎ (01694) 771400
Fax (01694) 771663
Email: griffiths@studio.enta.net

Country cottage adjoining family farm, in peaceful and beautiful countryside. Ideal for walking. Numerous places of interest nearby.

Bedrooms: 1 twin, 1 triple
Bathrooms: 1 public

Bed & breakfast per night:	£min	£max
Single	20.00	20.00
Double	34.00	36.00

Parking for 8
Open February–November

Grove Farm

Listed APPROVED

Cardington, Church Stretton SY6 7JZ
☎ (01694) 771451

27-acre mixed farm. Oak-beamed farmhouse built in 1667, in delightful village 5 miles from Church Stretton. Excellent walking country. Homely atmosphere, good food.

Bedrooms: 1 twin, 1 triple
Bathrooms: 1 public

Bed & breakfast per night:	£min	£max
Single	16.00	17.00
Double	28.00	32.00

Parking for 10

Malt House Farm

COMMENDED

Lower Wood, Church Stretton SY6 6LF
☎ (01694) 751379

100-acre mixed farm. Old, pretty, beamed farmhouse on the edge of a large area of unspoilt National Trust land.

Bedrooms: 1 double, 1 twin
Bathrooms: 2 en-suite

Bed & breakfast per night:	£min	£max
Single		17.50
Double		35.00

Half board per person:	£min	£max
Daily		30.00
Weekly		210.00

Evening meal 1800 (last orders 1900)
Parking for 4
Open March–October

Woolston Farm

COMMENDED

Church Stretton SY6 6QD
☎ (01694) 781201

350-acre mixed farm. Victorian farmhouse in the small hamlet of Woolston, off A49. Ideal position for touring Shropshire. Outstanding views and good farmhouse fare.

Bedrooms: 2 double, 1 twin
Bathrooms: 2 en-suite, 1 public

Bed & breakfast per night:	£min	£max
Single	19.00	19.00
Double	38.00	38.00

Half board per person:	£min	£max
Daily	46.50	

Evening meal 1850 (last orders 2000)
Parking for 2
Open January–November

OAP

CIRENCESTER

Gloucestershire
Map ref 2B1

"Capital of the Cotswolds", Cirencester was Britain's second most important Roman town with many finds housed in the Corinium Museum. It has a very fine Perpendicular church and old houses around the market place.
Tourist Information Centre ☎ (01285) 654180

Coleen Bed and Breakfast

Listed COMMENDED

Ashton Road, Siddington, Cirencester GL7 6HR
☎ (01285) 642203

Choice accommodation in a friendly, relaxed atmosphere. Close to Cotswold Water Park. Ideal location for walking and cycling.

Bedrooms: 2 double, 1 twin
Bathrooms: 1 en-suite, 1 public

Bed & breakfast per night:	£min	£max
Single	25.00	30.00
Double	35.00	40.00

Parking for 4

Eliot Arms Hotel Free House

COMMENDED

Clarks Hay, South Cerney, Cirencester GL7 5UA
☎ (01285) 860215
Fax (01285) 861121

Dating from the 16th C, a comfortable Cotswold freehouse hotel, 2.5 miles from Cirencester, just off the A419. Reputation for fine food and hospitality. Riverside gardens.

Bedrooms: 1 single, 5 double, 4 twin, 2 triple
Suites available
Bathrooms: 12 en-suite

Bed & breakfast per night:	£min	£max
Single	38.00	40.00
Double	49.50	55.00

Lunch available
Evening meal 1830 (last orders 2200)
Parking for 30
Cards accepted: Amex, Mastercard, Visa, Switch/Delta

50 OAP SP

The Masons Arms

COMMENDED

High Street, Meysey Hampton, Cirencester GL7 5JT
☎ (01285) 850164
Fax (01285) 850164

Seeking peace and tranquillity? Treat yourself to a break in this 17th C inn set beside the village green. Oak beams and log fire. A warm welcome awaits you.

Bedrooms: 6 double, 1 twin, 1 triple
Bathrooms: 8 en-suite

Bed & breakfast per night:	£min	£max
Single	32.00	38.00
Double	48.00	56.00

Lunch available
Evening meal 1900 (last orders 2130)

Continued ▶

CIRENCESTER

Continued

Parking for 8
Cards accepted: Mastercard, Visa, Switch/Delta

The Old Rectory

COMMENDED

Rodmarton, Cirencester GL7 6PE
☎ (01285) 841246
Fax (01285) 841246

17th C rectory set in three-quarters of an acre of gardens. Cirencester 6 miles, Tetbury 5 miles. Equidistant Swindon, Cheltenham and Gloucester. Oxford and Bath 40 minutes.

Bedrooms: 1 double, 1 twin
Bathrooms: 2 en-suite

Bed & breakfast per night:	£min	£max
Single	25.00	30.00
Double	40.00	45.00

Evening meal 1900 (last orders 2100)
Parking for 6

Smerrill Barns

COMMENDED

Kemble, Cirencester GL7 6BW
☎ (01285) 770907
Fax (01285) 770706

Accommodation in a converted barn, providing all modern facilities. On-site car parking. Situated 3 miles west of Cirencester on the A429.

Bedrooms: 1 single, 4 double, 1 twin, 1 family room
Bathrooms: 7 en-suite, 1 public

Bed & breakfast per night:	£min	£max
Single	35.00	40.00
Double	45.00	55.00

Parking for 7
Cards accepted: Mastercard, Visa, Switch/Delta

Please mention this guide when making your booking.

The Village Pub

Listed APPROVED

Barnsley, Cirencester GL7 5EF
☎ (01285) 740421

The Village Pub has 5 rooms, all with private facilities, and is situated in a pretty Cotswold village near Cirencester.

Bedrooms: 4 double, 1 twin
Bathrooms: 4 en-suite, 1 private

Bed & breakfast per night:	£min	£max
Single		30.00
Double		45.00

Lunch available
Evening meal 1900 (last orders 2130)
Parking for 40
Cards accepted: Amex, Mastercard, Visa

CLEOBURY MORTIMER

Shropshire
Map ref 4A3

Village with attractive timbered and Georgian houses and a church with a wooden spire. It is close to the Clee Hills with marvellous views.

Kings Arms Hotel

COMMENDED

Church Street, Cleobury Mortimer, Kidderminster, Worcestershire DY14 8BS
☎ (01299) 270252

16th C coaching inn, famous for fine food, in centre of picturesque village. Close to golf, fishing, safari park and Severn Valley Railway.

Bedrooms: 1 single, 2 double, 2 twin
Bathrooms: 4 en-suite, 1 private, 1 public

Bed & breakfast per night:	£min	£max
Single	25.00	30.00
Double	45.00	50.00

Lunch available
Evening meal 1900 (last orders 2100)
Parking for 4
Cards accepted: Mastercard, Visa

Information on accommodation listed in this guide has been supplied by the proprietors. As changes may occur you are advised to check details at the time of booking.

CLUN

Shropshire
Map ref 4A3

Small, ancient town on the Welsh border with flint and stone tools in its museum and Iron Age forts nearby. The impressive ruins of a Norman castle lie beside the River Clun and there are some interesting 17th C houses.

Birches Mill

HIGHLY COMMENDED

Birches Mill, Clun, Craven Arms SY7 8NL
☎ (01588) 640409
Fax (01588) 640409

17th C country house in secluded valley on river banks. Exposed beams, inglenook with open fire, traditional furnishings and pretty cottage garden.

Bedrooms: 2 double, 1 twin
Bathrooms: 1 public

Bed & breakfast per night:	£min	£max
Double	39.00	39.00

Half board per person:	£min	£max
Daily	35.00	35.00

Evening meal 1900 (last orders 2000)
Parking for 5
Open April–October

Clun Farm

Listed COMMENDED

High Street, Clun, Craven Arms SY7 8JB
☎ (01588) 640432

200-acre mixed farm. 16th C double cruck farmhouse situated in Clun High Street, within 200 metres of 3 public houses and restaurants.

Bedrooms: 2 single, 1 double, 1 triple
Bathrooms: 1 en-suite, 1 public

Bed & breakfast per night:	£min	£max
Single		16.00
Double	36.00	40.00

Half board per person:	£min	£max
Daily	24.00	28.00
Weekly	144.00	168.00

Evening meal (last orders 1800)
Parking for 6

You are advised to confirm your booking in writing.

Crown House

COMMENDED

Church Street, Clun, Craven Arms SY7 8JW
☎ (01588) 640780

Self-contained accommodation in charmingly converted stables and saddler's workshop at listed Georgian house. In Clun conservation area. Superb breakfasts and a warm welcome.

Bedrooms: 1 double, 1 twin
Bathrooms: 1 en-suite, 1 private

Bed & breakfast per night:	£min	£max
Single	18.00	19.00
Double	34.00	36.00

Parking for 2

8

Hurst Mill Farm

COMMENDED

Clun, Craven Arms SY7 0JA
☎ (01588) 640224

100-acre mixed farm. Attractive farmhouse and old mill in the lovely Clun Valley. River and woodland trails, 2 riding ponies, pets welcome. Previous winner of "Great Shropshire Breakfast" challenge.

Bedrooms: 1 double, 2 twin
Bathrooms: 1 en-suite, 2 public

Bed & breakfast per night:	£min	£max
Single	17.00	18.00
Double	34.00	36.00

Half board per person:	£min	£max
Daily	25.00	26.00
Weekly	170.00	175.00

Parking for 8

CLUNBURY

Shropshire
Map ref 4A3

Village near the River Clun and close to Hopton Castle with its ruins of a Norman moat and bailey.

Pool House Farm

Listed COMMENDED

Clunbury, Craven Arms SY7 0HG
☎ (01588) 660414
Fax (01588) 660414

Picturesque secluded farmhouse, with many friendly animals. Ideally situated for castles, pubs, walking or riding forgotten bridleways, in rolling Shropshire Borderlands.

Bedrooms: 1 single, 1 double
Bathrooms: 1 public

Bed & breakfast per night:	£min	£max
Single	17.00	17.00
Double	33.00	36.00

Evening meal 1900 (last orders 2030)
Parking for 6
Open March–September

12

CLUNGUNFORD

Shropshire
Map ref 4A3

Village near the River Clun and Stokesay Castle, a 13th C fortified manor house with an Elizabethan gatehouse.

Broadward Hall

Listed COMMENDED

Clungunford, Craven Arms SY7 0QA
☎ (01547) 530357

176-acre mixed farm. Grade II listed, castellated building, 9 miles west of Ludlow in rural Clun Valley surroundings.

Bedrooms: 2 twin, 1 triple
Bathrooms: 2 public

Bed & breakfast per night:	£min	£max
Single	15.00	15.00
Double	30.00	30.00

Half board per person:	£min	£max
Daily	24.00	24.00
Weekly	160.00	160.00

Evening meal 1900 (last orders 0900)
Parking for 15
Open March–November

COLEFORD

Gloucestershire
Map ref 2A1

Small town in the Forest of Dean with the ancient iron mines at Clearwell Caves nearby, where mining equipment and geological samples are displayed. There are several forest trails in the area.
Tourist Information Centre ☎ (01594) 812388

Millend House and Garden

HIGHLY COMMENDED

Newland, Coleford GL16 8NF
☎ (01594) 832128

250-year-old traditional stone-built house, in 2 acres of lovely hillside gardens and woodlands. Situated at the end of a valley looking down towards Newland and the "Cathedral of the Forest".

Bedrooms: 1 double, 2 twin
Bathrooms: 1 en-suite, 1 public

Bed & breakfast per night:	£min	£max
Double	40.00	44.00

Parking for 4

COTGRAVE

Nottinghamshire
Map ref 4C2

In 1934 an Anglo-Saxon burial ground was discovered on Mill Hill, in this interesting, historic village.

Jerico Farm

COMMENDED

Fosse Way, Cotgrave, Nottingham NG12 3HG
☎ (01949) 81733
Fax (01949) 81733

120-acre mixed farm. With lovely views over the Nottinghamshire Wolds, an excellent rural location for the business or holiday visitor yet only 8 miles from Nottingham with its universities, sports venues and tourist sites. Brochure available.

Bedrooms: 2 double, 1 twin
Bathrooms: 1 en-suite, 1 public

Bed & breakfast per night:	£min	£max
Single	20.00	27.00
Double	35.00	40.00

Parking for 4
Cards accepted: Mastercard, Visa, Switch/Delta

5

COTSWOLDS

See under Bibury, Birdlip, Bledington, Blockley, Bourton-on-the-Water, Broadway, Cheltenham, Chipping Campden, Cirencester, Donnington, Fairford, Gloucester, Great Rissington, Guiting Power, Lechlade, Long Compton, Minchinhampton, Moreton-in-Marsh, Nailsworth, Northleach, Nympsfield, Painswick, Stonehouse, Stow-on-the-Wold, Stroud, Teddington, Tetbury, Tewkesbury, Winchcombe, Wotton-under-Edge
See also Cotswolds in South of England region

COLOUR MAPS

Colour maps at the back of this guide pinpoint all places in which you will find accommodation listed.

COVENTRY

West Midlands
Map ref 4B3

Modern city with a long history. It has many places of interest including the post-war and ruined medieval cathedrals, art gallery and museums, some 16th C almshouses, St Mary's Guildhall, Lunt Roman fort and the Belgrade Theatre.
Tourist Information Centre ☎ (01203) 832303 or 832304

Abigail Guesthouse

COMMENDED
39 St. Patrick's Road, Coventry CV1 2LP
☎ (01203) 221378
Family-run establishment in centre of city, very clean and friendly. Convenient for station, cathedral and city centre shopping, also NEC and NAC.
Bedrooms: 3 single, 1 double, 1 twin, 1 triple
Bathrooms: 2 public

Bed & breakfast per night:	£min	£max
Single	17.00	22.00
Double	30.00	34.00

Acorn Lodge Private Guest House

COMMENDED
Pond Farm, Upper Eastern Green Lane, Coventry CV5 7DP
☎ (01203) 465182
300-year-old beamed farmhouse of character in secluded position. Ideally situated for touring Stratford and Warwick and 20 miles from National Exhibition Centre and Birmingham Airport. Friendly, informal atmosphere. Paddocks and ponies.
Bedrooms: 2 single, 1 double, 2 twin
Bathrooms: 1 en-suite, 2 public

Bed & breakfast per night:	£min	£max
Single	17.00	18.00
Double	34.00	36.00

Parking for 6

Mill Farmhouse

COMMENDED
Mill Lane, Fillongley, Coventry CV7 8EE
☎ (01676) 541898
Fax (01676) 541898
Beautiful farmhouse set in picturesque countryside, offering peace and tranquillity. Detached bed and breakfast apartments with en-suite bathrooms and colour TV. Private car park and gardens. 15 minutes from Coventry, NEC, Birmingham Airport.
Bedrooms: 1 double, 1 twin
Bathrooms: 2 en-suite

Bed & breakfast per night:	£min	£max
Single		25.00
Double	40.00	45.00

Half board per person:	£min	£max
Daily		35.00
Weekly		245.00

Lunch available
Evening meal 1800 (last orders 2000)
Parking for 4

Westwood Cottage

APPROVED
79 Westwood Heath Road, Westwood Heath, Coventry CV4 8GN
☎ (01203) 471084
Fax (01203) 471084
One of 4 sandstone farm cottages, circa 1834, in rural surroundings. Recently converted but with character maintained and offering comfortable accommodation for a small number of guests.
Bedrooms: 2 single, 1 double, 1 twin
Bathrooms: 4 en-suite

Bed & breakfast per night:	£min	£max
Single	18.00	20.00
Double	34.00	35.00

Parking for 5

Woodlands

COMMENDED
Oak Lane, Allesley, Coventry CV5 9BX
☎ (01676) 522688 & (0585) 520147
Comfortable, detached and privately situated in a beautiful country lane only 150 yards from the A45. Ten minutes from NEC and Birmingham Airport, ideal for Coventry, Stratford-upon-Avon and Warwick.
Bedrooms: 3 twin
Bathrooms: 1 en-suite, 1 public

Bed & breakfast per night:	£min	£max
Single	19.00	24.50
Double	36.00	42.00

Parking for 7

CRAVEN ARMS

Shropshire
Map ref 4A3

Busy village on A49 renowned for its sheep markets. Close to Wenlock Edge and the Longmynd and an ideal centre for walking with many fine views. Nearby Stokesay Castle, a 13th C fortified manor house, the ruins of Hopton Castle and Ludlow.

Castle View

Listed HIGHLY COMMENDED
148 Stokesay, Craven Arms SY7 9AL
☎ (01588) 673712
Large, comfortable stone-built Victorian house. Within easy walking distance of Stokesay Castle and on route of the Shropshire Way.
Bedrooms: 1 double, 1 twin
Bathrooms: 1 en-suite, 1 private

Bed & breakfast per night:	£min	£max
Single	17.00	19.00
Double	35.00	37.00

Parking for 3

CRESSBROOK

Derbyshire
Map ref 4B2

Delightful dale with stone hall and pleasant houses, steep wooded slopes and superb views.

Pancake Row Bed and Breakfast

Listed APPROVED
5 Dale Terrace, Cressbrook, Buxton SK17 8SY
☎ (01298) 872115
Charming and historic apprentice mill worker's terraced cottage facing Cressbrook Mill. Ideal location for walking, cycling, climbing, hacking, fishing and hangliding.
Bedrooms: 1 single, 2 double
Bathrooms: 1 public

Bed & breakfast per night:	£min	£max
Single	16.50	19.00
Double	33.00	38.00

The National Grading and Classification Scheme is explained at the back of this guide.

CRICH

Derbyshire
Map ref 4B2

Home of the National Tramway Museum where visitors can ride on trams along a 1 mile scenic route past reconstructed 19th C buildings. There are also workshops, a power station, an exhibition and a lead-mining display to be seen.

Upper Rosskeen Guesthouse

COMMENDED
Crich, Matlock DE4 5BP
☎ (01773) 857186
Large stone-built property, built 1843 and used as a surgery for 100 years, offering spacious bed and breakfast accommodation. Warm and friendly welcome.
Bedrooms: 2 double
Suite available
Bathrooms: 1 en-suite, 1 public

Bed & breakfast per night:	£min	£max
Single	20.00	25.00
Double	36.00	42.00

Parking for 2

DEDDINGTON

Oxfordshire
Map ref 2C1

Hill Barn
The Little House

See South of England region for full entry details

DEERHURST

Gloucestershire
Map ref 2B1

Deerhurst House

HIGHLY COMMENDED
Deerhurst, Gloucester GL19 4BX
☎ (01684) 292135 & 0850 520051
Fax (01242) 224019
Classical Georgian country house set in 3 acres on edge of ancient riverside village of Deerhurst, midway between Cheltenham, Tewkesbury and Gloucester.
Bedrooms: 1 double, 1 twin
Bathrooms: 2 en-suite

Bed & breakfast per night:	£min	£max
Single	25.00	30.00
Double	40.00	45.00

Parking for 10

DERBY

Derbyshire
Map ref 4B2

Modern industrial city but with ancient origins. There is a wide range of attractions including several museums (notably Royal Crown Derby), a theatre, a concert hall, and the cathedral with fine ironwork and Bess of Hardwick's tomb.
Tourist Information Centre ☎ (01332) 255802

Alambie

COMMENDED
189 Main Road, Morley, Derby
DE7 6DG
☎ (01332) 780349
Fax (01332) 780349
Friendly family bungalow in the country, facing the Rose & Crown public house on the Smalley crossroads, 6 miles from Derby. Non-smoking establishment.
Bedrooms: 1 double, 1 twin, 1 family room
Bathrooms: 3 en-suite

Bed & breakfast per night:	£min	£max
Single	20.00	
Double	35.00	

Half board per person:	£min	£max
Daily	28.00	

Parking for 4

Bonehill Farm

COMMENDED
Etwall Road, Mickleover, Derby
DE3 5DN
☎ (01332) 513553
120-acre mixed farm. Traditional farmhouse in a rural setting, 3 miles from Derby. Alton Towers, the Peak District, historic houses and the Potteries are all within easy reach.
Bedrooms: 1 double, 1 twin, 1 triple
Bathrooms: 1 en-suite, 1 public

Bed & breakfast per night:	£min	£max
Single	16.00	20.00
Double	32.00	36.00

Parking for 6

The symbol after an establishment name indicates that it is a Regional Tourist Board member.

DONNINGTON

Gloucestershire
Map ref 2B1

Holmleigh

Listed APPROVED
Donnington, Moreton-in-Marsh
GL56 0XX
☎ (01451) 830792
15-acre dairy farm. Farmhouse accommodation with friendly welcome. In a peaceful setting with own private lane from the village of Donnington, 1 mile from Stow-on-the-Wold.
Bedrooms: 2 twin
Bathrooms: 1 private, 1 public

Bed & breakfast per night:	£min	£max
Single	12.50	14.00
Double	25.00	28.00

Parking for 3
Open April–October
5

DUNCHURCH

Warwickshire
Map ref 4C3

The 14th C church has a sandstone tower, Norman doorway and Norman font. The northern chapel arcade is Victorian. Nearby is a statue of Lord John Scott, the seafaring sportsman, dating from 1867.

Toft Hill

Listed COMMENDED
Dunchurch, Rugby CV22 6NR
☎ (01788) 810342
Large country house set in mature gardens, half a mile from the centre of Dunchurch on Southam road.
Bedrooms: 1 single, 1 twin, 1 triple
Bathrooms: 1 en-suite, 1 public

Bed & breakfast per night:	£min	£max
Single	19.00	19.00
Double	38.00	38.00

Parking for 5
8

The symbols in each entry give information about services and facilities. A key to these symbols appears at the back of this guide.

DYMOCK

Gloucestershire
Map ref 2B1

Village with one of the most interesting churches in the area, which has extensive Norman work and a fragment of a manuscript copy of St John's Gospel of the 8th C. On the village green is the White House where John Kyrle, the Man of Ross, was born in 1637. Also noted for the Dymock poets.

The White House

Listed COMMENDED

Dymock GL18 2AQ
☎ (01531) 890516 & 890880
Fax (01531) 890333

17th C listed house in the centre of village, surrounded by lovely countryside. Family-run accommodation with a homely and relaxing atmosphere.

Bedrooms: 1 double, 1 triple
Bathrooms: 1 public

Bed & breakfast per night:	£min	£max
Single	16.00	18.00
Double	32.00	32.00

Parking for 4

EASTCOMBE

Gloucestershire
Map ref 2B1

Pretoria Villa

Listed HIGHLY COMMENDED

Wells Road, Eastcombe, Stroud GL6 7EE
☎ (01452) 770435

Cotswold-stone double-fronted detached house, built c1900, with private gardens. In quiet village lane with beautiful views.

Bedrooms: 1 single, 1 double, 1 twin
Bathrooms: 1 en-suite, 2 private, 1 public

Bed & breakfast per night:	£min	£max
Single	20.00	20.00
Double	40.00	40.00

Half board per person:	£min	£max
Daily	32.00	32.00
Weekly	210.00	210.00

Evening meal 1830 (last orders 2030)
Parking for 3
5

ECKINGTON

Hereford and Worcester
Map ref 2B1

Large and expanding village in a fruit growing and market gardening area beside the Avon, which is crossed here by a 15th C bridge. Half-timbered houses are much in evidence.

The Bell Inn

COMMENDED

Church Street, Eckington, Pershore, Worcestershire WR10 3AN
☎ (01386) 750205 & 751073
Fax (01386) 750205

In the centre of Eckington village, offering themed accommodation complemented by good food. Within easy reach of Worcester, Evesham and Cheltenham.

Bedrooms: 2 double, 1 twin, 1 triple
Bathrooms: 4 en-suite

Bed & breakfast per night:	£min	£max
Single	27.50	35.00
Double	50.00	60.00

Half board per person:	£min	£max
Daily	37.50	45.00
Weekly	209.50	252.00

Lunch available
Evening meal 1800 (last orders 2130)
Parking for 14
Cards accepted: Mastercard, Visa, Switch/Delta
90

EDWINSTOWE

Nottinghamshire
Map ref 4C2

Village close to Sherwood Forest, famous for the legend of Robin Hood.

Black Swan

COMMENDED

High Street, Edwinstowe, Mansfield NG21 9QR
☎ (01623) 822598

Built 1540 and in the centre of Robin Hood country. All rooms en-suite. Home-cooked food available all day until 9pm. Large car park at rear.

Bedrooms: 2 double, 1 twin
Bathrooms: 3 en-suite

Bed & breakfast per night:	£min	£max
Single		22.00
Double		36.00

Lunch available
Evening meal 1700 (last orders 2100)
Parking for 30

ELMESTHORPE

Leicestershire
Map ref 4C3

Silhouetted against the horizon, the picturesque church of St Mary has a 17th C tower and 12th or 13th C font and is set in a beautiful churchyard with lovely views.

Water Meadows Farm

Listed COMMENDED

22 Billington Road East, Elmesthorpe, Leicester LE9 7SB
☎ (01455) 843417

Tudor-style, oak-beamed farmhouse with extensive gardens, including 15-acre private conservation area, woodland and stream. Own produce, home cooking. On a private road. Central for visiting many places of scenic and historic interest.

Bedrooms: 2 double, 1 family room
Bathrooms: 1 public

Bed & breakfast per night:	£min	£max
Single	18.00	18.00
Double	30.00	30.00

Half board per person:	£min	£max
Daily	23.00	26.00
Weekly	149.94	171.99

Evening meal from 1900
Parking for 10
1

ENDON

Staffordshire
Map ref 4B2

Village between Stoke-on-Trent and Leek, noted for its well-dressing ceremony on Spring Bank Holiday.

Hollinhurst Farm

Listed COMMENDED

Park Lane, Endon, Stoke-on-Trent ST9 9JB
☎ (01782) 502633

116-acre dairy farm. 17th C farmhouse within easy reach of Potteries, Peak District and Alton Towers. Panoramic views, walking and touring.

Bedrooms: 1 double, 1 twin, 1 family room
Bathrooms: 2 en-suite, 1 private, 1 public

Bed & breakfast per night:	£min	£max
Double	32.00	36.00

Parking for 10
Open February–November

EVESHAM

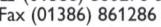

Hereford and Worcester
Map ref 2B1

Market town in the centre of a fruit-growing area. There are pleasant walks along the River Avon and many old houses and inns. A fine 16th C bell tower stands between 2 churches near the medieval Almonry Museum.
Tourist Information Centre ☎ (01386) 446944

Chequers Inn

COMMENDED

Fladbury, Pershore, Worcestershire WR10 2PZ
☎ (01386) 860276 & 860527
Fax (01386) 861286

14th C inn between Evesham and Pershore, on the edge of the Cotswolds. Off B4084 and A44, in a quiet village location, 17 miles from Stratford-upon-Avon.
Bedrooms: 4 double, 4 twin
Bathrooms: 8 en-suite

Bed & breakfast per night:	£min	£max
Single	42.50	
Double	55.00	65.00

Lunch available
Evening meal 1830 (last orders 2130)
Parking for 30
Cards accepted: Amex, Mastercard, Visa, Switch/Delta

Fircroft

COMMENDED

84 Greenhill, Evesham, Worcestershire WR11 4NH
☎ (01386) 45828
Comfortable B & B offering a relaxed and unobtrusive environment. Elegant house in attractive gardens, situated three-quarters of a mile north of town centre. No smoking.
Bedrooms: 1 double, 1 twin, 1 triple
Bathrooms: 1 en-suite, 2 public

Bed & breakfast per night:	£min	£max
Single	25.00	
Double	36.00	42.00

Parking for 6
Open March–October

Park View Hotel

APPROVED

Waterside, Evesham, Worcestershire WR11 6BS
☎ (01386) 442639
Email: mike.spires@btinternet.com
Family-run hotel offering comfortable accommodation in a friendly atmosphere. Riverside situation, close to town centre. Ideal base for touring the Cotswolds and Shakespeare country.
Bedrooms: 10 single, 4 double, 10 twin, 1 triple, 1 family room
Bathrooms: 7 public

Bed & breakfast per night:	£min	£max
Single	20.50	24.00
Double	37.00	41.00

Evening meal 1800 (last orders 1900)
Parking for 50
Cards accepted: Amex, Diners, Mastercard, Visa

EWEN

Gloucestershire
Map ref 2B1

Village in the South Cotswolds of attractive stone cottages and houses.

Wild Duck Inn

COMMENDED

Drakes Island, Ewen, Cirencester GL7 6BY
☎ (01285) 770310 & 770364
Fax (01285) 770924

15th C Cotswold-stone inn, set in a rural position in the village. Two four-poster rooms in the oldest part of the building. All rooms with private facilities. Delightful garden.
Bedrooms: 7 double, 3 twin
Bathrooms: 10 en-suite

Bed & breakfast per night:	£min	£max
Single	49.50	55.00
Double	69.50	90.00

Lunch available
Evening meal 1900 (last orders 2145)
Parking for 50
Cards accepted: Amex, Mastercard, Visa, Switch/Delta

EXHALL

Warwickshire
Map ref 2B1

Blossomfields

Listed COMMENDED

Exhall, Stratford-upon-Avon B49 6EA
☎ (01789) 490345
Fax (01789) 490345
Bed and breakfast in small village six miles north of Stratford-upon-Avon. Lovely country setting.
Bedrooms: 2 double
Bathrooms: 1 public

Bed & breakfast per night:	£min	£max
Single	17.50	
Double	35.00	

Parking for 4

EYAM

Derbyshire
Map ref 4B2

Attractive village famous for the courage it showed during the plague of 1665. The church has several memorials to this time and there is a well-dressing ceremony in August. The fine 17th C manor house of Eyam Hall is open in summer, and Chatsworth is nearby.

Royal Oak

APPROVED

Town Head, Eyam, Hope Valley S32 5RE
☎ (01433) 631390
Quaint pub in the historic and picturesque "plague village" of Eyam in the Peak Park, close to Bakewell and Buxton.
Bedrooms: 1 double, 1 twin, 1 triple
Bathrooms: 3 en-suite

Bed & breakfast per night:	£min	£max
Single	30.00	35.00
Double	40.00	50.00

Half board per person:	£min	£max
Daily	30.00	35.00
Weekly	200.00	240.00

Lunch available

Continued ▶

EYAM

Continued

Evening meal 1900 (last orders 2100)
Parking for 3

FAIRFORD

Gloucestershire
Map ref 2B1

Small town with a 15th C wool church famous for its complete 15th C stained glass windows, interesting carvings and original wall paintings. It is an excellent touring centre and the Cotswolds Wildlife Park is nearby.

East End House

HIGHLY COMMENDED
Fairford GL7 4AP
☎ (01285) 713715
Fax (01285) 713505
Email: 101625.1352comp.com

Spacious accommodation in large Georgian family home in peaceful conservation area. Private parking, gardens, tennis court. Listed building. Family run.
Bedrooms: 1 twin, 1 family room
Bathrooms: 2 private

Bed & breakfast per night:	£min	£max
Single	25.00	30.00
Double	45.00	50.00

Half board per person:	£min	£max
Daily	40.00	45.00
Weekly	295.00	315.00

Parking for 8

Waiten Hill Farm

COMMENDED
Fairford GL7 4JG
☎ (01285) 712652
Fax (01285) 712652
350-acre mixed farm. Imposing 19th C farmhouse, overlooking River Coln, old mill and famous church. Short walk to shops, pubs and restaurants. Ideal for touring the Cotswolds and water parks.
Bedrooms: 2 double, 1 twin
Bathrooms: 1 en-suite, 1 public

Bed & breakfast per night:	£min	£max
Single	20.00	25.00
Double	30.00	35.00

Parking for 8

FARTHINGHOE

Northamptonshire
Map ref 2C1

Greenfield

Listed HIGHLY COMMENDED
Baker Street, Farthinghoe, Brackley NN13 5PH
☎ (01295) 712380
Fax (01295) 712380
Modern, detached property in a picturesque village, close to a 16th C public house which serves meals.
Bedrooms: 1 double, 1 twin
Bathrooms: 1 public

Bed & breakfast per night:	£min	£max
Single	20.00	
Double	40.00	

Parking for 2
Open February–November

FIFIELD

Oxfordshire
Map ref 2B1

Merryfield

See South of England region for full entry details

FILLONGLEY

Warwickshire
Map ref 4B3

Small and tranquil farming village in leafy north Warwickshire, retaining its old character and with many old buildings and thatched cottages.

Hardingwood House

Hardingwood Lane, Fillongley, Coventry CV7 8EL
☎ (01676) 542579
Exquisite Warwickshire barn conversion, in open countryside. Easy access to National Exhibition Centre, airport and motorways.
Bedrooms: 1 double, 1 twin
Bathrooms: 2 en-suite

Bed & breakfast per night:	£min	£max
Single	30.00	30.00
Double	45.00	45.00

FOREST OF DEAN

See under Coleford, Lydney, Newent, Newland

FOWNHOPE

Hereford and Worcester
Map ref 2A1

Attractive village close to the River Wye with black and white cottages and other interesting houses. It has a large church with a Norman tower and a 14th C spire.

Green Man Inn

COMMENDED
Fownhope, Hereford HR1 4PE
☎ (01432) 860243
Fax (01432) 860207
15th C black and white coaching inn, midway between Ross-on-Wye and Hereford, in the picturesque village of Fownhope. On B4224, close to the River Wye and set in the beautiful Wye Valley.
Bedrooms: 1 single, 13 double, 1 twin, 4 triple
Bathrooms: 19 en-suite

Bed & breakfast per night:	£min	£max
Single	33.00	34.00
Double	52.50	54.00

Half board per person:	£min	£max
Daily	38.40	41.00
Weekly	250.00	263.00

Lunch available
Evening meal 1900 (last orders 2100)
Parking for 80
Cards accepted: Amex, Diners, Mastercard, Visa, Switch/Delta

FOXTON

Leicestershire
Map ref 4C3

Attractive village established in the 8th C. The 13th C church contains part of a Saxon Cross and a "Iepers window". The Grand Union Canal passes through the village. Within walking distance is historic Foxton Locks with its unique staircase flight of 10 locks, and Inclined Plane Museum.

The Old Manse

HIGHLY COMMENDED
Swingbridge Street, Foxton, Market Harborough LE16 7RH
☎ (01858) 545456
Period house in large gardens with warm and friendly atmosphere, on edge of conservation village, 3 miles north of Market Harborough. Good food at both local inns.
Bedrooms: 1 double, 2 twin

Bathrooms: 2 en-suite, 1 private

Bed & breakfast per night:	£min	£max
Single	25.00	25.00
Double	40.00	40.00

Parking for 6

FROGGATT

Derbyshire
Map ref 4B2

Small village above which to the east is Froggatt Edge where many well-known climbers have gained experience.

Chequers Inn

HIGHLY COMMENDED

Froggatt, Calver, Sheffield S30 1ZB
☎ (01433) 630231
Fax (01433) 631072

In the heart of the Peak District National Park, 3 miles from Chatsworth, 6 miles from Bakewell. Traditional ales, log fire and always a warm welcome.

Bedrooms: 4 double, 2 twin
Bathrooms: 6 en-suite

Bed & breakfast per night:	£min	£max
Single	44.00	51.00
Double	55.00	66.00

Lunch available
Evening meal 1900 (last orders 2130)
Parking for 60
Cards accepted: Mastercard, Visa, Switch/Delta

GLOUCESTER

Gloucestershire
Map ref 2B1

A Roman city and inland port, its cathedral is one of the most beautiful in Britain. Gloucester's many attractions include museums and the restored warehouses in the Victorian docks containing the National Waterways Museum, Robert Opie Packaging Collection and other attractions.
Tourist Information Centre ☎ (01452) 421188

Merrivale

COMMENDED

Tewkesbury Road, Norton, Gloucester GL2 9LQ
☎ (01452) 730412

Large private house with a pleasant garden, 3 miles north of Gloucester. TV and tea/coffee-making facilities in all bedrooms.

Bedrooms: 2 double, 3 twin, 1 triple
Bathrooms: 1 public, 2 private showers

Bed & breakfast per night:	£min	£max
Single	16.00	17.50
Double	32.00	35.00

Parking for 8

Notley House and Coach House

COMMENDED

93 Hucclecote Road, Hucclecote, Gloucester GL3 3TR
☎ (01452) 611584
Fax (01452) 371229

Affordable quality accommodation. Ideal for historic Gloucester and the Cotswolds. Tastefully furnished en-suite rooms, suites with four-poster bed.

Bedrooms: 1 single, 2 double, 2 twin, 1 triple, 1 family room
Bathrooms: 5 en-suite, 2 private showers

Bed & breakfast per night:	£min	£max
Single	23.50	41.50
Double	38.00	60.00

Half board per person:	£min	£max
Daily	26.00	70.00
Weekly	164.00	440.00

Evening meal 1900 (last orders 2000)
Parking for 8
Cards accepted: Mastercard, Visa

GOODRICH

Hereford and Worcester
Map ref 2A1

Village standing above the River Wye with the magnificent ruins of a red sandstone castle high above it, now in the care of English Heritage.

Brelston Court

COMMENDED

Marstow, Ross-on-Wye, Herefordshire HR9 6HF
☎ (01600) 890490

130-acre arable & livestock farm. Family farm in the Wye Valley. 18th C farmhouse with walled garden, overlooking the Garren. Peaceful rural location, yet easily accessible.

Bedrooms: 2 double
Bathrooms: 2 en-suite, 1 public

Bed & breakfast per night:	£min	£max
Single	25.00	
Double	38.00	45.00

Parking for 4
Open March–November

GOTHERINGTON

Gloucestershire
Map ref 2B1

Pardon Hill Farm

COMMENDED

Gotherington, Cheltenham GL52 4RD
☎ (01242) 672468
Fax (01242) 672468

300-acre mixed farm. Family-run farm. Outstanding views from all rooms. Ideal centre for walking and touring.

Bedrooms: 1 single, 1 double, 1 twin
Bathrooms: 3 en-suite

Bed & breakfast per night:	£min	£max
Single	25.00	25.00
Double	40.00	40.00

Parking for 10

GREAT RISSINGTON

Gloucestershire
Map ref 2B1

One of two villages overlooking the River Windrush near Bourton-on-the-Water.

Lower Farmhouse

Listed COMMENDED

Great Rissington, Cheltenham GL54 2LH
☎ (01451) 810163 & 810187

Grade II listed Georgian home with separate guest rooms in Cotswold barn conversion. On north-west edge of peaceful village, yet close to attractions.

Bedrooms: 1 single, 1 double
Bathrooms: 1 public

Bed & breakfast per night:	£min	£max
Single	16.00	18.00
Double	32.00	36.00

Parking for 4

For further information on accommodation establishments use the coupons at the back of this guide.

GUILSBOROUGH

Northamptonshire
Map ref 4C3

Lively village, situated 500 ft above sea level and close to two large reservoirs that have plenty of water activities. A very old village with much evidence of its history to be seen.

Seven Piers

Listed

Coton, Northampton NN6 8RF
☎ (01604) 740322

Detached, brick house with private garden, close to Ravensthorpe Reservoir, Althorpe House and Coton Manor Gardens. Quiet area.

Bedrooms: 2 single, 1 twin, 1 triple, 1 family room
Bathrooms: 2 en-suite, 1 private, 1 public

Bed & breakfast per night:	£min	£max
Single	15.00	16.00
Double	36.00	40.00

Parking for 3

GUITING POWER

Gloucestershire
Map ref 2B1

Unspoilt village with stone cottages and a green. The Cotswold Farm Park, with a collection of rare breeds, an adventure playground and farm trail, is nearby.

Halfway House

APPROVED

Kineton, Guiting Power, Cheltenham GL54 5UG
☎ (01451) 850344
Fax (01451) 850344

17th C inn serving good food and real ales. A warm retreat in the heart of the Cotswolds.

Bedrooms: 2 double, 1 twin
Bathrooms: 2 public

Bed & breakfast per night:	£min	£max
Single	20.00	20.00
Double	30.00	36.00

Half board per person:	£min	£max
Daily	35.00	35.00
Weekly	200.00	200.00

Lunch available
Evening meal 1830 (last orders 2130)
Parking for 15
Cards accepted: Mastercard, Visa, Switch/Delta

HAMPTON IN ARDEN

West Midlands
Map ref 4B3

Midway between Birmingham and Coventry and with the National Exhibition Centre on the doorstep.

Chelsea Lodge

COMMENDED

48 Meriden Road, Hampton in Arden, Solihull B92 0BT
☎ (01675) 442408
Fax (01675) 442408

Comfortable, refurbished detached property with delightful gardens. Walking distance to Hampton in Arden railway station (direct NEC/Birmingham Airport) and village pubs. Village location yet 3 miles NEC, 4 miles Solihull.

Bedrooms: 3 twin
Bathrooms: 2 en-suite, 1 private

Bed & breakfast per night:	£min	£max
Single	20.00	45.00
Double	40.00	45.00

Parking for 4

The Cottage Guest House

COMMENDED

Kenilworth Road, On A452 to Balsall Common, Hampton in Arden, Solihull B92 0LW
☎ (01675) 442323
Fax (01675) 443323

Charming cottage 2.5 miles from National Exhibition Centre and Birmingham Airport. All bedrooms en-suite with TV, radio alarms, tea and coffee facilities.

Bedrooms: 3 single, 3 double, 3 twin
Bathrooms: 9 en-suite

Bed & breakfast per night:	£min	£max
Single	20.00	28.00
Double	40.00	44.00

Parking for 15

Pear Tree House

HIGHLY COMMENDED

10 Station Road, Hampton in Arden, Solihull B92 0BJ
☎ (01675) 443993
Fax (01675) 443991

Comfortable Victorian house close to National Exhibition Centre and Birmingham Airport. All rooms en-suite and individually furnished. Near local railway station.

Bedrooms: 1 single, 2 twin
Bathrooms: 3 en-suite

Bed & breakfast per night:	£min	£max
Single	25.00	35.00
Double	40.00	45.00

Parking for 4
Cards accepted: Mastercard, Visa

HARTPURY

Gloucestershire
Map ref 2B1

Green Farm

Listed APPROVED

Blackwells End, Hartpury, Gloucester GL19 3DB
☎ (01452) 700048
Fax (01452) 700048

16-acre livestock farm. 17th C farmhouse in quiet location convenient for Forest of Dean, Gloucester, Cheltenham and the Malverns. Mohair centre and local produce.

Bedrooms: 1 single, 1 twin, 1 triple
Bathrooms: 1 private, 1 public

Bed & breakfast per night:	£min	£max
Single	15.00	17.50
Double	36.00	42.00

Parking for 6

HATHERSAGE

Derbyshire
Map ref 4B2

Hillside village in the Peak District, dominated by the church with many good brasses and monuments to the Eyre family which provide a link with Charlotte Bronte. Little John, friend of Robin Hood, is said to be buried here.

Hillfoot Farm

Listed COMMENDED

Castleton Road, Hathersage, Hope Valley S32 1EG
☎ (01433) 651673

Recently built accommodation on to the existing farmhouse. All rooms en-suite with colour TV, tea/coffee facilities. 2 rooms on ground floor, 2 on first floor. Telephone. Large car park.

Bedrooms: 2 double, 1 twin, 1 triple
Bathrooms: 4 en-suite

Bed & breakfast per night:	£min	£max
Single	20.00	37.00
Double	37.00	40.00

Lunch available
Evening meal 1800 (last orders 1900)
Parking for 13

The Old Vicarage

COMMENDED

Church Bank, Hathersage, Hope Valley S32 1AB
☎ (01433) 651099

In 1845 Charlotte Bronte stayed in this listed building which is beside Little John's grave overlooking the Hope Valley. Central for Chatsworth House, the caves, fishing and walking.
Bedrooms: 2 double, 1 twin
Bathrooms: 2 en-suite, 1 private, 2 public

Bed & breakfast per night:	£min	£max
Single	25.00	27.00
Double	44.00	54.00

Parking for 3

The Plough Inn

COMMENDED

Leadmill Bridge, Hathersage, Sheffield S30 1BA
☎ (01433) 650319 & 0850 609414

17th C stone-built inn, formerly a farmhouse, standing in 9 acres of land bounded by the River Derwent.
Bedrooms: 2 double, 1 triple
Bathrooms: 3 en-suite

Bed & breakfast per night:	£min	£max
Single	40.00	45.00
Double	55.00	60.00

Lunch available
Evening meal 1800 (last orders 2130)
Parking for 50
Cards accepted: Mastercard, Visa, Switch/Delta

HENLEY-IN-ARDEN

Warwickshire
Map ref 2B1

Old market town which in Tudor times stood in the Forest of Arden. It has many ancient inns, a 15th C Guildhall and parish church. Coughton Court with its Gunpowder Plot connections is nearby.

Holland Park Farm

COMMENDED

Buckley Green, Henley-in-Arden, Solihull, West Midlands B95 5QF
☎ (01564) 792625
Fax (01564) 792625
100-acre mixed farm. Georgian-style farmhouse situated off A3400 near Henley-in-Arden. Two large twin/family bedrooms en-suite. Good pubs and restaurants nearby.
Bedrooms: 2 triple
Bathrooms: 2 en-suite

Bed & breakfast per night:	£min	£max
Single	20.00	22.00
Double	36.00	38.00

Parking for 5

Irelands Farm

HIGHLY COMMENDED

Irelands Lane, Henley-in-Arden, Solihull, West Midlands B95 5SA
☎ (01564) 792476
220-acre arable farm. Secluded farmhouse in peaceful countryside. Close to Stratford, Warwick, National Exhibition Centre and the Cotswolds. 1 mile off A3400 between Henley and M42.
Bedrooms: 2 double, 1 twin
Bathrooms: 2 en-suite, 1 private

Bed & breakfast per night:	£min	£max
Single	20.00	22.00
Double	35.00	40.00

Parking for 6

National gradings and classifications were correct at the time of going to press but are subject to change. Please check at the time of booking.

HEREFORD

Hereford and Worcester
Map ref 2A1

Agricultural county town, its cathedral containing much Norman work and a large chained library. Among the city's varied attractions are several museums including the Cider Museum and the Old House.
Tourist Information Centre ☎ (01432) 268430

Ashgrove House

HIGHLY COMMENDED

Wellington Marsh, Hereford HR4 8DU
☎ (01432) 830608

Well-appointed accommodation with high standard of furnishings. Quiet, rural location overlooking cider apple orchards. Lovely gardens. 4 miles from Hereford centre.
Bedrooms: 1 single, 1 double, 1 twin
Bathrooms: 2 en-suite, 1 private

Bed & breakfast per night:	£min	£max
Single	20.00	23.00
Double	36.00	42.00

Parking for 3

Breinton Court Lodge

COMMENDED

Lower Breinton, Hereford, Herefordshire HR4 7PG
☎ (01432) 274523 & 760534
Charming country cottage, well maintained. Set in beautiful gardens, 2 miles west of Hereford city and on Wye Valley walk.
Bedrooms: 1 double
Bathrooms: 1 en-suite

Bed & breakfast per night:	£min	£max
Single	25.00	28.00
Double	35.00	40.00

Parking for 8
Cards accepted: Mastercard, Visa, Switch/Delta

Please check prices and other details at the time of booking.

HEREFORD

Continued

Cwm Craig Farm

COMMENDED

Little Dewchurch, Hereford HR2 6PS
☎ (01432) 840250

190-acre arable & livestock farm. Spacious Georgian farmhouse on edge of Wye Valley, surrounded by superb, unspoilt countryside. 5 miles south of Hereford. Easy access from M50.

Bedrooms: 1 double, 1 triple, 1 family room
Bathrooms: 2 en-suite, 2 public

Bed & breakfast per night:	£min	£max
Single	17.00	17.00
Double	30.00	36.00

Parking for 6

Felton House

HIGHLY COMMENDED

Felton, Hereford HR1 3PH
☎ (01432) 820366

The tranquil charm of a Victorian/Edwardian stone rectory. Four-poster and brass beds. Wide breakfast choice, warm welcome. Excellent local inns. Tiny hamlet 8 miles Hereford, Leominster, Bromyard, off A417.

Bedrooms: 1 single, 2 double, 1 twin
Bathrooms: 2 en-suite, 1 private, 1 public

Bed & breakfast per night:	£min	£max
Single	21.00	21.00
Double	42.00	42.00

Parking for 6

Grafton Villa Farm House

HIGHLY COMMENDED

Grafton, Hereford HR2 8ED
☎ (01432) 268689

180-acre mixed farm. Character farmhouse, beautifully furnished with antiques and lovely fabrics, surrounded by peaceful countryside. Ideal for touring Wye Valley. Set back off A49 Hereford/Ross-on-Wye road.

Bedrooms: 1 double, 2 twin
Bathrooms: 2 en-suite, 1 private, 3 public

Bed & breakfast per night:	£min	£max
Single	24.00	25.00
Double	39.00	41.00

Parking for 10
Open February–November

Hedley Lodge

COMMENDED

Belmont Abbey, Hereford HR2 9RZ
☎ (01432) 277475
Fax (01432) 277597

Guesthouse set within the historic estate of Belmont Abbey, a Benedictine monastery on the A465 Hereford to Abergavenny road.

Bedrooms: 8 twin
Bathrooms: 8 en-suite

Bed & breakfast per night:	£min	£max
Single	18.50	35.00
Double	50.00	55.00

Half board per person:	£min	£max
Daily	27.00	

Lunch available
Evening meal 1900 (last orders 1930)
Parking for 200
150

Sink Green Farm

COMMENDED

Rotherwas, Hereford HR2 6LE
☎ (01432) 870223

170-acre livestock farm. 16th C farmhouse on family-run farm. Overlooking River Wye and 3 miles from Hereford city centre. Establishment is non-smoking.

Bedrooms: 2 double, 1 twin
Bathrooms: 3 en-suite

Bed & breakfast per night:	£min	£max
Single	20.00	24.00
Double	38.00	44.00

Parking for 10

HOARWITHY

Hereford and Worcester
Map ref 2A1

Attractive village on the River Wye which is famous for fishing. Its church was built in the 19th C in Italianate style with the help of Italian workers. The interior contains gold mosaics and marble.

Aspen House

COMMENDED

Hoarwithy, Hereford HR2 6QP
☎ (01432) 840353 & 0860 709924
Fax (01432) 840353

Sandstone building dating back to the 1700s, set in attractive village alongside the River Wye amidst the beautiful countryside of the Wye Valley.

Bedrooms: 2 double, 1 twin
Bathrooms: 3 en-suite

Bed & breakfast per night:	£min	£max
Single	25.00	30.00
Double	36.00	40.00

Parking for 7

HOLBECK WOODHOUSE

Nottinghamshire
Map ref 4C2

Browns

Listed HIGHLY COMMENDED

The Old Orchard Cottage, Holbeck, Worksop S80 3NF
☎ (01909) 720659
Fax (01909) 720659

1730 country cottage in delightful 1-acre garden. Previous winner of East Midlands B&B of the Year. Separate lodge accommodation. Cross through the ford in the driveway and stay "somewhere special". 6 miles off junction 30 of M1.

Bedrooms: 1 double, 1 family room
Bathrooms: 2 en-suite

Bed & breakfast per night:	£min	£max
Single	17.00	30.00
Double	40.00	42.00

Parking for 6
8

HOLMESFIELD

Derbyshire
Map ref 4B2

Halfway between Sheffield and Bakewell with easy access to Chesterfield. Consists of 14 hamlets, each with its place within the story of the village.

Springwood House

HIGHLY COMMENDED

Cowley Lane, Holmesfield, Sheffield S18 5SD
☎ (0114) 289 0253 & 0831 398373
Fax (0114) 891365

Comfortable bungalow in 1.5 acres of

garden with glorious views from all windows, in a quiet rural position.
Bedrooms: 1 double, 1 twin
Bathrooms: 1 en-suite, 1 private

Bed & breakfast per night:	£min	£max
Single	20.00	25.00
Double	40.00	45.00

Parking for 12

HOW CAPLE

Hereford and Worcester
Map ref 2A1

Peaceful village in the wooded scenery of the Wye Valley, close to Brockhampton Church with its modern architecture and Burne-Jones' tapestry.

Garraway House

How Caple, Hereford HR1 4SS
☎ (01989) 740253
Fax (01989) 740253
18th C former rectory with Edwardian additions, standing in attractive gardens and grounds. All rooms have en-suite or adjacent private bathrooms. Sitting room with colour TV.
Bedrooms: 1 double, 2 twin
Bathrooms: 1 en-suite, 2 private

Bed & breakfast per night:	£min	£max
Single	18.00	18.00
Double	36.00	36.00

Parking for 3
Open April–September
Cards accepted: Amex

HUSBANDS BOSWORTH

Leicestershire
Map ref 4C3

Mrs J Armitage

APPROVED
31-33 High Street, Husbands Bosworth, Lutterworth LE17 6LJ
☎ (01858) 880066
Village centre home of character on A4304/A427, with wholesome cooking and warm welcome. Good choice of reasonably-priced evening meals at nearby inn.
Bedrooms: 3 twin
Bathrooms: 1 public

Bed & breakfast per night:	£min	£max
Single	15.00	16.50
Double	30.00	33.00

Parking for 6

IRONBRIDGE

Shropshire
Map ref 4A3

Small town on the Severn where the Industrial Revolution began. It has the world's first iron bridge built in 1779. The Ironbridge Gorge Museum, of exceptional interest, comprises a rebuilt turn-of-the-century town and sites spread over 6 square miles.
Tourist Information Centre ☎ (01952) 432166

Barberry Cottage Guesthouse

Listed APPROVED
71 Bower Yard, Ironbridge, Telford TF8 7AZ
☎ (01952) 882110
Set in elevated landscaped gardens on south side of the Severn.
Well-appointed and in a secluded spot.
Bedrooms: 2 single, 1 double, 1 twin
Bathrooms: 1 en-suite, 1 public

Bed & breakfast per night:	£min	£max
Single	22.00	24.00
Double	40.00	44.00

Half board per person:	£min	£max
Daily	27.00	29.00
Weekly	170.00	183.00

Evening meal 1730 (last orders 2030)
Parking for 8
3

Bird in Hand Inn

COMMENDED
Waterloo Street, Ironbridge, Telford TF8 7HG
☎ (01952) 432226
Family-run inn, circa 1774, in the centre of Ironbridge Gorge, with spectacular views over the River Severn and the gorge. All rooms are en-suite and can be adapted to double, twin or single. Extensive menu.
Bedrooms: 1 double, 1 twin, 1 family room
Bathrooms: 3 en-suite

Bed & breakfast per night:	£min	£max
Single	25.00	40.00
Double	35.00	50.00

Half board per person:	£min	£max
Daily	30.00	35.00

Lunch available
Evening meal 1200 (last orders 2200)
Parking for 30
Cards accepted: Mastercard, Visa

Bridge View

HIGHLY COMMENDED
10 Tontine Hill, Ironbridge, Telford TF8 7AL
☎ (01952) 432541 & (0402) 222203
Fax (01952) 432541
Right in the heart of Ironbridge with spectacular views of the bridge. All rooms with en-suite or private bathroom, colour TV, beverage tray. English breakfast. Private car park.
Bedrooms: 3 double, 1 twin, 1 triple
Bathrooms: 4 en-suite, 1 private, 1 public

Bed & breakfast per night:	£min	£max
Single	30.00	35.00
Double	40.00	45.00

Parking for 8

Lord Hill Guest House

Listed APPROVED
Duke Street, Broseley TF12 5LU
☎ (01952) 884270 & 580792
Former public house renovated to a high standard. Easy access to Ironbridge, Bridgnorth, Shrewsbury and Telford town centre.
Bedrooms: 1 single, 1 double, 5 twin
Bathrooms: 3 private, 2 public, 1 private shower

Bed & breakfast per night:	£min	£max
Single	15.00	18.00
Double	32.00	34.00

Parking for 9
8

All accommodation in this guide has been graded, or is awaiting a grading, by a trained Tourist Board inspector.

For farm holidays and accommodation suitable for young people and organised groups, please refer to the special sections at the back of this guide.

KENILWORTH

Warwickshire
Map ref 4B3

The main feature of the town is the ruined 12th C castle. It has many royal associations but was damaged by Cromwell. A good base for visiting Coventry, Leamington Spa and Warwick.
Tourist Information Centre ☎ (01926) 852595 or 850708

Oldwych House Farm

COMMENDED

Oldwych Lane, Fen End, Kenilworth CV8 1NR
☎ (01676) 533552
35-acre mixed farm. 14th C half-timbered farmhouse in open countryside. 2 pools, sheep, horses, abundant wildlife. Resident artist's gallery. 6 miles from NEC and NAC, 8 miles Warwick, 12 miles Stratford-upon-Avon, 4 miles junction 5 of M42.
Bedrooms: 2 double
Bathrooms: 2 en-suite

Bed & breakfast per night:	£min	£max
Single	25.00	30.00
Double	40.00	45.00

Parking for 6
Open February–December

KETTERING

Northamptonshire
Map ref 3A2

Ancient industrial town based on shoe-making. Wicksteed Park to the south has many children's amusements. The splendid 17th C ducal mansion of Boughton House is to the north.
Tourist Information Centre ☎ (01536) 410266

Dairy Farm

COMMENDED

Cranford St Andrew, Kettering NN14 4AQ
☎ (01536) 330273
350-acre mixed farm. 17th C thatched house with inglenook fireplaces and a garden with an ancient circular dovecote and mature trees. Good food.
Bedrooms: 2 double, 1 twin
Bathrooms: 2 en-suite, 1 public

Bed & breakfast per night:	£min	£max
Single	22.00	28.00
Double	44.00	56.00

Half board per person:	£min	£max
Daily	34.00	40.00

Evening meal 1900 (last orders 1200)
Parking for 5

KIDDERMINSTER

Hereford and Worcester
Map ref 4B3

The town is the centre for carpet manufacturing. It has a medieval church with good monuments and a statue of Sir Rowland Hill, a native of the town and founder of the penny post. West Midlands Safari Park is nearby. Severn Valley Railway station.

Cedars Hotel

COMMENDED

Mason Road, Kidderminster, Worcestershire DY11 6AG
☎ (01562) 515595
Fax (01562) 751103

Charming conversion of a Georgian building close to the River Severn, Severn Valley Railway and Worcestershire countryside. 15 minutes from M5.
Bedrooms: 2 single, 8 double, 6 twin, 4 triple, 2 family rooms
Bathrooms: 22 en-suite

Bed & breakfast per night:	£min	£max
Single	33.25	55.25
Double	45.75	67.50

Evening meal 1900 (last orders 2030)
Parking for 23
Cards accepted: Amex, Diners, Mastercard, Visa

ACCESSIBILITY

Look for the symbols which indicate accessibility for wheelchair users. These are described in detail at the front of this guide.

KINGSTONE

Hereford and Worcester
Map ref 2A1

Village near the Golden Valley, Abbey Dore Church and Kilpeck Church.

Mill Orchard

HIGHLY COMMENDED

Kingstone, Hereford HR2 9ES
☎ (01981) 250326
Email: handjcleveland @compuserve.com
Bed and breakfast with en-suite or private bathroom. Evening meals by arrangement.
Bedrooms: 2 double, 1 twin
Bathrooms: 2 en-suite, 1 private

Bed & breakfast per night:	£min	£max
Single	25.00	30.00
Double	36.00	40.00

Parking for 4
Open February–November

LEA MARSTON

West Midlands
Map ref 4B3

Water Park Lodge

COMMENDED

Kingsbury Road, Lea Marston, Sutton Coldfield B76 0DE
☎ (01675) 470533
Fax (01675) 470533
Bed and breakfast accommodation, all rooms en-suite.
Bedrooms: 1 single, 3 double, 1 twin, 1 triple
Bathrooms: 6 en-suite

Bed & breakfast per night:	£min	£max
Single	35.50	35.50
Double	55.00	55.00

Half board per person:	£min	£max
Daily	50.50	70.00

Parking for 24
Cards accepted: Mastercard, Visa

Information on accommodation listed in this guide has been supplied by the proprietors. As changes may occur you are advised to check details at the time of booking.

LEAMINGTON SPA

Warwickshire
Map ref 4B3

18th C spa town with many fine Georgian and Regency houses. Tea can be taken in the 19th C Pump Room. The attractive Jephson Gardens are laid out alongside the river and there is a museum and art gallery.
Tourist Information Centre ☎ (01926) 311470

Adelaide

COMMENDED

15 Adelaide Road, Leamington Spa CV31 3PN
☎ (01926) 450633
Fax (01926) 450633

Charming Victorian town house with original features, in beautiful town centre conservation area. Both rooms en-suite with colour TV and coffee-making facilities. Close to NEC and NAC.

Bedrooms: 1 double, 1 triple
Bathrooms: 2 en-suite

Bed & breakfast per night:	£min	£max
Single	17.50	27.50
Double	35.00	45.00

Parking for 3

Bungalow Farm

COMMENDED

Windmill Hill, Cubbington, Leamington Spa CV32 7LW
☎ (01926) 423276
Fax (01926) 887357

Attractive and spacious detached private residence, offering comfortable bed and breakfast accommodation. Both rooms have colour TV, radio/alarm clock and tea/coffee-making facilities.

Bedrooms: 1 double, 1 twin
Bathrooms: 1 en-suite, 1 public

Bed & breakfast per night:	£min	£max
Single	18.00	20.00
Double	36.00	50.00

Parking for 10

The symbols in each entry give information about services and facilities. A key to these symbols appears at the back of this guide.

8 Clarendon Crescent

HIGHLY COMMENDED

Leamington Spa CV32 5NR
☎ (01926) 429840

Elegant Regency house situated in a quiet backwater of Leamington Spa, 5 minutes' walk from town centre, overlooking private dell.

Bedrooms: 2 single, 1 double, 1 twin
Bathrooms: 3 en-suite, 1 private

Bed & breakfast per night:	£min	£max
Single	30.00	30.00
Double	50.00	50.00

Parking for 1

Corkhill Bed and Breakfast

APPROVED

27 Newbold Street, Leamington Spa CV32 4HN
☎ (01926) 336303
Fax (01926) 336303

Regency house with garden in town centre. Adjacent to Royal Spa Centre, Jephson Gardens, Newbold Comyn Park and River Leam. Close to bus, coach and railway station.

Bedrooms: 1 single, 1 double, 1 twin
Bathrooms: 3 en-suite

Bed & breakfast per night:	£min	£max
Single	20.00	30.00
Double	40.00	50.00

Parking for 1

The Guys Cliffe Guest House

COMMENDED

157 Rugby Road, Milverton, Leamington Spa CV32 6DJ
☎ (01926) 336217

Large Edwardian town house, centrally situated within walking distance of the town centre.

Bedrooms: 1 single, 2 double, 2 twin, 1 family room
Bathrooms: 6 en-suite

Bed & breakfast per night:	£min	£max
Single	22.50	27.50
Double	45.00	55.00

Parking for 4

Hill Farm

COMMENDED

Lewis Road, Radford Semele, Leamington Spa CV31 1UX
☎ (01926) 337571

350-acre mixed farm. Farmhouse set in large attractive garden, 2 miles from Leamington town centre and close to Warwick Castle and Stratford-upon-Avon.

Bedrooms: 3 double, 2 twin
Bathrooms: 3 en-suite, 1 public

Bed & breakfast per night:	£min	£max
Single	20.00	20.00
Double	36.00	40.00

Parking for 10

The Orchard

Listed APPROVED

3 Sherbourne Terrace, Clarendon Street, Leamington Spa CV32 5SP
☎ (01926) 428198

Victorian double-fronted terrace with walled garden. 5 minutes' walk to town centre. Overseas visitors and children welcome.

Bedrooms: 1 single, 1 twin, 1 triple
Bathrooms: 2 public

Bed & breakfast per night:	£min	£max
Single	17.00	18.00
Double	34.00	36.00

Half board per person:	£min	£max
Daily	22.00	23.00
Weekly	130.00	137.00

Lunch available
Evening meal from 1800

Snowford Hall

COMMENDED

Snowford Hall Farm, Hunningham, Leamington Spa CV33 9ES
☎ (01926) 632297
Fax (01926) 633599

200-acre arable farm. 18th C farmhouse off the Fosse Way, on the edge of Hunningham village. On elevated ground overlooking quiet surrounding countryside.

Bedrooms: 1 double, 2 twin
Bathrooms: 1 en-suite, 1 public, 1 private shower

Bed & breakfast per night:	£min	£max
Double	36.00	40.00

Parking for 4

LEAMINGTON SPA

Continued

Stonehouse Farm

Listed COMMENDED

Leicester Lane, Cubbington Heath, Leamington Spa CV32 6QZ
☎ (01926) 336370
Friendly, Grade II listed Queen Anne farmhouse, with extensive views over Warwickshire's beautiful countryside. A mile from the Royal Showground and close to Leamington Spa, Warwick and Stratford.
Bedrooms: 3 twin
Bathrooms: 1 en-suite, 1 public

Bed & breakfast per night:	£min	£max
Single	21.00	27.00
Double	36.00	43.00

Evening meal from 1930
Parking for 6

LECHLADE

Gloucestershire
Map ref 2B1

Attractive village on the River Thames and a popular spot for boating. It has a number of fine Georgian houses and a 15th C church. Nearby is Kelmscott Manor, with its William Morris furnishings, and 18th C Buscot House (National Trust).

Apple Tree House

Buscot, Faringdon, Oxfordshire SN7 8DA
☎ (01367) 252592
Listed property offering comfortable B & B in National Trust village near Lechlade. River Thames 5 minutes' walk through village. Large garden and car park.
Bedrooms: 2 double, 1 twin
Bathrooms: 1 en-suite, 1 public

Bed & breakfast per night:	£min	£max
Single	23.00	
Double	36.00	

Parking for 8

A key to symbols can be found inside the back cover flap.

Cambrai Lodge

Listed COMMENDED

Oak Street, Lechlade GL7 3AY
☎ (01367) 253173 & 0860 150467
Friendly, family-run guesthouse, recently modernised, close to River Thames. Ideal base for touring the Cotswolds. Four-poster bedroom, garden and ample parking.
Bedrooms: 2 single, 2 double
Bathrooms: 2 en-suite, 1 public

Bed & breakfast per night:	£min	£max
Single	21.00	30.00
Double	34.00	42.00

Parking for 11

LEDBURY

Hereford and Worcester
Map ref 2B1

Town with cobbled streets and many black and white timbered houses, including the 17th C market house and old inns. Nearby is Eastnor Castle with an interesting collection of tapestries and armour.
Tourist Information Centre ☎ (01531) 636147

Church Farm

Listed COMMENDED

Coddington, Ledbury, Herefordshire HR8 1JJ
☎ (01531) 640271

100-acre mixed farm. Black and white 16th C listed farmhouse in a quiet location. Malvern Hills 4 miles, Ledbury 4.5 miles. Warm welcome, log fires and home cooking.
Bedrooms: 2 double, 1 twin
Bathrooms: 1 public

Bed & breakfast per night:	£min	£max
Single	21.00	
Double	42.00	

Half board per person:	£min	£max
Daily	32.00	

Evening meal from 1830
Parking for 3
Open February–November

Kilmory

HIGHLY COMMENDED

Bradlow, Ledbury, Herefordshire HR8 1JF
☎ (01531) 631951
Detached dormer bungalow with attractive gardens, located on the outskirts of Ledbury and with wonderful views of the Malverns.
Bedrooms: 1 double, 1 twin
Bathrooms: 2 private

Bed & breakfast per night:	£min	£max
Single	20.00	20.00
Double	36.00	40.00

Parking for 4

Mainstone House

Listed COMMENDED

Trumpet, Ledbury, Herefordshire HR8 2RA
☎ (01531) 670230
Large 17th C former farmhouse with wealth of exposed beams. Four miles from Ledbury towards Hereford. Old world pub opposite.
Bedrooms: 1 double, 1 family room
Bathrooms: 2 private

Bed & breakfast per night:	£min	£max
Single	16.00	16.00
Double	32.00	32.00

Parking for 8

White House

COMMENDED

Aylton, Ledbury, Herefordshire HR8 2RQ
☎ (01531) 670349
Fax (01531) 670349

Listed 17th C old beamed farmhouse set in 2 acres of mature garden. Very comfortable and peaceful. Both bedrooms en-suite.
Bedrooms: 1 double, 1 triple
Bathrooms: 2 en-suite

Bed & breakfast per night:	£min	£max
Single	25.00	25.00
Double	40.00	40.00

Parking for 10

LEEK

Staffordshire
Map ref 4B2

Old silk and textile town, with some interesting buildings and a number of inns dating from the 17th C. Its art gallery has displays of embroidery. Brindley Mill, designed by James Brindley, has been restored as a museum.
Tourist Information Centre ☎ (01538) 483741

Abbey Inn

COMMENDED

Abbey Green Road, Leek ST13 8SA
☎ (01538) 382865
Fax (01538) 398604
Email: abbeyinn@fenetre.co.uk
17th C inn with accommodation in a separate annexe, set in beautiful countryside, 1 mile from the town and just off the main A523.
Bedrooms: 2 single, 4 double, 1 twin
Bathrooms: 7 en-suite

Bed & breakfast per night:	£min	£max
Single	27.00	30.00
Double	42.00	46.00

Lunch available
Evening meal 1830 (last orders 2100)
Parking for 60
Cards accepted: Amex, Diners, Mastercard, Visa, Switch/Delta

Three Horseshoes Inn & Restaurant

COMMENDED

Buxton Road, Blackshaw Moor, Leek ST13 8TW
☎ (01538) 300296
Fax (01538) 300320

Log fire, slate floor, oak and pine beams, good food and wines. Cottage-style rooms. Convenient for Peak District National Park and Alton Towers.
Bedrooms: 4 double, 2 twin
Bathrooms: 6 en-suite

Bed & breakfast per night:	£min	£max
Single	45.00	55.00
Double	50.00	65.00

Half board per person:	£min	£max
Daily	45.00	55.00

Lunch available
Evening meal 1900 (last orders 2100)
Parking for 100
Cards accepted: Amex, Mastercard, Visa, Switch/Delta

LEICESTER

Leicestershire
Map ref 4C3

Modern industrial city with a wide variety of attractions including Roman remains, ancient churches, Georgian houses and a Victorian clock tower. Excellent shopping precincts, arcades and market, museums, theatres, concert hall and sports and leisure centres.
Tourist Information Centre ☎ (0116) 265 0555

Stanfre' House Hotel

APPROVED

265 London Road, Leicester LE2 3BE
☎ (0116) 270 4294
Family-run hotel on the A6, 1 mile from the city centre and close to the university, racecourse, De Montfort Hall and railway station.
Bedrooms: 3 single, 1 double, 6 twin, 1 triple
Bathrooms: 2 public

Bed & breakfast per night:	£min	£max
Single	20.00	
Double	34.00	

Parking for 6

LEOMINSTER

Hereford and Worcester
Map ref 2A1

The town owed its prosperity to wool and has many interesting buildings, notably the timber-framed Grange Court, a former town hall. The impressive Norman priory church has 3 naves and a ducking stool. Berrington Hall (National Trust) is nearby.
Tourist Information Centre ☎ (01568) 616460

Heath House

HIGHLY COMMENDED

Stoke Prior, Leominster, Herefordshire HR6 0NF
☎ (01568) 760385
Fax (01568) 760385
Attractive stone farmhouse full of beams and history, set in peaceful countryside. Room to move and relax in comfort.
Bedrooms: 1 double, 2 twin
Bathrooms: 2 en-suite, 1 private

Bed & breakfast per night:	£min	£max
Single	25.00	27.00
Double	44.00	48.00

Half board per person:	£min	£max
Daily	37.00	39.00
Weekly	238.00	252.00

Evening meal 1900 (last orders 2000)
Parking for 6
Open March–November

Lower Bache House

HIGHLY COMMENDED

Kimbolton, Leominster, Herefordshire HR6 0ER
☎ (01568) 750304

Award-winning 17th C Herefordshire house, set in 14 acres of private nature reserve. Three suites, each with bedroom, bath/shower room and private sitting room. Renowned cuisine. Illustrated brochure.
Bedrooms: 3 double, 1 twin
Bathrooms: 4 en-suite

Bed & breakfast per night:	£min	£max
Single	31.50	
Double	53.00	

Half board per person:	£min	£max
Daily	36.00	45.00
Weekly	238.00	280.00

Lunch available
Evening meal (last orders 1230)
Parking for 6

National gradings and classifications were correct at the time of going to press but are subject to change. Please check at the time of booking.

LEOMINSTER

Continued

Tyn-Y-Coed

COMMENDED

Shobdon, Leominster, Herefordshire HR6 9NY
☎ (01568) 708277
Fax (01568) 708277
Country house in large garden on Mortimer Trail, close to Croft Castle and Berrington Hall (NT). Convenient for Leominster, Ludlow and Presteigne.
Bedrooms: 1 double, 1 twin
Bathrooms: 1 en-suite, 1 public

Bed & breakfast per night:	£min	£max
Single	16.00	20.00
Double	32.00	40.00

Parking for 2
Open April–October

Woonton Court Farm

COMMENDED

Leysters, Leominster, Herefordshire HR6 0HL
☎ (01568) 750232
Fax (01568) 750232
2-acre mixed farm. Tudor farmhouse offering warm welcome to all. Comfortable bedrooms and delicious breakfasts. Guernsey milk, free-range eggs. Freedom to walk on farm and enjoy wildlife.
Bedrooms: 1 double, 1 twin, 1 triple
Bathrooms: 2 en-suite, 1 private

Bed & breakfast per night:	£min	£max
Single	18.50	18.50
Double	36.00	

Half board per person:	£min	£max
Daily	25.00	
Weekly	175.00	200.00

Evening meal 1800 (last orders 2200)
Parking for 3

Please mention this guide when making your booking.

Half board prices are given per person, but in some cases these may be based on double/twin occupancy.

LICHFIELD

Staffordshire
Map ref 4B3

Lichfield is Dr Samuel Johnson's birthplace and commemorates him with a museum and statue. The 13th C cathedral has 3 spires and the west front is full of statues. Among the attractive town buildings is the Heritage Centre. The Regimental Museum is in Whittington Barracks.
Tourist Information Centre ☎ (01543) 252109

Altair House

Listed COMMENDED

21 Shakespeare Avenue, Lichfield WS14 9BE
☎ (01543) 252900 & 0973 688331
Semi-detached house in south Lichfield. Five minutes from rail and bus stations, 15 minutes from National Exhibition Centre.
Bedrooms: 1 single, 2 twin
Bathrooms: 2 public

Bed & breakfast per night:	£min	£max
Single	17.00	18.00
Double	33.00	33.00

Parking for 4

20 Beacon Street

Listed COMMENDED

Lichfield WS13 7AD
☎ (01543) 262338
Spacious and elegant Georgian town house with a welcoming atmosphere, conveniently situated near Lichfield Cathedral and all amenities. On Heart of England Way.
Bedrooms: 2 double
Bathrooms: 1 en-suite, 1 public, 1 private shower

Bed & breakfast per night:	£min	£max
Single	20.00	25.00
Double	38.00	40.00

Parking for 5

Coppers End

COMMENDED

Walsall Road, Muckley Corner, Lichfield WS14 0BG
☎ (01543) 372910
Fax (01543) 372910

Detached guesthouse of character and charm in its own grounds. Rural location with easy access to M6, Birmingham, Lichfield and M1. Residential licence. Telephone for weekly half-board rates.
Bedrooms: 1 single, 2 double, 2 twin
Bathrooms: 1 en-suite, 1 public

Bed & breakfast per night:	£min	£max
Single	23.00	30.00
Double	36.00	42.00

Half board per person:	£min	£max
Daily	30.50	37.50

Evening meal 1900 (last orders 2030)
Parking for 10
Cards accepted: Amex, Diners, Mastercard, Visa, Switch/Delta

For ideas on places to visit refer to the introduction at the beginning of this section.

The Farmhouse

HIGHLY COMMENDED

Lysway Lane, Longdon Green, Rugeley WS15 4PZ
☎ (0121) 378 4552 & (01543) 490416
Fax (0121) 311 2915
Country residence with elegant bedrooms, cosy lounge. Within easy reach of the National Exhibition Centre, Belfry sporting club, Shugborough Hall. Lichfield 3.5 miles. Evening meals by arrangement.
Bedrooms: 1 single, 1 double, 1 twin
Bathrooms: 1 private, 1 public

Bed & breakfast per night:	£min	£max
Single	25.00	30.00
Double	38.00	40.00

Evening meal 1900 (last orders 2100)
Parking for 6

LITTLE PRESTON

Northamptonshire
Map ref 2C1

Bee Close House

Listed COMMENDED

Little Preston, Daventry NN11 3TF
☎ (01327) 361641
Fax (01327) 361641
Detached modern house, in a quiet rural area, 6.5 miles from Daventry,

between Preston Cupes and Maidford Non-smokers only, please.
Wheelchair access category 3
Bedrooms: 1 double
Bathrooms: 1 en-suite, 1 public

Bed & breakfast per night:	£min	£max
Single	16.00	
Double	32.00	36.00

Parking for 3

LITTON

Derbyshire
Map ref 4B2

Hall Farm House

COMMENDED
Litton, Buxton SK17 8QP
☎ (01298) 872172
Friendly family home with spacious accommodation. Ideal base for touring by car or foot around the Peak District area.
Bedrooms: 1 double, 1 twin
Bathrooms: 1 en-suite, 1 private, 1 public

Bed & breakfast per night:	£min	£max
Double	36.00	40.00

Open January–November
2 SP

LLANGARRON

Hereford and Worcester
Map ref 2A1

Village near the splendid ruins of Goodrich Castle.

Panbrook House

Llangarron, Ross-on-Wye, Herefordshire HR9 6NW
☎ (01989) 770239
16th C country house set in mature gardens, paddocks adjoining. Quiet, relaxed atmosphere. Good home-cooked meals, vegetables fresh from garden when in season.
Bedrooms: 2 double, 1 twin
Bathrooms: 1 public

Bed & breakfast per night:	£min	£max
Single	17.50	22.00
Double	35.00	35.00

Half board per person:	£min	£max
Daily	30.00	34.50
Weekly	210.00	

Evening meal 1900 (last orders 1900)
Parking for 6
6

LONG BUCKBY

Northamptonshire
Map ref 4C3

Stretching for one and a half miles, this is a village with individuality and character.

Murcott Mill

COMMENDED
Murcott, Long Buckby, Northampton NN6 7QR
☎ (01327) 842236
100-acre livestock farm. Imposing Georgian mill house overlooking open countryside. Recently renovated to a high standard, with open fires and en-suite bedrooms. Ideal stopover for M1 travellers.
Bedrooms: 1 double, 2 twin
Bathrooms: 3 en-suite, 1 public

Bed & breakfast per night:	£min	£max
Single	18.00	20.00
Double	36.00	40.00

Evening meal 1900 (last orders 2030)
Parking for 12

LONG COMPTON

Warwickshire
Map ref 2B1

Village with a restored church displaying Norman doorways and a thatched room above the lych gate. Several interesting old houses exist in the area.

Butlers Road Farm

Listed COMMENDED
Long Compton, Shipston-on-Stour CV36 5JZ
☎ (01608) 684262
Fax (01608) 684262
115-acre dairy farm. Listed old stone farmhouse situated adjacent to A3400 between Oxford and Stratford-upon-Avon.
Bedrooms: 1 double, 1 twin
Bathrooms: 1 public

Bed & breakfast per night:	£min	£max
Single	18.00	
Double	34.00	

Parking for 4

Establishments should be open throughout the year, unless otherwise stated.

The Red Lion Hotel

COMMENDED
Main Street, Long Compton, Shipston-on-Stour CV36 5JS
☎ (01608) 684221
Fax (01608) 684221
Friendly village inn dating from 1748. Centrally located for places of interest in Stratford, Warwick and Cotswold areas.
Bedrooms: 1 single, 2 double, 1 twin, 1 triple
Bathrooms: 5 en-suite

Bed & breakfast per night:	£min	£max
Single		29.50
Double		45.00

Lunch available
Evening meal 1800 (last orders 2130)
Parking for 60
Cards accepted: Mastercard, Visa, Switch/Delta
10 SP

LONGHOPE

Gloucestershire
Map ref 2B1

Set in beautiful hilly countryside on the edge of the Forest of Dean, this ancient village is mentioned in the Domesday Book. The church is 12th C and other buildings of historic interest include the medieval Harts Barn.

Royal Spring Fruit Farm

COMMENDED
Longhope GL17 0PY
☎ (01452) 830550
14-acre fruit farm. Spacious 16th C beamed farmhouse backing on to own orchards and woodland. Local and home-grown produce. Centre for Forest of Dean, Gloucester, Wye Valley and Cotswolds.
Bedrooms: 1 single, 1 double, 1 twin
Bathrooms: 1 en-suite, 2 private

Bed & breakfast per night:	£min	£max
Single	17.00	19.00
Double	34.00	38.00

Half board per person:	£min	£max
Daily	23.00	25.00
Weekly		140.00

Evening meal 1900 (last orders 2100)
Parking for 20
4 OAP

LOUGHBOROUGH

Leicestershire
Map ref 4C3

Industrial town famous for its bell foundry and 47-bell Carillon Tower. The Great Central Railway operates steam railway rides of over 8 miles through the attractive scenery of Charnwood Forest.
Tourist Information Centre ☎ (01509) 218113

Garendon Park Hotel

COMMENDED

92 Leicester Road, Loughborough LE11 2AQ
☎ (01509) 236557
Fax (01509) 265559
You are assured of a warm, friendly welcome and high standards in bright, comfortable surroundings. Five minutes from town centre. Local attractions include Great Central Railway, Bell Foundry and surrounding countryside.
Bedrooms: 3 single, 2 double, 3 twin, 1 triple
Bathrooms: 7 en-suite, 1 public

Bed & breakfast per night:	£min	£max
Single	23.00	35.00
Double	30.00	45.00

Half board per person:	£min	£max
Daily	28.50	43.50

Evening meal 1830 (last orders 2030)
Cards accepted: Amex, Mastercard, Visa, Switch/Delta
15

LUDLOW

Shropshire
Map ref 4A3

Outstandingly interesting border town with a magnificent castle high above the River Teme, 2 half-timbered old inns and an impressive 15th C church. The Reader's House, with its 3-storey Jacobean porch, should also be seen.
Tourist Information Centre ☎ (01584) 875053

Bull Hotel

COMMENDED

14 The Bull Ring, Ludlow SY8 1AD
☎ (01584) 873611
Fax (01584) 873666
Oldest pub in Ludlow, earliest mention c1343. Was known as Peter of Proctors House and probably dates back to c1199.
Bedrooms: 2 double, 1 twin, 1 triple
Bathrooms: 4 en-suite

Bed & breakfast per night:	£min	£max
Single	30.00	30.00
Double	43.00	43.00

Lunch available
Parking for 8
Cards accepted: Amex, Mastercard, Visa
40

The Church Inn

COMMENDED

Butter Cross, Ludlow SY8 1AW
☎ (01584) 872174
Fax (01584) 877146
Georgian inn, centrally located on one of the most ancient sites in Ludlow. Good food and CAMRA listed for ales.
Bedrooms: 5 double, 2 twin, 1 triple
Bathrooms: 8 en-suite

Bed & breakfast per night:	£min	£max
Single	28.00	45.00
Double	45.00	45.00

Lunch available
Evening meal 1800 (last orders 2100)
Cards accepted: Mastercard, Visa

Corndene

COMMENDED

Coreley, Ludlow SY8 3AW
☎ (01584) 890324
Country house of character in the heart of rural Shropshire. Beautiful and secluded situation (Ludlow 7 miles). Spacious en-suite rooms, friendly and relaxing atmosphere. Visitors' kitchen for preparation of own snacks and light meals.
Wheelchair access category 1♿
Bedrooms: 3 twin
Bathrooms: 3 en-suite

Bed & breakfast per night:	£min	£max
Single	24.00	27.00
Double	42.00	46.00

Parking for 5
Open March–November

The Hen and Chickens

Listed APPROVED

103 Old Street, Ludlow SY8 1NU
☎ (01584) 874318
Small local pub built c1760. Family-run and offering clean, comfortable, friendly accommodation.
Bedrooms: 2 single, 2 double, 1 twin
Bathrooms: 2 public

Bed & breakfast per night:	£min	£max
Single	17.00	22.00
Double	34.00	44.00

Parking for 6

Longlands

COMMENDED

Woodhouse Lane, Richards Castle, Ludlow SY8 4EU
☎ (01584) 831636
35-acre livestock farm. Farmhouse set in lovely rural landscape. Home-grown produce. Convenient for Ludlow, Mortimer Forest and Croft Castle. Interesting 14th C church and remains of 11th C castle in village.
Bedrooms: 1 double, 1 twin
Suite available
Bathrooms: 1 en-suite, 1 private

Bed & breakfast per night:	£min	£max
Double	40.00	

Half board per person:	£min	£max
Daily	33.00	

Evening meal 1830 (last orders 1930)
Parking for 2

The Moor Hall

HIGHLY COMMENDED

Cleedownton, Ludlow SY8 3EG
☎ (01584) 823209 & 823333
Fax (01584) 823387

Built c1789 and set in 5 acres of mature grounds with pools, amid unspoilt countryside and yet close to Ludlow. Relaxed, informal atmosphere. Fishing.
Bedrooms: 2 double, 1 twin
Bathrooms: 3 en-suite

Bed & breakfast per night:	£min	£max
Single	22.00	28.00
Double	25.00	30.00

Half board per person:	£min	£max
Daily	40.00	45.00

Evening meal 1900 (last orders 2000)
Parking for 12
25

Number Twenty Eight

HIGHLY COMMENDED

28 Lower Broad Street, Ludlow
SY8 1PQ
☎ (01584) 876996
Fax (01584) 876996
Email: ross.no28@etinternet.com

Period town houses of great charm and character, centrally situated in old Ludlow town, near river. All rooms individually furnished, providing en-suite accommodation.

Bedrooms: 4 double, 1 twin, 1 triple
Bathrooms: 6 en-suite, 1 public

Bed & breakfast per night:	£min	£max
Single	35.00	60.00
Double	50.00	65.00

Evening meal 1930 (last orders 2030)
Cards accepted: Amex, Mastercard, Visa

Studley Cottage

COMMENDED

Studley, Clee Hill, Ludlow SY8 3NP
☎ (01584) 890990
Fax (01584) 891265

Comfortable spacious house, nestling on Clee Hill common. Enjoying magnificent views from landscaped gardens, offering immediate access to long country walks. Double and twin are en-suite, singles share bathroom.

Bedrooms: 2 single, 1 double, 1 twin
Bathrooms: 2 en-suite, 1 private, 1 public

Bed & breakfast per night:	£min	£max
Single	20.00	20.00
Double	40.00	40.00

Half board per person:	£min	£max
Daily	30.00	30.00
Weekly	190.00	190.00

Evening meal 1830 (last orders 1900)
Parking for 8
Open March–November

You are advised to confirm your booking in writing.

Map references apply to the colour maps at the back of this guide.

The Wheatsheaf Inn

COMMENDED

Lower Broad Street, Ludlow
SY8 1PQ
☎ (01584) 872980
Fax (01584) 877990

Family-run mid-17th C beamed inn, 100 yards from the town centre, nestling under Ludlow's historic 13th C Broad Gate, the last remaining of 7 town gates.

Bedrooms: 4 double, 1 twin
Bathrooms: 5 en-suite

Bed & breakfast per night:	£min	£max
Single	25.00	35.00
Double	40.00	40.00

Lunch available
Evening meal 1830 (last orders 2100)
Cards accepted: Mastercard, Visa, Switch/Delta

LYDNEY

Gloucestershire
Map ref 2B1

Small town in the Forest of Dean close to the River Severn, where Roman remains have been found. It has a steam centre with engines, coaches and wagons.

Treetops

HIGHLY COMMENDED

Viney Hill, Lydney GL15 4LZ
☎ (01594) 516149

You'll find a warm welcome at this country home. Relax in lovely garden with ponds and waterfalls. See unspoilt Forest of Dean and the Wye and Severn Valleys.

Bedrooms: 1 single, 1 double, 1 twin
Bathrooms: 1 en-suite, 2 private

Bed & breakfast per night:	£min	£max
Single	18.00	20.00
Double	36.00	40.00

Parking for 3

Please check prices and other details at the time of booking.

LYONSHALL

Hereford and Worcester
Map ref 2A1

Village close to the Welsh border. Hergest Croft Gardens, with their beautiful displays of rhododendrons and azaleas in May and June, are nearby.

Royal George Inn

COMMENDED

Lyonshall, Kington, Herefordshire
HR5 3JN
☎ (01544) 340210
Fax (01544) 340417

Charming 16th C black and white country inn offering quaint, comfortable accommodation. Delicious home-cooked food in bars and restaurant. Real ale, beer garden.

Bedrooms: 1 single, 2 double, 2 twin
Bathrooms: 2 public

Bed & breakfast per night:	£min	£max
Single	22.50	30.00
Double	40.00	50.00

Half board per person:	£min	£max
Daily	28.00	45.00
Weekly	150.00	255.00

Lunch available
Evening meal 1900 (last orders 2130)
Parking for 50
Cards accepted: Mastercard, Visa, Switch/Delta

MADELEY

Shropshire
Map ref 4A2

Woodlands

COMMENDED

Park Lane, Madeley, Telford TF7 5HJ
☎ (01952) 580693

Modern detached bungalow, both rooms en-suite. TV, car parking. Centrally located for museums, bridge and Telford centre.

Bedrooms: 1 double, 1 twin
Bathrooms: 2 en-suite

Bed & breakfast per night:	£min	£max
Single	20.00	25.00
Double	32.00	35.00

Parking for 6

MALVERN

Hereford and Worcester
Map ref 2B1

Spa town in Victorian times, its water is today bottled and sold worldwide. 6 resorts, set on the slopes of the Hills, form part of Malvern. Great Malvern Priory has splendid 15th C windows. It is an excellent walking centre.
Tourist Information Centre ☎ (01684) 892289 or 862345

Sunnydale

COMMENDED

69 Tanhouse Lane, Malvern, Worcestershire WR14 1LQ
☎ (01886) 832066
Attractive, modern, centrally heated bungalow with en-suite facilities. Set in private gardens with off-road parking.
Bedrooms: 2 double
Bathrooms: 2 en-suite

Bed & breakfast per night:	£min	£max
Single		25.00
Double		40.00

Half board per person:	£min	£max
Daily	35.00	40.00
Weekly	220.00	252.00

Parking for 3
Open January–November

The Wyche Inn

APPROVED

74 Wyche Road, Malvern, Worcestershire WR14 4EQ
☎ (01684) 575396 & 0976 271467
The highest inn in Worcestershire, nestling on top of the Malvern Hills and with spectacular views across the Severn Valley.
Bedrooms: 1 single, 3 double, 1 twin
Bathrooms: 5 en-suite

Bed & breakfast per night:	£min	£max
Single		30.00
Double		45.00

Lunch available
Evening meal 1900 (last orders 2130)
Parking for 12
Cards accepted: Mastercard, Visa, Switch/Delta

A key to symbols can be found inside the back cover flap.

York House

COMMENDED

Walwyn Road, Colwall, Malvern, Worcestershire WR13 6QG
☎ (01684) 540449
Large Edwardian house in centre of picturesque village. Close to Malvern and the hills, in an Area of Outstanding Natural Beauty.
Bedrooms: 2 double, 1 twin
Bathrooms: 2 en-suite, 1 private

Bed & breakfast per night:	£min	£max
Single	28.00	30.00
Double	38.00	45.00

Parking for 4

MARKET DRAYTON

Shropshire
Map ref 4A2

Old market town with black and white buildings and 17th C houses, also acclaimed for its gingerbread. Hodnet Hall is in the vicinity with its beautiful landscaped gardens covering 60 acres.
Tourist Information Centre ☎ (01630) 652139

Heath Farm Bed and Breakfast

Listed APPROVED

Heath Farm, Hodnet, Market Drayton TF9 3JJ
☎ (01630) 685570
Fax (01743) 249970
60-acre mixed farm. Traditional farmhouse welcome. Situated 1.5 miles south of Hodnet off the A442, approached by private drive.
Bedrooms: 1 double, 2 twin
Bathrooms: 1 public

Bed & breakfast per night:	£min	£max
Single	16.00	18.00
Double	30.00	36.00

Parking for 5

5

Please mention this guide when making your booking.

The National Grading and Classification Scheme is explained at the back of this guide.

MARKET HARBOROUGH

Leicestershire
Map ref 4C3

There have been markets here since the early 13th C, and the town was also an important coaching centre, with several ancient hostelries. The early 17th C grammar school was once the butter market.
Tourist Information Centre ☎ (01858) 821270

The Bell Inn

COMMENDED

Main Street, East Langton, Market Harborough LE16 7TW
☎ (01858) 545278
Fax (01858) 545748
17th C village inn in the heart of the village, serving fine ales, wines and food 7 days a week. Low beams and winter log fires.
Bedrooms: 1 double, 1 twin
Suites available
Bathrooms: 2 en-suite

Bed & breakfast per night:	£min	£max
Single	35.00	40.00
Double	45.00	50.00

Lunch available
Evening meal 1900 (last orders 2230)
Parking for 20
Cards accepted: Mastercard, Visa, Switch/Delta

The Fox Inn

COMMENDED

Church Street, Wilbarston, Market Harborough LE16 8QG
☎ (01536) 771270
Fax (01536) 771270
Old ironstone village inn offering home-cooked food, real ales and traditional pub games. Near Rockingham Castle and East Carlton Country Park.
Bedrooms: 2 double, 1 twin, 1 family room
Bathrooms: 4 en-suite

Bed & breakfast per night:	£min	£max
Single	24.00	30.00
Double	32.00	40.00

Lunch available
Evening meal 1830 (last orders 2145)
Parking for 10
Cards accepted: Mastercard, Visa

MATLOCK

Derbyshire
Map ref 4B2

The town lies beside the narrow valley of the River Derwent surrounded by steep wooded hills. Good centre for exploring Derbyshire's best scenery.

Farley Farm

APPROVED

Farley, Matlock DE4 5LR
☎ (01629) 582533 & 0860 625004

250-acre mixed farm. Built in 1610 of natural stone, set in open countryside close to Peak District and many places of interest.

Bedrooms: 1 double, 1 twin, 1 family room
Bathrooms: 1 en-suite, 2 public

Bed & breakfast per night:	£min	£max
Single	18.00	20.00
Double	32.00	36.00

Half board per person:	£min	£max
Daily	23.00	25.00
Weekly	161.00	175.00

Evening meal 1700 (last orders 1900)
Parking for 10

Home Farm

COMMENDED

Ible, Grange Mill, Matlock DE4 4HS
☎ (01629) 650349

A "retired farm", still retaining some small animals which guests are encouraged to feed. Quiet with plenty of walks and places to visit.

Bedrooms: 1 double, 1 family room
Bathrooms: 2 en-suite

Bed & breakfast per night:	£min	£max
Single	16.00	16.00
Double	32.00	32.00

Half board per person:	£min	£max
Daily		23.00

Evening meal 1800 (last orders 2000)
Parking for 4

For ideas on places to visit refer to the introduction at the beginning of this section.

MELTON MOWBRAY

Leicestershire
Map ref 4C3

Close to the attractive Vale of Belvoir and famous for its pork pies and Stilton cheese which are the subjects of special displays in the museum. It has a beautiful church with a tower 100 ft high.
Tourist Information Centre ☎ (01664) 480992

Hillside House

COMMENDED

27 Melton Road, Burton Lazars, Melton Mowbray LE14 2UR
☎ (01664) 66312 & 0585 068956; changing to (01664) 566312
Fax (01664) 501819

Comfortable, fully-modernised cottage in a small village with splendid views over rolling countryside. Homely and welcoming.

Bedrooms: 1 double, 2 twin
Bathrooms: 2 en-suite, 1 private

Bed & breakfast per night:	£min	£max
Single	20.00	23.00
Double	33.00	38.00

Parking for 4
10

MERIDEN

West Midlands
Map ref 4B3

Village halfway between Coventry and Birmingham. Said to be the centre of England, marked by a cross on the green.

Cooperage Farm Bed and Breakfast

APPROVED

Old Road, Meriden, Coventry CV7 7JP
☎ (01676) 523493
Fax (01676) 523876

6-acre mixed farm. 300-year-old red brick, Grade II listed farmhouse, set in beautiful countryside. Ideally situated for the National Exhibition Centre, airport and touring the centre of England.

Bedrooms: 2 double, 2 twin, 2 triple
Bathrooms: 4 en-suite, 1 public

Bed & breakfast per night:	£min	£max
Single	25.00	30.00
Double	45.00	50.00

Evening meal 1800 (last orders 1900)
Parking for 6
1

Innellan House

COMMENDED

Eaves Green Lane, Meriden, Coventry CV7 7JL
☎ (01676) 523005 & 522548

Detached country house surrounded by 18 acres of meadowland. Approximately one mile from Meriden village. Good touring centre, convenient for railway, airport and National Exhibition Centre. Non-smokers only, please.

Bedrooms: 3 twin
Bathrooms: 1 en-suite, 2 private

Bed & breakfast per night:	£min	£max
Single	26.00	28.00
Double	42.00	45.00

Parking for 10
7

MIDDLETON

Northamptonshire
Map ref 4C3

Valley View

COMMENDED

3 Camsdale Walk, Middleton, Market Harborough, Leicestershire LE16 8YR
☎ (01536) 770874

Elevated, stone-built house with panoramic views of the Welland Valley. Within easy distance of Market Harborough and Corby.

Bedrooms: 1 double, 1 twin
Bathrooms: 1 public

Bed & breakfast per night:	£min	£max
Single	16.00	16.00
Double	32.00	32.00

Parking for 2

The symbol after an establishment name indicates that it is a Regional Tourist Board member.

For farm holidays and accommodation suitable for young people and organised groups, please refer to the special sections at the back of this guide.

MINCHINHAMPTON

Gloucestershire
Map ref 2B1

Stone-built town, with many 17th/18th C buildings, owing its existence to the wool and cloth trades. A 17th C pillared market house may be found in the town square, near which is the Norman and 14th C church.

Hunters Lodge

HIGHLY COMMENDED

Dr Brown's Road, Minchinhampton, Stroud GL6 9BT
☎ (01453) 883588
Fax (01453) 731449
Cotswold-stone house adjoining Minchinhampton common and golf-course. Ideal centre for Bath, Gloucester, Cheltenham and Cotswolds. 2 miles from A419 Stroud-Cirencester road, 1.5 miles from A46 (first house on right going into Minchinhampton from common).
Bedrooms: 1 twin, 2 triple
Bathrooms: 1 en-suite, 2 private

Bed & breakfast per night:	£min	£max
Single	26.00	
Double	40.00	46.00

Parking for 8

MINSTERLEY

Shropshire
Map ref 4A3

Village with a curious little church of 1692 and a fine old black and white hall. The lofty ridge known as the Stiperstones is 4 miles to the south.

Cricklewood Cottage

HIGHLY COMMENDED

Plox Green, Minsterley, Shrewsbury SY5 0HT
☎ (01743) 791229
Delightful 18th C cottage with countryside views, at foot of Stiperstones Hills. Exposed beams, inglenook fireplace, traditional furnishings. Lovely cottage garden. Excellent restaurants and inns nearby.
Bedrooms: 2 double, 1 twin
Bathrooms: 3 en-suite

Bed & breakfast per night:	£min	£max
Single	19.50	33.00
Double	39.00	44.00

Parking for 4

MORETON PINKNEY

Northamptonshire
Map ref 2C1

Thriving village in the south west of the county. The annual summer fete is a major attraction.

Barewell Fields

Listed HIGHLY COMMENDED

Prestidge Row, Moreton Pinkney, Daventry NN11 3NJ
☎ (01295) 760754
200-acre mixed farm. In a peaceful corner of the conservation village of Moreton Pinkney, convenient for many National Trust properties, Stratford and Silverstone, M1 and M40.
Bedrooms: 1 single, 1 double, 1 twin
Bathrooms: 1 public

Bed & breakfast per night:	£min	£max
Single	18.00	25.00
Double	36.00	50.00

Parking for 4

10

MORETON-IN-MARSH

Gloucestershire
Map ref 2B1

Attractive town of Cotswold stone with 17th C houses, an ideal base for touring the Cotswolds. Some of the local attractions include Batsford Park Arboretum, the Jacobean Chastleton House and Sezincote Garden.

Dorn Priory

COMMENDED

Dorn, Moreton-in-Marsh GL56 9NS
☎ (01608) 650152

17th C Cotswold house in peaceful surroundings. Set in a small hamlet on edge of Cotswolds, within easy reach of Stratford-upon-Avon and Oxford.
Bedrooms: 1 twin, 1 family room
Bathrooms: 1 public

Bed & breakfast per night:	£min	£max
Double	35.00	

Parking for 10
Open April–October

Farriers Arms

COMMENDED

Todenham, Moreton-in-Marsh GL56 9PF
☎ (01608) 650901 & 0836 211025
Family-run bar and restaurant with comfortable, quiet spacious rooms. Picturesque Cotswold village with views over valley.
Bedrooms: 1 single, 2 double
Bathrooms: 1 public

Bed & breakfast per night:	£min	£max
Single	23.00	28.00
Double	40.00	45.00

Half board per person:	£min	£max
Daily	30.00	38.00
Weekly	200.00	240.00

Lunch available
Evening meal 1830 (last orders 2130)
Parking for 25
Cards accepted: Mastercard, Visa, Switch/Delta

Four Gables

COMMENDED

Little Compton, Moreton-in-Marsh GL56 0SQ
☎ (01608) 674233
Situated in peaceful Cotswold village, ideal for touring the Cotswolds. Within walking distance of local pub serving good evening meals.
Bedrooms: 2 double, 1 twin
Bathrooms: 3 en-suite

Bed & breakfast per night:	£min	£max
Single	25.00	25.00
Double	40.00	40.00

Parking for 6
Open February–November

2

For further information on accommodation establishments use the coupons at the back of this guide.

ACCESSIBILITY

Look for the symbols which indicate accessibility for wheelchair users. These are described in detail at the front of this guide.

New Farm

COMMENDED

Dorn, Moreton-in-Marsh GL56 9NS
☎ (01608) 650782

250-acre dairy farm. Old Cotswold farmhouse. All rooms spacious, en-suite and furnished with antiques and with colour TV, coffee and tea facilities. Dining room with large impressive fireplace. Full English breakfast served with hot crispy bread.

Bedrooms: 2 double, 1 twin
Bathrooms: 2 en-suite, 1 private

Bed & breakfast per night:	£min	£max
Single	17.00	20.00
Double	34.00	35.00

Parking for 10

Old Farm

COMMENDED

Dorn, Moreton-in-Marsh GL56 9NS
☎ (01608) 650394

250-acre mixed farm. Enjoy the delights of a 15th C farmhouse - a comfortable family home. Spacious bedrooms. Tennis and croquet. Children welcome. Surrounded by beautiful Cotswolds scenery.

Bedrooms: 2 double, 1 twin
Bathrooms: 2 en-suite, 1 public

Bed & breakfast per night:	£min	£max
Single	20.00	
Double	34.00	

Parking for 8
Open March–October

MOUNTSORREL

Leicestershire
Map ref 4C3

The Swan Inn

APPROVED

10 Loughborough Road, Mountsorrel, Loughborough LE12 7AT
☎ (0116) 230 2340
Fax (0116) 237 6115

Traditional 17th C coaching inn in the heart of historic Mountsorrel, on the banks of the River Soar.

Bedrooms: 1 single, 1 double, 1 twin
Bathrooms: 1 public

Bed & breakfast per night:	£min	£max
Single	20.00	20.00
Double	32.00	32.00

Lunch available
Evening meal 1900 (last orders 2130)
Parking for 12
Cards accepted: Amex, Mastercard, Visa

MUCH WENLOCK

Shropshire
Map ref 4A3

Small town close to Wenlock Edge in beautiful scenery and full of interest. In particular there are the remains of an 11th C priory with fine carving and the black and white 16th C Guildhall.

Talbot Inn

COMMENDED

Much Wenlock TF13 6AA
☎ (01952) 727077
Fax (01952) 728436

An inn since 1361, with beams, open fires and home-cooked food. Situated in an unspoilt medieval town near Ironbridge Gorge.

Bedrooms: 1 single, 3 double, 2 twin
Bathrooms: 6 en-suite

Bed & breakfast per night:	£min	£max
Single	40.00	80.00
Double	90.00	100.00

Half board per person:	£min	£max
Daily	45.00	50.00

Lunch available
Evening meal 1900 (last orders 2130)
Parking for 4
Cards accepted: Amex, Mastercard, Visa, Switch/Delta

Walton House

Listed COMMENDED

35 Barrow Street, Much Wenlock TF13 6EP
☎ (01952) 727139

Two minutes' walk from town centre. 5 miles from Ironbridge Gorge, 13 miles from Shrewsbury, 8 miles from Bridgnorth and 10 miles from Telford town centre. Lawns and patio.

Bedrooms: 1 single, 2 twin
Bathrooms: 1 public

Bed & breakfast per night:	£min	£max
Single	15.00	15.00
Double	30.00	30.00

Parking for 2
Open April–October

NAILSWORTH

Gloucestershire
Map ref 2B1

Ancient wool town with several elegant Jacobean and Georgian houses, surrounded by wooded hillsides with fine views.

Aaron Farm

COMMENDED

Nympsfield Road, Nailsworth, Stroud GL6 0ET
☎ (01453) 833598
Fax (01453) 833598
Email: pmulligan@sprynet.co.uk

Former farmhouse, with large en-suite bedrooms and panoramic views of the Cotswolds. Ideal touring centre. Many walks and attractions. Home cooking. Brochure on request.

Bedrooms: 1 double, 2 twin
Bathrooms: 3 en-suite

Bed & breakfast per night:	£min	£max
Single	26.00	28.00
Double	36.00	40.00

Half board per person:	£min	£max
Daily	38.00	40.00
Weekly	260.00	280.00

Evening meal 1800 (last orders 2000)
Parking for 4

Apple Orchard House

COMMENDED

Orchard Close, Springhill, Nailsworth, Stroud GL6 0LX
☎ (01453) 832503
Fax (01453) 836213

Elegant, spacious Cotswold house with pretty three-quarter acre garden. Good parking on site. Panoramic views of hills and town from bedrooms and sitting room. Dinner available, also 2 minutes' walk from 9 eating places. Wheelchair users welcome. Laundry facilities. Colour brochure.

Wheelchair access category 3
Bedrooms: 1 double, 2 twin

Continued ▶

NAILSWORTH

Continued

Bathrooms: 2 en-suite, 1 private

Bed & breakfast per night:	£min	£max
Single	20.00	28.00
Double	36.00	42.00

Evening meal 1800 (last orders 1700)
Parking for 3
Cards accepted: Amex, Mastercard, Visa

The Upper House

COMMENDED

Spring Hill, Nailsworth, Stroud GL6 0LX
☎ (01453) 836606
Fax (01453) 845004

Traditional Cotswold house in centre of small market town between Cheltenham and Bath. All bedrooms en-suite, TV, residents' lounge, garden. Children and dogs welcome. Excellent base for touring Cotswolds.

Bedrooms: 2 double, 1 twin
Bathrooms: 3 en-suite

Bed & breakfast per night:	£min	£max
Single	20.00	25.00
Double	38.00	40.00

Parking for 5

NEWENT

Gloucestershire
Map ref 2B1

Small town with the largest collection of birds of prey in Europe at the Falconry Centre. Flying demonstrations daily. Glass workshop where visitors can watch glass being blown. There is a "seconds" shop. North of the village are the Three Choirs Vineyards.
Tourist Information Centre ☎ (01531) 822468

Glendalough

Listed APPROVED

Kilcot, Newent GL18 1NN
☎ (01989) 720294
Fax (01989) 721710
Email: mikesteadman@msn,com

Situated on the edge of the Forest of Dean, close to Ross and Gloucester. Traditional English or vegetarian breakfast.

Bedrooms: 1 single, 1 double, 1 twin
Bathrooms: 1 public

Bed & breakfast per night:	£min	£max
Single	15.00	15.00
Double	30.00	30.00

Parking for 3

The Old Winery

HIGHLY COMMENDED

Welsh House Lane, Newent GL18 1LR
☎ (01531) 890824

Old winery converted to a high standard, offering very comfortable accommodation. Surrounded by beautiful countryside with views over vineyards - very peaceful. Evening meal and special diets by arrangement.

Bedrooms: 1 single, 1 twin
Suite available
Bathrooms: 1 en-suite, 1 private

Bed & breakfast per night:	£min	£max
Single	16.00	22.00
Double	40.00	50.00

Evening meal 1800 (last orders 2100)
Parking for 20

NEWLAND

Gloucestershire
Map ref 2A1

Probably the most attractive of the villages of the Forest of Dean. The church is often referred to as "the Cathedral of the Forest"; it contains a number of interesting monuments and the Forest Miner's Brass. Almshouses nearby were endowed by William Jones, founder of Monmouth School.

Scatterford Farm

HIGHLY COMMENDED

Newland, Coleford GL16 8NG
☎ (01594) 836562
Fax (01594) 836323

Beautiful 15th C farmhouse with spacious rooms, good views and delicious breakfasts with home-made bread. Ideal for walking, cycling and riding.

Bedrooms: 2 double, 1 twin
Bathrooms: 3 en-suite

Bed & breakfast per night:	£min	£max
Single	20.00	25.00
Double	40.00	46.00

Parking for 8

NEWPORT

Shropshire
Map ref 4A3

Small market town on the Shropshire Union Canal has a wide High Street and a church with some interesting monuments. Newport is close to Aqualate Mere which is the largest lake in Staffordshire.

Lane End Farm

COMMENDED

Chetwynd, Newport TF10 8BN
☎ (01952) 550337

5-acre livestock farm. Delightful period farmhouse set in lovely countryside. Located on A41 near Newport. Ideal touring base and beautiful local walks.

Bedrooms: 2 double
Bathrooms: 2 en-suite

Bed & breakfast per night:	£min	£max
Single	20.00	25.00
Double	36.00	38.00

Half board per person:	£min	£max
Daily	32.00	37.00

Evening meal 1800 (last orders 2100)
Parking for 5

NORTHAMPTON

Northamptonshire
Map ref 2C1

A bustling town and a shoe manufacturing centre, with excellent shopping facilities, several museums and parks, a theatre and a concert hall. Several old churches include 1 of only 4 round churches in Britain.
Tourist Information Centre ☎ (01604) 22677

Hollington Guesthouse

Listed

22 Abington Grove, Northampton NN1 4QW
☎ (01604) 32584

Comfortable guesthouse, close to town centre and with easy access to M1. TV and tea-making facilities in all rooms.

Bedrooms: 2 single, 2 double, 1 twin, 2 triple
Bathrooms: 2 public

Bed & breakfast per night:	£min	£max
Single	16.00	18.00
Double	30.00	35.00

Parking for 6
Cards accepted: Mastercard, Visa, Switch/Delta

NORTHLEACH

Gloucestershire
Map ref 2B1

Village famous for its beautiful 15th C wool church with its lovely porch and interesting interior. There are also some fine houses including a 17th C wool merchant's house containing Keith Harding's World of Mechanical Music. The Cotswold Countryside Collection is in the former prison.

Bank Villas Guesthouse

COMMENDED

West-end, Northleach, Cheltenham GL54 3HG
☎ (01451) 860464

Attractive residence with leaded windows, situated off the historic Fosse Way. An excellent base for exploring the beautiful Cotswolds and local places of interest.

Bedrooms: 2 single, 1 double, 1 twin, 1 triple
Bathrooms: 1 en-suite, 2 public

Bed & breakfast per night:	£min	£max
Single	18.00	20.00
Double	34.00	36.00

Cotteswold House

COMMENDED

Market Place, Northleach, Cheltenham GL54 3EG
☎ (01451) 860493
Fax (01451) 860493

Grade II listed 350-year-old home with exposed beams, original stonework and 13th C panelling in the dining room.

Bedrooms: 2 double, 1 twin
Bathrooms: 1 en-suite, 2 private

Bed & breakfast per night:	£min	£max
Double	45.00	70.00

Half board per person:	£min	£max
Daily	36.50	49.00
Weekly	219.00	294.00

Evening meal 1830 (last orders 2000)
Cards accepted: Mastercard, Visa, Switch/Delta

Northfield Bed & Breakfast

COMMENDED

Cirencester Road (A429), Northleach, Cheltenham GL54 3JL
☎ (01451) 860427
Email: nrth-fieldo@aol.com

Detached family house in the country with large gardens and home-grown produce. Excellent centre for visiting the Cotswolds and close to local services.

Bedrooms: 1 double, 2 family rooms
Bathrooms: 3 en-suite

Bed & breakfast per night:	£min	£max
Single	26.00	28.00
Double	45.00	48.00

Half board per person:	£min	£max
Daily	40.00	

Evening meal 1800 (last orders 1900)
Parking for 10

NOTTINGHAM

Nottinghamshire
Map ref 4C2

Attractive modern city with a rich history. Outside its castle, now a museum, is Robin Hood's statue. Attractions include "The Tales of Robin Hood"; the Lace Hall; Wollaton Hall; museums and excellent facilities for shopping, sports and entertainment.
Tourist Information Centre ☎ (0115) 947 0661

Grantham Hotel

COMMENDED

24-26 Radcliffe Road, West Bridgford, Nottingham NG2 5FW
☎ (0115) 981 1373
Fax (0115) 981 8567

Family-run licensed hotel offering modern accommodation in a comfortable atmosphere. Convenient for the centre of Nottingham, Trent Bridge and the National Water Sports Centre.

Bedrooms: 13 single, 2 double, 4 twin, 2 triple, 1 family room
Bathrooms: 14 en-suite, 2 public

Bed & breakfast per night:	£min	£max
Single	21.00	29.00
Double	39.00	42.00

Half board per person:	£min	£max
Daily	26.95	35.95
Weekly	135.00	155.00

Evening meal 1800 (last orders 1900)
Parking for 20
Cards accepted: Amex, Mastercard, Visa, Switch/Delta

NYMPSFIELD

Gloucestershire
Map ref 2B1

Pretty village high up in the Cotswolds, with a simple mid-Victorian church and a prehistoric long barrow nearby.

Rose and Crown Inn

COMMENDED

Nympsfield, Stonehouse GL10 3TU
☎ (01453) 860240
Fax (01453) 860240
Email: roseandcrowninn@btinternet

300-year-old inn, in quiet Cotswold village, close to Cotswold Way. Easy access to M4/M5.

Bedrooms: 1 double, 3 triple
Bathrooms: 3 en-suite, 1 private

Bed & breakfast per night:	£min	£max
Single	30.00	34.00
Double	51.00	58.00

Half board per person:	£min	£max
Daily	37.00	52.00

Lunch available
Evening meal (last orders 2130)
Parking for 30
Cards accepted: Amex, Diners, Mastercard, Visa, Switch/Delta

OAKAMOOR

Staffordshire
Map ref 4B2

Small village below a steep hill amid the glorious scenery of the Churnet Valley. Its industrial links have now gone, as the site of the factory which made 20,000 miles of copper wire for the first Atlantic cable has been transformed into an attractive picnic site on the riverside.

Beehive Guest House

Listed COMMENDED

Churnet View Road, Oakamoor, Stoke-on-Trent ST10 3AE
☎ (01538) 702420

Family-run guesthouse, overlooking river and parkland, in the beautiful Churnet Valley. Within walking distance of Alton Towers.

Bedrooms: 2 double, 1 twin, 2 family rooms
Bathrooms: 3 en-suite, 2 public

Continued ▶

OAKAMOOR

Continued

Bed & breakfast per night:	£min	£max
Double	30.00	36.00

Parking for 8
Open March–November
Cards accepted: Mastercard, Visa, Switch/Delta

Ribden Farm

HIGHLY COMMENDED

Oakamoor, Stoke-on-Trent
ST10 3BW
☎ (01538) 702830 & 702153
Fax (01538) 702830

98-acre livestock farm. Grade II listed 18th C farmhouse in open countryside, one and a half miles from Alton Towers. TV and tea/coffee in all rooms.
Bedrooms: 2 double, 1 triple, 3 family rooms
Bathrooms: 5 en-suite, 1 private

Bed & breakfast per night:	£min	£max
Double	40.00	42.00

Parking for 5
Cards accepted: Diners, Mastercard, Visa, Switch/Delta

OAKHAM

Leicestershire
Map ref 4C3

Pleasant former county town of Rutland. Fine 12th C Great Hall, part of its castle, with a historic collection of horseshoes. An octagonal Butter Cross stands in the market-place and Rutland County Museum, Rutland Farm Park and Rutland Water are of interest.
Tourist Information Centre ☎ (01572) 724329

Hall Farm

Listed APPROVED

Cottesmore Road, Exton, Oakham, Rutland LE15 8AN
☎ (01572) 812271 & 0385 915564
25-acre arable & horses farm. Early 19th C Grade II listed stone farmhouse in open countryside. Approximately 2 miles from Rutland Water north shore. TV, hairdryer, hot drinks in all rooms.
Bedrooms: 1 single, 1 twin, 1 triple
Bathrooms: 2 public

Bed & breakfast per night:	£min	£max
Single	17.50	
Double	30.00	

Parking for 6

The Tithe Barn

COMMENDED

Clatterpot Lane, Cottesmore, Oakham LE15 7DW
☎ (01572) 813591

Comfortable, stone-built house converted from a tithe barn with original dovecote. In the heart of Rutland, yet only 5 minutes from Rutland Water, Barnsdale Gardens and the A1.
Bedrooms: 1 double, 1 twin, 1 triple, 1 family room
Bathrooms: 3 en-suite, 1 private, 1 public

Bed & breakfast per night:	£min	£max
Single	15.00	25.00
Double	33.00	42.00

Parking for 6
Cards accepted: Mastercard, Visa, Switch/Delta

OMBERSLEY

Hereford and Worcester
Map ref 2B1

A particularly fine village full of black and white houses including the 17th C Dower House and some old inns. The church contains the original box pews.

The Crown and Sandys Arms

COMMENDED

Ombersley, Droitwich, Worcestershire WR9 0EW
☎ (01905) 620252
Fax (01905) 620769
Freehouse with comfortable bedrooms, draught beers and open fires. Home-cooked meals available lunchtimes and evenings, 7 days a week.
Bedrooms: 1 single, 3 double, 1 twin, 1 triple, 1 family room
Bathrooms: 6 en-suite, 1 public

Bed & breakfast per night:	£min	£max
Single	33.00	40.00
Double	45.00	50.00

Lunch available
Evening meal 1800 (last orders 2145)
Parking for 100
Cards accepted: Amex, Mastercard, Visa, Switch/Delta
30

ONNELEY

Staffordshire
Map ref 4A2

Village on the line between Shropshire and Staffordshire counties, within easy reach of Bridgemere Garden World.

The Wheatsheaf Inn at Onneley

COMMENDED

Bar Hill Road, Onneley, Madeley CW3 9QF
☎ (01782) 751581
Fax (01782) 751499
18th C country inn with bars, Spanish restaurant, conference and function facilities. On A525, 7 miles from Newcastle-under-Lyme. Close to Potteries, Keele University and M6. Convenient for Alton Towers and Chester.
Bedrooms: 4 double, 1 twin
Bathrooms: 5 en-suite

Bed & breakfast per night:	£min	£max
Single	45.00	45.00
Double	50.00	60.00

Half board per person:	£min	£max
Daily	57.50	

Lunch available
Evening meal 1800 (last orders 2130)
Parking for 150
Cards accepted: Amex, Diners, Mastercard, Visa, Switch/Delta
100

COLOUR MAPS

Colour maps at the back of this guide pinpoint all places in which you will find accommodation listed.

PAINSWICK

Gloucestershire
Map ref 2B1

Picturesque wool town with inns and houses dating from the 14th C. Painswick Rococo Garden is open to visitors from January to November, and the house is a Palladian mansion. The churchyard is famous for its yew trees.

Culvert Cottage

COMMENDED

Kingsmill Lane, Painswick, Stroud GL6 6RT
☎ (01452) 812293

Detached guesthouse standing in 1.5 acres of lovely gardens bordering a stream. Ideal base for touring or walking. Special rates for 3 nights or more.

Bedrooms: 1 double, 1 twin
Bathrooms: 1 en-suite, 1 private

Bed & breakfast per night:	£min	£max
Single	20.00	25.00
Double	35.00	40.00

Parking for 4
Open February–November

Hambutts Mynd

COMMENDED

Edge Road, Painswick, Stroud GL6 6UP
☎ (01452) 812352

Old corn windmill, c1700-50, with original beams. Panoramic views from all bedrooms. 200 yards from main road. Dogs accepted. Weekly rates available.

Bedrooms: 1 single, 1 double, 1 twin
Bathrooms: 1 private, 1 public

Bed & breakfast per night:	£min	£max
Single	21.00	23.00
Double	39.00	42.00

Parking for 3

Meadowcote

HIGHLY COMMENDED

Stroud Road, Painswick, Stroud GL6 6UT
☎ (01452) 813565

Pleasant spacious house with private parking, near centre of the village. Pretty, sheltered and secluded garden.

Bedrooms: 1 single, 2 double
Bathrooms: 2 en-suite, 1 private

Bed & breakfast per night:	£min	£max
Single	20.00	20.00
Double	40.00	40.00

Parking for 6
Open March–December

PEAK DISTRICT

See under Aldwark, Ashbourne, Ashford in the Water, Bakewell, Bamford, Butterton, Buxton, Castleton, Cressbrook, Eyam, Froggatt, Hathersage, Litton, Tideswell

PERSHORE

Hereford and Worcester
Map ref 2B1

Attractive Georgian town on the River Avon close to the Vale of Evesham, with fine houses and old inns. The remains of the beautiful Pershore Abbey form the parish church.
Tourist Information Centre ☎ (01386) 554262

The Barn

HIGHLY COMMENDED

Pensham Hill House, Pensham, Pershore, Worcestershire WR10 3HA
☎ (01386) 555270

Superior ground-floor accommodation in 19thC converted barn independent of main house. In private and tranquil setting with wonderful views of Pershore and surrounding areas.

Bedrooms: 2 double, 1 twin
Bathrooms: 3 en-suite

Bed & breakfast per night:	£min	£max
Single	29.00	35.00
Double	43.00	55.00

Parking for 6

PINXTON

Derbyshire
Map ref 4C2

Croftlands House

Listed APPROVED

4 West End, Pinxton NG16 6NN
☎ (01773) 510326

A warm welcome, good breakfast and comfortable rooms. Walkers and country people are especially welcome; walks and tours can be arranged.

Bedrooms: 1 single, 1 double, 1 twin
Bathrooms: 1 public

Bed & breakfast per night:	£min	£max
Single	13.00	14.50
Double	26.00	29.00

Parking for 4

PONTESBURY

Shropshire
Map ref 4A3

With views of the Rea Valley from nearby Pontesford Hill, this village is the site of a 7th C battle between a King of Mercia and a King of the West Saxons. Most of the village church was rebuilt in the last century, except for the 13th C chancel which retains its original roof.

Marehay Farm

HIGHLY COMMENDED

Ratlinghope, Pontesbury, Shrewsbury SY5 0SJ
☎ (01588) 650289

Splendid isolation at 1,100ft in the Long Mynd and Stiperstones environmentally sensitive area. Peace and quiet. Good walking and bird-watching.

Bedrooms: 2 twin
Bathrooms: 2 en-suite

Bed & breakfast per night:	£min	£max
Single	17.00	20.00
Double	34.00	40.00

Parking for 4

RAGNALL

Nottinghamshire
Map ref 4C2

Lying 4 miles north-east of Tuxford, close to the Trent. Pretty and interesting church.

Ragnall House

COMMENDED

Ragnall, Newark NG22 0UR
☎ (01777) 228575 & 0374 455792

Large listed Georgian family house in over an acre of grounds in a small village close to the River Trent. Good local inns and restaurants nearby.

Bedrooms: 1 single, 2 twin, 1 triple
Bathrooms: 1 en-suite, 1 public, 1 private shower

Bed & breakfast per night:	£min	£max
Single	16.00	18.00
Double	32.00	36.00

Parking for 8

RETFORD

Nottinghamshire
Map ref 4C2

Market town on the River Idle with a pleasant market square and Georgian houses. The surrounding villages were the homes and meeting places of the early Pilgrim Fathers.
Tourist Information Centre ☎ (01777) 860780

Rose Cottage

COMMENDED

South Street, Bole, Retford
DN22 9EJ
☎ (01427) 848572
Now extended from the original oak-beamed cottage built before 1650, Rose Cottage offers informal comfort and fresh home-grown produce. In village north-east of Retford.
Bedrooms: 1 double, 2 twin
Bathrooms: 3 en-suite, 1 public

Bed & breakfast per night:	£min	£max
Single	19.00	
Double	38.00	

Half board per person:	£min	£max
Daily	27.00	31.00

Evening meal 1730 (last orders 1930)
Parking for 3

ROCK

Hereford and Worcester
Map ref 4A3

The Old Forge

Listed COMMENDED

Gorst Hill, Rock, Kidderminster, Worcestershire DY14 9YG
☎ (01299) 266745
Recently renovated country cottage, near the Wyre Forest. Ideal for country walks and visiting local places of interest. Short and midweek breaks.
Bedrooms: 1 twin, 1 triple
Bathrooms: 1 public

Bed & breakfast per night:	£min	£max
Single	16.00	16.00

Parking for 5
Open January–November

ROSS-ON-WYE

Hereford and Worcester
Map ref 2A1

Attractive market town with a 17th C market hall, set above the River Wye. There are lovely views over the surrounding countryside from the Prospect and the town is close to Goodrich Castle and the Welsh border.
Tourist Information Centre ☎ (01989) 562768

The Arches Hotel

COMMENDED

Walford Road, Ross-on-Wye, Herefordshire HR9 5PT
☎ (01989) 563348
Small, family-run hotel, set in half an acre of lawned gardens, 10 minutes' walk from town centre. Warm, friendly atmosphere. All rooms furnished to a high standard and with views of the garden. Victorian-style conservatory in which to relax.
Bedrooms: 1 single, 4 double, 1 twin, 1 triple
Bathrooms: 4 en-suite, 2 public

Bed & breakfast per night:	£min	£max
Single	20.00	25.00
Double	38.00	44.00

Half board per person:	£min	£max
Daily	30.00	35.00
Weekly	191.00	227.00

Evening meal from 1900
Parking for 10

Bramley Cottage

Pencraig, Ross-on-Wye, Herefordshire HR9 6HP
☎ (01989) 770632
Self-contained bungalow accommodation with lovely views, 3 miles from Ross-on-Wye on A40 to Pencraig. (Turn right up lane at post office/shop.) Excellent breakfasts.
Bedrooms: 1 double
Bathrooms: 1 en-suite

Bed & breakfast per night:	£min	£max
Single		22.00
Double		40.00

Parking for 4

Brookfield House

APPROVED

Over Ross, Ross-on-Wye, Herefordshire HR9 7AT
☎ (01989) 562188
Queen Anne/Georgian listed building close to the town centre. Private car park. Easy reach of M50 and A40.
Bedrooms: 2 single, 3 double, 3 twin
Bathrooms: 3 en-suite, 3 public

Bed & breakfast per night:	£min	£max
Single	17.00	20.00
Double	30.00	40.00

Parking for 11
Cards accepted: Amex, Mastercard, Visa

Lea House Bed and Breakfast

COMMENDED

Lea House, The Lea, Ross-on-Wye, Herefordshire HR9 7JZ
☎ (01989) 750652 & (0589) 521797
Email: philnjo@vossnet.co.uk
16th C former coaching inn, tastefully converted and retaining many original features.
Bedrooms: 2 double, 1 twin
Bathrooms: 1 en-suite, 1 public

Bed & breakfast per night:	£min	£max
Double	28.00	35.00

Parking for 3

Merrivale Place

COMMENDED

The Avenue, Ross-on-Wye, Herefordshire HR9 5AW
☎ (01989) 564929
Fine Victorian house in quiet tree-lined avenue. Large comfortable rooms and lovely views. Home cooking. Near town and river.
Bedrooms: 2 double, 1 twin
Bathrooms: 2 public

Bed & breakfast per night:	£min	£max
Single	19.00	20.00
Double	34.00	36.00

Half board per person:	£min	£max
Daily	27.00	30.00
Weekly	185.00	200.00

Evening meal 1830 (last orders 1600)
Parking for 6
Open March–October

Norton House

HIGHLY COMMENDED

Whitchurch, Ross-on-Wye, Herefordshire HR9 6DJ
☎ (01600) 890046
Fax (01600) 890045
Email: jackson@osconwhi.source.co.uk

300-year-old listed building with oak beams, log fires and a wealth of character. Freshly prepared meals, friendly hospitality, quality and comfort our top priority.

Bedrooms: 3 double
Bathrooms: 3 en-suite

Bed & breakfast per night:	£min	£max
Single	25.00	30.00
Double	40.00	44.00

Half board per person:	£min	£max
Daily	29.50	31.50

Evening meal from 1930
Parking for 3

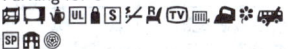

The Old Rectory

COMMENDED

Hope Mansell, Ross-on-Wye, Herefordshire HR9 5TL
☎ (01989) 750382
Fax (01989) 750382

Georgian house in beautiful rural surroundings near Ross-on-Wye. Friendly atmosphere, comfortable rooms with period furniture. Lovely mature gardens and all-weather tennis court.

Bedrooms: 2 double, 1 twin
Bathrooms: 1 private, 1 public

Bed & breakfast per night:	£min	£max
Single	18.50	20.00
Double	37.00	40.00

Parking for 4

Thatch Close

COMMENDED

Llangrove, Ross-on-Wye, Herefordshire HR9 6EL
☎ (01989) 770300

13-acre mixed farm. Secluded Georgian country farmhouse midway between Ross-on-Wye and Monmouth. Home-produced vegetables and meat. Ideal for country lovers of any age. Guests welcome to help with animals. Map sent on request. Ordnance Survey: 51535196.

Bedrooms: 2 double, 1 twin
Bathrooms: 2 en-suite, 1 private

Bed & breakfast per night:	£min	£max
Double	32.00	38.00

Half board per person:	£min	£max
Daily	28.00	31.00
Weekly	175.00	210.00

Lunch available
Evening meal 1830 (last orders 1800)
Parking for 7

RUGBY

Warwickshire
Map ref 4C3

Town famous for its public school which gave its name to Rugby Union football and which featured in "Tom Brown's Schooldays".
Tourist Information Centre ☎ (01788) 535348

White Lion Inn

APPROVED

Coventry Road, Pailton, Rugby CV23 0QD
☎ (01788) 832359
Fax (01788) 832359

17th C coaching inn, recently refurbished but retaining all old world features. Close to Rugby, Coventry and Stratford. Within 2 miles of motorways.

Bedrooms: 9 twin
Bathrooms: 3 en-suite, 2 public

Bed & breakfast per night:	£min	£max
Single	18.50	25.00
Double	37.00	45.00

Lunch available
Evening meal 1830 (last orders 2200)
Parking for 60
Cards accepted: Mastercard, Visa

30

You are advised to confirm your booking in writing.

Establishments should be open throughout the year, unless otherwise stated.

RUGELEY

Staffordshire
Map ref 4B3

Town close to Cannock Chase which has over 2000 acres of heath and woodlands with forest trails and picnic sites. Nearby is Shugborough Hall (National Trust) with a fine collection of 18th C furniture and interesting monuments in the grounds.

Park Farm

COMMENDED

Hawkesyard, Armitage Lane, Rugeley WS15 1ED
☎ (01889) 583477

40-acre livestock farm. While convenient for towns and attractions in the area, Park Farm is quietly tucked away in scenic hills.

Bedrooms: 2 triple
Bathrooms: 2 en-suite

Bed & breakfast per night:	£min	£max
Single	16.00	18.00
Double	32.00	36.00

Parking for 23

RUSHTON SPENCER

Staffordshire
Map ref 4B2

Village with an interesting church built in the 14th C of wood, some of which still remains. It is close to the pleasant Rudyard Reservoir.

Barnswood Farm

Listed COMMENDED

Rushton Spencer, Macclesfield, Cheshire SK11 0RA
☎ (01260) 226261

100-acre dairy farm. In a lovely setting overlooking Rudyard Lake 400 yards down the field. Alton Towers, Peak District and the Potteries all within a 15-mile radius. Homely welcome, English breakfast.

Bedrooms: 1 single, 1 double, 1 triple, 1 family room
Bathrooms: 2 public

Bed & breakfast per night:	£min	£max
Single		17.00
Double		30.00

Parking for 5

RUTLAND WATER

Rutland

See under Oakham

RUYTON-XI-TOWNS

Shropshire
Map ref 4A3

Town got its name from the time when, at the beginning of the 14th C, it was one of 11 towns "joined" into 1 manor. It is situated above the River Perry and has the remains of a castle in the churchyard.

Brownhill House

COMMENDED

Ruyton-XI-Towns, Shrewsbury
SY4 1LR
☎ (01939) 260626
Fax (01939) 260626
Email: ruyton@cityscape.uk

Quality accommodation, with first-class service. Good food and conversation, bring your own wine, extensive breakfast menu, non-stop tea/coffee. Local pubs. Unique hillside garden. Phone/fax for details.

Bedrooms: 1 single, 1 double, 1 twin
Bathrooms: 2 en-suite, 1 private

Bed & breakfast per night:	£min	£max
Single	18.00	26.00
Double	34.00	38.00

Half board per person:	£min	£max
Daily	28.00	37.00
Weekly	189.00	231.00

Lunch available
Evening meal 1800 (last orders 1300)
Parking for 5
Cards accepted: Mastercard, Visa, Switch/Delta

SHENINGTON

Oxfordshire
Map ref 2C1

Top Farm House

See South of England region for full entry details

SHERWOOD FOREST

See under Barnby Moor, Edwinstowe, Holbeck Woodhouse, Ragnall, Retford, Southwell

Please check prices and other details at the time of booking.

SHIPTON-UNDER-WYCHWOOD

Oxfordshire
Map ref 2B1

Courtlands

See South of England region for full entry details

SHREWSBURY

Shropshire
Map ref 4A3

Beautiful historic town on the River Severn retaining many fine old timber-framed houses. Its attractions include Rowley's Museum with Roman finds, remains of a castle, Clive House Museum, St Chad's 18th C round church, rowing on the river and the Shrewsbury Flower Show in August.
Tourist Information Centre ☎ (01743) 350761

Abbey Lodge Guest House

Listed COMMENDED

68 Abbey Foregate, Shrewsbury
SY2 6BG
☎ (01743) 235832 & 0860 335225

Georgian guesthouse. Friendly family-run business close to town centre. Some bedrooms en-suite. Car park at rear.

Bedrooms: 4 single, 3 double, 1 twin, 3 family rooms
Bathrooms: 4 en-suite, 3 public, 2 private showers

Bed & breakfast per night:	£min	£max
Single	16.00	18.00
Double	32.50	42.50

Parking for 11
Cards accepted: Mastercard, Visa

Ashton Lees

HIGHLY COMMENDED

Dorrington, Shrewsbury SY5 7JW
☎ (01743) 718378

Comfortable family home set in large secluded garden, 6 miles south of Shrewsbury on A49. Convenient for exploring the town and surrounding countryside.

Bedrooms: 2 double, 1 twin
Bathrooms: 1 en-suite, 1 public

Bed & breakfast per night:	£min	£max
Single	18.00	21.00
Double	36.00	42.00

Half board per person:	£min	£max
Daily	26.50	29.50

Evening meal 1830 (last orders 0900)
Parking for 6

Avonlea

Listed APPROVED

33 Coton Crescent, Coton Hill, Shrewsbury SY1 2NZ
☎ (01743) 359398

Built around 1900, an Edwardian house in a crescent of similar houses. Close to town centre and all public transport.

Bedrooms: 1 single, 2 twin
Bathrooms: 1 public, 1 private shower

Bed & breakfast per night:	£min	£max
Single	15.00	18.00
Double	28.00	32.00

10

Bancroft

Listed COMMENDED

17 Coton Crescent, Shrewsbury
SY1 2NY
☎ (01743) 231746
Fax (01743) 231746

This clean, friendly guesthouse, with central heating, welcome tray, and colour TV in rooms, is an easy walk to bus/railway and Brother Cadfael trail, alongside the river.

Bedrooms: 2 single, 1 twin, 1 triple
Bathrooms: 2 public

Bed & breakfast per night:	£min	£max
Single	17.00	20.00
Double	32.00	36.00

Half board per person:	£min	£max
Daily	27.00	

Evening meal 1830 (last orders 1600)
Parking for 3
Cards accepted: Mastercard, Visa

Chatford House

COMMENDED

Bayston Hill, Shrewsbury SY3 0AY
☎ (01743) 718301

5-acre mixed farm. Comfortable farmhouse built in 1776, 5.5 miles south of Shrewsbury off A49. Through Bayston Hill, take third right (Stapleton) then right to Chatford.

Bedrooms: 3 twin
Bathrooms: 1 public

Bed & breakfast per night:	£min	£max
Single	15.00	16.00
Double	30.00	32.00

Parking for 4
Open April–October

Hillsboro

Listed COMMENDED

1 Port Hill Gardens, Shrewsbury
SY3 8SH
☎ (01743) 231033

Charming Edwardian private house in quiet residential area, near park, river and Shrewsbury School. 5 minutes from town centre. Traditional breakfast a speciality. Parking.

Bedrooms: 1 double, 1 twin
Bathrooms: 1 public

Half board per person:	£min	£max
Daily	16.00	16.00
Weekly	112.00	112.00

Parking for 2

Merevale House

Listed COMMENDED

66 Ellesmere Road, Shrewsbury
SY1 2QP
☎ (01743) 243677

Lovely Victorian house. Attractive bedrooms with washbasins, TV, drinks and biscuits, hairdryer and many extra home comforts. Vegetarians catered for. 10 minutes from town. Private parking. Brochure.

Bedrooms: 1 single, 3 double
Bathrooms: 1 public

Bed & breakfast per night:	£min	£max
Single	16.00	16.00
Double	32.00	32.00

Parking for 8

Roseville

HIGHLY COMMENDED

12 Berwick Road, Shrewsbury
SY1 2LN
☎ (01743) 236470

Late Victorian detached town house, close to town centre. Comfortable, relaxed atmosphere and fine food. A no-smoking establishment.

Bedrooms: 1 single, 1 double, 1 twin
Bathrooms: 2 en-suite, 1 private

Bed & breakfast per night:	£min	£max
Single	20.00	22.00
Double	40.00	44.00

Parking for 3
Open February–December

Shorthill Lodge

HIGHLY COMMENDED

Shorthill, Lea Cross, Shrewsbury
SY5 8JE
☎ (01743) 860864

Comfortable country house in open setting. Centrally heated. Beautifully decorated rooms with TV/radio and hospitality tray. Full size en-suite bathrooms. Five miles south of Shrewsbury, off A488. Nearby pub/restaurant and golf-course. Brochure available.

Bedrooms: 1 double, 1 twin
Bathrooms: 2 en-suite, 1 public

Bed & breakfast per night:	£min	£max
Single	23.00	25.00
Double	34.00	38.00

Parking for 3

SILVERSTONE

Northamptonshire
Map ref 2C1

Old village with a lot of history to tell, including many stories of ghosts in the local buildings. Home of the world famous Silverstone Racing Circuit.

Silverthorpe Farm

Listed COMMENDED

Abthorpe Road, Silverstone, Towcester NN12 8TW
☎ (01327) 858020

5-acre organic farm. Large, spacious, modern bungalow with a warm and friendly atmosphere, standing in its own quiet, rural surroundings. 1.5 miles north of Silverstone.

Bedrooms: 2 twin, 1 family room
Bathrooms: 2 private, 2 public

Bed & breakfast per night:	£min	£max
Single	18.00	20.00
Double	36.00	40.00

Parking for 4

Please mention this guide when making your booking.

SOLIHULL

West Midlands
Map ref 4B3

On the outskirts of Birmingham. Some Tudor houses and a 13th C church remain amongst the new public buildings and shopping centre. The 16th C Malvern Hall is now a school and the 15th C Chester House at Knowle is now a library.
Tourist Information Centre ☎ (0121) 704 6130 or 704 6134

Acorn Guest House

COMMENDED

29 Links Drive, Solihull B91 2DJ
☎ (0121) 7055241

Quiet and comfortable family home with ample private facilities.

Bedrooms: 2 single, 1 double, 1 twin
Bathrooms: 1 en-suite, 2 public

Bed & breakfast per night:	£min	£max
Single	15.00	20.00
Double	40.00	45.00

Parking for 6

The Gate House

Listed COMMENDED

Barston Lane, Barston, Solihull
B92 0JN
☎ (01675) 443274

Early Victorian mansion house set in beautiful countryside. Close to National Exhibition Centre, International Convention Centre, airport and motorway.

Bedrooms: 1 single, 1 double, 2 twin
Bathrooms: 3 en-suite, 1 public

Bed & breakfast per night:	£min	£max
Single	20.00	30.00
Double	38.00	45.00

Parking for 20

SOULDERN

Oxfordshire
Map ref 2C1

Tower Fields
See South of England region for full entry details

All accommodation in this guide has been graded, or is awaiting a grading, by a trained Tourist Board inspector.

SOUTHWELL

Nottinghamshire
Map ref 4C2

Town dominated by the Norman minster which has some beautiful 13th C stone carvings in the Chapter House. Charles I spent his last night of freedom in one of the inns. The original Bramley apple tree can still be seen.

Barn Lodge

Listed COMMENDED

Duckers Cottage, Brinkley, Southwell NG25 0TP
☎ (01636) 813435

Smallholding with panoramic views, 1 mile from the centre of Southwell and close to the racecourse, railway station and River Trent.

Bedrooms: 1 double, 1 twin, 1 triple
Bathrooms: 3 en-suite

Bed & breakfast per night:	£min	£max
Single	20.00	20.00
Double	40.00	40.00

Parking for 3

STAFFORD

Staffordshire
Map ref 4B3

The town has a long history and some half-timbered buildings still remain, notably the 16th C High House. There are several museums in the town and Shugborough Hall and the famous angler Izaak Walton's cottage, now a museum, are nearby.
Tourist Information Centre ☎ (01785) 240204

Littywood Farm

COMMENDED

Bradley, Stafford ST18 9DW
☎ (01785) 780234 & 780770
Fax (01785) 780770

400-acre mixed farm. Beautiful 14th C manor offering country house accommodation, secluded yet easily accessible from the M6. Centrally heated.

Bedrooms: 1 double, 1 twin
Bathrooms: 1 en-suite, 1 public

Bed & breakfast per night:	£min	£max
Single	18.00	25.00
Double	36.00	40.00

Parking for 10

STAUNTON

Gloucestershire
Map ref 2B1

Village in attractive countryside, midway between Gloucester, Ledbury and Tewkesbury.

Kilmorie Guest House

APPROVED

Gloucester Road, Corse, Snigs End, Staunton, Gloucester GL19 3RQ
☎ (01452) 840224

7-acre livestock & fruit farm. Built by Chartists in 1847, Grade II listed smallholding in conservation area. All rooms ground floor with TV, tea tray, hot and cold water. Ideally situated for touring Cotswolds, Forest of Dean and Malvern Hills.

Bedrooms: 2 single, 2 double, 1 twin, 1 family room
Bathrooms: 1 en-suite, 1 private, 1 public

Bed & breakfast per night:	£min	£max
Single	15.00	
Double	30.00	

Half board per person:	£min	£max
Daily	22.50	
Weekly	150.50	

Lunch available
Evening meal from 1800
Parking for 8

STIPERSTONES

Shropshire
Map ref 4A3

Below the spectacular ridge of the same name, from which superb views over moorland, forest and hills may be enjoyed.

Sycamore Cottage

COMMENDED

5 Perkins Beach, Stiperstones, Minsterley, Shrewsbury SY5 0PQ
☎ (01743) 790914

Delightful accommodation in beamed cottage on Stiperstones Hills. Log fire. Friendly welcome. Wonderful views. Ideal walking country.

Bedrooms: 1 twin
Bathrooms: 1 en-suite

Bed & breakfast per night:	£min	£max
Single	17.50	21.50
Double	35.00	35.00

Half board per person:	£min	£max
Daily		27.00
Weekly		189.00

Evening meal 1930 (last orders 2200)
Parking for 3

Tankerville Lodge

COMMENDED

Stiperstones, Minsterley, Shrewsbury SY5 0NB
☎ (01743) 791401

Country house noted for warm hospitality, set in superb landscape which offers breathtaking views. Ideal touring base for Shropshire and Welsh borderland. Adjacent to Stiperstones Nature Reserve.

Bedrooms: 1 double, 3 twin
Bathrooms: 2 public

Bed & breakfast per night:	£min	£max
Single	16.50	19.50
Double	33.00	33.00

Half board per person:	£min	£max
Daily	26.00	29.00
Weekly	173.60	194.60

Evening meal 1900 (last orders 0900)
Parking for 5

STOKE BRUERNE

Northamptonshire
Map ref 2C1

Village on the Grand Union Canal at the southern end of the long Blisworth Tunnel. The Waterways Museum traces the history of the waterways and canals over the last 200 years and there are trips on the canal in summer.

Beam End

Listed COMMENDED

Stoke Park, Stoke Bruerne, Towcester NN12 7RZ
☎ (01604) 864638 & 864802
Fax (01604) 864638

Originally a stable for working horses on the Stoke Park Estate, now converted to provide secluded accommodation in a family home. On a private road.

Bedrooms: 1 double, 1 twin
Bathrooms: 1 public

Bed & breakfast per night:	£min	£max
Single	20.00	25.00
Double	40.00	50.00

Evening meal 1800 (last orders 2030)
Parking for 6

STOKE DOYLE

Northamptonshire
Map ref 3A2

Village whose church has a fine monument by the eminent 18th C sculptor Rysbrack.

Shuckburgh Arms

COMMENDED

Stoke Doyle, Peterborough
PE8 5TG
☎ (01832) 272339
Fax (01832) 275230
Fully licensed country inn, offering bed and breakfast, meals, real ales and a beer garden.
Bedrooms: 2 single, 1 double, 2 twin
Bathrooms: 5 en-suite

Bed & breakfast per night:	£min	£max
Single	27.50	30.00
Double	45.00	50.00

Half board per person:	£min	£max
Daily	40.00	40.00

Lunch available
Evening meal 1930 (last orders 2130)
Parking for 20
Cards accepted: Amex, Mastercard, Visa, Switch/Delta

STOKE-ON-TRENT

Staffordshire
Map ref 4B2

Famous for its pottery. Factories of several famous makers, including Josiah Wedgwood, can be visited. The City Museum has one of the finest pottery and porcelain collections in the world.
Tourist Information Centre ☎ (01782) 284600

Chestnut Grange

COMMENDED

Windmill Hill, Rough Close, Stoke-on-Trent ST3 7PJ
☎ (01782) 396084 & (0585) 847832
Fax (01782) 396084

18th C stone-clad cottage, set in rolling Staffordshire countryside, yet only 10 minutes from junction 15 of M6 and 5 minutes from Wedgwood.
Bedrooms: 2 double, 1 family room
Bathrooms: 3 en-suite

Bed & breakfast per night:	£min	£max
Single	18.00	24.00
Double	36.00	45.00

Parking for 5

The Hollies

COMMENDED

Clay Lake, Endon, Stoke-on-Trent
ST9 9DD
☎ (01782) 503252
Delightful Victorian house in a quiet country setting off B5051. Convenient for M6, the Potteries and Alton Towers. Spacious rooms - no smoking.
Bedrooms: 2 double, 3 triple
Bathrooms: 4 en-suite, 1 private

Bed & breakfast per night:	£min	£max
Single	20.00	30.00
Double	30.00	40.00

Parking for 5

The Old Dairy House

HIGHLY COMMENDED

Trentham Park, Stoke-on-Trent
ST4 8AE
☎ (01782) 641209
Fax (01782) 712904
Privately owned and family run former dairy, set in 2 acres of secluded wooded grounds with the benefit of a tennis court. Ample parking.
Bedrooms: 2 double
Bathrooms: 2 en-suite

Bed & breakfast per night:	£min	£max
Single	30.00	35.00
Double	42.00	45.00

Evening meal 1830 (last orders 1800)
Parking for 10

You are advised to confirm your booking in writing.

Trentside Private Hotel

260 Stone Road, Hanford,
Stoke-on-Trent ST4 8NJ
☎ (01782) 642443
Fax (01782) 641910
Situated by the River Trent on the A34. Offering homely, comfortable accommodation, convenient for all the local pottery manufacturers and Alton Towers.
Bedrooms: 2 single, 4 double, 2 twin, 1 triple, 1 family room
Bathrooms: 5 en-suite, 1 public

Bed & breakfast per night:	£min	£max
Single	16.00	20.00
Double	32.00	38.00

Parking for 10
Cards accepted: Mastercard, Visa

STONE

Staffordshire
Map ref 4B2

Town on the River Trent with the remains of a 12th C Augustinian priory. It is surrounded by pleasant countryside. Trentham Gardens with 500 acres of parklands and recreational facilities is within easy reach.

Couldreys

COMMENDED

8 Airdale Road, Stone ST15 8DW
☎ (01785) 812500
Fax (01785) 811761
Edwardian house quietly situated on town outskirts, providing every comfort plus home-made bread! Excellent restaurants within walking distance. Convenient for M6, Wedgwood and Potteries. Non-smokers only, please.
Bedrooms: 1 double, 1 twin
Bathrooms: 1 en-suite, 1 private

Bed & breakfast per night:	£min	£max
Single	22.00	
Double	34.00	

Parking for 2

Please check prices and other details at the time of booking.

Map references apply to the colour maps at the back of this guide.

STONEHOUSE

Gloucestershire
Map ref 2B1

Village in the Stroud Valley with an Elizabethan Court, later restored and altered by Lutyens.

Merton Lodge

APPROVED

8 Ebley Road, Stonehouse
GL10 2LQ
☎ (01453) 822018

Former gentleman's residence offering a warm welcome. Cotton and linen sheets only. No smoking. Three miles from M5 junction 13, over 4 roundabouts, straight on along Old Road, under foot bridge. Located virtually opposite garden centre. Short walk from carvery/pub.

Bedrooms: 3 double
Bathrooms: 1 en-suite, 2 public

Bed & breakfast per night:	£min	£max
Single	15.00	17.00

Parking for 6

STOULTON

Hereford and Worcester
Map ref 2B1

Caldewell

COMMENDED

Pershore Road, Stoulton, Worcester
WR7 4RL
☎ (01905) 840894

Country house set in woodland conservation area with lake. Farm animals kept. Miniature steam railway and excellent facilities for children.

Bedrooms: 2 double, 1 twin, 1 triple
Bathrooms: 2 en-suite, 1 private, 2 public

Bed & breakfast per night:	£min	£max
Single	20.00	24.00
Double	35.00	40.00

Parking for 6
Open March–December

Please mention this guide when making your booking.

A key to symbols can be found inside the back cover flap.

STOW-ON-THE-WOLD

Gloucestershire
Map ref 2B1

Attractive Cotswold wool town with a large market-place and some fine houses, especially the old grammar school. There is an interesting church dating from Norman times. Stow-on-the-Wold is surrounded by lovely countryside and Cotswold villages.
Tourist Information Centre ☎ (01451) 831082

Aston House

Listed COMMENDED

Broadwell, Stow-on-the-Wold, Moreton-in-Marsh GL56 0TJ
☎ (01451) 830475
Email: fja@netcomuk.co.uk

Quiet village location, 1.5 miles from Stow-on-the-Wold, central for touring Cotswolds. TV, tea-making facilities, bedtime drinks, good breakfast. Pub in walking distance. No smoking. Reduced rates for weekly stays.

Bedrooms: 2 double, 1 twin
Bathrooms: 2 en-suite, 1 private

Bed & breakfast per night:	£min	£max
Double	38.00	42.00

Parking for 3
Open February–November
10

Corsham Field Farmhouse

APPROVED

Bledington Road, Stow-on-the-Wold, Cheltenham GL54 1JH
☎ (01451) 831750

100-acre mixed farm. Homely farmhouse with breathtaking views. Ideally situated for exploring the Cotswolds. En-suite and standard rooms. TVs, guest lounge, tea/coffee facilities. Good pub food 5 minutes' walk away.

Bedrooms: 2 double, 2 twin, 3 family rooms
Bathrooms: 5 en-suite, 1 public

Bed & breakfast per night:	£min	£max
Single	15.00	25.00
Double	30.00	40.00

Parking for 10

For ideas on places to visit refer to the introduction at the beginning of this section.

Cross Keys Cottage

COMMENDED

Park Street, Stow-on-the-Wold, Cheltenham GL54 1AQ
☎ (01451) 831128

Just a few minutes' walk from Stow Square, this pretty 17th C cottage offers delightful accommodation and a warm welcome. Superb breakfasts and all facilities.

Bedrooms: 2 double, 1 twin
Bathrooms: 1 en-suite, 2 public

Bed & breakfast per night:	£min	£max
Single	25.00	36.00
Double	42.00	50.00

The Hollies

COMMENDED

Lower Swell Road, Stow-on-the-Wold, Cheltenham GL54 1LD
☎ (01451) 830577 & 0860 192017
Fax (01451) 830577
Email: hollies@mcmail.com

Cotswold family home, large garden with uninterrupted views across the Dikler Valley. Ample parking. Ten minutes to market square.

Bedrooms: 2 double, 1 twin
Bathrooms: 3 en-suite

Bed & breakfast per night:	£min	£max
Single	22.00	26.00
Double	37.00	42.00

Parking for 3

Horse and Groom Inn

COMMENDED

Upper Oddington, Moreton-in-Marsh GL56 0XH
☎ (01451) 830584
Fax (01451) 870494

16th C old world character inn off A436. In quiet village yet only 2 miles from Stow-on-the-Wold and close to motorway and trunk roads. En-suite rooms, lunchtime and evening meals. Families welcome.

Bedrooms: 5 double, 2 twin
Bathrooms: 7 en-suite

Bed & breakfast per night:	£min	£max
Single	40.00	50.00
Double	55.00	70.00

Lunch available
Evening meal 1830 (last orders 2130)
Parking for 40
Cards accepted: Mastercard, Visa, Switch/Delta

Old Farmhouse Hotel

COMMENDED

Lower Swell, Stow-on-the-Wold, Cheltenham GL54 1LF
☎ (01451) 830232 & 0500 657842
Fax (01451) 870962
Email: oldfarm@globalnet.co.uk

Sympathetically converted 16th C Cotswold-stone farmhouse in a quiet hamlet, 1 mile west of Stow-on-the-Wold. Warm and unpretentious hospitality.
http://www.scws.com/webcraft/hotels/Old_Farmhouse
Bedrooms: 7 double, 4 twin, 2 family rooms
Suites available
Bathrooms: 11 en-suite, 1 public

Bed & breakfast per night:	£min	£max
Single	20.00	75.00
Double	40.00	95.00

Half board per person:	£min	£max
Daily	37.00	92.00
Weekly	259.00	644.00

Lunch available
Evening meal 1900 (last orders 2100)
Parking for 25
Cards accepted: Mastercard, Visa, Switch/Delta
20

Woodlands

COMMENDED

Lower Swell, Stow-on-the-Wold, Cheltenham GL54 1EW
☎ (01451) 832346
Small guesthouse in quaint Cotswold village, 1 mile from Stow-on-the-Wold. Set in half-acre gardens with breathtaking views of the Cotswolds. All rooms en-suite. Guest lounge where light snacks can be served.
Bedrooms: 3 double
Bathrooms: 3 en-suite

Bed & breakfast per night:	£min	£max
Single	35.00	
Double	50.00	

Parking for 6
Cards accepted: Mastercard, Visa

Wyck Hill Lodge

HIGHLY COMMENDED

Burford Road, Stow-on-the-Wold, Cheltenham GL54 1HT
☎ (01451) 830141
Tastefully furnished Victorian lodge in peaceful rural surroundings. Renowned for comfort, fine breakfasts and hospitality. Extensive views. 1 mile from Stow-on-the-Wold. Ample parking. Non-smokers only, please.
Bedrooms: 2 double, 1 twin
Bathrooms: 3 en-suite

Bed & breakfast per night:	£min	£max
Double	42.00	46.00

Parking for 3
Open March–November

STRATFORD-UPON-AVON

Warwickshire
Map ref 2B1

Famous as Shakespeare's home town, Stratford's many attractions include his birthplace, New Place where he died, the Royal Shakespeare Theatre and Gallery, "The World of Shakespeare" 30 minute theatre and Hall's Croft (his daughter's house).
Tourist Information Centre ☎ (01789) 293127

Allors

Listed COMMENDED

62 Evesham Road, Stratford-upon-Avon CV37 9BA
☎ (01789) 269982
Detached house, comfortable rooms with en-suite facilities. Dining room overlooking secluded garden. TV, parking, non-smoking. Special rates for 3-night breaks.
Bedrooms: 2 double
Bathrooms: 2 en-suite

Bed & breakfast per night:	£min	£max
Double	36.00	44.00

Parking for 3

Braeside Guest House

COMMENDED

129 Shipston Road, Stratford-upon-Avon CV37 7LW
☎ (01789) 261648
Attractive detached family-run guesthouse, 10 minutes' walk from theatre and town centre along old tramway footpath. Double/family room and twin room are en-suite, single has private bathroom. Ample parking. Car service to coach and railway stations.
Bedrooms: 1 single, 1 twin, 1 triple
Bathrooms: 2 en-suite, 1 private, 1 public

Bed & breakfast per night:	£min	£max
Single	18.00	20.00
Double	36.00	40.00

Parking for 4

Bronhill House

Listed APPROVED

260 Alcester Road, Stratford-upon-Avon CV37 9JQ
☎ (01789) 299169
Detached family house in elevated position, 1 mile from Stratford-upon-Avon. Family-run with relaxed friendly atmosphere. A non-smoking establishment.
Bedrooms: 2 double, 1 twin
Bathrooms: 1 en-suite, 2 private, 2 public

Bed & breakfast per night:	£min	£max
Single	15.00	20.00
Double	27.00	34.00

Parking for 5
5

Burton Farm

COMMENDED

Bishopton, Stratford-upon-Avon CV37 0RW
☎ (01789) 293338
Fax (01789) 262877

150-acre mixed farm. Elizabethan farmhouse with large gardens, in rural surroundings 1.5 miles from Stratford-upon-Avon.
Bedrooms: 1 single, 2 double, 1 twin, 1 triple
Bathrooms: 4 en-suite, 1 private

Bed & breakfast per night:	£min	£max
Single	22.50	30.00
Double	45.00	50.00

Parking for 22

Cherangani

COMMENDED

61 Maidenhead Road, Stratford-upon-Avon CV37 6XU
☎ (01789) 292655
Pleasant detached house in a quiet,
Continued ▶

STRATFORD-UPON-AVON

Continued

residential area, offering warm, attractive accommodation. Within walking distance of the town and theatre.
Bedrooms: 1 twin
Bathrooms: 1 public

Bed & breakfast per night:	£min	£max
Single	18.00	20.00
Double	34.00	38.00

Parking for 3

Church Farm

COMMENDED

Dorsington, Stratford-upon-Avon CV37 8AX
☎ (01789) 720471 & 0831 504194
Fax (01789) 720830
127-acre mixed farm. Situated in beautiful countryside, most rooms en-suite, TV, tea and coffee facilities. Close to Stratford-upon-Avon, Warwick, the Cotswolds and Evesham.
Wheelchair access category 3
Bedrooms: 4 double, 1 twin, 2 family rooms
Bathrooms: 6 en-suite, 1 private

Bed & breakfast per night:	£min	£max
Double	33.00	39.00

Parking for 12

Clomendy Guest House

COMMENDED

157 Evesham Road,
Stratford-upon-Avon CV37 9BP
☎ (01789) 266957

Small, detached, mock-Tudor family-run guesthouse, convenient for town centre, Anne Hathaway's cottage and theatres. Stratford-in-Bloom commendation winner. Rail/coach guests met and returned. No smoking, please.
Bedrooms: 1 single, 1 double, 1 twin
Bathrooms: 1 public, 1 private shower

Bed & breakfast per night:	£min	£max
Single	16.00	19.00
Double	28.00	38.00

Parking for 5

Faviere

COMMENDED

127 Shipston Road,
Stratford-upon-Avon CV37 7LW
☎ (01789) 293764
Fax (01789) 269365
Email: favifajohn@ad.com

A warm, friendly welcome awaits you at this comfortable family-run guesthouse. Situated close to the river and a 10-minute walk will take you to the theatre and town centre.
Bedrooms: 1 single, 1 double, 1 triple
Bathrooms: 2 en-suite, 1 private

Bed & breakfast per night:	£min	£max
Single	17.00	20.00
Double	32.00	44.00

Parking for 6
Open January–February, April–December

Field View

APPROVED

35 Banbury Road, Stratford-upon-Avon CV37 7HW
☎ (01789) 292694

10 minutes' walk from Stratford town centre, offering comfortable, family-type accommodation.

Bedrooms: 1 double
Bathrooms: 1 public

Bed & breakfast per night:	£min	£max
Single	15.00	17.00
Double	30.00	34.00

Parking for 3

Glebe Farm

HIGHLY COMMENDED

Loxley, Warwick CV35 9JW
☎ (01789) 842501 & (0966) 236155
Fax (01789) 842501
Email: scorpiolimited@msn.com

Fine country house in 30 acres of Warwickshire countryside, only 2 miles from Stratford-upon-Avon. Both rooms have four-poster beds and are en-suite.

Bedrooms: 2 double
Bathrooms: 2 en-suite, 1 public

Bed & breakfast per night:	£min	£max
Double	58.00	80.00

Evening meal 1800 (last orders 2200)
Parking for 12
Cards accepted: Amex, Mastercard, Visa, Switch/Delta

Green Gables

COMMENDED

47 Banbury Road, Stratford-upon-Avon CV37 7HW
☎ (01789) 205557

Edwardian house in a residential area, within 10 minutes' walk of the town centre and theatre.

Bedrooms: 1 double
Bathrooms: 1 private, 1 public

Bed & breakfast per night:	£min	£max
Double	34.00	39.00

Parking for 3

Highcroft

COMMENDED

Banbury Road, Stratford-upon-Avon CV37 7NF
☎ (01789) 296293

Lovely country house in 2-acre garden, only 2 miles from Stratford-upon-Avon, on A422. Families welcome. Friendly, relaxed atmosphere.

Bedrooms: 1 double, 1 family room
Bathrooms: 2 en-suite

Bed & breakfast per night:	£min	£max
Single		20.00
Double		36.00

Parking for 3

Houndshill House

COMMENDED

Banbury Road, Ettington, Stratford-upon-Avon CV37 7NS
☎ (01789) 740267
Fax (01789) 740075

Family-run pub with restaurant, 4 miles from Stratford-upon-Avon. Informal and friendly atmosphere.

Bedrooms: 2 single, 3 double, 2 twin, 1 triple
Bathrooms: 8 en-suite

Bed & breakfast per night:	£min	£max
Single	30.00	
Double	50.00	

Lunch available
Evening meal 1900 (last orders 2200)
Parking for 50
Cards accepted: Mastercard, Visa, Switch/Delta

Moonraker House

COMMENDED

40 Alcester Road, Stratford-upon-Avon CV37 9DB
☎ (01789) 299346 & 267115
Fax (01789) 295504
Email: moonraker.spencer@virgin.net

Family-run, near town centre. Beautifully co-ordinated decor throughout. Some rooms with four-poster beds and garden terrace available for non-smokers.
www.stratford-upon-avon.co.uk/moonraker.htm

Bedrooms: 16 double, 2 twin, 4 triple
Bathrooms: 22 en-suite

Bed & breakfast per night:	£min	£max
Single	35.00	45.00
Double	45.00	70.00

Parking for 24
Cards accepted: Mastercard, Visa

Newlands

COMMENDED

7 Broad Walk, Stratford-upon-Avon CV37 6HS
☎ (01789) 298449
Fax (01789) 298449

Sue Boston's home is a short walk to the Royal Shakespeare Theatre, town centre and Shakespeare properties, and has some forecourt parking.

Bedrooms: 1 single, 1 double, 2 triple
Bathrooms: 3 en-suite, 1 public

Bed & breakfast per night:	£min	£max
Single	19.00	21.00
Double	40.00	46.00

Parking for 2
Cards accepted: Mastercard, Visa, Switch/Delta
10

Oxstalls Farm

COMMENDED

Warwick Road, Stratford-upon-Avon CV37 0NS
☎ (01789) 205277

Beautifully situated 60-acre stud farm overlooking the Welcome Hills and golf-course. 1 mile from Stratford-upon-Avon town centre and the Royal Shakespeare Theatre.

Bedrooms: 1 single, 11 double, 4 twin, 7 triple
Bathrooms: 16 en-suite, 1 public, 3 private showers

Bed & breakfast per night:	£min	£max
Single	17.50	35.00
Double	35.00	60.00

Parking for 20

Ad See display advertisement on page 184

STRATFORD-UPON-AVON

Continued

Peartree Cottage

HIGHLY COMMENDED

7 Church Road, Wilmcote, Stratford-upon-Avon CV37 9UX
☎ (01789) 205889
Fax (01789) 262862

Elizabethan house, furnished with antiques, set in beautiful garden overlooking Mary Arden's house. Pub and restaurant within walking distance.

Bedrooms: 4 double, 2 twin, 1 triple
Bathrooms: 7 en-suite

Bed & breakfast per night:	£min	£max
Single	30.00	32.00
Double	45.00	50.00

Parking for 8

Ravenhurst

COMMENDED

2 Broad Walk, Stratford-upon-Avon CV37 6HS
☎ (01789) 292515

Quietly situated, a few minutes' walk from the town centre and places of historic interest. Comfortable home, with substantial breakfast provided. Four-poster available.

Bedrooms: 4 double, 1 twin
Bathrooms: 5 en-suite

Bed & breakfast per night:	£min	£max
Double	40.00	50.00

Parking for 4
Cards accepted: Amex, Diners, Mastercard, Visa

Whitchurch Farm

COMMENDED

Wimpstone, Stratford-upon-Avon CV37 8NS
☎ (01789) 450275

260-acre mixed farm. Listed Georgian farmhouse set in park-like surroundings on the edge of the Cotswolds. Ideal for a touring holiday. Small village 4 miles south of Stratford-upon-Avon.

Bedrooms: 2 double, 1 twin
Bathrooms: 3 en-suite, 1 public

Bed & breakfast per night:	£min	£max
Single	18.00	19.00
Double	36.00	38.00

Half board per person:	£min	£max
Daily	28.00	29.00

Evening meal from 1830
Parking for 3

STROUD

Gloucestershire
Map ref 2B1

This old town, surrounded by attractive hilly country, has been producing broadcloth for centuries and the local museum has an interesting display on the subject. Many of the mills have been converted into craft centres and for other uses.
Tourist Information Centre ☎ (01453) 765768

The Dial Cottage

HIGHLY COMMENDED

Amberley, Stroud GL5 5AL
☎ (01453) 872563
Fax (01453) 873057

17th C Cotswold cottage situated in 600 acres of National Trust land, Minchinhampton Common, within the Royal Triangle.

Bedrooms: 2 double, 1 twin
Bathrooms: 3 en-suite

Bed & breakfast per night:	£min	£max
Single	38.50	
Double	70.00	

Parking for 8
Open March–November

Downfield Hotel

COMMENDED

134 Cainscross Road, Stroud GL5 4HN
☎ (01453) 764496
Fax (01453) 753150

Imposing hotel in quiet location. Home cooking. 1 mile from town centre, 5 miles from M5 motorway, junction 13, on main A419 road.

Bedrooms: 4 single, 9 double, 7 twin, 1 triple
Bathrooms: 11 en-suite, 3 public

Bed & breakfast per night:	£min	£max
Single	20.00	29.00
Double	33.00	39.00

Evening meal 1830 (last orders 2000)
Parking for 23
Cards accepted: Amex, Diners, Mastercard, Visa, Switch/Delta

The Laye-Bye

COMMENDED

7 Castlemead Road, Rodborough, Stroud GL5 3SF
☎ (01453) 751514
Fax (01453) 751514

Spacious elevated town house in discreet cul-de-sac. Attractive views, quiet garden, tastefully decorated. All modern facilities.

Bedrooms: 2 single, 2 double
Bathrooms: 4 en-suite, 1 public

Bed & breakfast per night:	£min	£max
Single	15.00	20.00
Double	30.00	40.00

Half board per person:	£min	£max
Daily	23.00	28.00
Weekly	150.00	175.00

Evening meal from 1800
Parking for 4

Whitegates Farm

COMMENDED

Cowcombe Hill, Chalford, Stroud GL6 8HP
☎ (01285) 760758

Peaceful hillside farmhouse with lovely views, gardens, orchards and 16 rambling acres. Good walking, central for touring. Non-smokers only, please. Spanish spoken.

Bedrooms: 1 double, 1 twin
Bathrooms: 1 en-suite, 1 private

Bed & breakfast per night:	£min	£max
Single	27.00	33.00
Double	38.00	46.00

Parking for 6

Information on accommodation listed in this guide has been supplied by the proprietors. As changes may occur you are advised to check details at the time of booking.

STUDLEY

Warwickshire
Map ref 2B1

This town has been producing needles for several centuries and has some old houses and inns. The Elizabethan Coughton Court (National Trust), the Palladian Ragley Hall with its beautiful plasterwork and Stratford-upon-Avon are easily reached.

Ardendane Manor

Listed COMMENDED

Henley Road, Outhill, Studley
B80 7DT
☎ (01527) 852808

Accommodation in large, comfortable house with peaceful gardens and commanding views. Traditional English breakfast. Easy access to motorway network.
Bedrooms: 1 double, 1 twin
Bathrooms: 2 en-suite

Bed & breakfast per night:	£min	£max
Single	40.00	40.00
Double	50.00	50.00

Half board per person:	£min	£max
Daily	65.00	100.00

Parking for 10

TEDDINGTON

Gloucestershire
Map ref 2B1

Village a few miles east of Tewkesbury and north of Cheltenham, with just a few farms and houses, but an interesting church.

Bengrove Farm

COMMENDED

Bengrove, Teddington, Tewkesbury
GL20 8JB
☎ (01242) 620332
Fax (01242) 620851
10-acre mixed farm. Large, interesting 17th C farmhouse with attractive rooms, timbered and beamed. 2 twin rooms, lounge and guests' bathroom. Comfortably furnished. In Area of Outstanding Natural Beauty.
Bedrooms: 2 twin
Bathrooms: 1 public

Bed & breakfast per night:	£min	£max
Single	20.00	20.00
Double	33.00	33.00

Parking for 10

TELFORD

Shropshire
Map ref 4A3

New Town named after Thomas Telford, the famous engineer who designed many of the country's canals, bridges and viaducts. It is close to Ironbridge with its monuments and museums to the Industrial Revolution, including restored 18th C buildings.
Tourist Information Centre ☎ (01952) 291370

Allscott Inn

APPROVED

Walcot, Wellington, Telford
TF6 5EQ
☎ (01952) 248484
Homely country inn offering delicious food and comfortable accommodation. Beer garden. Easy access Shrewsbury, Ironbridge and Telford.
Bedrooms: 1 double, 2 twin, 1 triple
Bathrooms: 2 en-suite, 1 public

Bed & breakfast per night:	£min	£max
Single	20.00	26.00
Double	32.00	40.00

Lunch available
Evening meal 1900 (last orders 2200)
Parking for 50
Cards accepted: Amex, Mastercard, Visa

Half board prices are given per person, but in some cases these may be based on double/twin occupancy.

The symbols in each entry give information about services and facilities. A key to these symbols appears at the back of this guide.

Old Rectory

Stirchley Village, Telford TF3 1DT
☎ (01952) 596308 & 596518
Fax (01952) 596308
Large, comfortable guesthouse dating from 1734. Set in an acre of secluded gardens, on edge of town park. Convenient for town centre and Ironbridge museums. Three miles from M54, junction 4.
Bedrooms: 2 single, 1 double, 2 twin, 1 family room
Bathrooms: 3 en-suite, 3 private

Bed & breakfast per night:	£min	£max
Single	23.00	25.00
Double	35.00	40.00

Half board per person:	£min	£max
Daily	31.00	33.00
Weekly	196.00	208.00

Evening meal 1800 (last orders 2100)
Parking for 6

TENBURY WELLS

Hereford and Worcester
Map ref 4A3

Small market town on the Teme possessing many fine black and white buildings. In 1839 mineral springs were found here and there were hopes of a spa centre developing. The waters never became fashionable and today only the old Pump Room remains.

Peacock Inn

HIGHLY COMMENDED

Boraston, Tenbury Wells, Worcestershire WR15 8LL
☎ (01584) 810506 & 811236
Fax (01584) 811236
14th C inn with oak-panelled walls, beamed ceilings and open log fires. Fine cuisine with fish a speciality.
Bedrooms: 3 double
Bathrooms: 3 en-suite

Bed & breakfast per night:	£min	£max
Single	55.00	55.00
Double	70.00	70.00

Lunch available
Evening meal 1900 (last orders 2130)
Parking for 30
Cards accepted: Mastercard, Visa, Switch/Delta

TETBURY

Gloucestershire
Map ref 2B2

Small market town with 18th C houses and an attractive 17th C Town Hall. It is a good touring centre with many places of interest nearby including Badminton House and Westonbirt Arboretum.

Tavern House

DE LUXE

Willesley, Tetbury GL8 8QU
☎ (01666) 880444
Fax (01666) 880254

Grade II listed Cotswold stone house (formerly a staging post) on the A433 Bath road, 1 mile from Westonbirt Arboretum and 4 miles from Tetbury.
Bedrooms: 3 double, 1 twin
Bathrooms: 4 en-suite

Bed & breakfast per night:	£min	£max
Single	42.50	47.50
Double	57.00	67.00

Parking for 4
Cards accepted: Mastercard, Visa

TEWKESBURY

Gloucestershire
Map ref 2B1

Tewkesbury's outstanding possession is its magnificent church, built as an abbey, with a great Norman tower and beautiful 14th C interior. The town stands at the confluence of the Severn and Avon and has many medieval houses, inns and several museums.
Tourist Information Centre ☎ (01684) 295027

Abbots Court Farm

COMMENDED

Church End, Twyning, Tewkesbury GL20 6DA
☎ (01684) 292515
Fax (01684) 292515

You are advised to confirm your booking in writing.

450-acre arable & dairy farm. Large, comfortable farmhouse in excellent touring area. Most rooms en-suite. 3 games rooms, grass tennis court, fishing available.
Bedrooms: 1 single, 1 double, 2 twin, 2 triple, 2 family rooms
Bathrooms: 6 en-suite, 1 public

Bed & breakfast per night:	£min	£max
Single	19.00	22.00
Double	32.00	36.00

Parking for 20

Lampitt House

COMMENDED

Lampitt Lane, Bredon's Norton, Tewkesbury GL20 7HB
☎ (01684) 772295
Fax (01684) 772295

Comfortable house set in 1.5 acre garden in picturesque Cotswold village at the foot of Bredon Hill. Extensive views. Tewkesbury 4 miles. Beautiful hill and riverside walks.
Bedrooms: 2 double, 1 twin
Bathrooms: 3 en-suite

Bed & breakfast per night:	£min	£max
Single	26.00	34.00
Double	36.00	40.00

Evening meal 1800 (last orders 2000)
Parking for 6

Please check prices and other details at the time of booking.

Establishments should be open throughout the year, unless otherwise stated.

Town Street Farm

COMMENDED

Tirley, Gloucester GL19 4HG
☎ (01452) 780442
Fax (01452) 780890

500-acre mixed farm. 18th C farmhouse set in beautiful surroundings and within half a mile of the River Severn.
Bedrooms: 1 double, 1 triple
Bathrooms: 2 en-suite, 1 public

Bed & breakfast per night:	£min	£max
Single	24.00	25.00
Double	36.00	37.00

Parking for 4

TIDESWELL

Derbyshire
Map ref 4B2

Small town with a large 14th C church known as the "Cathedral of the Peak". There is a well-dressing ceremony each June with Morris dancing, and many choral events throughout the year.

Poppies

Listed APPROVED

Bank Square, Tideswell, Buxton SK17 8LA
☎ (01298) 871083
Poppies offers a warm welcome, comfortable accommodation and good vegetarian and traditional home cooking in a small restaurant, at the centre of this picturesque mid-Peak District village.
Bedrooms: 1 double, 1 twin, 1 triple
Bathrooms: 1 en-suite, 1 public

Bed & breakfast per night:	£min	£max
Single	15.00	19.50
Double	30.00	39.00

Half board per person:	£min	£max
Daily	25.00	40.50
Weekly	160.00	260.00

Lunch available
Evening meal 1845 (last orders 1915)
Open February–December
Cards accepted: Amex, Diners, Mastercard, Visa

TOWCESTER

Northamptonshire
Map ref 2C1

Town built on the site of a Roman settlement. It has some interesting old buildings, including an inn featured in one of Dickens' novels. The racecourse lies alongside the A5 Watling Street, and motor racing takes place at nearby Silverstone.

Cutchems End

HIGHLY COMMENDED

Yorks Farm, Watling Street,
Towcester NN12 8EU
☎ (01327) 830640 & 830645
Fax (01327) 830645

Converted 19th C barn, retaining interesting features and utilising old materials. Delightful rural setting with extensive views over open countryside.

Bedrooms: 2 double
Bathrooms: 2 en-suite

Bed & breakfast per night:	£min	£max
Single	22.00	22.00
Double	37.00	37.00

Half board per person:	£min	£max
Daily	32.00	32.00

Lunch available
Evening meal 1900 (last orders 2100)
Parking for 12
10

TWO DALES

Derbyshire
Map ref 4B2

Village set in beautiful Derbyshire scenery and with easy access to the country houses of Haddon and Chatsworth.

Top 'O The Hill

Listed COMMENDED

Sydnope Hill, Two Dales, Matlock
DE4 2FN
☎ (01629) 734548

Modern, country residence overlooking the Peak Park border with superb views. On the B5057, Darley Dale to Chesterfield road.

Bedrooms: 2 double, 1 twin
Bathrooms: 1 public

Bed & breakfast per night:	£min	£max
Single	20.00	21.00
Double	32.00	34.00

Half board per person:	£min	£max
Daily	26.00	27.00
Weekly	182.00	189.00

Evening meal 1800 (last orders 2000)
Parking for 4

UPPER BROUGHTON

Nottinghamshire
Map ref 4C3

Nestling attractively into the steep hillside with extensive views of the Vale of Belvoir, this village has two greens with beautiful flowers and ornaments.

Swan Lodge

Listed COMMENDED

Station Road, Upper Broughton,
Melton Mowbray, Leicestershire
LE14 3BH
☎ (01664) 823686 & 822346
Fax (01664) 823860

200-acre mixed farm. 19th C farmhouse, 2 miles from the nearest village. Horse riding, fishing and miles of walking available.

Bedrooms: 1 triple
Bathrooms: 1 en-suite

Bed & breakfast per night:	£min	£max
Single	15.00	20.00
Double	30.00	40.00

Half board per person:	£min	£max
Daily	25.00	30.00
Weekly	175.00	210.00

Lunch available
Evening meal 1730 (last orders 1900)
Parking for 20
Cards accepted: Mastercard, Visa

UPPINGHAM

Leicestershire
Map ref 4C3

Quiet market town dominated by its famous public school which was founded in 1584. It has many stone houses and is surrounded by attractive countryside.

The Old Rectory

COMMENDED

New Road, Belton in Rutland,
Oakham, Rutland LE15 9LE
☎ (01572) 717279
Fax (01572) 717343

Victorian country house and guest annexe on 14-acre smallholding. Conservation village overlooking the EyeBrook Valley and rolling Rutland countryside. Cottage-style en-suite rooms, quiet friendly atmosphere. Families welcome. Excellent local pubs and restaurants.

Bedrooms: 1 single, 2 double, 3 twin, 2 triple
Bathrooms: 4 en-suite, 3 private, 2 public

Bed & breakfast per night:	£min	£max
Single	27.00	
Double	38.00	

Evening meal 1800 (last orders 1900)
Parking for 10
Cards accepted: Mastercard, Visa
10

Rutland House

COMMENDED

61 High Street East, Uppingham
LE15 9PY
☎ (01572) 822497
Fax (01572) 822497

Family-run B & B. All rooms en-suite. Close to Rutland Water. Full English or continental breakfast. Well-placed for exploring Rutland's villages and countryside.

Bedrooms: 2 double, 2 twin, 1 triple
Bathrooms: 5 en-suite

Bed & breakfast per night:	£min	£max
Single	30.00	30.00
Double	40.00	40.00

Parking for 3
Cards accepted: Mastercard, Visa
5

Please mention this guide when making your booking.

The National Grading and Classification Scheme is explained at the back of this guide.

UPTON-UPON-SEVERN

Hereford and Worcester
Map ref 2B1

Attractive country town on the banks of the Severn and a good river cruising centre. It has many pleasant old houses and inns, and the pepperpot landmark is now the Heritage Centre.
Tourist Information Centre ☎ (01684) 594200

Tiltridge Farm and Vineyard

HIGHLY COMMENDED

Upper Hook Road, Upton-upon-Severn, Worcester WR8 0SA
☎ (01684) 592906
Fax (01684) 594142
9-acre vineyard and farm. Fully renovated period farmhouse close to Upton and Malvern showground. Warm welcome, bumper breakfast and wine from our own vineyard!
Bedrooms: 2 double, 1 twin
Bathrooms: 3 en-suite

Bed & breakfast per night:	£min	£max
Single	23.00	25.00
Double	36.00	40.00

Parking for 12

Welland Court

HIGHLY COMMENDED

Upton-upon-Severn, Worcester WR8 0ST
☎ (01684) 594426 & 594413
Fax (01684) 594426
Built c.1450 and enlarged in the 18th C. Rescued from a dilapidated state and modernised to a high standard. It lies at the foot of the Malvern Hills and is an ideal base for touring the Wye and Teme valleys.
Bedrooms: 1 double, 2 twin
Bathrooms: 3 en-suite

Bed & breakfast per night:	£min	£max
Single	42.50	
Double	65.00	

Half board per person:	£min	£max
Daily	62.50	72.50

Parking for 13
Cards accepted: Mastercard, Visa

WADENHOE

Northamptonshire
Map ref 3A2

The Kings Head

Listed COMMENDED

Church Street, Wadenhoe, Peterborough PE8 5ST
☎ (01832) 720024
Fax (01832) 720024
Thatched 17th C building with traditional unspoilt interior and open fires. Northamptonshire skittles table. Home-made food. Acre of paddock edging river.
Bedrooms: 1 double, 1 twin
Bathrooms: 2 private

Bed & breakfast per night:	£min	£max
Single	25.00	35.00
Double	50.00	60.00

Lunch available
Evening meal 1900 (last orders 2100)
Parking for 20
Cards accepted: Mastercard, Visa, Switch/Delta

WARWICK

Warwickshire
Map ref 2B1

Castle rising above the River Avon, 15th C Beauchamp Chapel attached to St Mary's Church, medieval Lord Leycester's Hospital almshouses and several museums. Nearby is Ashorne Hall Nickelodeon and the National Heritage museum at Gaydon.
Tourist Information Centre ☎ (01926) 492212

Austin House

COMMENDED

96 Emscote Road, Warwick CV34 5QJ
☎ (01926) 493583
Fax (01926) 493583
Black and white Victorian house 1 mile from Warwick Castle and Royal Leamington Spa, 8 miles from Stratford-upon-Avon.
Bedrooms: 1 single, 1 double, 1 twin, 4 triple
Bathrooms: 5 en-suite, 1 public

Bed & breakfast per night:	£min	£max
Single	16.00	19.00
Double	32.00	38.00

Parking for 8
Cards accepted: Mastercard, Visa, Switch/Delta

Avon Lodge

HIGHLY COMMENDED

Watery Lane, Sherbourne, Warwick CV35 8AL
☎ (01926) 624295
Country house in large gardens, situated between Stratford-upon-Avon and Warwick, offering comfortable en-suite accommodation, private parking and a hearty breakfast.
Bedrooms: 1 double, 1 twin
Bathrooms: 2 en-suite

Bed & breakfast per night:	£min	£max
Single	35.00	45.00
Double	44.00	52.00

Parking for 2

The Croft

COMMENDED

Haseley Knob, Warwick CV35 7NL
☎ (01926) 484447
Fax (01926) 484447
Friendly family atmosphere in picturesque rural setting. In Haseley Knob village off the A4177 between Balsall Common and Warwick, convenient for NEC, National Agricultural Centre, Stratford and Coventry. 15 minutes from Birmingham Airport.
Bedrooms: 1 single, 1 double, 1 twin, 2 triple
Bathrooms: 5 en-suite, 2 public

Bed & breakfast per night:	£min	£max
Single	21.00	32.00
Double	39.00	44.00

Evening meal 1800 (last orders 1900)
Parking for 10
Cards accepted: Mastercard, Visa, Switch/Delta

30 Eastley Crescent

HIGHLY COMMENDED

Warwick CV34 5RX
☎ (01926) 496480
Next to A46 and 5 minutes from M40. A comfortable, non-smoking establishment.
Bedrooms: 1 single, 1 double
Bathrooms: 1 en-suite, 1 private, 1 public

Bed & breakfast per night:	£min	£max
Single	16.00	18.00
Double	32.00	34.00

Parking for 2

Forth House

HIGHLY COMMENDED

44 High Street, Warwick CV34 4AX
☎ (01926) 401512
Fax (01926) 490809

Ground floor and first floor guest suites with private sitting rooms and bathrooms. At the back of the house, overlooking peaceful garden, in town centre.

Bedrooms: 1 double, 1 twin
Suite available
Bathrooms: 2 en-suite

Bed & breakfast per night:	£min	£max
Single	36.00	40.00
Double	46.00	52.00

Parking for 2

High House

COMMENDED

Old Warwick Road, Rowington, Warwick CV35 7AA
☎ (01926) 843270 & 0385 748134
Fax (01203) 257943

Grade II listed Queen Anne farmhouse in beautiful secluded position with outstanding views, north-west of Warwick. Evening meals by prior arrangement.

Bedrooms: 1 double, 1 twin
Bathrooms: 2 en-suite

Bed & breakfast per night:	£min	£max
Single	25.00	30.00
Double	45.00	60.00

Parking for 20

Lower Rowley

HIGHLY COMMENDED

Wasperton, Warwick CV35 8EB
☎ (01926) 624937
Fax (01926) 624937

Non-smoking, en-suite accommodation in peaceful rural surroundings, with River Avon at bottom of garden. In village dating back over 5,000 years, between Warwick and Stratford-upon-Avon.

Bedrooms: 1 double, 1 twin
Bathrooms: 1 en-suite, 1 private, 1 public

Bed & breakfast per night:	£min	£max
Single	25.00	30.00
Double	38.00	45.00

Parking for 3

Lower Watchbury Farm

HIGHLY COMMENDED

Wasperton Lane, Barford, Warwick CV35 1DH
☎ (01926) 624772 & (0589) 478795

50-acre mixed farm. Well-appointed accommodation on working farm, in rural surroundings outside Barford. M40 2 miles, Stratford-upon-Avon 7 miles, Warwick 3 miles. All rooms en-suite, large garden. Good pubs nearby.

Bedrooms: 1 single, 1 double, 1 triple
Bathrooms: 2 en-suite, 1 private

Bed & breakfast per night:	£min	£max
Single	22.50	25.00
Double	40.00	45.00

Parking for 3

Northleigh House

HIGHLY COMMENDED

Five Ways Road, Hatton, Warwick CV35 7HZ
☎ (01926) 484203 & 0374 101894
Fax (01926) 484006

Comfortable, peaceful country house where the elegant rooms are individually designed and have en-suite bathroom, fridge, kettle and remote-control TV.

Bedrooms: 1 single, 5 double, 1 twin
Bathrooms: 7 en-suite

Bed & breakfast per night:	£min	£max
Single	33.00	40.00
Double	46.00	58.00

Parking for 8
Open February–November
Cards accepted: Mastercard, Visa

You are advised to confirm your booking in writing.

Shrewley Pools Farm

COMMENDED

Haseley, Warwick CV35 7LD
☎ (01926) 484315

260-acre mixed farm. Traditional mid-17th C beamed farmhouse set in 1 acre of gardens. 5 miles north of Warwick on the A4177.

Bedrooms: 1 twin, 1 triple
Bathrooms: 2 en-suite

Bed & breakfast per night:	£min	£max
Single	25.00	30.00
Double	40.00	45.00

Half board per person:	£min	£max
Daily	30.00	40.00
Weekly	200.00	270.00

Evening meal 1800 (last orders 2000)
Parking for 10

WATERHOUSES

Staffordshire
Map ref 4B2

Village in the valley of the River Hamps, once the terminus of the Leek and Manifold Light Railway, 8 miles of which is now a macadamised walkers' path.

Ye Olde Crown

APPROVED

Leek Road, Waterhouses, Stoke-on-Trent ST10 3HL
☎ (01538) 308204

17th C coaching inn, on the edge of the Peak District National Park and at the start of the beautiful Manifold Valley. It is built of natural stone and has a wealth of original oak beams.

Bedrooms: 2 single, 3 double, 1 twin, 1 family room
Bathrooms: 5 en-suite, 1 public

Bed & breakfast per night:	£min	£max
Single	15.00	23.50
Double	37.00	37.00

Lunch available
Evening meal 1900 (last orders 2130)
Parking for 50
Cards accepted: Mastercard, Visa

The symbol after an establishment name indicates that it is a Regional Tourist Board member.

WEEDON

Northamptonshire
Map ref 2C1

Old village steeped in history, with thatched cottages and several antique shops.

Globe Hotel

COMMENDED

High Street, Weedon, Northampton NN7 4QD
☎ (01327) 340336
Fax (01327) 349058

19th C countryside inn. Old world atmosphere and freehouse hospitality with good English cooking, available all day. Meeting rooms. Close to M1, Stratford and many tourist spots. Send for information pack.

Bedrooms: 4 single, 6 double, 5 twin, 3 triple
Bathrooms: 18 en-suite

Bed & breakfast per night:	£min	£max
Single	32.00	45.00
Double	45.00	55.00

Half board per person:	£min	£max
Daily	40.00	56.00

Lunch available
Evening meal (last orders 2200)
Parking for 40
Cards accepted: Amex, Diners, Mastercard, Visa, Switch/Delta

WEM

Shropshire
Map ref 4A3

Small town connected with Judge Jeffreys who lived in Lowe Hall. Well known for its ales.

Forncet

Listed COMMENDED

Soulton Road, Wem, Shrewsbury SY4 5HR
☎ (01939) 232996

Spacious, centrally heated Victorian house on the edge of this small market town, 200 yards from rail station.

Bedrooms: 1 single, 1 twin, 1 triple
Bathrooms: 2 public

Bed & breakfast per night:	£min	£max
Single	16.00	
Double	32.00	

Half board per person:	£min	£max
Daily	26.00	

Evening meal 1830 (last orders 1930)
Parking for 6

Soulton Hall

COMMENDED

Wem, Shrewsbury SY4 5RS
☎ (01939) 232786
Fax (01939) 234097

Super home cooking and en-suite rooms at this Tudor manor house ensure a relaxing holiday. Moated Domesday site in grounds, private riverside and woodland walks.

Bedrooms: 1 single, 3 double, 1 twin, 1 triple
Suite available
Bathrooms: 5 en-suite, 1 private

Bed & breakfast per night:	£min	£max
Single	33.50	40.50
Double	52.00	66.00

Half board per person:	£min	£max
Daily	51.50	58.50
Weekly	278.00	321.50

Evening meal 1900 (last orders 2030)
Parking for 23
Cards accepted: Diners, Mastercard, Visa

WENTNOR

Shropshire
Map ref 4A3

Village near the lovely countryside of the Long Mynd and close to the Welsh border and Offa's Dyke.

Crown Inn

Listed COMMENDED

Wentnor, Bishop's Castle SY9 5EE
☎ (01588) 650613
Fax (01588) 650436
Email: crown @lydbury.compulink.co.uk

Traditional 16th C country inn set in the rolling hills of South Shropshire. Easy access to Midland gliding club, several golf clubs, trout fishing, horse riding and hill walking. A warm welcome, fresh home-cooked food and real ales.

Bedrooms: 2 double, 2 twin
Bathrooms: 2 public

Bed & breakfast per night:	£min	£max
Single	24.50	
Double	44.00	

Lunch available
Evening meal 1900 (last orders 2100)
Parking for 20
Cards accepted: Mastercard, Visa, Switch/Delta

WEOBLEY

Hereford and Worcester
Map ref 2A1

One of the most beautiful Herefordshire villages, full of framed houses, at the heart of the Black and White Trail. It is dominated by the church which has a fine spire.

Hill Top Farm

COMMENDED

Wormsley, Hereford HR4 8LZ
☎ (01981) 590246 & (0421) 533807
Fax (01981) 590246

200-acre arable & livestock farm. Comfortable stone-built farmhouse under brow of hill, deep in the Herefordshire countryside. Magnificent views over fields and woods to Black Mountains. On Black and White Trail.

Bedrooms: 1 twin, 1 triple
Bathrooms: 1 en-suite, 1 private

Bed & breakfast per night:	£min	£max
Double	32.00	36.00

Parking for 6

For further information on accommodation establishments use the coupons at the back of this guide.

WESSINGTON

Derbyshire
Map ref 4B2

Small village between Alfreton and Matlock on the A615.

Crich Lane Farm

COMMENDED

Moorwood Moor Lane, Wessington, Alfreton, Derby DE55 6DU
☎ (01773) 835186

44-acre mixed farm. Beautiful stone farmhouse, easy walking distance of village and pubs. Pet attractions and a warm and friendly welcome to all. Easy access to M1 and A38.

Bedrooms: 1 single, 3 double, 2 twin, 2 family rooms
Bathrooms: 5 en-suite, 1 private, 2 public

Bed & breakfast per night:	£min	£max
Single	17.00	22.50
Double	34.00	45.00

Parking for 10

WHALEY BRIDGE

Derbyshire
Map ref 4B2

Old textile town, whose canal warehouses are a reminder of its former importance, at the junction of the Peak Forest Canal and the Cromford and High Peak Railway. Surrounded by hills and with splendid views.

The Old Bakery Guesthouse

COMMENDED

80 Buxton Road, Whaley Bridge, High Peak SK23 7JE
☎ (01663) 732359

A small, family-run guesthouse with traditional home cooking. Ideally situated for exploring the Goyt Valley in the Western Peak.

Bedrooms: 2 double, 1 twin
Bathrooms: 2 public

Bed & breakfast per night:	£min	£max
Single	17.50	19.50
Double	35.00	35.00

Half board per person:	£min	£max
Daily	24.50	27.50
Weekly	150.00	170.00

Lunch available
Evening meal 1830 (last orders 2000)
Parking for 3

WHITBOURNE

Hereford and Worcester
Map ref 2B1

Large parish on both sides of the Worcester to Bromyard road, the location of a medieval moated building, once the palace of the Bishops of Hereford. In the delightfully peaceful village are some houses of cruck construction and some unusual 16th C brick chimneys.

Upper Elmores End Farm

HIGHLY COMMENDED

Linley Green Road, Whitbourne, Worcester WR6 5RE
☎ (01886) 821245

50-acre mixed farm. Well-renovated 16th C black and white farmhouse set in orchards and wooded countryside. Ideally situated for touring Malvern Hills, Wye and Severn Valleys.

Bedrooms: 2 double, 1 twin
Bathrooms: 1 en-suite, 1 public

Bed & breakfast per night:	£min	£max
Double	33.00	39.00

Half board per person:	£min	£max
Daily	29.00	34.00

Evening meal from 1830
Parking for 5
Open April–October

WINCHCOMBE

Gloucestershire
Map ref 2B1

Ancient town with a folk museum and railway museum. To the south lies Sudeley Castle with its fine collection of paintings and toys and an Elizabethan garden.

Manor Farm

HIGHLY COMMENDED

Greet, Winchcombe, Cheltenham GL54 5BJ
☎ (01242) 602423

400-acre mixed farm. Cotswolds manor in quiet hamlet. Good views of Cotswold Escarpment. Picturesque, well-equipped self-catering cottages and small camp/caravan site with facilities available.

Bedrooms: 2 double, 1 twin
Bathrooms: 3 en-suite, 1 public

Bed & breakfast per night:	£min	£max
Single	25.00	30.00
Double	50.00	50.00

Parking for 10
Open January–November

Mercia

HIGHLY COMMENDED

Hailes Street, Winchcombe, Cheltenham GL54 5HU
☎ (01242) 602251

Black and white Cotswold-stone Tudor cottage with beamed walls and ceilings. Private parking at rear. Pleasant garden and views. 15 minutes from M5.

Bedrooms: 2 double, 1 twin
Bathrooms: 2 en-suite, 1 private

Bed & breakfast per night:	£min	£max
Single	19.00	22.00
Double	36.00	38.00

Parking for 3

The Old Stables

COMMENDED

Hill View, Farmcote, Winchcombe, Cheltenham GL54 5AU
☎ (01242) 603860

230-acre arable & livestock farm. A delightful stable conversion, situated on a working farm with magnificent views towards the Malvern Hills.

Bedrooms: 1 double, 1 twin
Bathrooms: 1 en-suite, 1 private

Bed & breakfast per night:	£min	£max
Single	20.00	25.00
Double	35.00	40.00

Half board per person:	£min	£max
Daily	30.00	35.00

WINCHCOMBE

Continued

Parks Farm

Listed COMMENDED

Sudeley, Winchcombe, Cheltenham GL54 5BX
☎ (01242) 603874
600-acre livestock farm. Listed buildings on Cotswold hill farm, with spectacular views. Family atmosphere. Close to Wardens, Windrush and Cotswold Way footpaths.
Bedrooms: 2 twin
Bathrooms: 1 public

Bed & breakfast per night:	£min	£max
Double	35.00	35.00

Half board per person:	£min	£max
Daily	27.00	27.00

Parking for 2

WITNEY

Oxfordshire
Map ref 2C1

The Court Inn
Field View
Quarrydene
See South of England region for full entry details

WOLVERHAMPTON

West Midlands
Map ref 4B3

Modern industrial town with a long history, a fine parish church and an excellent art gallery. There are several places of interest in the vicinity including Moseley Old Hall and Wightwick Manor with its William Morris influence.
Tourist Information Centre ☎ (01902) 312051

Fox Hotel International

APPROVED

118 School Street, Wolverhampton WV3 0NR
☎ (01902) 21680
Fax (01902) 711654
Town centre, free parking, nearby shopping. All rooms en-suite, satellite TV, direct-dial telephone. Bar, restaurant and conference room.
Bedrooms: 26 single, 6 double
Bathrooms: 32 en-suite

Bed & breakfast per night:	£min	£max
Single	30.00	43.00
Double	49.00	59.00

Half board per person:	£min	£max
Daily	40.00	45.00
Weekly	210.00	260.00

Lunch available
Evening meal 1700 (last orders 2200)
Parking for 20
Cards accepted: Amex, Diners, Mastercard, Visa, Switch/Delta
100

WOODSTOCK

Oxfordshire
Map ref 2C1

Gorselands Farmhouse Auberge
The Kings Head Inn
The Laurels
Punch Bowl Inn
The Ridings
Shepherds Hall Inn
Shipton Glebe
See South of England region for full entry details

WORCESTER

Hereford and Worcester
Map ref 2B1

Lovely riverside city dominated by its Norman and Early English cathedral, King John's burial place. Many old buildings including the 15th C Commandery and the 18th C Guildhall. There are several museums and the Royal Worcester porcelain factory.
Tourist Information Centre ☎ (01905) 726311 or 722480

Burgage House

Listed COMMENDED

4 College Precincts, Worcester WR1 2LG
☎ (01905) 25396
Fax (01905) 25396

Comfortable accommodation in elegant Georgian mews house in cobbled street next to cathedral. Close to River Severn, cricket ground, shops and restaurants
Bedrooms: 1 single, 1 double, 1 twin, 1 family room
Bathrooms: 2 en-suite, 1 public

Bed & breakfast per night:	£min	£max
Single	28.00	32.00
Double	40.00	50.00

Ivy Cottage

COMMENDED

Sinton Green, Hallow, Worcester WR2 6NP
☎ (01905) 641123
Charming cottage in quiet village, 4 miles north of Worcester, off A443 Worcester to Tenbury road. Good local restaurants.
Bedrooms: 1 single, 1 double, 1 twin
Bathrooms: 1 en-suite, 2 private

Bed & breakfast per night:	£min	£max
Single	18.00	25.00
Double	36.00	36.00

Parking for 4

Little Lightwood Farm

COMMENDED

Lightwood Lane, Cotheridge, Worcester WR6 5LT
☎ (01905) 333236
Fax (01905) 333468
56-acre dairy farm. Farmhouse accommodation with en-suite rooms, tea-making facilities and heating in all bedrooms. Delightful views of the Malvern Hills. Just off the A44 from Worcester to Leominster, 3.5 miles from Worcester.
Bedrooms: 2 double, 1 twin
Bathrooms: 3 en-suite

Bed & breakfast per night:	£min	£max
Single	21.50	24.00
Double	36.00	38.50

Parking for 6
Open February–December

WELCOME HOST

This is a nationally recognised customer care programme which aims to promote the highest standards of service and a warm welcome. Establishments who are taking part in this initiative are indicated by the symbol.

Loch Ryan Hotel

COMMENDED

119 Sidbury, Worcester WR5 2DH
☎ (01905) 351143
Fax (01905) 351143

Historic hotel, once home of Bishop Gore, close to cathedral, Royal Worcester Porcelain factory and Commandery. Attractive terraced garden. Imaginative food. Holders of Heartbeat and Worcester City clean food awards.

Bedrooms: 1 single, 4 double, 4 twin, 1 family room
Bathrooms: 10 en-suite

Bed & breakfast per night:	£min	£max
Single	42.00	
Double	58.00	

Half board per person:	£min	£max
Daily	45.00	

Evening meal 1800 (last orders 1900)
Parking for 10
Cards accepted: Amex, Diners, Mastercard, Visa

Oaklands

COMMENDED

Claines, Worcester WR3 7RR
☎ (01905) 458871 & (0585) 378771
Fax (01905) 458871

150-year-old cottage (renovated stables). Pleasant rural outlook yet close to the M5 and Worcester. City bus stops outside.

Bedrooms: 1 double, 1 twin
Bathrooms: 2 en-suite

Bed & breakfast per night:	£min	£max
Single	25.00	30.00
Double	40.00	50.00

Parking for 6

The Old Smithy

Listed HIGHLY COMMENDED

Pirton, Worcester WR8 9EJ
☎ (01905) 820482

17th C country house of historic interest, in peaceful countryside, only 4.5 miles from M5 motorway (junction 7) and Worcester city. Ideal central base for touring Cotswolds, Stratford-upon-Avon, Warwick and Potteries.

Bedrooms: 1 double, 1 twin
Bathrooms: 1 private, 1 public

Bed & breakfast per night:	£min	£max
Double	33.00	39.00

Half board per person:	£min	£max
Daily	25.00	29.00
Weekly	169.00	189.00

Evening meal from 1830
Parking for 6

Retreat Farm

Listed HIGHLY COMMENDED

Camp Lane, Grimley, Worcester WR2 6LX
☎ (01905) 640266

60-acre arable & livestock farm. 17th C farmhouse, overlooking River Severn and Bevere Lock. Within walking distance of the Camp House Inn and Wagon Wheel Restaurant.

Bedrooms: 2 double
Bathrooms: 2 en-suite

Bed & breakfast per night:	£min	£max
Single	25.00	35.00
Double	43.00	46.00

Parking for 14

12

WOTTON-UNDER-EDGE

Gloucestershire
Map ref 2B2

Small town in the southern Cotswolds. Berkeley Castle is within easy reach.

Burrows Court

COMMENDED

Nibley Green, North Nibley, Dursley GL11 6AZ
☎ (01453) 546230

18th C country house in idyllic setting. Peaceful, quiet and relaxing. All en-suite, exposed beams, acre of gardens. Ideal for Cotswolds and Bath.

Bedrooms: 3 double, 1 twin, 2 triple
Bathrooms: 6 en-suite

Bed & breakfast per night:	£min	£max
Single	29.00	34.00
Double	40.00	50.00

Parking for 20
Open February–November
Cards accepted: Mastercard, Visa

All accommodation in this guide has been graded, or is awaiting a grading, by a trained Tourist Board inspector.

Hillesley Mill

COMMENDED

Alderley, Wotton-under-Edge GL12 7QT
☎ (01453) 843258

Easily accessible converted cotton/woollen mill, nestling in undulating fields and prolific woodland, overlooking a mill lake and stream.

Bedrooms: 1 double, 1 twin
Bathrooms: 1 en-suite, 1 private

Bed & breakfast per night:	£min	£max
Single	20.00	24.00
Double	36.00	42.00

Parking for 8

WYE VALLEY

See under Fownhope, Goodrich, Hereford, Ross-on-Wye

WYMONDHAM

Leicestershire
Map ref 4C3

Old market town close to the Lincolnshire and Rutland border. Handsome cross-shaped church with parts from the 13th C.

The Old Rectory

COMMENDED

Sycamore Lane, Wymondham, Melton Mowbray LE14 2AZ
☎ (01572) 787583 & 787226
Fax (01572) 787347

Georgian rectory within its own secluded grounds, 5 miles west of the A1, offering comfortable self-contained accommodation. Evening meal available by prior arrangement.

Bedrooms: 2 double, 1 twin
Bathrooms: 2 en-suite, 1 private

Bed & breakfast per night:	£min	£max
Single	30.00	
Double	50.00	

Half board per person:	£min	£max
Daily	37.50	42.50

Parking for 4

1

WYRE PIDDLE

Hereford and Worcester
Map ref 2B1

On the north bank of the River Avon between Pershore and Evesham, with an ancient village cross.

Arbour House Bed and Breakfast

HIGHLY COMMENDED

Main Road, Wyre Piddle, Pershore, Worcestershire WR10 2HU
☎ (01386) 555833

Oak beams, real fires and flagstone floors. Exceptionally comfortable accommodation in relaxed home. Great breakfasts. A home full of personal touches.

Bedrooms: 1 double, 2 twin
Bathrooms: 3 en-suite

Bed & breakfast per night:	£min	£max
Single	25.00	26.00
Double	40.00	44.00

Half board per person:	£min	£max
Daily	35.00	36.00
Weekly	220.00	226.00

Evening meal 1800 (last orders 1900)
Parking for 5

YARKHILL

Hereford and Worcester
Map ref 2B1

Thatched cottages, oasthouses and a medieval church among the old hopfields and orchards.

Garford Farm

COMMENDED

Yarkhill, Hereford HR1 3ST
☎ (01432) 890226
Fax (01432) 890707

190-acre mixed farm. Picturesque black and white farmhouse on working farm. Very quiet but with easy access to the A4103 Hereford to Worcester road.

Bedrooms: 1 double, 1 twin
Bathrooms: 1 en-suite, 1 private

Bed & breakfast per night:	£min	£max
Single		17.50
Double		34.00

Parking for 6

YOXALL

Staffordshire
Map ref 4B3

Small village near the Needwood Forest north of Lichfield. Once the home of Thomas Gisborne, booklover and campaigner against slavery.

Thimble Hall

Listed COMMENDED

School Green, Yoxall, Burton upon Trent DE13 8NB
☎ (01543) 472226
Fax (01543) 472550

Listed 16th C timber-framed detached cottage with pleasant garden, central heating, oak beams and a warm welcome.

Bedrooms: 1 single, 2 twin
Bathrooms: 1 public

Bed & breakfast per night:	£min	£max
Single	20.00	20.00
Double	38.00	40.00

Parking for 4

AT-A-GLANCE SYMBOLS

Symbols at the end of each accommodation entry give useful information about services and facilities. A key to symbols can be found inside the back cover flap.

Keep this open for easy reference.

EAST OF ENGLAND

Traditional seaside resorts from Skegness to Southend-on-Sea, beautiful Constable country, the Norfolk Broads, lavender fields and heritage towns - these and much more await you in the East of England.

Discover some of the country's richest treasures - Lincoln and Norwich cathedrals, Cambridge, Royal Sandringham and Woburn Abbey. Or take a leisurely cruise on the region's waterways, teeming with wildlife. It's ideal cycling country, too.

Events to enjoy include a day at Newmarket races, plus a chance to tour the National Stud. Spalding, in the heart of the Lincolnshire fenland, stages a spectacular floral festival each Spring. There's also the famous music festival at Aldeburgh, or cheese rolling at Stilton!

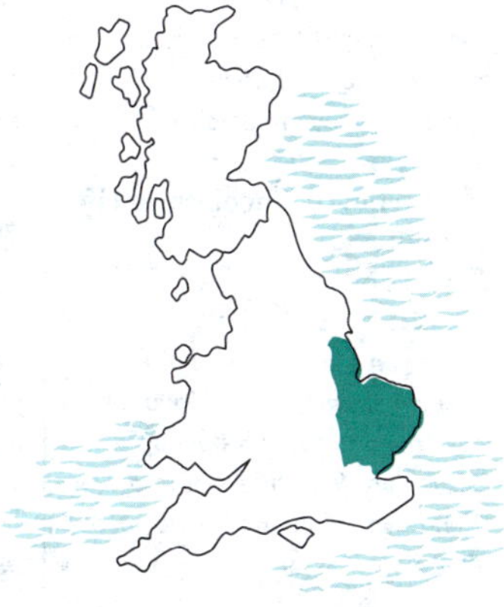

The counties of Bedforshire, Cambridgeshire, Essex, Hertfordshire, Lincolnshire, Norfolk and Suffolk

FOR MORE INFORMATION CONTACT:
East of England Tourist Board
Toppesfield Hall, Hadleigh, Suffolk IP7 5DN
Tel: (01473) 822922 **Fax:** (01473) 823063

Where to Go in the East of England – see pages 198-201
Where to Stay in the East of England – see pages 202-227

EAST OF ENGLAND

Where to Go and What to See

You will find hundreds of interesting places to visit during your stay in the East of England, just some of which are listed in these pages. The number against each name will help you locate it on the map (page 201). Contact any Tourist Information Centre in the region for more ideas on days out in the East of England.

1 Gainsborough Old Hall
Parnell Street, Gainsborough,
Lincolnshire DN21 2NB
Tel: (01427) 612669
A late medieval timber-framed manor house, built about 1460 with a fine medieval kitchen.

2 Museum of Lincolnshire Life
Burton Road,
Lincoln LN1 3LY
Tel: (01522) 528448
The region's largest social history museum showing the agricultural, industrial and social history of Lincolnshire from a teapot to a World War I tank and a Victorian room.

3 Belton House, Park and Gardens
Belton,
Lincolnshire NG32 2LS
Tel: (01476) 566116
The crowning achievement of restoration country house architecture, built in 1685-88 for Sir John Brownlow with alterations by James Wyatt in 1777.

4 Springfields Show Gardens
Camelgate, Spalding,
Lincolnshire PE12 6ET
Tel: (01775) 724843/713253
One of Britain's premier show gardens; in spring there is a spectacle of tulips, daffodils and hyacinths and in summer, a bedding plant display.

5 The African Violet Centre
Station Road,
Terrington St Clement,
Norfolk PE34 4PL
Tel: (01553) 828374
Cultivation and display of a unique collection of African Violets, plus a selection of seasonal garden plants.

6 Sandringham
Sandringham, King's Lynn,
Norfolk PE35 6EN
Tel: (01553) 772675
The country retreat of HM The Queen. Delightful house and 60 acres of grounds and lakes. Museum of royal vehicles and royal memorabilia.

7 Tales of the Old Gaol House
The Old Gaol House,
Saturday Market Place,
King's Lynn, Norfolk PE30 5DQ
Tel: (01553) 763044
A personal stereo tour of the Old Gaol House tells the true stories of Lynn's infamous murderers, highwaymen and witches.

8 Pensthorpe Waterfowl Park

Pensthorpe, Fakenham,
Norfolk NR21 0LN
Tel: (01328) 851465

One of the largest waterfowl and wildfowl collections in the world with information centre, conservation shop, adventure play area, walks, nature trails and a licensed restaurant.

9 Inspire Hands-On-Science Centre

St Michael's Church,
Coslany Street, Norwich,
Norfolk NR3 3DT
Tel: (01603) 612612

Hands-on science centre housed in a medieval church. Suitable for all ages, it allows everyone to explore and discover the wonders of science.

10 Pleasurewood Hills Family Theme Park

Corton, Lowestoft,
Suffolk NR32 5DZ
Tel: (01502) 508200

Log flume, chair lift, cine 180, two railways, pirate ship, fort, Aladdin's cave, parrot, sealion shows, roller coaster, waveswinger, Eye in the Sky and Star Ride Enterprise.

11 Ely Cathedral

The College, Ely,
Cambridgeshire CB7 4DL
Tel: (01353) 667735

One of England's finest cathedrals with fine buildings. Guided tours and tours of the Monastic Octagon and West Tower. Brass rubbing centre and stained glass museum.

12 Oliver Cromwell's House

29 St Marys Street, Ely,
Cambridgeshire CB7 4HF
Tel: (01353) 662062

The family home of Oliver Cromwell with a 17thC kitchen, parlour and a 'haunted bedroom'. Tourist Information Centre, souvenirs and a craft shop.

13 West Stow Country Park and Anglo Saxon Village

Icklingham Road, West Stow,
Bury St Edmunds,
Suffolk IP28 6HG
Tel: (01284) 728718

Reconstructions of six pagan Anglo-Saxon buildings with a seventh in the process of reconstruction. Information point with displays of excavation plans.

14 Bruisyard Vineyard and Herb Centre

Church Road, Bruisyard,
Saxmundham,
Suffolk IP17 2EF
Tel: (01728) 638281

A 10-acre vineyard showing summer work and maintenance of the vines, a tour of the winery and herb garden. A video show and display of winemaking is also provided.

15 Framlingham Castle

Framlingham, Woodbridge,
Suffolk IP13 9BP
Tel: (01728) 724189/621448

12thC curtain walls, 13 towers, Tudor brick chimneys and a wall walk. Built by the Bigod family, the Earls of Norfolk. Home of Mary Tudor in 1553.

16 National Horseracing Museum

99 High Street, Newmarket,
Suffolk CB8 8JL
Tel: (01638) 667333

Five galleries telling the development of horseracing and the individuals involved. A display of sporting art includes loans from the Tate gallery. Also a 'hands-on' gallery.

17 Imperial War Museum

Duxford Airfield, Duxford,
Cambridgeshire CB2 4QR
Tel: (01223) 835000

Over 140 aircraft on display with tanks, vehicles and guns, a ride on the simulator, an adventure playground, shops and a restaurant.

18 **Shuttleworth Collection**
Old Warden Aerodrome,
Biggleswade,
Bedfordshire SG18 9EP
Tel: (01767) 627288/627502
A unique historical collection of aircraft from a 1909 Bleriot to a 1942 Spitfire in flying condition. Cars dating from an 1898 Panhard in running order.

19 **The Swiss Garden**
Biggleswade Road, Old Warden,
Biggleswade, Bedfordshire
Tel: (01234) 228671
An attractive garden dating from the 19thC, taking its name from the tiny Swiss thatched cottage in the centre.

20 **Colne Valley Railway**
Yeldham Road,
Castle Hedingham,
Essex CO9 3DZ
Tel: (01787) 461174
An award-winning station and a ride in the loveliest part of the Colne Valley. A large, interesting collection of operational heritage rolling stock.

21 **Colchester Zoo**
Stanway, Maldon Road,
Colchester,
Essex CO3 5SL
Tel: (01206) 330253/331292
See 170 species of animals, 40 acres of gardens and lakes and award-winning animal enclosures. Picnic areas, a road train, two play areas, pony rides and a large soft play area.

22 **The Working Silk Museum**
New Mills, South Street,
Braintree, Essex CM7 3GB
Tel: (01376) 553393
A show of textiles (ancient textile machines restored and working) a mill shop and looms. Working looms with weaving demonstrations on the hour on Monday - Friday and Saturday mornings.

23 **Hyde Hall**
Rettendon,
Chelmsford,
Essex CM3 8ET
Tel: (01245) 400256
Royal Horticultural Society 8-acre garden with all-year-round interest including greenhouses, roses, flowering shrubs, perennial borders and alpines.

24 **Paradise Wildlife Park**
White Stubbs Lane,
Broxbourne,
Hertfordshire EN10 7QA
Tel: (01992) 468001
Britain's most interactive wildlife park with many animal activities daily. Also an adventure playground, children's rides, woodland railway and catering facilities.

25 **Hatfield House**
Hatfield Park, Hatfield,
Hertfordshire AL9 5NQ
Tel: (01707) 262823
Jacobean house built in 1611 and Old Palace built in 1497. Famous paintings, fine furniture and the possessions of Queen Elizabeth I. Extensive park and gardens.

26 **The Gardens of the Rose**
Chiswell Green, St Albans,
Hertfordshire AL2 3NR
Tel: (01727) 850461
Royal National Rose Society garden with 20 acres of showground and trial grounds for new varieties of rose. Roses of all types displayed, with 1,700 different varieties.

27 **Luton Hoo - The Wernher Collection**
The Mansion House, Luton Hoo,
Luton, Bedfordshire LU1 3TQ
Tel: (01582) 22955
An historic house built in 1767 exhibiting paintings, tapestries, bronzes, ivories, porcelain, jewellery by Carl Faberge and mementoes of the Russian imperial family.

28 **Stockwood Craft Museum and Gardens**
Stockwood Park, Farley, Hill,
Luton, Bedfordshire LU1 4BH
Tel: (01582) 738714/746739
Housed in an 18thC stable block and featuring Bedfordshire craft displays and workshops, including a blacksmith, wheelwright, saddler, shoemaker and thatcher.

29 Leighton Buzzard Railway
Page's Park Station,
Billington Road, Leighton
Buzzard, Bedfordshire LU7 8TN
Tel: (01525) 373888

A preserved industrial railway with steam locomotives from around the world and a diesel collection. This 2ft guage railway, built in 1919, offers a return trip of 5.5 miles.

FIND OUT MORE

Further information about holidays and attractions in the East of England is available from:

East of England Tourist Board,
Toppesfield Hall,
Hadleigh, Suffolk IP7 5DN.
Tel: (01473) 822922

These publications are available from the East of England Tourist Board (post free):

- **Touring Map** - Bed & Breakfast and Camping and Caravaning
- **Places to Stay**

Also available are (prices include postage and packaging):

- **East Anglia Guide 1998** *£4.50*

WHERE TO STAY (EAST OF ENGLAND)

Accommodation entries in this region are listed in alphabetical order of place name, and then in alphabetical order of establishment.

Map references refer to the colour location maps at the back of this guide. The first number indicates the map to use; the letter and number which follow refer to the grid reference on the map.

At-a-glance symbols at the end of each accommodation entry give useful information about services and facilities. A key to symbols can be found inside the back cover flap. Keep this open for easy reference.

ALDEBURGH

Suffolk
Map ref 3C2

A prosperous port in the 16th C, now famous for the Aldeburgh Music Festival held annually in June. The 16th C Moot Hall, now a museum, is a timber-framed building once used as an open market.

Faraway

Listed COMMENDED

28 Linden Close, Aldeburgh IP15 5JL
☎ (01728) 452571

Bungalow with CH, garden and car parking. Quiet, being off the main road. TV in all rooms, full English breakfast. Dogs welcome.

Bedrooms: 1 single, 1 twin, 1 triple
Bathrooms: 2 public

Bed & breakfast per night:	£min	£max
Single	15.00	16.00
Double	30.00	32.00

Parking for 4

Gorse Hill

Leiston Road, Aldeburgh IP15 5QD
☎ (01728) 452162 & 0860 585190
Fax (01728) 452162

Beautiful Grade II listed house set in 25 acres between Aldeburgh golf-course and the beach. Charming country house accommodation.

Bedrooms: 1 double, 1 twin
Suites available
Bathrooms: 1 public, 2 private showers

Bed & breakfast per night:	£min	£max
Single	35.00	35.00
Double	50.00	60.00

Parking for 7
Cards accepted: Mastercard, Visa

ALDRINGHAM

Suffolk
Map ref 3C2

Fern House

Listed COMMENDED

6 The Follies, Aldringham, Leiston IP16 4LU
☎ (01728) 830759

Large semi-detached house on Aldringham common near Aldeburgh. Peaceful, secluded situation but with easy access to all local amenities.

Bedrooms: 2 double
Bathrooms: 1 en-suite, 1 private, 1 public

Bed & breakfast per night:	£min	£max
Single	17.00	17.00
Double	34.00	34.00

Parking for 4
Open March–November

A key to symbols can be found inside the back cover flap.

ATTLEBOROUGH

Norfolk
Map ref 3B1

Market town, mostly destroyed in 1559 by fire, now a cider-making centre. Church with fine Norman tower.

Hill House Farm

COMMENDED

Deopham Road, Great Ellingham, Attleborough NR17 1AQ
☎ (01953) 453113
Fax (01953) 453113

100-acre mixed farm. Friendly, comfortable accommodation just off the B1077 at Great Ellingham. Easy reach of all local attractions. Children welcome.

Bedrooms: 1 double, 1 twin, 1 triple
Bathrooms: 1 public

Bed & breakfast per night:	£min	£max
Single	16.00	
Double	32.00	

Parking for 5

Scales Farm

Listed COMMENDED

Old Buckenham, Attleborough NR17 1PE
☎ (01953) 860324

400-acre arable & dairy farm. Thatched farmhouse conveniently situated for Norwich, the Broads, Bressingham Gardens, Breckland and touring East Anglia.

Bedrooms: 1 single, 1 twin
Bathrooms: 1 public

Bed & breakfast per night:	£min	£max
Single	20.00	20.00
Double	30.00	30.00

Parking for 4

AYLSHAM

Norfolk
Map ref 3B1

Small town on the River Bure with an attractive market place and interesting church. Nearby is Blickling Hall (National Trust). Also the terminus of the Bure Valley narrow gauge steam railway which runs on 9 miles of the old Great Eastern trackbed, between Wroxham and Aylsham.
Tourist Information Centre ☎ (01263) 733903

The Old Bank House

HIGHLY COMMENDED

3 Norwich Road, Aylsham, Norwich NR11 6BN
☎ (01263) 733843

Relax in the comfort and traditional Victorian atmosphere of Aylsham's former private bank. We offer guests a friendly break, spacious welcoming bedrooms with TV and home-cooked meals. Lovely countryside nearby.
Bedrooms: 1 double, 1 twin, 1 triple
Bathrooms: 1 en-suite, 2 public

Bed & breakfast per night:	£min	£max
Single	25.00	25.00
Double	38.00	38.00

Half board per person:	£min	£max
Daily	32.00	38.00
Weekly	192.00	228.00

Evening meal 1800 (last orders 2000)
Parking for 3

For further information on accommodation establishments use the coupons at the back of this guide.

BECCLES

Suffolk
Map ref 3C1

Fire destroyed the town in the 16th C and it was rebuilt in Georgian red brick. The River Waveney, on which the town stands, is popular with boating enthusiasts and has an annual regatta. Home of Beccles and District Museum.

Catherine House

COMMENDED

2 Ringsfield Road, Beccles NR34 9PQ
☎ (01502) 716428
Family home, tastefully decorated to high standard in quiet position overlooking Waveney Valley. Five minutes' walk to town centre.
Bedrooms: 1 single, 1 double, 1 triple
Bathrooms: 1 en-suite, 1 public

Bed & breakfast per night:	£min	£max
Single	17.50	18.50
Double	35.00	45.00

Evening meal 1800 (last orders 2000)
Parking for 4

BEDFORD

Bedfordshire
Map ref 2D1

Busy county town with interesting buildings and churches near the River Ouse which has pleasant riverside walks. Many associations with John Bunyan including Bunyan Meeting House, museum and statue. The Bedford Museum and Cecil Higgins Art Gallery are of interest.
Tourist Information Centre ☎ (01234) 215226

Firs Farm

COMMENDED

Stagsden, Bedford MK43 8TB
☎ (01234) 822344
Fax (01234) 822344
504-acre arable farm. Family-run, set in quiet surroundings quarter-of-a-mile south of A422, midway between Bedford and Milton Keynes (M1 junction 14).
Bedrooms: 2 double, 1 twin
Bathrooms: 1 en-suite, 1 public

Bed & breakfast per night:	£min	£max
Single	18.50	25.00
Double	34.00	40.00

Parking for 4

BEETLEY

Norfolk
Map ref 3B1

Peacock House

HIGHLY COMMENDED

Peacock Lane, Old Beetley, Dereham NR20 4DG
☎ (01362) 860371
Beautiful period farmhouse with lovely garden in rural setting, 3.5 miles from Dereham. Ideal for Norwich, Sandringham and coast. Good home cooking and a warm welcome.
Bedrooms: 2 double, 1 twin
Bathrooms: 3 en-suite

Bed & breakfast per night:	£min	£max
Single	18.00	22.00
Double	36.00	40.00

Parking for 4

BEYTON

Suffolk
Map ref 3B2

Manorhouse

HIGHLY COMMENDED

The Green, Beyton, Bury St Edmunds IP30 9AF
☎ (01359) 270960
Fax (01284) 761611

Lovely, timbered 15th C farmhouse with relaxed, welcoming atmosphere, overlooking village green. Spacious, quality accommodation, all en-suite. Non-smoking. Good local inns. 4 miles east of Bury St Edmunds, off A14.
Bedrooms: 1 double, 1 twin
Bathrooms: 2 en-suite

Bed & breakfast per night:	£min	£max
Single	25.00	35.00
Double	43.00	48.00

Continued ▶

BEYTON

Continued

Evening meal from 1900
Parking for 5

BLAKENEY

Norfolk
Map ref 3B1

Picturesque village on the north coast of Norfolk and a former port and fishing village. 15th C Guildhall. Marshy creeks extend towards Blakeney Point (National Trust) and are a paradise for naturalists, with trips to the reserve and to see the seals from Blakeney Quay.

Flintstones Guesthouse

Listed COMMENDED

Wiveton, Holt NR25 7TL
☎ (01263) 740337
Attractive licensed guesthouse in picturesque rural surroundings near village green. 1 mile from Cley and Blakeney with good sailing and bird-watching. All rooms with private facilities. Non-smokers only, please.
Bedrooms: 1 single, 1 double, 3 triple
Bathrooms: 3 en-suite, 2 private

Bed & breakfast per night:	£min	£max
Single	21.00	22.00
Double	34.00	38.00

Evening meal 1900 (last orders 1700)
Parking for 5

BLYTHBURGH

Suffolk
Map ref 3C2

Little Thorbyns

COMMENDED

The Street, Blythburgh, Halesworth IP19 9LS
☎ (01502) 478664
Good, comfortable accommodation and a warm welcome. Close to Minsmere RSPB sanctuary and Southwold, Walberswick and Dunwich beaches. Three-night mini-break from £70 per person.
Bedrooms: 1 single, 1 double, 1 twin
Bathrooms: 2 en-suite, 2 public

Bed & breakfast per night:	£min	£max
Single	17.50	18.00
Double	36.00	36.00

Half board per person:	£min	£max
Daily	25.00	25.00
Weekly	175.00	175.00

Evening meal 1800 (last orders 1900)
Parking for 4

BRADFIELD

Essex
Map ref 3B2

Emsworth House

Listed COMMENDED

Ship Hill, Bradfield, Manningtree CO11 2UP
☎ (01255) 870860
Formerly a vicarage, the spacious rooms look out over stunning countryside and the River Stour. 2 minutes' walk to shore. Near Colchester, Ipswich and Harwich. On business, holiday or en-route to the continent, it's perfect. Art tuition available.
Bedrooms: 2 double, 1 twin
Bathrooms: 1 private, 3 public

Bed & breakfast per night:	£min	£max
Single	26.00	30.00
Double	38.00	48.00

Lunch available
Evening meal 1830 (last orders 2200)
Parking for 12

BRAINTREE

Essex
Map ref 3B2

The Heritage Centre in the Town Hall describes Braintree's former international importance in wool, silk and engineering. St Michael's parish church includes some Roman bricks. Braintree market was first chartered in 1199.
Tourist Information Centre ☎ (01376) 550066

Spicers Farm

HIGHLY COMMENDED

Rotten End, Wethersfield, Braintree CM7 4AL
☎ (01371) 851021
70-acre arable farm. Attractive farmhouse set in delightful, peaceful position overlooking beautiful countryside. Comfortable and welcoming, all rooms en-suite. North-west of Braintree, convenient for Harwich, Stansted and Cambridge.
Bedrooms: 1 double, 2 twin
Bathrooms: 3 en-suite

Bed & breakfast per night:	£min	£max
Single	20.00	22.00
Double	32.00	36.00

Parking for 10

BULPHAN

Essex
Map ref 3B3

Bonny Downs Farm

Listed APPROVED

Doesgate Lane, Bulphan, Upminster RM14 3TB
☎ (01268) 542129
60-acre mixed farm. Large comfortable farmhouse offering home-cooked food. Conveniently placed for road links: M25, A13 and A127 to London and south-east England.
Bedrooms: 2 twin, 1 triple
Bathrooms: 1 private, 2 public

Bed & breakfast per night:	£min	£max
Single	20.00	20.00
Double	30.00	30.00

Half board per person:	£min	£max
Daily	30.00	30.00
Weekly	210.00	210.00

Parking for 4

BUNGAY

Suffolk
Map ref 3C1

Market town and yachting centre on the River Waveney with the remains of a great 12th C castle. In the market-place stands the Butter Cross, rebuilt in 1689 after being largely destroyed by fire. Nearby at Earsham is the Otter Trust.

Dove Restaurant

APPROVED

Wortwell, Harleston, Norfolk IP20 0EN
☎ (01986) 788315
Former railway hotel, now an established international restaurant offering accommodation. Norfolk/Suffolk border. Good centre for the Waveney Valley and coast.
Bedrooms: 1 double, 1 twin, 1 triple
Bathrooms: 1 en-suite, 1 private, 1 public

Bed & breakfast per night:	£min	£max
Single	17.50	

Lunch available
Evening meal 1900 (last orders 2130)
Parking for 16
Cards accepted: Mastercard, Visa

Shoo-Devil Farmhouse

COMMENDED

Ilketshall Saint Margaret, Bungay NR35 1QU
☎ (01986) 781303

16th C thatched farmhouse with attractive gardens, set in peaceful surroundings. Ideal for touring East Anglia. Comfortable, spacious bedrooms with en-suite facilities.

Bedrooms: 1 double, 1 twin
Bathrooms: 2 en-suite

Bed & breakfast per night:	£min	£max
Single	18.50	20.00
Double	35.00	35.00

Half board per person:	£min	£max
Daily	25.50	29.50

Evening meal 1800 (last orders 2000)
Parking for 4
Open March–November

BUNTINGFORD

Hertfordshire
Map ref 2D1

Southfields Farm

Listed COMMENDED

Throcking, Buntingford SG9 9RD
☎ (01763) 281224 & (0589) 646759
Fax (01763) 281224

Warm, comfortable farmhouse 1.5 miles off A10 midway between London and Cambridge. TV, tea and coffee facilities. Closed at Christmas. No smoking in bedrooms.

Bedrooms: 1 single, 1 twin
Bathrooms: 1 public

Bed & breakfast per night:	£min	£max
Single	20.00	22.00
Double	40.00	44.00

Parking for 5

COLOUR MAPS

Colour maps at the back of this guide pinpoint all places in which you will find accommodation listed.

BURNHAM OVERY STAITHE

Norfolk
Map ref 3B1

Unspoilt scenic village, steeped in naval history, Lord Nelson's playground as a boy. Captain Woodgett of the Cutty Sark once lived here and cargo ships visited the harbour. Wonderful tidal inlet with great variety of natural history. Close to Roman fort at Brancaster and famous Peddars Way.

Domville Guesthouse

COMMENDED

Glebe Lane, Burnham Overy Staithe, King's Lynn PE31 8JQ
☎ (01328) 738298

Standing in own grounds in a quiet lane, close to the sea. Closed for Christmas.

Bedrooms: 3 single, 2 double, 2 twin
Bathrooms: 2 en-suite, 2 public

Bed & breakfast per night:	£min	£max
Single	18.00	21.00
Double	36.00	42.00

Half board per person:	£min	£max
Daily	27.50	29.75
Weekly	170.00	205.00

Evening meal 1900 (last orders 1200)
Parking for 10

BURY ST EDMUNDS

Suffolk
Map ref 3B2

Ancient market and cathedral town which takes its name from the martyred Saxon King, St Edmund. Bury St Edmunds has many fine buildings including the Athenaeum and Moyses Hall, reputed to be the oldest Norman house in the county.
Tourist Information Centre ☎ (01284) 764667 or 757083

Craufurd House

Howe Lane, Cockfield, Bury St Edmunds IP30 OHA
☎ (01284) 828216

Self-contained unit comprising bedroom, sitting-room and bathroom in detached country house. TV and tea/coffee facilities. In pleasant countryside overlooking fields. Easy drive from Bury St Edmunds. Lavenham 4 miles.

Bedrooms: 1 twin
Bathrooms: 1 private

Bed & breakfast per night:	£min	£max
Single	17.50	
Double	35.00	

Parking for 4
Open April–October

The Gables

COMMENDED

107 Fornham Road, Bury St Edmunds IP32 6AS
☎ (01284) 754257

Warm and cosy atmosphere. Situated within 5 minutes' walking distance of station and 10 minutes from town centre.

Bedrooms: 1 single, 1 double, 1 triple
Bathrooms: 1 public

Bed & breakfast per night:	£min	£max
Single	18.00	18.00
Double	36.00	36.00

Parking for 3

Maundrell House

COMMENDED

109 Fornham Road, Bury St Edmunds IP32 6AS
☎ (01284) 705884
Fax (01284) 705884

Large Edwardian semi-detached town house. Twin rooms overlook garden. Close to town centre, station and A45. Guests are assured of a warm welcome and good food. Meeting from coach or train by arrangement.

Bedrooms: 1 single, 2 twin
Bathrooms: 1 en-suite, 2 public

Bed & breakfast per night:	£min	£max
Single	18.00	
Double	34.00	39.00

Parking for 2

South Hill House

Listed COMMENDED

43 Southgate Street, Bury St Edmunds IP33 2AZ
☎ (01284) 755650
Fax (01284) 752718

Grade II listed townhouse, reputed to be the school mentioned in Charles Dickens' "Pickwick Papers". 10 minutes' walk from town centre, 2 minutes' drive from A14.*

Bedrooms: 1 double, 1 twin, 1 family room
Bathrooms: 3 en-suite

Continued ▶

BURY ST EDMUNDS

Continued

Bed & breakfast per night:	£min	£max
Single	25.00	32.00
Double	40.00	44.00

Parking for 4

CAMBRIDGE

Cambridgeshire
Map ref 2D1

A most important and beautiful city on the River Cam with 31 colleges forming one of the oldest universities in the world. Numerous museums, good shopping centre, restaurants, theatres, cinema and fine bookshops.
Tourist Information Centre ☎ (01223) 322640

Antwerp Guest House

APPROVED

36 Brookfields, Mill Road, Cambridge CB1 3NW
☎ (01223) 247690
On A1134 ring road between Addenbrookes Hospital and Cambridge Airport. Near the city's amenities and bus and railway stations. Pleasant gardens.
Bedrooms: 4 double, 4 twin
Bathrooms: 2 en-suite, 2 public

Bed & breakfast per night:	£min	£max
Single	25.00	30.00
Double	35.00	40.00

Parking for 8
Open February–November

Bridge Hotel (Motel)

APPROVED

Clayhythe, Waterbeach, Cambridge CB5 9NZ
☎ (01223) 860252
Fax (01223) 440448

Picturesque 17th C riverside hotel with motel rooms, between A45 and A10 (B1047), 4 miles from Cambridge. Fishing, walking, boating.
Bedrooms: 3 single, 20 double, 5 twin
Suites available
Bathrooms: 28 en-suite

Bed & breakfast per night:	£min	£max
Single	35.00	
Double	55.00	65.00

Lunch available
Evening meal 1830 (last orders 2130)
Parking for 50
Cards accepted: Amex, Mastercard, Visa, Switch/Delta

Cristinas

COMMENDED

47 St Andrews Road, Cambridge CB4 1DH
☎ (01223) 365855 & 327700
Fax (01223) 365855
Small family-run business in quiet location, a short walk from city centre and colleges.
Bedrooms: 5 double, 3 twin, 1 triple
Bathrooms: 7 en-suite, 1 public

Bed & breakfast per night:	£min	£max
Single	35.00	42.00
Double	42.00	49.00

Parking for 8

Dykelands Guesthouse

COMMENDED

157 Mowbray Road, Cambridge CB1 4SP
☎ (01223) 244300
Fax (01223) 566746
Detached guesthouse offering modern accommodation. On south side of city, ideally located for city centre and for touring. Children welcome. Two bedrooms on ground floor.
Bedrooms: 1 single, 2 double, 2 twin, 2 triple, 1 family room
Bathrooms: 3 en-suite, 1 public, 2 private showers

Bed & breakfast per night:	£min	£max
Single	20.00	27.50
Double	34.00	40.00

Parking for 7
Cards accepted: Amex, Diners, Mastercard, Visa, Switch/Delta

Foxhounds

Listed COMMENDED

71 Cambridge Road, New Wimpole/Orwell, Royston, Hertfordshire SG8 5QD
☎ (01223) 207344
Former pub, part 17th C, now a family home. On A603, 9 miles from Cambridge and within easy reach of Wimpole Hall (National Trust). Sitting room for guests, large garden.
Bedrooms: 1 single, 2 twin
Bathrooms: 2 public

Bed & breakfast per night:	£min	£max
Single	18.00	18.00
Double	36.00	36.00

Evening meal 1930 (last orders 1930)
Parking for 3

Gransden Lodge Farm

HIGHLY COMMENDED

Little Gransden, Nr Longstowe, Cambridge, Bedfordshire SG19 3EB
☎ (01767) 677365
Fax (01767) 677647
860-acre arable & livestock farm. West of Cambridge on B1046. Two miles west of A1198, between Longstowe and Little Gransden.
Bedrooms: 1 double, 1 twin, 1 triple
Bathrooms: 3 en-suite, 1 public

Bed & breakfast per night:	£min	£max
Single	17.00	20.00
Double	34.00	38.00

Parking for 6

264 Hills Road

HIGHLY COMMENDED

Cambridge CB2 2QE
☎ (01223) 248369
Fax (01223) 441276
Email: davido@dial.pipex.com
Elegant 1920s detached house on main bus route, 1 mile from city centre and 2 miles from M11.
Bedrooms: 1 double
Bathrooms: 1 en-suite

Bed & breakfast per night:	£min	£max
Single	38.00	38.00
Double	58.00	58.00

Parking for 4
Cards accepted: Visa

Home From Home

COMMENDED

39 Milton Road, Cambridge CB4 1XA
☎ (01223) 323555 & (0589) 990698
Fax (01223) 565660
Small, friendly B & B, with spacious rooms, 10 minutes' walk from bus station and city centre.
Bedrooms: 2 double, 1 twin
Bathrooms: 1 private, 2 private showers

Bed & breakfast per night:

	£min	£max
Single	25.00	30.00
Double	36.00	45.00

Parking for 3

King's Tithe

HIGHLY COMMENDED

13a Comberton Road, Barton, Cambridge CB3 7BA
☎ (01223) 263610
Fax (01223) 263610

Guest often return to this up-market home in quiet surroundings. The rooms have an open view over the countryside. Breakfast has many choices and the village pubs have excellent meals. Close to M11 junction 12, on the B1046 off the A603.

Bedrooms: 2 twin
Bathrooms: 1 public

Bed & breakfast per night:

	£min	£max
Single	29.00	34.00
Double	40.00	50.00

Parking for 3
Open February–December

Leys Cottage

APPROVED

56 Wimpole Road, Barton, Cambridge CB3 7AB
☎ (01223) 262482
Fax (01223) 264166

Part 17th C house with modern extension in a quiet and secluded spot but within easy reach of Cambridge, M11 and A14. On A603 Cambridge-Sandy road, off junction 12 of M11.

Bedrooms: 1 single, 1 double, 1 twin
Bathrooms: 2 en-suite, 1 public

Bed & breakfast per night:

	£min	£max
Single	25.00	35.00
Double	40.00	48.00

Half board per person:

	£min	£max
Daily	32.50	36.50
Weekly	227.50	255.50

Evening meal 1900 (last orders 2030)
Parking for 4

Segovia Lodge

APPROVED

2 Barton Road, Newnham, Cambridge CB3 9JZ
☎ (01223) 354105
Fax (01223) 323011

Within walking distance of the city centre and colleges. Next to cricket and tennis fields. Warm welcome, personal service and both rooms with private facilities. Non-smokers only, please.

Bedrooms: 1 double, 1 twin
Bathrooms: 2 private, 1 public

Bed & breakfast per night:

	£min	£max
Double	45.00	50.00

Parking for 4

The White House

COMMENDED

196 Barton Road, Comberton, Cambridge CB3 7BU
☎ (01223) 262886
Fax (01223) 262886

Comfortable family home, warm and inviting, only 10 minutes from Cambridge city. Welcome, and welcome again.

Bedrooms: 1 double, 1 twin
Bathrooms: 2 private showers

Bed & breakfast per night:

	£min	£max
Single	20.00	30.00
Double	35.00	48.00

Parking for 6

CAPEL ST MARY

Suffolk
Map ref 3B2

Grove Farmhouse

COMMENDED

Little Wenham, Colchester CO7 6QB
☎ (01473) 310341

190-acre arable farm. Comfortable listed farmhouse in quiet rural setting, 15 minutes from Ipswich. Convenient for Constable country and the coast.

Bedrooms: 1 single, 1 double, 1 twin
Bathrooms: 1 public

Bed & breakfast per night:

	£min	£max
Single	17.50	
Double	35.00	

Evening meal 1830 (last orders 2000)
Parking for 5

CHATTERIS

Cambridgeshire
Map ref 3A2

Cross Keys Inn Hotel

COMMENDED

12-16 Market Hill, Chatteris PE16 6BA
☎ (01354) 693036 & 692644
Fax (01354) 693036

Elizabethan coaching inn built around 1540, Grade II listed. A la carte menu and bar meals. Friendly atmosphere, oak-beamed lounge with log fires. Ideally placed in the heart of the Fens.

Bedrooms: 2 double, 4 twin, 1 triple
Bathrooms: 5 en-suite, 1 public

Bed & breakfast per night:

	£min	£max
Single	21.00	32.50
Double	32.50	55.00

Half board per person:

	£min	£max
Daily	40.00	40.00

Lunch available
Evening meal 1900 (last orders 2200)
Parking for 10
Cards accepted: Amex, Diners, Mastercard, Visa, Switch/Delta

CHELMSFORD

Essex
Map ref 3B3

The county town of Essex, originally a Roman settlement, Caesaromagus, thought to have been destroyed by Boudicca. Growth of the town's industry can be traced in the excellent museum in Oaklands Park. 15th C parish church has been Chelmsford Cathedral since 1914.
Tourist Information Centre ☎ (01245) 283400

Crossways

COMMENDED

Main Road, Rettendon Common, Chelmsford CM3 8DY
☎ (01245) 400539
Fax (01245) 400539

Secluded south-facing home in charming,well-kept garden, set well back from A130 dual carriageway.

Continued ▶

CHELMSFORD

Continued

Bedrooms: 1 twin
Bathrooms: 1 private

Bed & breakfast per night:	£min	£max
Single	20.00	25.00
Double	40.00	50.00

Parking for 2

Neptune Cafe Motel

Listed APPROVED

Burnham Road, Latchingdon, Chelmsford CM3 6EX
☎ (01621) 740770
Cafe with adjoining chalet block, which includes 2 units suitable for physically disabled. Village location between Maldon and Burnham-on-Crouch.
Bedrooms: 4 double, 2 twin, 4 triple
Bathrooms: 10 en-suite

Bed & breakfast per night:	£min	£max
Single	20.00	24.00
Double	30.00	34.00

Half board per person:	£min	£max
Daily	25.00	30.00

Lunch available
Parking for 40

Old Bakery

Listed COMMENDED

Waltham Road, Terling, Chelmsford CM3 2QR
☎ (01245) 233363
Converted bakery in small village, 4 miles from A12 overlooking open farmland and on the Essex Way.
Bedrooms: 1 single, 1 twin
Bathrooms: 2 en-suite

Bed & breakfast per night:	£min	£max
Single	20.00	22.50
Double	40.00	45.00

Parking for 2
Open January–November

CHOSELEY

Norfolk
Map ref 3B1

Choseley Farmhouse

Listed COMMENDED

Choseley, Docking, King's Lynn PE31 8PQ
☎ (01485) 512331
17th C Norfolk farmhouse with Tudor chimneys. Foundations are thought to date back to original abbey of 1250.
Bedrooms: 1 double, 1 twin
Bathrooms: 1 public

Bed & breakfast per night:	£min	£max
Single	15.00	
Double	30.00	30.00

Parking for 10
Open July–September

COLCHESTER

Essex
Map ref 3B2

Britain's oldest recorded town standing on the River Colne and famous for its oysters. Numerous historic buildings, ancient remains and museums. Plenty of parks and gardens, extensive shopping centre, theatre and zoo.
Tourist Information Centre ☎ (01206) 282920

8 Broadmead Road

Listed APPROVED

Parsons Heath, Colchester CO4 3HB
☎ (01206) 861818
Fax (01206) 861818
Friendly, family home in quiet residential area, only 10 minutes from town centre, bus station, leisure complex and Colchester Castle.
Bedrooms: 1 double
Bathrooms: 1 public

Bed & breakfast per night:	£min	£max
Single	25.00	
Double	35.00	

Parking for 2

Darcy House

COMMENDED

3-5 Culver Street East, Colchester CO1 1LD
☎ (01206) 768111 & 763938
Fax (01206) 763938
Beautiful, restored Georgian town house in centre of town. Elegant licensed cafe/restaurant, very comfortable en-suite rooms (all double size) with CH, colour TV. Special weekend break offers.
Bedrooms: 3 double
Bathrooms: 3 en-suite

Bed & breakfast per night:	£min	£max
Single	30.00	35.00
Double	45.00	52.00

Half board per person:	£min	£max
Daily	42.00	47.00
Weekly	270.00	300.00

Lunch available
Evening meal 1730 (last orders 2130)
Parking for 3
Cards accepted: Mastercard, Visa

The Globe Hotel

APPROVED

71 North Station Road, Colchester CO1 1RQ
☎ (01206) 573881 & 502502
Fax (01206) 797265
Victorian pub/hotel, now fully restored. All rooms en-suite, car park, restaurant. Close to A12, mainline station and all local amenities.
Bedrooms: 4 single, 2 double, 2 twin, 2 triple, 2 family rooms
Bathrooms: 12 en-suite

Bed & breakfast per night:	£min	£max
Single	30.00	40.00
Double	50.00	60.00

Lunch available
Evening meal 1800 (last orders 2000)
Parking for 20
Cards accepted: Amex, Diners, Mastercard, Visa

11 Harvest End

Listed COMMENDED

Stanway, Colchester CO3 5YX
☎ (01206) 543202
Comfortable family home with friendly atmosphere. Colour TV and tea/coffee facilities in rooms. Many local restaurants and take-aways nearby. No smoking, please.
Bedrooms: 1 single, 1 double, 1 twin
Bathrooms: 1 public

Bed & breakfast per night:	£min	£max
Single	18.00	18.00
Double	35.00	36.00

Parking for 2

11a Lincoln Way

Listed COMMENDED

Colchester C01 2RL
☎ (01206) 867192 & (0410) 208168
Fax (01206) 867192
Accommodation in quiet residential area, close to town centre, bus station, castle, leisure complex and Charter Hall.
Bedrooms: 1 single, 1 twin
Bathrooms: 1 public

Bed & breakfast per night:	£min	£max
Single	18.00	20.00
Double	36.00	40.00

Evening meal 1800 (last orders 1930)
Parking for 1

Old House

COMMENDED

Ford Street, Aldham, Colchester CO6 3PH
☎ (01206) 240456

Bed and breakfast in 14th C family home, listed as historic building, with friendly atmosphere, oak beams, log fires, large garden and ample parking. Between Harwich and Cambridge, Felixstowe and London. On A604, 5 miles west of Colchester.

Bedrooms: 1 single, 1 twin, 1 triple
Bathrooms: 1 en-suite, 2 private

Bed & breakfast per night:	£min	£max
Single	25.00	32.50
Double	35.00	45.00

Parking for 8
Cards accepted: Mastercard, Visa

CONINGSBY

Lincolnshire
Map ref 4D2

Large thriving village on the edge of the Lincolnshire Fens. It is within easy reach of main towns and has a pleasing church with an unusual one-handed clock.

White Bull Inn

APPROVED

55 High Street, Coningsby, Lincoln LN4 4RB
☎ (01526) 342439

A warm welcome awaits at this friendly pub with real ale, riverside beer garden and large children's playground. Children's Certificate. Traditional home-made meals available every day, lunch time and evening. Half a mile from RAF Coningsby. Family Pub of the Year finalist, 1995.

Bedrooms: 2 single, 1 double, 1 twin
Bathrooms: 2 en-suite, 4 public

Bed & breakfast per night:	£min	£max
Single	14.00	16.00
Double	30.00	38.00

Half board per person:	£min	£max
Daily	18.00	20.00
Weekly	110.00	

Lunch available
Evening meal 1900 (last orders 2200)
Parking for 60

CORBY GLEN

Lincolnshire
Map ref 3A1

Stonepit Farmhouse

Listed COMMENDED

Swinstead Road, Corby Glen, Grantham NG33 4NU
☎ (01476) 550614
Fax (01476) 550614

Picturesque stone house on edge of village. 4 miles east of A1. Separate ground floor guest wing facing "Mediterranean style" courtyard.

Bedrooms: 1 single, 1 twin
Bathrooms: 1 public

Bed & breakfast per night:	£min	£max
Single	20.00	25.00
Double	40.00	40.00

Parking for 3

CROMER

Norfolk
Map ref 3C1

Once a small fishing village and now famous for its fishing boats that still work off the beach and offer freshly caught crabs. Excellent bathing on sandy beaches fringed by cliffs. The town boasts a fine pier, theatre, museum and a lifeboat station.
Tourist Information Centre ☎ (01263) 512497

The Crowmere

Listed COMMENDED

4 Vicarage Road, Cromer NR27 9DQ
☎ (01263) 513056

Charming Victorian residence in quiet road close to beach/town centre and all amenities. Tea/coffee making facilities and TV in all rooms. Most rooms en-suite. Family suites available.

Bedrooms: 1 single, 4 double, 2 twin, 1 triple
Bathrooms: 6 en-suite, 1 public

Bed & breakfast per night:	£min	£max
Single	18.00	28.00
Double	28.00	38.00

Parking for 6

Shrublands Farm

HIGHLY COMMENDED

Northrepps, Cromer NR27 0AA
☎ (01263) 579297
Fax (01263) 579297

300-acre arable farm. A warm welcome awaits you at this traditional Norfolk farmhouse in centre of Northrepps village, 1 mile off A149 and 2 miles from Cromer. Full central heating. Evening meals available.

Bedrooms: 1 double, 2 twin
Bathrooms: 1 en-suite, 2 private

Bed & breakfast per night:	£min	£max
Single	24.00	28.00
Double	40.00	44.00

Half board per person:	£min	£max
Daily	30.50	42.00

Evening meal 1900 (last orders 2000)
Parking for 4

The map references refer to the colour maps towards the end of the guide. The first figure is the map number; the letter and figure which follow indicate the grid reference on the map.

WELCOME HOST

This is a nationally recognised customer care programme which aims to promote the highest standards of service and a warm welcome. Establishments who are taking part in this initiative are indicated by the symbol.

DANBURY

Essex
Map ref 3B3

Southways

Listed COMMENDED

Copt Hill, Danbury, Chelmsford CM3 4NN
☎ (01245) 223428

Pleasant country house with large garden adjoining an area of National Trust common land.

Bedrooms: 2 twin
Bathrooms: 1 public

Bed & breakfast per night:	£min	£max
Single	18.00	18.00
Double	32.00	32.00

Parking for 2

DEBDEN GREEN

Essex
Map ref 2D1

Wigmores Farm

Listed COMMENDED

Debden Green, Saffron Walden CB11 3LX
☎ (01371) 830050

1000-acre arable farm. 16th C thatched farmhouse in open countryside, 2.5 miles from Thaxted, just off the Thaxted to Debden road.

Bedrooms: 3 double
Bathrooms: 2 public

Bed & breakfast per night:	£min	£max
Single	20.00	20.00
Double	36.00	36.00

Half board per person:	£min	£max
Daily	31.00	33.00
Weekly	217.00	231.00

Lunch available
Evening meal 1900 (last orders 2000)
Parking for 12

12

Please mention this guide when making your booking.

Half board prices are given per person, but in some cases these may be based on double/twin occupancy.

DEDHAM

Essex
Map ref 3B2

A former wool town. Dedham Vale is an Area of Outstanding Natural Beauty and there is a countryside centre in the village. This is John Constable country and Sir Alfred Munnings lived at Castle House which is open to the public.

May's Barn Farm

HIGHLY COMMENDED

May's Lane, Off Long Road West, Dedham, Colchester CO7 6EW
☎ (01206) 323191

300-acre arable farm. Tranquil old farmhouse with outstanding views over Dedham Vale in Constable country. Quarter mile down private lane. Comfortable, spacious rooms, with private facilities.

Bedrooms: 1 double, 1 twin
Bathrooms: 1 en-suite, 1 private

Bed & breakfast per night:	£min	£max
Single	22.00	25.00
Double	39.00	40.00

Parking for 5

10

DEREHAM

Norfolk
Map ref 3B1

East Dereham is famous for its associations with the poet William Cowper and also Bishop Bonner, chaplain to Cardinal Wolsey. His home is now a museum. Around the charming market-place are many notable buildings.

Clinton House

Listed HIGHLY COMMENDED

Well Hill, Clint Green, Yaxham, Dereham NR19 1RX
☎ (01362) 692079

Charming 18th C country house, full of character, in peaceful location. Tennis/croquet. Good touring centre. Breakfast served in beautiful conservatory.

Bedrooms: 1 double, 1 twin, 1 triple
Bathrooms: 1 private, 2 public

Bed & breakfast per night:	£min	£max
Single	20.00	22.00
Double	32.00	34.00

Parking for 10

DISS

Norfolk
Map ref 3B2

Old market town built around 3 sides of the Mere, a 6-acre stretch of water. Although modernised, some interesting Tudor, Georgian and Victorian buildings around the market-place remain. St Mary's church has a fine knapped flint chancel.
Tourist Information Centre ☎ (01379) 650523

Oxfootstone Granary

COMMENDED

Low Common, South Lopham, Diss IP22 2JS
☎ (01379) 687490

Converted barn in open countryside, erected in 1822. Guest rooms are situated in a single-storey wing, formerly cart-sheds, overlooking a large pond with waterfowl.

Bedrooms: 1 double, 1 twin
Bathrooms: 2 en-suite

Bed & breakfast per night:	£min	£max
Single		20.00
Double		36.00

Parking for 5

5

Rose Cottage

COMMENDED

Diss Road, Burston, Diss IP22 3TP
☎ (01379) 740602
Fax (01379) 740602

Delightful timber-framed 18th C house, situated on Church Green, opposite famous Burston Strike School. Parking and garden.

Bedrooms: 2 single, 1 double
Bathrooms: 1 public

Bed & breakfast per night:	£min	£max
Single	20.00	
Double	40.00	

Parking for 3

Strenneth

COMMENDED

Airfield Road, Fersfield, Diss IP22 2BP
☎ (01379) 688182
Fax (01379) 688260
Email: webb.strenneth@btinternet.com

Family-run, 17th C period property. Log fires, oak beams. Executive and four-poster, all en-suite, some ground floor. Licensed. Pets most welcome. Close Bressingham Gardens.

Bedrooms: 4 double, 2 twin
Bathrooms: 6 en-suite, 1 public

Bed & breakfast per night:	£min	£max
Single	25.00	
Double	40.00	

Parking for 10
Cards accepted: Amex, Diners, Mastercard, Visa

EARLS COLNE

Essex
Map ref 3B2

Riverside Motel

COMMENDED

40 Lower Holt Street A604, Earls Colne, Colchester CO6 2PH
☎ (01787) 223487

Converted farm buildings in village, on A604 at Earls Colne by the bridge over River Colne. All en-suite.

Wheelchair access category 3
Bedrooms: 2 double, 7 twin, 2 family rooms
Bathrooms: 11 en-suite

Bed & breakfast per night:	£min	£max
Single	30.50	32.50
Double	40.00	44.00

Lunch available
Evening meal 1930 (last orders 2200)
Parking for 40
Cards accepted: Mastercard, Visa

EAST BERGHOLT

Suffolk
Map ref 3B2

John Constable, the famous East Anglian artist, was born here in 1776 and at the church of St Mary are reminders of his family's associations with the area. 1 mile south of the village are Flatford Mill and Willy Lott's cottage, both made famous by Constable in his paintings.

Rosemary

Listed COMMENDED

Rectory Hill, East Bergholt, Colchester CO7 6TH
☎ (01206) 298241

Pleasant family house in lovely 1-acre garden in the National Garden Scheme. Wide variety of plants and old-fashioned roses. In centre of Constable country. A non-smoking establishment.

Bedrooms: 1 single, 2 twin
Bathrooms: 1 public

Bed & breakfast per night:	£min	£max
Single	19.00	19.00
Double	38.00	38.00

Parking for 2

ELY

Cambridgeshire
Map ref 3A2

Until the 17th C, when the Fens were drained, Ely was an island. The cathedral, completed in 1189, dominates the surrounding area. One particular feature is the central octagonal tower with a fan-vaulted timber roof and wooden lantern.
Tourist Information Centre ☎ (01353) 662062

Cathedral House

17 St Mary's Street, Ely CB7 4ER
☎ (01353) 662124

Grade II listed elegant town house offering comfortable accommodation in the shadow of Ely Cathedral. Parking. Walled garden. No smoking, please.

Bedrooms: 1 double, 1 twin, 1 family room
Suite available
Bathrooms: 3 en-suite

Bed & breakfast per night:	£min	£max
Single	30.00	40.00
Double	40.00	60.00

Parking for 4

2 Eastwood Close

Listed COMMENDED

Sutton, Ely CB6 2RH
☎ (01353) 778423 & (0421) 682357

Modern family house in quiet location on edge of village. A142 from Ely, turn left at roundabout to Sutton, left into Church Lane, then 2nd left into Eastwood Close.

Bedrooms: 1 single, 1 double, 1 twin
Bathrooms: 2 public

Bed & breakfast per night:	£min	£max
Single	16.00	16.00
Double	32.00	32.00

Parking for 2

Hill House Farm

HIGHLY COMMENDED

9 Main Street, Coveney, Ely CB6 2DJ
☎ (01353) 778369

240-acre arable farm. High quality en-suite accommodation and food, in fine Victorian farmhouse. In unspoilt Fenland village 3 miles west of Ely, with open views of surrounding countryside and easy access to Cambridge. No smoking and no pets, please.

Bedrooms: 2 double, 1 twin
Bathrooms: 3 en-suite

Bed & breakfast per night:	£min	£max
Single	25.00	36.00
Double	38.00	40.00

Parking for 4

Quarterway House

COMMENDED

Ely Road, Little Thetford, Ely CB6 3HP
☎ (01353) 648964
Fax (01353) 648964

Traditional-style CH house set in open countryside 2 miles from Ely. Relaxed, friendly atmosphere. Log fires, books, conservatory and garden. Private parking. Evening meals and special diets available.

Bedrooms: 1 double, 1 twin
Suites available
Bathrooms: 1 en-suite, 1 private, 1 public

Bed & breakfast per night:	£min	£max
Single	20.00	30.00
Double	35.00	40.00

Half board per person:	£min	£max
Daily	22.50	26.00

Parking for 7
Cards accepted: Mastercard, Visa

WELCOME HOST

This is a nationally recognised customer care programme which aims to promote the highest standards of service and a warm welcome. Establishments who are taking part in this initiative are indicated by the symbol.

ELY

Continued

Spinney Abbey

COMMENDED

Stretham Road, Wicken, Ely
CB7 5XQ
☎ (01353) 720971

150-acre dairy farm. Spacious Georgian farmhouse set in 1 acre of garden with tennis court. All rooms with private facilities. Farm borders Wicken Fen Nature Reserve.

Bedrooms: 1 double, 1 twin, 1 triple
Bathrooms: 2 en-suite, 1 private

Bed & breakfast per night:	£min	£max
Single	25.00	
Double	38.00	40.00

Parking for 4

EYKE

Suffolk
Map ref 3C2

The Old House

HIGHLY COMMENDED

Eyke, Woodbridge IP12 2QW
☎ (01394) 460213

Lovely Grade II listed house, c1600. Comfortable and friendly, with beams, open fires, large, interesting garden and views over Deben Valley. Centre of village and edge of heritage coast. Good choice of food. All rooms also let as singles.

Bedrooms: 1 double, 2 twin
Bathrooms: 3 en-suite

Bed & breakfast per night:	£min	£max
Single	25.00	30.00
Double	42.00	45.00

Half board per person:	£min	£max
Daily	33.00	42.00

Evening meal 1800 (last orders 1000)
Parking for 8

FELIXSTOWE

Suffolk
Map ref 3C2

Seaside resort that developed at the end of the 19th C. Lying in a gently curving bay with a 2-mile-long beach and backed by a wide promenade of lawns and floral gardens.
Tourist Information Centre ☎ (01394) 276770

Fludyer Arms Hotel

APPROVED

Undercliff Road East, Felixstowe
IP11 7LU
☎ (01394) 283279
Fax (01394) 670754

Closest hotel to the sea in Felixstowe. Two fully licensed bars and family room overlooking the sea. All rooms have superb sea views. Colour TV. Specialises in home-cooked food, with children's and vegetarian menus available.

Bedrooms: 3 single, 4 double, 2 twin
Bathrooms: 5 en-suite, 1 public

Bed & breakfast per night:	£min	£max
Single	18.00	26.00
Double	32.00	40.00

Lunch available
Evening meal 1900 (last orders 2100)
Parking for 14
Cards accepted: Mastercard, Visa

Sandlings

Listed COMMENDED

107 Cliff Road, Felixstowe IP11 9SA
☎ (01394) 672036

Modern detached house with ground floor bedrooms and 1st floor lounge with balcony giving panoramic sea views. Felixstowe Golf Club 100 yards, sailing and fishing close by. Ideal for exploring Suffolk coast and East Anglia generally.

Bedrooms: 1 single, 2 twin
Bathrooms: 1 en-suite, 1 public

Bed & breakfast per night:	£min	£max
Single	20.00	22.00
Double	37.00	42.00

Parking for 5

FILLINGHAM

Lincolnshire
Map ref 4C2

Church Farm

Listed HIGHLY COMMENDED

Fillingham, Gainsborough DN21 5BS
☎ (01427) 668279
Fax (01427) 668025

Idyllic stone farmhouse set in a large, tranquil garden. Near historic Lincoln and midway between Norwich and York.

Bedrooms: 1 single, 1 double, 1 twin
Suite available
Bathrooms: 1 en-suite, 2 public

Bed & breakfast per night:	£min	£max
Single	20.00	25.00
Double	32.00	38.00

Half board per person:	£min	£max
Daily	27.00	30.00
Weekly	189.00	210.00

FRAMLINGHAM

Suffolk
Map ref 3C2

Pleasant old market town with an interesting church, impressive castle and some attractive houses round Market Hill. The town's history can be traced at the Lanman Museum.

Shimmens Pightle

Listed COMMENDED

Dennington Road, Framlingham,
Woodbridge IP13 9JT
☎ (01728) 724036

Brian and Phyllis Collett's home is set in an acre of landscaped garden overlooking fields, on outskirts of Framlingham. Ground floor rooms with washbasins. Locally-cured bacon and home-made marmalade.

Bedrooms: 1 double, 2 twin
Bathrooms: 1 public

Bed & breakfast per night:	£min	£max
Single	20.00	
Double	37.00	39.00

Parking for 5

For ideas on places to visit refer to the introduction at the beginning of this section.

FRESSINGFIELD

Suffolk
Map ref 3C2

Chippenhall Hall

HIGHLY COMMENDED

Fressingfield, Eye IP21 5TD
☎ (01379) 588180 & 586733
Fax (01379) 586272

Listed Tudor manor, film location, heavily beamed and with inglenook fireplaces, in 7 secluded acres. Fine food and wines. 1 mile south of Fressingfield on B1116.

Bedrooms: 3 double
Bathrooms: 3 en-suite

Bed & breakfast per night:	£min	£max
Single	53.00	59.00
Double	59.00	65.00

Half board per person:	£min	£max
Daily	52.50	56.00
Weekly	348.00	375.00

Lunch available
Evening meal 1930 (last orders 1600)
Parking for 12
Cards accepted: Mastercard, Visa

GARBOLDISHAM

Norfolk
Map ref 3B2

Ingleneuk Lodge

COMMENDED

Hopton Road, Garboldisham, Diss IP22 2RQ
☎ (01953) 681541
Fax (01953) 681633

Modern single-level home, family-run. South-facing patio, riverside walk. Very friendly atmosphere. On B1111, 1 mile south of village.

Wheelchair access category 2♿
Bedrooms: 1 single, 1 double, 2 twin
Bathrooms: 4 en-suite

Bed & breakfast per night:	£min	£max
Single	33.00	33.00
Double	51.00	51.00

Parking for 20
Cards accepted: Amex, Mastercard, Visa, Switch/Delta

GREAT BIRCHAM

Norfolk
Map ref 3B1

King's Head Hotel

APPROVED

Great Bircham, King's Lynn PE31 6RJ
☎ (01485) 578265

Friendly village inn with 3 bars, Italian restaurant and beer gardens, near Sandringham, King's Lynn and the coast. English and Italian cuisine, fresh Norfolk seafood and produce, traditional Sunday lunch. Two-night or longer breaks available.

Bedrooms: 2 double, 3 twin
Bathrooms: 5 en-suite

Bed & breakfast per night:	£min	£max
Single	37.00	39.00
Double	57.00	59.00

Half board per person:	£min	£max
Daily	32.50	37.50
Weekly	227.50	262.50

Lunch available
Evening meal 1900 (last orders 2200)
Parking for 80
Cards accepted: Mastercard, Visa

GREAT DUNMOW

Essex
Map ref 3B2

On the main Roman road from Bishop's Stortford to Braintree. Doctor's Pond near the square was where the first lifeboat was tested in 1785. Home of the Dunmow Flitch trials held every 4 years on Whit Monday.

Yarrow

COMMENDED

27 Station Road, Felsted, Great Dunmow CM6 3HD
☎ (01371) 820878

Edwardian house with south-facing bedrooms, large garden and country views. Ample parking. Quarter of a mile to pubs and restaurants in lovely village. 20 minutes from Stansted/M11.

Bedrooms: 1 single, 1 double, 1 twin
Bathrooms: 1 en-suite, 1 public

Bed & breakfast per night:	£min	£max
Single	17.00	20.00
Double	30.00	34.00

Parking for 6

GREAT YARMOUTH

Norfolk
Map ref 3C1

One of Britain's major seaside resorts with 5 miles of seafront and every possible amenity including an award winning leisure complex offering a huge variety of all-weather facilities. Busy harbour and fishing centre.

The Britannia Guesthouse

Listed APPROVED

119 Wellesley Road, Great Yarmouth NR30 2AP
☎ (01493) 856488 & 857952

Small family-run Victorian terraced guesthouse situated 2 minutes from seafront and shops. Perfect base for exploring the Broads.

Bedrooms: 4 double, 2 family rooms
Bathrooms: 1 private, 1 public

Bed & breakfast per night:	£min	£max
Single	11.50	16.50
Double	23.00	35.00

Half board per person:	£min	£max
Daily	16.50	21.50
Weekly	115.00	150.00

Cards accepted: Visa, Switch/Delta

Spindrift Private Hotel

APPROVED

36 Wellesley Road, Great Yarmouth NR30 1EU
☎ (01493) 858674
Fax (01493) 858674

Attractively situated small private hotel, close to all amenities and with Beach Coach Station and car park at rear. Front bedrooms overlook gardens and sea.

Bedrooms: 2 single, 2 double, 1 twin, 1 triple, 1 family room
Bathrooms: 5 en-suite, 2 private

Continued ▶

Establishments should be open throughout the year, unless otherwise stated.

GREAT YARMOUTH

Continued

Bed & breakfast per night:	£min	£max
Single	20.00	32.00
Double	34.00	42.00

Cards accepted: Amex, Mastercard, Visa

GREAT YELDHAM

Essex
Map ref 3B2

Famous for its "gospel" oak tree.

The Waggon & Horses

Listed COMMENDED

High Street, Great Yeldham, Halstead CO9 4EX
☎ (01787) 237936

Traditional 16th C pub with a restaurant and comfortable accommodation.
Bedrooms: 1 single, 2 double, 3 twin
Bathrooms: 2 public

Bed & breakfast per night:	£min	£max
Single	17.50	22.50
Double	30.00	40.00

Lunch available
Evening meal 1900 (last orders 2100)
Parking for 40
Cards accepted: Amex, Diners, Mastercard, Visa, Switch/Delta

HADLEIGH

Suffolk
Map ref 3B2

Former wool town, lying on a tributary of the River Stour. The church of St Mary stands among a remarkable cluster of medieval buildings.
Tourist Information Centre ☎ (01473) 822922

French's Farm

COMMENDED

Hadleigh, Ipswich IP7 5PQ
☎ (01473) 824215
Fax (01473) 824215
20-acre farm with horses. Large period country house set in magnificent grounds, offering well-appointed, peaceful accommodation and friendly service. Horse riding facilities available.
Bedrooms: 1 double, 2 triple
Suites available
Bathrooms: 2 en-suite, 1 private

Bed & breakfast per night:	£min	£max
Single	20.00	25.00
Double	40.00	52.00

Evening meal 1800 (last orders 2000)
Parking for 15

The Marquis of Cornwallis

COMMENDED

Upper Layham, Hadleigh, Ipswich IP7 5JZ
☎ (01473) 822051 & 0850 559335
Fax (01473) 822051
Large public house in 2 acres of grounds leading down to River Brett, between Constable country and Lavenham.
Bedrooms: 2 double, 1 twin
Bathrooms: 2 en-suite, 1 private, 1 public

Bed & breakfast per night:	£min	£max
Single	29.00	29.00
Double	41.00	47.00

Lunch available
Evening meal 1900 (last orders 2130)
Parking for 22
Cards accepted: Amex, Diners, Mastercard, Visa, Switch/Delta

HARPENDEN

Hertfordshire
Map ref 2D1

Delightful country town with many scenic walks through surrounding woods and fields. Harpenden train station provides a fast service into London.

Carlton Guesthouse

8 Carlton Bank, Harpenden AL5 4SU
☎ (01582) 765756
Edwardian semi. Two minutes' walk from Thameslink Railway Station and 4 minutes from Harpenden high street. Decorated and furnished in period style.
Bedrooms: 2 single, 1 double
Bathrooms: 1 public

Bed & breakfast per night:	£min	£max
Single	16.00	20.00
Double	40.00	40.00

Evening meal 1800 (last orders 2030)

HARTEST

Suffolk
Map ref 3B2

Giffords Hall

COMMENDED

Hartest, Bury St Edmunds IP29 4EX
☎ (01284) 830464
Fax (01284) 830229

Georgian farmhouse just outside Hartest village, operating a vineyard and small country living with flowers and animals on 33 acres.
Bedrooms: 1 double, 2 twin
Bathrooms: 3 en-suite

Bed & breakfast per night:	£min	£max
Single	22.00	24.00
Double	38.00	42.00

Parking for 20
Cards accepted: Amex, Mastercard, Visa

HARWICH

Essex
Map ref 3C2

Port where the Rivers Orwell and Stour converge and enter the North Sea. The old town still has a medieval atmosphere with its narrow streets. To the south is the seaside resort of Dovercourt with long sandy beaches.
Tourist Information Centre ☎ (01255) 506139

Una House

COMMENDED

1 Una Road, Parkeston, Harwich CO12 4PP
☎ (01255) 551390
Fax (01255) 551390
A warm welcome awaits you at this modernised end-of-terrace Victorian house. All rooms are immaculate and en-suite. A short walk from Harwich International port and British Rail station.
Bedrooms: 1 single, 1 twin, 1 triple

Bathrooms: 3 en-suite

Bed & breakfast per night:	£min	£max
Single	20.00	25.00
Double	40.00	45.00

Parking for 4

HAUGHLEY

Suffolk
Map ref 3B2

Red House Farm

COMMENDED

Station Road, Haughley, Stowmarket
IP14 3QP
☎ (01449) 673323
Fax (01449) 673323

108-acre arable & fruit farm. Attractive farmhouse in rural location on small grassland farm. First class breakfast. Central heating and large garden.

Bedrooms: 2 single, 1 double, 1 twin
Bathrooms: 3 en-suite, 1 public

Bed & breakfast per night:	£min	£max
Single	18.00	20.00
Double	38.00	40.00

Parking for 3
Open January–November
8

HETHERSETT

Norfolk
Map ref 3B1

Magnolia House

Listed APPROVED

Cromwell Close, Hethersett
NR9 3HD
☎ (01603) 810749
Fax (01603) 810749

Family-run B & B. All rooms centrally heated, colour TV, hot and cold water, tea/coffee making facilities, own key. Laundry, public telephone and fax available. Private car park. Special discount rates for weekend breaks.

Bedrooms: 3 single, 1 double, 1 twin
Bathrooms: 4 public

Bed & breakfast per night:	£min	£max
Single	16.00	20.00
Double	30.00	36.00

Parking for 7
Cards accepted: Diners
6 OAP SP

You are advised to confirm your booking in writing.

HEVINGHAM

Norfolk
Map ref 3B1

Marsham Arms Inn

COMMENDED

Holt Road, Hevingham, Norwich
NR10 5NP
☎ (01603) 754268
Fax (01603) 754839

Set in peaceful Norfolk countryside within reach of Norwich, the Broads and the coast. Comfortable and spacious accommodation, good food and a fine selection of ales.

Bedrooms: 3 double, 5 twin
Bathrooms: 8 en-suite

Bed & breakfast per night:	£min	£max
Single	38.00	45.00
Double	49.50	55.00

Lunch available
Evening meal 1800 (last orders 2200)
Parking for 100
Cards accepted: Amex, Mastercard, Visa, Switch/Delta
50 SP

HILLINGTON

Norfolk
Map ref 3B1

Ffolkes Arms Hotel

COMMENDED

Lynn Road, Hillington, King's Lynn
PE31 6BJ
☎ (01485) 600210
Fax (01485) 601196

2 miles from Sandringham, family-run hotel with en-suite facilities on A148. Landscaped gardens in rural setting. Bar meals, carvery, restaurant.

Wheelchair access category 3
Bedrooms: 11 double, 7 twin, 2 triple
Bathrooms: 20 en-suite

Bed & breakfast per night:	£min	£max
Single	29.00	45.00
Double	45.00	60.00

Half board per person:	£min	£max
Daily	34.50	39.50
Weekly	240.00	275.00

Lunch available
Evening meal 1730 (last orders 2200)
Parking for 200
Cards accepted: Amex, Mastercard, Visa, Switch/Delta
200 OAP SP

HUNTINGDON

Cambridgeshire
Map ref 3A2

Attractive, interesting town which abounds in associations with the Cromwell family. The town is connected to Godmanchester by a beautiful 14th C bridge over the River Great Ouse.
Tourist Information Centre ☎ (01480) 388588

Prince of Wales

COMMENDED

Potton Road, Hilton, Huntingdon
PE18 9NG
☎ (01480) 830257
Fax (01480) 830257

Traditional village inn renowned for its traditional ales and good value food. Convenient for St Ives, Huntingdon, St Neots and Cambridge. On B1040, south-east of Huntingdon.

Bedrooms: 2 single, 1 double, 1 twin
Bathrooms: 4 en-suite

Bed & breakfast per night:	£min	£max
Single	25.00	37.50
Double	40.00	50.00

Lunch available
Evening meal 1900 (last orders 2115)
Parking for 9
Cards accepted: Amex, Diners, Mastercard, Visa, Switch/Delta
5 SP T

KELVEDON

Essex
Map ref 3B3

Village on the old Roman road from Colchester to London. Many of the buildings are 18th C but there is much of earlier date. The famous preacher Charles Spurgeon was born here in 1834.

Highfields Farm

COMMENDED

Kelvedon, Colchester CO5 9BJ
☎ (01376) 570334
Fax (01376) 570334

700-acre arable & horses farm. Farmhouse in quiet location in open

Continued ▶

KELVEDON

Continued

countryside. Easy access to A12. Heating in all rooms.
Bedrooms: 3 twin
Bathrooms: 2 en-suite, 1 private

Bed & breakfast per night:	£min	£max
Single	20.00	20.00
Double	36.00	36.00

Parking for 6

KERSEY

Suffolk
Map ref 3B2

A most picturesque village, which was famous for cloth-making, set in a valley with a water-splash. The church of St Mary is an impressive building at the top of the hill.

Fair View

HIGHLY COMMENDED

Priory Hill, Kersey, Ipswich IP7 6DU
☎ (01473) 828606
Converted 17th C cottages with beams and inglenooks. Village location, stunning views of church. Convenient for Constable country and coast.
Bedrooms: 1 double
Bathrooms: 1 en-suite

Bed & breakfast per night:	£min	£max
Single	24.00	26.00
Double	36.00	42.00

Parking for 1

Red House Farm

Listed COMMENDED

Kersey, Ipswich IP7 6EY
☎ (01787) 210245
Listed farmhouse between Kersey and Boxford, central for Constable country. Rooms have TV and tea-making facilities. Swimming pool.
Bedrooms: 1 single, 1 double, 1 twin
Bathrooms: 2 en-suite, 1 public

Bed & breakfast per night:	£min	£max
Single	22.00	25.00
Double	38.00	40.00

Half board per person:	£min	£max
Daily	27.50	29.00

Evening meal 1900 (last orders 1000)
Parking for 5
Cards accepted: Diners

KEXBY

Lincolnshire
Map ref 4C2

Kexby Grange

Listed COMMENDED

Kexby, Gainsborough DN21 5PJ
☎ (01427) 788265
300-acre mixed farm. Pleasant, Victorian farmhouse offering a warm welcome. In rural surroundings, 4 miles from Gainsborough. Convenient for Lincoln, Hemswell Antique Centre and Lincolnshire Wolds.
Bedrooms: 1 double
Bathrooms: 1 private

Bed & breakfast per night:	£min	£max
Single	14.00	14.00
Double	28.00	28.00

Half board per person:	£min	£max
Daily	24.00	
Weekly	168.00	

Lunch available
Evening meal 1700 (last orders 2100)
Parking for 4

KING'S LYNN

Norfolk
Map ref 3B1

A busy town with many outstanding buildings. The Guildhall and Town Hall are both built of flint in a striking chequer design. Behind the Guildhall in the Old Gaol House the sounds and smells of prison life 2 centuries ago are recreated.
Tourist Information Centre ☎ (01553) 763044

Ashwicken Hall

Listed COMMENDED

Church Lane, Ashwicken, King's Lynn PE32 1LN
☎ (01553) 630330

Secluded country house set in woods and garden, with duck pond and various animals. Heated indoor pool for guests' enjoyment. 5 miles east of King's Lynn.
Bedrooms: 2 double, 1 twin, 1 triple
Bathrooms: 4 en-suite

Bed & breakfast per night:	£min	£max
Single		27.50
Double		45.00

Parking for 10

Fairlight Lodge

HIGHLY COMMENDED

79 Goodwins Road, King's Lynn PE30 5PE
☎ (01553) 762234
Fax (01553) 770280
Lovely owner-run Victorian house with friendly atmosphere and well appointed rooms. Ground floor en-suite rooms available. Private parking. Closed Christmas.
Bedrooms: 2 single, 1 double, 3 twin, 1 triple
Bathrooms: 4 en-suite, 2 public

Bed & breakfast per night:	£min	£max
Single	17.00	25.00
Double	34.00	40.00

Parking for 6

Maranatha Guesthouse

APPROVED

115 Gaywood Road, Gaywood, King's Lynn PE30 2PU
☎ (01553) 774596
Large carrstone and brick residence with gardens front and rear, 10 minutes' walk from town centre, Lynnsport and Queen Elizabeth Hospital. Direct road to Sandringham and the coast.
Bedrooms: 2 single, 2 double, 2 twin, 1 triple
Bathrooms: 3 en-suite, 1 private, 1 public

Bed & breakfast per night:	£min	£max
Single	17.00	
Double	30.00	

Half board per person:	£min	£max
Daily	20.00	

Lunch available
Evening meal 1800 (last orders 1800)
Parking for 9

Marsh Farm

COMMENDED

Wolferton, King's Lynn PE31 6HB
☎ (01485) 540265
Fax (01485) 543143
Email: keithlarrington@farmline.com
755-acre arable farm. Relaxing and comfortable farmhouse on working farm in quiet village of Wolferton, on

the Norfolk coast, close to Sandringham. Coastal and countryside walks.
Bedrooms: 2 double, 1 twin
Bathrooms: 1 en-suite, 2 private

Bed & breakfast per night:	£min	£max
Single	20.00	20.00
Double	40.00	40.00

Parking for 5

KINGS LANGLEY

Hertfordshire
Map ref 2D1

Woodcote House

COMMENDED

7 The Grove, Chipperfield Road, Kings Langley WD4 9JF
☎ (01923) 262077
Fax (01923) 266198
Timber-framed house, sitting in 1 acre of landscaped gardens with quiet rural aspect. Convenient for M1 and M25 and close to Watford and Hemel Hempstead.
Bedrooms: 2 single, 1 double, 1 twin
Bathrooms: 4 en-suite

Bed & breakfast per night:	£min	£max
Single	20.00	24.00
Double	38.00	44.00

Evening meal 1800 (last orders 2100)
Parking for 8

LAVENHAM

Suffolk
Map ref 3B2

A former prosperous wool town of timber-framed buildings with the cathedral-like church and its tall tower. The market-place is 13th C and the Guildhall now houses a museum.

The Red House

COMMENDED

29 Bolton Street, Lavenham, Sudbury CO10 9RG
☎ (01787) 248074 & (0585) 536148
Attractive Victorian house. Comfortable en-suite bedrooms, pretty sitting room, country garden. Evening meal by prior arrangement. Only a step from the market square and the guildhall.
Bedrooms: 2 double, 1 twin
Bathrooms: 3 en-suite

Bed & breakfast per night:	£min	£max
Single	30.00	45.00
Double	45.00	45.00

Parking for 8
Open February–December

LAWSHALL

Suffolk
Map ref 3B2

Brighthouse Farm

COMMENDED

Melford Road, Lawshall, Bury St Edmunds IP29 4PX
☎ (01284) 830385
300-acre arable & livestock farm. A warm welcome awaits you at this 200-year-old farmhouse set in 3 acres of gardens. Close to many places of historic interest. Good pubs and restaurants nearby.
Bedrooms: 2 double, 1 twin
Bathrooms: 3 en-suite, 1 public

Bed & breakfast per night:	£min	£max
Single	20.00	28.00
Double	36.00	44.00

Parking for 10

LINCOLN

Lincolnshire
Map ref 4C2

Ancient city dominated by the magnificent 11th C cathedral with its triple towers. A Roman gateway is still used and there are medieval houses lining narrow, cobbled streets. Other attractions include the Norman castle, several museums and the Usher Gallery.
Tourist Information Centre ☎ (01522) 529828

Damon's Motel

HIGHLY COMMENDED

997 Doddington Road, Lincoln LN6 3SE
☎ (01522) 887733
Fax (01522) 887734
Purpose-built, 2-storey motel on the Lincoln ring road. Adjacent restaurant, indoor pool, gym, solarium. Satellite TV.
Wheelchair access category 3
Bedrooms: 24 double, 18 twin, 5 triple
Bathrooms: 47 en-suite

Bed & breakfast per night:	£min	£max
Single	42.00	45.00
Double	46.50	49.50

Lunch available
Evening meal 1500 (last orders 2200)
Parking for 47
Cards accepted: Amex, Diners, Mastercard, Visa, Switch/Delta

D'Isney Place Hotel

Listed COMMENDED

Eastgate, Lincoln LN2 4AA
☎ (01522) 538881
Fax (01522) 511321
Small family-run hotel near the cathedral, with individually styled bedrooms and an emphasis on comfort and privacy.
Bedrooms: 1 single, 10 double, 3 twin, 2 triple, 1 family room
Bathrooms: 17 en-suite

Bed & breakfast per night:	£min	£max
Single	57.00	67.00
Double	72.00	92.00

Parking for 20
Cards accepted: Amex, Diners, Mastercard, Visa, Switch/Delta

LITTLE WALSINGHAM

Norfolk
Map ref 3B1

Little Walsingham is larger than its neighbour Great Walsingham and more important because of its long history as a religious shrine to which many pilgrimages were made. The village has many picturesque buildings of the 16th C and later.

St David's House

APPROVED

Friday Market, Little Walsingham, Walsingham NR22 6BY
☎ (01328) 820633 & (0589) 594605
16th C brick house in a delightful medieval village. The village is fully signposted from Fakenham (A148).
Bedrooms: 1 double, 1 twin, 3 triple
Bathrooms: 4 private, 2 public

Bed & breakfast per night:	£min	£max
Single	18.00	20.00
Double	36.00	40.00

Half board per person:	£min	£max
Daily	27.50	29.50
Weekly	165.00	177.00

Lunch available
Evening meal 1800 (last orders 2100)

LOWESTOFT

Suffolk
Map ref 3C1

Seaside town with wide sandy beaches. Important fishing port with picturesque fishing quarter. Home of the famous Lowestoft porcelain and birthplace of Benjamin Britten. East Point Pavilion's exhibition describes the Lowestoft story.
Tourist Information Centre ☎ (01502) 523000

Church Farm

Listed HIGHLY COMMENDED

Corton, Lowestoft NR32 5HX
☎ (01502) 730359
Fax (01502) 730359

220-acre arable farm. Victorian farmhouse with clean and comfortable accommodation of high standard and a warm, welcoming atmosphere. Situated 3 miles north of Lowestoft near quiet, rural coastline and within easy reach of beautiful Broadland and many local attractions. Traditional English breakfast. Non-smoking establishment. German spoken.
Bedrooms: 3 double
Bathrooms: 3 en-suite

Bed & breakfast per night:	£min	£max
Single	25.00	
Double	36.00	38.00

Parking for 4
Open March–October

Hall Farm

Listed COMMENDED

Jay Lane, Church Lane, Lound, Lowestoft NR32 5LJ
☎ (01502) 730415
101-acre arable farm. Traditional 16th C Suffolk farmhouse within 2 miles of the sea. Clean, comfortable accommodation with generous English breakfast. Farm down a quiet, private lane half-a-mile from A12.
Bedrooms: 1 single, 1 double, 1 triple
Bathrooms: 2 private, 1 public

Bed & breakfast per night:	£min	£max
Single	16.00	18.00
Double	35.00	40.00

Parking for 6
Open March–September

MARGARET RODING

Essex
Map ref 2D1

Greys

Listed COMMENDED

Ongar Road, Margaret Roding, Dunmow CM6 1QR
☎ (01245) 231509
340-acre arable and mixed farm. Formerly 2 cottages pleasantly situated on family farm just off A1060 at telephone kiosk. Beamed throughout, large garden. Tea/coffee available..
Bedrooms: 2 double, 1 twin
Bathrooms: 1 public

Bed & breakfast per night:	£min	£max
Single	20.00	
Double	37.00	

Parking for 6

MUNDESLEY

Norfolk
Map ref 3C1

Small seaside resort with a superb sandy beach and excellent bathing. Nearby is a smock-mill still with cap and sails.

The Grange

HIGHLY COMMENDED

High Street, Mundesley, Norwich NR11 8JL
☎ (01263) 721556
Beautiful, well-furnished house with friendly atmosphere, in attractive garden. Ideal for the Broads and Norwich, bird-watching, fishing and beach.
Bedrooms: 1 double, 1 twin, 1 triple
Bathrooms: 2 public

Bed & breakfast per night:	£min	£max
Single	16.00	18.00
Double	32.00	36.00

Parking for 10

Information on accommodation listed in this guide has been supplied by the proprietors. As changes may occur you are advised to check details at the time of booking.

NAYLAND

Suffolk
Map ref 3B2

Charmingly located village on the River Stour owing its former prosperity to the cloth trade. The hub of the village is 15th C Alston Court. The altar-piece of St James Church was painted by John Constable.

Gladwins Farm

COMMENDED

Harpers Hill, Nayland, Colchester CO6 4NU
☎ (01206) 262261
Fax (01206) 263001
Email: 106302.725@compuserve.com

22-acre smallholding. Timbered farmhouse in peaceful wooded surroundings in Constable country. Entrance on A134. Trout fishing, tennis, heated indoor pool and sauna. Home and local produce. Colour brochure.
Bedrooms: 1 single, 1 double, 1 twin, 1 family room
Bathrooms: 2 en-suite, 1 public

Bed & breakfast per night:	£min	£max
Single	18.00	20.00
Double	52.00	56.00
Half board per person:	**£min**	**£max**
Daily	28.00	38.00
Weekly	180.00	196.00

Evening meal 1900 (last orders 2030)
Parking for 14
Cards accepted: Mastercard, Visa, Switch/Delta

Please check prices and other details at the time of booking.

The National Grading and Classification Scheme is explained at the back of this guide.

NEWMARKET

Suffolk
Map ref 3B2

Centre of the English horse-racing world and the headquarters of the Jockey Club and National Stud. Racecourse and horse sales. The National Horse Racing Museum traces the history and development of the Sport of Kings.
Tourist Information Centre ☎ (01638) 667200

Westley House

Listed

Westley Waterless, Newmarket CB8 0RQ
☎ (01638) 508112
Fax (01638) 508113
18th C former rectory, now a spacious Georgian country home with 5 acres, in a peaceful small village 5 miles south of Newmarket. Convenient for Cambridge and other East Anglian places of interest. Large, well furnished rooms. Visitors are our guests. Advance bookings please
Bedrooms: 2 single, 2 twin
Bathrooms: 1 private, 2 public

Bed & breakfast per night:	£min	£max
Single	22.00	25.00
Double	42.00	45.00

Half board per person:	£min	£max
Daily	36.00	39.00
Weekly	230.00	248.00

Evening meal 1930 (last orders 2100)
Parking for 6

NORFOLK BROADS

See under Aylsham, Beccles, Bungay, Great Yarmouth, Hevingham, Lowestoft, Norwich, Rackheath, Wroxham

NORWICH

Norfolk
Map ref 3C1

Beautiful cathedral city and county town on the River Wensum with many fine museums and medieval churches. Norman castle, Guildhall and interesting medieval streets. Good shopping centre and market.
Tourist Information Centre ☎ (01603) 666071

Cavell House

Listed COMMENDED

Swardeston, Norwich NR14 8D2
☎ (01508) 578195
Birthplace of nurse Edith Cavell. Georgian farmhouse on edge of Swardeston village. Off B1113 south of Norwich, 5 miles from centre. Rural setting. Close to university.
Bedrooms: 1 single, 1 double, 1 twin
Bathrooms: 2 public

Bed & breakfast per night:	£min	£max
Single	12.50	18.00
Double	30.00	36.00

Lunch available
Parking for 10

Kingsley Lodge

COMMENDED

3 Kingsley Road, Norwich NR1 3RB
☎ (01603) 615819
Fax (01603) 615819

Quiet, friendly Edwardian house near bus station, under 10 minutes' walk to city centre. Spacious bedrooms with en-suite bathrooms, TV, tea/coffee making facilities. No smoking.
Bedrooms: 1 single, 1 double, 1 twin
Bathrooms: 3 en-suite

Bed & breakfast per night:	£min	£max
Single	23.00	26.00
Double	36.00	40.00

Open February–December

Oakfield

HIGHLY COMMENDED

Yelverton Road, Framingham Earl, Norwich NR14 7SD
☎ (01508) 492605
Superior accommodation in beautiful, quiet setting on edge of village, 4 miles south-east of Norwich. Splendid breakfasts. Local pubs serve good evening meals.
Bedrooms: 1 single, 1 double, 1 twin
Bathrooms: 1 en-suite, 1 public

Bed & breakfast per night:	£min	£max
Single	20.00	25.00
Double	38.00	44.00

Parking for 6

The Old Rectory

Listed HIGHLY COMMENDED

Hall Road, Framingham Earl, Norwich NR14 7SB
☎ (01508) 493590
Beautifully renovated and extended 17th C family house set in 2 acres of country garden. Wealth of beams in lounge and dining room. Village 4.5 miles south-east of Norwich.
Bedrooms: 1 double, 1 twin
Bathrooms: 1 public

Bed & breakfast per night:	£min	£max
Single	21.00	25.00
Double	38.00	42.00

Parking for 6

Rosedale

Listed APPROVED

145 Earlham Road, Norwich NR2 3RG
☎ (01603) 453743
Friendly, family-run Victorian guesthouse and restaurant on main B1108, 1 mile from city centre. Shopping centre, restaurants and university nearby.
Bedrooms: 3 single, 1 double, 2 twin, 2 triple
Bathrooms: 2 public

Bed & breakfast per night:	£min	£max
Single	16.00	20.00
Double	32.00	36.00

Parking for 2

Witton Hall Farm

COMMENDED

Witton, Norwich NR13 5DN
☎ (01603) 714580
500-acre dairy farm. Elegant Georgian farmhouse in the heart of Norfolk. Peaceful, mature grounds. Swimming pool in walled garden.
Bedrooms: 2 double, 1 twin
Bathrooms: 3 en-suite

Bed & breakfast per night:	£min	£max
Single	16.00	30.00
Double	36.00	40.00

Parking for 4
Cards accepted: Diners

The symbol after an establishment name indicates that it is a Regional Tourist Board member.

PETERBOROUGH

Cambridgeshire
Map ref 3A1

Prosperous and rapidly expanding cathedral city on the edge of the Fens on the River Nene. Catherine of Aragon is buried in the cathedral. City Museum and Art Gallery. Ferry Meadows Country Park has numerous leisure facilities.
Tourist Information Centre ☎ (01733) 452336

Stoneacre

COMMENDED

Elton Road, Wansford, Peterborough PE8 6JT
☎ (01780) 783283
Modern country house in rural and secluded position with delightful views across the Nene Valley. Half a mile from A1, 10 minutes from Peterborough and Stamford. Large grounds with mini golf-course.
Bedrooms: 4 double, 1 twin
Bathrooms: 3 en-suite, 2 public

Bed & breakfast per night:	£min	£max
Single	24.00	40.00
Double	30.00	46.00

Parking for 24

POTTER HEIGHAM

Norfolk
Map ref 3C1

On the River Thurne, the village is one of the most popular of the Broadland centres and is well known for its 13th C bridge and boatyard. The thatched church has a rare octagonal font made of brick.

Falgate Inn

COMMENDED

Main Road, Potter Heigham, Great Yarmouth NR29 5HZ
☎ (01692) 670003 & (0585) 735068
Bed and breakfast, with restaurant, bar snacks and beer garden. Open 7 days a week, full on-licence.
Bedrooms: 1 single, 1 double, 2 twin, 1 triple
Bathrooms: 2 en-suite, 1 public

Bed & breakfast per night:	£min	£max
Single	17.00	21.00
Double	34.00	40.00

Lunch available
Evening meal 1900 (last orders 2130)
Cards accepted: Mastercard, Visa, Switch/Delta

RACKHEATH

Norfolk
Map ref 3C1

Barn Court

Listed COMMENDED

6 Back Lane, Rackheath, Norwich NR13 6NN
☎ (01603) 782536
Fax (01603) 782536
Spacious accommodation in a traditional Norfolk barn conversion, built around a courtyard. Ideal base for exploring Norfolk - 3 miles Norwich. Friendly atmosphere and good home cooking.
Bedrooms: 2 double, 1 twin
Bathrooms: 1 en-suite, 2 public

Bed & breakfast per night:	£min	£max
Single	18.00	21.00
Double	36.00	42.00

Parking for 4

RAITHBY

Lincolnshire
Map ref 4D2

Red Lion Inn/Le Baron Restaurant

Main Road, Raithby, Spilsby PE23 4DS
☎ (01790) 753727

16th C listed country inn providing comfortable accommodation. Restaurant with traditional and continental cuisine. Micro-brewery.
Bedrooms: 2 double, 2 twin
Bathrooms: 2 en-suite, 1 public

Bed & breakfast per night:	£min	£max
Single	20.00	27.00
Double	32.00	39.00

Half board per person:	£min	£max
Daily	26.00	37.00
Weekly	172.00	242.00

Lunch available
Evening meal 1900 (last orders 2130)
Parking for 20
Cards accepted: Amex, Mastercard, Visa, Switch/Delta

REEDHAM

Norfolk
Map ref 3C1

This pleasant riverside village is one of the few places to get beside the water in southern Broadland. A vehicle chain ferry crosses the River Yare here.

Briars

COMMENDED

10 Riverside, Reedham, Norwich NR13 3TF
☎ (01493) 700054 & (0370) 276456
Fax (01493) 700054
This welcoming home has a wonderful location with comfortable pine furnished accommodation over a traditional tea room and hair salon. A 1st floor lounge, conservatory and balcony have fabulous views of a Broadland river and marshland. Station close by.
Bedrooms: 3 double
Bathrooms: 3 en-suite

Bed & breakfast per night:	£min	£max
Single	34.00	34.00
Double	47.50	47.50

Lunch available
Evening meal 1800 (last orders 2000)
Parking for 6
Cards accepted: Mastercard, Visa, Switch/Delta

The Old Post Office

26 The Hills, Reedham, Norwich NR13 3AR
☎ (01493) 701262
Converted country post office in rural setting, thoughtfully equipped and with en-suite facilities. Off-road parking, attractive gardens and swimming pool.
Bedrooms: 2 double, 1 twin
Bathrooms: 3 en-suite

Bed & breakfast per night:	£min	£max
Single	30.00	30.00
Double	40.00	45.00

Parking for 12

ROYSTON

Hertfordshire
Map ref 2D1

Old town lying at the crossing of the Roman road Ermine Street and the Icknield Way. It has many interesting old houses and inns.

Hall Farm

COMMENDED

Great Chishill, Royston SG8 8SH
☎ (01763) 838263
Fax (01763) 838263

805-acre arable farm. Beautiful farmhouse accommodation on working farm, in secluded gardens on the highest point in Cambridgeshire. Royston 5 miles, Duxford Museum 4 miles, Cambridge 11 miles.

Bedrooms: 2 double, 1 twin
Bathrooms: 1 public

Bed & breakfast per night:	£min	£max
Single	20.00	25.00
Double	35.00	45.00

Parking for 8

SAFFRON WALDEN

Essex
Map ref 2D1

Takes its name from the saffron crocus once grown around the town. The church of St Mary has superb carvings, magnificent roofs and brasses. A town maze can be seen on the common. Two miles south-west is Audley End, a magnificent Jacobean mansion owned by English Heritage.
Tourist Information Centre ☎ (01799) 510444

Rowley Hill Lodge

COMMENDED

Little Walden, Saffron Walden CB10 1UZ
☎ (01799) 525975
Fax (01799) 516622

Quiet farm lodge with large garden, 1 mile from centre of Saffron Walden. Stansted Airport, Cambridge and Duxford 20 minutes.

Bedrooms: 1 double, 1 twin
Bathrooms: 2 en-suite

Bed & breakfast per night:	£min	£max
Single	25.00	25.00
Double	39.00	39.00

Parking for 4

Saxons

COMMENDED

Water Lane, Radwinter, Saffron Walden CB10 2TX
☎ (01799) 599565

Charming and comfortable modernised 16th C thatched house. Large garden, covered swimming pool - very peaceful countryside. Ideal base for exploring East Anglia. 30 minutes to Stansted Airport, 1 hour to London via M11 or train.

Bedrooms: 1 single, 1 twin
Bathrooms: 2 private

Bed & breakfast per night:	£min	£max
Single	22.00	22.00
Double	44.00	44.00

Parking for 5

ST ALBANS

Hertfordshire
Map ref 2D1

As Verulamium this was one of the largest towns in Roman Britain and its remains can be seen in the museum. The Norman cathedral was built from Roman materials to commemorate Alban, the first British Christian martyr.
Tourist Information Centre ☎ (01727) 864511

Care Inns

COMMENDED

29 Alma Road, St Albans AL1 3AT
☎ (01727) 867310

Comfortable family atmosphere. Ideally located close to station, city centre and cathedral. All rooms have en-suite bath/shower and toilet.

Bedrooms: 1 single, 1 double, 1 twin
Bathrooms: 3 en-suite

Bed & breakfast per night:	£min	£max
Single	25.00	30.00
Double	40.00	40.00

Parking for 5

76 Clarence Road

Listed COMMENDED

St Albans AL1 4NG
☎ (01727) 864880

Spacious Edwardian house with comfortable rooms and pleasant conservatory. Park nearby. Seven minutes' walk to station.

Bedrooms: 1 single, 1 twin
Bathrooms: 1 public

Bed & breakfast per night:	£min	£max
Single	20.00	25.00
Double	36.00	40.00

Parking for 2

2 The Limes

Listed APPROVED

Spencer Gate, St Albans AL1 4AT
☎ (01727) 831080

Modern, detached house in a quiet cul-de-sac, within 10 minutes' walk of the city centre. Home-baked bread. Friendly atmosphere.

Bedrooms: 1 single, 1 twin
Bathrooms: 1 public

Bed & breakfast per night:	£min	£max
Single	15.00	17.00
Double	30.00	34.00

Parking for 2

The Squirrels

Listed APPROVED

74 Sandridge Road, St Albans AL1 4AR
☎ (01727) 840497

Edwardian terraced house, 10 minutes' walk from town centre.

Bedrooms: 1 twin
Bathrooms: 1 private

Bed & breakfast per night:	£min	£max
Single	20.00	22.00
Double	30.00	32.00

ST IVES

Cambridgeshire
Map ref 3A2

Picturesque market town with a narrow 6-arched bridge spanning the River Ouse on which stands a bridge chapel. There are numerous Georgian and Victorian buildings and the Norris Museum has a good local collection.

The Old Ferry Boat Inn

COMMENDED

Holywell, St Ives, Huntingdon PE17 3TG
☎ (01480) 463227
Fax (01480) 494885

Thatched riverside inn with low beamed ceilings and log fires. Extensive, interesting menu, real ales, garden. From main A14 head for St Ives, then Needingworth, then Holywell.

Bedrooms: 6 double, 1 twin
Suites available
Bathrooms: 7 en-suite

Continued ▶

ST IVES

Continued

Bed & breakfast per night:	£min	£max
Single	44.50	55.00
Double	54.50	72.00

Lunch available
Evening meal 1800 (last orders 2200)
Parking for 150
Cards accepted: Mastercard, Visa, Switch/Delta

SANDRINGHAM

Norfolk
Map ref 3B1

Famous as the country retreat of Her Majesty the Queen. The house and grounds are open to the public at certain times.

Mill Cottage, by Sandringham

HIGHLY COMMENDED

Mill Road, Dersingham, King's Lynn
PE31 6HY
☎ (01485) 544411

"Seek peace and pursue it" - Psalm 34:14. By Sandringham, set amidst quiet picturesque countryside with distant sea views, a Georgian cottage with lawned gardens, paddock and barn. Children a focus. Vegetarian and special diets catered for.
Bedrooms: 1 single, 1 double, 1 twin
Bathrooms: 1 en-suite, 2 private

Bed & breakfast per night:	£min	£max
Single	21.00	42.00
Double	39.00	64.00

Parking for 4

The symbols in each entry give information about services and facilities. A key to these symbols appears at the back of this guide.

SANDY

Bedfordshire
Map ref 2D1

Small town on the River Ivel on the site of a Roman settlement. Sandy is mentioned in Domesday.
Tourist Information Centre ☎ (01767) 682728

Highfield Farm

HIGHLY COMMENDED

Great North Road, Sandy
SG19 2AQ
☎ (01767) 682332
Fax (01767) 692503

300-acre arable farm. Beautifully peaceful, comfortable farmhouse. Most rooms en-suite. Cambridge, the Shuttleworth Collection, RSPB and London all within easy reach. A warm welcome awaits you. Most guests return.
Bedrooms: 1 double, 3 twin, 2 family rooms
Bathrooms: 4 en-suite, 1 private, 1 public

Bed & breakfast per night:	£min	£max
Single	22.50	30.00
Double	38.00	45.00

Parking for 14

SAXILBY

Lincolnshire
Map ref 4C2

A picturesque village offering easy access to Lincoln and Gainsborough. The "Sun Inn" is said to be haunted by a former local murderer.

Orchard Cottage

HIGHLY COMMENDED

3 Orchard Lane, Saxilby, Lincoln
LN1 2HT
☎ (01522) 703192

Cottage-style house, with a guest annexe in a pleasant garden, 6 miles from Lincoln. Non-smokers only, please.
Bedrooms: 1 double, 1 twin, 1 triple
Bathrooms: 2 en-suite, 1 private, 1 public

Bed & breakfast per night:	£min	£max
Single	22.00	22.00
Double	36.00	36.00

Parking for 2

SAXMUNDHAM

Suffolk
Map ref 3C2

The church of St John the Baptist has a hammer-beam roof and contains a number of good monuments.

Little Orchard

Listed HIGHLY COMMENDED

Middleton, Saxmundham IP17 3NT
☎ (01728) 648385
Charming early 18th C house with open views all around. Ideally situated for sea and countryside, Snape Maltings and Concert Hall and Minsmere nature reserve. First house on left on B1125 coming from Theberton off the B1122.
Bedrooms: 2 double
Bathrooms: 2 en-suite

Bed & breakfast per night:	£min	£max
Single	17.50	20.00
Double	35.00	40.00

Parking for 3

Stratford Hall

Listed COMMENDED

Stratford St Andrew, Saxmundham
IP17 1LH
☎ (01728) 602025
Spacious family home with parts dating back to 17th C. In extensive gardens with dry moat and tennis court. Dinner by arrangement. Perfect for Snape, Aldeburgh and Heritage Coast.
Bedrooms: 1 double, 1 twin
Bathrooms: 2 private

Bed & breakfast per night:	£min	£max
Single	21.00	21.00
Double	42.00	42.00

Half board per person:	£min	£max
Daily	30.50	33.50
Weekly	200.00	200.00

Evening meal 2000 (last orders 2100)
Parking for 10

SAXTEAD

Suffolk
Map ref 3C2

Ivy Forge

Listed COMMENDED

The Green, Saxtead, Woodbridge IP13 9QG
☎ (01728) 685054
Spacious and comfortable modern bungalow on The Green opposite a working windmill. Close to Framlingham, Woodbridge, Snape and Heritage Coast.
Bedrooms: 1 double, 1 twin
Bathrooms: 1 en-suite, 1 private

Bed & breakfast per night:	£min	£max
Single	18.00	18.00
Double	36.00	36.00

Half board per person:	£min	£max
Daily	26.00	28.00
Weekly	160.00	175.00

Evening meal 1800 (last orders 1930)
Parking for 6

SHERINGHAM

Norfolk
Map ref 3B1

Holiday resort with Victorian and Edwardian hotels and a sand and shingle beach where the fishing boats are hauled up. The North Norfolk Railway operates from Sheringham station during the summer. Other attractions include museums, theatre and Splash Fun Pool.

Camberley Guesthouse

COMMENDED

62 Cliff Road, Sheringham NR26 8BJ
☎ (01263) 823101
In its own grounds, overlooking sea, town and surrounding countryside. Slipway to beach directly opposite. Family-run.
Bedrooms: 2 double, 2 twin
Bathrooms: 4 en-suite, 1 public

Bed & breakfast per night:	£min	£max
Single	17.00	24.00
Double	34.00	48.00

Parking for 6

SKEGNESS

Lincolnshire
Map ref 4D2

Famous seaside resort with 6 miles of sandy beaches and bracing air. Attractions include swimming pools, bowling greens, gardens, Natureland Marine Zoo, golf-courses and a wide range of entertainment at the Embassy Centre. Nearby is Gibraltar Point Nature Reserve.
Tourist Information Centre ☎ (01754) 764821

Victoria Inn

APPROVED

Wainfleet Road, Skegness PE25 3RG
☎ (01754) 767333
Friendly, traditional inn with hotel annexe, providing home-cooked food. Central for town and beach facilities.
Bedrooms: 1 single, 3 double, 1 twin, 2 family rooms
Bathrooms: 4 en-suite, 1 public

Bed & breakfast per night:	£min	£max
Single	14.00	16.00
Double	25.00	30.00

Lunch available
Evening meal 1900 (last orders 2200)
Parking for 20
Cards accepted: Mastercard, Visa

SKILLINGTON

Lincolnshire
Map ref 3A1

Hidden away on the edge of the Leicestershire border, still with a fragment of the old cross on its green. The pretty abbey is a small 17th C stone manor house.

Sproxton Lodge Farm

Listed APPROVED

Skillington, Grantham NG33 5HJ
☎ (01476) 860307
230-acre arable farm. Quiet family farmhouse. Large lawns. Good breakfast, large TV lounge with open fire. Located about 3 miles off the A1.
Bedrooms: 1 single, 1 double, 1 triple
Bathrooms: 1 public

Bed & breakfast per night:	£min	£max
Single	16.00	16.00
Double	32.00	32.00

Parking for 4

SOUTH MIMMS

Hertfordshire
Map ref 2D1

Best known today for its location at the junction of the M25 and the A1M.
Tourist Information Centre ☎ (01707) 643233

The Black Swan

Listed COMMENDED

62-64 Blanche Lane, South Mimms, Potters Bar EN6 3PD
☎ (01707) 644180
Comfortable accommodation in oak-beamed bedrooms or self-contained flats in quietly located listed building. Breakfast provided.
Bedrooms: 1 triple
Bathrooms: 1 private

Bed & breakfast per night:	£min	£max
Single	20.00	25.00
Double	30.00	35.00

Parking for 7

SOUTH WITHAM

Lincolnshire
Map ref 3A1

The Blue Cow Inn

Listed COMMENDED

29 High Street, South Witham, Grantham NG33 5QB
☎ (01572) 768432
Fax (01572) 768432
13th C beamed freehouse with log fires, real ales and home-cooked meals. Restaurant and bar meals 7 days a week. Convenient for A1, Grantham, Oakham, Stamford and Melton Mowbray. Own brewery on premises.
Bedrooms: 1 single, 1 double, 2 twin
Suite available
Bathrooms: 1 en-suite, 2 public

Bed & breakfast per night:	£min	£max
Single	17.50	27.50
Double	35.00	45.00

Half board per person:	£min	£max
Daily	22.50	26.00
Weekly	150.00	180.00

Lunch available
Evening meal 1800 (last orders 2130)
Parking for 45
Cards accepted: Mastercard, Visa
50

SOUTHWOLD

Suffolk
Map ref 3C2

Pleasant and attractive seaside town with a triangular market square and spacious greens around which stand flint, brick and colour-washed cottages. The parish church of St Edmund is one of the greatest churches in Suffolk.

The Angel Inn

COMMENDED

39 High Street, Wangford, Beccles
NR34 8RL
☎ (01502) 578636
Fax (01502) 578535

16th C, Grade II listed village inn, carefully renovated in 1995, with log fires and en-suite rooms.
Bedrooms: 4 double, 1 family room
Bathrooms: 5 en-suite

Bed & breakfast per night:	£min	£max
Single	40.00	40.00
Double	49.00	58.00

Half board per person:	£min	£max
Daily	25.00	30.00

Lunch available
Evening meal 1800 (last orders 2200)
Parking for 30
Cards accepted: Amex, Diners, Mastercard, Visa, Switch/Delta

No 3 Cautley Road

COMMENDED

Southwold IP18 6DD
☎ (01502) 723611
Elegant Edwardian family house. All en-suite rooms. Near beach, shops, church and theatre. Colour TV in all rooms.
Bedrooms: 2 double, 1 twin
Bathrooms: 3 en-suite

Bed & breakfast per night:	£min	£max
Single	25.00	35.00
Double	35.00	50.00

21 North Parade

COMMENDED

Southwold IP18 6LT
☎ (01502) 722573 & 724326
Fax (01502) 724326
Seafront Victorian townhouse overlooking promenade and Blue Flag beach. Panoramic sea views. Convenient for Suffolk's Heritage Coast. Guest lounge. High tea available.
Bedrooms: 2 double, 1 twin
Bathrooms: 2 en-suite, 1 private

Bed & breakfast per night:	£min	£max
Single	25.00	30.00
Double	40.00	50.00

STAMFORD

Lincolnshire
Map ref 3A1

Exceptionally beautiful and historic town with many houses of architectural interest, several notable churches and other public buildings all in the local stone. Burghley House, built by William Cecil, is a magnificent Tudor mansion on the edge of the town.
Tourist Information Centre ☎ (01780) 755611

Birch House

Listed COMMENDED

4 Lonsdale Road, Stamford
PE9 2RW
☎ (01780) 754876 & 0850 185759
Comfortable home in mature residential location, 1 mile west of Stamford centre. TV and tea/coffee facilities in rooms. Parking. Non-smoking.
Bedrooms: 2 single, 1 double, 1 twin
Bathrooms: 1 public

Bed & breakfast per night:	£min	£max
Single	17.00	17.00
Double	34.00	34.00

Parking for 3

Rock Lodge

COMMENDED

1 Empingham Road, Stamford
PE9 2RH
☎ (01780) 764211
Fax (01780) 482442
Victorian stone "hunting lodge" style mansion, set within huge walled gardens, close to heart of Stamford. En-suite rooms.
Bedrooms: 2 double, 1 twin
Bathrooms: 2 en-suite, 1 private

Bed & breakfast per night:	£min	£max
Single	25.00	40.00
Double	40.00	50.00

Parking for 3

STOKE HOLY CROSS

Norfolk
Map ref 3C1

Salamanca Farm

COMMENDED

116-118 Norwich Road, Stoke Holy Cross, Norwich NR14 8QJ
☎ (01508) 492322

175-acre mixed farm. Picturesque village near Norwich. Comfortable Victorian farmhouse in a flower arranger's garden. Guests have been welcomed for 20 years.
Bedrooms: 3 double, 1 twin
Bathrooms: 3 en-suite, 1 private, 1 public

Bed & breakfast per night:	£min	£max
Single	20.00	22.00
Double	36.00	40.00

Parking for 8
Cards accepted: Diners

STOKE-BY-NAYLAND

Suffolk
Map ref 3B2

Picturesque village with a fine group of half-timbered cottages near the church of St Mary, the tower of which was one of Constable's favourite subjects. In School Street are the Guildhall and the Maltings, both 16th C timber-framed buildings.

Ryegate House

HIGHLY COMMENDED

Stoke-by-Nayland, Colchester
CO6 4RA
☎ (01206) 263679
Comfortable friendly house in Suffolk village within Dedham Vale. On the B1068, 5.5 miles from A12 and 2.5 miles from A134. All rooms en-suite.
Bedrooms: 2 double, 1 twin
Bathrooms: 3 en-suite

Bed & breakfast per night:	£min	£max
Single	25.00	29.00
Double	36.00	42.00

Parking for 6

SUDBURY

Suffolk
Map ref 3B2

Former important cloth and market town on the River Stour. Birthplace of Thomas Gainsborough whose home is now an art gallery and museum. The Corn Exchange is an excellent example of early Victorian civic building.
Tourist Information Centre ☎ (01787) 881320

The Boathouse Hotel

Listed COMMENDED

Ballingdon Bridge, Sudbury
CO10 6DA
☎ (01787) 379090
Family-owned and operated hotel set on the banks of the River Stour, offering good food and service in picturesque surroundings.
Bedrooms: 4 double, 1 triple
Bathrooms: 3 en-suite, 1 public

Bed & breakfast per night:	£min	£max
Single	31.00	37.00
Double	49.00	55.00

Half board per person:	£min	£max
Daily	37.00	40.00
Weekly	210.00	231.00

Lunch available
Evening meal 1830 (last orders 2130)
Parking for 14
Cards accepted: Mastercard, Visa

SWAFFHAM

Norfolk
Map ref 3B1

Busy market town with a triangular market-place, a domed rotunda built in 1783 and a number of Georgian houses. The 15th C church possesses a large library of ancient books.

Glebe Bungalow

COMMENDED

8a Princes Street, Swaffham
PE37 7BP
☎ (01760) 722764

Quiet secluded town centre location on no-through road. Home-from-home accommodation with private parking. Ideal for discovering Norfolk.
Wheelchair access category 3
Bedrooms: 1 double, 1 twin, 1 triple
Bathrooms: 3 en-suite

Bed & breakfast per night:	£min	£max
Single	18.00	20.00
Double	36.00	40.00

Evening meal 1700 (last orders 1900)
Parking for 6

Lodge Farm

Listed COMMENDED

Castle Acre, King's Lynn PE32 2BS
☎ (01760) 755506
Fax (01760) 755103
Spacious country farmhouse with garden and paddocks, 1 mile north of historic Castle Acre. Peddars Way, Sandringham, walking country nearby.
Bedrooms: 3 twin
Bathrooms: 1 en-suite, 1 public

Bed & breakfast per night:	£min	£max
Single	19.00	23.00
Double	38.00	46.00

Parking for 7

SWAYFIELD

Lincolnshire
Map ref 3A1

The Royal Oak Inn

Listed COMMENDED

High Street, Swayfield, Grantham
NG33 4LL
☎ (01476) 550247
Fax (01476) 550996
Old world inn in country setting, 3.5 miles from A1. Well-appointed 1650 property with chalet accommodation. Separate restaurant.
Bedrooms: 2 double, 2 twin, 1 family room
Bathrooms: 5 en-suite

Bed & breakfast per night:	£min	£max
Single	33.00	33.00
Double	44.00	44.00

Half board per person:	£min	£max
Daily	38.00	48.00
Weekly	196.00	259.00

Lunch available
Evening meal 1830 (last orders 2230)
Parking for 40
Cards accepted: Amex, Diners, Mastercard, Visa

THAXTED

Essex
Map ref 3B2

Small town rich in outstanding buildings and dominated by its hilltop medieval church. The magnificent Guildhall was built by the Cutlers' Guild in the late 14th C. A windmill built in 1804 has been restored and houses a rural museum.

Crossways Guesthouse

COMMENDED

32 Town Street, Thaxted, Dunmow
CM6 2LA
☎ (01371) 830348
Elegant 16th C house with Georgian additions, situated on B184 in centre of Thaxted opposite the Guildhall.
Bedrooms: 1 double, 1 twin
Bathrooms: 1 en-suite, 1 private

Bed & breakfast per night:	£min	£max
Single	27.50	30.00
Double	45.00	50.00

Piggots Mill

HIGHLY COMMENDED

Watling Lane, Thaxted, Dunmow
CM6 2QY
☎ (01371) 830379
Fax (01371) 831309
850-acre arable farm. Traditional Essex barn, now a secluded farmhouse offering excellent accommodation in the centre of Thaxted. Garden leads into meadow giving access to attractive walks.
Bedrooms: 1 double, 1 twin
Bathrooms: 2 en-suite

Bed & breakfast per night:	£min	£max
Single	31.00	34.00
Double	46.00	50.00

Parking for 10

THORNHAM

Norfolk
Map ref 3B1

The Lifeboat Inn

COMMENDED

Ship Lane, Thornham, Hunstanton PE36 6LT
☎ (01485) 512236
Fax (01485) 512323
16th C smugglers' alehouse with views across Thornham harbour to the sea.
Bedrooms: 3 double, 7 twin, 3 triple
Bathrooms: 13 en-suite

Bed & breakfast per night:	£min	£max
Single	45.00	55.00
Double	60.00	70.00

Half board per person:	£min	£max
Daily	52.00	46.50
Weekly	255.50	260.50

Lunch available
Evening meal 1900 (last orders 2200)
Parking for 80
Cards accepted: Diners, Mastercard, Visa, Switch/Delta

THURSFORD

Norfolk
Map ref 3B1

Noted for its collection of steam locomotives, mechanical musical organs and fairground engines.

The Old Forge Bistro and Fish Restaurant

Listed COMMENDED

Fakenham Road, Thursford, Fakenham NR21 0BD
☎ (01328) 878345
A 14th C forge with original beams and ironwork for tethering horses. All rooms and restaurant have been fully refurbished.
Bedrooms: 2 double, 1 twin
Bathrooms: 1 en-suite, 2 private showers

Bed & breakfast per night:	£min	£max
Single	17.50	20.00
Double	35.00	45.00

Half board per person:	£min	£max
Daily	27.50	45.00
Weekly	192.50	300.00

Lunch available
Evening meal 1900 (last orders 2200)
Parking for 10
Open February–December
Cards accepted: Mastercard, Visa, Switch/Delta

UPWELL

Cambridgeshire
Map ref 3A1

The Olde Mill Hotel

APPROVED

Town Street, Upwell, Wisbech PE14 9AF
☎ (01945) 772614
Fax (01945) 772614

Converted mill which has been tastefully extended. In a small town on the outskirts of Wisbech, providing a good base for touring the Fens. Close to Norfolk coast. Minimum B&B prices below do not include breakfast.
Bedrooms: 3 double, 1 twin, 3 triple
Bathrooms: 7 en-suite

Bed & breakfast per night:	£min	£max
Single	25.00	31.00
Double	40.00	52.00

Half board per person:	£min	£max
Daily	41.00	50.00
Weekly	275.00	300.00

Lunch available
Evening meal 1830 (last orders 2145)
Parking for 150
Cards accepted: Amex, Diners, Mastercard, Visa, Switch/Delta

WARE

Hertfordshire
Map ref 2D1

Interesting riverside town with picturesque summer-houses lining the tow-path of the River Lea. The town has many timber-framed and Georgian houses and the famous Great Bed of Ware is now in the Victoria and Albert Museum.

Ashridge

COMMENDED

3 Belle Vue Road, Ware SG12 7BD
☎ (01920) 463895
Comfortable, Edwardian residence in quiet cul-de-sac. 10 minutes' walk from Ware and station. Non-smokers only, please.
Bedrooms: 2 single, 1 double, 1 twin
Bathrooms: 2 public

Bed & breakfast per night:	£min	£max
Single	17.50	20.00
Double	35.00	40.00

Parking for 4

WEST BARKWITH

Lincolnshire
Map ref 4D2

The Manor House

HIGHLY COMMENDED

Louth Road, West Barkwith, Market Rasen LN8 5LF
☎ (01673) 858253 & (0402) 460537
Fax (01673) 858253
In extensive landscaped gardens. All rooms have a view over lake, very private and secluded by a screen of mature trees.
Bedrooms: 1 double, 1 twin
Bathrooms: 2 en-suite

Bed & breakfast per night:	£min	£max
Double	45.00	45.00

Half board per person:	£min	£max
Daily	36.00	36.00

Parking for 10
Open February–December

WIX

Essex
Map ref 3B2

New Farm House

COMMENDED

Spinnell's Lane, Wix, Manningtree CO11 2UJ
☎ (01255) 870365
Fax (01255) 870837

Modern comfortable farmhouse in large garden, 10 minutes' drive to Harwich and convenient for Constable country. From Wix village crossroads, take Bradfield Road, turn right at top of hill; first house on left.
Bedrooms: 3 single, 1 double, 3 twin, 5 family rooms
Bathrooms: 7 en-suite, 2 public

Bed & breakfast per night:	£min	£max
Single	22.00	26.00
Double	42.00	45.00

Half board per person:	£min	£max
Daily	35.00	39.00

Evening meal 1830 (last orders 1730)
Parking for 18
Cards accepted: Amex, Mastercard, Visa

WOODHAM FERRERS

Essex
Map ref 3B3

Woolfe's Cottage

Listed

The Street, Woodham Ferrers, Chelmsford CM3 8RG
☎ (01245) 320037

Large converted Victorian cottage in historic village, 12 miles from Chelmsford on the B1418. Many excellent walking trails for ramblers.

Bedrooms: 1 double, 2 twin
Bathrooms: 1 public

Bed & breakfast per night:	£min	£max
Single	18.00	20.00
Double	30.00	32.00

Parking for 2

WOOLPIT

Suffolk
Map ref 3B2

Village with a number of attractive timber-framed Tudor and Georgian houses. St Mary's Church is one of the most beautiful churches in Suffolk and has a fine porch. The brass eagle lectern is said to have been donated by Elizabeth I.

The Bull Inn & Restaurant

COMMENDED

The Street, Woolpit, Bury St Edmunds IP30 9SA
☎ (01359) 240393

Public house and restaurant offering good accommodation in centre of pretty village. Large garden, ample parking. Ideal base for touring Suffolk.

Bedrooms: 1 single, 2 double
Suites available
Bathrooms: 3 en-suite

Bed & breakfast per night:	£min	£max
Single	20.00	
Double	38.00	

Half board per person:	£min	£max
Daily	25.00	

Lunch available
Evening meal 1800 (last orders 2130)
Parking for 50
Cards accepted: Amex, Diners, Mastercard, Visa, Switch/Delta

WROXHAM

Norfolk
Map ref 3C1

Yachting centre on the River Bure which houses the headquarters of the Norfolk Broads Yacht Club. The church of St Mary has a famous doorway and the manor house nearby dates back to 1623.

Manor Barn House

COMMENDED

Back Lane, Rackheath, Wroxham, Norwich NR13 6NN
☎ (01603) 783543

Traditional Norfolk barn conversion with exposed beams, in quiet setting with pleasant gardens. Just off the A1151, 2 miles from Wroxham.

Bedrooms: 3 double, 2 twin
Bathrooms: 4 en-suite, 1 private

Bed & breakfast per night:	£min	£max
Single	18.00	25.00
Double	36.00	40.00

Parking for 8

Wroxham Park Lodge

HIGHLY COMMENDED

142 Norwich Road, Wroxham, Norwich NR12 8SA
☎ (01603) 782991

Comfortable Victorian house in lovely gardens. All rooms en-suite. In Broads capital of Wroxham, central for all Broads amenities. Private parking.

Bedrooms: 2 double, 1 twin
Bathrooms: 3 en-suite

Bed & breakfast per night:	£min	£max
Single	25.00	30.00
Double	40.00	44.00

Parking for 6

Please mention this guide when making your booking.

WYMONDHAM

Norfolk
Map ref 3B1

Thriving historic market town of charm and architectural interest. The octagonal market cross, 12th C abbey and 15th C Green Dragon inn blend with streetscapes spanning three centuries. An excellent touring base.

Home Farm

Listed COMMENDED

Golf Links Road, Morley, Wymondham NR18 9SU
☎ (01953) 602581
Fax (01953) 602581

Quiet, comfortable rural location. Three miles from Wymondham and 20 minutes from Norwich.

Bedrooms: 1 single, 2 double
Bathrooms: 1 public

Bed & breakfast per night:	£min	£max
Single	16.00	17.00
Double	32.00	34.00

Parking for 5

Rose Farm

Listed APPROVED

School Lane, Suton, Wymondham NR18 9JN
☎ (01953) 603512

Homely farmhouse accommodation within easy reach of Norwich, Broads and Breckland. Quiet, rural location, but only three-quarters of a mile from A11 London/Norwich trunk road.

Bedrooms: 2 single, 1 double, 1 family room
Bathrooms: 2 public

Bed & breakfast per night:	£min	£max
Single	19.00	22.00
Double	38.00	40.00

Parking for 4
Cards accepted: Diners

For ideas on places to visit refer to the introduction at the beginning of this section.

USE YOUR *i*'s

There are more than 550 Tourist Information Centres throughout England offering friendly help with accommodation and holiday ideas as well as suggestions of places to visit and things to do. There may well be a centre in your home town which can help you before you set out. You'll find addresses in the local Phone Book or simply call Freepages 0800 192 192.

COUNTRY CODE

Always follow the Country Code

- Enjoy the countryside and respect its life and work
- Guard against all risk of fire
- Fasten all gates
- Keep your dogs under close control
- Keep to public paths across farmland
- Use gates and stiles to cross fences, hedges and walls
- Leave livestock, crops and machinery alone
- Take your litter home
- Help to keep all water clean
- Protect wildlife, plants and trees
- Take special care on country roads
- Make no unnecessary noise

West Country

Go west for an area of natural beauty that's rich in history, legend and perhaps magic too. Land's End, vast Exmoor and Dartmoor, Tintagel, home of King Arthur, and prehistoric Stonehenge wait to be explored. Thatched cottages, coastal artists' colonies, and elegant cities like Bath or Wells are typical of this unspoilt area.

Spring comes early to the delightful Isles of Scilly, while the magnificent coastline of Devon and Cornwall is home to beach resorts as well as tiny, sheltered coves and, for the adventurous, the best surfing in the country.

For the true flavour of the west, don't forget those tasty local delights - Devon cream, scrumpy and Cheddar cheese.

The counties of Bath and North East Somerset, Bristol, Cornwall, Devon, Dorset (Western), Isles of Scilly, North Somerset, Somerset, South Gloucestershire and Wiltshire

FOR MORE INFORMATION CONTACT:
West Country Tourist Board
60 St Davids Hill, Exeter EX4 4SY
Tel: (01392) 425426 **Fax:** (01392) 420891
Email: post@wctb.co.uk

Where to Go in the West Country – see pages 230-234
Where to Stay in the West Country – see pages 235-288

West Country

Where to Go and What to See

You will find hundreds of interesting places to visit during your stay in the West Country, just some of which are listed in these pages. The number against each name will help you locate it on the map (pages 232-233). Contact any Tourist Information Centre in the region for more ideas on days out in the West Country.

1 Sheldon Manor
Chippenham,
Wiltshire SN14 0RG
Tel: (01249) 653120
Ancient manor house with fine example of 13thC porch. Early English oak furniture and Nailsea glass. A 15thC detached chapel and connoisseur gardens.

2 Bowood House & Gardens
Calne,
Wiltshire SN11 OLZ
Tel: (01249) 812102
An 18thC house by Robert Adam with collections of paintings, watercolours, Victoriana, Indiana and porcelain. Landscaped park with lake, terraces, waterfall and grottos.

3 The Exploratory Hands-on Science Centre
Bristol Old Station,
Temple Meads,
Bristol BS1 6QU
Tel: (0117) 907 9000
Exhibition of lights, lenses, lasers, bubbles, bridges, illusions, gyroscopes and much more all housed in Brunel's original engine shed and drawing office.

4 Harveys Wine Museum
12 Denmark Street,
Bristol BS1 5DQ
Tel: (0117) 9275036
Wine museum in original 13thC cellars displaying artefacts connected with the production and enjoyment of wines, especially glass, silver and corkscrews.

5 Museum of Costume
Assembly Rooms,
Bennett Street, Bath BA1 2QH
Tel: (01225) 477789
Displays of fashionable dress for men, women and children, from 16thC to present day.

6 Roman Baths Museum
Pump Room,
Abbey Church Yard,
Bath BA1 1LZ
Tel: (01225) 477000/477785
Roman baths and temple precinct, hot springs and Roman temple. Jewellery, coins, curses and votive offerings from the sacred spring.

7 Weston-super-Mare Sea Life Centre
Marine Parade,
Weston-super-Mare BS23 1BE
Tel: (01934) 641603
All aspects of British marine life housed on Britain's first pier for 85 years.

8 Rode Bird Gardens
Rode, Bath,
Somerset BA3 6QW
Tel: (01373) 830326
Hundreds of exotic birds in lovely natural surroundings, 17 acres of woodland, gardens, lakes, children's play area, pets corner, clematis collection. Miniature steam railway.

9 Wookey Hole Caves and Papermill
Wookey Hole, Wells,
Somerset BA5 1BB
Tel: (01749) 672243
Spectacular caves and legendary home of the Witch of Wookey. Working Victorian papermill including Fairground Memories, Old Penny Arcade, Magical Mirror Maze and Cave Diving Museum.

10 Wells Cathedral
Wells
Somerset BA5 2PA
Tel: (01749) 674483
Dating from the 12thC and built in the Early English Gothic style. Magnificent West Front with 296 medieval groups of sculpture. Chapter House and Lady Chapel.

11 Longleat
Warminster,
Wiltshire BA12 7NW
Tel: (01985) 844400
Great Elizabethan house with lived-in atmosphere. Important libraries and Italian ceilings. Capability Brown designed parkland. Safari Park.

12 Stonehenge
Amesbury, Salisbury,
Wiltshire SP4 7DE
Tel: (01980) 23108/624715
World famous pre-historic monument built as a ceremonial centre. Started 5,000 years ago and remodelled several times.

13 Wilton House
Wilton, Salisbury,
Wiltshire SP2 OBJ
Tel: (01722) 743115
Home of the Earls of Pembroke for nearly 450 years. Famous Double and Single Cube rooms. Art collection. Adventure playground. Woodland walk. Wareham Bears.

14 Clarks Village
Farm Road, Street,
Somerset BA16 0BB
Tel: (01458) 840064
Factory shopping village including over 40 high street name outlets plus a variety of attractions including shoe museum, landscaped walkways, children's play area, pottery, studio.

15 Cannington College Heritage Gardens and Plant Centre
Cannington, Bridgwater,
Somerset TA5 2LS
Tel: (01278) 652226
The gardens have been established for 75 years and house extensive plant collections including eight national collections. Glasshouses open to visitors.

16 Sheppy's Cider Farm Centre
Three Bridges,
Bradford-on-Tone, Taunton,
Somerset TA4 1ER
Tel: (01823) 461233
Wander through orchards, visit the press room and farm/cider museum. Three farm trails. Children's play area. Licensed tea room open in season.

17 Fleet Air Arm Museum
Royal Naval Air Station,
Yeovilton, Ilchester,
Somerset BA22 8HT
Tel: (01935) 840565
Forty historic naval aircraft, displays, models, uniforms and other artefacts. Concorde, WWI, WWII, Wrens, Kamikaze, Harrier, Korea and Aircraft Carrier exhibitions.

18 Clovelly Village
Clovelly, Bideford,
Devon EX39 5SY
Tel: (01237) 431200/431781
Unspoilt fishing village on North Devon coast with steep cobbled street and no vehicular access. Donkeys and sledges are the only means of transport.

19 Rosemoor Garden
Rosemoor, Torrington,
Devon EX38 8PH
Tel: (01805) 624067
Royal Horticultural Society garden with trees, shrubs, roses, alpines and arboretum. Nursery of uncommon and rare plants. Eight acres being expanded to 40 acres.

20 Sherborne Castle
Sherborne,
Dorset
Tel: (01935) 813182
Built by Sir Walter Raleigh in 1594 to replace the old castle. The Elizabethan Hall and Jacobean Oak Room show two of the many styles of architecture.

21 Forde Abbey and Gardens
Chard,
Somerset TA20 4LU
Tel: (01460) 220231
A 12thC Cistercian abbey converted during Commonwealth. Mortlake tapestries, pictures. Thirty acres of outstanding gardens. Crucifixion painting dated 1320 in undercroft.

22 Athelhampton House and Gardens
Athelhampton, Dorchester, Dorset
DT2 7LG Tel: (01305) 848363
Legendary site of King Athelstan's Palace. Family home for five centuries. Fine example of 15thC architecture. Gardens with fountains, pools and waterfalls.

23 **Hardy's Cottage and Garden**
Higher Bockhampton,
Dorchester, Dorset DT2 8QJ
Tel: (01305) 262366
A small thatched cottage where the novelist and poet Thomas Hardy was born in 1840, built by his great grandfather and little altered.

24 **The Tutankhamun Exhibition**
High West Street, Dorchester,
Dorset DT1 1UW
Tel: (01305) 269571
Tutankhamun's tomb perfectly reconstructed for the first time outside of Egypt. Facsimiles of his magnificent treasures including his golden burial mask.

25 **Abbotsbury Sub-Tropical Gardens**
Bullers Way, Abbotsbury,
Weymouth, Dorset DT3 4LA
Tel: (01305) 871387
Twenty acres of woodland valley. Exotic plants from all over the world thrive. Bird aviary and children's play area.

26 Crealy Park

Sidmouth Road, Clyst St Mary,
Exeter,
Devon EX5 1DR
Tel: (01395) 233200
One of Devon's largest animal farms. Milk a cow, feed a lamb and pick up a piglet. Adventure playgrounds. Dragonfly lake and farm trails.

27 Castle Drogo

Drewsteignton,
Exeter,
Devon EX6 6PB
Tel: (01647) 433306
Granite castle, built between 1910 and 1930 by Sir Edwin Lutyens, overlooking the wooded gorge of the River Teign. Views of Dartmoor.

28 Babbacombe Model Village

Hampton Avenue,
Babbacombe,
Torquay,
Devon TQ1 3LA
Tel: (01803) 315315/328669
Over 400 models, many with sound and animation, within four acres of award-winning gardens. See modern towns, villages, railways and rural areas. 'City of Lights' - illuminations.

29 Dobwalls Family Adventure Park

Dobwalls, Liskeard,
Cornwall PL14 6HD
Tel: (01579) 320325/320578
Two miles of scenically dramatic miniature railway based on an American railroad. Children's Adventureland. Krazee Kavern.

30 Lanhydrock

Bodmin,
Cornwall PL30 5AD
Tel: (01208) 73320
A 17thC house largely rebuilt after fire in 1881. 116ft gallery with magnificent plaster ceiling illustrating scenes from the Old Testament. Park, gardens, walks.

31 Newquay Sea Life Centre

Towan Promenade, Newquay,
Cornwall TR7 1DU
Tel: (01637) 878134
Journey beneath the ocean waves and encounter thousands of marine creatures - everything from shrimps and starfish to conger eels and octopus.

32 The Lost Gardens of Heligan

Heligan, Pentewan, St Austell,
Cornwall PL26 6EN
Tel: (01726) 844157/843566
The largest garden restoration project undertaken since the war. New attraction, The Lost Valley, covers 35 acres.

33 Pendennis Castle

Falmouth, Cornwall TR11 4LP
Tel: (01326) 316594
Well-preserved coastal fort erected in 1540s by Henry VIII, and added to by Elizabeth I.

34 St Michael's Mount

Marazion, Cornwall TR17 0HT
Tel: (01736) 710507
Originally the site of a Benedictine chapel, the castle on its rock dates from the 14thC. Fine views towards Land's End and the Lizard. Reached by foot, or ferry at high tide in summer.

35 Tate Gallery - St Ives

Porthmeor Beach, St Ives,
Cornwall TR26 1TG
Tel: (01736) 796226
A major new gallery showing changing groups of work from the Tate Gallery's pre-eminent collection of St Ives painting and sculpture.

36 The Minack Theatre and Exhibition Centre

Porthcurno, Penzance,
Cornwall TR19 6JU
Tel: (01736) 810694/810181
Open-air cliffside theatre with breathtaking views, presenting a 16-week season of plays and musicals. Exhibition centre telling the theatre's story.

37 Lands End

The Custom House,
Sennen, Penzance,
Cornwall TR19 7AA
Tel: (01736) 871501/871780
Spectacular cliffs with breathtaking vistas. Superb multi-sensory Last Labyrinth Show, Land's End Hotel, art gallery, exhibitions and much more.

FIND OUT MORE

Further information about holidays and attractions in the West Country is available from:

West Country Tourist Board,
60 St Davids Hill,
Exeter EX4 4SY.
Tel: (01392) 425426
Fax: (01392) 420891
Email: post@wctb.co.uk

These publications are available free from the West Country Tourist Board:

- **Great Escapes in England's West Country**
- **Bed & Breakfast Touring Map**
- **West Country Inspected Holiday Homes**
- **Commended Hotels and Guesthouses**
- **Glorious Gardens of the West Country**
- **Camping and Caravan Touring Map**
- **Tourist Attraction Touring Map**
- **Trencherman's West Country, Good Food Guide**

WHERE TO STAY (WEST COUNTRY)

Accommodation entries in this region are listed in alphabetical order of place name, and then in alphabetical order of establishment.

Map references refer to the colour location maps at the back of this guide. The first number indicates the map to use; the letter and number which follow refer to the grid reference on the map.

At-a-glance symbols at the end of each accommodation entry give useful information about services and facilities. A key to symbols can be found inside the back cover flap. Keep this open for easy reference.

ABBOTSBURY

Dorset
Map ref 2A3

Beautiful village near Chesil Beach, with a long main street of mellow stone and thatched cottages and the ruins of a Benedictine monastery. High above the village on a hill is a prominent 15th C chapel. Abbotsbury's famous swannery and sub-tropical gardens lie just outside the village.

Swan Lodge

COMMENDED

Rodden Row, Abbotsbury, Weymouth DT3 4JL
☎ (01305) 871249
Fax (01305) 871249

Situated on the B3157 coastal road between Weymouth and Bridport. Swan Inn public house opposite, where food is served all day, is under the same ownership.

Bedrooms: 2 double, 2 twin, 1 triple
Bathrooms: 4 en-suite, 1 public

Bed & breakfast per night:	£min	£max
Single	30.00	36.00
Double	44.00	56.00

Lunch available
Evening meal 1800 (last orders 2200)
Parking for 10
Cards accepted: Mastercard, Visa

ALDERTON

Wiltshire
Map ref 2B2

Manor Farm

HIGHLY COMMENDED

Alderton SN14 6NL
☎ (01666) 840271
Fax (01666) 840271

540-acre arable & livestock farm. Beautiful 17th C family home offers warm hospitality, lovely en-suite bedrooms. Super pubs. Ideal for Bath and Cotswolds - a fabulous area.

Bedrooms: 2 double, 1 twin
Bathrooms: 3 en-suite

Bed & breakfast per night:	£min	£max
Single	30.00	30.00
Double	50.00	50.00

Lunch available
Parking for 10

Information on accommodation listed in this guide has been supplied by the proprietors. As changes may occur you are advised to check details at the time of booking.

AMESBURY

Wiltshire
Map ref 2B2

Standing on the banks of the River Avon, this is the nearest town to Stonehenge on Salisbury Plain. The area is rich in prehistoric sites.
Tourist Information Centre ☎ (01980) 622833

Church Cottage

HIGHLY COMMENDED

Church Street, Amesbury, Salisbury SP4 7EY
☎ (01980) 624650 & (0585) 633245

Your own bathroom, beautiful quiet bedrooms, spotlessly clean, excellent 3-course breakfasts, Stonehenge 2 miles, restaurants only 2 minutes. In short, superb value.

Bedrooms: 1 single, 2 double
Suite available
Bathrooms: 2 en-suite, 1 private

Bed & breakfast per night:	£min	£max
Single	25.00	29.00
Double	36.00	40.00

Epworth House Bed and Breakfast

HIGHLY COMMENDED

21 Edwards Road, Amesbury, Salisbury SP4 7LT
☎ (01980) 624242
Fax (01980) 624242

Restful detached house in quiet cul-de-sac, two minutes' level walk from

Continued ▶

AMESBURY

Continued

Amesbury centre. Lovely enclosed garden, excellent breakfasts. Stonehenge nearby.
Bedrooms: 2 double, 2 twin
Bathrooms: 2 en-suite, 2 private

Bed & breakfast per night:	£min	£max
Double	36.00	40.00

Parking for 5

Mandalay Guest House

HIGHLY COMMENDED

15 Stonehenge Road, Amesbury, Salisbury SP4 7BA
☎ (01980) 623733
Beautiful bedrooms in house of great character. Fine breakfast served in classical breakfast room overlooking the garden temple. No-smoking policy.
Bedrooms: 1 single, 1 double, 2 twin, 1 triple
Bathrooms: 5 en-suite

Bed & breakfast per night:	£min	£max
Single		28.00
Double		38.00

Parking for 5
Cards accepted: Amex, Diners, Mastercard, Visa, Switch/Delta

The Old Bakery

COMMENDED

Netton, Salisbury SP4 6AW
☎ (01722) 782351
Pleasantly modernised former village bakery in the Woodford Valley. Five miles north of Salisbury and 5 miles from Stonehenge. Local inn within walking distance. Open all year.
Bedrooms: 1 single, 1 double, 1 twin
Bathrooms: 1 public, 1 private shower

Bed & breakfast per night:	£min	£max
Single	15.00	18.00
Double	30.00	36.00

Parking for 3

COLOUR MAPS

Colour maps at the back of this guide pinpoint all places in which you will find accommodation listed.

ASHBURTON

Devon
Map ref 1C2

Formerly a thriving wool centre and important as one of Dartmoor's four stannary towns. Today's busy market town has many period buildings. Ancient tradition is maintained in the annual ale-tasting and bread-weighing ceremony. Good centre for exploring Dartmoor or the south Devon coast.

New Cott Farm

COMMENDED

Poundsgate, Newton Abbot TQ13 7PD
☎ (01364) 631421
Fax (01364) 631421

130-acre mixed farm. Enjoy the freedom, peace and tranquillity of moorland and valleys in the Dartmoor National Park. A warm welcome and lots of lovely home-made food to complete your stay.
Wheelchair access category 3
Bedrooms: 2 double, 1 twin, 1 triple
Bathrooms: 4 en-suite

Bed & breakfast per night:	£min	£max
Double	35.00	37.00

Half board per person:	£min	£max
Daily	28.00	30.00
Weekly	180.00	

Evening meal 1830 (last orders 1700)
Parking for 4

Wellpritton Farm

HIGHLY COMMENDED

Holne, Newton Abbot TQ13 7RX
☎ (01364) 631273
15-acre mixed farm. Plenty of mouth-watering farm-produced food in a tastefully modernised farmhouse on the edge of Dartmoor. Special diets catered for by arrangement. A warm welcome and caring personal attention.
Bedrooms: 2 twin, 2 family rooms
Bathrooms: 3 en-suite, 1 private

Bed & breakfast per night:	£min	£max
Single	18.00	18.00
Double	36.00	36.00

Half board per person:	£min	£max
Daily	26.00	26.00
Weekly	175.00	175.00

Evening meal 1900 (last orders 1200)
Parking for 6

ASHTON KEYNES

Wiltshire
Map ref 2B2

Village beside the River Thames, with houses standing along the edge of the stream reached by bridges from the road on the opposite bank. Nearby stands the manor, Ashton House.

Corner Cottage

COMMENDED

Fore Street, Ashton Keynes, Swindon SN6 6NP
☎ (01285) 861454
Homely 17th C stone cottage in centre of best kept village within the Cotswold Water Park and on route of Thames Path. Ideal for touring Cotswolds.
Bedrooms: 1 double, 1 family room
Suite available
Bathrooms: 2 en-suite

Bed & breakfast per night:	£min	£max
Single	22.00	25.00
Double	37.00	45.00

Parking for 4

BAMPTON

Devon
Map ref 1D1

Riverside market town, famous for its fair each October.

Newhouse Farm

COMMENDED

Oakford, Tiverton EX16 9JE
☎ (01398) 351347

42-acre livestock farm. Charming 16th C farmhouse featuring oak beams and inglenook fireplace. Pretty en-suite bedrooms with colour TV. Home-baked bread, delicious country cooking, warm hospitality.
Bedrooms: 3 double
Bathrooms: 3 en-suite

Bed & breakfast per night:	£min	£max
Single	18.00	22.00
Double	32.00	40.00

Half board per person:	£min	£max
Daily	28.00	31.00

Evening meal 1930 (last orders 1700)
Parking for 3

BARNSTAPLE

Devon
Map ref 1C1

At the head of the Taw Estuary, once a ship-building and textile town, now an agricultural centre with attractive period buildings, a modern civic centre and leisure centre. Attractions include Queen Anne's Walk, a charming colonnaded arcade and Pannier Market.
Tourist Information Centre ☎ (01271) 375000

Bradiford Cottage

COMMENDED
Bradiford, Barnstaple EX31 4DP
☎ (01271) 45039
Fax (01271) 45039
17th C cottage in quiet, rural setting. Own garden and car parking. Well placed for exploring the Atlantic coast and the moors of North Devon.
Bedrooms: 2 single, 1 double, 1 twin
Bathrooms: 2 public

Bed & breakfast per night:	£min	£max
Single	15.00	17.00
Double	30.00	34.00

Parking for 3

Home Park Farm Accommodation

COMMENDED
Lower Blakewell, Muddiford, Barnstaple EX31 4ET
☎ (01271) 42955
Fax (01271) 42955
70-acre livestock farm. Paradise for country and garden lovers. Warm hospitality, a relaxing tranquil atmosphere and genuine farmhouse cooking await you. All rooms en-suite with colour TV, hairdryer, hospitality tray. Two miles north of Barnstaple. Laundry facilities and many extras.
Bedrooms: 1 double, 2 triple
Bathrooms: 3 en-suite

Bed & breakfast per night:	£min	£max
Single	15.00	20.00
Double	30.00	40.00

Half board per person:	£min	£max
Daily	22.50	29.50

Lunch available
Evening meal 1800 (last orders 1800)
Parking for 3

The Red House

HIGHLY COMMENDED
Brynsworthy, Roundswell, Barnstaple EX31 3NP
☎ (01271) 45966
Country house, panoramic views. Both rooms colour TV, shower, hairdryer, tea/coffee facilities, central heating. Good pub food nearby.
Bedrooms: 1 double, 1 twin
Bathrooms: 1 public, 2 private showers

Bed & breakfast per night:	£min	£max
Single	17.00	21.00
Double	32.00	36.00

Parking for 6
Open February–November

The Spinney

COMMENDED
Shirwell, Barnstaple EX31 4JR
☎ (01271) 850282
Former rectory with views towards Exmoor. Spacious accommodation. Delicious meals prepared by chef/proprietor, served in restored Victorian conservatory under the ancient vine.
Bedrooms: 1 single, 1 double, 1 twin, 2 triple
Bathrooms: 1 en-suite, 2 public

Bed & breakfast per night:	£min	£max
Single	17.00	20.00
Double	34.00	40.00

Half board per person:	£min	£max
Daily	25.00	28.00
Weekly	144.00	162.00

Evening meal 1900 (last orders 1700)
Parking for 7

Waytown Farm

COMMENDED
Shirwell, Barnstaple EX31 4JN
☎ (01271) 850396
Fax (01271) 850396
240-acre mixed farm. Set in beautiful Devon countryside, 3 miles north of Barnstaple. 17th C farmhouse offering comfortable en-suite bedrooms, convenient for exploring Exmoor and visiting local beaches.
Bedrooms: 1 single, 1 twin, 1 triple, 1 family room
Suites available
Bathrooms: 3 en-suite, 1 public

Bed & breakfast per night:	£min	£max
Single	17.50	
Double	38.00	

Half board per person:	£min	£max
Daily	26.00	29.00
Weekly	170.00	180.00

Evening meal 1830 (last orders 1600)
Parking for 6

BATH

Bath & North East Somerset
Map ref 2B2

Georgian spa city beside the River Avon. Important Roman site with impressive reconstructed baths, uncovered in 19th C. Bath Abbey built on site of monastery where first king of England was crowned (AD 973). Fine architecture in mellow local stone. Pump Room and museums.
Tourist Information Centre ☎ (01225) 477101

Astor House

COMMENDED
14 Oldfield Road, Bath BA2 3ND
☎ (01225) 429134
Fax (01225) 429134
Comfortable, spacious Victorian home with lovely views of the city and countryside yet only a short walk to the centre. Friendly welcome, varied delicious breakfasts.
Bedrooms: 3 double, 2 twin, 1 triple
Bathrooms: 4 en-suite, 2 public
Parking for 6
Open March–December
Cards accepted: Mastercard, Visa

BATH

Continued

Bailbrook Lodge Hotel

COMMENDED

35/37 London Road West, Bath
BA1 7HZ
☎ (01225) 859090
Fax (01225) 852299

Fine Georgian house with many original features - ceilings, staircase and fireplaces. All rooms en-suite, some with four posters. Close to centre of Bath, M4 and many historic attractions.

Bedrooms: 4 double, 4 twin, 4 family rooms
Bathrooms: 12 en-suite

Bed & breakfast per night:	£min	£max
Single	35.00	46.00
Double	50.00	70.00

Half board per person:	£min	£max
Daily	37.50	45.00
Weekly	220.00	240.00

Evening meal 1930 (last orders 2130)
Parking for 20
Cards accepted: Amex, Diners, Mastercard, Visa

Barrow Castle

COMMENDED

Rush Hill, Bath BA2 2QR
☎ (01225) 480725

A Victorian castle with panoramic rural views, lovely grounds and a sweeping drive. Secluded and peaceful, yet so close to all the city amenities. An unusual family home with a relaxed and friendly atmosphere.

Bedrooms: 2 double, 1 twin
Bathrooms: 1 en-suite, 2 private

Bed & breakfast per night:	£min	£max
Single	35.00	40.00
Double	45.00	75.00

Half board per person:	£min	£max
Daily	50.00	60.00
Weekly	350.00	420.00

Evening meal 1900 (last orders 2100)
Parking for 6

9 Charlotte Street

Listed APPROVED

Bath BA1 2NE
☎ (01225) 424193

Grade II listed Georgian house, 3 minutes from city centre, with public car park at rear. All rooms have hot and cold water, colour TV, tea and coffee-making facilities.

Bedrooms: 2 double, 1 twin, 1 triple, 1 family room
Bathrooms: 2 public

Bed & breakfast per night:	£min	£max
Double	33.00	35.00

Church Farm

APPROVED

Monkton Farleigh,
Bradford-on-Avon, Wiltshire
BA15 2QJ
☎ (01225) 858583 & (0589) 596929

52-acre mixed farm. Sympathetically converted barn. Horses, golf and swimming. Ideal base for walking, or touring south-west England, 10 minutes from Bath.

Bedrooms: 3 double
Bathrooms: 2 en-suite, 1 private, 1 public

Bed & breakfast per night:	£min	£max
Single	25.00	25.00
Double	35.00	40.00

Parking for 5

Fern Cottage

HIGHLY COMMENDED

Monkton Farleigh,
Bradford-on-Avon, Wiltshire
BA15 2QJ
☎ (01225) 859412
Fax (01225) 859018

Delightful stone-built 17th C cottage, set in fine gardens in peaceful conservation village between Bath and Bradford-on-Avon. Well-appointed rooms.

Bedrooms: 3 double
Bathrooms: 2 en-suite, 1 public

Bed & breakfast per night:	£min	£max
Single	30.00	36.00
Double	48.00	58.00

Parking for 5

Flaxley Villa

APPROVED

9 Newbridge Hill, Bath BA1 3PW
☎ (01225) 313237

Comfortable Victorian house, just a few minutes by car to city centre and within easy reach of Royal Crescent and main attractions.

Bedrooms: 2 double, 1 twin
Bathrooms: 2 en-suite, 1 public, 1 private shower

Bed & breakfast per night:	£min	£max
Single	18.00	25.00
Double	34.00	42.00

Parking for 3

Gainsborough Hotel

COMMENDED

Weston Lane, Bath BA1 4AB
☎ (01225) 311380
Fax (01225) 447411

Spacious and comfortable country house hotel in own lovely grounds, near the botanical gardens and within easy walking distance of the city. High ground, nice views, own large car park. 5-course breakfast, friendly staff, warm welcome.

Bedrooms: 2 single, 6 double, 6 twin, 2 triple, 1 family room
Bathrooms: 17 en-suite

Bed & breakfast per night:	£min	£max
Single	30.00	46.00
Double	50.00	70.00

Parking for 18
Cards accepted: Amex, Mastercard, Visa

Georgian Guest House

Listed APPROVED

34 Henrietta Street, Bath BA2 6LR
☎ (01225) 424103

Central Bath. Grade I listed Georgian town house, next to Henrietta Park and

only 2 minutes' walk to town centre. 1 minute from famous Pulteney Bridge and restaurants.
Bedrooms: 2 single, 3 double, 2 twin, 2 triple, 1 family room
Bathrooms: 3 en-suite, 1 public, 4 private showers

Bed & breakfast per night:	£min	£max
Single	20.00	35.00
Double	40.00	60.00

Cards accepted: Amex, Mastercard, Visa

Hermitage

COMMENDED

Bath Road, Box, Corsham, Wiltshire SN13 8DT
☎ (01225) 744187
Fax (01225) 743447
Email: hermitage@telecall.co.uk
Six miles from Bath on A4 to Chippenham, 1st drive on left by 30 mph sign. 16th C house with heated pool in summer. Dining room with vaulted ceiling.
Bedrooms: 4 double, 1 triple
Bathrooms: 5 en-suite

Bed & breakfast per night:	£min	£max
Single	30.00	40.00
Double	42.00	50.00

Parking for 9

Holly Lodge

DE LUXE

8 Upper Oldfield Park, Bath BA2 3JZ
☎ (01225) 424042
Fax (01225) 481138
Elegant Victorian house set in its own grounds, enjoying magnificent views of the city.
Bedrooms: 1 single, 4 double, 2 twin
Bathrooms: 7 en-suite

Bed & breakfast per night:	£min	£max
Single	48.00	55.00
Double	75.00	89.00

Parking for 8
Cards accepted: Amex, Diners, Mastercard, Visa, Switch/Delta

Kennard Hotel

HIGHLY COMMENDED

11 Henrietta Street, Bath BA2 6LL
☎ (01225) 310472
Fax (01225) 460054
Email: kennard@dircon.co.uk
Georgian town house hotel of charm and character in a quiet street. A few minutes' level walk to the Abbey and Roman Baths.
Bedrooms: 2 single, 9 double, 1 twin, 1 family room
Bathrooms: 11 en-suite, 1 public

Bed & breakfast per night:	£min	£max
Single	35.00	45.00
Double	65.00	85.00

Cards accepted: Amex, Diners, Mastercard, Visa, Switch/Delta

Leighton House

HIGHLY COMMENDED

139 Wells Road, Bath BA2 3AL
☎ (01225) 314769 & 420210
Fax (01225) 443079

Marilyn and Colin extend a warm welcome at their elegant, spacious, detached Victorian home, with car park and just a 10 minute walk to the city centre.
Bedrooms: 3 double, 4 twin, 1 family room
Bathrooms: 8 en-suite

Bed & breakfast per night:	£min	£max
Single	47.00	60.00
Double	62.00	75.00

Parking for 8
Cards accepted: Mastercard, Visa, Switch/Delta

Meadowland

DE LUXE

36 Bloomfield Park, Bath BA2 2BX
☎ (01225) 311079
Fax (01452) 304507
Set in quiet, secluded grounds and offering the highest standard in de-luxe en-suite accommodation, Meadowland is elegantly furnished and decorated. Private parking, lovely gardens, non-smoking only. A peaceful retreat for discerning travellers.
Bedrooms: 2 double, 1 twin
Bathrooms: 3 en-suite

Bed & breakfast per night:	£min	£max
Single	40.00	45.00
Double	58.00	65.00

Parking for 6
Cards accepted: Mastercard, Visa

Midway Cottage

COMMENDED

10 Farleigh Wick, Bradford-on-Avon, Wiltshire BA15 2PU
☎ (01225) 863932
Friendly, relaxed cottage with high standards of comfort and service. On A363 between Bath and Bradford-on-Avon, next door to a country inn serving excellent food.
Bedrooms: 2 double, 1 twin
Bathrooms: 3 en-suite, 1 public

Bed & breakfast per night:	£min	£max
Double	36.00	40.00

Parking for 5

Hotel Saint Clair

COMMENDED

1 Crescent Gardens, Upper Bristol Road, Bath BA1 2NA
☎ (01225) 425543 & (01378) 834592
Fax (01225) 425543
Small family hotel 5 minutes' walk from city, 2 minutes from Royal Crescent. Large public car park 1 minute away. One-night stays welcome.
Bedrooms: 4 double, 2 twin, 2 triple, 1 family room
Bathrooms: 7 en-suite, 1 public

Bed & breakfast per night:	£min	£max
Single	22.00	38.00
Double	34.00	52.00

Cards accepted: Mastercard, Visa

Sampford

APPROVED

11 Oldfield Road, Bath BA2 3ND
☎ (01225) 310053
In a quiet residential area half a mile south of city centre off the A367 Exeter/Radstock/Shepton Mallet road.
Bedrooms: 1 double, 1 twin, 1 triple
Bathrooms: 1 public, 3 private showers

Bed & breakfast per night:	£min	£max
Double	36.00	40.00

Parking for 2

Please mention this guide when making your booking.

BATH

Continued

Seven Springs

Listed COMMENDED

4 High Street, Woolley, Bath
BA1 8AR
☎ (01225) 858001

In small country hamlet of Woolley, 3 miles from Bath city centre and 4 miles from M4. Lovely walks on public footpaths. Ideal for touring West Country. Bedrooms can be let as twins, doubles or family rooms.

Bedrooms: 1 double, 2 family rooms
Bathrooms: 3 en-suite

Bed & breakfast per night:	£min	£max
Double	35.00	40.00

Parking for 8

Toghill House Farm

Listed COMMENDED

Doynton, Bristol BS15 5RT
☎ (01225) 891261

50-acre mixed farm. Bath 5 minutes. Warm and cosy 17th C farmhouse, formerly a resting home for monks travelling from Malmesbury to Glastonbury. Views over historic Bath, Bristol and Welsh hills.

Bedrooms: 1 double, 1 triple, 1 family room
Bathrooms: 3 en-suite

Bed & breakfast per night:	£min	£max
Single	25.00	29.00
Double	44.00	44.00

Parking for 50

Walton Villa

COMMENDED

3 Newbridge Hill, Bath BA1 3PW
☎ (01225) 482792

Late Victorian semi, family-run bed and breakfast offering en-suite accommodation. One mile from city centre.

Bedrooms: 2 double, 1 twin
Bathrooms: 3 en-suite, 1 public

Bed & breakfast per night:	£min	£max
Double	40.00	50.00

Parking for 5

The Wheatsheaf Inn

Listed COMMENDED

Combe Hay, Bath BA2 7EG
☎ (01225) 833504
Fax (01225) 833504

Set in glorious Somerset countryside, a traditional country pub, famous for its delicious home-cooked food and cask-conditioned ales. With its wonderful terraced gardens, the perfect choice for a peaceful break in the country.

Bedrooms: 3 double
Bathrooms: 3 en-suite

Bed & breakfast per night:	£min	£max
Single	39.00	45.00
Double	68.00	75.00

Evening meal 1830 (last orders 2130)
Parking for 150
Cards accepted: Mastercard, Visa, Switch/Delta

BEAMINSTER

Dorset
Map ref 2A3

Old country town of mellow local stone set amid hills and rural vales. Mainly Georgian buildings; attractive almshouses date from 1603. The 17th C church with its ornate, pinnacled tower was restored inside by the Victorians. Parnham, a Tudor manor house, lies 1 mile south.

Beam Cottage

COMMENDED

16 North Street, Beaminster
DT8 3DZ
☎ (01308) 863639

Attractive, Grade II listed cottage in centre of Beaminster, with secluded and pretty garden.

Bedrooms: 1 double, 1 twin, 1 family room
Bathrooms: 2 en-suite, 1 private

Bed & breakfast per night:	£min	£max
Single	20.00	22.00
Double	40.00	45.00

Half board per person:	£min	£max
Daily	28.00	30.00

Evening meal 1900 (last orders 2100)
Parking for 2

BIDEFORD

Devon
Map ref 1C1

The home port of Sir Richard Grenville, the town with its 17th C merchants' houses flourished as a shipbuilding and cloth town. The bridge of 24 arches was built about 1460. Charles Kingsley stayed here while writing Westward Ho!
Tourist Information Centre ☎ (01237) 477676 or 421853

Sunset Hotel

COMMENDED

Landcross, Bideford EX39 5JA
☎ (01237) 472962

Small, quality country hotel in peaceful, picturesque location, specialising in home cooking. Delightful en-suite bedrooms with beverages and colour TV. Book with confidence. A non-smoking establishment.

Bedrooms: 1 double, 1 twin, 1 triple, 1 family room
Bathrooms: 4 en-suite

Bed & breakfast per night:	£min	£max
Single	25.00	30.00
Double	46.00	50.00

Half board per person:	£min	£max
Daily	34.50	35.50
Weekly	220.00	224.00

Evening meal 1900 (last orders 1900)
Parking for 10
Open March–October
Cards accepted: Mastercard, Visa

The symbols in each entry give information about services and facilities. A key to these symbols appears at the back of this guide.

BISHOP'S LYDEARD

Somerset
Map ref 1D1

Village 5 miles north-west of Taunton, the county town. Terminus for the West Somerset steam railway.

West View

COMMENDED

Minehead Road, Bishop's Lydeard, Taunton TA4 3BS
☎ (01823) 432223
Fax (01823) 432223

Attractive Victorian house in the village close to the privately-owned West Somerset Steam Railway. Your hosts were formerly at Slimbridge Station Farm.

Bedrooms: 1 double, 2 twin
Bathrooms: 1 en-suite, 1 public

Bed & breakfast per night:	£min	£max
Single	16.50	25.00
Double	33.00	44.00

Parking for 4

BODMIN

Cornwall
Map ref 1B2

County town south-west of Bodmin Moor with a ruined priory and church dedicated to St Petroc. Nearby are Lanhydrock House and Pencarrow House.
Tourist Information Centre ☎ (01208) 76616

Bokiddick Farm

HIGHLY COMMENDED

Lanivet, Bodmin PL30 5HP
☎ (01208) 831481
Fax (01208) 831481

185-acre dairy farm. Lovely oak-beamed farmhouse in beautiful countryside. Magnificent views, central for coast and moors. Close to National Trust Lanhydrock House.

Bedrooms: 1 double, 1 triple
Bathrooms: 2 en-suite

Bed & breakfast per night:	£min	£max
Single	25.00	
Double	38.00	42.00

Evening meal 1830 (last orders 1200)
Parking for 4
Open April–October

Colliford Tavern

COMMENDED

Colliford Lake, St Neot, Liskeard PL14 6PZ
☎ (01208) 821335
Fax (01208) 821335

"An oasis on Bodmin Moor". Friendly country pub, ideally situated for exploring Cornwall. Immaculate facilities. Good home-cooked meals and fine traditional ales. Take A30 from Launceston to Bodmin, take left turn signed to Colliford Lake then first left for Colliford Tavern, follow the lane and bear left at the fork.

Bedrooms: 3 double, 2 twin
Bathrooms: 5 en-suite

Bed & breakfast per night:	£min	£max
Single	27.50	35.00
Double	35.00	50.00

Lunch available
Evening meal 1900 (last orders 2130)
Parking for 50
Open April–September
Cards accepted: Amex, Mastercard, Visa, Switch/Delta

BOSCASTLE

Cornwall
Map ref 1B2

Small, unspoilt village in Valency Valley. Active as a port until onset of railway era, its natural harbour affords rare shelter on this wild coast. Attractions include spectacular blow-hole, Celtic field strips, part-Norman church. Nearby St Juliot Church was restored by Thomas Hardy.

Tolcarne House Hotel and Restaurant

HIGHLY COMMENDED

Tintagel Road, Boscastle PL35 0AS
☎ (01840) 250654
Fax (01840) 250654

Delightful late Victorian house in spacious grounds with lovely views to the dramatic Cornish coastline. All rooms en-suite. Restaurant and bar. Warm welcome.

Bedrooms: 1 single, 5 double, 2 twin
Bathrooms: 8 en-suite, 1 public

Bed & breakfast per night:	£min	£max
Single	28.00	30.00
Double	44.00	60.00

Half board per person:	£min	£max
Daily	36.00	41.00
Weekly	230.00	280.00

Evening meal 1900 (last orders 2100)
Parking for 15
Open March–October
Cards accepted: Mastercard, Visa

BOVEY TRACEY

Devon
Map ref 1D2

Standing by the river just east of Dartmoor National Park, this old town has good moorland views. Its church, with a 14th C tower, holds one of Devon's finest medieval rood screens.

Frost Farmhouse

COMMENDED

Frost Farm, Hennock Road, Bovey Tracey, Newton Abbot TQ13 9PP
☎ (01626) 833266
Fax (01626) 833266

220-acre mixed farm. Come and stay in this pretty pink-washed thatched farmhouse. Excellent en-suite bedrooms (shower/bath). Quiet location, country views.

Bedrooms: 2 double, 1 twin
Bathrooms: 3 en-suite

Bed & breakfast per night:	£min	£max
Single	18.00	20.00
Double	36.00	40.00

Evening meal from 1900
Parking for 6

For further information on accommodation establishments use the coupons at the back of this guide.

National gradings and classifications were correct at the time of going to press but are subject to change. Please check at the time of booking.

BOX

Wiltshire
Map ref 2B2

Village in an Area of Outstanding Natural Beauty, 7 miles south-west of Chippenham. It is famed for Box ground stone, used for centuries on buildings of national importance.

Lorne House

COMMENDED

London Road, Box, Corsham
SN13 8NA
☎ (01225) 742597
Fax (01225) 742597

Victorian property, recently refurbished, on main A4 road opposite Brunel's famous Box tunnel between Bath and Chippenham. Warm and welcoming.

Bedrooms: 1 double, 3 triple
Bathrooms: 4 en-suite

Bed & breakfast per night:	£min	£max
Single	20.00	27.50
Double	35.00	45.00

Parking for 6
Cards accepted: Mastercard, Visa

BRADFORD-ON-AVON

Wiltshire
Map ref 2B2

Huddled beside the river, the buildings of this former cloth-weaving town reflect continuing prosperity from the Middle Ages. There is a tiny Anglo-Saxon church, part of a monastery. The part-14th C bridge carries a medieval chapel, later used as a gaol.
Tourist Information Centre ☎ (01225) 865797

Brookfield House

HIGHLY COMMENDED

Vaggs Hill, Southwick, Trowbridge
BA14 9NA
☎ (01373) 830615

150-acre dairy farm. Delightful converted country barn in quiet rural setting. Relaxed, warm and friendly atmosphere. Dairy farm 200 yards away.

Bedrooms: 2 double, 1 twin
Bathrooms: 1 en-suite, 2 public

Bed & breakfast per night:	£min	£max
Single	15.00	35.00
Double	36.00	45.00

Parking for 10

BRAUNTON

Devon
Map ref 1C1

Large village just north of the Taw Estuary and close to botanically-important dunelands, National Nature Reserve, at Braunton Burrows on Devon's north coast. Braunton Great Field shows rare example of ancient field-strip cultivation.
Tourist Information Centre ☎ (01271) 816400

Poyers Hotel

Listed APPROVED

Wrafton, Braunton, North Devon
EX33 2DN
☎ (01271) 812149

16th C thatched longhouse with all en-suite accommodation. On edge of pretty village, 2 miles from coast.

Bedrooms: 2 single, 3 double, 3 twin, 1 triple
Bathrooms: 9 en-suite

Bed & breakfast per night:	£min	£max
Single	25.00	25.00
Double	44.00	44.00

Parking for 20
Cards accepted: Amex, Mastercard, Visa

BRIDESTOWE

Devon
Map ref 1C2

Small Dartmoor village with a much restored 15th C church, and Great Links Tor rising to the south-east.

White Hart Inn

COMMENDED

Fore Street, Bridestowe,
Okehampton EX20 4EL
☎ (01837) 861318
Fax (01837) 861318
Email: whihartinn@aol.com

17th C village inn, family-run for 36 years, primarily noted for good food. En-suite accommodation. Close to Dartmoor National Park, Lydford Gorge and fishing at Roadford Lake.

Bedrooms: 2 double
Bathrooms: 2 en-suite

Bed & breakfast per night:	£min	£max
Single	27.00	
Double	44.00	

Lunch available
Evening meal 1900 (last orders 2130)
Parking for 20
Cards accepted: Amex, Diners, Mastercard, Visa

BRIDGWATER

Somerset
Map ref 1D1

Former medieval port on the River Parrett, now small industrial town with mostly 19th C or modern architecture. Georgian Castle Street leads to West Quay and site of 13th C castle razed to the ground by Cromwell. Birthplace of Cromwellian Admiral Robert Blake is now museum. Arts centre.

Moxhill Farmhouse

HIGHLY COMMENDED

Moxhill Farm, Combwich,
Bridgwater TA5 2PN
☎ (01278) 652285 & 0802 382870
Fax (01278) 653942
Email: nigel.venner@ukonline.co.uk

136-acre dairy farm. Spacious 17th C farmhouse in peaceful countryside setting near Quantock Hills and sea, 4 miles from Bridgwater.

Bedrooms: 1 double, 2 family rooms
Bathrooms: 2 en-suite, 1 private

Bed & breakfast per night:	£min	£max
Single	21.00	25.00
Double	38.00	42.00

Half board per person:	£min	£max
Daily	27.50	40.00
Weekly	166.00	245.00

Evening meal 1900 (last orders 1800)
Parking for 4

Woodlands

HIGHLY COMMENDED

35 Durleigh Road, Bridgwater
TA6 7HX
☎ (01278) 423442

Beautiful listed house in 2 acres of

landscaped gardens, in convenient location for exploring Quantocks and north Somerset coastline. Tranquillity and seclusion yet close to town centre, only 3 miles from junction 24 of M5. Country house hotel quality at B & B prices.
Bedrooms: 1 single, 2 double, 1 twin
Bathrooms: 3 en-suite, 1 private, 1 public

Bed & breakfast per night:	£min	£max
Single	22.00	32.00
Double	44.00	50.00

Half board per person:	£min	£max
Daily	36.00	46.00

Evening meal 1830 (last orders 1400)
Parking for 4
Cards accepted: Mastercard, Visa
10

BRIDPORT

Dorset
Map ref 2A3

Market town and chief producer of nets and ropes just inland of dramatic Dorset coast. Old, broad streets built for drying and twisting and long gardens for rope-walks. Grand arcaded Town Hall and Georgian buildings. Local history museum has Roman relics.
Tourist Information Centre ☎ (01308) 424901

Bridport Arms Hotel

APPROVED
West Bay, Bridport DT6 4EN
☎ (01308) 422994
Fax (01308) 425141
16th C thatched hotel on beach. Restaurant specialising in local sea food. 2 bars, real local ales and bar meals.
Bedrooms: 3 single, 4 double, 3 twin, 1 triple, 2 family rooms
Bathrooms: 6 en-suite, 3 public

Bed & breakfast per night:	£min	£max
Single	22.00	30.00
Double	42.00	60.00

Half board per person:	£min	£max
Daily	38.00	42.00
Weekly	200.00	250.00

Lunch available
Evening meal 1900 (last orders 2100)
Parking for 10
Cards accepted: Mastercard, Visa, Switch/Delta

Britmead House

HIGHLY COMMENDED
West Bay Road, Bridport DT6 4EG
☎ (01308) 422941
Fax (01308) 422516

Elegant, spacious, tastefully decorated house. Lounge and dining room overlooking garden. West Bay Harbour/Coastal Path, 10 minutes' walk away. Renowned for hospitality, delicious meals and comfort.
Bedrooms: 4 double, 3 twin
Bathrooms: 6 en-suite, 1 private

Bed & breakfast per night:	£min	£max
Single	25.00	36.00
Double	40.00	58.00

Half board per person:	£min	£max
Daily	33.50	42.50
Weekly	206.50	241.50

Evening meal 1900 (last orders 1700)
Parking for 8
Cards accepted: Amex, Diners, Mastercard, Visa
5

New House Farm

APPROVED
Mangerton Lane, Bradpole, Bridport DT6 3SF
☎ (01308) 422884
50-acre beef farm. Modern, comfortable, peaceful farmhouse set in rural Dorset hills, close to the sea. Historic Area of Outstanding Natural Beauty.
Bedrooms: 1 double, 1 family room
Bathrooms: 2 en-suite

Bed & breakfast per night:	£min	£max
Single	20.00	25.00
Double	34.00	38.00

Half board per person:	£min	£max
Daily	28.00	35.00

Lunch available
Evening meal 1800 (last orders 2000)
Parking for 10
Open March–November

117 South Street

Listed APPROVED
Bridport DT6 3PA
☎ (01308) 424864
Fax (01308) 456747
Comfortable, spacious, Grade II cottage in historic part of town, close to town centre and near sea. Garden and views.
Bedrooms: 1 twin
Bathrooms: 1 private

Bed & breakfast per night:	£min	£max
Single	17.00	22.00
Double	30.00	45.00

Open March–October

Urella

COMMENDED
65 Burton Road, Bridport DT6 4JE
☎ (01308) 422450
Family home in Hardy country. Ramblers' delight - or relax in our garden. Golf course nearby, West Bay 15 minutes.
Bedrooms: 2 double, 1 twin
Bathrooms: 3 en-suite

Bed & breakfast per night:	£min	£max
Single		24.00
Double		34.00

Half board per person:	£min	£max
Daily	26.00	
Weekly	168.00	

Lunch available
Evening meal 1900 (last orders 2100)
Parking for 5

BRISTOL

Map ref 2A2

Famous for maritime links, historic harbour, Georgian terraces and Brunel's Clifton suspension bridge. Many attractions including SS Great Britain, Bristol Zoo, museums and art galleries and top name entertainments. Events include Balloon Fiesta and Regatta.
Tourist Information Centre ☎ (0117) 926 0767

Harpenden

Listed HIGHLY COMMENDED
149 Richmond Road, Montpelier, Bristol BS6 5ES
☎ (0117) 9240016
Quiet, comfortable Victorian character family house. One mile city

Continued ▶

BRISTOL

Continued

centre/motorway. Television and tea/coffee-making facilities in bedrooms.
Bedrooms: 1 single, 1 double
Bathrooms: 1 public

Bed & breakfast per night:	£min	£max
Single	15.99	17.99
Double	32.00	36.00

Westbury Park Hotel

HIGHLY COMMENDED

37 Westbury Road, Bristol BS9 3AU
☎ (0117) 9620465
Fax (0117) 9628607
Friendly, family-run hotel on Durdham Downs, close to city centre and M5, junction 17.
Bedrooms: 1 single, 5 double, 2 twin
Bathrooms: 8 en-suite

Bed & breakfast per night:	£min	£max
Single	29.00	39.00
Double	45.00	52.00

Parking for 5
Cards accepted: Amex, Diners, Mastercard, Visa
20

BROOMFIELD

Somerset
Map ref 1D1

Westleigh Farm

Listed COMMENDED

Broomfield, Bridgwater TA5 2EH
☎ (01823) 451773
Fax (01823) 451772
30-acre farm with horses. Quiet farmhouse in Quantock Hills, between Bridgwater and Taunton. Backing on to Broomfield Common. Plenty of good walking and fishing nearby, 20 minutes from the seaside. Evening meal by arrangement.
Bedrooms: 1 single, 3 double
Bathrooms: 3 en-suite, 1 public

Bed & breakfast per night:	£min	£max
Single		20.00
Double		40.00

Evening meal 1800 (last orders 2000)
Parking for 20

BUCKFASTLEIGH

Devon
Map ref 1C2

Small manufacturing and market town just south of Buckfast Abbey on the fringe of Dartmoor. Trips can be taken by steam train on a reopened line along the beautiful Dart Valley to the historic town of Totnes.

Dartbridge Inn

HIGHLY COMMENDED

Totnes Road, Buckfastleigh TQ11 OJR
☎ (01364) 642214
Fax (01364) 643977
Picturesque inn on the banks of the River Dart, 200 yards off the A38 between Plymouth and Exeter. 1 mile from Buckfast Abbey.
Bedrooms: 7 double, 4 twin
Bathrooms: 11 en-suite

Bed & breakfast per night:	£min	£max
Single	37.50	42.00
Double	50.00	59.00

Lunch available
Evening meal 1900 (last orders 2130)
Parking for 100
Cards accepted: Mastercard, Visa, Switch/Delta
100

Wellpark Farm

Listed HIGHLY COMMENDED

Dean Prior, Buckfastleigh TQ11 OLY
☎ (01364) 643775
Fax (01364) 643775
500-acre arable & dairy farm. Set on the edge of Dartmoor near Buckfast Abbey. Very comfortable rooms with colour TV and tea/coffee facilities. Relaxing lounge with log fire, delicious farmhouse breakfasts, enclosed garden. A warm and friendly welcome assured. Excellent local 11th C inn. Reductions for children and weekly bookings.
Bedrooms: 1 double, 1 family room
Bathrooms: 1 public

Bed & breakfast per night:	£min	£max
Single	14.00	17.00
Double	28.00	34.00

Parking for 3

You are advised to confirm your booking in writing.

BUCKLAND MONACHORUM

Devon
Map ref 1C2

Village just north of Buckland Abbey, home of Sir Francis Drake. Founded by Cistercians, the building is of unique interest through its conversion into a country home by Sir Richard Grenville. Now a museum of Drake and Grenville mementoes, including Drake's drum. Beautiful gardens.

Store Cottage Bed & Breakfast

HIGHLY COMMENDED

19 The Village, Buckland Monachorum, Yelverton PL20 7NA
☎ (01822) 853117
Fax (01822) 853117

South-facing listed stone house in centre of village. Excellent meals at village pub. Unspoilt countryside at western edge of Dartmoor National Park.
Bedrooms: 1 double, 1 twin
Bathrooms: 2 en-suite

Bed & breakfast per night:	£min	£max
Single	20.00	20.00
Double	40.00	40.00

Parking for 2
12

BUCKLAND NEWTON

Dorset
Map ref 2B3

Village in an Area of Outstanding Natural Beauty, on the edge of the Dorset Downs midway between Dorchester and Sherborne.

Holyleas House

Listed HIGHLY COMMENDED

Buckland Newton, Dorchester DT2 7DP
☎ (01300) 345214 & (01305) 264488
Charming, period country house, set in walled gardens. Peaceful village within easy reach of Sherborne, Dorchester and coast. Pretty rooms, glorious views and walks.
Bedrooms: 1 single, 1 double, 1 twin
Bathrooms: 3 private

Bed & breakfast per night:	£min	£max
Single	19.00	20.00
Double	38.00	40.00

Parking for 12

Rew Cottage

COMMENDED

Buckland Newton, Dorchester DT2 7DN
☎ (01300) 345467

Comfortable, peaceful farmhouse with pretty garden and breathtaking views. Within easy reach of Dorchester and Sherborne. One mile east of Buckland Newton on Mappowder road.

Bedrooms: 1 double, 1 twin
Bathrooms: 2 private

Bed & breakfast per night:	£min	£max
Single	19.00	21.00
Double	38.00	42.00

Parking for 4

BUCKLAND ST MARY

Somerset
Map ref 1D2

Keymer Cottage

Listed HIGHLY COMMENDED

Buckland St Mary, Chard TA20 3JF
☎ (01460) 234460
Fax (01460) 234226

Victorian farmhouse. Fully centrally heated, attractively furnished, recently subject to full renovation. The gardens are stocked with mature shrubs and trees and have been restored by the owners.

Bedrooms: 1 single, 1 double, 1 twin
Bathrooms: 1 en-suite, 1 private, 1 public

Bed & breakfast per night:	£min	£max
Single	20.00	30.00
Double	40.00	50.00

Half board per person:	£min	£max
Daily	35.00	45.00

Evening meal 1900 (last orders 2100)
Parking for 6

BUDE

Cornwall
Map ref 1C2

Resort on dramatic Atlantic coast. High cliffs give spectacular sea and inland views. Golf-course, cricket pitch, folly, surfing, coarse-fishing and boating. Mother-town Stratton was base of Royalist Sir Bevil Grenville.
Tourist Information Centre ☎ (01288) 354240

Cliff Hotel

HIGHLY COMMENDED

Crooklets Beach, Bude EX23 8NG
☎ (01288) 353110
Fax (01288) 353110

Indoor pool, mini-gym, putting, tennis court, bowling green, 5 acres next to National Trust cliffs, 200 yards from the beach. Chef/proprietor.

Bedrooms: 2 single, 3 double, 1 twin, 9 triple
Bathrooms: 15 en-suite

Bed & breakfast per night:	£min	£max
Single	22.50	28.50
Double	45.00	57.00

Half board per person:	£min	£max
Daily	31.50	38.50
Weekly	215.00	265.00

Lunch available
Evening meal 1830 (last orders 2030)
Parking for 15
Open April–September
Cards accepted: Mastercard, Visa, Switch/Delta

Clovelly House

4 Burn View, Bude EX23 8BY
☎ (01288) 352761

In a level location, opposite golf club and close to all amenities. All rooms with tea/coffee facilities, satellite TV, some en-suite.

Bedrooms: 2 single, 2 double, 1 twin, 1 triple
Bathrooms: 3 en-suite, 1 public

Bed & breakfast per night:	£min	£max
Single	14.50	19.00
Double	29.00	40.00

Parking for 2

Lower Northcott Farm

COMMENDED

Poughill, Bude EX23 9EL
☎ (01288) 352350
Fax (01288) 352350

400-acre mixed farm. Georgian farmhouse in secluded grounds with children's safe play area. Visitors welcome to wander around and meet the animals.

Bedrooms: 1 single, 1 twin, 3 family rooms
Bathrooms: 4 en-suite, 1 public

Bed & breakfast per night:	£min	£max
Single	18.00	
Double	36.00	

Half board per person:	£min	£max
Daily	26.00	
Weekly	175.00	

Evening meal 1830 (last orders 1830)
Parking for 4

BURNHAM-ON-SEA

Somerset
Map ref 1D1

Small Victorian resort famous for sunsets and sandy beaches, a few minutes from junction 22 of the M5. Ideal base for touring Somerset, Cheddar and Bath. Good sporting facilities, championship golf-course.
Tourist Information Centre ☎ (01278) 787852

Prospect Farm Guest House

Listed COMMENDED

Strowlands, East Brent, Highbridge TA9 4JH
☎ (01278) 760507

17th C Somerset farmhouse with inglenook fireplaces, bread ovens, beamed ceilings and a colourful history.

Continued ▶

Please check prices and other details at the time of booking.

BURNHAM-ON-SEA

Continued

3 miles from Burnham-on-Sea. Variety of small farm animals and pets. Children welcome.
Bedrooms: 2 double, 2 triple
Bathrooms: 1 en-suite, 1 public

Bed & breakfast per night:	£min	£max
Single	18.00	21.00
Double	36.00	42.00

Parking for 12

BURTON BRADSTOCK

Dorset
Map ref 2A3

Lying amid fields beside the River Bride, a village of old stone houses, a 14th C church and a village green. The beautiful coast road from Abbotsbury to Bridport passes by and Iron Age forts top the surrounding hills. The sheltered river valley makes a staging post for migrating birds.

Bridge Cottage Stores

Listed COMMENDED

87 High Street, Burton Bradstock, Bridport DT6 4RA
☎ (01308) 897222
Self-contained en-suite accommodation in rooms above village shop and tea room. Close to beach, on Bridport to Weymouth road.
Bedrooms: 2 double, 1 twin
Bathrooms: 3 en-suite

Bed & breakfast per night:	£min	£max
Single	14.14	24.50
Double	28.28	39.00

Lunch available
Parking for 8

Pebble Beach Lodge

Coast Road, Burton Bradstock, Bridport DT6 4RJ
☎ (01308) 897428 & (0467) 201383
Located on B3157 coast road, affording panoramic views of heritage coastline. Direct access to beach.
Bedrooms: 8 double, 2 twin
Bathrooms: 9 en-suite, 1 private

Bed & breakfast per night:	£min	£max
Single	19.00	25.00
Double	38.00	44.00

Evening meal 1830 (last orders 1730)
Parking for 10
Open May–September
Cards accepted: Mastercard, Visa

Three Horseshoes

COMMENDED

Mill Street, Burton Bradstock, Bridport DT6 4QZ
☎ (01308) 897259
Thatched inn with car park and garden on the B3157 Bridport to Weymouth road. Menu available AM/PM daily. Log fire in winter.
Bedrooms: 2 double, 1 twin
Suites available
Bathrooms: 3 en-suite

Bed & breakfast per night:	£min	£max
Single	27.00	27.00
Double	40.00	40.00

Lunch available
Evening meal 1830 (last orders 2115)
Parking for 14
Cards accepted: Mastercard, Visa, Switch/Delta

CALNE

Wiltshire
Map ref 2B2

Prosperity from wool in the 15th C endowed this ancient market town with a fine church in the Perpendicular style. To the east are chalk downlands and at Oldbury Castle, an Iron Age fort, a 17th C white horse is carved into the hillside.

Maundrell House

COMMENDED

Horsebrook, The Green, Calne SN11 8DL
☎ (01249) 821267
Fax (01249) 821267

Attractive Grade II stone house in conservation area in cul-de-sac off The Green. Two comfortable rooms which share a bathroom.
Bedrooms: 2 double
Bathrooms: 1 public

Bed & breakfast per night:	£min	£max
Single	28.00	28.00
Double	38.00	38.00

CARBIS BAY

Cornwall
Map ref 1B3

Overlooking St Ives Bay and with fine beaches.

White House Hotel

COMMENDED

The Valley, Carbis Bay, St Ives TR26 2QY
☎ (01736) 797405 & 797426
Relaxed and friendly family-run hotel situated at the bottom of a woody valley, 150 yards to Carbis Bay beach. Cosy a la carte restaurant.
Bedrooms: 4 double, 2 twin, 1 triple, 1 family room
Bathrooms: 8 en-suite, 1 public

Bed & breakfast per night:	£min	£max
Single	30.00	40.00
Double	40.00	60.00

Half board per person:	£min	£max
Daily	33.00	43.00
Weekly	199.50	238.00

Lunch available
Evening meal 1900 (last orders 2130)
Parking for 10
Open March–October
Cards accepted: Mastercard, Visa, Switch/Delta

CHALLACOMBE

Devon
Map ref 1C1

Small, attractive village surrounded by the stunning countryside of the Exmoor National Park. Close to the North Devon coast, a number of National Trust properties and family attractions.

Twitchen Farm

COMMENDED

Challacombe, Barnstaple EX31 4TT
☎ (01598) 763568
Fax (01598) 763310
Email: kdenby@easynet.co.uk

18th C stone-built courtyard farm with unusual arched windows, characteristic of the Fortescue Estate. Enjoy the peace and panoramic views whilst staying in our newly converted accommodation. Web site address http://www.castlelink.co.uk/gratton/twitchen
Bedrooms: 3 double, 2 twin, 2 triple, 1 family room
Bathrooms: 8 en-suite

Bed & breakfast per night:	£min	£max
Single	19.00	25.00
Double	38.00	50.00

Half board per person:	£min	£max
Daily	31.50	37.50
Weekly	201.50	237.50

Evening meal 1900 (last orders 1930)
Parking for 10

CHARMINSTER

Dorset
Map ref 2B3

Three Compasses Inn

COMMENDED

Charminster, Dorchester DT2 9QT
☎ (01305) 263618

Traditional village public house/inn with skittle alley, set in village square.
Bedrooms: 1 single, 1 double, 1 twin, 1 triple
Bathrooms: 2 en-suite, 1 public

Bed & breakfast per night:	£min	£max
Single	17.50	
Double	37.50	

Lunch available
Evening meal 1900 (last orders 2200)
Parking for 50

CHEDDAR

Somerset
Map ref 1D1

Large village at foot of Mendips just south of the spectacular Cheddar Gorge. Close by are Roman and Saxon sites and famous show caves. Traditional Cheddar cheese is still made here.

Constantine

Listed COMMENDED

Lower New Road, Cheddar BS27 3DY
☎ (01934) 742732
Very friendly family home with beautiful views, close to village and Gorge. Large garden available to guests. Children welcome. Private sitting room.
Bedrooms: 1 single, 1 double, 1 triple
Bathrooms: 1 public, 1 private shower

Bed & breakfast per night:	£min	£max
Single	15.00	15.00
Double	30.00	30.00

Parking for 6

Tor Farm

HIGHLY COMMENDED

Nyland, Cheddar BS27 3UP
☎ (01934) 743710
Fax (01934) 743710
33-acre mixed farm. On A371 between Cheddar and Draycott (take the road signposted Nyland). Quiet and peaceful on Somerset Levels. Ideally situated for visiting Cheddar, Bath, Wookey Hole, Glastonbury, Wells and coast.
Bedrooms: 1 single, 5 double, 1 twin, 1 family room
Bathrooms: 5 en-suite, 2 public

Bed & breakfast per night:	£min	£max
Single	19.00	25.00
Double	33.00	44.00

Evening meal from 1800
Parking for 10
Cards accepted: Mastercard, Visa

COLOUR MAPS

Colour maps at the back of this guide pinpoint all places in which you will find accommodation listed.

CHEW MAGNA

Bath & North East Somerset
Map ref 2A2

Prosperous redstone village in the Mendip Hills with fine houses, cottages and inns of varying periods. High Street rises between railed, raised pavements from a part-Norman church with lofty 15th C tower.

Woodbarn Farm

COMMENDED

Denny Lane, Chew Magna, Bristol BS18 8SZ
☎ (01275) 332599
70-acre mixed farm. Central for touring Bath, Bristol, Wells and Cheddar. 3 minutes from Chew Valley Lake. En-suite bedrooms. Large farmhouse breakfasts. Warm welcome.
Bedrooms: 1 double, 1 family room
Bathrooms: 2 en-suite

Bed & breakfast per night:	£min	£max
Single	20.00	22.00
Double	36.00	40.00

Parking for 4
Open March–December

CHIPPENHAM

Wiltshire
Map ref 2B2

Ancient market town with modern industry. Notable early buildings include the medieval Town Hall and the gabled 15th C Yelde Hall, now a local history museum. On the outskirts Hardenhuish has a charming hilltop church by the Georgian architect John Wood of Bath.
Tourist Information Centre ☎ (01249) 657733

Frogwell House

COMMENDED

132 Hungerdown Lane, Chippenham SN14 0BD
☎ (01249) 650328
Fax (01249) 650328
Imposing late 19th C house built of local stone, modernised to provide comfortable and appealing accommodation.
Bedrooms: 1 single, 1 double, 2 twin
Bathrooms: 2 en-suite, 2 private

Bed & breakfast per night:	£min	£max
Single	16.00	22.00
Double	32.00	37.00

Continued ▶

CHIPPENHAM

Continued

Half board per person:	£min	£max
Daily	22.00	28.00

Evening meal from 1800
Parking for 6

75 Rowden Hill

APPROVED

Chippenham SN15 2AL
☎ (01249) 652981

Near National Trust village of Lacock and attractive Castle Combe. Corsham Court also nearby. Friendly welcome assured.

Bedrooms: 2 double, 1 twin
Bathrooms: 1 public

Bed & breakfast per night:	£min	£max
Single		16.00
Double		26.00

Parking for 5

5

CHISELDON

Wiltshire
Map ref 2B2

Large village occupying a steep hilly site on the south side of Swindon.

Norton House

Listed COMMENDED

46 Draycott Road, Chiseldon, Swindon SN4 0LS
☎ (01793) 741210 & 0973 406669

Executive country house in rural location with easy access from M4. Central for Bath, Oxford, Stonehenge and Cotswolds. TV, tea/coffee. Garden, parking.

Bedrooms: 1 single, 2 double, 1 twin
Bathrooms: 2 en-suite, 1 public

Bed & breakfast per night:	£min	£max
Single	20.00	22.00
Double	38.00	44.00

Parking for 4
Open January–October, December

5

COLOUR MAPS

Colour maps at the back of this guide pinpoint all places in which you will find accommodation listed.

CHULMLEIGH

Devon
Map ref 1C2

Small, hilly town above the Little Dart River, long since by-passed by the main road. The large 15th C church is noted for its splendid rood screen and 38 carved wooden angels on the roof.

The Old Bakehouse

HIGHLY COMMENDED

South Molton Street, Chulmleigh EX18 7BW
☎ (01769) 580074 & 580137

16th C merchant's house with licensed restaurant. En-suite bedrooms in converted bakehouse. Situated in beautiful Taw Valley between Dartmoor and Exmoor National Parks. Unique atmosphere, caring hosts. Excellent cuisine using local produce and drinks.

Bedrooms: 2 double, 2 twin
Bathrooms: 4 en-suite

Bed & breakfast per night:	£min	£max
Single	23.00	23.00
Double	46.00	46.00

Half board per person:	£min	£max
Daily	37.00	37.00
Weekly	231.00	231.00

Lunch available
Evening meal 1945 (last orders 2030)
Cards accepted: Mastercard, Visa, Switch/Delta

2

CLAWTON

Devon
Map ref 1C2

Small village on the road between Holsworthy and Launceston.

Claw House

Listed COMMENDED

Clawton, Holsworthy EX22 6QJ
☎ (01409) 253930

Georgian farmhouse in pretty village. Spacious and comfortable. Lovely views. Ideal for touring Devon and Cornwall. Home cooking. Off-road parking.

Bedrooms: 1 single, 1 double, 1 twin
Bathrooms: 1 en-suite, 2 public

Bed & breakfast per night:	£min	£max
Single	16.00	
Double	32.00	

Evening meal 1800 (last orders 2000)
Parking for 8

CLOVELLY

Devon
Map ref 1C1

Clinging to wooded cliffs, fishing village with steep cobbled street zigzagging, or cut in steps, to harbour. Carrying sledges stand beside whitewashed flower-decked cottages. Charles Kingsley's father was rector of the church set high up near the Hamlyn family's Clovelly Court.

Dyke Green Farm

COMMENDED

Clovelly, Bideford EX39 5RU
☎ (01237) 431699 & 431279

50-acre arable farm. Tastefully converted barn offering good quality bed and breakfast in lovely, fully-equipped en-suite rooms. Full English breakfast. Warm welcome. Non-smoking.

Bedrooms: 2 double, 1 twin
Bathrooms: 2 en-suite, 1 private, 1 public

Bed & breakfast per night:	£min	£max
Single	20.00	25.00
Double	38.00	42.00

Parking for 6
Open February–November

Fuchsia Cottage

Listed COMMENDED

Burscott, Clovelly, Bideford EX39 5RR
☎ (01237) 431398

Private house with comfortable ground and first floor en-suite accommodation. Surrounded by beautiful views of sea and country. Good walking area. Ample parking.

Bedrooms: 2 single, 1 double, 1 triple
Bathrooms: 2 en-suite, 1 public

Bed & breakfast per night:	£min	£max
Single		13.00
Double		34.00

Evening meal from 1830
Parking for 3
Open April–October

COLD ASHTON

South Gloucestershire
Map ref 2B2

Rectory Farm

Cold Ashton, Chippenham, Wiltshire SN14 8JS
☎ (01225) 891218
Farmhouse situated on the Cotswold Way and only 5 minutes from M4, Bath and Bristol.
Bedrooms: 1 double, 1 twin
Bathrooms: 2 en-suite

Bed & breakfast per night:	£min	£max
Single	29.95	35.00
Double	38.00	42.00

Parking for 10

COLYTON

Devon
Map ref 1D2

Surrounded by fertile farmland, this small riverside town was an early Saxon settlement. Medieval prosperity from the wool trade built the grand church tower with its octagonal lantern and the church's fine west window.

Smallicombe Farm

COMMENDED
Northleigh, Colyton EX13 6BU
☎ (01404) 831310
Fax (01404) 831431
25-acre mixed farm. Escape the fast lane and unwind watching traditional farm animals in idyllic rural setting. Meet our prize-winning pigs. Explore the coast from Lyme to Sidmouth or walk the East Devon Way.
Bedrooms: 1 double, 1 family room
Suites available
Bathrooms: 2 en-suite

Bed & breakfast per night:	£min	£max
Single	18.50	21.00
Double	37.00	42.00

Parking for 10

For farm holidays and accommodation suitable for young people and organised groups, please refer to the special sections at the back of this guide.

CORSHAM

Wiltshire
Map ref 2B2

Growing town with old centre showing Flemish influence, legacy of former prosperity from weaving. The church, restored last century, retains Norman features. The Elizabethan Corsham Court, with additions by Capability Brown, has fine furniture.

Halfway Firs

Listed COMMENDED
5 Halfway Firs, Corsham SN13 0PJ
☎ (01225) 810552
Situated 7 miles from Bath on A4, 5 miles from Chippenham and 1 mile from Corsham, overlooking open farmland.
Bedrooms: 1 single, 1 double, 1 triple
Bathrooms: 1 public

Bed & breakfast per night:	£min	£max
Single	18.00	20.00
Double	30.00	34.00

Parking for 4

Heatherly Cottage

COMMENDED
Ladbrook Lane, Gastard, Corsham SN13 9PE
☎ (01249) 701402
Fax (01249) 701412
Delightful 17th C cottage in 1.5 acres with views over open countryside. Rooms with TV and hospitality trays. Many pubs serving food nearby. Bath 9 miles. Ample parking.
Bedrooms: 2 double, 1 twin
Bathrooms: 3 en-suite

Bed & breakfast per night:	£min	£max
Single	21.00	22.00
Double	36.00	39.00

Parking for 10

CRACKINGTON HAVEN

Cornwall
Map ref 1C2

Tiny village on the North Cornwall coast, with a small sandy beach and surf bathing. The highest cliffs in Cornwall lie to the south.

Coombe Barton Inn

APPROVED
Crackington Haven EX23 0JG
☎ (01840) 230345
Fax (01840) 230788
Warm and friendly inn beside the beach, serving good food, local ales, fine wines and offering comfortable accommodation.
Bedrooms: 1 single, 2 double, 1 twin, 1 family room
Bathrooms: 3 en-suite, 2 public

Bed & breakfast per night:	£min	£max
Single	20.50	24.50
Double	38.00	58.00

Lunch available
Evening meal 1800 (last orders 2200)
Parking for 40
Open March–October
Cards accepted: Amex, Diners, Mastercard, Visa, Switch/Delta

Hallagather Farmhouse

COMMENDED
Crackington Haven, Bude EX23 0LA
☎ (01840) 230276
184-acre livestock farm. Ancient farmhouse, 4 miles north of Boscastle and one and a quarter miles from beach, spectacular heritage coast scenery and footpaths. Substantial Cornish breakfasts, informality, warmth and individual attention.
Bedrooms: 1 single, 1 double, 1 triple
Bathrooms: 2 en-suite, 1 private

Bed & breakfast per night:	£min	£max
Single	17.00	24.00
Double	30.00	44.00

Parking for 6
Open January–November

CREDITON

Devon
Map ref 1D2

Ancient town in fertile valley, once prosperous from wool, now active in cider-making. Said to be the birthplace of St Boniface. The 13th C Chapter House, the church governors' meeting place, holds a collection of armour from the Civil War.

Birchmans Farm

COMMENDED
Colebrooke, Crediton EX17 5AD
☎ (01363) 82393
200-acre mixed farm. In the centre of Devon within easy reach of Exeter and Dartmoor. All rooms en-suite with tea

Continued ▶

CREDITON

Continued

and coffee-making facilities. Log fire in lounge. Panoramic views of unspoilt countryside.

Bedrooms: 2 double, 1 twin
Bathrooms: 3 en-suite

Bed & breakfast per night:	£min	£max
Single	16.00	
Double	30.00	

Half board per person:	£min	£max
Daily	24.00	
Weekly	156.00	

Evening meal (last orders 1830)
Parking for 6

CREWKERNE

Somerset
Map ref 1D2

This charming little market town on the Dorset border nestles in undulating farmland and orchards in a conservation area. Built of local sandstone with Roman and Saxon origins. The magnificent St Bartholomew's Church dates from 15th C; St Bartholomew's Fair is held in September.

Broadview Gardens

DE LUXE

East Crewkerne, Crewkerne
TA18 7AG
☎ (01460) 73424
Fax (01460) 73424

Unusual Colonial bungalow, a winner of awards for quality, friendliness and traditional English cooking. En-suite rooms overlooking acre of beautiful secluded gardens. Dorset border, perfect touring base.

Bedrooms: 1 double, 2 twin
Bathrooms: 2 en-suite, 1 private

Bed & breakfast per night:	£min	£max
Single	35.00	46.00
Double	50.00	56.00

Half board per person:	£min	£max
Daily	39.00	42.00
Weekly	273.00	294.00

Evening meal 1830 (last orders 1200)
Parking for 6
Cards accepted: Mastercard, Visa, Switch/Delta

CROYDE

Devon
Map ref 1C1

Pretty village with thatched cottages near Croyde Bay. To the south stretch Saunton Sands and their dunelands Braunton Burrows with interesting flowers and plants, nature reserve and golf-course. Cliff walks and bird-watching at Baggy Point, west of the village.

Denham Farm and Country House

COMMENDED

North Buckland, Braunton
EX33 1HY
☎ (01271) 890297
Fax (01271) 890297

160-acre mixed farm. Sample home cooking in this delightful country house, a "little gem" off the beaten track. Enjoy peace and tranquillity amid beautiful unspoilt countryside, near miles of golden sands.

Bedrooms: 6 double, 1 twin, 1 triple, 2 family rooms
Bathrooms: 10 en-suite, 1 public

Bed & breakfast per night:	£min	£max
Single	30.00	
Double	50.00	54.00

Half board per person:	£min	£max
Daily	37.00	39.00
Weekly	215.00	240.00

Evening meal 1900 (last orders 1900)
Parking for 11
Cards accepted: Mastercard, Visa

Please mention this guide when making your booking.

All accommodation in this guide has been graded, or is awaiting a grading, by a trained Tourist Board inspector.

CROYDE BAY

Devon
Map ref 1C1

Hamlet on the North Devon coast, west of Croyde village, with fine surfing beaches and magnificent cliff scenery.

West Winds

COMMENDED

Moor Lane, Croyde Bay, Braunton
EX33 1PA
☎ (01271) 890489 & 0831 211247
Fax (01271) 890489

Picturesque water's edge location, private access to Croyde beach. Ideal for walking, touring and golf. Comfortable and relaxing atmosphere.

Bedrooms: 1 single, 3 double, 1 twin
Bathrooms: 4 en-suite, 1 public, 1 private shower

Bed & breakfast per night:	£min	£max
Single	31.00	35.00
Double	46.00	52.00

Half board per person:	£min	£max
Daily	35.00	38.00

Evening meal 1830 (last orders 1800)
Parking for 6
Open March–November
Cards accepted: Mastercard, Visa

CULLOMPTON

Devon
Map ref 1D2

Market town on former coaching routes, with pleasant tree-shaded cobbled pavements and some handsome 17th C houses. Earlier prosperity from the wool industry is reflected in the grandness of the church with its fan-vaulted aisle built by a wool-stapler in 1526.

Aller Barton Farm

COMMENDED

Cullompton EX15 1QQ
☎ (01884) 32275
Fax (01884) 35837

250-acre dairy farm. Ideal centre from which to experience glorious Devon. Delightful, spacious farmhouse on family farm. Relax in garden. Tennis court, games room. Brochure available.
Bedrooms: 1 twin, 1 triple
Bathrooms: 2 en-suite

Bed & breakfast per night:	£min	£max
Single	17.00	
Double	32.00	

Half board per person:	£min	£max
Daily	24.00	
Weekly	145.00	

Evening meal from 1900

Weir Mill Farm

HIGHLY COMMENDED
Jaycroft, Willand, Cullompton EX15 2RE
☎ (01884) 820803
Fax (01884) 820973

105-acre livestock farm. Farmhouse accommodation in the beautiful Culm Valley. Only 3 miles from junction 27 of M5, giving easy access to coast, moors and National Trust properties.
Bedrooms: 2 double, 1 family room
Bathrooms: 1 private, 1 public

Bed & breakfast per night:	£min	£max
Single	18.00	20.00
Double	32.00	36.00

Half board per person:	£min	£max
Daily	26.00	30.00
Weekly	167.00	180.00

Evening meal 1830 (last orders 0900)
Parking for 5

DARTMOOR

See under Ashburton, Bovey Tracey, Bridestowe, Buckfastleigh, Buckland Monachorum, Lustleigh, Manaton, Moretonhampstead, Okehampton, Peter Tavy, Tavistock, Widecombe-in-the-Moor, Yelverton

DARTMOUTH

Devon
Map ref 1D3

Ancient port at mouth of Dart. Has fine period buildings, notably town houses near Quay and Butterwalk of 1635. Harbour castle ruin. In 12th C Crusader fleets assembled here. Royal Naval College dominates from Hill. Carnival, June; Regatta, August.
Tourist Information Centre ☎ (01803) 834224

The Captains House

HIGHLY COMMENDED
18 Clarence Street, Dartmouth TQ6 9NW
☎ (01803) 832133
18th C listed house. Tasteful decor and personal service. Close to river and shops.
Bedrooms: 1 single, 3 double, 1 twin
Bathrooms: 4 en-suite, 1 private

Bed & breakfast per night:	£min	£max
Single	28.00	35.00
Double	42.00	55.00

Ford House

HIGHLY COMMENDED
44 Victoria Road, Dartmouth TQ6 9DX
☎ (01803) 834047 & 0378 771971
Fax (01803) 834047

All the assets of a hotel but the intimacy of a guesthouse. Centrally located. Twin or king-sized beds. Breakfast served until noon.
Bedrooms: 3 double, 1 twin
Bathrooms: 3 en-suite, 1 private

Bed & breakfast per night:	£min	£max
Single	35.00	70.00
Double	50.00	70.00

Half board per person:	£min	£max
Daily	60.00	95.00
Weekly	420.00	665.00

Lunch available
Evening meal 1900 (last orders 2100)
Parking for 5
Open March–October
Cards accepted: Amex, Mastercard, Visa

Woodside Cottage

HIGHLY COMMENDED
Blackawton, Totnes TQ9 7BL
☎ (01803) 712375
Fax (01803) 712605
Email: john@woodside-cottage.demon.co.uk
18th C Devon house, formerly a gamekeeper's cottage. Set on side of beautiful valley, west of Dartmouth. Panoramic views. Log fires, beamed ceilings, guests' lounge. Ample parking.
Bedrooms: 3 double
Bathrooms: 3 en-suite

Bed & breakfast per night:	£min	£max
Single	24.00	26.66
Double	36.00	40.00

Parking for 6
Open February–November

DAWLISH

Devon
Map ref 1D2

Small resort, developed in Regency and Victorian periods beside Dawlish Water. Town centre has ornamental riverside gardens with black swans. One of England's most scenic stretches of railway was built by Brunel alongside jagged red cliffs between the sands and the town.
Tourist Information Centre ☎ (01626) 863589

West Hatch Hotel

HIGHLY COMMENDED
34 West Cliff, Dawlish EX7 9DN
☎ (01626) 864211 & 862948
Fax (01626) 864211
Recently refurbished, quality, licensed hotel. Centrally situated overlooking sea. All rooms en-suite, some ground floor, four-poster. Excellent breakfast menu.
Bedrooms: 7 double, 1 twin, 2 triple
Suite available
Bathrooms: 10 en-suite, 1 public

Bed & breakfast per night:	£min	£max
Single	30.00	36.00
Double	44.00	64.00

Parking for 12
Cards accepted: Mastercard, Visa, Switch/Delta

A key to symbols can be found inside the back cover flap.

DEVIZES

Wiltshire
Map ref 2B2

Old market town standing on the Kennet and Avon Canal. Rebuilt Norman castle, good 18th C buildings. St John's church has 12th C work and Norman tower. Museum of Wiltshire's archaeology and natural history reflects wealth of prehistoric sites in the county. *Tourist Information Centre ☎ (01380) 729408*

Eastcott Manor

APPROVED

Easterton, Devizes SN10 4PL
☎ (01380) 813313
Grade II listed Elizabethan manor house in own 20-acre grounds. Tranquil situation on edge of Salisbury Plain. Nearest road B3098.*
Bedrooms: 1 single, 2 double
Bathrooms: 2 en-suite, 1 private

Bed & breakfast per night:	£min	£max
Single	19.00	25.00
Double	40.00	42.00

Half board per person:	£min	£max
Daily	34.00	40.00

Evening meal 1930 (last orders 1930)
Parking for 20

The Gate House

Listed COMMENDED

Wick Lane, Devizes SN10 5DW
☎ (01380) 725283
Fax (01380) 725283
Family home, comfortable and clean. Log fire in winter. Short walk to town. Friendly welcome. No dogs and no smoking please.
Bedrooms: 1 single, 1 double, 1 twin
Bathrooms: 1 en-suite, 1 public

Bed & breakfast per night:	£min	£max
Single	16.50	
Double		40.00

Parking for 8
Open January–November and Christmas

For ideas on places to visit refer to the introduction at the beginning of this section.

Heathcote House

The Green, Devizes SN10 2JG
☎ (01380) 725080
Georgian family house dated 1786 with lots of original features. Situated on the green in the market town of Devizes near the sports centre (swimming pool, etc) and near the canal.
Bedrooms: 2 double
Bathrooms: 1 en-suite, 1 private

Bed & breakfast per night:	£min	£max
Single	20.00	20.00
Double	35.00	40.00

The Old Coach House

COMMENDED

21 Church Street, Market Lavington, Devizes SN10 4DU
☎ (01380) 812879
Fax (01380) 812879
Comfortable, spacious 18th C home south of Devizes. All rooms en-suite. Delicious breakfast. Convenient Salisbury, Bath and many places of interest. Ideal for short breaks.
Bedrooms: 1 double, 2 twin
Bathrooms: 3 en-suite

Bed & breakfast per night:	£min	£max
Single		26.00
Double		43.50

Parking for 5

Pinecroft

Potterne Road (A360), Devizes SN10 5DA
☎ (01380) 721433
Fax (01380) 721229
Comfortable Georgian family house with spacious rooms, exquisite garden and private parking. Only 3 minutes' walk from town centre.
Wheelchair access category 3
Bedrooms: 2 double, 2 twin, 1 family room
Suite available
Bathrooms: 4 en-suite, 1 private

Bed & breakfast per night:	£min	£max
Single	30.00	30.00
Double	45.00	45.00

Parking for 7
Cards accepted: Amex, Mastercard, Visa

Stroud Hill Farm

Listed HIGHLY COMMENDED

Potterne Wick, Potterne, Devizes SN10 5QR
☎ (01380) 720371
Delightful farmhouse, set in 140 acres of Wiltshire countryside, just 2.5 miles south of Devizes. An ideal base from which to explore. Private sitting room with open fire.
Bedrooms: 1 double, 1 twin
Bathrooms: 2 private

Bed & breakfast per night:	£min	£max
Single		18.00
Double		35.00

Parking for 6

DODDISCOMBSLEIGH

Devon
Map ref 1D2

Riverside village amid hilly countryside just east of Dartmoor. Former manor house stands beside granite church. Spared from the Roundheads by its remoteness, the church's chief interest lies in glowing 15th C windows said to contain Devon's finest collection of medieval glass.

Whitemoor Farm

APPROVED

Doddiscombsleigh, Exeter EX6 7PU
☎ (01647) 252423
284-acre mixed farm. Homely 16th C thatched farmhouse, surrounded by garden and own farmland. Within easy reach of Dartmoor, the coast, Exeter, forest walks, birdwatching and Haldon Racecourse. Evening meal on request with good local inn nearby. Swimming pool available.
Bedrooms: 2 single, 1 double, 1 twin
Bathrooms: 1 public

Bed & breakfast per night:	£min	£max
Single	17.50	18.00
Double	35.00	36.00

Half board per person:	£min	£max
Daily	26.00	28.00
Weekly	119.50	121.50

Evening meal 1900 (last orders 2000)
Parking for 5

DORCHESTER

Dorset
Map ref 2B3

Busy medieval county town destroyed by fires in 17th and 18th C. Cromwellian stronghold and scene of Judge Jeffreys' Bloody Assize after Monmouth Rebellion of 1685. Tolpuddle Martyrs were tried in Shire Hall. Museum has Roman and earlier exhibits and Hardy relics.

Tourist Information Centre ☎ (01305) 267992

Mountain Ash

APPROVED

30 Mountain Ash Road, Dorchester DT1 2PB
☎ (01305) 264811

Comfortable accommodation close to transport, Records Office and museums. Washbasins, TV, beverage facilities in bedrooms. Owner knowledgeable about Dorset.

Bedrooms: 1 single, 1 double, 1 twin
Bathrooms: 1 public

Bed & breakfast per night:	£min	£max
Single	15.00	18.00
Double	30.00	36.00

Parking for 5

The Old Rectory

HIGHLY COMMENDED

Winterbourne Steepleton, Dorchester DT2 9LG
☎ (01305) 889468
Fax (01305) 889737
Email: trees@zynet.co.uk

Built 1850 - 8 miles from beaches, 6 miles from historic Dorchester. Surrounded by spectacular walks. Excellent local pubs or private dining facilities. French spoken.

Bedrooms: 3 double, 1 twin, 1 family room
Bathrooms: 4 en-suite, 1 private

Bed & breakfast per night:	£min	£max
Single	28.00	30.00
Double	38.00	90.00

Parking for 10

Tarkaville

COMMENDED

30 Shaston Crescent, Manor Park, Dorchester DT1 2EB
☎ (01305) 266253

Lovely accommodation in attractive modern house on edge of town. Quiet area, close to all amenities. Warm welcome, many facilities.

Bedrooms: 1 double, 1 twin
Bathrooms: 1 public

Bed & breakfast per night:	£min	£max
Single	16.00	20.00
Double	32.00	35.00

Parking for 3

DULVERTON

Somerset
Map ref 1D1

Set among woods and hills of south-west Exmoor, a busy riverside town with a 13th C church. The Rivers Barle and Exe are rich in salmon and trout. The information centre at the Exmoor National Park Headquarters at Dulverton is open throughout the year.

Scatterbrook Farm

APPROVED

Hinam Cross, Dulverton TA22 9QQ
☎ (01398) 323857

28-acre mixed farm. Small working farm in Exmoor National Park. Ideal walking, riding (stabling available). Dogs welcome and, of course, children. Beautiful scenery.

Wheelchair access category 1
Bedrooms: 1 single, 2 double
Bathrooms: 2 en-suite, 1 public

Bed & breakfast per night:	£min	£max
Single	15.00	20.00
Double	25.00	30.00

Half board per person:	£min	£max
Daily	24.00	29.00
Weekly	168.00	203.00

Evening meal 1800 (last orders 1900)
Parking for 6

COLOUR MAPS

Colour maps at the back of this guide pinpoint all places in which you will find accommodation listed.

Town Mills

HIGHLY COMMENDED

High Street, Dulverton TA22 9HB
☎ (01398) 323124

Secluded 19th C millhouse in centre of town. Spacious bedrooms, some with log fires, providing bedsitting facilities with breakfast served in rooms.

Bedrooms: 3 double, 2 twin
Suite available
Bathrooms: 3 en-suite, 1 public

Bed & breakfast per night:	£min	£max
Single	21.00	36.00
Double	35.00	44.00

Parking for 5

DUNSTER

Somerset
Map ref 1D1

Ancient town with views of Exmoor. The hilltop castle has been continuously occupied since 1070. Medieval prosperity from cloth built 16th C octagonal Yarn Market and the church. A riverside mill, packhorse bridge and 18th C hilltop folly occupy other interesting corners in the town.

Woodville House

Listed COMMENDED

25 West Street, Dunster, Minehead TA24 6SN
☎ (01643) 821228

Georgian house in the residential end of the village. Warm welcome, comfortable accommodation, good breakfast, homely relaxing atmosphere assured. Parking available in courtyard.

Bedrooms: 1 single, 1 double, 1 twin
Bathrooms: 1 public

Bed & breakfast per night:	£min	£max
Single	17.00	19.00
Double	36.00	40.00

Parking for 4
Open March–November

The map references refer to the colour maps towards the end of the guide. The first figure is the map number; the letter and figure which follow indicate the grid reference on the map.

EAST TYTHERTON

Wiltshire
Map ref 2B2

Village 3 miles east of Chippenham.

Barnbridge

Listed APPROVED

East Tytherton, Chippenham
SN15 4LT
☎ (01249) 740280
Self-contained wing of country farmhouse enjoying beautiful views. Tennis court and private heated indoor/outdoor swimming pool.
Bedrooms: 1 single, 1 twin, 1 triple
Bathrooms: 1 public

Bed & breakfast per night:	£min	£max
Single	16.00	20.00
Double	32.00	40.00

Half board per person:	£min	£max
Daily	22.00	26.00

Evening meal 1900 (last orders 2100)
Parking for 6

ENFORD

Wiltshire
Map ref 2B2

Village beside the River Avon, on Salisbury Plain, 2 miles south of Upavon. Stonehenge 9 miles south.

Enford House

COMMENDED

Enford, Pewsey SN9 6DJ
☎ (01980) 670414
Listed country house with pretty garden. In attractive village 7 miles from Stonehenge. Good food at local village pub. Quiet and comfortable.
Bedrooms: 1 double, 2 twin
Bathrooms: 3 public

Bed & breakfast per night:	£min	£max
Single	18.00	
Double	32.00	

Evening meal 1830 (last orders 1300)
Parking for 8
Cards accepted: Amex

Establishments should be open throughout the year, unless otherwise stated.

ERLESTOKE

Wiltshire
Map ref 2B2

Village on Salisbury Plain, 6 miles east of Westbury.

Longwater

COMMENDED

Lower Road, Erlestoke, Devizes
SN10 5UE
☎ (01380) 830095
Fax (01380) 830095

160-acre beef farm. Lakes, woods, coarse fishing and adjacent to golf-course. Traditional farm fare, with local produce and wines. Wheelchair friendly.
Wheelchair access category 2
Bedrooms: 2 double, 2 twin, 1 triple
Bathrooms: 5 en-suite

Bed & breakfast per night:	£min	£max
Single	25.00	30.00
Double	40.00	44.00

Half board per person:	£min	£max
Daily	31.00	42.00
Weekly	200.00	290.00

Lunch available
Evening meal 1900 (last orders 1000)
Parking for 8

EXETER

Devon
Map ref 1D2

University city rebuilt after the 1940s around its cathedral. Attractions include 13th C cathedral with fine west front; notable waterfront buildings; Guildhall; Royal Albert Memorial Museum; underground passages; Northcott Theatre.
Tourist Information Centre ☎ (01392) 265700

Danson House

COMMENDED

Marsh Green, Exeter EX5 2ES
☎ (01404) 823260

Large country house in rural location. Excellent award-winning en-suite accommodation. 2 miles from A30 and with easy access from M5. http://www.webscape.co.uk/danson/
Bedrooms: 1 double, 2 triple
Bathrooms: 3 en-suite

Bed & breakfast per night:	£min	£max
Single	20.00	22.00
Double	34.00	38.00

Half board per person:	£min	£max
Daily	28.00	32.00
Weekly	165.00	180.00

Evening meal 1900 (last orders 2000)
Parking for 4

The Grange

COMMENDED

Stoke Hill, Exeter EX4 7JH
☎ (01392) 259723
Country house set in 3 acres of woodlands, 1.5 miles from the city centre. Ideal for holidays and off-season breaks. En-suite rooms.
Bedrooms: 2 double, 1 twin
Bathrooms: 3 en-suite

Bed & breakfast per night:	£min	£max
Single	20.00	22.00
Double	30.00	37.00

Parking for 11

Hayne Barton

COMMENDED

Whitestone, Exeter EX4 2JN
☎ (01392) 811268
16-acre mixed farm. Listed farmhouse dating from 1086 (Domesday Book), set in gardens, woodland and fields overlooking Alphinbrook Valley. 4 miles from Exeter Cathedral and convenient for Dartmoor and Torquay.
Bedrooms: 2 double, 1 twin
Bathrooms: 3 en-suite

Bed & breakfast per night:	£min	£max
Single	24.00	26.00
Double	44.00	48.00

Half board per person:	£min	£max
Daily	34.00	36.00
Weekly	210.00	224.00

Evening meal 1930 (last orders 2030)
Parking for 10

Lochinvar

COMMENDED

Shepherds Park Farm, Woodbury, Exeter EX5 1LA
☎ (01395) 232185

250-acre dairy farm. Near Woodbury village, in beautiful countryside. Spacious rooms, furnished to a high standard, with colour TV, tea/coffee facilities. Off-road parking.
Bedrooms: 1 double, 1 twin, 1 triple
Bathrooms: 2 en-suite, 1 private

Bed & breakfast per night:	£min	£max
Single	19.00	20.00
Double	36.00	40.00

Parking for 4

EXMOOR

See under Challacombe, Dulverton, Dunster, Lynmouth, Lynton, Timberscombe, West Anstey, Wheddon Cross, Winsford

EXMOUTH

Devon
Map ref 1D2

Developed as a seaside resort in George III's reign, set against the woods of the Exe Estuary and red cliffs of Orcombe Point. Extensive sands, small harbour, chapel and almshouses, a model railway and A la Ronde, a 16-sided house.
Tourist Information Centre ☎ (01395) 222299

The Mews

COMMENDED

Knappe Cross, Brixington Lane, Exmouth EX8 5DL
☎ (01395) 272198
Large part of a delightfully secluded mews building in a country setting. Midway between Exmouth and Woodbury Common. We ask that guests refrain from smoking.
Bedrooms: 1 single, 1 double, 1 twin
Bathrooms: 1 public

Bed & breakfast per night:	£min	£max
Single	15.50	16.50
Double	31.00	33.00

Parking for 10

FALMOUTH

Cornwall
Map ref 1B3

Busy port and fishing harbour, popular resort on the balmy Cornish Riviera. Henry VIII's Pendennis Castle faces St Mawes Castle across the broad natural harbour and yacht basin Carrick Roads, which receives 7 rivers.
Tourist Information Centre ☎ (01326) 312300

Ivanhoe Guest House

COMMENDED

7 Melvill Road, Falmouth TR11 4AS
☎ (01326) 319083
Charming Edwardian town house situated minutes from the beaches and town centre. Most rooms are en-suite with colour TV and all amenities.
Bedrooms: 2 single, 1 double, 1 twin, 2 triple, 1 family room
Bathrooms: 4 en-suite, 2 public

Bed & breakfast per night:	£min	£max
Single	18.00	22.00
Double	36.00	44.00

Parking for 4
Cards accepted: Amex, Diners, Mastercard, Visa, Switch/Delta

FENNY BRIDGES

Devon
Map ref 1D2

Village on the River Otter, 2 miles north-east of Ottery St Mary.

Skinners Ash Farm

Listed COMMENDED

Fenny Bridges, Honiton EX14 0BH
☎ (01404) 850231
127-acre mixed farm. Family-run rare breeds farm on A30, 3 miles from Honiton and close to beaches. Home cooking, pony rides. Brochure available.
Bedrooms: 1 twin, 1 family room
Bathrooms: 2 public

Bed & breakfast per night:	£min	£max
Single		16.00
Double		32.00

Half board per person:	£min	£max
Daily		24.00
Weekly		160.00

Lunch available
Evening meal 1900 (last orders 2100)
Parking for 7

FIGHELDEAN

Wiltshire
Map ref 2B2

Village on the River Avon, 4 miles north of Amesbury. Stonehenge 6 miles south west.

Vale House

COMMENDED

Figheldean, Salisbury SP4 8JJ
☎ (01980) 670713
Secluded house in centre of picturesque village, 4 miles north of Amesbury on A345. Pub food nearby. Stonehenge 2 miles.
Bedrooms: 1 single, 2 twin
Bathrooms: 1 en-suite, 1 private, 1 public

Bed & breakfast per night:	£min	£max
Single	15.00	17.00
Double	29.00	33.00

Parking for 3

FONTHILL GIFFORD

Wiltshire
Map ref 2B2

Village north of Tisbury. The 18th C architect, James Wyatt, built the now ruined Fonthill Abbey. Old Wardour Castle, 4 miles south.

Beckford Arms

COMMENDED

Fonthill Gifford, Tisbury, Salisbury SP3 6PX
☎ (01747) 870385
Fax (01747) 851496
Tasteful refurbished, stylish and comfortable 18th C inn, between Tisbury and Hindon in area of outstanding beauty. 2 miles A303. Convenient for Salisbury and Shaftesbury.
Bedrooms: 3 single, 4 double, 1 twin
Bathrooms: 5 en-suite, 3 private showers

Continued ▶

FONTHILL GIFFORD

Continued

Bed & breakfast per night:	£min	£max
Single	34.50	34.50
Double	54.50	59.50

Half board per person:	£min	£max
Daily	39.00	
Weekly	227.50	

Lunch available
Evening meal 1900 (last orders 2200)
Parking for 42
Cards accepted: Amex, Mastercard, Visa, Switch/Delta

FROME

Somerset
Map ref 2B2

Old market town with modern light industry, its medieval centre watered by the River Frome. Above Cheap Street with its flagstones and watercourse is the church showing work of varying periods. Interesting buildings include 18th C wool merchants' houses.
Tourist Information Centre ☎ (01373) 467271

Fourwinds Guest House

COMMENDED

19 Bath Road, Frome BA11 2HJ
☎ (01373) 462618
Fax (01373) 453029
Comfortable and friendly guesthouse with all the amenities of a small hotel. Half a mile north of town centre.
Wheelchair access category 3
Bedrooms: 1 single, 2 double, 2 twin, 1 family room
Bathrooms: 4 en-suite, 2 public

Bed & breakfast per night:	£min	£max
Single	25.00	30.00
Double	40.00	50.00

Half board per person:	£min	£max
Daily	35.00	42.00

Evening meal 1800 (last orders 1900)
Parking for 12
Cards accepted: Mastercard, Visa, Switch/Delta

GLASTONBURY

Somerset
Map ref 2A2

Market town associated with Joseph of Arimathea and the birth of English Christianity. Built around its 7th C abbey said to be the site of King Arthur's burial. Glastonbury Tor with its ancient tower gives panoramic views over flat country and the Mendip Hills.
Tourist Information Centre ☎ (01458) 832954

Little Orchard

Listed COMMENDED

Ashwell Lane, Glastonbury
BA6 8BG
☎ (01458) 831620
On the A361 Glastonbury to Shepton Mallet road. Good central position for touring the West Country. At the foot of historic Glastonbury Tor, with views over the Vale of Avalon.
Bedrooms: 1 single, 1 double, 1 triple, 1 family room
Bathrooms: 1 public

Bed & breakfast per night:	£min	£max
Single	15.00	17.00
Double	30.00	34.00

Parking for 4

Meadow Barn

COMMENDED

Middlewick Farm, Wick Lane, Glastonbury BA6 8JW
☎ (01458) 832351
Fax (01458) 832351
20-acre beef farm. Idyllically situated amidst apple orchards and gardens, Meadow Barn has country-style ground-floor accommodation with indoor heated swimming pool. From Glastonbury take A361 Shepton Mallet road for 1.5 miles, take left turn signposted Wick, continue for 1.5 miles.
Bedrooms: 2 double, 1 twin
Bathrooms: 3 en-suite

Bed & breakfast per night:	£min	£max
Single	22.00	24.00
Double	36.00	38.00

Half board per person:	£min	£max
Daily	30.50	35.50
Weekly	213.50	248.50

Evening meal 1900 (last orders 2030)
Parking for 20

Wick Hollow House

HIGHLY COMMENDED

8 Wick Hollow, Glastonbury
BA6 8JJ
☎ (01458) 833595
Fax (01458) 834244
Peaceful, self-contained accommodation with private sitting room, on ground floor of lovely house overlooking Chalice Hill and the Tor. Special rates for stays of more than 3 nights. Children half price.
Bedrooms: 1 family room
Suite available
Bathrooms: 1 en-suite

Bed & breakfast per night:	£min	£max
Single	28.00	30.00
Double	40.00	45.00

Parking for 3

Wyrrall House

HIGHLY COMMENDED

78 The Roman Way, Glastonbury
BA6 8AD
☎ (01458) 835510 & 0976 978060

Beautiful Victorian house in elevated, peaceful gardens backing on to fields of historic Weanfall Hill. Spacious, well-appointed rooms, breakfast menu, car park. 15 minutes' walk to Glastonbury.
Bedrooms: 1 double, 1 twin, 1 triple
Bathrooms: 1 en-suite, 2 private

Bed & breakfast per night:	£min	£max
Single	25.00	
Double	39.00	

Parking for 10

You are advised to confirm your booking in writing.

Half board prices are given per person, but in some cases these may be based on double/twin occupancy.

GOONHAVERN

Cornwall
Map ref 1B3

September Lodge

COMMENDED

Wheal Hope, Goonhavern, Truro
TR4 9QJ
☎ (01872) 571435

Warm relaxed atmosphere. Spacious rooms in lovely setting, close to beautiful beaches, golf courses and coarse fishing lakes. Breakfasts at flexible times.

Bedrooms: 1 double, 1 family room
Bathrooms: 2 en-suite

Bed & breakfast per night:	£min	£max
Single	18.00	25.00
Double	36.00	38.00

Parking for 4

GORRAN HAVEN

Cornwall
Map ref 1B3

Once important in the pilchard fisheries, now a seaside village gathered at the mouth of its valley. A medieval chapel and Methodist church stand among the cottages overlooking the quay and beautiful unspoilt cliffs spread south-west of Dodman Point.

Llawnroc Inn

COMMENDED

Gorran Haven, St Austell PL26 6NU
☎ (01726) 843461

Small, family-run pub/hotel with a local inn atmosphere and fresh, home-cooked food. All bedrooms face the sea and have magnificent views.

Bedrooms: 4 double, 2 twin, 1 triple, 1 family room
Bathrooms: 5 en-suite, 1 private, 1 public

Bed & breakfast per night:	£min	£max
Single	22.00	28.00
Double	40.00	48.00

Lunch available
Evening meal 1900 (last orders 2130)
Parking for 36
Cards accepted: Amex, Diners, Mastercard, Visa

40

Please check prices and other details at the time of booking.

GRAMPOUND

Cornwall
Map ref 1B3

Village on the River Fal, 6 miles south-west of St Austell. Probus Gardens 3 miles south-west.

Perran House

APPROVED

Fore Street, Grampound, Truro
TR2 4RS
☎ (01726) 882066

Delightful listed cottage in the pretty village of Grampound, between St Austell and Truro. Central for touring.

Bedrooms: 2 single, 3 double, 1 twin
Bathrooms: 3 en-suite, 1 public

Bed & breakfast per night:	£min	£max
Single	15.00	16.00
Double	32.00	36.00

Parking for 6
Cards accepted: Mastercard, Visa, Switch/Delta

GREAT BEDWYN

Wiltshire
Map ref 2B2

The Cross Keys Inn

Listed APPROVED

High Street, Great Bedwyn, Marlborough SN8 3NU
☎ (01672) 870678

18th C oak-beamed pub with log fire, in centre of pretty village, close to Kennet and Avon Canal.

Bedrooms: 2 twin, 1 family room
Bathrooms: 1 en-suite, 1 private, 1 public

Bed & breakfast per night:	£min	£max
Single	27.00	30.00
Double	39.00	42.00

Lunch available
Evening meal 1800 (last orders 2100)
Cards accepted: Amex, Mastercard, Visa

50

ACCESSIBILITY

Look for the symbols which indicate accessibility for wheelchair users. These are described in detail at the front of this guide.

GREINTON

Somerset
Map ref 1D1

Village on the southern slopes of the Polden Hills, within easy reach of Bridgwater and the historic town of Glastonbury.

West Town Farm

COMMENDED

Greinton, Bridgwater TA7 9BW
☎ (01458) 210277

Original part of house is over 200 years old, with large inglenook fire and bread oven, flagstone floors and Georgian front. Listed building. Non-smoking establishment.

Bedrooms: 1 double, 1 twin
Bathrooms: 2 en-suite

Bed & breakfast per night:	£min	£max
Single	20.00	24.00
Double	38.00	42.00

Parking for 2
Open March–September

03

GRITTLETON

Wiltshire
Map ref 2B2

The Neeld Arms Inn

COMMENDED

The Street, Grittleton, Chippenham
SN14 6AP
☎ (01249) 782470
Fax (01249) 782470

Charming 17th C inn, in picturesque village near Castle Combe. Comfortable en-suite rooms, four-poster and family room. Excellent home-cooked food, real ales, log fires. Easy access from M4.

Bedrooms: 2 double, 3 twin, 1 family room
Bathrooms: 6 en-suite

Bed & breakfast per night:	£min	£max
Single	34.50	
Double	46.50	

Continued ▶

GRITTLETON

Continued

Lunch available
Evening meal 1900 (last orders 2130)
Parking for 20
Cards accepted: Mastercard, Visa, Switch/Delta

HARBERTONFORD

Devon
Map ref 1D2

The Hungry Horse Restaurant

COMMENDED

Old Road, Harbertonford, Totnes TQ9 7TA
☎ (01803) 732441
Fax (01803) 732780

John and Caroline invite you to stay in this delightful old building and sample some of the finest food in the south west. Only local produce used - fish a speciality.

Bedrooms: 3 double
Bathrooms: 3 en-suite

Bed & breakfast per night:	£min	£max
Single	25.00	32.00
Double	45.00	50.00

Evening meal 1800 (last orders 2130)
Parking for 8
Open February–December
Cards accepted: Mastercard, Visa, Switch/Delta

Information on accommodation listed in this guide has been supplied by the proprietors. As changes may occur you are advised to check details at the time of booking.

The symbols in each entry give information about services and facilities. A key to these symbols appears at the back of this guide.

HARTLAND

Devon
Map ref 1C1

Hamlet on high, wild country near Hartland Point. Just west, the parish church tower makes a magnificent landmark; the light, unrestored interior holds one of Devon's finest rood screens. There are spectacular cliffs around Hartland Point and the lighthouse.

Elmscott Farm

HIGHLY COMMENDED

Hartland, Bideford EX39 6ES
☎ (01237) 441276

650-acre mixed farm. In a coastal setting, quietly situated near the Devon/Cornwall border. Signposted from the main A39, about 4 miles away.

Bedrooms: 2 double, 1 twin
Bathrooms: 2 en-suite, 1 public

Bed & breakfast per night:	£min	£max
Single	20.00	
Double	40.00	

Half board per person:	£min	£max
Daily	28.50	

Evening meal 1800 (last orders 2000)
Parking for 8
Open January–October

HATCH BEAUCHAMP

Somerset
Map ref 1D1

Village with wooded slopes in the heart of rural Somerset. Hatch Court, a fine Bath stone Palladian mansion, is close by.

Hatch Inn

Village Road, Hatch Beauchamp, Taunton TA3 6SG
☎ (01823) 480245

In village on A358, 6 miles or 10 minutes from the centre of Taunton and 5 minutes from junction 25 of M5.

Bedrooms: 1 double, 2 triple, 2 family rooms
Bathrooms: 2 public

Bed & breakfast per night:	£min	£max
Single	17.50	
Double	33.00	

Lunch available
Evening meal 1900 (last orders 2200)
Parking for 20

HATHERLEIGH

Devon
Map ref 1C2

Set in pastoral countryside, small town with thatched cottages and a cattle market. There are trout and salmon streams close by.

George Hotel

APPROVED

Market Street, Hatherleigh, Okehampton EX20 3JN
☎ (01837) 810454
Fax (01837) 810901

14th C coaching inn with cobbled courtyard, thatched roof, cob walls, blackened beams and blazing log fires. A la carte restaurant, 3 character bars, heated swimming pool in summer. Traditional four-poster beds.

Bedrooms: 1 single, 7 double, 3 twin
Bathrooms: 9 en-suite, 2 private, 1 public

Bed & breakfast per night:	£min	£max
Single	28.50	48.50

Half board per person:	£min	£max
Daily	42.00	62.00
Weekly	250.00	360.00

Lunch available
Evening meal 1900 (last orders 2145)
Parking for 40
Cards accepted: Amex, Mastercard, Visa, Switch/Delta

The National Grading and Classification Scheme is explained at the back of this guide.

HELSTON

Cornwall
Map ref 1B3

Handsome town with steep, main street and narrow alleys. In medieval times it was a major port and stannary town. Most buildings date from Regency and Victorian periods. The famous May dance, the Furry, is thought to have pre- Christian origins. A museum occupies the old Butter Market.
Tourist Information Centre ☎ (01326) 565431

Longstone Farm

COMMENDED
Trenear, Helston TR13 0HG
☎ (01326) 572483

57-acre beef farm. In peaceful countryside in west Cornwall. Ideal for touring and beaches. Flambards and swimming pool nearby. B3297 to Redruth, left for Coverack Bridges. Right at bottom of hill, continue left for about 1.5 miles to the farm.
Bedrooms: 1 double, 1 twin, 2 triple, 1 family room
Bathrooms: 3 en-suite, 2 private

Bed & breakfast per night:	£min	£max
Single	18.00	20.00
Double	36.00	40.00

Half board per person:	£min	£max
Daily	26.50	28.50
Weekly	145.00	155.00

Evening meal 1800 (last orders 0900)
Parking for 6
Open February–October

HENSTRIDGE

Somerset
Map ref 2B3

Village with a rebuilt church containing the Tudor Carent tomb.

Fountain Inn Motel

APPROVED
High Street, Henstridge, Templecombe BA8 0RA
☎ (01963) 362722
Just off the A30 on the A357 Henstridge to Stalbridge road. Country inn (1700) with modern en-suite motel-type accommodation.
Wheelchair access category 3
Bedrooms: 6 double
Bathrooms: 6 en-suite

Bed & breakfast per night:	£min	£max
Single	18.00	25.00
Double	25.00	35.00

Lunch available
Evening meal 1800 (last orders 2230)
Parking for 28
Cards accepted: Amex, Diners, Mastercard, Visa, Switch/Delta

HIGHWORTH

Wiltshire
Map ref 2B2

Small town 6 miles north-east of Swindon with square of 17th C and 18th C buildings close to the church.

Roves Farm

COMMENDED
Sevenhampton, Highworth, Swindon SN6 7QG
☎ (01793) 763939
Fax (01793) 763939
450-acre arable & livestock farm. Spacious, comfortable, quiet accommodation surrounded by beautiful countryside. Panoramic views, farm trails and full range of farm animals. Signposted in Sevenhampton village.
Bedrooms: 1 twin, 1 triple
Bathrooms: 2 en-suite

Bed & breakfast per night:	£min	£max
Single	22.00	23.00
Double	35.00	36.00

Parking for 5

HOLSWORTHY

Devon
Map ref 1C2

Busy rural town and centre of a large farming community. Market day attracts many visitors.

The Barton

COMMENDED
Pancrasweek, Holsworthy EX22 7JT
☎ (01288) 381315
200-acre dairy farm. At the Devon/Cornwall border on the A3072, 3.5 miles from Holsworthy and 6 miles from the Cornish coast. Friendly atmosphere and home cooking with home-produced vegetables.
Bedrooms: 2 double, 1 twin
Bathrooms: 3 en-suite

Bed & breakfast per night:	£min	£max
Single	16.00	17.00
Double	32.00	34.00

Half board per person:	£min	£max
Daily	24.00	25.00
Weekly	168.00	175.00

Evening meal 1800 (last orders 1600)
Parking for 5
Open April–September

The Bickford Arms

COMMENDED
Brandis Corner, Holsworthy EX22 7XY
☎ (01409) 221318
Fax (01409) 221781

17th C thatched inn, newly renovated but retaining beautiful old world appeal. Old-fashioned wood fires in lounge and restaurant. Elegant bedrooms.
Bedrooms: 5 family rooms
Bathrooms: 5 en-suite

Bed & breakfast per night:	£min	£max
Single	35.00	39.00
Double	50.00	60.00

Half board per person:	£min	£max
Daily	33.00	47.00

Lunch available
Evening meal 1730 (last orders 2130)
Parking for 47
Cards accepted: Mastercard, Visa

For farm holidays and accommodation suitable for young people and organised groups, please refer to the special sections at the back of this guide.

HONITON

Devon
Map ref 1D2

Old coaching town in undulating farmland. Formerly famous for lace-making, it is now an antiques trade centre and market town. Small museum.
Tourist Information Centre ☎ (01404) 43716

Barn Park Farm

COMMENDED

Stockland Hill, Nr Cotleigh, Honiton EX14 9JA
☎ (01404) 861297
140-acre dairy farm. Barn Park farmhouse is full of character. Sloping floors and exposed beams all add to the homely atmosphere. Farm walks.
Bedrooms: 1 double, 1 twin
Bathrooms: 1 public

Bed & breakfast per night:	£min	£max
Single	16.00	18.00
Double	32.00	32.00

Half board per person:	£min	£max
Daily	25.00	27.00
Weekly	160.00	160.00

Lunch available
Evening meal 1800 (last orders 2100)
Parking for 20

ILFRACOMBE

Devon
Map ref 1C1

Resort of Victorian grandeur set on hillside between cliffs with sandy coves. At the mouth of the harbour stands an 18th C lighthouse, built over a medieval chapel. There are fine formal gardens and a museum. Chambercombe Manor, an interesting old house, is nearby.
Tourist Information Centre ☎ (01271) 863001

Belvedere

HIGHLY COMMENDED

12 Broad Park Avenue, Ilfracombe EX34 8DZ
☎ (01271) 862710
Beautiful, balconied Victorian house. Hill and valley views, garden, ample parking, close to walks. Friendly personal service. Evening dinner by request. No smoking except on balconies.
Bedrooms: 2 double, 1 twin
Bathrooms: 2 en-suite, 1 private

Bed & breakfast per night:	£min	£max
Single	20.00	26.00
Double	34.00	44.00

Half board per person:	£min	£max
Daily	30.00	36.00
Weekly	172.00	200.00

Evening meal from 1730
Parking for 7

IVYBRIDGE

Devon
Map ref 1C2

Town set in delightful woodlands on the River Erme. Brunel designed the local railway viaduct. South Dartmoor Leisure Centre.
Tourist Information Centre ☎ (01752) 897035

Hillhead Farm

COMMENDED

Ugborough, Ivybridge PL21 0HQ
☎ (01752) 892674 & 0385 915612
Fax (01752) 690111
77-acre mixed farm. Spacious family farmhouse, surrounded by fields. All home-cooked and largely home-grown food. From A38 turn off at Wrangaton Cross, turn left, take third right over crossroads, after half a mile go straight over next crossroads, after three-quarters of a mile turn left, farm is 75 yards on left.
Bedrooms: 2 double, 1 twin
Bathrooms: 2 en-suite, 1 private

Bed & breakfast per night:	£min	£max
Single	18.00	20.00
Double	36.00	40.00

Half board per person:	£min	£max
Daily	28.00	30.00
Weekly	182.00	196.00

Evening meal 1900 (last orders 2100)
Parking for 5

ACCESSIBILITY

Look for the symbols which indicate accessibility for wheelchair users. These are described in detail at the front of this guide.

KINGSBRIDGE

Devon
Map ref 1C3

Formerly important as a port, now a market town overlooking head of beautiful, wooded estuary winding deep into rural countryside. Summer art exhibitions; Cookworthy Museum.
Tourist Information Centre ☎ (01548) 853195

Globe Inn

COMMENDED

Frogmore, Kingsbridge TQ7 2NR
☎ (01548) 531351
Friendly village freehouse at the head of Frogmore Creek. Atmospheric restaurant and bars. Real ales, good food, open fires, beer garden and parking.
Bedrooms: 3 double, 1 twin, 2 family rooms
Bathrooms: 3 en-suite, 2 public

Bed & breakfast per night:	£min	£max
Single	18.00	26.00
Double	32.00	42.00

Lunch available
Evening meal 1800 (last orders 2200)
Parking for 20
Cards accepted: Mastercard, Visa, Switch/Delta

LACOCK

Wiltshire
Map ref 2B2

Village of great charm. Medieval buildings of stone, brick or timber-frame have jutting storeys, gables, oriel windows. Magnificent church has perpendicular fan-vaulted chapel with grand tomb to benefactor who, after Dissolution, bought Augustinian nunnery, Lacock Abbey.

Lacock Pottery Bed and Breakfast

COMMENDED

1 The Tanyard, Church Street, Lacock, Chippenham SN15 2LB
☎ (01249) 730266
A 200-year-old workhouse, now a working pottery in a National Trust medieval village.
Bedrooms: 1 double, 1 twin
Bathrooms: 1 en-suite, 1 private

Bed & breakfast per night:	£min	£max
Single	25.00	35.00
Double	50.00	60.00

Parking for 3

LANGPORT

Somerset
Map ref 1D1

Small market town with Anglo-Saxon origins, sloping to River Parrett. Well-known for glove making and, formerly, for eels. Interesting old buildings include some fine local churches.

Tuckers Hill

HIGHLY COMMENDED

Frog Lane, Langport TA10 ONE
☎ (01458) 250413

Secluded stone cottages close to historic Langport. Magnificent views across Somerset Levels. Ideal for touring, walking, wildlife or that well-deserved rest. Acclaimed cooking.

Bedrooms: 1 double, 1 triple
Bathrooms: 2 en-suite

Bed & breakfast per night:	£min	£max
Single	19.50	23.00
Double	35.00	39.00

Half board per person:	£min	£max
Daily	30.40	37.40

Lunch available
Evening meal 1900 (last orders 2100)
Parking for 6
Open April–October and Christmas

LAUNCESTON

Cornwall
Map ref 1C2

Medieval "Gateway to Cornwall", county town until 1838, founded by the Normans under their hilltop castle near the original monastic settlement. This market town, overlooked by its castle ruin, has a square with Georgian houses and an elaborately-carved granite church.
Tourist Information Centre ☎ (01566) 772321 or 772333

Lower Dutson Farm

COMMENDED

Lower Dutson Farm, Launceston PL15 9SP
☎ (01566) 776456

200-acre mixed farm. 17th C listed farmhouse, right on the Devon/Cornwall border, ideal for touring both counties, moors and coasts.

Bedrooms: 1 double, 1 family room
Bathrooms: 1 en-suite, 1 private

Bed & breakfast per night:	£min	£max
Single	17.00	
Double	30.00	36.00

Parking for 6

The Old Vicarage

HIGHLY COMMENDED

Treneglos, Launceston PL15 8UQ
☎ (01566) 781351

Elegant Georgian vicarage in idyllic rural setting near spectacular North Cornwall coast. Renowned for hospitality and good food. Highest standards throughout. Organic kitchen gardens. Non-smoking.

Bedrooms: 2 double
Bathrooms: 2 en-suite

Bed & breakfast per night:	£min	£max
Double	46.00	48.00

Half board per person:	£min	£max
Daily	38.00	39.00

Evening meal 1800 (last orders 2130)
Parking for 10
Open March–October and Christmas

LERRYN

Cornwall
Map ref 1C2

Ship Inn

Listed COMMENDED

Lerryn, Lostwithiel PL22 0PT
☎ (01208) 872374

17th C riverside country inn in a rural village location. Central for coast and moors. Golf, horse riding, coarse/fly/sea fishing and beaches within 5 miles.

Bedrooms: 4 double
Bathrooms: 4 en-suite

Bed & breakfast per night:	£min	£max
Double	40.00	45.00

Half board per person:	£min	£max
Daily		33.00

Lunch available
Evening meal 1830 (last orders 2100)
Cards accepted: Mastercard, Visa, Switch/Delta

LEWDOWN

Devon
Map ref 1C2

Small village on the very edge of Dartmoor. Lydford Castle is 4 miles to the east.

Old Cottage

Listed COMMENDED

Dippertown, Lewdown, Okehampton EX20 4PT
☎ (01566) 783250

Stone-built house. Old part with original beams and fireplaces, rest modern. Quiet rural location with lovely woodland walks and close to Dartmoor. Good home cooking on Aga.

Bedrooms: 1 double
Bathrooms: 1 en-suite, 1 public

Bed & breakfast per night:	£min	£max
Single	18.00	
Double	36.00	40.00

Half board per person:	£min	£max
Daily	26.00	35.00
Weekly	182.00	245.00

Evening meal 1800 (last orders 2130)
Parking for 5

LISKEARD

Cornwall
Map ref 1C2

Former stannary town with a livestock market and light industry, at the head of a valley running to the coast. Handsome Georgian and Victorian residences and a Victorian Guildhall reflect the prosperity of the mining boom. The large church has an early 20th C tower and a Norman font.

Tregondale Farm

HIGHLY COMMENDED

Menheniot, Liskeard PL14 3RG
☎ (01579) 342407
Fax (01579) 342407

200-acre mixed farm. Characteristic farmhouse in beautiful countryside. En-suite bedrooms with TV and tea/coffee. Home-produced food our

Continued ▶

LISKEARD

Continued

speciality. Log fires, tennis court. North east of Menheniot, between A38 and A390.
Bedrooms: 1 double, 1 twin, 1 triple
Bathrooms: 2 en-suite, 1 private

Bed & breakfast per night:	£min	£max
Single	20.00	22.00
Double	36.00	39.00

Half board per person:	£min	£max
Daily	28.00	29.50
Weekly	189.00	195.00

Evening meal 1900 (last orders 1800)
Parking for 3

Tresulgan Farm

HIGHLY COMMENDED

Menheniot, Liskeard PL14 3PU
☎ (01503) 240268
Fax (01503) 240268

145-acre mixed farm. Picturesque views from 17th C farmhouse of character, with original beams. Lots to explore in this beautiful area. A friendly welcome awaits.
Bedrooms: 1 double, 1 triple, 1 family room
Bathrooms: 3 en-suite

Bed & breakfast per night:	£min	£max
Single	19.00	21.00
Double	38.00	40.00

Half board per person:	£min	£max
Daily	26.00	28.00
Weekly	182.00	196.00

Evening meal 1830 (last orders 1900)
Parking for 3

The symbol after an establishment name indicates that it is a Regional Tourist Board member.

LODDISWELL

Devon
Map ref 1C3

Millside

Listed HIGHLY COMMENDED

Avon Mill, Loddiswell, Kingsbridge TQ7 4DD
☎ (01548) 550409
Fax (01548) 550147
Friendly, family home, serving good food and evening meals by arrangement. Situated in peaceful hamlet with superb valley views.
Bedrooms: 1 single, 1 double, 1 twin
Suite available
Bathrooms: 1 public, 1 private shower

Bed & breakfast per night:	£min	£max
Single	23.00	26.00
Double	35.00	39.00

Half board per person:	£min	£max
Daily	28.50	37.00
Weekly	187.00	240.00

Parking for 4

LONGDOWN

Devon
Map ref 1D2

Willhayes Farm

COMMENDED

Longdown, Exeter EX6 7BN
☎ (01392) 832636
45-acre mixed farm. Mainly sheep grazing. Carp and trout ponds. Wild flowers and butterflies abound and birds of prey are often seen.
Bedrooms: 1 double, 1 twin, 1 triple
Bathrooms: 3 en-suite

Bed & breakfast per night:	£min	£max
Double	33.00	36.00

Half board per person:	£min	£max
Daily	25.00	26.50
Weekly	163.45	172.90

Evening meal 1900 (last orders 1600)
Parking for 6
Open February–November

Map references apply to the colour maps at the back of this guide.

LOOE

Cornwall
Map ref 1C2

Small resort developed around former fishing and smuggling ports occupying the deep estuary of the East and West Looe Rivers. Narrow winding streets, with old inns; museum and art gallery are housed in interesting old buildings. Shark fishing centre, boat trips; busy harbour.

Bucklawren Farm

HIGHLY COMMENDED

St Martin-by-Looe, Looe PL13 1NZ
☎ (01503) 240738
Fax (01503) 240481

534-acre arable & dairy farm. Set in glorious countryside with beautiful sea views. Only 1.5 miles from beach. Family and en-suite accommodation with colour TV. Delicious farmhouse cooking.
Bedrooms: 2 double, 1 twin, 2 triple, 1 family room
Bathrooms: 5 en-suite, 1 public

Bed & breakfast per night:	£min	£max
Single	25.00	25.00
Double	38.00	42.00

Half board per person:	£min	£max
Daily	30.00	31.00
Weekly	196.00	203.00

Evening meal 1800 (last orders 1800)
Parking for 10
Open March–October
Cards accepted: Mastercard, Visa

Coombe Farm

HIGHLY COMMENDED

Widegates, Looe PL13 1QN
☎ (01503) 240223
Fax (01503) 240895

Lovely country house in wonderful tranquil setting with superb views to

the sea. Delicious food, log fires and warm, friendly hospitality. 3.5 miles east of Looe on B3253.
Bedrooms: 3 double, 3 twin, 2 triple, 2 family rooms
Bathrooms: 10 en-suite

Bed & breakfast per night:	£min	£max
Single	23.00	29.00
Double	46.00	58.00

Half board per person:	£min	£max
Daily	38.00	44.00
Weekly	252.00	294.00

Evening meal 1900 (last orders 1900)
Parking for 12
Open March–October
Cards accepted: Amex, Diners, Mastercard, Visa, Switch/Delta

Hall Barton Farm

COMMENDED

Pelynt, Looe PL13 2LG
☎ (01503) 220203
Fax (01503) 220203

275-acre arable & livestock farm. Grade II listed farmhouse overlooking fields in village of Pelynt on B3359. 3 miles from Looe and Polperro. Close to coarse fishing. Pony trekking, woodland walks.
Bedrooms: 2 double, 1 twin
Bathrooms: 2 en-suite, 1 private, 1 public

Bed & breakfast per night:	£min	£max
Single	15.00	24.00
Double	30.00	40.00

Parking for 7
Open March–December

Kantara Guest House

COMMENDED

7 Trelawney Terrace, Looe PL13 2AG
☎ (01503) 262093
Licensed guesthouse close to beach and shops. Informal, friendly atmosphere. Ideal family holiday setting and touring base. Satellite TV in all rooms.
Bedrooms: 1 single, 1 double, 1 twin, 1 triple, 2 family rooms
Bathrooms: 2 public

Bed & breakfast per night:	£min	£max
Single	12.00	15.50
Double	24.00	31.00

Half board per person:	£min	£max
Daily	22.00	25.50
Weekly	150.00	174.00

Evening meal 1800 (last orders 1900)
Parking for 1
Cards accepted: Amex, Mastercard, Visa

Little Larnick Farm

COMMENDED

Pelynt, Looe PL13 2NB
☎ (01503) 262837
Fax (01503) 262837
200-acre mixed & dairy farm. Spacious, character en-suite accommodation in the beautiful West Looe River Valley. Peaceful and relaxing. Superb farmhouse breakfast.
Bedrooms: 1 double, 1 twin, 1 triple
Bathrooms: 3 en-suite

Bed & breakfast per night:	£min	£max
Double	36.00	40.00

Parking for 3
Open February–November

Stonerock Cottage

COMMENDED

Portuan Road, Hannafore, Looe PL13 2DN
☎ (01503) 263651
Modernised, old world cottage facing south to the Channel. Ample free parking. 2 minutes from the beach, shops, tennis and other amenities.
Bedrooms: 1 single, 2 double, 1 triple
Bathrooms: 3 private, 1 public

Bed & breakfast per night:	£min	£max
Single	15.00	16.00
Double	34.00	40.00

Parking for 4
Open February–October

For further information on accommodation establishments use the coupons at the back of this guide.

LUSTLEIGH

Devon
Map ref 1D2

Riverside village of pretty thatched cottages gathered around its 15th C church. The traditional Mayday festival has dancing round the maypole. Just west is Lustleigh Cleave, where Dartmoor is breached by the River Bovey which flows through a deep valley of boulders and trees.

The Mill

Listed COMMENDED

Lustleigh, Newton Abbot TQ13 9SS
☎ (01647) 277357
12-acre smallholding. Historic riverside millhouse on edge of beautiful Dartmoor village. Exposed beams, antique furniture, home-grown produce.
Bedrooms: 1 single, 2 double
Suite available
Bathrooms: 1 en-suite, 1 public

Bed & breakfast per night:	£min	£max
Single		22.00
Double	37.00	39.00

Parking for 3

LUXBOROUGH

Somerset
Map ref 1D1

Royal Oak of Luxborough

Luxborough, Watchet TA23 0SH
☎ (01984) 640319 & 640216

14th C unspoilt country inn, with flagstone floors, low beams and inglenook fireplaces. Fresh fish and game specialities.
Bedrooms: 6 double, 2 twin
Bathrooms: 6 en-suite, 2 private, 1 public

Bed & breakfast per night:	£min	£max
Single	25.00	30.00
Double	45.00	45.00

Lunch available
Evening meal 1900 (last orders 2200)
Parking for 8

LYME REGIS

Dorset
Map ref 1D2

Pretty, historic fishing town and resort set against the fossil-rich cliffs of Lyme Bay. In medieval times it was an important port and cloth centre. The Cobb, a massive stone breakwater, shelters the ancient harbour which is still lively with boats.
Tourist Information Centre ☎ (01297) 442138

Coverdale Guest House

COMMENDED

Woodmead Road, Lyme Regis
DT7 3AB
☎ (01297) 442882

Bright, spacious, non-smoking house. Well furnished, comfortable bedrooms with excellent en-suite facilities and sea/country views. Short walk to town, restaurants and beach. Parking.

Bedrooms: 2 single, 2 double, 1 twin, 3 triple
Bathrooms: 6 en-suite, 1 public

Bed & breakfast per night:	£min	£max
Single	16.00	20.00
Double	30.00	40.00

Parking for 9
Open March–October
8

Higher Spence

Listed APPROVED

Wootton Fitzpaine, Bridport
DT6 6DF
☎ (01297) 560556

Rural farm cottage with country and sea views. 3 miles Charmouth, 5 miles Lyme Regis.

Bedrooms: 1 double, 1 triple
Bathrooms: 1 public

Bed & breakfast per night:	£min	£max
Single	14.00	16.00
Double	28.00	32.00

Parking for 3
3

Lydwell House

COMMENDED

Lyme Road, Uplyme, Lyme Regis
DT7 3TJ
☎ (01297) 443522

Delightful Victorian house in attractive gardens, ideally located for coast and country walks. Short distance to Lyme Regis town centre and beaches.

Bedrooms: 1 single, 1 double, 1 twin, 2 family rooms
Bathrooms: 2 en-suite, 1 public

Bed & breakfast per night:	£min	£max
Single	17.00	19.00
Double	36.00	44.00

Half board per person:	£min	£max
Daily	29.00	32.00
Weekly	149.00	210.00

Evening meal 1800 (last orders 2000)
Parking for 7

Old Lyme Guest House

COMMENDED

29 Coombe Street, Lyme Regis
DT7 3PP
☎ (01297) 442929

Historic 18th C building in a quiet street in the old town. 3 minutes' walk to sea, shops, restaurants and recently restored town corn mill.

Bedrooms: 4 double, 1 triple
Bathrooms: 4 en-suite, 1 private

Bed & breakfast per night:	£min	£max
Double	40.00	44.00

4

The Red House

HIGHLY COMMENDED

Sidmouth Road, Lyme Regis
DT7 3ES
☎ (01297) 442055

Superb coastal views, large garden, parking. All rooms en-suite.

Bedrooms: 2 twin, 1 triple
Bathrooms: 3 en-suite

Bed & breakfast per night:	£min	£max
Single	30.00	36.00
Double	40.00	50.00

Parking for 4
Open March–November
Cards accepted: Mastercard, Visa, Switch/Delta
8

COLOUR MAPS

Colour maps at the back of this guide pinpoint all places in which you will find accommodation listed.

Southernhaye

COMMENDED

Pound Road, Lyme Regis DT7 3HX
☎ (01297) 443077
Fax (01297) 443077

Distinctive Edwardian house in quiet location with panoramic views over Lyme Bay, about 10 minutes' walk from town and beach. Off-road parking.

Bedrooms: 1 single, 1 double, 1 twin
Bathrooms: 1 public

Bed & breakfast per night:	£min	£max
Single	18.00	18.00
Double	32.00	34.00

Parking for 2

Springfield

COMMENDED

Woodmead Road, Lyme Regis
DT7 3LJ
☎ (01297) 443409

Elegant Georgian house and conservatory in partly walled garden, with well-proportioned rooms, many enjoying views over the sea. Close to major footpaths.

Bedrooms: 1 single, 2 double, 2 twin, 1 triple, 1 family room
Bathrooms: 3 en-suite, 2 public

Bed & breakfast per night:	£min	£max
Single	15.00	20.00
Double	30.00	40.00

Parking for 9
Open February–November

White House

COMMENDED

47 Silver Street, Lyme Regis
DT7 3HR
☎ (01297) 443420

Fine views of Dorset coastline from rear of this 18th C guesthouse. A short walk from beach, gardens and shops.

Bedrooms: 5 double, 2 twin
Bathrooms: 7 en-suite

Bed & breakfast per night:	£min	£max
Double	34.00	42.00

Parking for 6
Open April–September

LYNMOUTH

Devon
Map ref 1C1

Resort set beneath bracken-covered cliffs and pinewood gorges where 2 rivers meet, and cascade between boulders to the town. Lynton, set on cliffs above, can be reached by water-operated cliff railway from the Victorian esplanade. Valley of the Rocks, to the west, gives dramatic walks.

Coombe Farm

COMMENDED

Countisbury, Lynton EX35 6NF
☎ (01598) 741236
365-acre hill farm. Located half a mile off the A39 and 2.5 miles from Lynmouth.
Bedrooms: 2 double, 3 twin, 2 triple, 1 family room
Bathrooms: 4 en-suite, 2 public

Bed & breakfast per night:	£min	£max
Double	35.50	48.00

Parking for 6
Open March–November

LYNTON

Devon
Map ref 1C1

Hilltop resort on Exmoor coast linked to its seaside twin, Lynmouth, by a water-operated cliff railway which descends from the town hall. Spectacular surroundings of moorland cliffs with steep chasms of conifer and rocks through which rivers cascade.
Tourist Information Centre ☎ (01598) 752225

Ingleside Hotel

COMMENDED

Lynton EX35 6HW
☎ (01598) 752223
Family-run hotel with high standards in elevated position overlooking village. Ideal centre for exploring Exmoor.
Bedrooms: 4 double, 1 twin, 2 triple
Bathrooms: 7 en-suite

Bed & breakfast per night:	£min	£max
Single	24.00	27.00
Double	48.00	54.00

Half board per person:	£min	£max
Daily	36.00	39.00
Weekly	238.00	259.00

Evening meal 1900 (last orders 1800)
Parking for 10
Open March–October
Cards accepted: Mastercard, Visa

Kingford House

HIGHLY COMMENDED

Longmead, Lynton EX35 6DQ
☎ (01598) 752361
Private hotel close to Valley of Rocks. Attractive, comfortable rooms, good home-cooked meals with choice of menu. Individual attention assured.
Bedrooms: 2 single, 3 double, 1 twin
Bathrooms: 5 en-suite, 1 private

Bed & breakfast per night:	£min	£max
Single	18.00	21.00
Double	36.00	42.00

Half board per person:	£min	£max
Daily	29.50	32.50

Evening meal 1900 (last orders 1700)
Parking for 8
Open February–December

Sandrock Hotel

COMMENDED

Longmead, Lynton EX35 6DH
☎ (01598) 753307
Fax (01598) 752665

Relaxing Edwardian hotel with modern comforts, in delightful sunny position close to Exmoor's superb coastal scenery and beauty spots.
Bedrooms: 2 single, 4 double, 3 twin
Bathrooms: 7 en-suite, 1 public

Bed & breakfast per night:	£min	£max
Single	19.50	23.00
Double	43.00	49.00

Half board per person:	£min	£max
Daily	31.00	37.50
Weekly	217.00	262.50

Evening meal 1900 (last orders 2000)
Parking for 9
Cards accepted: Amex, Mastercard, Visa, Switch/Delta

South Cheriton Farm

COMMENDED

Barbrook, Lynton EX35 6LJ
☎ (01598) 753280
9-acre mixed farm. 17th C farmhouse with inglenook fireplaces and extensive exposed beams. Set high up in the beautiful Exmoor countryside and offering a traditional welcome.
Bedrooms: 2 double, 1 twin
Bathrooms: 3 en-suite

Bed & breakfast per night:	£min	£max
Single	20.00	22.00
Double	36.00	40.00

Half board per person:	£min	£max
Daily	28.00	30.00

Evening meal from 1900
Parking for 6
Open April–October

South View Guest House

COMMENDED

23 Lee Road, Lynton EX35 6BP
☎ (01598) 752289
Friendly village centre guesthouse offering comfortable bed and breakfast accommodation. All rooms en-suite, overnight guests welcome, private parking. Open all year.
Bedrooms: 3 double, 2 triple
Bathrooms: 5 en-suite

Bed & breakfast per night:	£min	£max
Single	15.00	20.00
Double	30.00	40.00

Parking for 5

All accommodation in this guide has been graded, or is awaiting a grading, by a trained Tourist Board inspector.

WELCOME HOST

This is a nationally recognised customer care programme which aims to promote the highest standards of service and a warm welcome. Establishments who are taking part in this initiative are indicated by the symbol.

MALMESBURY

Wiltshire
Map ref 2B2

Overlooking the River Avon, an old town dominated by its great church, once a Benedictine abbey. The surviving Norman nave and porch are noted for fine sculptures, 12th C arches and musicians' gallery.
Tourist Information Centre ☎ (01666) 823748

Manor Farm

COMMENDED

Corston, Malmesbury SN16 0HF
☎ (01666) 822148 & 0374 675783
Fax (01666) 822148

436-acre mixed farm. Relax and unwind in this award-winning 17th C Cotswold farmhouse. Ideally situated for visiting Cotswolds, Bath and Stonehenge. Just 3 miles from junction 17 of M4.
Bedrooms: 1 single, 2 double, 1 twin, 1 triple, 1 family room
Bathrooms: 4 en-suite, 1 public, 2 private showers

Bed & breakfast per night:	£min	£max
Single	18.00	26.00
Double	36.00	48.00

Parking for 12
Cards accepted: Mastercard, Visa

Winkworth Farm

Listed COMMENDED

Lea, Malmesbury SN16 9NH
☎ (01666) 823267

230-acre beef farm. Enjoy the warm, friendly atmosphere of this 17th C Cotswold-stone farmhouse set in a secluded walled garden. Comfortable rooms, oak beams, log fires. Ideal for a quiet holiday or as a touring base, just 3 miles from Malmesbury. No smoking, please.
Bedrooms: 2 double
Bathrooms: 1 en-suite, 1 private, 1 public

Bed & breakfast per night:	£min	£max
Single	25.00	25.00
Double	36.00	40.00

Half board per person:	£min	£max
Daily	32.50	32.50

Parking for 10

MANATON

Devon
Map ref 1C2

Scattered village with whitewashed cottages and a tree-shaded green, set in rugged country on the eastern edge of Dartmoor. Becka Brook with its waterfall flows through the Bovey Valley nearby and there are good moorland walks to Bowerman's Nose, a lofty, jutting rock stack.

Sandy Meadow

Listed COMMENDED

Manaton, Newton Abbot
TQ13 9UN
☎ (01647) 221263
Bungalow set in tranquil countryside with moorland views. At crossroads in Manaton by Kestor Inn take lane signposted Southcott. Bungalow is approximately one-third of a mile.
Bedrooms: 1 single, 1 double
Bathrooms: 2 public

Bed & breakfast per night:	£min	£max
Single	14.00	14.00
Double	28.00	32.00

Parking for 2
12

MARTINSTOWN

Dorset
Map ref 2B3

Village 3 miles west of Dorchester. Maiden Castle Iron Age fort lies to the east of the village and the Hardy Monument stands on Black Down to the south west.

Old Post Office

Listed APPROVED

Martinstown, Dorchester DT2 9LF
☎ (01305) 889254
Grade II listed Georgian cottage tastefully modernised throughout. Large garden with many small animals. Good rural base, children and pets welcome.
Bedrooms: 1 double, 2 twin
Bathrooms: 1 public

Bed & breakfast per night:	£min	£max
Single	17.50	20.00
Double	30.00	35.00

Half board per person:	£min	£max
Daily	27.50	

Evening meal 1900 (last orders 1630)
Parking for 3

MARTOCK

Somerset
Map ref 2A3

Small town with many handsome buildings of Ham stone and a beautiful old church with tie-beam roof. Medieval treasurer's house, Georgian market house, 17th C manor.

Wychwood

HIGHLY COMMENDED

7 Bearley Road, Martock TA12 6PG
☎ (01935) 825601
Fax (01935) 825601
Small, quality B&B just off A303 between Montacute and Tintinhull. Ideal for visiting the ten Classic gardens of South Somerset. Visit Glastonbury/Wells.
Bedrooms: 2 double, 1 twin
Suites available
Bathrooms: 2 en-suite, 1 private

Bed & breakfast per night:	£min	£max
Single	28.00	32.00
Double	38.00	42.00

Parking for 3
Cards accepted: Mastercard, Visa

MEVAGISSEY

Cornwall
Map ref 1B3

Small fishing town, a favourite with holidaymakers. Earlier prosperity came from pilchard fisheries, boat-building and smuggling. By the harbour are fish cellars, some converted, and a local history museum is housed in an old boat-building shed. Handsome Methodist chapel; shark fishing, sailing.

Kerry Anna Country House

HIGHLY COMMENDED

Treleaven Farm, Mevagissey, St Austell PL26 6RZ
☎ (01726) 843558
Fax (01726) 843558

200-acre arable farm. Country house overlooking village, surrounded by rambling farmland, wild flowers and wildlife. Outdoor swimming pool, games barn, putting green. Farm cooking.
Bedrooms: 4 double, 1 twin, 1 family room
Bathrooms: 6 en-suite

Bed & breakfast per night:

	£min	£max
Double	40.00	50.00

Half board per person:

	£min	£max
Daily	31.00	36.00

Evening meal 1900 (last orders 1200)
Parking for 6
Open April–October
5 S TV SP

Mevagissey House

COMMENDED

Vicarage Hill, Mevagissey, St Austell PL26 6SZ
☎ (01726) 842427
Fax (01726) 842427
Georgian country house in woodland setting on a hillside, set in 4 acres. Sea views, elegant spacious rooms, many facilities, licensed bar. Also, self-catering cottages.
Bedrooms: 1 double, 1 twin, 2 triple
Bathrooms: 3 en-suite, 1 private, 1 public

Bed & breakfast per night:

	£min	£max
Single	25.00	33.00
Double	38.00	54.00

Parking for 12
Open March–October
Cards accepted: Mastercard, Visa, Switch/Delta
7 S TV SP

Polrudden Farm

HIGHLY COMMENDED

Pentewan, St Austell PL26 6BJ
☎ (01726) 843213 & 842051
75-acre mixed farm. Modern farmhouse with fantastic views and walks, 3 miles from St Austell and 2 miles from Mevagissey. Peace and tranquillity.
Bedrooms: 1 double, 2 twin
Bathrooms: 1 en-suite, 2 public

Bed & breakfast per night:

	£min	£max
Single	25.00	27.50
Double	36.00	40.00

Parking for 13
Open March–November
10 UL S TV SP T

Steep House

Portmellon Cove, Mevagissey, St Austell PL26 6PH
☎ (01726) 843732

Comfortable house with large garden and covered (summertime) pool. Superb seaside views, licensed, free off-road parking.
Bedrooms: 1 single, 5 double, 1 twin, 1 triple
Bathrooms: 2 en-suite, 1 private, 2 public

Bed & breakfast per night:

	£min	£max
Single	20.00	24.00
Double	36.00	

Parking for 12
Cards accepted: Amex, Mastercard, Visa
10 TV SP

MINEHEAD

Somerset
Map ref 1D1

Victorian resort with spreading sands developed around old fishing port on the coast below Exmoor. Former fishermen's cottages stand beside the 17th C harbour; cobbled streets climb the hill in steps to the church. Boat trips, steam railway. Hobby Horse festival 1 May.
Tourist Information Centre ☎ (01643) 702624

Hillside

HIGHLY COMMENDED

Higher Allerford, Allerford, Minehead TA24 8HS
☎ (01643) 862831

Thatched cottage owned by the National Trust. Wonderful views overlooking the picturesque village of Allerford. Ideally situated for exploring Exmoor.
Bedrooms: 1 double, 1 twin
Bathrooms: 1 public

Bed & breakfast per night:

	£min	£max
Single	19.00	20.00
Double	38.00	40.00

Parking for 4
2 UL S TV

Kildare Lodge

COMMENDED

Townsend Road, Minehead TA24 5RQ
☎ (01643) 702009
Fax (01643) 706516
Family-run, Edwin Lutyens designed, Grade II listed building. Elegant a la carte restaurant; character-filled licensed bar; bar meals; well appointed en-suite accommodation, including family rooms.
Bedrooms: 1 single, 4 double, 2 twin, 2 family rooms
Bathrooms: 9 en-suite, 1 public

Bed & breakfast per night:

	£min	£max
Single	19.00	37.00
Double	38.00	74.00

Half board per person:

	£min	£max
Daily	26.00	45.00
Weekly	170.00	260.00

Lunch available
Evening meal 1900 (last orders 2100)
Parking for 28
Cards accepted: Amex, Diners, Mastercard, Visa
S TV 50 OAP SP T

MORETONHAMPSTEAD

Devon
Map ref 1C2

Small market town with a row of 17th C almshouses standing on the Exeter road. Surrounding moorland is scattered with ancient farmhouses, prehistoric sites.

Great Doccombe Farm

COMMENDED

Doccombe, Moretonhampstead, Newton Abbot TQ13 8SS
☎ (01647) 440694
8-acre mixed farm. 300-year-old farmhouse in Dartmoor National Park. Comfortable rooms, farmhouse cooking. Ideal for walking the Teign Valley and Dartmoor.
Bedrooms: 1 double, 1 triple
Bathrooms: 2 private, 2 public

Continued ▶

MORETONHAMPSTEAD

Continued

Bed & breakfast per night:	£min	£max
Double	34.00	40.00

Parking for 6

Great Sloncombe Farm

HIGHLY COMMENDED

Moretonhampstead, Newton Abbot TQ13 8QF
☎ (01647) 440595
Fax (01647) 440595

170-acre dairy farm. 13th C Dartmoor farmhouse. Comfortable rooms, central heating, en-suite. Large wholesome farmhouse breakfasts and delicious dinners. Friendly Devonshire welcome.

Bedrooms: 2 double, 1 twin
Bathrooms: 3 en-suite

Bed & breakfast per night:	£min	£max
Single	20.00	21.00
Double	40.00	42.00

Half board per person:	£min	£max
Daily	31.00	32.00

Evening meal 1830 (last orders 1000)
Parking for 3

Wooston Farm

HIGHLY COMMENDED

Moretonhampstead, Newton Abbot TQ13 8QA
☎ (01647) 440367
Fax (01647) 440367

280-acre mixed farm. Situated within Dartmoor National Park above the Teign Valley, with scenic views and walks. Two rooms are en-suite, one with four-poster bed.

Bedrooms: 2 double, 1 twin
Bathrooms: 2 en-suite, 1 private

Bed & breakfast per night:	£min	£max
Single	19.00	21.00
Double	38.00	42.00

Evening meal 1800 (last orders 1850)
Parking for 3

MORWENSTOW

Cornwall
Map ref 1C2

Scattered parish on the wild north Cornish coast. The church, beautifully situated in a deep combe by the sea, has a fine Norman doorway and 15th C bench-ends. Its unique vicarage was built by the 19th C poet-priest Robert Hawker. Nearby are Cornwall's highest cliffs.

Cornakey Farm

Listed COMMENDED

Morwenstow, Bude EX23 9SS
☎ (01288) 331260

220-acre mixed farm. Convenient coastal walking area with extensive views of sea and cliffs from bedrooms. Home cooking, games room. Reduced rates for children. Good touring centre.

Bedrooms: 1 double, 2 triple
Bathrooms: 1 en-suite, 2 private, 1 public

Bed & breakfast per night:	£min	£max
Single	15.50	
Double	31.00	

Half board per person:	£min	£max
Daily	23.50	
Weekly	161.00	

Evening meal 1830 (last orders 1730)
Parking for 2

MULLION

Cornwall
Map ref 1B3

Small holiday village with a golf-course, set back from the coast. The church has a serpentine tower of 1500, carved roof and beautiful medieval bench-ends. Beyond Mullion Cove, with its tiny harbour, wild untouched cliffs stretch south-eastward toward Lizard Point.

Polurrian Hotel, Apartments and Leisure Club

HIGHLY COMMENDED

Polurrian Cove, Mullion, Helston TR12 7EN
☎ (01326) 240421
Fax (01326) 240083

Idyllic setting for family-run hotel with own beach, surrounded by National Trust coastline. Indoor leisure club and outdoor amenities. Personal service.

Bedrooms: 18 double, 17 twin, 4 triple
Suite available
Bathrooms: 39 en-suite, 1 public

Bed & breakfast per night:	£min	£max
Single	35.00	50.00
Double	70.00	100.00

Half board per person:	£min	£max
Daily	45.00	90.00
Weekly	270.00	575.00

Lunch available
Evening meal 1900 (last orders 2100)
Parking for 60
Open February–December
Cards accepted: Amex, Diners, Mastercard, Visa

MYLOR BRIDGE

Cornwall
Map ref 1B3

Penmere Guest House

COMMENDED

Rosehill, Mylor Bridge, Falmouth TR11 5LZ
☎ (01326) 374470
Fax (01326) 378828

Beautifully restored Victorian property enjoying splendid creek views, close to yachting centres. Lovely garden, perfect for a relaxing stay.

Bedrooms: 3 double, 2 twin, 1 triple
Bathrooms: 4 en-suite, 2 private

Bed & breakfast per night:	£min	£max
Single	25.00	30.00
Double	44.00	52.00

Parking for 6

NETHER STOWEY

Somerset
Map ref 1D1

Winding village below east slopes of Quantocks with attractive old cottages of varying periods. A Victorian clock tower stands at its centre, where a village road climbs the hill beside a small stream.

Rose and Crown

St Mary Street, Nether Stowey, Bridgwater TA5 1LJ
☎ (01278) 732265

A coaching inn written about by John

Taylor (the Water Poet) in 1649 when it was old and dirty. Now even older but a lot cleaner!
Bedrooms: 2 double, 2 twin
Bathrooms: 2 en-suite, 2 private, 1 public

Bed & breakfast per night:	£min	£max
Single	14.00	18.00
Double	25.00	30.00

Half board per person:	£min	£max
Daily	19.00	23.00

Lunch available
Evening meal 1900 (last orders 2100)
Parking for 4

NEWQUAY

Cornwall
Map ref 1B2

Popular resort spread over dramatic cliffs around its old fishing port. Many beaches with abundant sands, caves and rock pools; excellent surf. Pilots' gigs are still raced from the harbour and on the headland stands the stone Huer's House from the pilchard-fishing days.
Tourist Information Centre ☎ (01637) 871345

Degembris Farmhouse

HIGHLY COMMENDED
St Newlyn East, Newquay TR8 5HY
☎ (01872) 510555
Fax (01872) 510230
165-acre arable farm. Cosy south-facing farmhouse offering welcoming log fires in winter, comfortable en-suite bedrooms and delicious home cooking. "A wonderful oasis from 23 million cars".
Bedrooms: 1 single, 1 double, 1 twin, 1 triple, 1 family room
Bathrooms: 3 en-suite, 1 public

Bed & breakfast per night:	£min	£max
Single	18.00	20.00
Double	36.00	40.00

Half board per person:	£min	£max
Daily	28.00	30.00
Weekly	196.00	210.00

Evening meal from 1830
Parking for 8
Cards accepted: Mastercard, Visa, Switch/Delta

Rose Cottage

HIGHLY COMMENDED
Shepherds Farm, St Newlyn East, Newquay TR8 5NW
☎ (01872) 540502
600-acre mixed farm. Come and share our warm and friendly atmosphere, with first class service and quality accommodation. Cleanliness guaranteed. All rooms en-suite, colour TV and tea-making facilities. Ideal touring and beaches, 1 mile from A30 in little hamlet of Fiddlers Green. Free horse riding (seasonal) and games room.
Bedrooms: 2 double, 1 twin
Bathrooms: 3 en-suite

Bed & breakfast per night:	£min	£max
Single	15.00	18.00
Double	30.00	36.00

Parking for 3

NORTH PETHERWIN

Cornwall
Map ref 1C2

The Old Granary

Listed COMMENDED
North Petherwin, Launceston PL15 8LR
☎ (01566) 785593
Unique converted family home, situated close to the village church, with 4 of the best beaches in Cornwall 12-13 miles away.
Bedrooms: 1 double, 1 twin
Bathrooms: 1 public

Bed & breakfast per night:	£min	£max
Single	16.00	18.00
Double	32.00	36.00

Half board per person:	£min	£max
Daily	26.00	30.00
Weekly	170.00	190.00

Evening meal 1800 (last orders 1930)
Parking for 4
Open January–November

NOSS MAYO

Devon
Map ref 1C3

Slade Barn

Listed COMMENDED
Netton Farm, Noss Mayo, Plymouth PL8 1HA
☎ (01752) 872235
Fax (01752) 872235
50-acre arable farm. Attractive coastal barn conversion 10 miles from Plymouth. Indoor pool, games room, tennis court, gardens. Fabulous National Trust walks. Up-market B & B and self-catering. Ideal family holiday.
Bedrooms: 2 double, 1 twin
Bathrooms: 2 public, 1 private shower

Bed & breakfast per night:	£min	£max
Double	40.00	44.00

Parking for 6

OKEHAMPTON

Devon
Map ref 1C2

Busy market town near the high tors of northern Dartmoor. The Victorian church, with William Morris windows and a 15th C tower, stands on the site of a Saxon church. A Norman castle ruin overlooks the river to the west of the town. Museum of Dartmoor Life in a restored mill.

Higher Cadham Farm

HIGHLY COMMENDED
Jacobstowe, Okehampton EX20 3RB
☎ (01837) 851647
Fax (01837) 851410

139-acre mixed farm. For a real Devonshire welcome come to our farm in the secluded Okement Valley near Dartmoor. Central heating, farmhouse food.
Bedrooms: 1 single, 3 double, 2 twin, 3 family rooms
Bathrooms: 6 en-suite, 1 public

Bed & breakfast per night:	£min	£max
Single	17.00	23.00
Double	34.00	46.00

Half board per person:	£min	£max
Daily	27.00	33.00
Weekly	170.00	210.00

Lunch available
Evening meal 1900 (last orders 2000)
Parking for 6
Cards accepted: Mastercard, Visa, Switch/Delta

OKEHAMPTON

Continued

Oxenham Arms

COMMENDED

South Zeal, Okehampton EX20 2JT
☎ (01837) 840244
Fax (01837) 840791

In the centre of Dartmoor village, originally built in the 12th C. Wealth of granite fireplaces, oak beams, mullion windows. Various diets available on request.

Bedrooms: 3 double, 3 twin, 3 triple
Bathrooms: 8 en-suite, 1 private

Bed & breakfast per night:	£min	£max
Single	40.00	45.00
Double	50.00	60.00

Half board per person:	£min	£max
Daily	40.00	45.00
Weekly	245.00	280.00

Lunch available
Evening meal 1930 (last orders 2100)
Parking for 8
Cards accepted: Amex, Diners, Mastercard, Visa

Staddlestones

Listed COMMENDED

Thorndon, Thorndon Cross, Okehampton EX20 4NG
☎ (01837) 861389

Converted barn and round house in peaceful, rural position ideal for exploring the West Country. Use of delightful garden and complete privacy. Fishing, golf, riding and countless walks close to hand. Warm welcome assured.

Bedrooms: 1 twin
Bathrooms: 1 private

Bed & breakfast per night:	£min	£max
Single	19.00	21.00
Double	38.00	42.00

Parking for 4
Open January–November

Information on accommodation listed in this guide has been supplied by the proprietors. As changes may occur you are advised to check details at the time of booking.

Week Farm

COMMENDED

Bridestowe, Okehampton
EX20 4HZ
☎ (01837) 861221
Fax (01837) 861221

180-acre dairy & livestock farm. A warm welcome awaits you at this homely 17th C farmhouse, three-quarters of a mile from the old A30 and 6 miles from Okehampton. Home cooking and every comfort. Outdoor heated pool. Come and spoil yourselves.

Wheelchair access category 3
Bedrooms: 3 double, 1 triple, 1 family room
Bathrooms: 5 en-suite

Bed & breakfast per night:	£min	£max
Single	22.00	24.00
Double	44.00	48.00

Half board per person:	£min	£max
Daily	32.00	34.00
Weekly	224.00	238.00

Evening meal 1900 (last orders 1700)
Parking for 10
Cards accepted: Visa

PADSTOW

Cornwall
Map ref 1B2

Old town encircling its harbour on the Camel Estuary. The 15th C church has notable bench-ends. There are fine houses on North Quay and Raleigh's Court House on South Quay. Tall cliffs and golden sands along the coast and ferry to Rock. Famous 'Obby 'Oss Festival on 1 May.
Tourist Information Centre ☎ (01841) 533449

Trevorrick Farm

COMMENDED

St Issey, Wadebridge PL27 7QH
☎ (01841) 540574

11-acre mixed farm. Farmhouse by footpath to Camel Trail offers en-suite rooms and welcomes families and pets. Indoor heated swimming pool. Near sandy beaches.

Bedrooms: 2 double, 1 twin
Bathrooms: 3 en-suite, 1 public

Bed & breakfast per night:	£min	£max
Single	25.00	30.00
Double	35.00	44.00

Half board per person:	£min	£max
Daily	27.45	31.95

Evening meal 1800 (last orders 1930)
Parking for 20

PAIGNTON

Devon
Map ref 1D2

Lively seaside resort with a pretty harbour on Torbay. Bronze Age and Saxon sites are occupied by the 15th C church, which has a Norman door and font. The beautiful Chantry Chapel was built by local landowners, the Kirkhams.
Tourist Information Centre ☎ (01803) 558383

South Sands Hotel

COMMENDED

12 Alta Vista Road, Paignton
TQ4 6BZ
☎ (01803) 557231 & 0500 432153
Fax (01803) 529947

Family-run, wonderful fresh food. Superb, peaceful location overlooking sea, beach, park and close to harbour. Large car park. Dogs and children very welcome.

Bedrooms: 2 single, 3 double, 1 twin, 5 triple, 8 family rooms
Bathrooms: 17 en-suite, 2 private

Bed & breakfast per night:	£min	£max
Single	20.00	30.00
Double	40.00	60.00

Half board per person:	£min	£max
Daily	28.00	38.00
Weekly	165.00	230.00

Lunch available
Evening meal 1800 (last orders 2130)
Parking for 17
Open April–October and Christmas
Cards accepted: Mastercard, Visa

A key to symbols can be found inside the back cover flap.

PENSFORD

Bath & North East Somerset
Map ref 2A2

Green Acres

Listed APPROVED

Stanton Wick, Pensford BS18 4BX
☎ (01761) 490397
Fax (01761) 490397

A friendly welcome awaits you in peaceful setting, off A37/A368. Relax and enjoy panoramic views across Chew Valley to Dundry Hills.

Bedrooms: 2 single, 1 double, 1 twin
Bathrooms: 2 public

Bed & breakfast per night:	£min	£max
Single	16.00	18.00
Double	32.00	36.00

Parking for 22

PENZANCE

Cornwall
Map ref 1A3

Resort and fishing port on Mount's Bay with mainly Victorian promenade and some fine Regency terraces. Former prosperity came from tin trade and pilchard fishing. Grand Georgian style church by harbour. Grand Georgian Egyptian building at head of Chapel Street and Morrab Gardens.
Tourist Information Centre ☎ (01736) 362207

Menwidden Farm

Listed APPROVED

Ludgvan, Penzance TR20 8BN
☎ (01736) 740415

40-acre mixed farm. Centrally situated in west Cornwall. Warm family atmosphere and home cooking. Turn right at Crowlas crossroads on the A30 from Hayle, signpost Vellanoweth on right turn. Last farm on left.

Bedrooms: 1 single, 2 double, 1 twin, 1 family room
Bathrooms: 2 public

Bed & breakfast per night:	£min	£max
Single	16.00	
Double	32.00	

Half board per person:	£min	£max
Daily	23.00	
Weekly	140.00	

Evening meal 1800 (last orders 1800)
Parking for 8
Open March–October

Rose Farm

COMMENDED

Chyanhal, Buryas Bridge, Penzance TR19 6AN
☎ (01736) 731808
Fax (01736) 731808

25-acre livestock & horses farm. Small farm with many animals. Near beaches and shops. Land's End 7 miles, Mousehole 2 miles. Lovely walks. Four-poster bed available. Cosy and relaxing.

Bedrooms: 2 double, 1 family room
Bathrooms: 3 en-suite

Bed & breakfast per night:	£min	£max
Single	24.00	25.50
Double	38.00	41.00

Parking for 10

PERRANUTHNOE

Cornwall
Map ref 1B3

Small village on Mount's Bay, with lovely cliff walks.

Ednovean House

APPROVED

Perranuthnoe, Penzance TR20 9LZ
☎ (01736) 711071

Stands in 1 acre of gardens, with superb views of St Michael's Mount and Mount's Bay. Ideal centre for touring and walking.

Bedrooms: 2 single, 4 double, 2 twin, 1 triple
Bathrooms: 6 en-suite, 1 public

Bed & breakfast per night:	£min	£max
Single	23.00	25.00
Double	40.00	50.00

Half board per person:	£min	£max
Daily	35.00	40.00
Weekly	220.00	250.00

Evening meal 1900 (last orders 2000)
Parking for 12
Cards accepted: Amex, Mastercard, Visa

PETER TAVY

Devon
Map ref 1C2

Churchtown

Listed APPROVED

Peter Tavy, Tavistock PL19 9NN
☎ (01822) 810477 & 810094
Fax (01822) 810094

Peaceful Victorian house in own grounds on edge of village. Beautiful moorland views. 5 minutes' walk to excellent pub food.

Bedrooms: 1 single, 2 double
Bathrooms: 2 public, 2 private showers

Bed & breakfast per night:	£min	£max
Single	13.00	15.00
Double	26.00	30.00

Parking for 6

PIDDLETRENTHIDE

Dorset
Map ref 2B3

The Poachers Inn

COMMENDED

Piddletrenthide, Dorchester DT2 7QX
☎ (01300) 348358

Inn situated in lovely Piddle Valley on B3143. En-suite rooms with colour TV, telephone, tea/coffee. Restaurant. Stay 2 nights half board October-March, get third night free.

Bedrooms: 9 double, 1 twin, 2 family rooms
Bathrooms: 12 en-suite

Bed & breakfast per night:	£min	£max
Double	46.00	50.00

Half board per person:	£min	£max
Daily	33.00	35.00
Weekly	230.00	245.00

Lunch available
Evening meal 1700 (last orders 2130)
Parking for 30
Cards accepted: Mastercard, Visa

PLYMOUTH

Devon
Map ref 1C2

Devon's largest city, major port and naval base. Old houses on the Barbican and ambitious architecture in modern centre, with aquarium, museum and art gallery, the Dome - a heritage centre on the Hoe. Superb coastal views over Plymouth Sound from the Hoe.
Tourist Information Centre ☎ (01752) 264849 or 266030

Bowling Green Hotel

HIGHLY COMMENDED

9-10 Osborne Place, Lockyer Street, Plymouth PL1 2PU
☎ (01752) 209090
Fax (01752) 209092

Rebuilt Victorian property with views of Dartmoor. Overlooking Sir Francis Drake's bowling green on beautiful Plymouth Hoe. Centrally situated for the Barbican, Theatre Royal and leisure/conference centre.
Bedrooms: 1 single, 9 double, 1 twin, 1 triple
Bathrooms: 12 en-suite

Bed & breakfast per night:	£min	£max
Single	34.00	36.00
Double	46.00	50.00

Parking for 4
Cards accepted: Amex, Diners, Mastercard, Visa, Switch/Delta

Gabber Farm

COMMENDED

Down Thomas, Plymouth PL9 0AW
☎ (01752) 862269
120-acre mixed & dairy farm. On the south Devon coast, near Bovisand and Wembury. Lovely walks in the area. Near diving centre. Directions are provided. Friendly welcome assured. Special weekly rates, especially for OAPs and children.
Bedrooms: 1 double, 2 twin, 1 triple, 1 family room
Bathrooms: 2 en-suite, 1 public

Bed & breakfast per night:	£min	£max
Single	16.00	18.00
Double	32.00	36.00

Half board per person:	£min	£max
Daily	25.00	27.00
Weekly	155.00	165.00

Evening meal 1900 (last orders 1800)
Parking for 4

POLPERRO

Cornwall
Map ref 1C3

Picturesque fishing village clinging to steep valley slopes about its harbour. A river splashes past cottages and narrow lanes twist between. The harbour mouth, guarded by jagged rocks, is closed by heavy timbers during storms.

Brent House

APPROVED

1 Brent House, Talland Hill, Polperro, Looe PL13 2RY
☎ (01503) 272495
Amazing bird's eye view of Polperro Harbour, the village and out to sea. Sun terraces, car parking. Good restaurants, pubs and shops in village, just a short walk away. Good walking area.
Bedrooms: 1 double
Bathrooms: 1 en-suite

Bed & breakfast per night:	£min	£max
Single	20.00	20.00
Double	37.00	37.00

Parking for 50

PORTLAND

Dorset
Map ref 2B3

Joined by a narrow isthmus to the coast, a stony promontory sloping from the lofty landward side to a lighthouse on Portland Bill at its southern tip. Villages are built of the white limestone for which the "isle" is famous.

Alessandria Hotel and Italian Restaurant

APPROVED

71 Wakeham Easton, Portland, Weymouth DT5 1HW
☎ (01305) 822270 & 820108
Fax (01305) 820561
Italy on Portland. Warm and friendly Italian hospitality from chef/proprietor Giovanni. Spacious en-suite bedrooms with all facilities. Food prepared and cooked to order. Three bedrooms on ground floor.
Bedrooms: 6 single, 3 double, 3 twin, 2 triple, 1 family room
Suite available
Bathrooms: 10 en-suite, 1 private, 3 public, 1 private shower

Bed & breakfast per night:	£min	£max
Single	25.00	35.00
Double	45.00	60.00

Half board per person:	£min	£max
Daily	40.00	50.00
Weekly	220.00	245.00

Evening meal 1900 (last orders 2100)
Parking for 19
Cards accepted: Amex, Mastercard, Visa, Switch/Delta
20

ST AUSTELL

Cornwall
Map ref 1B3

Leading market town, the meeting point of old and new Cornwall. One mile from St Austell Bay with its sandy beaches, old fishing villages and attractive countryside. Ancient narrow streets, pedestrian shopping precincts. Fine church of Pentewan stone and Italianate Town Hall.

Hembal Manor

HIGHLY COMMENDED

Hembal Lane, Trewoon, St Austell PL25 5TD
☎ (01726) 72144
Fax (01726) 72144

Dating from the 16th C, Hembal Manor is set in 6 acres of gardens. Ideally situated for beaches and places of interest and easy travelling distance of main Cornish towns. All rooms tastefully decorated and furnished.
Bedrooms: 2 double, 1 twin
Bathrooms: 3 en-suite, 1 public

Bed & breakfast per night:	£min	£max
Single	25.00	28.00
Double	45.00	50.00

Parking for 6
12

Poltarrow Farm

HIGHLY COMMENDED

St Mewan, St Austell PL26 7DR
☎ (01726) 67111

45-acre mixed farm. Ideal central base for touring, close to coast and Heligan Gardens. Charming farmhouse, delightful accommodation and peaceful countryside.

Bedrooms: 3 double, 1 twin, 1 family room
Bathrooms: 4 en-suite, 1 private

Bed & breakfast per night:	£min	£max
Single	22.00	25.00
Double	38.00	44.00

Parking for 5
Cards accepted: Mastercard, Visa

ST IVES

Cornwall
Map ref 1B3

Old fishing port, artists' colony and holiday town with good surfing beach. Fishermen's cottages, granite fish cellars, a sandy harbour and magnificent headlands typify a charm that has survived since the 19th C pilchard boom. Tate Gallery opened in 1993.

Tourist Information Centre ☎ (01736) 796297

The Anchorage Guest House

COMMENDED

5 Bunkers Hill, St Ives TR26 1LJ
☎ (01736) 797135

18th C fisherman's cottage, 30 yards from harbour front and beaches, full of old world charm. Two minutes from Tate Gallery.

Bedrooms: 1 single, 4 double, 1 twin
Bathrooms: 4 en-suite, 1 public

Bed & breakfast per night:	£min	£max
Single	15.00	22.00
Double	30.00	42.00

Cards accepted: Amex, Mastercard, Visa

The symbols in each entry give information about services and facilities. A key to these symbols appears at the back of this guide.

ST KEW

Cornwall
Map ref 1B2

Old village sheltered by trees standing beside a stream. The church is noted for its medieval glass showing the Passion and the remains of a scene of the Tree of Jesse.

Tregellist Farm

COMMENDED

Tregellist, St Kew, Bodmin PL30 3HG
☎ (01208) 880537

130-acre mixed farm. Farmhouse, built in 1989, offering old-fashioned hospitality. Set in tiny hamlet with lovely views and pleasant walks. Central for coast and moors. Children welcome. 1.5 miles from A39.

Bedrooms: 1 double, 1 twin, 1 family room
Bathrooms: 3 en-suite

Bed & breakfast per night:	£min	£max
Single	21.00	23.00
Double	40.00	46.00

Half board per person:	£min	£max
Daily	31.00	31.00
Weekly	217.00	217.00

Evening meal from 1800
Parking for 6
Open March–October

ST MAWGAN

Cornwall
Map ref 1B2

Pretty village of great historic interest, on wooded slopes in the Vale of Lanherne. At its centre, an old stone bridge over the River Menahyl is overlooked by the church with its lofty buttressed tower. Among ancient stone crosses in the churchyard is a 15th C lantern cross with carved figures.

The Falcon Inn

COMMENDED

St Mawgan, Newquay TR8 4EP
☎ (01637) 860225
Fax (01637) 860884

16th C wisteria-covered inn with beautiful gardens in the Vale of Lanherne. Unspoilt peaceful situation.

Bedrooms: 2 double, 1 twin
Bathrooms: 2 en-suite, 1 private, 1 public

Bed & breakfast per night:	£min	£max
Single	15.00	32.00
Double	42.00	52.00

Lunch available
Evening meal 1830 (last orders 2200)
Parking for 25
Cards accepted: Diners, Mastercard, Visa, Switch/Delta

ST WENN

Cornwall
Map ref 1B2

Tregolls Farm

Listed COMMENDED

St Wenn, Bodmin PL30 5PG
☎ (01208) 812154

107-acre mixed farm. Set in a picturesque, tranquil valley, this Grade II listed house has bright airy rooms and a feature fireplace.

Bedrooms: 1 single, 2 double, 1 twin
Bathrooms: 1 en-suite, 1 public

Bed & breakfast per night:	£min	£max
Single	12.75	16.25
Double	25.50	32.50

Half board per person:	£min	£max
Daily	20.50	24.00
Weekly	143.00	154.00

Evening meal from 1900
Parking for 5

Half board prices are given per person, but in some cases these may be based on double/twin occupancy.

National gradings and classifications were correct at the time of going to press but are subject to change. Please check at the time of booking.

SALCOMBE

Devon
Map ref 1C3

Sheltered yachting resort of whitewashed houses and narrow streets in a balmy setting on the Salcombe Estuary. Palm, myrtle and other Mediterranean plants flourish. There are sandy bays and creeks for boating.
Tourist Information Centre ☎ (01548) 843927

Burton Farm

HIGHLY COMMENDED
Galmpton, Kingsbridge TQ7 3EY
☎ (01548) 561210
Fax (01548) 561210

325-acre dairy & livestock farm. In coastal valley, 1 mile from the beach. 16th C farmhouse, tastefully restored. A warm welcome is assured. En-suite rooms.
Bedrooms: 2 single, 2 double, 2 twin, 3 family rooms
Bathrooms: 5 en-suite, 1 private, 1 public

Bed & breakfast per night:	£min	£max
Single	21.00	25.00
Double	42.00	50.00

Half board per person:	£min	£max
Daily	32.00	36.00

Evening meal 1830 (last orders 1930)
Parking for 10
Cards accepted: Amex, Mastercard, Visa, Switch/Delta

Torre View Hotel

COMMENDED
Devon Road, Salcombe TQ8 8HJ
☎ (01548) 842633
Fax (01548) 842633
Detached Victorian residence with every modern comfort, commanding extensive views of the estuary and surrounding countryside. Congenial atmosphere. No smoking, please.
Bedrooms: 6 double, 2 twin
Suites available
Bathrooms: 5 en-suite, 3 private

Bed & breakfast per night:	£min	£max
Single	25.00	29.00
Double	46.50	53.00

Half board per person:	£min	£max
Daily	35.00	39.00
Weekly	228.00	255.00

Evening meal 1900 (last orders 1800)
Parking for 5
Open March–October
Cards accepted: Mastercard, Visa

SALISBURY

Wiltshire
Map ref 2B3

Beautiful city and ancient regional capital set amid water meadows. Buildings of all periods are dominated by the cathedral whose spire is the tallest in England. Built between 1220 and 1258, it is one of the purest examples of Early English architecture.
Tourist Information Centre ☎ (01722) 334956

Barlings

COMMENDED
41 Gravel Close, Downton, Salisbury SP5 3JQ
☎ (01725) 510310
Well-appointed bungalow, in quiet lane, with fine views overlooking water meadows towards church. All en-suite. Old world village with good local inns, south of Salisbury.
Bedrooms: 2 double, 1 twin
Bathrooms: 3 en-suite

Bed & breakfast per night:	£min	£max
Single	25.00	30.00
Double	35.00	40.00

Parking for 12

The Bell Inn

APPROVED
Warminster Road, South Newton, Salisbury SP2 OQD
☎ (01722) 743336
300-year-old roadside inn offering full en-suite facilities. Extensive range of bar meals. 6 miles north-west of Salisbury.
Bedrooms: 1 single, 1 double, 1 twin
Bathrooms: 3 en-suite

Bed & breakfast per night:	£min	£max
Single	20.00	25.00
Double	36.00	38.00

Lunch available
Evening meal 1900 (last orders 2100)
Parking for 60

Beulah

Listed APPROVED
144 Britford Lane, Salisbury SP2 8AL
☎ (01722) 333517
Bungalow in quiet road, 1.25 miles from city centre and overlooking meadows. Tea/coffee making and colour TV in bedrooms. No-smoking establishment.
Bedrooms: 1 single, 1 family room
Bathrooms: 1 public

Bed & breakfast per night:	£min	£max
Single	16.00	16.00
Double	32.00	32.00

Parking for 4

Byways House

APPROVED
31 Fowlers Road, City Centre, Salisbury SP1 2QP
☎ (01722) 328364
Fax (01722) 322146

Attractive family-run Victorian house close to cathedral in quiet area of city centre. Car park. Bedrooms with private bathrooms and colour satellite TV. Traditional English and vegetarian breakfasts.
Bedrooms: 4 single, 7 double, 3 twin, 2 triple, 7 family rooms
Bathrooms: 19 en-suite, 1 public

Bed & breakfast per night:	£min	£max
Single	24.00	
Double	39.00	

Parking for 15
Cards accepted: Mastercard, Visa

Castleavon

COMMENDED
15 Wyndham Road, Salisbury SP1 3AA
☎ (01722) 339087
Large, comfortable Victorian house, furnished with antiques. Close to city centre and cathedral. Traditional breakfasts, evening meals provided to

Cordon Bleu trained standard. Smoking permitted in lounge.
Bedrooms: 1 double, 1 twin
Bathrooms: 1 private, 1 public

Bed & breakfast per night:	£min	£max
Single	16.00	20.00
Double	29.00	31.00

Half board per person:	£min	£max
Daily	22.00	23.00
Weekly	145.00	150.00

Evening meal from 1800

2 The Farriers

HIGHLY COMMENDED

Middleton, Middle Winterslow, Salisbury SP5 1QS
☎ (01980) 862881
Fax (01980) 862881

Traditionally built large family house, situated in a peaceful village, providing accommodation in a relaxed atmosphere.
Bedrooms: 1 double, 1 twin
Suite available
Bathrooms: 1 en-suite, 1 private

Bed & breakfast per night:	£min	£max
Single	25.00	
Double	45.00	

Parking for 4
10

The Gallery

Listed COMMENDED

36 Wyndham Road, Salisbury SP1 3AB
☎ (01722) 324586 & 500956
Fax (01722) 324586
Experience our warm hospitality and delicious breakfasts in a non-smoking environment. Well situated for exploring Salisbury and the many attractions in the area.
Bedrooms: 1 double, 2 twin
Bathrooms: 3 en-suite

Bed & breakfast per night:	£min	£max
Double	33.00	36.00

12

Harvest Moon

Listed COMMENDED

31 Hillside Drive, Gomeldon, Salisbury SP4 6LF
☎ (01980) 610126 & (0468) 241494
Fax (01980) 610126
Friendly family home with beautiful gardens situated in the Bourne Valley. Only 15 minutes' drive to Stonehenge and Salisbury.
Bedrooms: 1 single, 1 double, 1 twin
Bathrooms: 1 public

Bed & breakfast per night:	£min	£max
Double	30.00	36.00

Half board per person:	£min	£max
Daily	22.00	25.00

Lunch available
Parking for 4

Hayburn Wyke Guest House

COMMENDED

72 Castle Road, Salisbury SP1 3RL
☎ (01722) 412627
Fax (01722) 412627
Family-run spacious guesthouse adjacent to Victoria Park. A short riverside walk from the cathedral and city centre. Old Sarum 1 mile, Stonehenge 9 miles.
Bedrooms: 2 double, 2 twin, 2 triple
Bathrooms: 2 en-suite, 1 public

Bed & breakfast per night:	£min	£max
Single	24.00	37.00
Double	36.00	42.00

Parking for 6
Cards accepted: Mastercard, Visa, Switch/Delta

Leena's Guest House

COMMENDED

50 Castle Road, Salisbury SP1 3RL
☎ (01722) 335419
Fax (01722) 335419
Friendly, family-run guesthouse with pretty bedrooms and delightful public areas. Close to riverside walk to city centre and cathedral.
Bedrooms: 1 single, 2 double, 2 twin, 1 family room
Bathrooms: 5 en-suite, 1 public, 1 private shower

Bed & breakfast per night:	£min	£max
Single	19.00	21.00
Double	35.00	41.00

Parking for 7

Manor Farm

COMMENDED

Burcombe, Salisbury SP2 0EJ
☎ (01722) 742177
Fax (01722) 744600
960-acre mixed farm. Comfortable farmhouse set in pretty village 0.25 miles off A30 west of Salisbury. Ideal location for touring the area. Pub with good food 5 minutes away.
Bedrooms: 1 double, 1 twin
Bathrooms: 2 en-suite

Bed & breakfast per night:	£min	£max
Single	25.00	30.00
Double	40.00	44.00

Parking for 6
Open March–November

Newton Farm House

COMMENDED

Southampton Road, Whiteparish, Salisbury SP5 2QL
☎ (01794) 884416

Historic 16th C farmhouse, 10 minutes from Salisbury. Delightful en-suite rooms, 3 four-posters. Beamed and flagstoned dining room with bread oven and Nelson memorabilia. Superb gardens and swimming pool.
Bedrooms: 3 double, 2 twin, 2 triple, 1 family room
Bathrooms: 8 en-suite

Bed & breakfast per night:	£min	£max
Single	25.00	30.00
Double	36.00	50.00

Half board per person:	£min	£max
Daily	34.00	46.00

Evening meal from 1900
Parking for 10

The Old Inn

The Ridge, Woodfalls, Salisbury SP5 2LH
☎ (01725) 510422
Comfortable country inn on edge of New Forest. Public and lounge bars with traditional pub games and separate dining area. Friendly family atmosphere.
Bedrooms: 2 double, 1 twin

Continued ▶

SALISBURY

Continued

Suite available
Bathrooms: 2 en-suite, 1 private, 1 public

Bed & breakfast per night:	£min	£max
Single	20.00	25.00
Double	38.00	42.00

Lunch available
Evening meal 1700 (last orders 2200)
Parking for 50

Richburn Guest House

APPROVED

23 and 25 Estcourt Road, Salisbury SP1 3AP
☎ (01722) 325189

Large, tastefully renovated Victorian house with homely family atmosphere. All modern amenities and large car park. Close to city centre and parks.

Bedrooms: 2 single, 4 double, 2 twin, 1 triple, 1 family room
Bathrooms: 2 en-suite, 2 public

Bed & breakfast per night:	£min	£max
Single	18.00	18.50
Double	32.00	42.00

Parking for 10

Swaynes Firs Farm

APPROVED

Grimsdyke, Coombe Bissett, Salisbury SP5 5RF
☎ (01725) 519240

15-acre mixed farm. Country farmhouse with en-suite rooms, in pleasant position with good views. Ancient Roman ditch on farm. Peacocks, ducks, chickens and horses are reared on the farm.

Bedrooms: 2 twin, 1 family room
Bathrooms: 3 en-suite

Bed & breakfast per night:	£min	£max
Single	20.00	20.00
Double	40.00	40.00

Parking for 9

Websters

Listed COMMENDED

11 Hartington Road, Salisbury SP2 7LG
☎ (01722) 339779
Fax (01722) 339779

Arrive as strangers, leave as friends from our end Victorian terraced home. Ample parking. Easy walk to town. HCS award 1996.

Wheelchair access category 1
Bedrooms: 1 single, 2 double, 2 twin
Bathrooms: 5 en-suite

Bed & breakfast per night:	£min	£max
Single	20.00	24.00
Double	33.00	36.00

Parking for 5

48 Wyndham Road

Listed COMMENDED

Salisbury SP1 3AB
☎ (01722) 327757

Large, tastefully restored Edwardian house in quiet area, within easy reach of city centre and all amenities. En-suite facilities available. On-street parking.

Bedrooms: 2 double, 1 twin
Bathrooms: 1 en-suite, 1 public

Bed & breakfast per night:	£min	£max
Single	18.00	25.00
Double	30.00	36.00

SALISBURY PLAIN

See under Amesbury, Figheldean, Salisbury, Shrewton, Warminster

SENNEN COVE

Cornwall
Map ref 1A3

The Old Success Inn

COMMENDED

Sennen Cove, Penzance TR19 7DG
☎ (01736) 871232
Fax (01736) 871457

Attractively modernised fishermen's inn, nestling in one of Cornwall's most beautiful bays. Well known for meals, snacks and seafood specialities. Friendly staff. Small, well-behaved dogs welcome. Bay ideal for swimmers, surfers. Great cliff walks, golf-course nearby. 2 self-catering apartments available.

Bedrooms: 2 single, 8 double, 2 twin
Bathrooms: 8 en-suite, 2 private, 1 public

Bed & breakfast per night:	£min	£max
Single	25.00	36.00
Double	50.00	73.00

Half board per person:	£min	£max
Daily	40.00	51.00

Lunch available
Evening meal 1900 (last orders 2130)
Parking for 14
Cards accepted: Mastercard, Visa

SHEPTON MALLET

Somerset
Map ref 2A2

Historic town in the Mendip foothills, important in Roman times and site of many significant archaeological finds. Cloth industry reached its peak in the 17th C, and many fine examples of cloth merchants' houses remain. Beautiful parish church, market cross, local history museum, Collett Park.

Hurlingpot Farm

COMMENDED

Chelynch, Shepton Mallet BA4 4PY
☎ (01749) 880256

Lovely 300-year-old farmhouse in a peaceful country setting, 2 miles east of Shepton Mallet. A361 to Doulting, then take Chelynch road. Turn left past Poachers Pocket pub and left again into farm entrance.

Bedrooms: 1 double, 2 twin
Suites available
Bathrooms: 3 en-suite

Bed & breakfast per night:	£min	£max
Single	20.00	25.00
Double	35.00	40.00

Parking for 6

Temple House Farm

COMMENDED

Doulting, Shepton Mallet BA4 4RQ
☎ (01749) 880294
Fax (01749) 880688

200-acre dairy farm. 400-year-old listed farmhouse with all facilities. In rural area within easy reach of Wells, Bath, Shepton Mallet, the walking delights of the Mendips and plenty of tourist attractions.

Bedrooms: 2 triple

Bathrooms: 2 en-suite

Bed & breakfast per night:	£min	£max
Single		20.00
Double		36.00

Half board per person:	£min	£max
Daily		30.00
Weekly		210.00

Parking for 4

SHERBORNE

Dorset
Map ref 2B3

Dorset's "Cathedral City" of medieval streets, golden hamstone buildings and great abbey church, resting place of Saxon kings. Formidable 12th C castle ruins and Sir Walter Raleigh's splendid Tudor mansion and deer park. Street markets, leisure centre, many cultural activities.
Tourist Information Centre ☎ (01935) 815341

The Alders

HIGHLY COMMENDED

Sandford Orcas, Sherborne DT9 4SB
☎ (01963) 220666
Secluded stone house set in old walled garden, in picturesque conservation village near Sherborne. Excellent food available in friendly village pub.
Bedrooms: 1 double, 1 twin
Bathrooms: 2 en-suite

Bed & breakfast per night:	£min	£max
Double	40.00	45.00

Parking for 6

The Carpenters Arms

Listed COMMENDED

Leigh, Sherborne DT9 6HJ
☎ (01935) 872438
Fax (01935) 872438
18th C building, en-suite rooms, restaurant, bars. In beautiful countryside, ideal for walking and close to riding and fishing. 7 miles from Yeovil and Sherborne, 11 miles from Dorchester.
Bedrooms: 2 double, 1 twin
Bathrooms: 3 en-suite

Bed & breakfast per night:	£min	£max
Double	40.00	45.00

Half board per person:	£min	£max
Daily	25.00	30.00
Weekly	150.00	180.00

Lunch available
Evening meal 1900 (last orders 2130)

Crown Inn

APPROVED

Green Hill, Sherborne DT9 4EP
☎ (01935) 812930
Fax (01935) 812930
Friendly and comfortable freehouse. Excellent English and French cuisine.
Bedrooms: 1 double, 2 twin, 1 triple, 1 family room
Bathrooms: 1 public

Bed & breakfast per night:	£min	£max
Single	20.00	
Double	37.00	

Half board per person:	£min	£max
Daily	25.00	
Weekly	175.00	

Lunch available
Evening meal 1830 (last orders 2130)
Parking for 10
Cards accepted: Mastercard, Visa

Heartsease Cottage

HIGHLY COMMENDED

North Street, Bradford Abbas, Sherborne DT9 6SA
☎ (01935) 475480

Delightful old honey coloured stone cottage in country village. Idyllic garden. Evening meals. Themed bedrooms, Guests' private sitting room.
Bedrooms: 1 double, 1 twin
Bathrooms: 1 en-suite, 1 private

Bed & breakfast per night:	£min	£max
Single	17.50	22.50
Double	35.00	45.00

Half board per person:	£min	£max
Daily	27.50	32.50

Lunch available
Evening meal 1900 (last orders 2130)
Parking for 4
Open May-November

The Queens Head

APPROVED

High Street, Milborne Port, Sherborne DT9 5DQ
☎ (01963) 250314
Grade II village inn offering comfortable accommodation. In Good Beer Guide and Good Pub Food Guide - 7 real ales. Conservatory/restaurant and bar meals.
Bedrooms: 1 single, 2 double
Bathrooms: 1 public, 1 private shower

Bed & breakfast per night:	£min	£max
Single		21.00
Double		35.00

Lunch available
Evening meal 1900 (last orders 2130)
Parking for 10
Cards accepted: Amex, Diners, Mastercard, Visa

SHREWTON

Wiltshire
Map ref 2B2

Ashwick House

COMMENDED

Upper Backway, Shrewton, Salisbury SP3 4DE
☎ (01980) 621138
Fax (01980) 620152
Large village house in quiet position. Ideal touring centre for Salisbury, Bath, New Forest, Stonehenge (2 miles). Walking distance of 2 pubs. Parking in driveway.
Bedrooms: 1 single, 2 twin
Bathrooms: 1 private, 1 public

Bed & breakfast per night:	£min	£max
Single	15.00	18.00
Double	32.00	36.00

Half board per person:	£min	£max
Daily	20.00	26.00
Weekly	120.00	150.00

Evening meal 1900 (last orders 2030)
Parking for 5

SHREWTON

Continued

Maddington House

Listed COMMENDED

Maddington Street, Shrewton, Salisbury SP3 4JD
☎ (01980) 620406
Fax (01980) 620406

Beautiful listed 17th C family home, with attractive period hall and dining room. Stonehenge 2 miles, Salisbury 9 miles.

Bedrooms: 1 double, 1 twin, 1 family room
Bathrooms: 1 public, 3 private showers

Bed & breakfast per night:	£min	£max
Single	23.00	25.00
Double	36.00	40.00

Parking for 7

SIDMOUTH

Devon
Map ref 1D2

Charming resort set amid lofty red cliffs where the River Sid meets the sea. The wealth of ornate Regency and Victorian villas recalls the time when this was one of the south coast's most exclusive resorts. Museum; August International Festival of Folk Arts.
Tourist Information Centre ☎ (01395) 516441

Lower Pinn Farm

COMMENDED

Pinn, Sidmouth EX10 0NN
☎ (01395) 513733 & 0374 694776

220-acre mixed farm. Situated 2 miles west of Sidmouth, comfortable accommodation with substantial breakfast. Bedrooms have TV, tea/coffee facilities, central heating. Access at all times.

Bedrooms: 2 double, 1 triple
Bathrooms: 2 en-suite, 1 public

Bed & breakfast per night:	£min	£max
Single	18.00	21.00
Double	38.00	42.00

Parking for 3

For ideas on places to visit refer to the introduction at the beginning of this section.

SLAPTON

Devon
Map ref 1D3

Little Pittaford

HIGHLY COMMENDED

Slapton, Kingsbridge TQ7 2QG
☎ (01548) 580418
Fax (01548) 580406

Spacious stone cottage with south-facing light rooms, each with TV and pretty en-suite bathroom. A rural retreat, log fires, a tinkling stream.

Bedrooms: 2 double, 1 family room
Bathrooms: 3 en-suite

Bed & breakfast per night:	£min	£max
Double	50.00	50.00

Evening meal from 2000
Parking for 5
Open April–November

Start House

COMMENDED

Start, Slapton, Kingsbridge TQ7 2QD
☎ (01548) 580254

Comfortable Georgian house, overlooking beautiful valley in quiet hamlet 1 mile from Slapton. Attractive terraced garden. Ideal for wildlife and walking.

Bedrooms: 1 single, 2 double, 1 twin
Bathrooms: 2 en-suite, 1 public

Bed & breakfast per night:	£min	£max
Single	17.00	19.00
Double	19.00	21.00

Half board per person:	£min	£max
Daily	31.00	34.00

Evening meal 1830 (last orders 1000)
Parking for 4
Open January–November

For farm holidays and accommodation suitable for young people and organised groups, please refer to the special sections at the back of this guide.

SOUTH MOLTON

Devon
Map ref 1C1

Busy market town at the mouth of the Yeo Valley near southern Exmoor. Wool, mining and coaching brought prosperity between the Middle Ages and the 19th C and the fine square with Georgian buildings, a Guildhall and Assembly Rooms reflect this former affluence.

Kerscott Farm

HIGHLY COMMENDED

Ash Mill, South Molton EX36 4QG
☎ (01769) 550262

130-acre livestock farm. Peaceful, welcoming, working farm mentioned in Domesday Book, overlooking Exmoor. Superb views. Beautiful old world antique interior. Excellent home farm cooking. Non-smokers only.

Bedrooms: 2 double, 1 twin
Bathrooms: 3 en-suite

Bed & breakfast per night:	£min	£max
Double	35.00	38.00

Half board per person:	£min	£max
Daily	26.00	29.00

Evening meal 1830 (last orders 1400)
Parking for 8
10

SOUTH PETHERTON

Somerset
Map ref 1D2

Small town with a restored 15th C house, King Ina's Palace. The Roman Fosse Way crosses the River Parrett to the east by way of an old bridge on which there are 2 curious carved figures.

September House

COMMENDED

Lopen, South Petherton TA13 5JU
☎ (01460) 240647

Feel comfortable and at ease in this warm and friendly home. Enjoy the attractive and well stocked garden, high standards, good English breakfast.

Bedrooms: 2 double, 1 twin
Bathrooms: 1 en-suite, 1 public

Bed & breakfast per night:	£min	£max
Single	15.00	19.00
Double	34.00	38.00

Parking for 3

SUTTON MANDEVILLE

Wiltshire
Map ref 2B3

The Lancers Inn

COMMENDED

Sutton Mandeville, Salisbury
SP3 5NL
☎ (01722) 714220 & 714374

Built in 1933 to cater for trade/travel on main A30 road to West Country. Large, imposing 2-storey building in open country with views.

Bedrooms: 3 double, 1 triple
Bathrooms: 4 en-suite

Bed & breakfast per night:	£min	£max
Single	25.00	30.00
Double	40.00	45.00

Lunch available
Evening meal 1800 (last orders 2130)
Parking for 30
Cards accepted: Amex, Mastercard, Visa, Switch/Delta

SUTTON POYNTZ

Dorset
Map ref 2B3

Selwyns

Listed COMMENDED

Puddledock Lane, Sutton Poyntz, Weymouth DT3 6LZ
☎ (01305) 832239

Chalet bungalow in pretty village, 1 mile inland, near Weymouth and White Horse, Osmington. A353 to Preston, turn into Seven Acres Road, right at top of hill into Pudledock Lane.

Bedrooms: 2 double, 1 twin
Bathrooms: 1 public

Bed & breakfast per night:	£min	£max
Single	20.00	20.00
Double	30.00	35.00

Half board per person:	£min	£max
Daily	22.50	27.50
Weekly	157.50	192.50

Evening meal 1800 (last orders 2000)
Parking for 4
Open February–October

SWINDON

Wiltshire
Map ref 2B2

Wiltshire's industrial and commercial centre, an important railway town in the 19th C, situated just north of the Marlborough Downs. The railway village created in the mid-19th C has been preserved. Railway museum, art gallery, theatre and leisure centre. Designer shopping village.
Tourist Information Centre ☎ (01793) 530328 or 493007

Courtleigh House

COMMENDED

40 Draycott Road, Chiseldon, Swindon SN4 OLS
☎ (01793) 740246

Large detached village house with downland views, ample parking, tennis court and gardens. Easy access to Marlborough, Swindon and M4.

Bedrooms: 2 twin
Bathrooms: 1 en-suite, 1 private, 2 public

Bed & breakfast per night:	£min	£max
Single	20.00	24.00
Double	32.00	37.00

Parking for 3

Internos

APPROVED

3 Turnpike Road, Blunsdon, Swindon, Wilshire SN2 4EA
☎ (01793) 721496
Fax (01793) 721496

Detached red brick house off A419, 4 miles north of Swindon and 6 miles from M4 junction 15.

Bedrooms: 1 single, 1 twin, 1 triple
Bathrooms: 2 public

Bed & breakfast per night:	£min	£max
Single	20.00	23.00
Double	32.00	32.00

Parking for 6

ACCESSIBILITY

Look for the symbols which indicate accessibility for wheelchair users. These are described in detail at the front of this guide.

The Live and Let Live

HIGHLY COMMENDED

Upper Pavenhill, Purton, Swindon SN5 9DQ
☎ (01793) 770627

Converted stable, 5 miles west of Swindon, north of M4 (junction 16) and Wootton Bassett. At "One Stop" shop turn into Pavenhill. Proceed for half a mile to right turning - Upper Pavenhill. House is 200 yards on left. Non-smokers preferred.

Bedrooms: 1 twin, 1 triple
Bathrooms: 1 public

Bed & breakfast per night:	£min	£max
Single		20.00
Double		35.00

Parking for 3

The School House Hotel and Restaurant

COMMENDED

Hook Street, Hook, Swindon
SN4 8EF
☎ (01793) 851198
Fax (01793) 851025

Charming country house hotel in a converted 1860 school house. Combining modern facilities and Victorian decor. In rural hamlet but close to M4, Swindon and Cotswolds.

Bedrooms: 9 double, 1 twin
Bathrooms: 10 en-suite

Bed & breakfast per night:	£min	£max
Single	59.00	79.00
Double	69.00	89.00

Half board per person:	£min	£max
Daily	79.00	99.00
Weekly	475.00	595.00

Lunch available
Evening meal 1800 (last orders 2200)
Parking for 40
Cards accepted: Amex, Diners, Mastercard, Visa, Switch/Delta

Establishments should be open throughout the year, unless otherwise stated.

TAUNTON

Somerset
Map ref 1D1

County town, well-known for its public schools, sheltered by gentle hill-ranges on the River Tone. Medieval prosperity from wool has continued in marketing and manufacturing and the town retains many fine period buildings.
Tourist Information Centre ☎ (01823) 336344

Higher Dipford Farm

Trull, Taunton TA3 7NU
☎ (01823) 275770 & 257916
120-acre dairy farm. 14th C listed Somerset longhouse with magnificent walks and views. Antique furniture, log fires and spacious en-suite rooms. Renowned for high class cuisine using fresh dairy produce.
Bedrooms: 1 double, 2 twin
Bathrooms: 3 en-suite

Bed & breakfast per night:	£min	£max
Single	30.00	35.00
Double	46.00	54.00

Half board per person:	£min	£max
Daily	42.00	50.00
Weekly	266.00	315.00

Lunch available
Evening meal 1900 (last orders 2130)
Parking for 6
Cards accepted: Amex

Prockters Farm

West Monkton, Taunton TA2 8QN
☎ (01823) 412269
Fax (01823) 412269
300-acre mixed farm. 300-year-old farmhouse, 3 miles from M5. Inglenook fireplaces, brass beds, collection of farm antiques. Large garden. Ground floor en-suite bedrooms. Tea and cake on arrival.
Bedrooms: 1 single, 2 double, 1 twin, 1 triple
Bathrooms: 2 en-suite, 2 public

Bed & breakfast per night:	£min	£max
Single	18.00	21.00
Double	36.00	42.00

Parking for 6
Cards accepted: Amex

The Spinney

HIGHLY COMMENDED
Curland, Taunton TA3 5SE
☎ (01460) 234362
Fax (01460) 234362
Modern detached house in quiet countryside. Lovely garden with panoramic views from slopes of Blackdown Hills.
Bedrooms: 1 twin, 2 triple
Bathrooms: 3 en-suite, 1 public

Bed & breakfast per night:	£min	£max
Single	25.00	25.00
Double	39.00	44.00

Half board per person:	£min	£max
Daily	30.00	34.50
Weekly	210.00	241.50

Evening meal 1900 (last orders 2000)
Parking for 6

TAVISTOCK

Devon
Map ref 1C2

Old market town beside the River Tavy on the western edge of Dartmoor. Developed around its 10th C abbey, of which some fragments remain, it became a stannary town in 1305 when tin-streaming thrived on the moors. Tavistock Goose Fair, October.
Tourist Information Centre ☎ (01822) 612938

Acorn Cottage

COMMENDED
Heathfield, Tavistock PL19 0LQ
☎ (01822) 810038
17th C Grade II listed with many original features. Set in lovely, peaceful rural location close to Lydford Gorge and Brent Tor medieval church. Just 3 miles from Tavistock on Chillaton road.
Bedrooms: 1 double, 2 twin
Bathrooms: 3 en-suite

Bed & breakfast per night:	£min	£max
Single	20.00	30.00
Double	27.00	40.00

Parking for 20

Map references apply to the colour maps at the back of this guide.

April Cottage

HIGHLY COMMENDED
Mount Tavy Road, Tavistock PL19 9JB
☎ (01822) 613280

Award-winning bed and breakfast. Victorian character cottage in picturesque garden setting on the banks of the River Tavy. 2 minutes' walk to Tavistock with its excellent pubs and restaurants. As featured in "Sunday People" 101 Best B&Bs.
Bedrooms: 2 double, 1 twin
Bathrooms: 3 en-suite

Bed & breakfast per night:	£min	£max
Single	14.00	24.00
Double	28.00	36.00

Parking for 5

Kingfisher Cottage

COMMENDED
Mount Tavy Road, Vigo Bridge, Tavistock PL19 9JB
☎ (01822) 613801 & (0421) 772095
Riverside accommodation in newly built stone cottage, comfortable and convenient. Close to town centre and Dartmoor. Ideal base for touring Devon and Cornwall.
Bedrooms: 2 double, 1 twin
Bathrooms: 1 en-suite, 1 public

Bed & breakfast per night:	£min	£max
Single	15.00	30.00
Double	28.00	36.00

Parking for 5

TIMBERSCOMBE

Somerset
Map ref 1D1

Wellum

COMMENDED
Brook Street, Timberscombe, Minehead TA24 7TG
☎ (01643) 841234
Spacious stone-built 18th C house in Exmoor National Park. Commanding views towards Dunkery Beacon and surrounding rural landscape.
Bedrooms: 1 single, 1 double, 1 twin
Bathrooms: 1 public

Bed & breakfast per night:	£min	£max
Single	15.00	19.00
Double	30.00	38.00

Half board per person:	£min	£max
Daily	24.00	30.00
Weekly	168.00	210.00

Evening meal 1930 (last orders 2000)
Open February–November

TINTAGEL

Cornwall
Map ref 1B2

Coastal village near the legendary home of King Arthur. There is a lofty headland with the ruin of a Norman castle and traces of a Celtic monastery are still visible in the turf.

The Cornishman Inn

COMMENDED

Fore Street, Tintagel PL34 0DB
☎ (01840) 770238
Fax (01840) 770078

Beautiful old world inn offering en-suite bedrooms with TV and tea/coffee-making facilities. Three bars, extensive menus, beautiful gardens.

Bedrooms: 4 double, 4 twin, 1 triple, 1 family room
Suites available
Bathrooms: 10 en-suite

Bed & breakfast per night:	£min	£max
Single	25.00	30.00
Double	45.00	55.00

Lunch available
Evening meal 1800 (last orders 2130)
Parking for 30
Cards accepted: Amex, Diners, Mastercard, Visa, Switch/Delta

Port William Inn

COMMENDED

Trebarwith Strand, Tintagel
PL34 0HB
☎ (01840) 770230
Fax (01840) 770936
Email: phale@william.zynet.co.uk

Probably the best located inn in Cornwall, overlooking sea and beach. All rooms en-suite with TV and telephone. Extensive menu, including local seafood. Open all day, all year.

Bedrooms: 2 double, 1 twin, 1 triple, 2 family rooms
Bathrooms: 6 en-suite

Bed & breakfast per night:	£min	£max
Single	35.00	55.00
Double	50.00	90.00

Lunch available
Evening meal 1800 (last orders 2130)
Parking for 50
Cards accepted: Amex, Mastercard, Visa, Switch/Delta

TIVERTON

Devon
Map ref 1D2

Busy market and textile town, settled since the 9th C, at the meeting of 2 rivers. Town houses, Tudor almshouses and parts of the fine church were built by wealthy cloth merchants; a medieval castle is incorporated into a private house; Blundells School.
Tourist Information Centre ☎ (01884) 255827

Lower Collipriest Farm

HIGHLY COMMENDED

Tiverton EX16 4PT
☎ (01884) 252321
Fax (01884) 252321

221-acre dairy & livestock farm. Thatched farmhouse built around courtyard garden. All rooms en-suite. Super fresh home cooking using local produce. Walks on farm by pond and river. Brochure.

Bedrooms: 1 single, 2 twin
Bathrooms: 3 en-suite

Bed & breakfast per night:	£min	£max
Single	20.00	22.00
Double	40.00	44.00

Half board per person:	£min	£max
Daily	30.00	32.00
Weekly		205.00

Evening meal 1900 (last orders 1200)
Parking for 4
Open February–November

Please mention this guide when making your booking.

TORQUAY

Devon
Map ref 1D2

Devon's grandest resort, developed from a fishing village. Smart apartments and terraces rise from the seafront and Marine Drive along the headland gives views of beaches and colourful cliffs.
Tourist Information Centre ☎ (01803) 297428

Barn Hayes Country Hotel

HIGHLY COMMENDED

Brim Hill, Maidencombe, Torquay
TQ1 4TR
☎ (01803) 327980
Fax (01803) 327980

Warm, friendly and comfortable country house hotel in an Area of Outstanding Natural Beauty overlooking countryside and sea. Relaxation is guaranteed in these lovely surroundings by personal service, good food and fine wines.

Bedrooms: 2 single, 4 double, 2 twin, 2 triple, 2 family rooms
Bathrooms: 10 en-suite, 2 private

Bed & breakfast per night:	£min	£max
Single	25.00	30.00
Double	50.00	60.00

Half board per person:	£min	£max
Daily	38.00	44.00

Lunch available
Evening meal 1830 (last orders 1900)
Parking for 16
Open February–December
Cards accepted: Mastercard, Visa

You are advised to confirm your booking in writing.

The National Grading and Classification Scheme is explained at the back of this guide.

TORQUAY

Continued

Chelston Manor Hotel

Old Mill Road, Torquay TQ2 6HW
☎ (01803) 605142
Fax (01803) 605142

Old world bed and breakfast inn. Reputation for good pub food and hospitality. Sun-trap gardens with heated swimming pool.
Bedrooms: 1 single, 10 double, 3 twin, 1 triple
Bathrooms: 10 en-suite, 1 private, 1 public, 1 private shower

Bed & breakfast per night:	£min	£max
Single	21.00	30.00
Double	42.00	60.00

Lunch available
Evening meal 1800 (last orders 2130)
Parking for 40
Open April–October

Gainsboro Hotel

COMMENDED

22 Rathmore Road, Torquay TQ2 6NY
☎ (01803) 292032
Fax (01803) 292032
Family-run hotel providing friendly atmosphere. Close to station, seafront and amenities.
Bedrooms: 1 single, 5 double
Bathrooms: 4 private, 1 public

Bed & breakfast per night:	£min	£max
Single	13.00	18.00
Double	26.00	36.00

Parking for 5
Open March–September
Cards accepted: Mastercard, Visa

Kingston House

HIGHLY COMMENDED

75 Avenue Road, Torquay TQ2 5LL
☎ (01803) 212760

Combines Victorian elegance with modern amenities, ensuring a fulfilling, relaxed holiday. Conveniently situated for seafront, harbour, town. Private car park.
Bedrooms: 1 single, 2 double, 1 twin, 1 triple, 1 family room
Bathrooms: 6 en-suite

Bed & breakfast per night:	£min	£max
Single	17.50	20.00
Double	29.00	39.00

Parking for 6
Cards accepted: Diners, Mastercard, Visa

Maple Lodge

COMMENDED

36 Ash Hill Road, Torquay TQ1 3JD
☎ (01803) 297391
Detached guesthouse with beautiful views. Relaxed atmosphere, home cooking, en-suite rooms. Centrally situated for town and beaches.
Bedrooms: 1 single, 2 double, 1 twin, 2 triple, 1 family room
Bathrooms: 6 en-suite, 1 private, 1 public

Bed & breakfast per night:	£min	£max
Single	15.00	18.00
Double	30.00	36.00

Evening meal from 1800
Parking for 5
Open March–October

TOTNES

Devon
Map ref 1D2

Old market town steeply built near the head of the Dart Estuary. Remains of medieval gateways, a noble church, 16th C Guildhall and medley of period houses recall former wealth from cloth and shipping, continued in rural and water industries.
Tourist Information Centre ☎ (01803) 863168

Buckyette Farm

COMMENDED

Buckyette, Totnes TQ9 6ND
☎ (01803) 762638
51-acre arable farm. Victorian farmhouse in large garden in Devon valley. Children welcome. Central heating.
Bedrooms: 1 double, 2 twin, 3 triple
Bathrooms: 4 en-suite, 2 private

Bed & breakfast per night:	£min	£max
Single	22.00	23.00
Double	36.00	38.00

Parking for 8
Open March–October

Old Church House Inn

COMMENDED

Torbryan, Newton Abbot TQ12 5UR
☎ (01803) 812372 & 812180
Fax (01803) 812180
13th C coaching house of immense character and old world charm with inglenook fireplaces, stone walls and oak beamed ceilings. Situated in a beautiful valley between Dartmoor and Torquay.
Bedrooms: 5 double, 5 triple, 1 family room
Bathrooms: 11 en-suite

Bed & breakfast per night:	£min	£max
Single	40.00	50.00
Double	55.00	65.00

Half board per person:	£min	£max
Daily	40.00	47.50
Weekly	250.00	300.00

Lunch available
Evening meal 1800 (last orders 2130)
Parking for 30
Cards accepted: Mastercard, Visa

The Old Forge at Totnes

HIGHLY COMMENDED

Seymour Place, Totnes TQ9 5AY
☎ (01803) 862174
Fax (01803) 865385
Delightful 600-year-old stone building, with walled garden and working smithy. Cottage suite suitable for family or disabled guests. No smoking indoors. Extensive breakfast menu (traditional, vegetarian, fish and continental). Whirlpool spa. Speciality: golf breaks.
Bedrooms: 1 single, 5 double, 2 twin, 2 family rooms
Suites available
Bathrooms: 9 en-suite, 1 private, 1 public

Bed & breakfast per night:	£min	£max
Single	40.00	50.00
Double	50.00	70.00

Parking for 10

Cards accepted: Mastercard, Visa, Switch/Delta

The Watermans Arms

HIGHLY COMMENDED

Bow Bridge, Ashprington, Totnes TQ9 7EG
☎ (01803) 732214
Fax (01803) 732214

Famous riverside inn noted for award-winning accommodation and beautiful location in a sheltered valley at the head of Bow Creek on the River Dart.
Bedrooms: 10 double, 3 twin, 2 triple
Bathrooms: 15 en-suite

Bed & breakfast per night:	£min	£max
Single	36.00	40.00
Double	56.00	76.00

Half board per person:	£min	£max
Daily	41.00	55.00
Weekly	287.00	385.00

Lunch available
Evening meal 1830 (last orders 2130)
Parking for 60
Cards accepted: Amex, Mastercard, Visa, Switch/Delta
30

TREGASWITH

Cornwall
Map ref 1B2

Twas-A-Barn

Tregaswith, Newquay TR8 4HY
☎ (01637) 880907
Barn converted to character living accommodation, in small hamlet just off the beaten track. Extensive country views. En-suite bedrooms.
Bedrooms: 2 double, 1 triple, 1 family room
Bathrooms: 3 en-suite, 1 private

Bed & breakfast per night:	£min	£max
Single	20.00	25.00
Double	40.00	40.00

Parking for 4
3

TROWBRIDGE

Wiltshire
Map ref 2B2

Wiltshire's administrative centre, a handsome market and manufacturing town with a wealth of merchants' houses and other Georgian buildings.
Tourist Information Centre ☎ (01225) 777054

Welam House

COMMENDED

Bratton Road, West Ashton, Trowbridge BA14 6AZ
☎ (01225) 755908
Located in quiet village. Garden with trees and lawn with a view of Westbury White Horse. Ideally situated for touring. Bowls and mini-golf for guests.
Bedrooms: 1 double, 1 twin, 1 triple
Bathrooms: 3 en-suite, 1 public

Bed & breakfast per night:	£min	£max
Double	32.00	32.00

Parking for 6
Open March–November

TRURO

Cornwall
Map ref 1B3

Cornwall's administrative centre and cathedral city, set at the head of Truro River on the Fal Estuary. A medieval stannary town, it handled mineral ore from west Cornwall; fine Georgian buildings recall its heyday as a society haunt in the second mining boom.
Tourist Information Centre ☎ (01872) 274555

Arrallas

HIGHLY COMMENDED

Ladock, Truro TR2 4NP
☎ (01872) 510379
Fax (01872) 510200
320-acre arable farm. Signed from opposite the Clock Garage, Summercourt. Farmhouse accommodation set in truly rural situation. Good food, warm welcome, attention to detail. Listed building.
Bedrooms: 2 double, 1 twin
Bathrooms: 3 en-suite

Bed & breakfast per night:	£min	£max
Double	40.00	48.00

Half board per person:	£min	£max
Daily	32.00	36.00
Weekly	214.00	227.00

Evening meal from 1900
Parking for 8
Open February–October

Marcorrie Hotel

APPROVED

20 Falmouth Road, Truro TR1 2HX
☎ (01872) 277374
Fax (01872) 241666
Family-run hotel 5 minutes' walk from city centre and cathedral. Ideal for business or holiday, central for visiting the country houses and gardens of Cornwall.
Bedrooms: 3 single, 3 double, 2 twin, 1 triple, 3 family rooms
Bathrooms: 12 en-suite, 1 public

Bed & breakfast per night:	£min	£max
Single	33.00	35.00
Double	44.00	46.00

Half board per person:	£min	£max
Daily	42.00	
Weekly	280.00	

Evening meal 1900 (last orders 1700)
Parking for 16
Cards accepted: Amex, Diners, Mastercard, Visa, Switch/Delta
20

Rock Cottage

HIGHLY COMMENDED

Blackwater, Truro TR4 8EU
☎ (01872) 560252
Fax (01872) 560252

18th C beamed cottage, old world charm. Formerly village schoolmaster's home. Haven for non-smokers. Comfort, hospitality, friendly service, a la carte menu.
Bedrooms: 2 double, 1 twin
Bathrooms: 3 en-suite

Bed & breakfast per night:	£min	£max
Single	26.00	
Double	44.00	

Evening meal 1900 (last orders 1500)
Parking for 4

TRURO

Continued

Trevispian-Vean Farm Guest House

COMMENDED

St Erme, Truro TR4 9BL
☎ (01872) 279514
Fax (01872) 263730

300-acre arable farm. Beautifully situated 7 miles from the coast in the heart of the countryside, the farmhouse combines modern comforts with all the charm of a 300-year-old farm. Ideal for touring Cornwall. Non-smokers only, please.

Bedrooms: 4 double, 2 twin, 4 triple, 2 family rooms
Bathrooms: 12 en-suite, 2 public

Bed & breakfast per night:	£min	£max
Single	20.00	22.00
Double	36.00	40.00

Half board per person:	£min	£max
Daily	26.00	28.00
Weekly	151.00	165.00

Evening meal 1830 (last orders 1600)
Parking for 15
Open April–September

WARMINSTER

Wiltshire
Map ref 2B2

Attractive stone-built town high up to the west of Salisbury Plain. A market town, it originally thrived on cloth and wheat. Many prehistoric camps and barrows nearby, along with Longleat House and Safari Park.
Tourist Information Centre ☎ (01985) 218548

Belmont Bed & Breakfast

COMMENDED

9 Boreham Road, Warminster BA12 9JP
☎ (01985) 212799

Enjoy a friendly welcome in comfortable, spacious and well-appointed accommodation. Ideally placed for shops, restaurants and rail station. Ideal location for Stonehenge, Longleat, Stourhead and Bath. Non-smoking.

Bedrooms: 2 double, 1 twin
Bathrooms: 1 public

Bed & breakfast per night:	£min	£max
Single	20.00	30.00
Double	30.00	36.00

Parking for 4

WELLINGTON

Somerset
Map ref 1D1

Hangeridge Farm

Wrangway, Wellington TA21 9QG
☎ (01823) 662339

55-acre mixed farm. Personal service and home cooking. Scenic walk and lovely gardens. 1 hour's drive to West Country coast.

Bedrooms: 2 double, 1 twin
Bathrooms: 2 private

Bed & breakfast per night:	£min	£max
Single		15.00
Double		30.00

Half board per person:	£min	£max
Daily		23.00

Parking for 4

WELLS

Somerset
Map ref 2A2

Small city set beneath the southern slopes of the Mendips. Built between 1180 and 1424, the magnificent cathedral is preserved in much of its original glory and with its ancient precincts forms one of our loveliest and most unified groups of medieval buildings.
Tourist Information Centre ☎ (01749) 672552

Bekynton House

COMMENDED

7 St Thomas Street, Wells BA5 2UU
☎ (01749) 672222 & 672061
Fax (01749) 672222

This attractive period house with cathedral views is well appointed with charming antique furniture and comfortable en-suite rooms. Desmond and Rosaleen Gripper offer a warm welcome and delicious breakfasts. Excellent location close to cathedral and Bishop's Palace.

Bedrooms: 3 double, 2 twin, 1 triple
Bathrooms: 4 en-suite, 2 private, 1 public

Bed & breakfast per night:	£min	£max
Single	30.00	
Double	45.00	49.00

Parking for 6
Cards accepted: Mastercard, Visa

Burcott Mill

COMMENDED

Burcott, Wells BA5 1NJ
☎ (01749) 673118 & (0421) 378773
Fax (01749) 673118

Restored working watermill with attached house and craft workshops. Friendly country atmosphere. Birds and animals. Home cooking. Opposite good country pub. Accommodation available for wheelchair user.

Wheelchair access category 1♿
Bedrooms: 1 single, 1 double, 3 triple, 1 family room
Suite available
Bathrooms: 5 en-suite, 1 private

Bed & breakfast per night:	£min	£max
Single	19.00	30.00
Double	33.00	50.00

Half board per person:	£min	£max
Daily	27.50	36.00
Weekly	181.00	234.00

Evening meal 1800 (last orders 2200)
Parking for 10
Cards accepted: Diners, Mastercard, Visa

Franklyns Farm

HIGHLY COMMENDED

Chewton Mendip, Bath BA3 4NB
☎ (01761) 241372

350-acre arable & dairy farm. Comfortable and cosy modern farmhouse in heart of Mendips, in a peaceful setting with superb views. Situated on Emborough B3114 road. Ideal for touring Wells, Cheddar and Bath. Delicious breakfast.

Bedrooms: 1 double, 2 twin
Suites available
Bathrooms: 2 en-suite, 1 private, 1 public

Bed & breakfast per night:	£min	£max
Single	25.00	
Double	38.00	

Parking for 5

Littlewell Farm Guest House

HIGHLY COMMENDED

Coxley, Wells BA5 1QP
☎ (01749) 677914

Delightful 18th C farmhouse nestling in pretty garden and enjoying extensive views over beautiful countryside. Charming bedrooms with antique furniture offer comfort and pleasing style coupled with high standards. 1 mile south-west of Wells.

Bedrooms: 1 single, 2 double, 2 twin
Bathrooms: 4 en-suite, 1 private

Bed & breakfast per night:	£min	£max
Single	21.00	24.00
Double	37.00	46.00
Half board per person:	£min	£max
Daily	27.00	40.00

Evening meal 1900 (last orders 2000)
Parking for 12
Open February–December

Milton Manor Farm

COMMENDED

Old Bristol Road, Upper Milton, Wells BA5 3AH
☎ (01749) 673394

130-acre beef farm. Elizabethan manor house, Grade II listed, on the southern slopes of the Mendips, 1 mile north of Wells. Superb view.*

Bedrooms: 1 double, 1 twin, 1 triple
Bathrooms: 1 public

Bed & breakfast per night:	£min	£max
Single	17.50	18.50
Double	31.00	32.00

Parking for 6

Tor House

HIGHLY COMMENDED

20 Tor Street, Wells BA5 2US
☎ (01749) 672322 & 672084
Fax (01749) 672322

Historic, sympathetically restored 17th C building in delightful grounds overlooking the cathedral and Bishop's Palace. Attractive, comfortable and tastefully furnished throughout. 3 minutes' walk to town centre. Ample parking.

Bedrooms: 1 single, 3 double, 1 twin, 3 family rooms
Bathrooms: 5 en-suite, 2 public

Bed & breakfast per night:	£min	£max
Single	22.00	40.00
Double	38.00	55.00

Evening meal 1830 (last orders 1000)
Parking for 12
Cards accepted: Mastercard, Visa, Switch/Delta

WEST ANSTEY

Devon
Map ref 1D1

Partridge Arms Farm

COMMENDED

Yeo Mill, West Anstey, South Molton EX36 3NU
☎ (01398) 341217
Fax (01398) 341217

200-acre mixed farm. Old world farmhouse set within established family farm, offering genuine hospitality and traditional farmhouse fare. Ideal for touring, outdoor pursuits and coastal resorts.

Bedrooms: 3 double, 2 twin, 2 family rooms
Bathrooms: 4 en-suite, 1 public

Bed & breakfast per night:	£min	£max
Single	20.00	24.50
Double	40.00	49.00
Half board per person:	£min	£max
Daily	29.50	34.00
Weekly	199.50	231.00

Evening meal 1930 (last orders 1600)
Parking for 10

WESTON-SUPER-MARE

North Somerset
Map ref 1D1

Large, friendly resort developed in the 19th C. Traditional seaside attractions include theatres and a dance hall. The museum has a Victorian seaside gallery and Iron Age finds from a hill fort on Worlebury Hill in Weston Woods.
Tourist Information Centre ☎ (01934) 888800

Braeside Hotel

COMMENDED

2 Victoria Park, Weston-super-Mare BS23 2HZ
☎ (01934) 626642
Fax (01934) 626642

Delightful, family-run hotel, ideally situated near seafront. All rooms en-suite. Single rooms always available. Unrestricted on-street parking.

Bedrooms: 1 single, 5 double, 1 twin, 2 triple
Bathrooms: 9 en-suite

Bed & breakfast per night:	£min	£max
Single	24.00	24.00
Double	40.00	48.00
Half board per person:	£min	£max
Daily	34.00	34.00
Weekly	196.00	196.00

Lunch available
Evening meal 1830 (last orders 1800)

Conifers

COMMENDED

63 Milton Road, Weston-super-Mare BS23 2SP
☎ (01934) 624404
Fax (01934) 624404

Semi-detached corner guesthouse standing back in a large garden. Completely refurbished for bed and breakfast use. 27 years' experience.

Bedrooms: 2 double, 1 twin
Bathrooms: 1 en-suite, 1 public

Bed & breakfast per night:	£min	£max
Single	18.00	22.00
Double	32.00	40.00

Parking for 4
Open January–November

Purn House Farm

COMMENDED

Bleadon, Weston-super-Mare BS24 0QE
☎ (01934) 812324
Fax (01934) 811029

700-acre mixed farm. Comfortable 17th C farmhouse only 3 miles from Weston-super-Mare. En-suite available with TV. 1 ground floor room. Peaceful yet not isolated, on bus route to town centre and station.

Bedrooms: 1 single, 1 twin, 2 triple, 3 family rooms
Bathrooms: 2 en-suite, 2 private, 1 public

Bed & breakfast per night:	£min	£max
Single	22.50	27.00
Double	35.00	44.00

Parking for 10
Open February–November

The symbol after an establishment name indicates that it is a Regional Tourist Board member.

WESTWARD HO!

Devon
Map ref 1C1

Small resort, whose name comes from the title of Charles Kingsley's famous novel, on Barnstaple Bay, close to the Taw and Torridge Estuary. There are good sands and a notable golf-course - one of the oldest in Britain.

The Puffins Inn

APPROVED

123 Bay View Road, Westward Ho!, Bideford EX39 1BJ
☎ (01237) 473970
Former gentleman's residence overlooking Northam Burrows Country Park. Car park and garden.
Bedrooms: 1 double, 1 twin, 2 triple, 1 family room
Bathrooms: 5 en-suite, 1 public

Bed & breakfast per night:	£min	£max
Single	18.50	19.50
Double	37.00	39.00

Lunch available
Evening meal 1800 (last orders 2100)
Parking for 12
Cards accepted: Mastercard, Visa

WEYMOUTH

Dorset
Map ref 2B3

Ancient port and one of the south's earliest resorts. Curving beside a long, sandy beach, the elegant Georgian esplanade is graced with a statue of George III and a cheerful Victorian Jubilee clock tower.
Tourist Information Centre ☎ (01305) 785747

New Salsudas

COMMENDED

22 Lennox Street, Weymouth DT4 7HE
☎ (01305) 771903
Private B&B close to town centre, in quiet position 300 yards from beach, station and gardens. Convenient for nature reserve, windsurfing and many attractions. Warm and friendly, winter or summer. JCB card also accepted.
Bedrooms: 1 double, 2 twin
Bathrooms: 3 en-suite, 1 public

Bed & breakfast per night:	£min	£max
Single	20.00	30.00
Double	32.00	45.00

Parking for 3
Cards accepted: Mastercard, Visa, Switch/Delta

WHEDDON CROSS

Somerset
Map ref 1D1

Crossroads hamlet in the heart of Exmoor National Park.

Exmoor House

HIGHLY COMMENDED

Wheddon Cross TA24 7DU
☎ (01643) 841432
Fax (01643) 841432
Edwardian house. Elegant spacious accommodation. Excellent meals from local produce. Good wines. Exclusively for non-smokers. Perfect centre for touring and walking in Exmoor National Park.
Bedrooms: 2 double, 3 twin, 1 triple
Bathrooms: 4 en-suite, 2 private, 1 public

Bed & breakfast per night:	£min	£max
Single	31.00	32.00
Double	42.00	44.00
Half board per person:	**£min**	**£max**
Daily	34.50	35.50
Weekly	217.00	224.00

Evening meal 1900 (last orders 1800)
Parking for 9
Open March–November
Cards accepted: Mastercard, Visa, Switch/Delta
10

WIDECOMBE-IN-THE-MOOR

Devon
Map ref 1C2

Old village in pastoral country under the high tors of East Dartmoor. The "Cathedral of the Moor" stands near a tiny square, once used for archery practice, which has a 16th C Church House among other old buildings.

Higher Venton Farm

Listed APPROVED

Widecombe-in-the-Moor, Newton Abbot TQ13 7TF
☎ (01364) 621235
40-acre beef farm. 17th C thatched farmhouse with a homely atmosphere and farmhouse cooking. Ideal for touring Dartmoor. 16 miles from the coast.
Bedrooms: 2 double, 1 twin
Bathrooms: 1 en-suite, 1 public

Bed & breakfast per night:	£min	£max
Single	20.00	21.00
Double	32.00	40.00
Half board per person:	**£min**	**£max**
Daily	24.00	25.00
Weekly	160.00	185.00

Parking for 5
5

Sheena Tower

APPROVED

Widecombe-in-the-Moor, Newton Abbot TQ13 7TE
☎ (01364) 621308
Comfortable moorland guesthouse overlooking Widecombe village, offering a relaxed holiday in picturesque surroundings. Well placed for discovering Dartmoor.
Bedrooms: 1 single, 2 double, 1 twin, 1 triple, 1 family room
Bathrooms: 2 en-suite, 2 public

Bed & breakfast per night:	£min	£max
Single	16.00	18.00
Double	32.00	36.00

Evening meal 1900 (last orders 1200)
Parking for 6
Open February–October

WINSFORD

Somerset
Map ref 1D1

Small village on the River Exe in splendid walking country under Winsford Hill. On the other side of the hill is a Celtic standing stone, the Caratacus Stone, and nearby across the River Barle stretches an ancient packhorse bridge, Tarr Steps, built of great stone slabs.

Larcombe Foot

HIGHLY COMMENDED

Winsford, Minehead TA24 7HS
☎ (01643) 851306
Comfortable country house in tranquil, beautiful setting, overlooking River Exe. Lovely walks on doorstep. Ideal for touring Exmoor and north Devon coast.
Bedrooms: 1 double, 1 twin
Bathrooms: 2 private

Bed & breakfast per night:	£min	£max
Single		18.00
Double		36.00
Half board per person:	**£min**	**£max**
Daily		30.00

Evening meal (last orders 1930)
Parking for 3
Open April–October

WIVELISCOMBE

Somerset
Map ref 1D1

Small, friendly town at the foot of the Brendon Hills, leading to the wonderful wilderness of Exmoor National Park. Well served with local facilities, it is an ideal centre for walking, fishing, riding and relaxing.

Alpine House

HIGHLY COMMENDED

10 West Road, Wiveliscombe, Taunton TA4 2TF
☎ (01984) 623526

Elegant Victorian house in the rolling countryside of the Brendons. Excellent base for enjoying the beauty of West Somerset, including Exmoor and the coastline. Evening meals can be arranged.

Bedrooms: 3 double, 1 twin
Bathrooms: 3 en-suite, 1 private

Bed & breakfast per night:	£min	£max
Single	30.00	30.00
Double	50.00	50.00

Cards accepted: Mastercard, Visa, Switch/Delta

YARCOMBE

Devon
Map ref 1D2

Tiny village between Honiton and Chard.

Crawley Farm

COMMENDED

Yarcombe, Honiton EX14 9AX
☎ (01460) 64760
Fax (01460) 64760

200-acre mixed farm. 17th C thatched farmhouse in Blackdown Hills. Tea-making, TV, hot and cold in bedrooms. En-suite available. Excellent pub food locally.

Bedrooms: 1 double, 1 twin, 1 triple
Bathrooms: 1 en-suite, 2 public

Bed & breakfast per night:	£min	£max
Single	15.00	19.00
Double	32.00	34.00

Parking for 6
Open March–November

YELVERTON

Devon
Map ref 1C2

Village on the edge of Dartmoor, where ponies wander over the flat common. Buckland Abbey is 2 miles south-west, while Burrator Reservoir is 2 miles to the east.

Greenwell Farm

COMMENDED

Meavy, Yelverton PL20 6PY
☎ (01822) 853563
Fax (01822) 853563

220-acre livestock farm. Fresh country air, breathtaking views and scrumptious farmhouse cuisine. This busy family farm welcomes you to share the countryside and wildlife.

Bedrooms: 2 double, 1 twin
Bathrooms: 2 en-suite, 1 private

Bed & breakfast per night:	£min	£max
Double	40.00	46.00

Half board per person:	£min	£max
Daily	32.50	36.00
Weekly	205.00	218.00

Evening meal 1830 (last orders 1200)
Parking for 8

Peek Hill Farm

COMMENDED

Dousland, Yelverton PL20 6PD
☎ (01822) 854808 & 852908
Fax (01822) 854808

300-acre livestock farm. Relax on an antique brass bed, experience a proper farmhouse breakfast, then wander down mossy moorland ways.

Bedrooms: 1 double, 1 family room
Bathrooms: 2 en-suite, 1 public

Bed & breakfast per night:	£min	£max
Single	20.00	20.00
Double	34.00	34.00

Half board per person:	£min	£max
Daily	27.00	30.00
Weekly	175.00	185.00

Lunch available
Evening meal from 1800
Parking for 4

YEOVIL

Somerset
Map ref 2A3

Lively market town, famous for glove making, set in dairying country beside the River Yeo. Interesting parish church. Museum of South Somerset at Hendford Manor.
Tourist Information Centre ☎ (01935) 471279

Holywell House

HIGHLY COMMENDED

Holywell, East Coker, Yeovil BA22 9NQ
☎ (01935) 862612
Fax (01935) 863035

Delightful country home with fine amenities. Three acres of gardens (National Gardens Scheme), tennis court. Idyllic rural setting in quiet location off A30, 2 miles west of Yeovil.

Bedrooms: 2 double, 1 twin
Suite available
Bathrooms: 3 en-suite

Bed & breakfast per night:	£min	£max
Single	35.00	40.00
Double	60.00	65.00

Half board per person:	£min	£max
Daily	52.00	57.00
Weekly	330.00	360.00

Evening meal 1900 (last orders 2030)
Parking for 15

Please check prices and other details at the time of booking.

A key to symbols can be found inside the back cover flap.

YEOVILTON

Somerset
Map ref 2A3

Cary Fitzpaine

COMMENDED

Yeovilton, Yeovil BA22 8JB
☎ (01458) 223250 & (0402) 166841
Fax (01458) 223372

600-acre mixed farm. Elegant Georgian manor farmhouse in idyllic setting. Large gardens. High standard of accommodation, all bedrooms with en-suite bath. Four-poster bed.

Bedrooms: 1 double, 1 twin, 1 triple
Bathrooms: 2 en-suite, 1 private, 1 public

Bed & breakfast per night:	£min	£max
Single	20.00	24.00
Double	36.00	40.00

Parking for 14
Cards accepted: Amex, Diners, Mastercard, Visa, Switch/Delta

Courtry Farm

Listed APPROVED

Bridgehampton, Yeovil BA22 8HF
☎ (01935) 840327

590-acre mixed farm. Farmhouse with ground floor rooms, en-suite, TV, tea-making facilities. Tennis court. Fleet Air Arm Museum half a mile.

Bedrooms: 1 twin, 1 triple
Bathrooms: 2 en-suite

Bed & breakfast per night:	£min	£max
Single	20.00	
Double	35.00	

Parking for 20

AT-A-GLANCE SYMBOLS

Symbols at the end of each accommodation entry give useful information about services and facilities. A key to symbols can be found inside the back cover flap.

Keep this open for easy reference.

CHECK THE MAPS

The colour maps at the back of this guide show all the cities, towns and villages for which you will find accommodation entries.

Refer to the town index to find the page on which it is listed.

SOUTH OF ENGLAND

England's south is ideal for a coast and countryside holiday. Enjoy the lively resorts of Poole and Swanage, or visit Portsmouth, at the heart of England's ancient naval heritage. Then it's a short trip to the delightful Isle of Wight or inland to the lovely New Forest.

The region's packed with English tradition. Historic cities include magnificent Oxford, Windsor and Winchester - home of King Arthur's Round Table. The recently-restored Kennet and Avon canal and nearby waterways offer trips in a traditional horse-drawn canal boat. And attractive spots can be found all along the Thames, perfect for a picnic lunch.

Henley Regatta and the Ascot race meeting are just two of the area's famed annual events.

The counties of Berkshire, Buckinghamshire, Dorset (Eastern), Hampshire, Isle of Wight and Oxfordshire

FOR MORE INFORMATION CONTACT:
Southern Tourist Board
40 Chamberlayne Road, Eastleigh,
Hampshire SO50 5JH
Tel: (01703) 620555 **Fax:** (01703) 620010

Where to Go in the South of England –
see pages 290-293
Where to Stay in the South of England –
see pages 294-325

SOUTH OF ENGLAND

Where to Go and What to See

You will find hundreds of interesting places to visit during your stay in the South of England, just some of which are listed in these pages. The number against each name will help you locate it on the map (page 293). Contact any Tourist Information Centre in the region for more ideas on days out in the South of England.

1 Blenheim Palace
Woodstock,
Oxfordshire OX20 1PX
Tel: (01993) 811091
Home of the 11th Duke of Marlborough. Birthplace of Sir Winston Churchill. Designed by Vanbrugh in the English baroque style. Landscaped by Capability Brown.

2 Waterperry Gardens
Waterperry,
Oxford OX33 1JZ
Tel: (01844) 339254
Ornamental gardens covering six acres of the 83-acre 18thC Waterperry House estate. Saxon village church, garden shop, teashop, art and craft gallery.

3 Sheldonian Theatre
Broad Street, Oxford OX1 3AZ
Tel: (01865) 277299
One of Sir Christopher Wren's earliest works. Built in 1664-1669 it is the Ceremonial Hall of the University.

4 Didcot Railway Centre
Great Western Society,
Didcot, Oxfordshire OX11 7NJ
Tel: (01235) 817200
Living museum recreating the golden age of the Great Western Railway. Steam locomotives and trains, engine shed and small relics museum.

5 Bekonscot Model Village
Warwick Road, Beaconsfield,
Buckinghamshire HP9 2PL
Tel: (01494) 672919
A complete model village of the 1930s, with outdoor gauge 1 model railway. The world's first model village with zoo, cinema, minster, cricket match and 1,400 inhabitants.

6 Legoland Windsor
Winkfield Road, Windsor,
Berkshire SL4 4AY
Tel: (0990) 626375
A unique family park with hands-on activities, rides, themed playscapes and more Lego bricks than you ever dreamed possible.

7 **The Vyne**
Sherborne St John, Basingstoke,
Hampshire RG24 9HL
Tel: (01256) 881337
Original house dating back to Henry VIII's time, extensively altered in the mid 17thC. Tudor chapel, beautiful gardens and lake.

8 **Whitchurch Silk Mill**
28 Winchester Street,
Whitchurch,
Hampshire RG28 7AL
Tel: (01256) 893882
A working silk mill situated on Frog Island on the River Test. See historic looms weaving silk, waterwheel powering machinery, video on silk production.

9 **Jane Austen's House**
Chawton, Alton, Hampshire
GU34 1SD Tel: (01420) 83262
17thC house where Jane Austen lived from 1809-1817 and wrote or revised her six great novels. Letters, pictures, memorabilia, garden with old fashioned flowers.

10 **Gilbert White's House and Garden and The Oates Museum**
The Wakes, High Street,
Selborne, Alton,
Hampshire GU34 3JH
Tel: (01420) 511275
Historic house and garden, home of Gilbert White, author of The Natural History of Selborne. *Exhibition on Frank Oates, explorer, and Captain Lawrence Oates of Antarctic fame.*

11 **The Sir Harold Hillier Gardens and Arboretum**
Jermyns Lane, Ampfield, Romsey,
Hampshire SO51 0QA
Tel: (01794) 368787
The largest collection of trees and shrubs of its kind in the British Isles, planted within an attractive landscape of over 166 acres. Rhododendrons, camellias and other plants.

12 **Marwell Zoological Park**
Colden Common,
Winchester,
Hampshire SO21 1JH
Tel: (01962) 777407
Conservation zoo set in 100 acres of parkland with over 150 rare species including Siberian tiger, jaguar, hippo and rhino. Road and rail trains, children's amusements and restaurant.

13 **Broadlands**
Romsey,
Hampshire SO51 9ZD
Tel: (01794) 517888
Home of late Lord Mountbatten. Magnificent 18thC house and contents. Superb views across the River Test. Mountbatten exhibition and audio-visual presentation.

14 **The Dorset Heavy Horse Centre**
Grains Hill, Edmondsham,
Verwood, Wimborne
Minster,
Dorset BH21 5RJ
Tel: (01202) 824040
Various breeds of heavy horses plus miniature and shetland ponies. Old farm wagons and implements. Demonstrations of plaiting and harnessing. Information, pets and aviaries.

15 **New Forest Nature Quest**
Longdown,
Ashurst,
Southampton
SO4 4UH
Tel: (01703)
292166
Situated in a beautiful part of the New Forest, this is your chance to become a nature detective and discover Britain's wealth of wildlife.

16 **The New Forest Owl Sanctuary**
Crow Lane, Crow,
Ringwood, Hampshire BH24 1EA
Tel: (01425) 476487
All the barn owls are destined to be released into the wild. The sanctuary includes an incubation room, hospital unit and 100 aviaries of various sizes.

17 **Royal Signals Museum**
Blandford Camp,
Blandford Forum,
Dorset DT11 8RH
Tel: (01258) 482248
History of army communication from Crimean War to Gulf War. Vehicles, uniforms, medals and badges on display.

18 National Motor Museum
John Montagu Building,
Beaulieu, Brockenhurst,
Hampshire SO42 7ZN
Tel: (01590) 612345
Motor museum with over 250 exhibits showing the history of motoring from 1895. Palace House, Wheels Experience, abbey ruins, and a display of monastic life.

19 The D Day Museum and Overlord Embroidery
Clarence Esplanade,
Portsmouth PO5 3NT
Tel: (01705) 827261/875276
Incorporates Overlord Embroidery depicting allied invasion of Normandy. Displays of D-Day action with some of the vehicles that took part.

20 HMS Victory
HM Naval Base,
Portsmouth PO1 3LJ
Tel: (01705) 839766/295252
Vice Admiral Lord Nelson's flagship at Trafalgar. See his cabin, the 'cockpit' where he died. Memorable tours of the sombre gun decks where men lived.

21 Mary Rose Ship Hall & Exhibition
HM Naval Base,
Portsmouth PO1 3PZ
Tel: (01705) 812931
See the restoration and conservation of Henry VIII's warship exhibition. Plus the ship's treasures with film and slide presentation on the sinking and raising of the Mary Rose.

22 Bembridge Windmill
High Street, Bembridge,
Isle of Wight PO35 5SQ
Tel: (01983) 873945
Dating from 1700, it is the only remaining windmill on the Island. Last used in 1913 it contains much of its original wooden machinery. Delightful views from the Cap.

23 Butterfly World and Fountain World
Staplers Road, Wootton,
Isle of Wight PO33 4RW
Tel: (01983) 883430
Tropical indoor garden with butterflies from around the world. Many fountains, water features and huge fish. Italian and Japanese garden.

24 Barton Manor Gardens and Vineyards
Whippingham, East Cowes,
Isle of Wight PO32 6LB
Tel: (01983) 292835/293923
Vineyard, 20-acre gardens, wine bar, shop. Island's largest rose maze, art and music memorabilia collection.

25 Osborne House
East Cowes,
Isle of Wight PO32 6JY
Tel: (01983) 200022
Queen Victoria and Prince Albert's seaside holiday home. Swiss Cottage where royal children learnt cooking and gardening. Victorian carriage service to the cottage.

26 Calbourne Watermill and Rural Museum
Newport,
Isle of Wight PO30 4JN
Tel: (01983) 531227
Fine example of an early 17thC watermill still in working order. Granary, waterwheel, water and pea fowl.

27 The Needles Pleasure Park
Alum Bay,
Isle of Wight PO39 0JD
Tel: (01983) 752401
Chairlift to beach. Famous coloured sand cliffs. Glasswork studio. View of Needles lighthouse. Adventure playground. Super X motion simulator and carousel. Vision 180 cinema.

28 The Alice in Wonderland Family Park
Merritown Lane,
Hurn, Christchurch,
Dorset BH23 6BA
Tel: (01202) 483444
Hedge maze, Mad Hatter's restaurant, Queen of Hearts croquet lawn, Cheshire Cat's adventure playground, Duchess' rose and herb garden, Alice Theatre, Alice shop, animals.

29 Compton Acres

Canford Cliffs Road, Poole,
Dorset BH13 7ES
Tel: (01202) 700778

Nine separate and distinct gardens of the world. The gardens include Italian, Japanese, sub tropical glen, rock, water and heather garden. Collection of statues.

30 Poole Pottery

The Quay, Poole,
Dorset BH15 1RF
Tel: (01202) 666200

Factory tour, self-guided commentary includes museum, cinema, factory and craft area where visitors can 'have a go'. Craft village, throwing, painting, plus craft demonstrations.

FIND OUT MORE

Further information about holidays and attractions in the South of England is available from:

Southern Tourist Board,
40 Chamberlayne Road,
Eastleigh, Hampshire SO50 5JH.
Tel: (01703) 620555

WHERE TO STAY (SOUTH OF ENGLAND)

Accommodation entries in this region are listed in alphabetical order of place name, and then in alphabetical order of establishment.

Map references refer to the colour location maps at the back of this guide. The first number indicates the map to use; the letter and number which follow refer to the grid reference on the map.

At-a-glance symbols at the end of each accommodation entry give useful information about services and facilities. A key to symbols can be found inside the back cover flap. Keep this open for easy reference.

ABBOTTS ANN

Hampshire
Map ref 2C2

Virginia Lodge

HIGHLY COMMENDED

Salisbury Road, Abbotts Ann, Andover SP11 7NX
☎ (01264) 710713

Genuine welcome at comfortable bungalow (non-smoking), with large gardens, on edge of picturesque Abbotts Ann. On A343, 1 mile from A303 and central for Salisbury, Winchester, Stonehenge. "Heartbeat" award for healthy-option breakfasts.

Bedrooms: 1 double, 2 twin
Bathrooms: 1 en-suite, 1 public

Bed & breakfast per night:	£min	£max
Single	22.00	27.00
Double	34.00	40.00

Parking for 6

WELCOME HOST

This is a nationally recognised customer care programme which aims to promote the highest standards of service and a warm welcome. Establishments who are taking part in this initiative are indicated by the symbol.

ALTON

Hampshire
Map ref 2C2

Pleasant old market town standing on the Pilgrim's Way, with some attractive Georgian buildings. The parish church still bears the scars of bullet marks, evidence of a bitter struggle between the Roundheads and the Royalists.
Tourist Information Centre ☎ (01420) 88448

Glen Derry

Listed COMMENDED

52 Wellhouse Road, Beech, Alton GU34 4AG
☎ (01420) 83235 & 0378 406084

Peaceful, secluded family home set in 3.5 acres of garden. Warm welcome assured. Ideal base for Watercress Steam Railway, Winchester and Portsmouth.

Bedrooms: 1 twin, 1 family room
Bathrooms: 1 en-suite, 1 public

Bed & breakfast per night:	£min	£max
Single	20.00	26.00
Double	30.00	36.00

Parking for 13

AMERSHAM

Buckinghamshire
Map ref 2D1

Old town with many fine buildings, particularly in the High Street. There are several interesting old inns.

The Barn

Listed HIGHLY COMMENDED

Rectory Hill, Old Amersham, Amersham HP7 0BT
☎ (01494) 722701
Fax (01494) 728826

Restored 17th C heavily beamed tithe barn with warm friendly atmosphere. Short walk from Amersham station, good pubs and restaurants. Easy access to M25 and M40.

Bedrooms: 1 single, 2 twin
Bathrooms: 1 public

Bed & breakfast per night:	£min	£max
Single	32.00	32.00
Double	50.00	50.00

Parking for 9

Information on accommodation listed in this guide has been supplied by the proprietors. As changes may occur you are advised to check details at the time of booking.

AMPORT

Hampshire
Map ref 2C2

Broadwater

HIGHLY COMMENDED

Amport, Andover SP11 8AY
☎ (01264) 772240
Fax (01264) 772240

Grade II listed thatched cottage. From A303 (from Andover) take turn off to Hawk Conservancy/Amport. At T-junction, turn right, take first road right (East Cholderton). Broadwater is first cottage on the right.
Bedrooms: 2 twin
Bathrooms: 2 en-suite, 1 public

Bed & breakfast per night:	£min	£max
Single	22.50	25.00
Double	45.00	45.00

Parking for 3

ANDOVER

Hampshire
Map ref 2C2

Town that achieved importance from the wool trade and now has much modern development. A good centre for visiting places of interest.
Tourist Information Centre ☎ (01264) 324320

The Old Barn

HIGHLY COMMENDED

Amport, Andover SP11 8AE
☎ (01264) 710410 & 0860 844772
Fax (01264) 710410
Converted old barn, in small village approximately 3 miles south west of Andover. Secluded, but only three-quarters of a mile from A303.
Bedrooms: 1 double, 1 triple
Bathrooms: 2 en-suite

Bed & breakfast per night:	£min	£max
Single	25.00	26.00
Double	39.00	41.00

Parking for 4

ASCOT

Berkshire
Map ref 2C2

Small country town famous for its racecourse which was founded by Queen Anne. The race meeting each June is attended by the Royal Family.

Tanglewood

COMMENDED

Birch Lane, off Longhill Road, Chavey Down, Ascot SL5 8RF
☎ (01344) 882528
Spacious, modern bungalow. Quiet, secluded location, large wooded garden, safe parking. 4 miles Windsor, 15 miles Heathrow. Easy access M4, M40, M3, M25. Convenient for Wentworth, Sunningdale, Ascot, Bracknell, Thames Valley and London. Telephone for directions/map as hidden away.
Bedrooms: 1 single, 2 twin
Bathrooms: 3 en-suite, 1 public

Bed & breakfast per night:	£min	£max
Single	22.50	35.00
Double	40.00	60.00

Evening meal 1900 (last orders 2000)
Parking for 6

ASCOTT-UNDER-WYCHWOOD

Oxfordshire
Map ref 2C1

Village with stone houses and Norman church, set in lovely Oxfordshire countryside and close to the ancient Forest of Wychwood.

The Mill

Listed COMMENDED

Ascott-under-Wychwood, Chipping Norton OX7 6AP
☎ (01993) 831282 & (0421) 842538
Former watermill and cottage on the edge of the Cotswolds, in unique idyllic rural location on the River Evenlode.
Bedrooms: 1 single, 1 double, 1 twin
Bathrooms: 3 private, 1 public

Bed & breakfast per night:	£min	£max
Single	16.00	20.00
Double	32.00	35.00

Parking for 12

ASHURST

Hampshire
Map ref 2C3

Small village on the A35, on the edge of the New Forest and three miles north-east of Lyndhurst. Easy access to beautiful forest lawns.

Forest Gate Lodge

Listed COMMENDED

161 Lyndhurst Road, Ashurst, Lyndhurst SO40 7AW
☎ (01703) 293026
Large, comfortable house, with direct access to New Forest. Restaurants and public houses nearby. Central to all forest attractions.
Bedrooms: 2 double
Bathrooms: 2 en-suite, 1 public

Bed & breakfast per night:	£min	£max
Single	16.00	18.00
Double	36.00	40.00

Parking for 8

AYLESBURY

Buckinghamshire
Map ref 2C1

Historic county town in the Vale of Aylesbury. The cobbled market square has a Victorian clock tower and the 15th C King's Head Inn (National Trust). Interesting county museum and 13th C parish church. Twice-weekly livestock market.
Tourist Information Centre ☎ (01296) 330559

Longmoor Farm

HIGHLY COMMENDED

Cublington Road, Aston Abbotts, Aylesbury HP22 4ND
☎ (01296) 681010
Fax (01296) 688594
Spacious, Victorian country house, completely refurbished, built around handsome enclosed courtyard. Four acres of lovely gardens including 2 giant cedar trees.
Bedrooms: 2 double, 1 twin
Bathrooms: 1 public

Bed & breakfast per night:	£min	£max
Single	25.00	
Double	45.00	

Parking for 10

AYLESBURY

Continued

The Seasons

HIGHLY COMMENDED

9 Ballard Close, Aylesbury
HP21 9UY
☎ (01296) 84465

Comfortable, friendly, quality accommodation in quiet close. Good centre for Chilterns, London, Oxford and National Trust properties. Ideal for business or holiday.

Bedrooms: 1 single, 1 double, 1 twin
Bathrooms: 1 public

Bed & breakfast per night:	£min	£max
Single	18.00	25.00
Double	36.00	40.00

Parking for 8

10

BAMPTON

Oxfordshire
Map ref 2C1

Small market town, well known for its Spring Bank Holiday Monday Fete with Morris Dance Festival.

Cedars

COMMENDED

Mill Lane, Black Bourton, Bampton
OX18 2PJ
☎ (01993) 841368

Large, comfortable village house in secluded position on edge of Cotswolds. Located between Burford and Witney, 2 miles outside Bampton.

Bedrooms: 2 double
Bathrooms: 2 en-suite

Bed & breakfast per night:	£min	£max
Double	30.00	40.00

Parking for 6
Open March–November

A key to symbols can be found inside the back cover flap.

For further information on accommodation establishments use the coupons at the back of this guide.

BANBURY

Oxfordshire
Map ref 2C1

Famous for its cattle market, cakes and nursery rhyme Cross. Founded in Saxon times, it has some fine houses and interesting old inns. A good centre for touring Warwickshire and the Cotswolds.
Tourist Information Centre ☎ (01295) 259855

The Lodge

HIGHLY COMMENDED

Main Road, Middleton Cheney, Banbury OX17 2PP
☎ (01295) 710355

200-year-old lodge in lovely countryside, on outskirts of historic village, 3 miles east of Banbury on A422 and 1 mile from M40.

Bedrooms: 1 double, 1 twin
Bathrooms: 2 en-suite

Bed & breakfast per night:	£min	£max
Double	50.00	50.00

Parking for 5

3

Roxtones

Listed COMMENDED

Malthouse Lane, Shutford, Banbury OX15 6PB
☎ (01295) 788240

Stone-fronted semi-bungalow with garden surrounds, orchard and lawns. 6 miles from Banbury, 16 miles from Stratford-upon-Avon and 2 miles from Broughton Castle.

Bedrooms: 2 single, 1 double
Bathrooms: 1 public

Bed & breakfast per night:	£min	£max
Single	15.00	17.00
Double	25.00	27.00

Half board per person:	£min	£max
Daily		35.00
Weekly		150.00

Parking for 3
Open April–September

Information on accommodation listed in this guide has been supplied by the proprietors. As changes may occur you are advised to check details at the time of booking.

BARTON ON SEA

Hampshire
Map ref 2B3

Seaside village with views of the Isle of Wight. Within easy driving distance of the New Forest.

Bank Cottage

COMMENDED

Grove Road, Barton on Sea, New Milton BH25 7DN
☎ (01425) 613677
Fax (01425) 613677

Enjoy our B&B, designed to make your stay with us a relaxing and memorable experience. Lots to see and do in fresh air and peaceful surroundings.

Bedrooms: 2 double, 1 twin
Bathrooms: 3 en-suite, 1 public

Bed & breakfast per night:	£min	£max
Single	20.00	25.00
Double	35.00	42.00

Half board per person:	£min	£max
Daily	29.00	35.00
Weekly	180.00	245.00

Evening meal from 1800
Parking for 6
Open March–October and Christmas

5

BEACONSFIELD

Buckinghamshire
Map ref 2C2

Former coaching town with several inns still surviving. The old town has many fine houses and an interesting church. Beautiful countryside and beech woods nearby.

Beacon House

Listed APPROVED

113 Maxwell Road, Beaconsfield
HP9 1RF
☎ (01494) 672923
Fax (01494) 672923

Extended, semi-detached house, with gardens front and back and use of patio. On Heathrow bus route and close to railway station. German/French spoken.

Bedrooms: 1 single, 1 twin, 1 triple
Bathrooms: 2 en-suite, 1 public

Bed & breakfast per night:	£min	£max
Single	17.00	25.00
Double	30.00	36.00

Half board per person:	£min	£max
Daily	25.00	33.00
Weekly	155.00	210.00

Evening meal 1830 (last orders 1930)
Parking for 3

Highclere Farm

COMMENDED

Newbarn Lane, Seer Green, Beaconsfield HP9 2QZ
☎ (01494) 875665 & 874505
Fax (01494) 875238

En-suite twin-bedded rooms with views to horse paddock. Quiet location, close to M25, M40 and only half an hour by train to London (Marylebone).

Bedrooms: 1 single, 6 twin, 2 family rooms
Bathrooms: 9 en-suite

Bed & breakfast per night:	£min	£max
Single	35.00	45.00
Double	48.00	56.00

Parking for 12
Open January, March–December
Cards accepted: Mastercard, Visa, Switch/Delta

BEAULIEU

Hampshire
Map ref 2C3

Beautifully situated among woods and hills on the Beaulieu river, the village is both charming and unspoilt. The 13th C ruined Cistercian abbey and 14th C Palace House stand close to the National Motor Museum. There is a maritime museum at Bucklers Hard.

Dale Farm House

COMMENDED

Manor Road, Applemore Hill, Dibden, Southampton SO45 5TJ
☎ (01703) 849632
Fax (01703) 840285

Beautiful 18th C converted farmhouse in wooded setting. Large garden with play area. 250 yards from A326, adjacent to riding stables. Convenient for beaches, Beaulieu and Exbury Gardens.

Bedrooms: 3 double, 1 twin, 1 family room
Bathrooms: 2 en-suite, 1 public

Bed & breakfast per night:	£min	£max
Single	22.00	25.00
Double	36.00	42.00

Half board per person:	£min	£max
Weekly		185.00

Evening meal 1800 (last orders 1900)
Parking for 20

Leygreen Farm House

COMMENDED

Lyndhurst Road, Beaulieu, Brockenhurst SO42 7YP
☎ (01590) 612355

Comfortable Victorian farmhouse with large garden. Convenient for Beaulieu, Bucklers Hard museums and Exbury Gardens. Reductions for 3 days or more.

Bedrooms: 2 double, 1 twin
Bathrooms: 3 en-suite, 1 public

Bed & breakfast per night:	£min	£max
Single	18.00	20.00
Double	36.00	40.00

Parking for 6

BICESTER

Oxfordshire
Map ref 2C1

Market town with large army depot and well-known hunting centre with hunt established in the late 18th C. The ancient parish church displays work of many periods. Nearby is the Jacobean mansion of Rousham House with gardens landscaped by William Kent.
Tourist Information Centre ☎ (01869) 369055

Manor Farm

COMMENDED

Poundon, Bicester OX6 0BB
☎ (01869) 277212
Fax (01869) 277166

300-acre arable and mixed farm. 400-year-old farmhouse, tranquil, spacious, comfortable, and with a warm welcome for all. Take A421 Bicester to Buckingham road. Poundon turn is 3 miles along on right.

Bedrooms: 1 single, 1 double, 1 triple
Bathrooms: 2 public

Bed & breakfast per night:	£min	£max
Single	20.00	25.00
Double	36.00	45.00

Parking for 12

BLANDFORD FORUM

Dorset
Map ref 2B3

Almost completely destroyed by fire in 1731, the town was rebuilt in a handsome Georgian style. The church is large and grand and the town is the hub of a rich farming area.
Tourist Information Centre ☎ (01258) 454770

Farnham Farm House

Listed COMMENDED

Farnham, Blandford Forum DT11 8DG
☎ (01725) 516254
Fax (01725) 516254

350-acre arable farm. 19th C farmhouse in the Cranborne Chase with extensive views to the south. Within easy reach of the coast.

Bedrooms: 2 double, 1 twin
Bathrooms: 1 en-suite, 1 public

Bed & breakfast per night:	£min	£max
Single	20.00	25.00
Double	40.00	50.00

Parking for 7

Meadow House

HIGHLY COMMENDED

Tarrant Hinton, Blandford Forum DT11 8JG
☎ (01258) 830498

17th-18th C brick and flint farmhouse set in 4.5 acres. Warm welcome in peaceful, clean and comfortable family home. Noted for delicious home-produced English breakfast. Excellent base for touring.

Bedrooms: 1 single, 1 double, 1 triple
Bathrooms: 3 public

Bed & breakfast per night:	£min	£max
Single	18.00	25.00
Double	36.00	50.00

Parking for 6

BOURNEMOUTH

Dorset
Map ref 2B3

Seaside town set among the pines with a mild climate, sandy beaches and fine coastal views. The town has wide streets with excellent shops, a pier, a pavilion, museums and conference centre.
Tourist Information Centre ☎ (01202) 451700

The Cottage Hotel

COMMENDED

12 Southern Road, Southbourne, Bournemouth BH6 3SR
☎ (01202) 422764
Charming character family-run hotel. Restful location. Noted for home-prepared fresh cooking, cleanliness and tastefully furnished accommodation. Ample parking. Non-smoking.
Bedrooms: 1 single, 1 double, 2 twin, 1 triple, 2 family rooms
Bathrooms: 4 en-suite, 2 public, 1 private shower

Bed & breakfast per night:	£min	£max
Single	18.50	25.00
Double	37.00	46.00

Half board per person:	£min	£max
Daily	26.50	33.00
Weekly	170.00	182.00

Evening meal 1800 (last orders 1800)
Parking for 8
Open March–October

The Golden Sovereigns Hotel

COMMENDED

97 Alumhurst Road, Alum Chine, Bournemouth BH4 8HR
☎ (01202) 762088
Attractively decorated Victorian character hotel. Quiet, convenient location; beach 4 minutes' walk. Comfortable rooms, traditional home-cooking. Early booking special discounts.
Bedrooms: 2 single, 2 double, 1 twin, 2 triple, 2 family rooms
Bathrooms: 6 en-suite, 1 private, 1 public

Bed & breakfast per night:	£min	£max
Single	15.50	30.00
Double	30.00	50.00

Half board per person:	£min	£max
Daily	23.00	37.50
Weekly	140.00	190.00

Lunch available
Evening meal 1800 (last orders 1600)
Parking for 9
Cards accepted: Mastercard, Visa

Mayfield Private Hotel

COMMENDED

46 Frances Road, Bournemouth BH1 3SA
☎ (01202) 551839
Overlooking public gardens with tennis, bowling greens, crazy-golf. Central for sea, shops and main rail/coach stations. Some rooms have shower or toilet/shower. Licensed.
Bedrooms: 1 single, 4 double, 2 twin, 1 family room
Bathrooms: 5 en-suite, 2 public, 2 private showers

Bed & breakfast per night:	£min	£max
Single	15.00	17.00
Double	30.00	34.00

Half board per person:	£min	£max
Daily	21.00	23.00
Weekly	110.00	131.00

Evening meal from 1800
Parking for 5
Open January–November

Northover Hotel

COMMENDED

10 Earle Road, Alum Chine, Bournemouth BH4 8JQ
☎ (01202) 767349

Facing Alum Chine, 400 yards from sea and sandy beaches and only 20 minutes' walk from Bournemouth pier.
Bedrooms: 4 double, 2 twin, 2 triple, 2 family rooms
Suites available
Bathrooms: 7 en-suite, 2 public

Bed & breakfast per night:	£min	£max
Single	19.50	27.50
Double	39.00	55.00

Half board per person:	£min	£max
Daily	28.00	35.00
Weekly	168.00	210.00

Evening meal 1800 (last orders 1700)
Parking for 11

Pinewood

Listed COMMENDED

197 Holdenhurst Road, Bournemouth BH8 8DG
☎ (01202) 292684
Friendly guesthouse, close to rail, coach stations and all amenities. Satellite TV in all rooms. Traditional or vegetarian breakfast available.
Bedrooms: 1 single, 3 double, 1 twin, 3 triple
Bathrooms: 2 public

Bed & breakfast per night:	£min	£max
Single	16.00	18.00
Double	32.00	36.00

Parking for 8

Sandy Beach Hotel

COMMENDED

43 Southwood Avenue, Southbourne, Bournemouth BH6 3QB
☎ (01202) 424385
Fax (01202) 424385

Family-run hotel with panoramic views over Bournemouth Bay. Friendly personal service, scrumptious home-cooked food, licensed bar, ample car parking. Ideal base for touring New Forest and Dorset.
Bedrooms: 2 single, 7 double, 1 twin, 2 triple
Bathrooms: 12 en-suite, 1 public

Bed & breakfast per night:	£min	£max
Single	20.00	25.00
Double	38.00	52.00

Half board per person:	£min	£max
Daily	27.50	34.50
Weekly	173.50	215.50

Evening meal from 1800
Parking for 12
Open March–October
Cards accepted: Mastercard

BRANSGORE

Hampshire
Map ref 2B3

Situated in extensive woodlands. In the church of St Mary is a lovely Perpendicular font which is said to have come from Christchurch.

Wiltshire House

HIGHLY COMMENDED

West Road, Bransgore, Christchurch, Dorset BH23 8BD
☎ (01425) 672450

Friendly, informal accommodation including 1 four poster bedroom. Early Victorian residence set in large secluded garden with easy access to forest and beach.

Bedrooms: 1 double, 1 family room
Bathrooms: 2 en-suite, 1 public

Bed & breakfast per night:	£min	£max
Single	22.00	26.00
Double	38.00	44.00

Parking for 4

BRIGHSTONE

Isle of Wight
Map ref 2C3

Excellent centre for visitors who want somewhere quiet. Calbourne nearby is ideal for picnics and the sea at Chilton Chine has safe bathing at high tide.

The Lodge

Listed HIGHLY COMMENDED

Main Road, Brighstone, Newport PO30 4DJ
☎ (01983) 741272

Beautiful Victorian, family-run manor house, set in large gardens. Offering quality bed and breakfast accommodation and service. Delightful village location.

Bedrooms: 7 double, 2 triple
Bathrooms: 5 en-suite, 2 public

Bed & breakfast per night:	£min	£max
Single	20.00	25.00
Double	10.00	50.00

Parking for 9

For ideas on places to visit refer to the introduction at the beginning of this section.

BROCKENHURST

Hampshire
Map ref 2C3

Attractive village with thatched cottages and a ford in its main street. Well placed for visiting the New Forest.

The Cottage Hotel

HIGHLY COMMENDED

Sway Road, Brockenhurst SO42 7SH
☎ (01590) 622296
Fax (01590) 623014
Email: 100604.22@compuserve.com

Delightfully converted cosy oak-beamed forester's cottage, noted for comfort and service. Two minutes' walk from forest and village centre. http://ourworld.compuserve.com/homepages/terry-eisner

Bedrooms: 1 single, 5 double, 1 twin
Bathrooms: 6 en-suite, 1 private shower

Bed & breakfast per night:	£min	£max
Single	49.00	69.00
Double	69.00	83.00

Parking for 12
Open February–November
Cards accepted: Mastercard, Visa, Switch/Delta
10

BUCKINGHAM

Buckinghamshire
Map ref 2C1

Interesting old market town surrounded by rich farmland. It has many Georgian buildings, including the Town Hall and Old Jail and many old almshouses and inns. Stowe School nearby has magnificent 18th C landscaped gardens.
Tourist Information Centre ☎ (01280) 823020

Folly Farm

COMMENDED

Padbury, Buckingham MK18 2HS
☎ (01296) 712413

500-acre arable farm. On A413 between Winslow and Padbury, 2 miles south of Buckingham. Substantial farmhouse opposite Folly Inn. Convenient for Stowe Landscape Gardens, Silverstone circuit, Addington Equestrian Centre, Waddesdon Manor and Claydon House. Evening meals by arrangement.

Bedrooms: 3 double
Bathrooms: 3 en-suite

Bed & breakfast per night:	£min	£max
Single	20.00	20.00
Double	34.00	35.00

Half board per person:	£min	£max
Daily	27.00	29.00
Weekly	189.00	196.00

Evening meal 1830 (last orders 1200)
Parking for 10
12

BURFORD

Oxfordshire
Map ref 2B1

One of the most beautiful Cotswold wool towns with Georgian and Tudor houses, many antique shops and a picturesque High Street sloping to the River Windrush.
Tourist Information Centre ☎ (01993) 823558

Bee Cottage

COMMENDED

Fulbrook, Burford OX18 4BZ
☎ (01993) 822070

Stone-built, self-contained annexe with outstanding views. Take the A361 from Burford, through Fulbrook up the hill and on the left, down Waterloo Farm drive.

Bedrooms: 1 double
Bathrooms: 1 en-suite

Bed & breakfast per night:	£min	£max
Double	45.00	50.00

Parking for 8

All accommodation in this guide has been graded, or is awaiting a grading, by a trained Tourist Board inspector.

BURFORD

Continued

The Bird in Hand

HIGHLY COMMENDED

Whiteoak Green, Hailey, Witney
OX8 5XP
☎ (01993) 868321 & 868811
Fax (01993) 868702

Recently restored inn, with attractive cottage-style bedrooms surrounding a quiet courtyard. Home-cooked food, real ales and open fires.

Bedrooms: 10 double, 4 twin, 2 family rooms
Bathrooms: 16 en-suite

Bed & breakfast per night:	£min	£max
Single	52.50	60.00
Double	60.00	75.00

Half board per person:	£min	£max
Daily	45.00	55.00

Lunch available
Evening meal 1900 (last orders 2130)
Parking for 100
Cards accepted: Mastercard, Visa, Switch/Delta

30

Hillborough House

COMMENDED

The Green,
Milton-under-Wychwood, Oxford
OX7 6JH
☎ (01993) 830501
Fax (01993) 832005

Facing village green in delightful Cotswold village. Warm, spacious en-suite accommodation, cosy lounge, gardens. Dinner can be arranged Tue-Sat in our separately run and adjoining Willows Restaurant.

Bedrooms: 4 double, 3 twin, 3 triple
Bathrooms: 10 en-suite

Bed & breakfast per night:	£min	£max
Single	35.00	
Double	52.00	

Half board per person:	£min	£max
Daily	38.00	43.00
Weekly	230.00	

Lunch available
Evening meal 1900 (last orders 2130)
Parking for 15
Open February–December
Cards accepted: Mastercard, Visa

Romany Inn

APPROVED

Bridge Street, Bampton, Oxford
OX18 2HA
☎ (01993) 850237

19th C listed Georgian building, recently refurbished, at nearby Bampton. Lounge bar, separate restaurant, chef/proprietor. Noted in pub and beer guides. Brochure available.

Bedrooms: 4 double, 2 twin, 3 triple
Bathrooms: 9 en-suite, 1 public

Bed & breakfast per night:	£min	£max
Single	25.00	30.00
Double	35.00	40.00

Lunch available
Evening meal 1830 (last orders 2200)
Parking for 6
Cards accepted: Mastercard, Visa, Switch/Delta

St Winnow

COMMENDED

160 The Hill, Burford OX18 4QY
☎ (01993) 823843

Comfortable 16th C Cotswold house, in conservation area on hill above the high street. Garden, garage and parking at rear.

Bedrooms: 1 single, 1 double, 1 twin
Bathrooms: 1 public

Bed & breakfast per night:	£min	£max
Single	20.00	25.00
Double	35.00	40.00

Parking for 2

Half board prices are given per person, but in some cases these may be based on double/twin occupancy.

BURLEY

Hampshire
Map ref 2B3

Attractive centre from which to explore the south-west part of the New Forest. There is an ancient earthwork on Castle Hill nearby, which also offers good views.

Pikes Post

HIGHLY COMMENDED

Chapel Lane, Burley, Ringwood
BH24 4DJ
☎ (01425) 402285

Pretty bungalow, quietly situated, offering high quality accommodation. Ideally placed for forest walks, country activities and South Coast beaches.

Bedrooms: 2 double, 1 twin
Bathrooms: 3 en-suite

Bed & breakfast per night:	£min	£max
Single	25.00	28.00
Double	36.00	42.00

Parking for 5
Open February–November

CADNAM

Hampshire
Map ref 2C3

Village with numerous attractive cottages and an inn close to the entrance of the M27.

The Old Well Restaurant

COMMENDED

Copythorne, Southampton
SO40 2PE
☎ (01703) 812321 & 812700

Family-owned business for over 30 years. Spacious accommodation and friendly service, with good access to New Forest and Southampton ferries.

Bedrooms: 4 double, 2 triple
Bathrooms: 3 en-suite, 2 public

Bed & breakfast per night:	£min	£max
Single	22.50	30.00
Double	35.00	45.00

Lunch available
Evening meal 1900 (last orders 2200)
Parking for 50
Cards accepted: Diners, Mastercard, Visa, Switch/Delta

Establishments should be open throughout the year, unless otherwise stated.

CHALFONT ST GILES

Buckinghamshire
Map ref 2D2

Pretty, old village in wooded Chiltern Hills yet only 20 miles from London and a good base for visiting the city. Excellent base for Windsor, Henley, the Thames Valley, Oxford and the Cotswolds.

Gorelands Corner

Listed COMMENDED

Gorelands Lane, Chalfont St Giles
HP8 4HQ
☎ (01494) 872689
Fax (01494) 872689

Family home set in large garden. Easy access to M25, M40, M4 and London underground.

Bedrooms: 1 triple
Bathrooms: 1 en-suite

Bed & breakfast per night:	£min	£max
Single	20.00	25.00
Double	40.00	45.00

Parking for 3

CHALGROVE

Oxfordshire
Map ref 2C1

Cornerstones

Listed

1 Cromwell Close, Chalgrove
OX44 7SE
☎ (01865) 890298

Bungalow in pretty village with thatched cottages. The Red Lion (half a mile away) serves good and reasonably priced food.

Bedrooms: 2 twin
Bathrooms: 1 public

Bed & breakfast per night:	£min	£max
Single	23.00	23.00
Double	35.00	35.00

Parking for 2

TOWN INDEX

This can be found at the back of the guide. If you know where you want to stay, the index will give you the page number listing all accommodation in your chosen town, city or village.

CHARLBURY

Oxfordshire
Map ref 2C1

Large Cotswold village with beautiful views of the Evenlode Valley just outside the village and close to the ancient Forest of Wychwood.

Banbury Hill Farm

COMMENDED

Enstone Road, Charlbury, Oxford
OX7 3JH
☎ (01608) 810314
Fax (01608) 811891

54-acre mixed farm. Cotswold-stone farmhouse with extensive views across Evenlode Valley. Ideal touring centre for Blenheim Palace, Oxford and the Cotswolds.

Bedrooms: 1 single, 2 double, 1 twin, 1 triple
Bathrooms: 3 en-suite, 1 public

Bed & breakfast per night:	£min	£max
Single	20.00	30.00
Double	40.00	50.00

Parking for 6
Open March–October
Cards accepted: Mastercard, Visa, Switch/Delta

CHIPPING NORTON

Oxfordshire
Map ref 2C1

Old market town set high in the Cotswolds and an ideal touring centre. The wide market-place contains many 16th C and 17th C stone houses and the Town Hall and Tudor Guildhall.
Tourist Information Centre ☎ (01608) 644379

Oak House

HIGHLY COMMENDED

Chalford Park, Old Chalford, Chipping Norton OX7 5QR
☎ (01608) 641435
Fax (01608) 641435

Converted Cotswold-stone farmhouse of character, set in courtyard. Decorated and furnished to high standard. Bridleway walks in open country.

Bedrooms: 1 double, 1 twin
Bathrooms: 1 en-suite, 1 private

Bed & breakfast per night:	£min	£max
Single	30.00	35.00
Double	45.00	50.00

Parking for 4
Open March–November

CHRISTCHURCH

Dorset
Map ref 2B3

Tranquil town lying between the Avon and Stour just before they converge and flow into Christchurch Harbour. A fine 11th C church and the remains of a Norman castle and house can be seen.
Tourist Information Centre ☎ (01202) 471780

Stour Lodge Guest House

COMMENDED

54 Stour Road, Christchurch
BH23 1LW
☎ (01202) 486902

Very comfortable accommodation, with all bedrooms to very high standard. Very clean. Near railway station and bus route.

Bedrooms: 4 double
Bathrooms: 3 en-suite, 1 private, 1 public

Bed & breakfast per night:	£min	£max
Single	20.00	25.00
Double	30.00	35.00

Parking for 5
Open January–November

COLWELL BAY

Isle of Wight
Map ref 2C3

2-mile curving stretch of sand.

Chine Cottage

COMMENDED

Colwell Chine Road, Colwell Bay, Freshwater PO40 9NP
☎ (01983) 752808

150-year-old stone cottage, 200 yards from beach. Spacious bedrooms with en-suite facilities. Ideal situation for lovely walks.

Bedrooms: 3 twin
Bathrooms: 3 en-suite

Bed & breakfast per night:	£min	£max
Single	17.50	20.00
Double	35.00	40.00

Half board per person:	£min	£max
Daily	25.50	29.00
Weekly	165.50	185.50

Continued ▶

COLWELL BAY

Continued

Evening meal 1800 (last orders 2030)
Parking for 20

COMPTON

Hampshire
Map ref 2C3

Manor House

Listed COMMENDED

Place Lane, Compton, Winchester SO21 2BA
☎ (01962) 712162

Comfortable country house, 8 minutes from Shawford railway station and 2 miles from city of Winchester. Non-smokers preferred.

Bedrooms: 1 double
Bathrooms: 1 public

Bed & breakfast per night:	£min	£max
Single	13.00	13.00
Double	26.00	26.00

Parking for 1

COOKHAM

Berkshire
Map ref 2C2

The Inn on the Green

COMMENDED

The Old Cricket Common, Cookham Dean, Cookham, Maidenhead SL6 9NZ
☎ (01628) 482638
Fax (01628) 487474

An extensive restaurant menu is available, offering freshly cooked dishes for all meals. Residents' menu available from midday until midnight.

Bedrooms: 1 single, 3 double, 2 twin
Bathrooms: 6 en-suite

Bed & breakfast per night:	£min	£max
Single	45.00	75.00
Double	80.00	100.00

Half board per person:	£min	£max
Daily	60.00	90.00
Weekly	380.00	570.00

Lunch available
Evening meal 1930 (last orders 2200)
Parking for 40
Cards accepted: Amex, Mastercard, Visa, Switch/Delta

14

CORFE CASTLE

Dorset
Map ref 2B3

One of the most spectacular ruined castles in Britain. Norman in origin, the castle was a Royalist stronghold during the Civil War and held out until 1645. The village had a considerable marble-carving industry in the Middle Ages.

Bradle Farmhouse

COMMENDED

Bradle Farm, Church Knowle, Wareham BH20 5NU
☎ (01929) 480712
Fax (01929) 481144

550-acre mixed farm. Picturesque farmhouse in the heart of Purbeck. Superb views of castle and surrounding countryside, beach 2 miles. Warm family atmosphere; evening meals available at local inn.

Bedrooms: 2 double, 1 twin
Bathrooms: 2 en-suite, 1 private

Bed & breakfast per night:	£min	£max
Single	20.00	27.00
Double	38.00	41.00

Parking for 3

COTSWOLDS

See under Ascott-under-Wychwood, Bampton, Burford, Charlbury, Chipping Norton, Deddington, Fifield, Shipton-under-Wychwood, Witney, Woodstock
See also Cotswolds in Heart of England region

WELCOME HOST

This is a nationally recognised customer care programme which aims to promote the highest standards of service and a warm welcome. Establishments who are taking part in this initiative are indicated by the symbol.

COWES

Isle of Wight
Map ref 2C3

Regular ferry and hydrofoil services cross the Solent to Cowes. The town is the headquarters of the Royal Yacht Squadron and Cowes Week is held every August.
Tourist Information Centre ☎ (01983) 291914

Noss Mayo

COMMENDED

66a Baring Road, Cowes PO31 8DW
☎ (01983) 200266

Modern, detached bungalow with garden and patio. Limited views of Solent. Parking spaces. Within walking distance of Cowes and Esplanade.

Bedrooms: 1 double, 1 twin
Bathrooms: 1 public

Bed & breakfast per night:	£min	£max
Single	16.00	26.00
Double	32.00	52.00

Evening meal from 1800
Parking for 2
Open May–September

CROOKHAM VILLAGE

Hampshire
Map ref 2C2

Orchard House

Listed COMMENDED

Crondall Road, Crookham Village, Fleet GU13 0SY
☎ (01252) 850333

Listed, small country house, part Tudor, William and Mary, Regency and Victorian. Set in beautiful, mature gardens and grounds with stunning views.

Bedrooms: 1 double, 1 twin
Bathrooms: 2 private, 1 public

Bed & breakfast per night:	£min	£max
Single	20.00	25.00
Double	40.00	50.00

Parking for 10

COLOUR MAPS

Colour maps at the back of this guide pinpoint all places in which you will find accommodation listed.

CUDDESDON

Oxfordshire
Map ref 2C1

The Bat & Ball Inn

28 High Street, Cuddesdon, Oxford OX44 9HJ
☎ (01865) 874379
Fax (01865) 873363
Old coaching inn with scenic views and interesting collection of cricket memorabilia. Cuddesdon is an attractive small village, well placed for Oxford and the M40.
Bedrooms: 2 single, 3 double, 1 twin, 1 triple
Bathrooms: 7 en-suite

Bed & breakfast per night:	£min	£max
Single	30.00	40.00
Double	35.00	50.00

Lunch available
Evening meal 1830 (last orders 2130)
Parking for 15
Cards accepted: Mastercard, Visa, Switch/Delta

DEDDINGTON

Oxfordshire
Map ref 2C1

On the edge of the Cotswolds and settled since the Stone Age, this is the only village in England to have been granted a full Coat of Arms, displayed on the 16th C Town Hall in the picturesque market square. Many places of interest include the Church of St Peter and St Paul.

Hill Barn

Listed COMMENDED

Milton Gated Road, Deddington, Banbury OX15 0TS
☎ (01869) 338631
Converted barn set in open countryside, convenient for Stratford, Warwick, Oxford and Cotswolds. Banbury-Oxford road, half a mile before Deddington, turn right to Milton Gated Road. Hill Barn is 100 yards on the right.
Bedrooms: 1 double, 2 twin
Bathrooms: 1 public

Bed & breakfast per night:	£min	£max
Single	20.00	20.00
Double	36.00	36.00

Parking for 6

The Little House

HIGHLY COMMENDED

Clifton Road, Deddington, Banbury OX15 0TP
☎ (01869) 337319
Stone country house in 6 acres of pasture and gardens. En-suite accommodation in adjacent barn conversion, with galleried landing and flagstoned breakfast/sitting room.
Bedrooms: 1 double, 1 twin
Suites available
Bathrooms: 2 en-suite, 1 public

Bed & breakfast per night:	£min	£max
Single	30.00	35.00
Double	45.00	50.00

Parking for 6
Open January–November

DENMEAD

Hampshire
Map ref 2C3

Comparatively modern village, south-west of the original settlement.

Forest Gate

Listed COMMENDED

Hambledon Road, Denmead, Waterlooville PO7 6EX
☎ (01705) 255901
Listed Georgian house in large garden, on outskirts of village. Within easy reach of maritime Portsmouth and continental ferries. Dinner by arrangement.
Bedrooms: 2 twin
Bathrooms: 2 en-suite

Bed & breakfast per night:	£min	£max
Single	22.00	24.00
Double	36.00	40.00

Half board per person:	£min	£max
Daily	32.00	35.50
Weekly	202.00	224.00

Evening meal from 1930
Parking for 4

The symbols in each entry give information about services and facilities. A key to these symbols appears at the back of this guide.

EDGCOTT

Buckinghamshire
Map ref 2C1

Perry Manor Farm

HIGHLY COMMENDED

Buckingham Road, Edgcott, Aylesbury HP18 0TR
☎ (01296) 770257
200-acre livestock farm. Working sheep farm, offering peaceful and comfortable accommodation, with en-suite toilet and basin. Extensive views over Aylesbury Vale. Walkers welcome. Non-smokers only, please.
Bedrooms: 1 single, 1 double, 1 twin
Bathrooms: 1 public

Bed & breakfast per night:	£min	£max
Single	18.00	18.00
Double	32.00	32.00

Parking for 10

FAREHAM

Hampshire
Map ref 2C3

Lies on a quiet backwater of Portsmouth Harbour. The High Street is lined with fine Georgian buildings.
Tourist Information Centre ☎ (01329) 221342

Manor House

HIGHLY COMMENDED

Church Path, Fareham PO16 7DT
☎ (01329) 287775 & (0589) 665847
Fax (01329) 287775

Grade II listed Victorian manor house, quietly situated in town centre. Quality accommodation with all facilities. Easy access to M27.
Bedrooms: 1 single, 2 twin
Bathrooms: 1 en-suite, 1 public, 2 private showers

Bed & breakfast per night:	£min	£max
Single	25.00	34.00
Double	45.00	65.00

Evening meal 1800 (last orders 2200)
Parking for 12
Cards accepted: Mastercard, Visa

FIFIELD

Oxfordshire
Map ref 2B1

Charming village with a gabled manor and a fortified house set in a beautiful park, once the site of a Norman abbey.

Merryfield

Listed COMMENDED

High Street, Fifield, Oxford OX7 6HL
☎ (01993) 830517

Stone chalet bungalow with magnificent views and access to the Cotswolds. Midway between Burford and Stow-on-the-Wold. Non-smokers preferred.

Bedrooms: 2 twin
Bathrooms: 1 en-suite, 1 private

Bed & breakfast per night:	£min	£max
Single	18.50	21.50
Double	37.00	39.50

Parking for 4

FORDINGBRIDGE

Hampshire
Map ref 2B3

On the north-west edge of the New Forest. A medieval bridge crosses the Avon at this point and gave the town its name. A good centre for walking, exploring and fishing.

Hillbury

Listed COMMENDED

2 Fir Tree Hill, Camel Green Road, Alderholt, Fordingbridge SP6 3AY
☎ (01425) 652582
Fax (01425) 657587

Bungalow in quiet situation with easy access to M27. Ideal touring base for New Forest and South Coast. Riding, swimming, golf and fishing nearby. Sorry, no pets or smokers.

Bedrooms: 1 single, 1 twin, 1 triple
Bathrooms: 1 public

Bed & breakfast per night:	£min	£max
Single	16.00	18.00
Double	32.00	36.00

Parking for 5

OAP T

Map references apply to the colour maps at the back of this guide.

GORING

Oxfordshire
Map ref 2C2

Riverside town on the Oxfordshire/Berkshire border, linked by an attractive bridge to Streatley with views to the Goring Gap.

The John Barleycorn

APPROVED

Manor Road, Goring, Reading, Berkshire RG8 9DP
☎ (01491) 872509

16th C inn with exposed beams. Real ale, home-cooked food. Close to the river, lovely walks.

Bedrooms: 1 single, 2 double, 1 triple
Bathrooms: 1 public

Bed & breakfast per night:	£min	£max
Single	25.00	
Double	42.00	

Lunch available
Evening meal 1900 (last orders 2200)
Parking for 2
Cards accepted: Mastercard, Visa

HAMBLEDON

Hampshire
Map ref 2C3

In a valley, surrounded by wooded downland and marked by an air of Georgian prosperity. It was here that cricket was given its first proper rules. The Bat and Ball Inn at Broadhalfpenny Down is the cradle of cricket.

Cams

COMMENDED

Hambledon, Waterlooville PO7 4SP
☎ (01705) 632865
Fax (01705) 632691

Comfortable, listed family house in beautiful setting with large garden on the edge of Hambledon village. Two pubs within walking distance. Evening meal by arrangement.

Bedrooms: 1 double, 2 twin
Bathrooms: 1 en-suite, 1 public, 1 private shower

Bed & breakfast per night:	£min	£max
Single	17.00	20.00
Double	31.00	40.00

Half board per person:	£min	£max
Daily	23.50	30.00

Evening meal from 1900
Parking for 6

Mornington House

Listed COMMENDED

Speltham Hill, Hambledon, Waterlooville PO7 4RU
☎ (01705) 632704

18th C private house with 2 acres of garden and paddock, in the centre of Hambledon behind the George Inn, 2 miles from famous Bat and Ball Inn.

Bedrooms: 2 twin
Bathrooms: 1 public

Bed & breakfast per night:	£min	£max
Single	20.00	20.00
Double	32.00	32.00

Parking for 6

HAVANT

Hampshire
Map ref 2C3

Once a market town famous for making parchment. Nearby at Leigh Park extensive early 19th C landscape gardens and parklands are open to the public. Right in the centre of the town stands the interesting 13th C church of St Faith.
Tourist Information Centre ☎ (01705) 480024

High Towers

COMMENDED

14 Portsdown Hill Road, Bedhampton, Havant PO9 3JY
☎ (01705) 471748

On Wayfarers Walk and near Palmerston's Forts. Modern residence near A3M/A27, with superb views overlooking Portsmouth, countryside and sea. Portsmouth centre and ferries 15 minutes, Havant 5 minutes. Non-smokers only, please.

Bedrooms: 2 single, 2 double
Bathrooms: 3 en-suite, 1 private, 1 public

Bed & breakfast per night:	£min	£max
Single	20.00	26.00
Double	36.00	40.00

Parking for 6

HENLEY-ON-THAMES

Oxfordshire
Map ref 2C2

The famous Thames Regatta is held in this prosperous and attractive town at the beginning of July each year. The town has many Georgian buildings and old coaching inns and the parish church has some fine monuments.
Tourist Information Centre ☎ (01491) 578034

Alftrudis

HIGHLY COMMENDED

8 Norman Avenue, Henley-on-Thames RG9 1SQ
☎ (01491) 573099 & 0802 408643
Fax (01494) 573099

Friendly detached Victorian house in quiet, private cul-de-sac, centrally situated two minutes' walk from the station, town centre and river. Easy parking.

Bedrooms: 2 double, 1 twin
Bathrooms: 2 en-suite, 1 private

Bed & breakfast per night:	£min	£max
Single	30.00	35.00
Double	40.00	50.00

Parking for 2

8

Crowsley House

Listed COMMENDED

Crowsley Road, Shiplake, Henley-on-Thames RG9 3JT
☎ (01189) 403197

Attractive house in quiet riverside village, close to Henley-on-Thames. Convenient for Oxford, London, Windsor and Heathrow.

Bedrooms: 1 double, 2 twin
Bathrooms: 2 public

Bed & breakfast per night:	£min	£max
Single	20.00	25.00
Double	40.00	50.00

Parking for 4

TOWN INDEX

This can be found at the back of the guide. If you know where you want to stay, the index will give you the page number listing all accommodation in your chosen town, city or village.

Holmwood

HIGHLY COMMENDED

Shiplake Row, Binfield Heath, Henley-on-Thames RG9 4DP
☎ (0118) 947 8747
Fax (0118) 947 8637

Large Georgian country house in beautiful surroundings. In Binfield Heath, equidistant from Henley and Reading, off A4155. Binfield Heath is signposted.

Wheelchair access category 3
Bedrooms: 1 single, 2 double, 2 twin
Bathrooms: 5 en-suite

Bed & breakfast per night:	£min	£max
Single	30.00	30.00
Double	50.00	50.00

Parking for 8

12 UL
20

Lenwade

HIGHLY COMMENDED

3 Western Road, Henley-on-Thames RG9 1JL
☎ (01491) 573468 & 0374 941629
Fax (01494) 573468

Victorian house in quiet surroundings, within walking distance of the River Thames and town centre. Children welcome. Parking available.

Bedrooms: 2 double, 1 twin
Bathrooms: 2 en-suite, 2 public

Bed & breakfast per night:	£min	£max
Single	28.00	40.00
Double	40.00	50.00

Parking for 2

New Lodge

COMMENDED

Henley Park, Henley-on-Thames RG9 6HU
☎ (01491) 576340

Victorian lodge in parkland in Area of Outstanding Natural Beauty. Lovely walks and views. Only 1 mile from Henley, 45 minutes from Heathrow.

Bedrooms: 2 double
Bathrooms: 1 en-suite, 1 private

Bed & breakfast per night:	£min	£max
Single	23.00	27.00
Double	33.00	41.00

Parking for 7

A key to symbols can be found inside the back cover flap.

HIGH WYCOMBE

Buckinghamshire
Map ref 2C2

Famous for furniture-making, historic examples of which feature in the museum. The 18th C Guildhall and the octagonal market house were designed by the Adam brothers. West Wycombe Park and Hughenden Manor (National Trust) are nearby.
Tourist Information Centre ☎ (01494) 421892

The Birches

Listed APPROVED

30 Lucas Road, High Wycombe HP13 6QG
☎ (01494) 533547

Nice, friendly home. All guests welcomed with tea and biscuits. Children welcome. Quiet road, 5 minutes from railway station.

Bedrooms: 1 single, 1 twin, 1 triple
Bathrooms: 1 public

Bed & breakfast per night:	£min	£max
Single	16.00	20.00
Double	25.00	35.00

Parking for 4

HILTON

Dorset
Map ref 2B3

Village with thatched cottages grouped against a background of woods and downs. The church is a blend of Decorated and Perpendicular styles.

Stocklands House

HIGHLY COMMENDED

Hilton, Blandford Forum DT11 0DE
☎ (01258) 880580 & 881188
Fax (01258) 881188

In secluded position with stunning views. Log fires. Heated pool (June-September). Professional chef. Well situated for sightseeing.

Bedrooms: 1 double, 1 twin
Bathrooms: 2 en-suite

Bed & breakfast per night:	£min	£max
Single	18.50	28.50
Double	37.00	57.00

Lunch available
Evening meal 1930 (last orders 2100)
Parking for 15

12 10

HINTON ST MARY

Dorset
Map ref 2B3

The Old Post Office Guest House

COMMENDED

Hinton St Mary, Sturminster Newton DT10 1NG
☎ (01258) 472366
Fax (01258) 472173

Cosy and welcoming guesthouse, where your comfort is top priority. Ideally situated for exploring beautiful Dorset by car, cycle or foot. Large, attractive garden. Traditional, satisfying home cooking. Lovely old pub in village.

Bedrooms: 2 double, 1 twin
Bathrooms: 1 en-suite, 1 public

Bed & breakfast per night:	£min	£max
Single	17.00	19.00
Double	32.00	38.00

Half board per person:	£min	£max
Daily	23.00	27.00
Weekly	140.00	160.00

Evening meal 1800 (last orders 1930)
Parking for 5

HUNGERFORD

Berkshire
Map ref 2C2

Attractive town on the Avon Canal and the River Kennet, famous for its fishing. It has a wide High Street and many antique shops. Nearby is the Tudor manor of Littlecote with its large Roman mosaic.

Marshgate Cottage Hotel

COMMENDED

Marsh Lane, Hungerford RG17 0QX
☎ (01488) 682307
Fax (01488) 685475

Family-run canalside hotel, linked to 350-year-old thatched cottage at end of quiet country lane. Overlooks marshland and trout streams. Lovely walks, bird watching. Important antiques centre. 1 hour from Heathrow and 5 minutes from M4.

Bedrooms: 3 double, 2 twin, 3 triple
Bathrooms: 8 en-suite, 1 public

Bed & breakfast per night:	£min	£max
Single		35.50
Double	48.50	55.00

Parking for 9
Cards accepted: Amex, Mastercard, Visa

20

HYTHE

Hampshire
Map ref 2C3

Changri-La

HIGHLY COMMENDED

12 Ashleigh Close, Hythe, Southampton SO45 3QP
☎ (01703) 846664

Spacious comfortable home, in unique position on edge of New Forest, a few minutes' drive from Beaulieu and other places of interest. Golf-course, pony trekking and sports complex nearby.

Bedrooms: 1 double, 1 twin
Bathrooms: 2 public

Bed & breakfast per night:	£min	£max
Single	16.00	
Double	32.00	

Parking for 3

ISLE OF WIGHT

See under Brighstone, Colwell Bay, Cowes, Ryde, Sandown, Shanklin, Wellow

KIDLINGTON

Oxfordshire
Map ref 2C1

Village with a beautiful old church flanked by a row of gabled almshouses. Has now become dormitory satellite of Oxford.

Breffni House

Listed APPROVED

9 Lovelace Drive, Kidlington OX5 2LY
☎ (01865) 372569

Detached property, very homely, close to Woodstock and 2.5 miles from M40. Sports facilities close by. Lovely gardens and ample off-road parking.

Bedrooms: 1 single, 1 double
Bathrooms: 1 public

Bed & breakfast per night:	£min	£max
Single	20.00	25.00
Double	36.00	40.00

Evening meal 1800 (last orders 2000)
Parking for 6
Cards accepted: Visa

5

KINGSCLERE

Hampshire
Map ref 2C2

Cleremede

HIGHLY COMMENDED

Fox's Lane, Kingsclere, Newbury, Berkshire RG20 5SL
☎ (01635) 297298 & 0374 280716
Fax (01635) 297298

Near Watership Down and Wayfarers Walk. Breakfast in conservatory in summer overlooking large garden.

Bedrooms: 1 single, 2 twin
Suites available
Bathrooms: 2 en-suite, 1 private

Bed & breakfast per night:	£min	£max
Single	21.00	26.00
Double	40.00	46.00

Parking for 6

10

11 Hook Road

Listed COMMENDED

Kingsclere, Newbury, Berkshire RG20 5PD
☎ (01635) 298861
Fax (01635) 298861

Comfortable, modern house in historic Kingsclere at the foot of the beautiful Hampshire Downs. Convenient for M3, M4, A34 and all local amenities. Hook Road is off Basingstoke Road, half a mile east of Kingsclere village square.

Bedrooms: 1 single, 2 twin
Suite available
Bathrooms: 1 public

Bed & breakfast per night:	£min	£max
Single	18.00	19.00
Double	30.00	31.00

Half board per person:	£min	£max
Daily	26.00	31.00

Lunch available
Evening meal 1900 (last orders 2100)
Parking for 6

LANE END

Buckinghamshire
Map ref 2C2

Orchid House

Listed HIGHLY COMMENDED

Spring Coppice, Lane End, High Wycombe HP14 3NU
☎ (01494) 881032 & 0860 314438
Fax (01494) 882100

Set in three-quarters of an acre of landscaped gardens, completely surrounded by woodland plentiful in

wildlife. 5 minutes from M40 motorway, close to Marlow-on-Thames, the Chiltern Hills and within 30 minutes of Windsor and Oxford.
Bedrooms: 2 double
Bathrooms: 2 private, 1 public

Bed & breakfast per night:	£min	£max
Single	25.00	30.00
Double	35.00	40.00

Parking for 6

LITTLE WITTENHAM

Oxfordshire
Map ref 2C2

Rooks Orchard

HIGHLY COMMENDED

Little Wittenham, Abingdon
OX14 4QY
☎ (01865) 407765
Attractive, peaceful and welcoming listed 17th C family house and garden, in pretty Thameside village next to nature reserve and Wittenham Clumps. "Splendid breakfasts". Abingdon, Didcot and Wallingford approximately 4 miles, Oxford 9 miles.
Bedrooms: 2 double
Bathrooms: 1 en-suite, 1 private

Bed & breakfast per night:	£min	£max
Single	26.00	29.00
Double	42.00	49.00

Parking for 6

LONGHAM

Dorset
Map ref 2B3

Astride the A348 Poole to Ringwood road and on the north bank of the River Stour. The river floods its banks in this area when the weather is severe.

Bridge House Hotel

COMMENDED

2 Ringwood Road, Longham, Ferndown BH22 9AN
☎ (01202) 578828
Fax (01202) 572620

Located between Poole and Bournemouth. Garden on the banks of the beautiful River Stour. A la carte restaurant, carvery bar. Four-poster beds available.
Bedrooms: 4 single, 21 double, 11 twin, 1 triple
Bathrooms: 37 en-suite

Bed & breakfast per night:	£min	£max
Single	30.00	40.00
Double	40.00	50.00

Lunch available
Evening meal 1900 (last orders 2200)
Parking for 200
Cards accepted: Amex, Diners, Mastercard, Visa
100

LYMINGTON

Hampshire
Map ref 2C3

Small, pleasant town with bright cottages and attractive Georgian houses, lying on the edge of the New Forest with a ferry service to the Isle of Wight. A sheltered harbour makes it a busy yachting centre.

Altworth

Listed COMMENDED

12 North Close, Lymington
SO41 9BT
☎ (01590) 674082
Fax (01590) 674082
Near centre of town in quiet residential street, 5 minutes from bus/railway stations and Isle of Wight ferry. Brockenhurst and New Forest area only 10 minutes away. Lock-up for bicycles.
Bedrooms: 1 single, 1 double, 1 triple
Bathrooms: 1 public

Bed & breakfast per night:	£min	£max
Single	15.50	15.50
Double	28.00	28.00

Open April–October

Auplands

Listed COMMENDED

22 Southampton Road, Lymington
SO41 9GG
☎ (01590) 675944 & 0958 214448
Detached house close to shops, restaurants, pubs and town quay. Short drive sea, Isle of Wight ferry and forest. En-suites, TV, parking and friendly welcome.
Bedrooms: 2 double
Bathrooms: 2 en-suite

Bed & breakfast per night:	£min	£max
Single	20.00	30.00
Double	32.00	40.00

Parking for 3

Cedars

Listed COMMENDED

2 Linden Way, Highfield, Lymington
SO41 9JU
☎ (01590) 676468
Bungalow accommodation in quiet, secluded area, ideal for forest and coastal walks. Ground floor annexe rooms, free access, off-street garage parking. Close to High Street, marinas and ferry.
Bedrooms: 1 double, 2 twin
Bathrooms: 2 en-suite, 1 private, 1 public

Bed & breakfast per night:	£min	£max
Single	20.00	25.00
Double	36.00	40.00

Parking for 4
12

Efford Cottage

COMMENDED

Everton, Lymington SO41 0JD
☎ (01590) 642315 & 0374 703075
Fax (01590) 642315

Friendly, spacious, Georgian cottage forming award-winning guesthouse. Four-course, multi-choice breakfast, home-made bread and preserves. Traditional country cooking by qualified chef using home-grown produce.
Bedrooms: 3 double
Bathrooms: 3 en-suite

Bed & breakfast per night:	£min	£max
Double	40.00	42.00

Half board per person:	£min	£max
Daily	30.00	36.00
Weekly	203.00	245.00

Lunch available
Evening meal 1800 (last orders 1900)
Parking for 4
12

LYMINGTON

Continued

Hideaway

COMMENDED

Middle Common Road, Pennington, Lymington SO41 8LE
☎ (01590) 676974

Quiet country house, tucked away. Pretty rooms, all en-suite with TV and tea/coffee.
Bedrooms: 2 double, 1 triple
Bathrooms: 3 en-suite

Bed & breakfast per night:	£min	£max
Single	25.00	25.00
Double	40.00	44.00

Parking for 5

Our Bench

COMMENDED

9 Lodge Road, Pennington, Lymington SO41 8HH
☎ (01590) 673141
Fax (01590) 673141
Email: ourbench @newforest.demon.co.uk

All en-suite bedrooms with TV. Indoor heated pool, jacuzzi and sauna. Non-smokers only, please. Sorry, no children. Large quiet garden. Close to forest. Nominee for Southern Tourist Board regional heat in England for Excellence awards 1997.
Wheelchair access category 3
Bedrooms: 2 double, 1 twin
Bathrooms: 3 en-suite

Bed & breakfast per night:	£min	£max
Single	20.00	26.00
Double	40.00	48.00

Half board per person:	£min	£max
Daily	27.00	36.00
Weekly	187.00	252.00

Evening meal 1800 (last orders 1800)
Parking for 5
Cards accepted: Mastercard, Visa, Switch/Delta

LYNDHURST

Hampshire
Map ref 2C3

The "capital" of the New Forest, surrounded by attractive woodland scenery and delightful villages. The town is dominated by the Victorian Gothic-style church where the original Alice in Wonderland is buried.
Tourist Information Centre ☎ (01703) 282269

Burwood Lodge

COMMENDED

Romsey Road, Lyndhurst SO43 7AA
☎ (01703) 282445
Fax (01703) 282445
Lovely house in half-acre garden, near the village centre. All rooms with en-suite shower, WC and washbasin. Parking in grounds.
Bedrooms: 1 single, 3 double, 1 triple, 1 family room
Bathrooms: 6 en-suite

Bed & breakfast per night:	£min	£max
Single	22.00	26.00
Double	40.00	50.00

Parking for 8

Forest Cottage

Listed COMMENDED

High Street, Lyndhurst SO43 7BH
☎ (01703) 283461
Charming 300-year-old cottage with welcoming atmosphere, in the village, yet open forest only yards away. Guest lounge with open fire and TV.
Bedrooms: 1 single, 1 double, 1 twin
Bathrooms: 2 public

Bed & breakfast per night:	£min	£max
Single	20.00	20.00
Double	36.00	36.00

Parking for 3
14

The Penny Farthing Hotel

COMMENDED

Romsey Road, Lyndhurst SO43 7AA
☎ (01703) 284422
Fax (01703) 284488
Perfectly situated, cheerful, small hotel, 1 minute's walk from village centre, shops, restaurants, 2 minutes from open forest. Tastefully furnished rooms ensure a comfortable stay. New cottage annexe.
Bedrooms: 3 single, 5 double, 1 twin, 1 triple, 1 family room
Bathrooms: 10 en-suite, 1 private

Bed & breakfast per night:	£min	£max
Single	25.00	40.00
Double	49.00	75.00

Parking for 15
Cards accepted: Amex, Mastercard, Visa, Switch/Delta

Ad See display advertisement on this page

MAIDENHEAD

Berkshire
Map ref 2C2

Attractive town on the River Thames which is crossed by an elegant 18th C bridge and by Brunel's well-known railway bridge. It is a popular place for boating with delightful riverside walks. The Courage Shire Horse Centre is nearby.
Tourist Information Centre ☎ (01628) 781110

Cartlands Cottage

APPROVED

Kings Lane, Cookham Dean, Cookham, Maidenhead SL6 9AY
☎ (01628) 482196
Family room in self-contained garden studio. Meals in delightful timbered character cottage with exposed beams. Traditional cottage garden. National Trust common land. Very quiet.
Bedrooms: 1 triple
Bathrooms: 1 en-suite, 1 public

Bed & breakfast per night:	£min	£max
Single	18.50	22.50
Double	35.00	45.00

Parking for 4

Moor Farm

HIGHLY COMMENDED

Ascot Road, Holyport, Maidenhead SL6 2HY
☎ (01628) 33761
Fax (01628) 33761
100-acre mixed farm. 700-year-old medieval manor in picturesque Holyport village. 4 miles from Windsor.
Bedrooms: 1 double, 2 twin
Bathrooms: 3 en-suite

Bed & breakfast per night:	£min	£max
Double	45.00	55.00

Parking for 4

The map references refer to the colour maps towards the end of the guide. The first figure is the map number; the letter and figure which follow indicate the grid reference on the map.

MARLOW

Buckinghamshire
Map ref 2C2

Attractive Georgian town on the River Thames, famous for its 19th C suspension bridge. The High Street contains many old houses and there are connections with writers including Shelley and T S Eliot.

Acorn Lodge

COMMENDED

79 Marlow Bottom Road, Marlow Bottom, Marlow SL7 3NA
☎ (01628) 472197
House with outdoor swimming pool, backing on to woodland. Large en-suite bedrooms with TV. Children welcome. Within easy reach of M40, M4. London 30 miles, Heathrow/Windsor 30 minutes.
Bedrooms: 1 double, 1 family room
Bathrooms: 1 en-suite, 1 private

Bed & breakfast per night:	£min	£max
Single	30.00	40.00
Double	45.00	50.00

Parking for 6

OAP SP

2 Hyde Green

Listed COMMENDED

Marlow SL7 1QL
☎ (01628) 483526 & 0378 178802
Comfortable family home. Quietly situated yet only a few minutes' level walk from town centre, River Thames and station (Paddington 1 hour).
Bedrooms: 1 double, 2 twin
Bathrooms: 2 en-suite, 1 public

Bed & breakfast per night:	£min	£max
Single	25.00	28.00
Double	35.00	38.00

Parking for 2

Monkton Farmhouse

Listed COMMENDED

Monkton Farm, Little Marlow, Marlow SL7 3RF
☎ (01494) 521082
Fax (01494) 443905
150-acre dairy farm. 14th C cruckhouse set in beautiful countryside. Easily reached by motorway and close to shopping and sporting facilities.
Bedrooms: 1 single, 1 twin, 1 triple
Bathrooms: 1 public

Bed & breakfast per night:	£min	£max
Single	25.00	30.00
Double	45.00	50.00

Parking for 6

5 30

5 Pound Lane

Listed COMMENDED

Marlow SL7 2AE
☎ (01628) 482649
Older style house, just off town centre, 2 minutes from River Thames and leisure complex. Double room has own balcony with delightful view.
Bedrooms: 1 double, 1 twin
Bathrooms: 1 public

Bed & breakfast per night:	£min	£max
Single	25.00	28.00
Double	38.00	40.00

Parking for 2

10

Red Barn Farm

COMMENDED

Marlow Road, Marlow SL7 3DQ
☎ (01494) 882820
Fax (01494) 883545
10-acre mixed farm. Large detached farmhouse on small farm with sheep, horses and free-range hens. Baby sitting/listening service available by arrangement. Heated swimming pool.
Bedrooms: 1 single, 1 twin, 1 family room
Bathrooms: 1 en-suite, 2 private, 1 public

Bed & breakfast per night:	£min	£max
Single	20.00	25.00
Double	40.00	50.00

Parking for 4

Sneppen House

Listed HIGHLY COMMENDED

Henley Road, Marlow SL7 2DF
☎ (01628) 485227
Large modern house within a few minutes' level walk of town centre. Convenient for Thames Walk. Off-street parking. Good pub food nearby.
Bedrooms: 1 double, 1 twin
Bathrooms: 1 public

Bed & breakfast per night:	£min	£max
Single	20.00	22.00
Double	35.00	40.00

Parking for 3

4 SP

MARNHULL

Dorset
Map ref 2B3

Has a fine church and numerous attractive houses.

The Old Bank

Listed COMMENDED

Burton Street, Marnhull, Sturminster Newton DT10 1PH
☎ (01258) 821019
Fax (01258) 821019

Stone-built (1730) house in quiet Dorset country village. Attractive courtyard bordered by barns, leading to pretty garden. Pub approximately 100 yards away. Expect friendly Dorset country hospitality.

Bedrooms: 2 double, 1 twin
Bathrooms: 3 private, 2 public

Bed & breakfast per night:	£min	£max
Single	18.00	18.00
Double	36.00	36.00

Parking for 5

MILTON KEYNES

Buckinghamshire
Map ref 2C1

Designated a New Town in 1967, Milton Keynes offers a wide range of housing and is abundantly planted with trees. It has excellent shopping facilities and 3 centres for leisure and sporting activities. The Open University is based here.
Tourist Information Centre ☎ (01908) 232525

Haversham Grange

COMMENDED

Haversham, Milton Keynes MK19 7DX
☎ (01908) 312389
Fax (01908) 312389

Large 14th C stone house with many interesting features. Set in own gardens backing on to lakes.

Bedrooms: 3 twin
Suite available
Bathrooms: 2 en-suite, 1 private, 1 public

Bed & breakfast per night:	£min	£max
Single	25.00	25.00
Double	46.00	50.00

Half board per person:	£min	£max
Daily	40.00	40.00

Parking for 4

Michelville House

Newton Road, Bletchley, Milton Keynes MK3 5BN
☎ (01908) 371578

Clean, compact establishment within easy reach of railway station, M1, shopping and sporting facilities. 10 minutes from Milton Keynes shopping centre.

Bedrooms: 10 single, 6 twin
Bathrooms: 4 public

Bed & breakfast per night:	£min	£max
Single	15.00	22.00
Double	30.00	40.00

Parking for 16

Mill Farm

COMMENDED

Gayhurst, Newport Pagnell MK16 8LT
☎ (01908) 611489
Fax (01908) 611489

505-acre mixed farm. 17th C farmhouse. Hard tennis court, riding, fishing on River Ouse, which flows through farm. Good touring centre.

Bedrooms: 1 single, 1 double, 1 twin, 1 family room
Bathrooms: 1 en-suite, 3 private, 1 public

Bed & breakfast per night:	£min	£max
Single	15.00	20.00
Double	30.00	40.00

Parking for 12

The Old Rectory

COMMENDED

Drayton Road, Newton Longville, Milton Keynes MK17 0BH
☎ (01908) 375794

Brick-built, listed Georgian house (1769), in village setting to the south of Milton Keynes.

Bedrooms: 2 single, 1 double, 1 twin
Bathrooms: 1 en-suite, 2 public, 1 private shower

Bed & breakfast per night:	£min	£max
Single	17.00	18.00
Double	40.00	44.00

Half board per person:	£min	£max
Daily	24.00	25.00
Weekly	150.00	160.00

Evening meal 1800 (last orders 2000)
Parking for 6

Rose Cottage Guest Accommodation

Listed HIGHLY COMMENDED

Broughton Road, Salford, Milton Keynes MK17 8BQ
☎ (01908) 582239 & (0402) 587648
Fax (01908) 282029

Restored 16th C cottage and outbuildings, with 2.5 acre garden, in rural village between Milton Keynes and Woburn. Aga cooking.

Bedrooms: 4 double, 1 triple
Suites available
Bathrooms: 5 en-suite

Bed & breakfast per night:	£min	£max
Single	35.00	40.00
Double	45.00	55.00

Parking for 8

Vignoble

Listed COMMENDED

2 Medland, Woughton Park, Milton Keynes MK6 3BH
☎ (01908) 666804
Fax (01908) 666626
Email: 101532,627 @compuserve.com

In a quiet cul-de-sac within walking distance of the Open University and 2.5 miles from the city centre. A warm welcome home from home in 3 languages.

Bedrooms: 1 single, 1 double, 1 twin
Bathrooms: 1 en-suite, 1 public

Bed & breakfast per night:	£min	£max
Single	23.00	39.00
Double	42.00	50.00

Parking for 3

The symbols in each entry give information about services and facilities. A key to these symbols appears at the back of this guide.

MINSTEAD

Hampshire
Map ref 2C3

Cluster of thatched cottages and detached period houses. The church, listed in the Domesday Book, has private boxes - one with its own fireplace.

Grove House

Listed COMMENDED

Newtown, Minstead, Lyndhurst SO43 7GG
☎ (01703) 813211

9-acre smallholding. Lovely, quiet country home set in heart of the New Forest. Superb walking, cycling, riding (stabling available). Ideal base for touring.

Bedrooms: 1 triple
Bathrooms: 1 private

Bed & breakfast per night:	£min	£max
Double	35.00	40.00

Parking for 1

MOULSFORD ON THAMES

Oxfordshire
Map ref 2C2

White House

HIGHLY COMMENDED

Moulsford on Thames, Wallingford OX10 9JD
☎ (01491) 651397

Attractive detached family home with large, peaceful garden in Thames-side village. Ground floor accommodation with own front door. Convenient for Oxford, Henley and the Ridgeway.

Bedrooms: 1 double, 1 twin
Bathrooms: 1 public

Bed & breakfast per night:	£min	£max
Single	25.00	25.00
Double	45.00	45.00

Parking for 6

A key to symbols can be found inside the back cover flap.

Half board prices are given per person, but in some cases these may be based on double/twin occupancy.

NETHER WALLOP

Hampshire
Map ref 2C2

Winding lane leads to thatched cottages, cob walls of clay and straw and colourful gardens with the Wallop Brook running by St Andrew's Church. This has 11th C origins and a fine mural urging Sunday observance.

The Great Barn

HIGHLY COMMENDED

Five Bells Lane, Nether Wallop, Stockbridge SO20 8EN
☎ (01264) 782142

16th C barn, self-contained unit with en-suite rooms. In picturesque village of Nether Wallop, setting for Agatha Christie's "Miss Marple" stories.

Bedrooms: 1 double, 1 twin
Bathrooms: 2 en-suite

Bed & breakfast per night:	£min	£max
Single	26.00	26.00
Double	36.00	36.00

Parking for 2

NEW FOREST

See under Ashurst, Barton on Sea, Beaulieu, Bransgore, Brockenhurst, Burley, Cadnam, Fordingbridge, Hythe, Lymington, Lyndhurst, Minstead, New Milton, Ringwood, Sway

NEW MILTON

Hampshire
Map ref 2B3

New Forest residential town on the mainline railway.

Wayward Cottage

HIGHLY COMMENDED

New Lane, Bashley, New Milton, Hamphire BH25 5TD
☎ (01425) 611500
Fax (01425) 611500

Comfortable, friendly forest cottage down country lane, run by local family. Delightful secluded garden. Forest walks 1 mile, sea 3 miles. En-suite rooms. Good food nearby.

Bedrooms: 1 double, 1 twin
Bathrooms: 2 en-suite

Bed & breakfast per night:	£min	£max
Double	34.00	40.00

Parking for 3
Open February–November
6

NEWBURY

Berkshire
Map ref 2C2

Ancient town surrounded by the Downs and on the Kennet and Avon Canal. It has many buildings of interest, including the 17th C Cloth Hall. The racecourse is nearby.
Tourist Information Centre ☎ (01635) 30267

15 Dalby Crescent

Listed COMMENDED

Newbury RG14 7JR
☎ (01635) 522405

In quiet cul-de-sac within half a mile of town centre and station. Within walking distance of Newbury racecourse and 4 miles from M4 motorway.

Bedrooms: 1 double, 1 twin
Bathrooms: 1 public

Bed & breakfast per night:	£min	£max
Single	20.00	30.00
Double	40.00	60.00

Half board per person:	£min	£max
Daily	27.00	38.00
Weekly	180.00	250.00

Evening meal 1800 (last orders 2000)
Parking for 2
12

The Old Farmhouse

COMMENDED

Downend Lane, Chieveley, Newbury RG20 8TN
☎ (01635) 248361 & (0370) 590844

Small country farmhouse on edge of village. Within 1 mile of M4/A34 (junction 13) and close to Newbury. Accommodation in self-contained annexe. Large garden.

Bedrooms: 1 family room
Suite available
Bathrooms: 1 private

Bed & breakfast per night:	£min	£max
Single	22.00	25.00
Double	42.00	45.00

Parking for 5
8

NEWBURY

Continued

Rookwood Farmhouse

HIGHLY COMMENDED

Stockcross, Newbury RG20 8JX
☎ (01488) 608676
Fax (01488) 608676

Newly converted self-contained coach house with period furniture. Beautifully decorated, conservatory overlooking outdoor heated swimming pool and large garden. Easy access to M4 and A4. No smoking and no pets, please.

Bedrooms: 1 double, 1 twin
Suites available
Bathrooms: 2 en-suite

Bed & breakfast per night:	£min	£max
Single	40.00	
Double	55.00	

Evening meal 1830 (last orders 2030)
Parking for 3
12

NORTHMOOR

Oxfordshire
Map ref 2C1

The Ferryman Inn

Bablock Hythe, Northmoor, Oxford OX8 1BL
☎ (01865) 880028
Fax (01865) 880028

Riverside inn on site of ancient ferry crossing. Recently renovated to give two bars, restaurant and en-suite bedrooms.

Bedrooms: 3 double, 1 twin, 2 triple
Bathrooms: 6 en-suite

Bed & breakfast per night:	£min	£max
Single	35.00	35.00
Double	40.00	40.00

Lunch available
Evening meal 1830 (last orders 2200)
Parking for 100
350 OAP SP

Please check prices and other details at the time of booking.

OXFORD

Oxfordshire
Map ref 2C1

Beautiful university town with many ancient colleges, some dating from the 13th C, and numerous buildings of historic and architectural interest. The Ashmolean Museum has outstanding collections. Lovely gardens and meadows with punting on the Cherwell.
Tourist Information Centre ☎ (01865) 726871

Acorn Guest House

Listed COMMENDED

260 Iffley Road, Oxford OX4 1SE
☎ (01865) 247998

Victorian house situated midway between the city centre and the ring-road. Convenient for all local amenities and more distant attractions.

Bedrooms: 4 single, 2 twin, 7 triple
Bathrooms: 4 public

Bed & breakfast per night:	£min	£max
Single	22.00	25.00
Double	34.00	40.00

Parking for 11
Cards accepted: Diners, Mastercard, Visa

The Athena Guest House

Listed

253-255 Cowley Road, Oxford OX4 1XQ
☎ (01865) 243124
Fax (01865) 791007

Large, comfortable Victorian guesthouse with colour TV and tea/coffee in all rooms. Close to shops and restaurants. Easy transport to station and city centre. Ideal for small or large groups.

Bedrooms: 3 single, 3 double, 3 twin, 3 triple, 1 family room
Bathrooms: 2 en-suite, 1 private, 3 public, 3 private showers

Bed & breakfast per night:	£min	£max
Single	18.00	25.00
Double	38.00	45.00

Parking for 7
5

The symbol after an establishment name indicates that it is a Regional Tourist Board member.

Becket House

Listed

5 Becket Street, Oxford OX1 7PP
☎ (01865) 724675
Fax (01865) 316859

Friendly guesthouse convenient for rail and bus station, within walking distance of city centre and colleges. Good, clean accommodation, en-suite rooms.

Bedrooms: 4 single, 1 double, 3 twin, 1 triple
Bathrooms: 6 private, 1 public

Bed & breakfast per night:	£min	£max
Single	25.00	45.00
Double	36.00	55.00

Cards accepted: Amex, Diners, Mastercard, Visa, Switch/Delta

The Bungalow

Listed

Cherwell Farm, Mill Lane, Old Marston, Oxford OX3 0QF
☎ (01865) 557171

Modern bungalow set in 5 acres, in quiet location with views over open countryside, but within 3 miles of city centre. No smoking.

Bedrooms: 2 double, 2 twin
Bathrooms: 1 en-suite, 1 public

Bed & breakfast per night:	£min	£max
Single	22.00	30.00
Double	38.00	47.00

Parking for 4
Open April–October
6

Cumnor Village B & B

Listed COMMENDED

Beinn Bheag, 96 Oxford Road, Cumnor, Oxford OX2 9PQ
☎ (01865) 864020
Fax (01865) 864020

Detached bungalow with large garden in quiet village just outside the city. Comfortable accommodation, warm welcome. Wide choice of breakfasts. Non-smoking.

Bedrooms: 1 single, 1 double, 1 family room
Bathrooms: 2 en-suite, 1 public

Bed & breakfast per night:	£min	£max
Single	20.00	30.00
Double	40.00	45.00

Parking for 4

Gables

HIGHLY COMMENDED

6 Cumnor Hill, Oxford OX2 9HA
☎ (01865) 862153
Fax (01865) 864054

Attractive detached house with beautiful garden. Close to city centre, bus and railway stations. High quality rooms with satellite TV and direct-dial telephones.

Bedrooms: 2 single, 2 double, 1 twin, 1 triple
Bathrooms: 5 en-suite, 1 private, 1 public

Bed & breakfast per night:	£min	£max
Single	22.00	28.00
Double	40.00	48.00

Parking for 8
Cards accepted: Mastercard, Visa

High Hedges

COMMENDED

8 Cumnor Hill, Oxford OX2 9HA
☎ (01865) 863395
Fax (01865) 863395

Close to city centre, offering a high standard of accommodation, including en-suite rooms with TV/Sky and tea/coffee facilities, making your stay a comfortable one.

Bedrooms: 2 double, 2 twin
Bathrooms: 4 en-suite, 1 public

Bed & breakfast per night:	£min	£max
Double	40.00	44.00

Parking for 6
Cards accepted: Mastercard, Visa

Highfield West

HIGHLY COMMENDED

188 Cumnor Hill, Oxford OX2 9PJ
☎ (01865) 863007

Comfortable home in residential location. Good access to city centre and ring road. Large outdoor pool, heated in summer.

Bedrooms: 2 single, 1 double, 1 twin, 1 family room
Bathrooms: 3 en-suite, 1 public

Bed & breakfast per night:	£min	£max
Single	21.00	27.00
Double	40.00	52.00

Parking for 6

Mount Pleasant

APPROVED

76 London Road, Headington, Oxford OX3 9AJ
☎ (01865) 62749
Fax (01865) 62749

Small, no smoking, family-run hotel offering full facilities. On the A40 and convenient for Oxford shopping, hospitals, colleges, visiting the Chilterns and the Cotswolds.

Bedrooms: 2 double, 5 twin, 1 triple
Bathrooms: 8 en-suite

Bed & breakfast per night:	£min	£max
Single	37.50	45.00
Double	48.00	75.00

Half board per person:	£min	£max
Daily	37.50	45.00

Lunch available
Evening meal 1800 (last orders 2130)
Parking for 6
Cards accepted: Amex, Diners, Mastercard, Visa

Newton House

82-84 Abingdon Road, Oxford OX1 4PL
☎ (01865) 240561 & (0585) 485656
Fax (01865) 244647

Centrally located Victorian town house within walking distance of city centre, university, meadows, River Isis and university boat houses.

Bedrooms: 7 double, 4 twin, 2 family rooms
Bathrooms: 5 private, 3 public

Bed & breakfast per night:	£min	£max
Single	22.00	30.00
Double	34.00	50.00

Parking for 8
Cards accepted: Amex, Mastercard, Visa, Switch/Delta

7 Princes Street

Listed

Oxford OX4 1DD
☎ (01865) 726755

Restored Victorian artisan's cottage, furnished with many antiques. Short walk from Magdalen Bridge and central Oxford.

Bedrooms: 2 single, 1 double
Bathrooms: 1 public

Bed & breakfast per night:	£min	£max
Single	17.00	20.00
Double	34.00	38.00

Parking for 2

Sportsview Guest House

APPROVED

106-110 Abingdon Road, Oxford OX1 4PX
☎ (01865) 244268 & 0378 657691
Fax (01865) 249270

Guesthouse with garden, located near the city centre. Views over tennis and cricket grounds and the River Thames.

Bedrooms: 6 single, 8 double, 5 twin, 1 triple
Bathrooms: 8 en-suite, 1 private, 5 public

Bed & breakfast per night:	£min	£max
Single	23.00	30.00
Double	35.00	48.00

Parking for 8
Cards accepted: Amex, Mastercard, Visa, Switch/Delta

West Farm

Listed COMMENDED

Eaton, Appleton, Abingdon OX13 5PR
☎ (01865) 862908

1100-acre arable & livestock farm. Comfortable, centrally heated farmhouse on working farm, 5 miles west of Oxford. Children welcome (equipment, toys, etc). Tennis court. Excellent centre for touring, also frequent cheap coaches from Oxford to London. Good local pubs.

Bedrooms: 1 single, 1 double, 1 triple
Bathrooms: 1 private, 1 public

Bed & breakfast per night:	£min	£max
Single	20.00	25.00
Double	40.00	50.00

Parking for 6
Open April–December

PETERSFIELD

Hampshire
Map ref 2C3

Grew prosperous from the wool trade and was famous as a coaching centre. Its attractive market square is dominated by a statue of William III. Close by are Petersfield Heath with numerous ancient barrows and Butser Hill with magnificent views.
Tourist Information Centre ☎ (01730) 268829

The Butts

Listed COMMENDED

Steep, Petersfield GU32 1AA
☎ (01730) 263878
Fax (01730) 263878
Interesting, architect-designed house in a rural setting with 10 acres of grounds and magnificent downland views. Good walking territory. Very quiet.
Bedrooms: 1 single, 1 double
Bathrooms: 1 en-suite, 1 private

Bed & breakfast per night:	£min	£max
Single	20.00	20.00
Double	40.00	40.00

Parking for 3

Heath Farmhouse

COMMENDED

Heath Road East, Petersfield GU31 4HU
☎ (01730) 264709
4-acre horses & poultry farm. Georgian farmhouse with lovely views, set in large garden. Surrounded by quiet farmland yet only three-quarters of a mile from town centre. Within easy reach of Portsmouth, Chichester, Winchester.
Bedrooms: 1 double, 1 twin, 1 family room
Bathrooms: 2 en-suite, 1 private, 1 public

Bed & breakfast per night:	£min	£max
Single	17.00	20.00
Double	34.00	36.00

Parking for 5

National gradings and classifications were correct at the time of going to press but are subject to change. Please check at the time of booking.

POOLE

Dorset
Map ref 2B3

Tremendous natural harbour makes Poole a superb boating centre. The harbour area is crowded with historic buildings including the 15th C Town Cellars housing a maritime museum.
Tourist Information Centre ☎ (01202) 253253

Fernway

COMMENDED

56 Fernside Road, Poole BH15 2JJ
☎ (01202) 252044 & 0802 351033
Fax (01202) 666587
Home-from-home environment, close to all amenities. Colour TV, refreshment and washing facilities in both rooms. Full English breakfast. Open all year.
Bedrooms: 1 double, 1 twin
Bathrooms: 1 public

Bed & breakfast per night:	£min	£max
Single	18.00	22.00
Double	30.00	36.00

Parking for 3

Homeleigh

COMMENDED

105 Wimborne Road, Poole BH15 2BP
☎ (01202) 777075
Small, friendly, non-smoking establishment, near town centre, harbour, beaches and bus/rail stations. Within easy reach of coast and New Forest.
Bedrooms: 2 twin
Bathrooms: 1 public

Bed & breakfast per night:	£min	£max
Single	16.00	18.00
Double	30.00	34.00

Parking for 2

WELCOME HOST

This is a nationally recognised customer care programme which aims to promote the highest standards of service and a warm welcome. Establishments who are taking part in this initiative are indicated by the symbol.

PORTSMOUTH & SOUTHSEA

Hampshire
Map ref 2C3

The first dock was built in 1194. HMS Victory, Nelson's flagship, is here and Charles Dickens' former home is open to the public. Neighbouring Southsea has a promenade with magnificent views of Spithead.
Tourist Information Centre ☎ (01705) 838382 or 826722

The Elms Guest House

COMMENDED

48 Victoria Road South, Southsea, Hampshire PO5 2BT
☎ (01705) 823924
Fax (01705) 823924
Small, family-run guesthouse, close to ferry port and local attractions. Family rooms available.
Bedrooms: 1 single, 4 triple, 1 family room
Bathrooms: 2 en-suite, 1 public

Bed & breakfast per night:	£min	£max
Single	16.00	18.00
Double	32.00	42.00

Parking for 2

Hamilton House

COMMENDED

95 Victoria Road North, Southsea, Portsmouth, Hampshire PO5 1PS
☎ (01705) 823502
Fax (01705) 823502
Delightful family-run guesthouse, 5 minutes by car to ferry terminals, university and tourist attractions. Some en-suite rooms are available. Breakfast served from 6am.
Bedrooms: 1 single, 2 double, 2 twin, 1 triple, 2 family rooms
Suites available
Bathrooms: 5 en-suite, 2 public

Bed & breakfast per night:	£min	£max
Single	17.00	19.00
Double	34.00	38.00

Half board per person:	£min	£max
Daily	23.00	25.00
Weekly	151.00	165.00

Evening meal from 1800

OAP SP

Establishments should be open throughout the year, unless otherwise stated.

QUARLEY

Hampshire
Map ref 2B2

Lains Cottage

HIGHLY COMMENDED

Quarley, Andover SP11 8PX
☎ (01264) 889697
Fax (01264) 889697

Charming thatched house combining modern comforts with traditional cottage-style. In a country setting less than half a mile from the A303, giving access to London and the West Country.

Bedrooms: 2 double, 1 twin
Bathrooms: 3 en-suite

Bed & breakfast per night:	£min	£max
Single	26.00	35.00
Double	42.00	46.00

Parking for 10

READING

Berkshire
Map ref 2C2

Busy, modern county town with large shopping centre and many leisure and recreation facilities. There are several interesting museums and the Duke of Wellington's Stratfield Saye is nearby.
Tourist Information Centre ☎ (0118) 956 6226

Belstone

Listed HIGHLY COMMENDED

36 Upper Warren Avenue, Caversham, Reading RG4 7EB
☎ (0118) 947 7435
Fax (0118) 946 1465

Friendly welcome in elegant Victorian family house. Quiet tree-lined avenue near river and farmland. Convenient for town centre by car. Non-smokers only, please.

Bedrooms: 1 double, 1 twin
Bathrooms: 1 public

Bed & breakfast per night:	£min	£max
Single	26.00	30.00
Double	42.00	46.00

Parking for 2

Dittisham Guest House

Listed COMMENDED

63 Tilehurst Road, Reading RG3 2JL
☎ (0118) 956 9483 & (0589) 605193

Renovated Edwardian property with garden, in a quiet but central location. Good value and quality. On bus routes for centre of town.

Bedrooms: 4 single, 1 twin
Bathrooms: 3 en-suite, 1 public

Bed & breakfast per night:	£min	£max
Single	22.00	30.00
Double	35.00	45.00

Parking for 7
Cards accepted: Mastercard, Visa

The Elms

COMMENDED

Gallowstree Road, Rotherfield Peppard, Henley-on-Thames, Oxfordshire RG9 5HT
☎ (01734) 723164

Bed and breakfast near Reading. Heated swimming pool. All normal services, large garden, good parking. Excellent pub close by.

Bedrooms: 1 single, 1 double, 1 twin
Bathrooms: 2 en-suite, 1 public

Bed & breakfast per night:	£min	£max
Single	15.00	25.00
Double	30.00	45.00

Evening meal 1930 (last orders 2000)
Parking for 13

10 Greystoke Road

Listed COMMENDED

Caversham, Reading RG4 0EL
☎ (01734) 475784

Private home in quiet, residential area. TV lounge, tea and coffee-making facilities. Non-smokers only, please.

Bedrooms: 2 single, 1 double
Bathrooms: 2 public

Bed & breakfast per night:	£min	£max
Single	19.00	25.00
Double	35.00	40.00

Parking for 2

Orchid Bed & Breakfast

1 Micklands Road, Caversham, Reading RG4 6LT
☎ (0118) 947 9635 & 0958 953582

Private house in quiet road, convenient for access to Henley or Reading. Residents' private lounge with open fire.

Bedrooms: 2 single, 2 double
Bathrooms: 1 public

Bed & breakfast per night:	£min	£max
Single	18.00	25.00
Double	35.00	40.00

Parking for 4

The Six Bells

COMMENDED

Beenham Village, Beenham, Reading RG7 5NX
☎ (0118) 971 3368

Village pub, overlooking farmland. Four miles from Theale M4 junction 12, 1 mile off A4. Newly-built bedrooms. Home cooking always available - varied menu.

Bedrooms: 1 single, 2 double, 1 twin
Bathrooms: 4 en-suite

Bed & breakfast per night:	£min	£max
Single	36.00	36.00
Double	49.00	49.00

Lunch available
Evening meal 1830 (last orders 2130)
Parking for 35
Cards accepted: Mastercard, Visa, Switch/Delta

RINGWOOD

Hampshire
Map ref 2B3

Market town by the River Avon comprising old cottages, many of them thatched. Although just outside the New Forest, there is heath and woodland nearby and it is a good centre for horse-riding and walking.

Beau Cottage

COMMENDED

1 Hiltom Road, Ringwood BH24 1PW
☎ (01425) 461274

Quiet, comfortable, friendly accommodation in modernised old cottage. Good English breakfast, TV and tea making facilities in each room. Ample parking.

Bedrooms: 2 double
Bathrooms: 2 en-suite

Bed & breakfast per night:	£min	£max
Single	16.00	20.00
Double	32.00	40.00

Parking for 4

RINGWOOD

Continued

Old Stacks

HIGHLY COMMENDED

154 Hightown Road, Ringwood
BH24 1NP
☎ (01425) 473840
Fax (01425) 473840

Home-from-home hospitality assured in this delightful, spacious bungalow set in a lovely garden. Wonderful breakfast. Close to country inn and New Forest. Beaches and Bournemouth 10 minutes by car.

Bedrooms: 1 double, 1 twin
Bathrooms: 1 en-suite, 1 private

Bed & breakfast per night:	£min	£max
Single	20.00	26.00
Double	36.00	42.00

Parking for 4

12

Picket Hill House

HIGHLY COMMENDED

Picket Hill, Ringwood BH24 3HH
☎ (01425) 476173
Fax (01425) 470022

Large country house, with direct access to New Forest, offering comfortable accommodation and good breakfast. Ideal for walkers/riders. Overseas guests particularly welcome. Accommodation for 2 horses by prior arrangement.

Bedrooms: 2 double, 1 twin
Bathrooms: 3 en-suite

Bed & breakfast per night:	£min	£max
Single	25.00	30.00
Double	36.00	44.00

Parking for 6

10

For farm holidays and accommodation suitable for young people and organised groups, please refer to the special sections at the back of this guide.

ROMSEY

Hampshire
Map ref 2C3

Town grew up around the important abbey and lies on the banks of the River Test, famous for trout and salmon. Broadlands House, home of the late Lord Mountbatten, is open to the public.
Tourist Information Centre ☎ (01794) 512987

Country Accommodation

COMMENDED

The Old Post Office, New Road, Michelmersh, Romsey SO51 0NL
☎ (01794) 368739 & 0374 734478

Character rooms in ground floor independent annexe. Quiet village, 3 miles from Romsey. All en-suite, tea/coffee, TV. Good local pubs and restaurants.

Bedrooms: 2 double, 1 twin
Bathrooms: 3 en-suite

Bed & breakfast per night:	£min	£max
Single	28.00	28.00
Double	45.00	45.00

Parking for 4
Cards accepted: Mastercard, Visa

Highfield House

HIGHLY COMMENDED

Newtown Road, Awbridge, Romsey
SO51 0GG
☎ (01794) 340727
Fax (01794) 341450

In unspoilt rural village, overlooking golf-course. Delightful setting and charming gardens. Home cooking a speciality. Close to Mottisfont Abbey National Trust and Hillier Arboretum.

Bedrooms: 1 double, 2 twin
Bathrooms: 3 en-suite, 1 public

Bed & breakfast per night:	£min	£max
Double	45.00	50.00

Evening meal from 1900
Parking for 10

12

RYDE

Isle of Wight
Map ref 2C3

The island's chief entry port, connected to Portsmouth by ferries and hovercraft. 7 miles of sandy beaches with a half-mile pier, esplanade and gardens.
Tourist Information Centre ☎ (01983) 562905

Sillwood Acre

HIGHLY COMMENDED

Church Road, Binstead, Ryde
PO33 3TB
☎ (01983) 563553

Large Victorian house near Ryde, convenient for the ferry and hovercraft terminals. Two spacious en-suite rooms. Non-smoking.

Bedrooms: 1 double, 1 triple
Bathrooms: 2 en-suite

Bed & breakfast per night:	£min	£max
Single	17.00	19.00
Double	34.00	38.00

Parking for 3

SANDOWN

Isle of Wight
Map ref 2C3

The 6-mile sweep of Sandown Bay is one of the island's finest stretches, with excellent sands. The pier has a pavilion and sun terrace; the esplanade has amusements, bars, eating-places and gardens.
Tourist Information Centre ☎ (01983) 403886

Annandale Guest House

Listed COMMENDED

30 St John's Road, Sandown
PO36 8HA
☎ (01983) 402955

Small, comfortable, family-run guesthouse, 2 to 3 minutes' walk from the shops, beach, pier and theatre.

Bedrooms: 1 double, 1 twin, 1 triple, 1 family room
Bathrooms: 1 public

Bed & breakfast per night:	£min	£max
Single	14.00	16.00
Double	28.00	32.00

SELBORNE

Hampshire
Map ref 2C2

Village made famous by Gilbert White, who was a curate here and is remembered for his classic book "The Natural History of Selborne", published in 1788. His house is now a museum.

8 Goslings Croft

Listed HIGHLY COMMENDED

Selborne, Alton GU34 3HZ
☎ (01420) 511285
Fax (01420) 587451

Family home, set on edge of historic village, adjacent to National Trust land. Ideal base for walking and touring. Non-smokers only, please.

Bedrooms: 1 twin
Bathrooms: 1 en-suite

Bed & breakfast per night:	£min	£max
Single	19.50	19.50
Double	32.50	32.50

Parking for 1

The Queen's & The Limes

COMMENDED

High Street, Selborne, Alton GU34 3JJ
☎ (01420) 511454
Fax (01420) 511272

The Queens, an old village inn, and the Limes, a thatched cottage, set in the village of Selborne, much loved by naturalist Gilbert White.

Bedrooms: 2 single, 3 double, 2 twin, 1 triple, 1 family room
Bathrooms: 5 en-suite, 1 private, 2 public

Bed & breakfast per night:	£min	£max
Single	32.00	40.00
Double	45.00	65.00

Half board per person:	£min	£max
Daily	44.50	52.50
Weekly	296.50	352.50

Lunch available
Evening meal 1800 (last orders 2200)
Parking for 26
Cards accepted: Amex, Mastercard, Visa, Switch/Delta

50

SHAFTESBURY

Dorset
Map ref 2B3

Hilltop town with a long history. The ancient and cobbled Gold Hill is one of the most attractive in Dorset. There is an excellent small museum containing a collection of buttons for which the town is famous.
Tourist Information Centre ☎ (01747) 853514

The Knoll

HIGHLY COMMENDED

Bleke Street, Shaftesbury SP7 8AH
☎ (01747) 855243

Spacious Victorian family house with outstanding views, set in large garden, but within level walking distance of town centre and famous Gold Hill. Ideal centre for artists. Non-smoking.

Bedrooms: 2 double, 1 twin
Bathrooms: 2 en-suite, 1 private

Bed & breakfast per night:	£min	£max
Single	26.00	30.00
Double	46.00	50.00

Parking for 4

SHANKLIN

Isle of Wight
Map ref 2C3

Set on a cliff with gentle slopes leading down to the beach, esplanade and marine gardens. The picturesque, old thatched village nestles at the end of the wooded chine.
Tourist Information Centre ☎ (01983) 862942

Culham Lodge Hotel

COMMENDED

31 Landguard Manor Road, Shanklin PO37 7HZ
☎ (01983) 862880
Fax (01983) 862880

Charming hotel in beautiful tree-lined road. Heated swimming pool, conservatory, home cooking and personal service. TV in all rooms with Sky movies and sport.

Bedrooms: 5 double, 5 twin
Bathrooms: 10 en-suite, 1 public

Bed & breakfast per night:	£min	£max
Single	21.00	22.00
Double	42.00	44.00

Half board per person:	£min	£max
Daily	27.00	28.00
Weekly	175.00	182.00

Evening meal 1800 (last orders 1600)
Parking for 8
Open February–October
Cards accepted: Mastercard, Visa

12

Hazelwood Hotel

COMMENDED

14 Clarence Road, Shanklin PO37 7BH
☎ (01983) 862824
Fax (01983) 862824

Detached, friendly, comfortable hotel in a quiet tree-lined road, close to all amenities. Daily bookings taken. Parking available.

Bedrooms: 2 single, 4 double, 2 twin, 1 triple, 1 family room
Bathrooms: 8 en-suite, 1 public

Bed & breakfast per night:	£min	£max
Single	16.00	20.00
Double	32.00	40.00

Half board per person:	£min	£max
Daily	22.50	27.00
Weekly	137.00	175.00

Evening meal 1800 (last orders 1600)
Parking for 5
Cards accepted: Amex, Diners, Mastercard, Visa

2

Ryedale Private Hotel

COMMENDED

3 Atherley Road, Shanklin PO37 7AT
☎ (01983) 862375 & 0831 413233

Small, friendly, private hotel situated near sea, station and all amenities. One child free until late July and from September onwards.

Bedrooms: 2 single, 2 double, 1 triple, 3 family rooms
Bathrooms: 4 en-suite, 2 public

Bed & breakfast per night:	£min	£max
Single	15.50	19.00
Double	31.00	38.00

Half board per person:	£min	£max
Daily	20.50	24.00
Weekly	128.00	150.00

Evening meal 1800 (last orders 1800)
Open April–October
Cards accepted: Mastercard, Visa, Switch/Delta

SHENINGTON

Oxfordshire
Map ref 2C1

Village notable for its fine location around a hilltop green with charming views across the valley.

Top Farm House

Listed COMMENDED

Shenington, Banbury OX15 6LZ
☎ (01295) 670226
Fax (01295) 678170

An 18th C Hornton stone farmhouse with gardens to front and rear. Ideally situated for exploring the Cotswolds, Stratford-upon-Avon. 6 miles M40 junction 11.

Bedrooms: 1 double, 1 twin
Bathrooms: 2 private

Bed & breakfast per night:	£min	£max
Single	20.00	25.00
Double	40.00	45.00

Parking for 4

SHIPTON BELLINGER

Hampshire
Map ref 2B2

Parsonage Farm

COMMENDED

Shipton Bellinger, Tidworth SP9 7UF
☎ (01980) 842404

Former farmhouse of 16th/17th C origins in quiet village. Walled garden, stables, paddocks. Situated off A338 opposite parish church and Boot Inn. Convenient for Stonehenge.

Bedrooms: 1 single, 1 twin, 1 triple
Bathrooms: 1 private, 2 public

Bed & breakfast per night:	£min	£max
Single	20.00	30.00
Double	35.00	40.00

Parking for 6
10

WELCOME HOST

This is a nationally recognised customer care programme which aims to promote the highest standards of service and a warm welcome. Establishments who are taking part in this initiative are indicated by the symbol.

SHIPTON-UNDER-WYCHWOOD

Oxfordshire
Map ref 2B1

Situated in the ancient Forest of Wychwood with many fine old houses and an interesting parish church. Nearby is Shipton Court, a gabled Elizabethan house set in beautiful grounds that include an ornamental lake and a tree-lined avenue approach.

Courtlands

COMMENDED

6 Courtlands Road, Shipton-under-Wychwood, Oxford OX7 6DF
☎ (01993) 830551

Relaxed, friendly house in centre of unspoilt village. Offering peace and tranquillity. Coffee/tea, TV. Close to Oxfordshire Way and 3 inns.

Bedrooms: 1 double, 1 twin
Bathrooms: 1 en-suite, 1 private, 1 public

Bed & breakfast per night:	£min	£max
Single	20.00	25.00
Double	38.00	40.00

Parking for 2

SIXPENNY HANDLEY

Dorset
Map ref 2B3

The Barleycorn House

COMMENDED

Deanland, Sixpenny Handley, Salisbury, Wiltshire SP5 5PD
☎ (01725) 552583
Fax (01725) 552090

Converted 17th C inn retaining original period features, in peaceful surroundings with many nearby walks. Relaxed atmosphere and home cooking.

Bedrooms: 1 single, 1 double, 1 twin
Bathrooms: 2 en-suite, 1 public

Bed & breakfast per night:	£min	£max
Single	18.50	18.50
Double	37.00	37.00

Half board per person:	£min	£max
Daily	27.50	27.50
Weekly	179.55	179.55

Evening meal from 1830
Parking for 5

SOULDERN

Oxfordshire
Map ref 2C1

Tower Fields

COMMENDED

Tusmore Road, Souldern, Bicester OX6 9HY
☎ (01869) 346554
Fax (01869) 345157

Converted 18th C cottages and 14-acre smallholding with rare breeds of poultry, sheep and cattle. Small collection of vintage cars.

Bedrooms: 1 single, 1 twin, 1 family room
Suites available
Bathrooms: 3 en-suite

Bed & breakfast per night:	£min	£max
Single	23.00	26.50
Double	48.00	50.00

Parking for 22

SOUTHAMPTON

Hampshire
Map ref 2C3

One of Britain's leading seaports with a long history, now a major container port. In the 18th C it became a fashionable resort with the assembly rooms and theatre. The old Guildhall and the Wool House are now museums. Sections of the medieval wall can still be seen.
Tourist Information Centre ☎ (01703) 221106

Ashelee Lodge

Listed COMMENDED

36 Atherley Road, Shirley, Southampton SO15 5DQ
☎ (01703) 222095
Fax (01703) 222095

Homely guesthouse, garden with pool. Half a mile from city centre, near station, M27 and Red Funnel ferryport. Good touring base for New Forest, Salisbury and Winchester. Near university.

Bedrooms: 1 single, 1 double, 1 twin, 1 triple
Bathrooms: 1 public

Bed & breakfast per night:	£min	£max
Single	15.00	17.00
Double	30.00	32.00

Evening meal from 1800
Parking for 2
Cards accepted: Mastercard, Visa

SOUTHSEA

Hampshire

See under Portsmouth & Southsea

SUTTON SCOTNEY

Hampshire
Map ref 2C2

Knoll House

HIGHLY COMMENDED

Wonston, Sutton Scotney, Winchester SO21 3LR
☎ (01962) 760273
Take Andover road from Winchester to Sutton Scotney. Turn right at village hall to Wonston. Situated on right hand side almost opposite Wonston Arms.
Bedrooms: 1 double, 1 twin
Bathrooms: 2 en-suite

Bed & breakfast per night:	£min	£max
Single	19.00	
Double	38.00	

Half board per person:	£min	£max
Daily	28.00	
Weekly		196.00

Evening meal 1830 (last orders 2030)
Parking for 2

SWAY

Hampshire
Map ref 2C3

Small village on the south-western edge of the New Forest. It is noted for its 220-ft tower, Peterson's Folly, built in the 1870s by a retired Indian judge to demonstrate the value of concrete as a building material.

Manor Farm

Listed COMMENDED

Coombe Lane, Sway, Lymington SO41 6BP
☎ (01590) 683542
30-acre beef farm. 18th C, Grade II listed farmhouse, surrounded by open fields and forest. Off B3055 Sway-Brockenhurst road.
Bedrooms: 1 double, 1 family room
Bathrooms: 2 en-suite, 1 public

Bed & breakfast per night:	£min	£max
Double	36.00	40.00

Parking for 20

Squirrels

COMMENDED

Broadmead, (off Silver Street), Sway, Lymington SO41 6DH
☎ (01590) 683163
Between forest, sea and yachting centre. Modern house with large woodland garden. Tranquil setting up footpath and bridleway, opposite Broadmead Cottages. No smoking please.
Bedrooms: 1 single, 1 double, 1 triple
Suite available
Bathrooms: 2 en-suite, 1 public

Bed & breakfast per night:	£min	£max
Single	18.00	20.00
Double	36.00	40.00

Parking for 8

THAME

Oxfordshire
Map ref 2C1

Historic market town on the River Thame. The wide, unspoilt High Street has many styles of architecture with medieval timber-framed cottages, Georgian houses and some famous inns.
Tourist Information Centre ☎ (01844) 212834

The Dairy

HIGHLY COMMENDED

Moreton, Thame OX9 2HX
☎ (01844) 214075
Fax (01844) 214075

Former milking parlour, set in 4.5 acres of lawns and native trees, enjoying a quiet village location with views of the Chilterns.
Bedrooms: 3 double
Suites available
Bathrooms: 3 en-suite

Bed & breakfast per night:	£min	£max
Single	50.00	
Double	60.00	

Parking for 6
Cards accepted: Amex

THRUXTON

Hampshire
Map ref 2B2

May Cottage

COMMENDED

Thruxton, Andover SP11 8LZ
☎ (01264) 771241 & (0468) 242166
Fax (01264) 771770

Set in tranquil, picturesque village and dating back to 1740. Ideal touring area, quarter of a mile off A303. Secluded, comfortable house with TV in bedrooms. Guests have own sitting/dining room. All home cooking.
Bedrooms: 1 single, 3 twin
Bathrooms: 2 en-suite, 2 private

Bed & breakfast per night:	£min	£max
Single	20.00	25.00
Double	40.00	50.00

Half board per person:	£min	£max
Daily	32.00	35.00

Evening meal from 1900
Parking for 4
Open January, March–December

WARNFORD

Hampshire
Map ref 2C3

Hayden Barn Cottage

HIGHLY COMMENDED

Warnford, Southampton SO32 3LF
☎ (01730) 829454
Late 19th C red brick house in lovely garden amid rolling countryside.
Bedrooms: 2 twin
Bathrooms: 2 en-suite

Bed & breakfast per night:	£min	£max
Single	20.00	25.00
Double	40.00	40.00

Parking for 4

WARNFORD

Continued

Paper Mill

Listed COMMENDED

Peake Lane, Warnford, Southampton SO32 3LA
☎ (01730) 829387

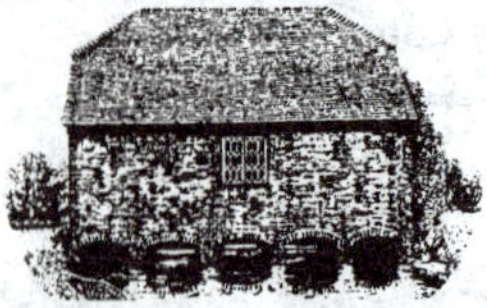

Self-contained mill house in unique setting on River Meon. Take A272 from Petersfield or Winchester to West Meon Hut traffic lights, turn south on A32, follow road to Warnford, past George and Falcon and turn left into Peake Lane.

Bedrooms: 1 double
Bathrooms: 1 en-suite

Bed & breakfast per night:	£min	£max
Single		28.00
Double		48.00

Parking for 1
Open April–September

WELLOW

Isle of Wight
Map ref 2C3

Mattingley Farm

COMMENDED

Main Road, Wellow, Yarmouth PO41 0SZ
☎ (01983) 760503
Fax (01983) 760503

5-acre smallholding. Comfortable 17th C island stone farmhouse, en-suite, oak beams, home cooking. Picturesque rural setting. Farm animals. 2 miles sea, bus route.

Bedrooms: 1 double
Bathrooms: 1 en-suite

Bed & breakfast per night:	£min	£max
Single	23.00	25.00
Double	46.00	50.00

Half board per person:	£min	£max
Daily	32.00	34.00
Weekly	195.00	250.00

Evening meal 1850 (last orders 1950)
Parking for 3

WEST LULWORTH

Dorset
Map ref 2B3

Well-known for Lulworth Cove, the almost landlocked circular bay of chalk and limestone cliffs.

Graybank Guest House

Listed COMMENDED

Main Road, West Lulworth, Wareham BH20 5RL
☎ (01929) 400256

Victorian guesthouse in beautiful countryside, 5 minutes' walk from Lulworth Cove and the coastal path. Ideal base for walking, touring or just unwinding. Excellent breakfast.

Bedrooms: 1 single, 2 double, 1 twin, 1 triple, 2 family rooms
Bathrooms: 3 public

Bed & breakfast per night:	£min	£max
Single	15.00	18.00
Double	30.00	36.00

Parking for 7
Open February–November

Newlands Farm

COMMENDED

West Lulworth, Wareham BH20 5PU
☎ (01929) 400376
Fax (01929) 400536

750-acre arable & livestock farm. 19th C farmhouse, with outstanding views to sea and distant Purbeck Hills. At Durdle Door, 1 mile west of Lulworth Cove.

Bedrooms: 1 double, 1 triple
Bathrooms: 1 public, 2 private showers

Bed & breakfast per night:	£min	£max
Double	44.00	44.00

Parking for 10
Open March–October

The Old Barn

Listed APPROVED

Lulworth Cove, West Lulworth, Wareham BH20 5RL
☎ (01929) 400305

Converted barn in peaceful, picturesque coastal village. Choice of rooms with continental breakfast or please-yourself-rooms with light self-catering facilities. Large gardens. Ideal base for touring Dorset. Restaurants nearby.

Bedrooms: 2 single, 2 double, 1 twin, 1 triple, 1 family room
Bathrooms: 3 public

Bed & breakfast per night:	£min	£max
Single	17.00	22.00
Double	34.00	44.00

Parking for 9
Cards accepted: Mastercard, Visa

WESTBURY

Buckinghamshire
Map ref 2C1

Mill Farm House

Westbury, Brackley, Northamptonshire NN13 5JS
☎ (01280) 704843

1000-acre mixed farm. Grade II listed farmhouse, overlooking a colourful garden including a covered heated swimming pool. Situated in the centre of Westbury village.

Bedrooms: 1 single, 1 double, 1 triple
Bathrooms: 1 en-suite, 2 private, 1 public

Bed & breakfast per night:	£min	£max
Single	20.00	25.00
Double	40.00	45.00

Half board per person:	£min	£max
Daily	30.00	40.00

Evening meal 1930 (last orders 2130)
Parking for 6

WICKHAM

Hampshire
Map ref 2C3

Lying in the Meon Valley, this market town is built around the Square and in Bridge Street can be seen some timber-framed cottages. Still the site of an annual horse fair.

Chiphall Acre

COMMENDED

Droxford Road, Wickham, Fareham PO17 5AY
☎ (01329) 833188 & 662182
Fax (01329) 664680

Beautifully situated, comfortable house, in large secluded garden full of interesting plants. All rooms on ground

floor. Non-smokers only, please. Ample secure parking. Wide choice of home-made/free range produce.
Bedrooms: 1 double, 1 twin, 1 triple
Suites available
Bathrooms: 1 en-suite, 1 public

Bed & breakfast per night:	£min	£max
Single	21.00	31.00
Double	41.00	45.00

Evening meal 1800 (last orders 2000)
Parking for 3

Montrose

HIGHLY COMMENDED

Solomons Lane, Shirrell Heath, Southampton SO32 2HU
☎ (01329) 833345
Attractive, comfortable accommodation in lovely Meon Valley, offering personal attention. Equidistant from main towns and convenient for continental ferries and motorway links.
Bedrooms: 2 double, 1 twin
Bathrooms: 1 en-suite, 1 public

Bed & breakfast per night:	£min	£max
Single	23.00	28.00
Double	42.00	48.00

Parking for 6
Cards accepted: Mastercard, Visa

WIMBORNE MINSTER

Dorset
Map ref 2B3

Market town centred on the twin-towered Minster Church of St Cuthberga which gave the town the second part of its name. Good touring base for the surrounding countryside, depicted in the writings of Thomas Hardy.
Tourist Information Centre ☎ (01202) 886116

Acacia House

HIGHLY COMMENDED

2 Oakley Road, Wimborne Minster BH21 1QJ
☎ (01202) 883958
Fax (01202) 881943

Beautifully decorated rooms are what the discerning traveller expects. What comes as a surprise is Eveline Stimpson's tea and cake welcome.
Bedrooms: 1 single, 1 double, 1 twin, 1 triple
Bathrooms: 2 en-suite, 1 private, 1 public

Bed & breakfast per night:	£min	£max
Single	17.00	25.00
Double	35.00	40.00

Parking for 3
Cards accepted: Mastercard, Visa, Switch/Delta

Ashton Lodge

COMMENDED

10 Oakley Hill, Merley, Wimborne Minster BH21 1QH
☎ (01202) 883423
Fax (01202) 886180
Large, detached, family house, with attractive gardens and relaxed, friendly atmosphere. Off-street parking available. Payphone. Children welcome.
Bedrooms: 2 single, 1 twin, 2 triple
Bathrooms: 2 en-suite, 2 public

Bed & breakfast per night:	£min	£max
Single	20.00	
Double	44.00	

Parking for 4
Cards accepted: Mastercard, Visa

Henbury Farm

COMMENDED

Dorchester Road, Sturminster Marshall, Wimborne Minster BH21 3RN
☎ (01258) 857306
Fax (01258) 857928

240-acre mixed & dairy farm. 300-year-old farmhouse facing large pond and lawn. Close to New Forest and 15 minutes from sandy beaches. Numerous local restaurants to meet your evening meal requirements.
Bedrooms: 1 single, 3 double, 1 twin
Suites available
Bathrooms: 2 en-suite, 1 public

Bed & breakfast per night:	£min	£max
Single	20.00	27.00
Double	40.00	46.00

Parking for 10

Homestay

Listed HIGHLY COMMENDED

22 West Borough, Wimborne Minster BH21 1NF
☎ (01202) 849015
Listed Georgian town house in centre of town. All rooms have colour TV and tea/coffee facilities. Just 5 miles from Poole, 8 miles from Bournemouth. Sorry, no children and no smoking.
Bedrooms: 2 double, 1 twin
Bathrooms: 1 en-suite, 2 private

Bed & breakfast per night:	£min	£max
Double	40.00	50.00

Peacehaven

Listed COMMENDED

282 Sopwith Crescent, Merley, Wimborne Minster BH21 1XL
☎ (01202) 880281
A warm welcome awaits you in this bungalow family home, with all rooms on the ground floor. On bus routes to Wimborne, Poole and Bournemouth.
Bedrooms: 1 double, 1 twin
Bathrooms: 1 public

Bed & breakfast per night:	£min	£max
Single	17.50	17.50
Double	35.00	35.00

Half board per person:	£min	£max
Daily	25.00	25.00
Weekly	157.50	157.50

Evening meal 1700 (last orders 2000)
Parking for 2

Twynham

Listed COMMENDED

67 Poole Road, Wimborne Minster BH21 1QB
☎ (01202) 887310
Friendly, family home, recently refurbished, with vanity unit, TV and beverages in rooms. Within walking distance of town centre.
Bedrooms: 2 double, 1 twin
Bathrooms: 2 public

Bed & breakfast per night:	£min	£max
Single	15.00	18.00
Double	25.00	30.00

Parking for 2

Map references apply to the colour maps at the back of this guide.

WINCHESTER

Hampshire
Map ref 2C3

King Alfred the Great made Winchester the capital of Saxon England. A magnificent Norman cathedral, with one of the longest naves in Europe, dominates the city. Home of Winchester College founded in 1382.
Tourist Information Centre ☎ (01962) 840500

Cathedral View

COMMENDED
9A Magdalen Hill, Winchester
SO23 0HJ
☎ (01962) 863802
Guesthouse with views across historic city and cathedral. 5 minutes' walk from city centre. En-suite facilities, TV, parking.
Bedrooms: 4 double, 1 twin, 1 family room
Bathrooms: 3 en-suite, 3 private

Bed & breakfast per night:	£min	£max
Single	33.00	35.00
Double	42.00	48.00

Parking for 4

The Farrells

COMMENDED
5 Ranelagh Road, St Cross,
Winchester SO23 9TA
☎ (01962) 869555
A warm welcome awaits you at this comfortable Victorian house close to city centre, St Cross Hospital and water meadows.
Bedrooms: 2 double, 1 twin
Bathrooms: 1 en-suite, 1 private, 2 public

Bed & breakfast per night:	£min	£max
Single	18.00	20.00
Double	34.00	42.00

Parking for 2

ACCESSIBILITY

Look for the symbols which indicate accessibility for wheelchair users. These are described in detail at the front of this guide.

32 Hyde Street

APPROVED
Winchester SO23 7DX
☎ (01962) 851621
Attractive 18th C town house close to city centre and recreational amenities.
Bedrooms: 1 double, 1 triple
Bathrooms: 1 public

Bed & breakfast per night:	£min	£max
Single	17.00	19.00
Double	30.00	32.00

54 St Cross Road

Listed COMMENDED
Winchester SO23 9PS
☎ (01962) 852073
Fax (01962) 852073
Victorian family house, with warm, welcoming atmosphere. Close to water meadows and 10 minutes' walk from city centre.
Bedrooms: 1 single, 1 double, 1 twin
Bathrooms: 1 public

Bed & breakfast per night:	£min	£max
Single	19.00	21.00
Double	36.00	40.00

Parking for 3

67 St Cross Road

COMMENDED
Winchester SO23 9RE
☎ (01962) 863002
Fax (01962) 863002
Large, terraced town house, with comfortable rooms, good food and a friendly atmosphere.
Bedrooms: 1 double, 1 family room
Bathrooms: 1 en-suite, 1 private

Bed & breakfast per night:	£min	£max
Single	20.00	
Double	36.00	

St Margaret's

Listed COMMENDED
3 St Michael's Road, Winchester
SO23 9JE
☎ (01962) 861450
Light and comfortable rooms in Victorian house, a short walk from cathedral, college and city centre. Delicious breakfasts, friendly atmosphere.
Bedrooms: 1 double, 1 twin
Bathrooms: 2 public

Bed & breakfast per night:	£min	£max
Double	36.00	38.00

Parking for 2

Shawlands

COMMENDED
46 Kilham Lane, Winchester
SO22 5QD
☎ (01962) 861166
Fax (01962) 861166

Attractive, modern house, situated in a quiet, elevated position overlooking open countryside. Delightful garden. 1.5 miles from city centre.
Wheelchair access category 3
Bedrooms: 2 double, 2 twin, 1 triple
Bathrooms: 1 private, 3 public

Bed & breakfast per night:	£min	£max
Single	24.00	30.00
Double	35.00	40.00

Parking for 4
Cards accepted: Mastercard, Visa, Switch/Delta

Stratton House

COMMENDED
Stratton Road, St Giles Hill,
Winchester SO23 0JQ
☎ (01962) 863919 & 864529
Fax (01962) 842095
Email: strattongroup
@btinternet.com
Lovely old Victorian house with an acre of grounds, in an elevated position on St Giles Hill.
Bedrooms: 1 single, 3 double, 2 twin, 1 triple
Bathrooms: 6 en-suite, 1 private

Bed & breakfast per night:	£min	£max
Single	33.00	39.00
Double	48.00	59.00

Half board per person:	£min	£max
Daily	41.00	47.00
Weekly	258.00	296.00

Evening meal 1800 (last orders 1600)
Parking for 8
Cards accepted: Mastercard, Visa, Switch/Delta

A key to symbols can be found inside the back cover flap.

WINDSOR

Berkshire
Map ref 2D2

Town dominated by the spectacular castle, home of the Royal Family for over 900 years. Parts are open to the public. There are many attractions including the Great Park, Eton and trips on the river.
Tourist Information Centre ☎ (01753) 852010

Chasela

Listed COMMENDED

30 Convent Road, Windsor SL4 3RB
☎ (01753) 860410
Warm, modern house 1 mile from the castle. Easy access M4, M40, M25, M3, Heathrow. TV, tea/coffee facilities in rooms. Breakfast room overlooks lovely garden. Payphone.
Bedrooms: 1 single, 1 twin
Bathrooms: 1 public

Bed & breakfast per night:	£min	£max
Single	18.00	22.00
Double	36.00	44.00

Parking for 5

The Crown & Cushion Inn

Listed APPROVED

84 High Street, Eton, Windsor
SL4 6AF
☎ (01753) 861531
Family-run establishment, 15th C in part, close to Eton College, Windsor Castle and River Thames. Traditional lunchtime/evening meals.
Bedrooms: 5 single, 2 double, 2 twin
Bathrooms: 1 public, 1 private shower

Bed & breakfast per night:	£min	£max
Single	27.50	27.50
Double	55.00	55.00

Half board per person:	£min	£max
Daily	33.50	33.50
Weekly	210.00	210.00

Lunch available
Evening meal 1730 (last orders 2030)
Parking for 10
Cards accepted: Amex, Mastercard, Visa

Please check prices and other details at the time of booking.

Halcyon House

COMMENDED

131 Clarence Road, Windsor
SL4 5AR
☎ (01753) 863262
Fax (01753) 863262
A warm welcome at a family-run guesthouse, 10 minutes' walk from the town centre and river. Ideal base for London. Off-street parking.
Bedrooms: 2 double, 1 twin
Bathrooms: 3 en-suite, 1 public

Bed & breakfast per night:	£min	£max
Single	42.00	42.00
Double	50.00	50.00

Parking for 6

Oscar Hotel

APPROVED

65 Vansittart Road, Windsor
SL4 5DB
☎ (01753) 830613
Fax (01753) 833744
Fully licensed bar, all rooms en-suite with direct-dial telephone, colour TV, tea/coffee facilities. Own car park. Minutes' drive to Legoland.
Bedrooms: 3 single, 4 double, 2 twin, 1 triple, 2 family rooms
Bathrooms: 12 en-suite

Bed & breakfast per night:	£min	£max
Single	45.00	55.00
Double	55.00	65.00

Half board per person:	£min	£max
Daily	37.50	40.00
Weekly	245.00	275.00

Evening meal 1800 (last orders 1930)
Parking for 10
Cards accepted: Amex, Diners, Mastercard, Visa, Switch/Delta

WELCOME HOST

This is a nationally recognised customer care programme which aims to promote the highest standards of service and a warm welcome. Establishments who are taking part in this initiative are indicated by the symbol.

Tanglewood

Listed HIGHLY COMMENDED

Oakley Green, Windsor SL4 4PZ
☎ (01753) 860034
Fax (01753) 860034
Picturesque chalet-style guesthouse in beautiful garden. Rural area overlooking open fields on B3024. Windsor 10 minutes' drive, Heathrow 15 miles. Excellent meals at nearby pub.
Bedrooms: 2 twin
Bathrooms: 1 public

Bed & breakfast per night:	£min	£max
Double	42.00	42.00

Parking for 2
Open May–September

WITNEY

Oxfordshire
Map ref 2C1

Town famous for its blanket-making and mentioned in the Domesday Book. The market-place contains the Butter Cross, a medieval meeting place, and there is a green with merchants' houses.
Tourist Information Centre ☎ (01993) 775802

The Court Inn

APPROVED

43 Bridge Street, Witney OX8 6DA
☎ (01993) 703228
Historic inn with dining room and 2 bars, featured in "Good Beer Guide". TV and telephone in all bedrooms.
Bedrooms: 3 single, 2 double, 3 twin, 2 triple
Bathrooms: 5 en-suite, 1 public, 1 private shower

Bed & breakfast per night:	£min	£max
Single	22.00	32.00
Double	34.00	42.00

Lunch available
Evening meal 1900 (last orders 2100)
Parking for 12
Cards accepted: Mastercard, Visa

Information on accommodation listed in this guide has been supplied by the proprietors. As changes may occur you are advised to check details at the time of booking.

WITNEY

Continued

Field View

HIGHLY COMMENDED

Wood Green, Witney OX8 6DE
☎ (01993) 705485 & (0468) 614347
Situated in 2 acres on edge of the bustling market town of Witney. Ideal for Oxford University and the Cotswolds.
Bedrooms: 1 double, 2 twin
Bathrooms: 3 en-suite

Bed & breakfast per night:	£min	£max
Single	25.00	25.00
Double	40.00	44.00

Parking for 10

Quarrydene

Listed COMMENDED

17 Dene Rise, Witney OX8 5LU
☎ (01993) 772152 & 0850 054786
My 1930s detached home will give you a friendly welcome. A few minutes' walk from town centre, but in a very quiet cul de sac. Good location for Oxford/Cotswolds/Stratford.
Bedrooms: 2 single, 1 double, 1 twin
Bathrooms: 1 en-suite, 2 public

Bed & breakfast per night:	£min	£max
Single	16.00	20.00
Double	32.00	40.00

Half board per person:	£min	£max
Daily	21.00	25.00
Weekly	147.00	175.00

Parking for 2

WOODCOTE

Oxfordshire
Map ref 2C2

Hedges

COMMENDED

South Stoke Road, Woodcote, Reading, Berkshire RG8 0PL
☎ (01491) 680461
Peaceful, rural situation on edge of village. Historic Area of Outstanding Natural Beauty. Good access Henley, Oxford, Reading (Heathrow link), M4, M40.
Bedrooms: 2 single, 2 twin
Bathrooms: 1 private, 2 public

Bed & breakfast per night:	£min	£max
Single	15.00	17.50
Double	30.00	35.00

Parking for 4

Please mention this guide when making your booking.

WOODSTOCK

Oxfordshire
Map ref 2C1

Small country town clustered around the park gates of Blenheim Palace, the superb 18th C home of the Duke of Marlborough. The town has well-known inns and an interesting museum. Sir Winston Churchill was born and buried nearby.
Tourist Information Centre ☎ (01993) 811038

Gorselands Farmhouse Auberge

Boddington Lane, Long Hanborough, Witney OX8 6PU
☎ (01993) 881895
Fax (01993) 882799
Cotswold stone country farmhouse with exposed beams, snooker room, conservatory. Convenient for Blenheim Palace, Oxford, Cotswold villages. Evening meals available. Licensed for wine and beer. Grass tennis court.
Bedrooms: 1 single, 2 double, 1 twin, 2 family rooms
Suite available
Bathrooms: 6 en-suite

Bed & breakfast per night:	£min	£max
Single	30.00	35.00
Double	42.00	50.00

Half board per person:	£min	£max
Daily	44.95	49.95
Weekly	250.00	350.00

Evening meal 1900 (last orders 2100)
Parking for 7
Cards accepted: Amex, Mastercard, Visa

The symbols in each entry give information about services and facilities. A key to these symbols appears at the back of this guide.

The Kings Head Inn

COMMENDED

Chapel Hill, Wootton, Woodstock, Oxford OX20 1DX
☎ (01993) 811340
Fax (01993) 811340

15th C Cotswold village inn with individually appointed cottage-style rooms. Acclaimed restaurant and bar serving freshly prepared food with fish specialities. Two miles north of Woodstock.
Bedrooms: 3 double
Suites available
Bathrooms: 3 en-suite

Bed & breakfast per night:	£min	£max
Single	39.95	54.00
Double	65.00	90.00

Half board per person:	£min	£max
Daily	45.00	55.00
Weekly	290.00	360.00

Lunch available
Evening meal 1900 (last orders 2200)
Parking for 8
Cards accepted: Mastercard, Visa, Switch/Delta
10

The Laurels

HIGHLY COMMENDED

Hensington Road, Woodstock OX20 1JL
☎ (01993) 812583
Fax (01993) 812583
Fine Victorian house, charmingly furnished with an emphasis on comfort and quality. Just off town centre and a short walk from Blenheim Palace.
Bedrooms: 2 double, 1 twin
Bathrooms: 2 en-suite, 1 private

Bed & breakfast per night:	£min	£max
Single	35.00	40.00
Double	45.00	50.00

Parking for 3
Cards accepted: Mastercard, Visa, Switch/Delta
7

A key to symbols can be found inside the back cover flap.

Punch Bowl Inn

Listed APPROVED

12 Oxford Street, Woodstock, Oxford OX20 1TR
☎ (01993) 811218
Fax (01993) 811393

Family-run pub in the centre of Woodstock, close to Blenheim Palace. A good touring centre for Oxford and the Cotswolds.

Bedrooms: 2 single, 5 double, 2 twin, 2 family rooms
Bathrooms: 6 en-suite, 2 public

Bed & breakfast per night:	£min	£max
Single	28.00	32.00
Double	38.00	42.00

Lunch available
Evening meal 1800 (last orders 2130)
Parking for 20
Cards accepted: Amex, Mastercard, Visa, Switch/Delta

The Ridings

COMMENDED

32 Banbury Road, Woodstock OX20 1LQ
☎ (01993) 811269

Detached house in a quiet, rural setting. 10 minutes' walk to town centre and Blenheim Palace. Go past the Tourist Information Centre for 300 yards then take left fork along Banbury Road.

Bedrooms: 1 double, 2 twin
Bathrooms: 1 en-suite, 1 public

Bed & breakfast per night:	£min	£max
Single	30.00	35.00
Double	40.00	45.00

Parking for 4

Shepherds Hall Inn

COMMENDED

Witney Road, Freeland, Witney OX8 8HQ
☎ (01993) 881256

Well-appointed inn offering good accommodation. All rooms en-suite. Ideally situated for Oxford, Woodstock and the Cotswolds, on the A4095 Woodstock to Witney road.

Bedrooms: 1 single, 1 double, 2 twin, 1 triple
Bathrooms: 5 en-suite

Bed & breakfast per night:	£min	£max
Single	25.00	30.00
Double	40.00	45.00

Lunch available
Evening meal 1900 (last orders 2200)
Parking for 50
Cards accepted: Mastercard, Visa

Shipton Glebe

HIGHLY COMMENDED

Woodstock, Oxford OX20 1QQ
☎ (01993) 812688
Fax (01993) 813142
Email: phase@patrol.i-way.co.uk

Lovely country house in 9 acres of garden. Conservatory lounge area, golf practice facility. Woodstock 1 mile, Oxford 6 miles.

Bedrooms: 1 double, 1 twin, 1 family room
Bathrooms: 3 en-suite, 1 public

Bed & breakfast per night:	£min	£max
Single	30.00	35.00
Double	60.00	75.00

Evening meal 1930 (last orders 2030)
Parking for 6
Open April–October
Cards accepted: Mastercard, Visa, Switch/Delta

AT-A-GLANCE SYMBOLS

Symbols at the end of each accommodation entry give useful information about services and facilities. A key to symbols can be found inside the back cover flap.

Keep this open for easy reference.

USE YOUR *i*'s

There are more than 550 Tourist Information Centres throughout England offering friendly help with accommodation and holiday ideas as well as suggestions of places to visit and things to do. There may well be a centre in your home town which can help you before you set out. You'll find addresses in the local Phone Book or simply call Freepages 0800 192 192.

COUNTRY CODE

Always follow the Country Code

- Enjoy the countryside and respect its life and work
- Guard against all risk of fire
- Fasten all gates
- Keep your dogs under close control
- Keep to public paths across farmland
- Use gates and stiles to cross fences, hedges and walls
- Leave livestock, crops and machinery alone
- Take your litter home
- Help to keep all water clean
- Protect wildlife, plants and trees
- Take special care on country roads
- Make no unnecessary noise

SOUTH EAST ENGLAND

The South East is brimming with bright holiday ideas. From seaside resorts to unhurried villages, open downland, grand cathedrals and historic houses - there's lots to interest everyone.

The charm of Kent's 'Garden of England' rolls gently on to the pretty South Downs of Sussex with their majestic chalk cliffs and excellent walking country. In the heart of historic 1066 Country tour the ruins of Battle Abbey or discover some of the region's many beautiful gardens.

There's a huge variety of sports, from golf and sailing to bowls and surfing. While entertainments range from the annual Glyndebourne Opera season to the Brighton Festival and end-of-the-pier fun.

The counties of East Sussex, Kent, Surrey and West Sussex

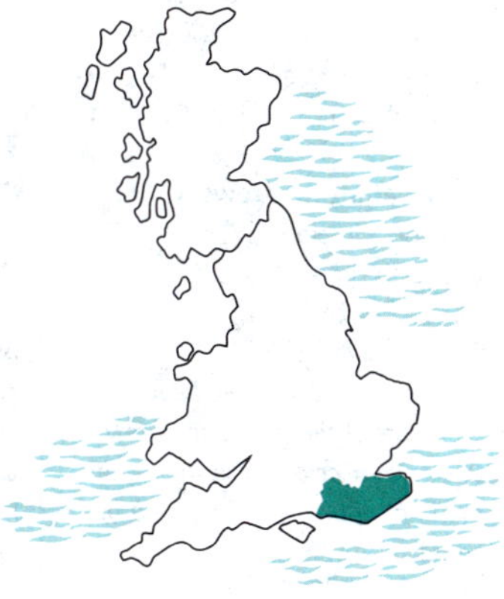

FOR MORE INFORMATION CONTACT:
South East England Tourist Board,
The Old Brew House, Warwick Park,
Tunbridge Wells, Kent TN2 5TU
Tel: (01892) 540766 **Fax:** (01892) 511008

Where to Go in South East England –
see pages 328-331
Where to Stay in South East England –
see pages 332-352

SOUTH EAST ENGLAND

Where to Go and What to See

You will find hundreds of interesting places to visit during your stay in South East England, just some of which are listed in these pages. The number against each name will help you locate it on the map (page 331). Contact any Tourist Information Centre in the region for more ideas on days out in South East England.

1 The Dickens Centre
Eastgate House,
High Street,
Rochester,
Kent ME1 1EW
Tel: (01634) 844176/827980
Unique experience of Dickens' life and novels. Life-size models, sound and light effects. New 'Dickens Dream' tableau/audio-visual presentation on Dickens' life.

2 Great Stour Brewery
75 Stour Street,
Canterbury,
Kent CT1 2NR
Tel: (01227) 763579
An historic 250-year-old building. Members of the public can brew their own beer and visit the on-site museum of brewing. Shop and beer garden.

3 St Augustine's Abbey
Longport,
Canterbury,
Kent CT1 1TF
Tel: (01227) 767345
A World Heritage Site founded in AD598 by St Augustine, first Archbishop of Canterbury. Remains include Norman church and ruins of the 7thC church of St Pancras.

4 Yalding Organic Gardens
Benover Road,
Yalding, Maidstone,
Kent ME18 6EX
Tel: (01622) 814650
Newly created 'green' history of gardening through the ages - 11thC herb garden, Tudor knot, 19thC cottage gardens, and Victorian herbaceous border with 1950s allotment.

5 Ightham Mote
Ivy Hatch,
Sevenoaks,
Kent TN15 0NT
Tel: (01732) 810378
Medieval moated manor house remodelled in the 16thC. Great hall, two chapels and 18thC drawing room. Garden. Woodland walk. Pretty courtyard.

6 Knole
Sevenoaks,
Kent TN15 0RP
Tel: (01732) 462100
Large house dating from 1456, home of the Sackvilles. Richly panelled and furnished. 17thC silk and velvet tapestries. State rooms, Old Master paintings. Deer park.

7 Godstone Vineyards
Quarry Road,
Godstone,
Surrey RH9 8ZA
Tel: (01883) 744590
Ten-acre vineyard with modern winery set in 50 acres of beautiful farmland. Vineyard shop. Coarse fishing lake (day tickets available) and pick-your-own crops (seasonal).

8 Brooklands Museum
Brooklands Road,
Weybridge,
Surrey KT13 0QN
Tel: (01932) 857381
Opened in 1991 on 30 acres of the original 1907 motor racing circuit. Features the most historic and steepest section of the old banked track and 1-in-4 Test Hill. Motoring village.

9 Painshill Park
Between Streets,
Cobham, Surrey KT11 1JE
Tel: (01932) 864674/868113
18thC landscape gardens with lake, lawns, woodland, specimen trees and shrubberies. Gothic temple, grotto, Chinese bridge, waterwheel, vineyard, historic plantings and Turkish tent.

10 Chapel Farm Animal Trail
Chapel Farm,
Westhumble,
Dorking,
Surrey RH5 6AY
Tel: (01306) 882865
See a full range of farm animals and follow marked routes through the farmyard. Rabbits, lambs, chicks and ducklings can be touched. Tractor trailer rides.

11 Clandon Park
West Clandon,
Guildford,
Surrey GU4 7RQ
Tel: (01483) 222482
Palladian-style house built for Lord Onslow circa 1730. Marble hall, Gubbay collection of furniture, needlework and porcelain. Royal Surrey Regiment Museum.

12 Rural Life Centre
Old Kiln Museum,
Reeds Road,
Tilford, Farnham,
Surrey GU10 2DL
Tel: (01252) 792300
Museum with farm machines, implements and waggons. Wheelwright's shop, working smith and displays on past village life. Hop press. Small arboretum and woodland walk.

13 Owl House Gardens
Mount Pleasant,
Lamberhurst,
Kent TN3 8LY
Tel: (01892) 890230/890963
Over 16 acres of romantic walks through woodland, dell and sunken gardens. Azaleas, rhododendrons, spring flowers and rare shrubs. Gardens surround 16thC wood-smuggler's cottage.

14 Lathe Barn
Donkey Street,
Burmarsh, Romney Marsh,
Kent TN29 0JN
Tel: (01303) 873618
Museum with collection of rural and domestic bygones. Children's farm with sheep, donkey, pigs, goats, geese, rabbits, calves, chickens and peacocks. Children's play area.

15 Romney, Hythe and Dymchurch Railway
New Romney Station,
New Romney, Kent TN28 8PL
Tel: (01797) 362353/363256
The world's only main line in miniature runs for 14 miles across Romney Marsh. Steam and diesel locomotives, yards, engine sheds, toy and model museum at New Romney.

16 The High Beeches Gardens
Handcross,
Haywards Heath,
West Sussex RH17 6HQ
Tel: (01444) 400589
Twenty acres of landscaped woodland and water gardens with many rare plants, a wildflower meadow and glorious autumn colour.

17 Borde Hill Garden

Balcombe Road,
Haywards Heath,
West Sussex RH16 1XP
Tel: (01444) 450326
Large private collection of champion trees. Peaceful gardens with rich variety of all season colour set in 200 acres of parkland and woods. Children's trout fishing and playground.

18 Lavender Line Steam Railway Museum

Isfield Station, Near Uckfield,
East Sussex TN22 5XB
Tel: (01825) 750515/
(01825) 750515
Fully-restored station buildings. Three standard-gauge steam engines pull carriages along one mile of track. Museum and signal box.

19 Battle Abbey and Battlefield

High Street, Battle,
East Sussex TN33 0AD
Tel: (01424) 773792
Abbey founded by William the Conqueror on the Battle of Hastings site. Church alter marks the spot where Harold was killed. Gatehouse exhibition and Monk's dormitory.

20 Herstmonceux Castle Gardens

Herstmonceux,
East Sussex BN27 1RP
Tel: (01323) 834444
Elizabethan courtyard. Flower garden and nature trail surrounding castle (tours daily). Walled and herbal gardens. Visitor and Science centres.

21 Michelham Priory

Upper Dicker, Hailsham,
East Sussex BN27 3QS
Tel: (01323) 844224
A 13th-16thC priory, country house and gatehouse, working watermill, physic garden, rope museum, blacksmith's and wheelwright's museum. Gardens, grounds, moat and play area.

22 Bentley Wildfowl and Motor Museum

Halland, Near Lewes,
East Sussex BN8 5AF
Tel: (01825) 840573
Over 1,000 wildfowl in parkland with lakes. Motor museum. Antiques and wildfowl paintings in house. Indoor children's activity centre, children's playground and woodland walk.

23 Anne of Cleves House Museum

52 Southover High Street,
Lewes,
East Sussex BN7 1JA
Tel: (01273) 474610
Old timber-framed house and workshops housing folk museum. 17th-18thC Wealden ironwork, furnished rooms with domestic utensils and trade equipment. Tudor-style garden.

24 Drusillas Park

Alfriston, Polegate,
East Sussex BN26 5QS
Tel: (01323) 870234/870656
Award-winning zoo with animals in natural habitats, farmyard, miniature railway and adventure playground. Japanese and rose gardens.

25 Filching Manor Motor Museum

Wannock,
Polegate,
East Sussex BN26 5QA
Tel: (01323) 487838/487124
Wealden hall house on site of 600AD priory. Over 100 veteran, vintage, sports and racing cars, Jupiter aircraft and racing motor boats.

26 Eastbourne Miniature Steam Railway Park

Lottbridge Drove, Eastbourne,
East Sussex BN23 6NS
Tel: (01323) 520229
Miniature steam and diesel-hauled passenger trains. New railway-style buildings, engine shed and large man-made lake. Children's playground. Fishing available.

27 The Body Shop Tour

Watersmead Business Park,
Littlehampton,
West Sussex BN17 6LS
Follow the life of a product from an idea to raw ingredients, testing, manufacturing, filling and distribution. Information on the environment.

28 Pulborough Brooks RSPB Nature Reserve

Wiggonholt,
Pulborough,
West Sussex RH20 2EL
Tel: (01798) 875851
Upperton's Barn visitor centre with displays, extensive nature reserve featuring nature trail, scenic views and viewing hides.

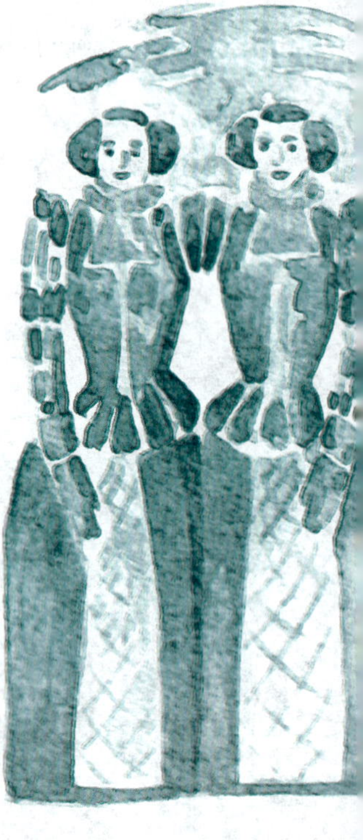

29 Chichester Harbour Water Tours
Itchenor,
Chichester,
West Sussex
Tel: (01243) 786418
Leisurely hour-and-a-half trips from Itchenor around the attractive Chichester Harbour - an Area of Outstanding Natural Beauty and wildlife reserve.

30 Fishbourne Roman Palace and Museum
Salthill Road,
Fishbourne,
Chichester,
West Sussex PO19 3QR
Tel: (01243) 785859
Remains of the largest Roman residence in Britain. Many beautiful mosaics now under cover. Hypocaust and restored formal garden. Museum of finds. Model and audio-visual programme.

31 Sculpture at Goodwood
Hat Hill Copse,
Goodwood,
Chichester,
West Sussex PO18 0QP
Tel: (01243) 538449
A changing collection of contemporary British sculpture set in 20 acres of beautiful grounds on the South Downs overlooking Chichester.

FIND OUT MORE

Further information about holidays and attractions in South East England is available from:
South East England Tourist Board,
The Old Brew House,
Warwick Park, Tunbridge Wells,
Kent TN2 5TU.
Tel: (01892) 540766

These publications are available free from the South East England Tourist Board:

- **Great Escapes**
- **Accommodation Guide**
- **Bed and Breakfast Touring Map**
- **Outstanding Churches and Cathedrals**

Also available is (price includes postage and packaging):

- **South East England Leisure Map** *£4*
- **Hundreds of Places to Visit in the South East** *UK £3.15, Overseas £3.50*
- **Villages to Visit** *UK £2.60, Overseas £2.95*

WHERE TO STAY (SOUTH EAST ENGLAND)

Accommodation entries in this region are listed in alphabetical order of place name, and then in alphabetical order of establishment.

Map references refer to the colour location maps at the back of this guide. The first number indicates the map to use; the letter and number which follow refer to the grid reference on the map.

At-a-glance symbols at the end of each accommodation entry give useful information about services and facilities. A key to symbols can be found inside the back cover flap.

Keep this open for easy reference.

ALDINGTON

Kent
Map ref 3B4

Once the home of Elizabeth Barton, the "Holy Maid" or "Nun of Kent".

Hogben Farm

Listed COMMENDED

Church Lane, Aldington, Ashford TN25 7EH
☎ (01233) 720219

Small 16th C country house, surrounded by pretty garden and 17 acres of farmland. Convenient for Channel ports, Channel Tunnel, Canterbury, Rye, Tenterden and Romney Marsh. Evening meals by prior arrangement.

Bedrooms: 1 double, 2 twin
Bathrooms: 1 en-suite, 1 private, 1 public, 1 private shower

Bed & breakfast per night:	£min	£max
Single	18.50	20.50
Double	37.00	41.00

Half board per person:	£min	£max
Daily	28.50	30.50
Weekly	110.00	123.00

Evening meal 1800 (last orders 2000)
Parking for 6

A key to symbols can be found inside the back cover flap.

ARDINGLY

West Sussex
Map ref 2D3

Famous for the South of England Agricultural Showground with its famous antique fairs and the public school. Nearby is Wakehurst Place (National Trust), the gardens of which are administered by the Royal Botanic Gardens, Kew.

Jordans

COMMENDED

Church Lane, Ardingly, Haywards Heath RH17 6UP
☎ (01444) 892681
Fax (01444) 414269

Victorian country house set in beautiful gardens opposite medieval village church. Behind South of England Showground, close to many facilities and 20 minutes from Gatwick.

Bedrooms: 1 single, 1 twin
Bathrooms: 1 public

Bed & breakfast per night:	£min	£max
Single	22.00	25.00
Double	40.00	42.00

Parking for 5

Information on accommodation listed in this guide has been supplied by the proprietors. As changes may occur you are advised to check details at the time of booking.

ARUNDEL

West Sussex
Map ref 2D3

Picturesque, historic town on the River Arun, dominated by Arundel Castle, home of the Dukes of Norfolk. There are many 18th C houses, the Toy and Military Museum, Wildfowl and Wetlands Centre and Museum and Heritage Centre.
Tourist Information Centre ☎ (01903) 882268

Arundel Vineyards

COMMENDED

The Vineyard, Church Lane, Lyminster, Arundel BN17 7QF
☎ (01903) 883393

3-acre vineyard & grazing farm. Quiet, friendly English vineyard close to historic Arundel, Chichester, Goodwood and the sea. Both rooms en-suite. Traditional breakfast. French and German spoken.

Bedrooms: 1 double, 1 twin
Bathrooms: 2 en-suite

Bed & breakfast per night:	£min	£max
Single	24.00	24.00
Double	38.00	38.00

Parking for 15

10

For ideas on places to visit refer to the introduction at the beginning of this section.

Mill Lane House

COMMENDED

Slindon, Arundel BN18 0RP
☎ (01243) 814440

17th C house in beautiful National Trust village. Magnificent views to coast. Pubs within easy walking distance. One mile from A29/A27 junction.

Wheelchair access category 3

Bedrooms: 1 single, 3 double, 2 twin, 1 triple
Suite available
Bathrooms: 7 en-suite, 1 public

Bed & breakfast per night:	£min	£max
Single	26.00	26.00
Double	40.00	40.00

Half board per person:	£min	£max
Daily	30.25	36.25
Weekly	196.75	237.75

Evening meal 1900 (last orders 1000)
Parking for 7

Pindars

HIGHLY COMMENDED

Lyminster, Arundel BN17 7QF
☎ (01903) 882628

Charming country house in small village offers comfortable bedrooms, good food and warm hospitality. Beautiful garden. Non-smoking. On A284 off A27.

Bedrooms: 2 double, 1 twin
Bathrooms: 1 en-suite, 1 public

Bed & breakfast per night:	£min	£max
Single	22.00	
Double	32.00	42.00

Evening meal from 1900
Parking for 7
Cards accepted: Mastercard, Visa
10

Establishments should be open throughout the year, unless otherwise stated.

The symbols in each entry give information about services and facilities. A key to these symbols appears at the back of this guide.

ASHFORD

Kent
Map ref 3B4

Once a market centre for the farmers of the Weald of Kent and Romney Marsh. The town centre has a number of Tudor and Georgian houses and a museum. Eurostar trains stop at Ashford International station.
Tourist Information Centre ☎ (01233) 629165

Fishponds Farm

HIGHLY COMMENDED

Pilgrims Way, Brook, Ashford TN25 5PP
☎ (01233) 812398

Rural farmhouse with lake in Wye Downs Nature Reserve, 3 miles south-east of Wye on lane to Brabourne.

Bedrooms: 1 double, 1 twin
Bathrooms: 2 en-suite

Bed & breakfast per night:	£min	£max
Single		20.00
Double		32.00

Parking for 10

Goldwell Manor

Listed APPROVED

Great Chart, Ashford TN23 3BY
☎ (01233) 631495
Fax (01233) 631495

Peaceful, historic 10th C family farmhouse surrounded by wonderful 10-mile country views. Large garden, beams galore, big log fires, cosy sitting room. Comfortable rooms with tea/coffee, TV. Easy M20, Canterbury, Dover. Warm traditional welcome. Evening meals by arrangement.

Bedrooms: 2 double, 1 twin
Bathrooms: 1 en-suite, 1 private, 1 public

Bed & breakfast per night:	£min	£max
Single	23.00	25.00
Double	40.00	50.00

Parking for 14
1

COLOUR MAPS

Colour maps at the back of this guide pinpoint all places in which you will find accommodation listed.

Mayflower House

Listed COMMENDED

61 Magazine Road, Ashford TN24 8NR
☎ (01233) 621959

Family-run establishment, all rooms with colour TV and tea/coffee making facilities. Friendly atmosphere.

Bedrooms: 2 single, 1 double
Bathrooms: 1 public

Bed & breakfast per night:	£min	£max
Single	16.00	
Double	30.00	

Half board per person:	£min	£max
Daily	23.00	
Weekly	161.00	

Evening meal 1830 (last orders 2000)

Warren Cottage Hotel

COMMENDED

136 The Street, Willesborough, Ashford TN24 0NB
☎ (01233) 621905 & 632929
Fax (01233) 623400

17th C hotel and restaurant, set in 2.5 acres, where a cosy atmosphere awaits. All rooms en-suite with colour TV, large car park. M20 junction 10 and minutes from Ashford International Station, Channel Tunnel, Dover and Folkestone.

Bedrooms: 2 single, 2 double, 1 twin, 1 triple, 1 family room
Bathrooms: 7 en-suite, 1 public

Bed & breakfast per night:	£min	£max
Single	34.90	39.90
Double	45.00	59.90

Half board per person:	£min	£max
Daily	44.90	
Weekly	314.30	

Lunch available
Evening meal 1830 (last orders 2130)
Parking for 23
Cards accepted: Diners, Mastercard, Visa, Switch/Delta
20

BATTLE

East Sussex
Map ref 3B4

The Abbey at Battle was built on the site of the Battle of Hastings, when William defeated Harold II and so became the Conqueror in 1066. The museum has a fine collection relating to the Sussex iron industry and there is a social history museum - Buckleys Yesterday's World.
Tourist Information Centre ☎ (01424) 773721

Moons Hill Farm

COMMENDED

The Green, Ninfield, Battle
TN33 9LH
☎ (01424) 892645
Fax (01424) 892645
10-acre mixed farm. Modernised farmhouse in Ninfield village centre, in the heart of "1066" country. A warm welcome and Sussex home cooking. Pub opposite.
Bedrooms: 1 double, 2 twin
Bathrooms: 3 en-suite, 1 public

Bed & breakfast per night:	£min	£max
Single	15.00	20.00
Double	30.00	35.00

Parking for 12
Open January–November

BEXHILL-ON-SEA

East Sussex
Map ref 3B4

Popular resort with beach of shingle and firm sand at low tide. The impressive 1930s designed De la Warr Pavilion has good entertainment facilities. Costume Museum in Manor Gardens.
Tourist Information Centre ☎ (01424) 732208

Treforfan Guest House

Listed COMMENDED

33 Woodville Road, Bexhill-on-Sea
TN39 3ET
☎ (01424) 223767
Comfortable, family-run guesthouse in quiet residential road overlooking Egerton park. Close to seafront/town centre. Easy parking. No smoking.
Bedrooms: 1 single, 1 double, 1 twin
Bathrooms: 1 public

Bed & breakfast per night:	£min	£max
Single	15.00	15.00
Double	30.00	30.00

Half board per person:	£min	£max
Daily	21.00	21.00
Weekly	147.00	147.00

Parking for 1

BIDDENDEN

Kent
Map ref 3B4

Perfect village with black and white houses, a tithe barn and a pond. Part of the village is grouped around a green with a village sign depicting the famous Biddenden Maids. It was an important centre of the Flemish weaving industry, hence the beautiful Old Cloth Hall. Vineyard nearby.

Bettmans Oast

HIGHLY COMMENDED

Hareplain Road, Biddenden, Ashford
TN27 8LJ
☎ (01580) 291463
Grade II listed oast house and converted barn set in 10 acres near Sissinghurst Castle, a quarter of a mile from Three Chimneys pub. Lovely gardens. Log fires in winter.
Bedrooms: 1 single, 1 twin, 1 family room
Bathrooms: 1 en-suite, 1 public

Bed & breakfast per night:	£min	£max
Single	24.00	24.00
Double	40.00	48.00

Half board per person:	£min	£max
Daily	32.00	39.00

Evening meal 1900 (last orders 2100)
Parking for 4
10

Bishopsdale Oast

HIGHLY COMMENDED

Biddenden, Ashford TN27 8DR
☎ (01580) 291027 & 292065
Fax (01580) 292321

18th C double kiln oast. Outstanding views, business facilities, professional cooks. Tenterden 2 miles, Cranbrook 5 miles. Signpost on bend.
Bedrooms: 3 double
Bathrooms: 2 en-suite, 1 private

Bed & breakfast per night:	£min	£max
Single	38.50	
Double	45.00	55.00

Half board per person:	£min	£max
Daily	55.50	72.00
Weekly	388.50	504.00

Lunch available
Evening meal 1830 (last orders 2000)
Parking for 6
Cards accepted: Mastercard, Visa, Switch/Delta

BIRCHINGTON

Kent
Map ref 3C3

Town on the north coast of Kent with sandy beaches and rock pools. Powell Cotton Museum is in nearby Quex Park.

Elmstead

HIGHLY COMMENDED

2 Kings Avenue, Minnis Bay, Birchington CT7 9QL
☎ (01843) 847407
Attractive accommodation overlooking Minnis Bay. Close to the ancient City of Canterbury, interesting towns, villages and coastlines. 2-night breaks available.
Bedrooms: 1 double, 1 twin
Bathrooms: 1 en-suite, 1 private

Bed & breakfast per night:	£min	£max
Single	15.00	18.00
Double	30.00	40.00

Parking for 2

BIRLING GAP

East Sussex
Map ref 2D3

Beauty spot on the famous Seven Sisters cliffs near Beachy Head, surrounded by magnificent National Trust downland. Ancient home of the Saxon tribe, the Boerls, who inhabited a gap in the cliffs. Famous for former smuggling activities.

Birling Gap Hotel

APPROVED

Birling Gap, Seven Sisters Cliffs, East Dean, Eastbourne, East Sussex
BN20 0AB
☎ (01323) 423197
Fax (01323) 423030

Magnificent Seven Sisters clifftop position, with views of country, sea, beach. Superb downland and beach walks. Old world "Thatched Bar" and "Oak Room Restaurant". Coffee shop and games room, function and conference suite. Off A259 coast road at East Dean, 1.5 miles west of Beachy Head.
Bedrooms: 1 single, 2 double, 3 twin, 3 triple
Bathrooms: 9 en-suite, 1 public

Bed & breakfast per night:	£min	£max
Single	20.00	50.00
Double	30.00	60.00

Half board per person:	£min	£max
Daily	29.00	38.00
Weekly	183.00	245.00

Lunch available
Evening meal 1830 (last orders 2115)
Parking for 100
Cards accepted: Amex, Diners, Mastercard, Visa, Switch/Delta
240 SP

BRASTED

Kent
Map ref 2D2

Standing in a park adjoining the village is 18th C Brasted Place. The work of Robert Adam, this fine house was once the home of Napoleon III.

The Mount House

Listed COMMENDED

Brasted, Westerham TN16 1JB
☎ (01959) 563617
Fax (01959) 561296
Large early Georgian family residence in centre of village. Listed Grade II.
Bedrooms: 1 single, 1 double, 1 twin
Bathrooms: 1 en-suite, 1 public

Bed & breakfast per night:	£min	£max
Single	25.00	30.00
Double	50.00	60.00

Parking for 3
10 UL TV

BRIGHTON & HOVE

East Sussex
Map ref 2D3

Brighton's attractions include the Royal Pavilion, Volks Electric Railway, Sea Life Centre and Marina Village, Conference Centre and "The Lanes" and several theatres. Neighbouring Hove is a resort in its own right.
Tourist Information Centre ☎ (01273) 323755; for Hove (01273) 778087

Brighton Marina House Hotel

APPROVED

8 Charlotte Street, Marine Parade, Brighton, East Sussex BN2 1AG
☎ (01273) 605349 & 679484
Fax (01273) 605349
Email: the21@pavilion.co.uk

Cosy, elegantly furnished, well-equipped, clean, comfortable, caring, family-run. Near sea, central for Palace Pier, Royal Pavilion, conference and exhibition halls, the famous Lanes, tourist attractions. Flexible breakfast, check-in/out times. Offering all facilities. Free street parking. Best in price range.
Bedrooms: 3 single, 3 double, 1 twin, 3 triple
Bathrooms: 7 en-suite, 1 public

Bed & breakfast per night:	£min	£max
Single	15.00	39.00
Double	35.00	59.00

Half board per person:	£min	£max
Daily	26.00	49.00
Weekly	167.00	371.00

Lunch available
Evening meal 1830 (last orders 1700)
Cards accepted: Amex, Diners, Mastercard, Visa
S OAP SP T

National gradings and classifications were correct at the time of going to press but are subject to change. Please check at the time of booking.

Brighton Twenty One Hotel

COMMENDED

21 Charlotte Street, Marine Parade, Brighton, East Sussex BN2 1AG
☎ (01273) 686450 & 681617
Fax (01273) 695560
Email: the21@pavilion.co.uk

Exquisite rooms, including the Green Room, the executive Victorian Room or the Suite. Discounts: 10% 2 nights, 15% 4 nights, 20% 7 nights.
Bedrooms: 4 double, 2 twin
Suite available
Bathrooms: 6 en-suite, 1 public

Bed & breakfast per night:	£min	£max
Single	25.00	65.00
Double	45.00	89.00

Half board per person:	£min	£max
Daily	43.00	81.00
Weekly	240.00	498.00

Evening meal 1830 (last orders 2000)
Cards accepted: Amex, Diners, Mastercard, Visa, Switch/Delta
10 UL S TV SP T

Diana House

Listed APPROVED

25 St Georges Terrace, Brighton, East Sussex BN2 1JJ
☎ (01273) 605797
Fax (01273) 600533
Email: diana@enterprise.co.uk
Large, friendly guesthouse close to sea, town and conference centre. All rooms have TV, hospitality tray, clock/radio, shaver point. Some rooms en-suite. 24-hour access.
Bedrooms: 2 double, 1 twin, 5 triple, 1 family room
Bathrooms: 4 en-suite, 1 public, 4 private showers

Bed & breakfast per night:	£min	£max
Single	18.00	20.00
Double	36.00	40.00

Cards accepted: Mastercard, Visa
UL S OAP SP T

BURWASH

East Sussex
Map ref 3B4

Village of old houses, many from the Tudor and Stuart periods. One of the old ironmasters' houses is Bateman's (National Trust) which was the home of Rudyard Kipling.

Glydwish Place

Listed HIGHLY COMMENDED

Fontridge Lane, Burwash
TN19 7DG
☎ (01435) 882869 & 0850 421732
Fax (01435) 882749
Tranquil setting with beautiful views. Numerous interesting places to visit. Excellent pubs in surrounding villages. Lovely walks. All bedrooms overlooking gardens. Sauna, solarium, gym.
Bedrooms: 1 single, 3 double
Suites available
Bathrooms: 2 en-suite, 2 private, 4 public

Bed & breakfast per night:	£min	£max
Single	20.00	30.00
Double	45.00	55.00

Parking for 14

CANTERBURY

Kent
Map ref 3B3

Place of pilgrimage since the martyrdom of Becket in 1170 and the site of Canterbury Cathedral. Visit St Augustine's Abbey, St Martin's (the oldest church in England), Royal Museum and Art Gallery and the Canterbury Tales. Nearby is Howletts Wild Animal Park. Good shopping centre.
Tourist Information Centre ☎ (01227) 451026

Abberley House

Listed COMMENDED

115 Whitstable Road, Canterbury
CT2 8EF
☎ (01227) 450265
Fax (01227) 450265
Comfortable family guesthouse. Easy walk to centre. Tea/coffee making. Shower in one double. Residential area. Parking. Non-smokers only, please.
Bedrooms: 2 double, 1 twin
Bathrooms: 1 public, 1 private shower

Bed & breakfast per night:	£min	£max
Single	19.00	25.00
Double	36.00	40.00

Parking for 3

Acacia Lodge

Listed COMMENDED

39 London Road, Canterbury
CT2 8LF
☎ (01227) 769955 & (0585) 489681
Delightful family house close to cathedral. Friendly and comfortable. Private facilities, TV, tea/coffee. English or vegetarian breakfast. Parking.
Bedrooms: 2 double, 1 twin
Bathrooms: 3 en-suite, 1 private

Bed & breakfast per night:	£min	£max
Double	30.00	40.00

Parking for 3

Bower Farm House

HIGHLY COMMENDED

Stelling Minnis, Canterbury
CT4 6BB
☎ (01227) 709430
Delightful heavily beamed 17th C farmhouse between the villages of Stelling Minnis and Bossingham. Canterbury and Hythe are approximately 7 miles away.
Bedrooms: 1 double, 1 twin
Bathrooms: 1 en-suite, 1 private

Bed & breakfast per night:	£min	£max
Single	19.50	19.50
Double	39.00	39.00

Parking for 8

Cathedral Gate Hotel

APPROVED

36 Burgate, Canterbury CT1 2HA
☎ (01227) 464381
Fax (01227) 462800
Email: 101336.430
@compuserve.com
Central position at main entrance to the cathedral. Car parking nearby. Old world charm at reasonable prices. English breakfast extra. A la carte dinner available.
Bedrooms: 4 single, 8 double, 7 twin, 3 triple, 2 family rooms
Bathrooms: 12 en-suite, 3 public

Bed & breakfast per night:	£min	£max
Single	22.00	50.00
Double	40.00	75.00

Evening meal 1900 (last orders 2100)
Cards accepted: Amex, Diners, Mastercard, Visa, Switch/Delta

Chislet Court Farm

Listed COMMENDED

Chislet, Canterbury CT3 4DU
☎ (01227) 860309
Fax (01227) 860444
800-acre arable farm. A Queen Anne farmhouse, with conservatory, overlooking attractive gardens, in a small village 6 miles north-east of Canterbury.
Bedrooms: 2 double
Bathrooms: 1 en-suite, 1 public

Bed & breakfast per night:	£min	£max
Single	25.00	30.00
Double	40.00	50.00

Parking for 4
12

Clare-Ellen Guest House

HIGHLY COMMENDED

9 Victoria Road, Wincheap, Canterbury CT1 3SG
☎ (01227) 760205
Fax (01227) 784482
Email: loraine.williams@virgin.net

Victorian house with large, elegant en-suite rooms, 6 minutes' walk to town centre. 5 minutes to Canterbury East train station. Car park and garage available.
Bedrooms: 1 single, 1 double, 1 twin, 1 triple, 1 family room
Bathrooms: 4 en-suite, 1 private, 1 public

Bed & breakfast per night:	£min	£max
Single	23.00	26.00
Double	42.00	48.00

Parking for 9
Cards accepted: Mastercard, Visa, Switch/Delta

A key to symbols can be found inside the back cover flap.

The Corner House

Listed COMMENDED

113 Whitstable Road, Canterbury
CT2 8EF
☎ (01227) 761352
Fax (01227) 761065

Just a few minutes' walking distance from city, university, shops and restaurants. Spacious family house with friendly hospitality.
http://forge.co.uk/cornerhouse
Bedrooms: 1 double, 2 twin
Bathrooms: 2 public

Bed & breakfast per night:	£min	£max
Single	20.00	26.00
Double	36.00	40.00

Parking for 4

The Farmhouse

HIGHLY COMMENDED

Upper Mystole Park Farm, Pennypot Lane, Mystole, Canterbury CT4 7BT
☎ (01227) 730589
90-acre fruit farm. Modern farmhouse in the heart of Kent and with magnificent views. Set between historic Canterbury and beautiful Chilham (A28). Dover 25 minutes. Ideal touring base.
Bedrooms: 2 double, 1 twin
Bathrooms: 2 en-suite, 1 private

Bed & breakfast per night:	£min	£max
Single	20.00	24.00
Double	40.00	45.00

Parking for 6

Magnolia House

HIGHLY COMMENDED

36 St Dunstans Terrace, Canterbury
CT2 8AX
☎ (01227) 765121 & (0585) 595970
Fax (01227) 765121

Quiet Georgian house in attractive city street. Close to university, gardens, river and city centre. Pretty walled garden in which to relax. Winner 1995 "Welcome to Kent Hospitality Award".
Bedrooms: 1 single, 4 double, 2 twin
Bathrooms: 7 en-suite

Bed & breakfast per night:	£min	£max
Single	36.00	50.00
Double	60.00	95.00

Evening meal 1800 (last orders 1900)
Parking for 5
Cards accepted: Amex, Mastercard, Visa, Switch/Delta

Old Stone House

Listed COMMENDED

The Green, Wickhambreaux, Canterbury CT3 1RQ
☎ (01227) 728591
One of the oldest houses in Kent, parts dating from 12th C. Once the home of Joan Plantagenet, wife of the Black Prince. Ten minutes east of Canterbury, 30 minutes from Folkestone and Dover.
Bedrooms: 1 single, 2 double, 1 twin
Bathrooms: 2 en-suite, 1 public

Bed & breakfast per night:	£min	£max
Single	25.00	30.00
Double	40.00	45.00

Parking for 4

Oriel Lodge

HIGHLY COMMENDED

3 Queens Avenue, Canterbury
CT2 8AY
☎ (01227) 462845
Fax (01227) 462845
In a tree-lined residential avenue, an attractive Edwardian house with private parking close to the city centre. Afternoon tea in the garden or lounge with log fire. Restricted smoking.
Bedrooms: 1 single, 3 double, 1 twin, 1 triple
Bathrooms: 2 en-suite, 2 public

Bed & breakfast per night:	£min	£max
Single	22.00	28.00
Double	38.00	58.00

Parking for 6
Cards accepted: Mastercard, Visa

National gradings and classifications were correct at the time of going to press but are subject to change. Please check at the time of booking.

The Willows

HIGHLY COMMENDED

Howfield Lane, Chartham Hatch, Canterbury CT4 7HG
☎ (01227) 738442
Fax (01227) 738442
Dr and Mrs Gough welcome you to The Willows, situated in a quiet country lane, 2 miles from Canterbury Cathedral. A garden for enthusiasts. No smoking.
Bedrooms: 1 double, 1 twin
Bathrooms: 1 en-suite, 1 private

Bed & breakfast per night:	£min	£max
Single	20.00	20.00
Double	45.00	45.00

Evening meal 1900 (last orders 2000)
Parking for 8

CHICHESTER

West Sussex
Map ref 2C3

The county town of West Sussex with a beautiful Norman cathedral. Noted for its Georgian architecture but also has modern buildings like the Festival Theatre. Surrounded by places of interest, including Fishbourne Roman Palace, Weald and Downland Open-Air Museum and West Dean Gardens.
Tourist Information Centre ☎ (01243) 775888

Abelands Barn

HIGHLY COMMENDED

Bognor Road, Merston, Chichester
PO20 6DY
☎ (01243) 533826
Fax (01243) 555533
Listed converted agricultural barns on A259 just 2 miles outside Chichester on coast road to Bognor Regis. Close to Festival Theatre and Goodwood.
Bedrooms: 2 double, 1 twin
Bathrooms: 3 en-suite

Bed & breakfast per night:	£min	£max
Double	45.00	50.00

Parking for 5
Cards accepted: Mastercard, Visa

For further information on accommodation establishments use the coupons at the back of this guide.

CHICHESTER

Continued

Hedgehogs

Listed COMMENDED

45 Whyke Lane, Chichester
PO19 2JT
☎ (01243) 780022

About two-thirds of a mile from city centre, bus/railway stations and theatre. Secluded garden, TV lounge. Parking. Weekly terms available. Cyclists and hikers welcome. No smoking.

Bedrooms: 2 double, 1 twin
Bathrooms: 2 public

Bed & breakfast per night:	£min	£max
Single	21.00	23.00
Double	32.00	36.00

Parking for 4

CHIDDINGSTONE

Kent
Map ref 2D2

Pleasant village of 16th and 17th C, preserved by the National Trust, with an 18th C "castle" and attractive Tudor inn.

Hoath Holidays

Listed APPROVED

Hoath House, Chiddingstone Hoath, Edenbridge TN8 7DB
☎ (01342) 850362

Tudor family house with beamed and panelled rooms and extensive gardens. Convenient for Chartwell, Hever, Penshurst, Gatwick and London.

Bedrooms: 1 double, 2 twin
Bathrooms: 1 en-suite, 1 public

Bed & breakfast per night:	£min	£max
Single	21.00	23.00
Double	40.00	45.00

Parking for 8

TOWN INDEX

This can be found at the back of the guide. If you know where you want to stay, the index will give you the page number listing all accommodation in your chosen town, city or village.

CHILHAM

Kent
Map ref 3B3

Extremely pretty village of mostly Tudor and Jacobean houses. The village rises to the spacious square with the castle and the 15th C church.

Julliеberrie House

COMMENDED

Canterbury Road, Chilham, Canterbury CT4 8DX
☎ (01227) 730488

Modern house with lovely views over lake and woodland. On the A28 Ashford to Canterbury road, close to Chilham village.

Bedrooms: 2 double, 2 twin
Bathrooms: 2 en-suite, 1 public

Bed & breakfast per night:	£min	£max
Single	21.00	26.00
Double	35.00	40.00

Parking for 5

The Woolpack Inn

COMMENDED

High Street, Chilham, Canterbury CT4 8DL
☎ (01227) 730208 & 730351
Fax (01227) 731053

Ancient inn, c 1422, with inglenook fireplaces and oak-beamed restaurant, in picturesque Chilham. Regional specialities, locally brewed ales. Half-board daily prices are based on a minimum 2-night stay.

Bedrooms: 7 double, 3 twin, 1 triple, 2 family rooms
Bathrooms: 13 en-suite

Bed & breakfast per night:	£min	£max
Single	38.50	41.00
Double	49.50	52.00

Half board per person:	£min	£max
Daily	37.50	40.00

Lunch available
Evening meal 1900 (last orders 2130)
Parking for 30
Cards accepted: Amex, Mastercard, Visa, Switch/Delta

CRANBROOK

Kent
Map ref 3B4

Old town, a centre for the weaving industry in the 15th C. The 72-ft high Union Mill is a 3-storey windmill, still in working order, and there is a museum. Sissinghurst Gardens (National Trust) nearby.

Old Rectory

HIGHLY COMMENDED

Frittenden, Cranbrook TN17 2DG
☎ (01580) 852313
Fax (01580) 852313

Near Sissinghurst and Leeds Castles. Peacefully situated Victorian former rectory. Spacious and comfortable, 3 large bedrooms with en-suite facilities. Secluded private parking. Large garden, lovely views. London 1 hour by train. Channel Tunnel 45 minutes. Evening meals by arrangement.

Bedrooms: 1 double, 2 twin
Bathrooms: 2 en-suite, 1 private

Bed & breakfast per night:	£min	£max
Single	24.00	26.00
Double	48.00	52.00

Evening meal from 1830
Parking for 8
Open April–October
Cards accepted: Amex

12

CRANLEIGH

Surrey
Map ref 2D2

White Hart Hotel

Listed APPROVED

Ewhurst Road, Cranleigh GU6 7AE
☎ (01483) 268647 & 267154
Fax (01483) 267154

Bed and breakfast in country village pub. En-suite facilities, satellite TV, lunch/evening meals available. 10 miles south of Guildford, off A281. Brochure available.

Bedrooms: 1 single, 5 double, 5 twin, 1 triple
Bathrooms: 12 en-suite, 3 public

Bed & breakfast per night:	£min	£max
Single	36.00	36.00
Double	45.00	45.00

Lunch available
Evening meal 1800 (last orders 2300)
Parking for 20
Cards accepted: Mastercard, Visa, Switch/Delta

CRAWLEY

West Sussex
Map ref 2D2

One of the first New Towns built after World War II, but it also has some old buildings. Set in magnificent wooded countryside.

The Manor House

COMMENDED

Bonnetts Lane, Ifield, Crawley RH11 0NY
☎ (01293) 510000 & 512298

100-year-old manor house in pleasant rural surroundings on Gatwick's doorstep. Family-run establishment offering comfortable and spacious accommodation.

Bedrooms: 1 single, 2 double, 2 twin, 1 family room
Bathrooms: 4 en-suite, 2 private, 1 public

Bed & breakfast per night:	£min	£max
Single	25.00	35.00
Double	35.00	45.00

Parking for 25
Cards accepted: Mastercard, Visa

Waterhall Country House

COMMENDED

Prestwood Lane, Ifield Wood, Crawley RH11 0LA
☎ (01293) 520002
Fax (01293) 539905

Attractive country house in open countryside, 5 minutes from Gatwick. Warm and friendly welcome. Off-road parking. Guest lounge/conservatory.

Bedrooms: 1 single, 1 double, 2 twin, 1 family room
Bathrooms: 4 en-suite, 1 private, 1 public

Bed & breakfast per night:	£min	£max
Single	25.00	25.00
Double	40.00	40.00

Parking for 25

DEAL

Kent
Map ref 3C4

Coastal town and popular holiday resort. Deal Castle was built by Henry VIII as a fort and the museum is devoted to finds excavated in the area. Also the Time-Ball Tower museum. Angling available from both beach and pier.
Tourist Information Centre ☎ (01304) 369576

Hardicot Guest House

COMMENDED

Kingsdown Road, Walmer, Deal CT14 8AW
☎ (01304) 373867

Large, quiet, detached Victorian house with Channel views and secluded garden. Ideal for sea fishing, cliff walks and golfing.

Bedrooms: 1 double, 2 twin
Bathrooms: 1 en-suite, 2 private

Bed & breakfast per night:	£min	£max
Single	18.00	20.00
Double	36.00	40.00

Parking for 4

Ilex Cottage

COMMENDED

Temple Way, Worth, Deal CT14 0DA
☎ (01304) 617026

Renovated 1736 house with lovely conservatory and country views. Secluded yet convenient village location north of Deal. Sandwich 5 minutes, Canterbury, Dover and Ramsgate 25 minutes.

Bedrooms: 1 double, 2 twin
Bathrooms: 3 en-suite

Bed & breakfast per night:	£min	£max
Single	20.00	26.00
Double	35.00	40.00

Half board per person:	£min	£max
Daily	30.00	38.00
Weekly		190.00

Evening meal 1900 (last orders 2030)
Parking for 6

DORKING

Surrey
Map ref 2D2

Ancient market town and a good centre for walking, delightfully set between Box Hill and the Downs. Denbies Wine Estate - England's largest vineyard - is situated here.

Bulmer Farm

COMMENDED

Holmbury St Mary, Dorking RH5 6LG
☎ (01306) 730210

30-acre beef farm. 17th C character farmhouse with beams and inglenook fireplace, in the Surrey hills. Choice of twin rooms in the house or double/twin en-suite rooms in tastefully converted barn adjoining the house. Village is 5 miles from Dorking.

Bedrooms: 3 double, 5 twin
Bathrooms: 5 en-suite, 2 public

Bed & breakfast per night:	£min	£max
Single	19.00	30.00
Double	38.00	42.00

Parking for 12

Sturtwood Farm

COMMENDED

Partridge Lane, Newdigate, Dorking RH5 5EE
☎ (01306) 631308
Fax (01306) 631908

140-acre mixed farm. Attractive 18th C farmhouse, 5 miles south of Dorking, where you are assured of a warm welcome. 12 minutes from Gatwick. Many National Trust properties in the area.

Bedrooms: 1 single, 1 double, 1 twin
Bathrooms: 1 en-suite, 1 public

Bed & breakfast per night:	£min	£max
Single	20.00	25.00
Double	35.00	45.00

Evening meal from 1900
Parking for 6

For ideas on places to visit refer to the introduction at the beginning of this section.

DOVER

Kent
Map ref 3C4

A Cinque Port and busiest passenger port in the world. Still a historic town and seaside resort beside the famous White Cliffs. The White Cliffs Experience attraction traces the town's history through the Roman, Saxon, Norman and Victorian periods.
Tourist Information Centre ☎ (01304) 205108

Amanda Guest House

Listed APPROVED

4 Harold Street, Dover CT16 1SF
☎ (01304) 201711
Fax (01304) 201711
Large Victorian semi-detached house in a quiet cul-de-sac off the main road. Close to town and ferries.
Bedrooms: 1 double, 2 twin, 2 family rooms
Bathrooms: 1 public

Bed & breakfast per night:	£min	£max
Double	26.00	32.00

Parking for 5

Coldred Court

HIGHLY COMMENDED

Church Road, Coldred, Dover CT15 5AQ
☎ (01304) 830816
Fax (01304) 830816
Dating from 1620, in picturesque rural location. Soak up the cosy, relaxed atmosphere of this tastefully restored and beautiful home. Private parking. Dover 10 minutes.
Bedrooms: 2 double, 1 twin
Bathrooms: 3 en-suite

Bed & breakfast per night:	£min	£max
Single	30.00	60.00
Double	45.00	65.00

Evening meal 1800 (last orders 2030)
Parking for 13

For farm holidays and accommodation suitable for young people and organised groups, please refer to the special sections at the back of this guide.

Elmo Guest House

APPROVED

120 Folkestone Road, Dover CT17 9SP
☎ (01304) 206236
Conveniently situated for ferries and Hoverport terminals and 10 minutes' drive to Channel Tunnel. Within easy reach of town centre and railway station. Overnight stops our speciality.
Bedrooms: 2 single, 2 double, 1 triple, 1 family room
Bathrooms: 2 public

Bed & breakfast per night:	£min	£max
Single	11.00	18.00
Double	22.00	36.00

Parking for 7
Cards accepted: Mastercard, Visa

Esther House

Listed COMMENDED

55 Barton Road, Dover CT16 2NF
☎ (01304) 241332
Fax (01304) 241332
Non-smoking B & B with warm Christian atmosphere. Close to ferries and town centre. Ideal base for touring and 15 minutes from Channel Tunnel. Early breakfasts. Evening meals by arrangement.
Bedrooms: 1 single, 1 twin, 1 triple
Bathrooms: 1 public

Bed & breakfast per night:	£min	£max
Single	15.00	18.00
Double	30.00	34.00

Evening meal 1830 (last orders 1930)

Owler Lodge

HIGHLY COMMENDED

Alkham Valley Road, Alkham, Dover CT15 7DF
☎ (01304) 826375
Small family-run guesthouse with inglenook and beams. In centre of village of Alkham on B2060 between Dover and Folkestone. 3 miles from Channel Tunnel, 4 miles from Dover Docks.
Bedrooms: 2 double, 1 family room
Bathrooms: 3 en-suite

Bed & breakfast per night:	£min	£max
Single	30.00	35.00
Double	42.00	45.00

Evening meal 1800 (last orders 2100)
Parking for 6

EASTBOURNE

East Sussex
Map ref 3B4

One of the finest, most elegant resorts on the south-east coast situated beside Beachy Head. Long promenade, well known Carpet Gardens on the seafront, Devonshire Park tennis and indoor leisure complex, theatres, Towner Art Gallery, "How We Lived Then" Museum of Shops and Social History.
Tourist Information Centre ☎ (01323) 411400

Bay Lodge Hotel

COMMENDED

61-62 Royal Parade, Eastbourne BN22 7AQ
☎ (01323) 732515
Fax (01323) 735009

Small seafront hotel opposite Pavilion Gardens, close to bowling greens and marina. Large sun-lounge. All double/twin bedrooms have en-suite or private facilities. Non-smokers' lounge.
Bedrooms: 3 single, 5 double, 3 twin
Bathrooms: 4 en-suite, 5 private, 2 public

Bed & breakfast per night:	£min	£max
Single	20.00	26.00
Double	38.00	45.00

Half board per person:	£min	£max
Daily	28.00	34.00
Weekly	165.00	225.00

Evening meal 1800 (last orders 1800)
Parking for 2
Open March–October and Christmas
Cards accepted: Mastercard, Visa

ACCESSIBILITY

Look for the symbols which indicate accessibility for wheelchair users. These are described in detail at the front of this guide.

FARNHAM

Surrey
Map ref 2C2

Town noted for its Georgian houses. Willmer House (now a museum) has a facade of cut and moulded brick with fine carving and panelling in the interior. The 12th C castle has been occupied by Bishops of both Winchester and Guildford.
Tourist Information Centre ☎ (01252) 715109

High Wray

Listed COMMENDED

73 Lodge Hill Road, Farnham GU10 3RB
☎ (01252) 715589 & 724386
Visitors welcome as family guests. Gracious house with interesting garden. Wing purpose-built for disabled guests. Home-grown vegetables and eggs.
Wheelchair access category 1
Bedrooms: 2 single, 1 double, 2 twin
Bathrooms: 1 en-suite, 3 public

Bed & breakfast per night:	£min	£max
Single	16.00	18.00
Double	40.00	44.00

Half board per person:	£min	£max
Daily	22.00	24.00
Weekly	142.00	196.00

Evening meal 1830 (last orders 2000)
Parking for 7

FAVERSHAM

Kent
Map ref 3B3

Historic town, once a port, dating back to prehistoric times. Abbey Street has more than 50 listed buildings. Roman and Anglo-Saxon finds and other exhibits can be seen in a museum in the Maison Dieu at Ospringe. Fleur de Lis Heritage Centre.
Tourist Information Centre ☎ (01795) 534542

Barnsfield

Listed COMMENDED

Hernhill, Faversham ME13 9JH
☎ (01227) 750973 & (0589) 836259
Listed Grade II country cottages, just off A299, set in 3 acres of orchards, 6 miles from Canterbury.
Bedrooms: 2 double, 1 twin
Bathrooms: 1 en-suite, 1 public

Bed & breakfast per night:	£min	£max
Single	15.00	28.00
Double	30.00	48.00

Half board per person:	£min	£max
Daily	23.00	38.00
Weekly	145.00	239.00

Parking for 10
Cards accepted: Mastercard, Visa

The Granary

HIGHLY COMMENDED

Plumford Lane, Ospringe, Faversham ME13 ODS
☎ (01795) 538416 & 0860 817713
Fax (01795) 538416
Email: thegranary @compuserve.com
Delightfully converted granary in peaceful setting with large garden. Own lounge with colour TV. Close to M2 and Canterbury. Friendly welcome.
Bedrooms: 1 double, 1 twin, 1 triple
Bathrooms: 2 en-suite, 1 private

Bed & breakfast per night:	£min	£max
Single	25.00	30.00
Double	44.00	44.00

Parking for 8
Cards accepted: Mastercard, Visa, Switch/Delta

Preston Lea

HIGHLY COMMENDED

Canterbury Road, Faversham ME13 8XA
☎ (01795) 535266 & (0421) 329442
Fax (01795) 533388

Beautiful, imposing Victorian house with turrets and other interesting features, set in large secluded grounds. Only 15 minutes from Canterbury and 30 minutes from Channel ports and Eurotunnel.
Bedrooms: 2 double, 1 twin
Bathrooms: 2 en-suite, 1 private

Bed & breakfast per night:	£min	£max
Single	30.00	35.00
Double	40.00	50.00

Parking for 11
Cards accepted: Mastercard, Visa

White Horse Inn

COMMENDED

Boughton, Faversham ME13 9AX
☎ (01227) 751700 & 751343
Fax (01227) 751090

15th C coaching inn with oak beams and inglenook fireplaces. Freshly prepared regional specialities, locally brewed award-winning ales. Half board daily prices are based on a minimum 2-night stay.
Bedrooms: 7 double, 4 twin, 2 triple
Bathrooms: 13 en-suite

Bed & breakfast per night:	£min	£max
Single	38.50	41.00
Double	49.50	52.00

Half board per person:	£min	£max
Daily	37.50	40.00

Lunch available
Evening meal 1900 (last orders 2130)
Parking for 50
Cards accepted: Amex, Mastercard, Visa, Switch/Delta

FINDON

West Sussex
Map ref 2D3

Downland village well-known for its annual sheep fair and its racing stables. The ancient landmarks, Cissbury Ring and Chanctonbury Ring, are nearby.

Findon Tower

COMMENDED

Cross Lane, Findon, Worthing BN14 0UG
☎ (01903) 873870
Elegant Edwardian country house in large secluded garden. Spacious accommodation with en-suite facilities. Warm, friendly welcome, relaxed and peaceful atmosphere. Rural views, snooker room. Strictly no smoking. Excellent food in village.
Bedrooms: 2 double, 1 twin
Bathrooms: 2 en-suite, 1 private

Bed & breakfast per night:	£min	£max
Single	25.00	35.00
Double	40.00	50.00

Parking for 10

FOLKESTONE

Kent
Map ref 3C4

Popular resort and important cross-channel port. The town has a fine promenade, the Leas, from where orchestral concerts and other entertainments are presented. Horse-racing at Westenhanger Racecourse nearby.
Tourist Information Centre ☎ (01303) 258594

Harbourside Bed and Breakfast Hotel

HIGHLY COMMENDED

14 Wear Bay Road, Folkestone CT19 6AT
☎ (01303) 256528 & (0468) 123884
Fax (01303) 241299
Email: r.j.pye@dial.pipex.com
Victorian houses, superior en-suite rooms. The service, hospitality and views are truly unique. Adult. Licensed. No smoking. See our web site: http://www.s-h-systems.co.uk/hotels/harbour.html
Bedrooms: 4 double, 2 twin
Bathrooms: 5 en-suite, 1 private

Bed & breakfast per night:	£min	£max
Single	35.00	60.00
Double	50.00	70.00

Parking for 1
Cards accepted: Amex, Mastercard, Visa, Switch/Delta
12

All accommodation in this guide has been graded, or is awaiting a grading, by a trained Tourist Board inspector.

WELCOME HOST

This is a nationally recognised customer care programme which aims to promote the highest standards of service and a warm welcome. Establishments who are taking part in this initiative are indicated by the symbol.

FULKING

West Sussex
Map ref 2D3

Small, pretty village nestling on the north side of the South Downs near the route of the South Downs Way.

Downers Vineyard

Listed APPROVED

Clappers Lane, Fulking, Henfield BN5 9NH
☎ (01273) 857484 & 0378 392367
Fax (01273) 857068
Email: downer@mistral.co.uk
Quiet rural position, 1 mile north of the South Downs and Devil's Dyke, 8 miles from Brighton.
Bedrooms: 2 triple
Bathrooms: 2 public

Bed & breakfast per night:	£min	£max
Single	20.00	22.00
Double	34.00	36.00

Parking for 6

GATWICK AIRPORT

West Sussex

See under Crawley, Horley

GUILDFORD

Surrey
Map ref 2D2

Bustling town with many historic monuments, one of which is the Guildhall clock jutting out over the old High Street. The modern cathedral occupies a commanding position on Stag Hill.
Tourist Information Centre ☎ (01483) 444333

Beevers Farm

Listed APPROVED

Chinthurst Lane, Bramley, Guildford GU5 0DR
☎ (01483) 898764
In peaceful surroundings 2 miles from Guildford, near villages with pubs and restaurants. Convenient for Heathrow and Gatwick. Friendly atmosphere. Non-smokers only.
Bedrooms: 3 twin
Bathrooms: 1 en-suite, 1 public

Bed & breakfast per night:	£min	£max
Double	30.00	40.00

Parking for 10
Open February–November

High Edser

Listed COMMENDED

Shere Road, Ewhurst, Cranleigh, Guildford GU6 7PQ
☎ (01483) 278214 & (01585) 379136
Fax (01483) 278200
Early 16th C family home set in Area of Outstanding Natural Beauty. 6 miles from Guildford and Dorking, within easy reach of airports and many tourist attractions. Non-smokers only, please.
Bedrooms: 2 double, 1 twin
Bathrooms: 1 public

Bed & breakfast per night:	£min	£max
Single	20.00	25.00
Double	40.00	40.00

Parking for 7

Littlefield Manor

COMMENDED

Littlefield Common, Guildford GU3 3HJ
☎ (01483) 233068 & 232687
Fax (01483) 233686
120-acre mixed farm. 17th C listed manor house with Tudor origins. Enjoy the walled rose garden in summer or the warmth of a blazing log fire in winter. Heathrow and Gatwick are 45 minutes away.
Bedrooms: 1 double, 1 twin
Bathrooms: 2 en-suite

Bed & breakfast per night:	£min	£max
Single		35.00
Double		55.00

Evening meal 1900 (last orders 2130)
Parking for 10
Cards accepted: Amex, Mastercard, Visa
10

Map references apply to the colour maps at the back of this guide.

Information on accommodation listed in this guide has been supplied by the proprietors. As changes may occur you are advised to check details at the time of booking.

HAILSHAM

East Sussex
Map ref 2D3

An important market town since Norman times and still one of the largest markets in Sussex. Two miles west, at Upper Dicker, is Michelham Priory, an Augustinian house founded in 1229.
Tourist Information Centre ☎ (01323) 844426

Sandy Bank

COMMENDED

Old Road, Magham Down, Hailsham BN27 1PW
☎ (01323) 842488
Fax (01323) 842488
Well-appointed en-suite rooms in recent development adjacent to cottage, plus one en-suite in cottage. In attractive Sussex countryside with easy access to Downs and sea. Ideal base for touring Sussex. Friendly atmosphere.
Bedrooms: 3 twin
Bathrooms: 3 en-suite

Bed & breakfast per night:	£min	£max
Single	25.00	
Double	44.00	48.00

Evening meal 1830 (last orders 2000)
Parking for 3

HARTFIELD

East Sussex
Map ref 2D2

Pleasant village in Ashdown Forest, the setting for A A Milne's "Winnie the Pooh" stories.

Stairs Farmhouse and Tea Room

Listed COMMENDED

High Street, Hartfield TN7 4AB
☎ (01892) 770793 & 770561
Fax (01892) 770793
17th C modernised farmhouse with various period features, in picturesque village. Close to Pooh Bridge and Hever Castle. Views over open countryside. Home produced additive-free meals provided. Tea room and farm shop.
Bedrooms: 1 double, 2 twin
Bathrooms: 1 private, 2 public

Bed & breakfast per night:	£min	£max
Single	25.00	35.00
Double	40.00	45.00

Half board per person:	£min	£max
Daily	35.00	45.00

Lunch available
Evening meal 1800 (last orders 1930)
Parking for 16
Cards accepted: Mastercard, Visa, Switch/Delta
6

HERSTMONCEUX

East Sussex
Map ref 3B4

Pleasant village noted for its woodcrafts and the beautiful 15th C moated Herstmonceux Castle, with its Science Centre and gardens open to the public.

Conquerors

HIGHLY COMMENDED

Stunts Green, Herstmonceux, Hailsham BN27 4PR
☎ (01323) 832446
13-acre mixed farm. Charming single-storey home set in own farmland with spectacular views over 1066 country to Eastbourne and the sea. Total tranquillity in complete comfort. Access for disabled.
Wheelchair access category 3
Bedrooms: 1 double, 2 twin
Bathrooms: 2 en-suite, 1 private

Bed & breakfast per night:	£min	£max
Single	22.00	24.00
Double	40.00	44.00

Parking for 25
10

The Stud Farm

COMMENDED

Bodle Street Green, Herstmonceux, Hailsham BN27 4RJ
☎ (01323) 833201
Fax (01323) 833201
70-acre mixed farm. Upstairs, 2 bedrooms and bathroom let as one unit to party of 2, 3 or 4. Downstairs, twin-bedded en-suite room. Guests' sitting room and sunroom.
Bedrooms: 1 double, 2 twin
Bathrooms: 1 en-suite, 1 public

Bed & breakfast per night:	£min	£max
Single	22.00	25.00
Double	36.00	40.00

Half board per person:	£min	£max
Daily	32.00	35.00
Weekly	224.00	245.00

Evening meal from 1830
Parking for 3

HOLLINGBOURNE

Kent
Map ref 3B3

Pleasant village near romantic Leeds Castle in the heart of orchard country at the foot of the North Downs. Some fine half-timbered houses and a flint and ragstone church.

Woodhouses

COMMENDED

49 Eyhorne Street, Hollingbourne, Maidstone ME17 1TR
☎ (01622) 880594
Fax (01622) 880594
Interconnected listed cottages dating from 17th C, with inglenook fireplace and exposed wooden beams. Well-stocked cottage garden.
Bedrooms: 1 double, 2 twin
Bathrooms: 3 en-suite

Bed & breakfast per night:	£min	£max
Single	18.00	18.00
Double	35.00	35.00

Parking for 4
10

HORLEY

Surrey
Map ref 2D2

Town on the London to Brighton road, just north of Gatwick Airport, with an ancient parish church and 15th C inn.

Aintree & Gables Guest House

Listed COMMENDED

50 Bonehurst Road, Horley RH6 8QG
☎ (01293) 774553
Approximately 2 miles from Gatwick and the railway station. Long term parking. Transport to the airport available.
Bedrooms: 3 single, 7 double, 9 twin, 5 triple
Bathrooms: 9 en-suite, 4 public

Bed & breakfast per night:	£min	£max
Single	25.00	25.00
Double	32.00	39.00

Parking for 25

You are advised to confirm your booking in writing.

HORLEY

Continued

The Lawn Guest House

HIGHLY COMMENDED

30 Massetts Road, Horley RH6 7DE
☎ (01293) 775751
Fax (01293) 821803

Classic Victorian house with mature garden, 2 minutes from Horley centre, restaurants, pubs and main rail station to London/Brighton. 5 minutes' drive to Gatwick, long-term parking. Non-smoking.

Bedrooms: 1 double, 2 twin, 4 triple
Bathrooms: 7 en-suite

Bed & breakfast per night:	£min	£max
Double	45.00	47.00

Parking for 10
Cards accepted: Amex, Mastercard, Visa

UL T

HOVE

East Sussex

See under Brighton & Hove

ICKLESHAM

East Sussex
Map ref 3B4

Small village between the ancient towns of Rye and Hastings. The village itself was first recorded in 772 AD.

Manor Farm Oast

HIGHLY COMMENDED

Windmill Orchard, Main Road, Icklesham, Winchelsea TN36 4AJ
☎ (01424) 813787
Fax (01424) 813787

Three-roundel oast house in the heart of 1066 country. Quiet and secluded, in orchards close to Rye, Battle and Hastings. JCB cards accepted.

Bedrooms: 2 double, 1 twin
Bathrooms: 2 en-suite, 1 private

Bed & breakfast per night:	£min	£max
Single	38.00	
Double	60.00	

Half board per person:	£min	£max
Daily	45.00	53.00
Weekly	350.00	371.00

Evening meal 1900 (last orders 2000)
Parking for 10
Open February–December
Cards accepted: Mastercard, Visa, Switch/Delta

12 S

LENHAM

Kent
Map ref 3B4

Shops, inns and houses, many displaying timber-work of the late Middle Ages, surround a square which is the centre of the village. The 14th C parish church has one of the best examples of a Kentish tower.

The Dog & Bear Hotel

COMMENDED

The Square, Lenham, Maidstone ME17 2PG
☎ (01622) 858219
Fax (01622) 859415

15th C coaching inn retaining its old world character and serving good Kent ale, lagers and fine wines with home cooking. En-suite rooms. 5 minutes' drive from Leeds Castle. Half board daily prices are based on a minimum 2-night stay.

Wheelchair access category 3
Bedrooms: 3 single, 13 double, 5 twin, 2 triple, 1 family room
Bathrooms: 24 en-suite

Bed & breakfast per night:	£min	£max
Single	38.50	41.00
Double	49.50	52.00

Half board per person:	£min	£max
Daily	37.50	40.00

Lunch available
Evening meal 1900 (last orders 2130)
Parking for 26
Cards accepted: Amex, Mastercard, Visa, Switch/Delta

S 50 SP T

All accommodation in this guide has been graded, or is awaiting a grading, by a trained Tourist Board inspector.

LINGFIELD

Surrey
Map ref 2D2

Wealden village with many buildings dating back to the 15th C. Nearby there is year-round horse racing at Lingfield Park.

The Old Cage

APPROVED

Plaistow Street, Lingfield RH7 6AU
☎ (01342) 834271
Fax (01342) 832112

Restored timbered English pub, dating from 1592, with restaurant and en-suite accommodation. Ideal for M25, Gatwick and London connections.

Bedrooms: 3 twin
Bathrooms: 3 en-suite

Bed & breakfast per night:	£min	£max
Single	30.00	30.00
Double	40.00	40.00

Lunch available
Evening meal (last orders 2100)
Parking for 30
Cards accepted: Amex, Mastercard, Visa, Switch/Delta

SP

LYMINSTER

West Sussex
Map ref 2D3

Links up with Littlehampton looking inland, and across the watermeadows to the churches and towers of Arundel. There is a vineyard here.

Sandfield House

COMMENDED

Lyminster, Littlehampton BN17 7PG
☎ (01903) 724129
Fax (01903) 715041

Spacious country-style family house in 2 acres. Between Arundel and sea, in area of great natural beauty.

Bedrooms: 1 double
Bathrooms: 1 public

Bed & breakfast per night:	£min	£max
Double	34.00	40.00

Parking for 4

UL S TV

MAIDSTONE

Kent
Map ref 3B3

Busy county town of Kent on the River Medway has many interesting features and is an excellent centre for excursions. Museum of Carriages, Museum and Art Gallery, Mote Park.
Tourist Information Centre ☎ (01622) 602169

Willington Court

HIGHLY COMMENDED
Willington Street, Maidstone ME15 8JW
☎ (01622) 738885
Fax (01622) 631790
Charming Grade II listed building. Antiques, four-poster bed. Friendly and relaxed atmosphere. Adjacent to Mote Park and near Leeds Castle.
Bedrooms: 2 double, 1 twin
Bathrooms: 2 en-suite, 1 private

Bed & breakfast per night:	£min	£max
Single	26.00	36.00
Double	40.00	50.00

Parking for 6
Cards accepted: Amex, Diners, Mastercard, Visa

NEW ROMNEY

Kent
Map ref 3B4

Capital of Romney Marsh. Now a mile from the sea, it was one of the original Cinque Ports. Romney, Hythe and Dymchurch Railway's main station is here.

Broadacre Hotel

COMMENDED
North Street, New Romney TN28 8DR
☎ (01797) 362381
Fax (01797) 362381
Small 16th C family-run hotel offering a warm, friendly welcome and personal attention. Intimate restaurants, lounge bar, garden. Weekend breaks.
Bedrooms: 3 single, 4 double, 2 twin, 1 family room
Bathrooms: 10 en-suite

Bed & breakfast per night:	£min	£max
Single	35.00	42.00
Double	45.00	60.00

Half board per person:	£min	£max
Daily	34.00	50.00
Weekly	210.00	

Lunch available
Evening meal 1900 (last orders 2100)
Parking for 9
Cards accepted: Mastercard, Visa, Switch/Delta

NEWICK

East Sussex
Map ref 2D3

Lies on one of the pilgrims' ways to Canterbury. There are some good period houses, a well-restored church, a village pump of wrought-iron and a village green.

Fairseat House

Listed HIGHLY COMMENDED
Newick, Lewes BN8 4PJ
☎ (01825) 722263
Email: bnbuk@pavilion.co.uk
Edwardian period house set in 5 acres with heated pool. Comfortable, prettily decorated rooms, including four-poster. Convenient for Bluebell Railway, Glyndebourne and many Sussex gardens.
Bedrooms: 2 double, 1 twin
Bathrooms: 2 en-suite, 1 private

Bed & breakfast per night:	£min	£max
Single	31.00	50.00
Double	44.00	85.00

Half board per person:	£min	£max
Daily	33.50	55.00

Lunch available
Evening meal 1930 (last orders 2030)
Parking for 6
Cards accepted: Mastercard, Visa

OXTED

Surrey
Map ref 2D2

Pleasant town on the edge of National Trust woodland and at the foot of the North Downs. Chartwell (National Trust), the former home of Sir Winston Churchill, is close by.

The New Bungalow

Listed APPROVED
Old Hall Farm, Tandridge Lane, Oxted RH8 9NS
☎ (01342) 892508
Fax (01342) 892508
40-acre livestock farm. Spacious, modern bungalow set in green fields and reached by a private drive. 5 minutes' drive from M25.
Bedrooms: 1 twin, 1 family room
Bathrooms: 1 public

Bed & breakfast per night:	£min	£max
Single	22.00	22.00
Double	34.00	36.00

Parking for 5

PARTRIDGE GREEN

West Sussex
Map ref 2D3

Small village between Henfield and Billingshurst.

Pound Cottage Bed & Breakfast

COMMENDED
Mill Lane, Littleworth, Partridge Green, Horsham RH13 8JU
☎ (01403) 710218 & 711285
Pleasant country house in quiet surroundings. 8 miles from Horsham, 25 minutes from Gatwick. Just off the B2135 West Grinstead to Steyning road.
Bedrooms: 1 single, 1 double, 1 twin
Bathrooms: 1 public

Bed & breakfast per night:	£min	£max
Single	17.00	17.00
Double	34.00	34.00

Parking for 8

PENSHURST

Kent
Map ref 2D2

Pretty village in a hilly wooded setting with Penshurst Place, the ancestral home of the Sidney family since 1552, standing in delightful grounds with a formal Tudor garden.

Swale Cottage

Listed HIGHLY COMMENDED
Off Poundsbridge Lane, Penshurst, Tonbridge TN11 8AH
☎ (01892) 870738

Charmingly converted Grade II listed barn overlooking medieval manor house and gardens. Idyllic and tranquil. Delightful bedrooms (1 with*

Continued ▶

PENSHURST

Continued

four-poster). Close to Penshurst Place, Hever and Chartwell. Near A26 off B2176.
Bedrooms: 2 double, 1 twin
Bathrooms: 2 en-suite, 1 private

Bed & breakfast per night:	£min	£max
Single	36.00	45.00
Double	52.00	63.00

Parking for 7

PETWORTH

West Sussex
Map ref 2D3

Town dominated by Petworth House (National Trust), the great 17th C mansion, set in 2000 acres of parkland laid out by Capability Brown. The house contains wood-carvings by Grinling Gibbons.
Tourist Information Centre ☎ (01798) 343523

The Horse Guards Inn

COMMENDED

Tillington, Petworth GU28 9AF
☎ (01798) 342332
Charming 300-year-old inn, with lots of low beams, inglenook area, 3 open fires, secluded garden and magnificent views over South Downs.
Bedrooms: 2 double, 1 twin
Bathrooms: 2 en-suite, 1 private

Bed & breakfast per night:	£min	£max
Double	57.50	62.50

Lunch available
Evening meal 1900 (last orders 2200)
Parking for 5
Cards accepted: Amex, Mastercard, Visa, Switch/Delta

White Horse Inn

HIGHLY COMMENDED

The Street, Sutton, Pulborough RH20 1PS
☎ (01798) 869221
Fax (01798) 869291

Pretty Georgian village inn close to South Downs Way. Roman villa 1 mile. Garden, log fires. 4 miles Petworth, 5 miles Pulborough.
Bedrooms: 4 double, 2 twin
Bathrooms: 5 en-suite, 1 private shower

Bed & breakfast per night:	£min	£max
Single	48.00	48.00
Double	58.00	68.00

Lunch available
Evening meal 1900 (last orders 2145)
Parking for 10
Cards accepted: Amex, Diners, Mastercard, Visa

ROGATE

West Sussex
Map ref 2C3

On the main road between Midhurst and Petersfield, Rogate probably gets its name from its position as gateway to wooded hill slopes, the habitat of deer.

Trotton Farm

COMMENDED

Trotton, Petersfield, Hampshire GU31 5EN
☎ (01730) 813618
Fax (01730) 816093
Farmhouse just off the A272, access through yard. Accommodation and lounge/games room in a converted cartshed adjoining farmhouse. All rooms with en-suite shower.
Bedrooms: 1 double, 2 twin
Bathrooms: 3 en-suite

Bed & breakfast per night:	£min	£max
Single	25.00	30.00
Double	35.00	40.00

ROTTINGDEAN

East Sussex
Map ref 2D3

The quiet High Street contains a number of fine old buildings and the village pond and green are close by.

Braemar Guest House

COMMENDED

Steyning Road, Rottingdean, Brighton BN2 7GA
☎ (01273) 304263
Family-run guesthouse, proud of its cheerful atmosphere, in an old world village where Rudyard Kipling once lived.
Bedrooms: 5 single, 5 double, 2 twin, 2 triple
Bathrooms: 3 public, 2 private showers

Bed & breakfast per night:	£min	£max
Single	15.00	17.50
Double	30.00	35.00

ROYAL TUNBRIDGE WELLS

Kent
Map ref 2D2

This "Royal" town became famous as a spa in the 17th C and much of its charm is retained, as in the Pantiles, a shaded walk lined with elegant shops. Heritage attraction "A Day at the Wells". Excellent shopping centre.
Tourist Information Centre ☎ (01892) 515675

Chequers

HIGHLY COMMENDED

Camden Park, Royal Tunbridge Wells TN2 5AD
☎ (01892) 532299
Fax (01892) 526448
Email: stubbs.family@btinternet.com
Friendly family house, origins 1840. Part-walled garden. Unique private location, 10 minutes from Pantiles, high street, railway station. Peaceful, comfortable, central base. Non-smokers only, please.
Bedrooms: 1 single, 1 twin
Bathrooms: 1 en-suite, 1 private

Bed & breakfast per night:	£min	£max
Single	18.00	20.00
Double	38.00	40.00

Parking for 5

Cheviots

COMMENDED

Cousley Wood, Wadhurst, East Sussex TN5 6HD
☎ (01892) 782952
Fax (01892) 782952
Email: cheviots.guesthouse @dial.pipex.com
On B2100 between Lamberhurst and Wadhurst. Comfortable bed and breakfast in modern country house with extensive garden. Home cooking. Convenient base for walking and motoring. Close to Bewl Water.
Bedrooms: 2 single, 2 twin
Bathrooms: 2 en-suite, 1 public

Bed & breakfast per night:	£min	£max
Single	20.00	30.00
Double	40.00	60.00

Half board per person:	£min	£max
Daily	35.00	45.00
Weekly	220.00	280.00

Evening meal from 1800
Parking for 4
Cards accepted: Mastercard, Visa, Switch/Delta

Hawkenbury Farm

COMMENDED

Hawkenbury Road, Royal Tunbridge Wells TN3 9AD
☎ (01892) 536977
Fax (01892) 536200
Comfortable accommodation on small working farm in quiet location one and a half miles south-east of Tunbridge Wells. Ample parking, views and walks. Many National Trust properties nearby.
Bedrooms: 1 double, 1 twin
Bathrooms: 1 en-suite, 1 private

Bed & breakfast per night:	£min	£max
Double	36.00	42.00

Parking for 7

Nightingales

Listed COMMENDED

London Road, Southborough, Royal Tunbridge Wells TN4 0UJ
☎ (01892) 528443
Fax (01892) 511376
Georgian house with lovely views over Kent countryside. Attractive, spacious bedrooms, good breakfasts (English or Continental). Families welcome, discounts for long stays. Garden, parking.
Bedrooms: 1 single, 1 double, 1 triple
Bathrooms: 1 public

Bed & breakfast per night:	£min	£max
Single	15.00	18.00
Double	32.00	36.00

Parking for 3

Please check prices and other details at the time of booking.

A key to symbols can be found inside the back cover flap.

189 Upper Grosvenor Road

Listed APPROVED

Royal Tunbridge Wells TN1 2EF
☎ (01892) 524017
Fax (01892) 517975
Victorian home with modern amenities, located 5 minutes' drive from town centre. Ideal base for historic Kent, London and Sussex.
Bedrooms: 3 twin
Bathrooms: 1 public

Bed & breakfast per night:	£min	£max
Single	18.00	20.00
Double	30.00	32.00

Parking for 4

RYE

East Sussex
Map ref 3B4

Cobbled, hilly streets and fine old buildings make Rye, once a Cinque Port, a most picturesque town. Noted for its church with ancient clock, potteries and antique shops. Town Model Sound and Light Show gives a good introduction to the town.
Tourist Information Centre ☎ (01797) 226696

Aviemore Guest House

APPROVED

28-30 Fishmarket Road, Rye TN31 7LP
☎ (01797) 223052
Fax (01797) 223052

Owner-run, friendly guesthouse offering a warm welcome and hearty breakfast. Overlooking "Town Salts" and the River Rother. 2 minutes from town centre.
Bedrooms: 1 single, 4 double, 3 twin
Bathrooms: 4 en-suite, 2 public

Bed & breakfast per night:	£min	£max
Single	20.00	25.00
Double	35.00	41.00

Half board per person:	£min	£max
Daily	26.00	29.00
Weekly	166.00	199.00

Evening meal 1800 (last orders 2200)
Cards accepted: Amex, Mastercard, Visa

Fiddlers Oast

Listed COMMENDED

Watermill Lane, Beckley, Rye TN31 6SH
☎ (01797) 252394 & 0836 621211
Fax (01797) 252394
Email: 106515,1552 @compuserve.com
Branch left after Rose and Crown in Beckley on B2165 for 350m, left opposite red letter box...then relax! Children and well behaved adults welcome.
Bedrooms: 1 double, 1 twin, 1 triple
Bathrooms: 3 en-suite, 1 public

Bed & breakfast per night:	£min	£max
Single	28.50	34.50
Double	37.00	45.00

Parking for 6
Open January–November
Cards accepted: Mastercard, Visa, Switch/Delta

Jeake's House

HIGHLY COMMENDED

Mermaid Street, Rye TN31 7ET
☎ (01797) 222828
Fax (01797) 222623
Email: jeakeshouse@btinternet.com

Recapture the past in this historic building, in a cobblestoned street at the heart of the old town. Honeymoon suite available.
Bedrooms: 1 single, 7 double, 1 twin, 2 triple, 1 family room
Bathrooms: 9 en-suite, 1 private, 2 public

Bed & breakfast per night:	£min	£max
Single	24.50	56.50
Double	45.00	63.00

Cards accepted: Amex, Mastercard, Visa

COLOUR MAPS

Colour maps at the back of this guide pinpoint all places in which you will find accommodation listed.

RYE

Continued

Kimblee

COMMENDED

Main Street, Peasmarsh, Rye TN31 6UL
☎ (01797) 230514 & 0831 841004

Country house with views from all aspects, 250 metres from pub/restaurant and 5 minutes' drive on the A268 from Rye. Warm welcome.

Bedrooms: 3 double
Bathrooms: 3 en-suite

Bed & breakfast per night:	£min	£max
Single	20.00	
Double	36.00	40.00

Parking for 4
Cards accepted: Mastercard, Visa

The Old Vicarage

Listed COMMENDED

Rye Harbour, Rye TN31 7TT
☎ (01797) 222088

Imposing Victorian former vicarage, quietly situated close to sea and nature reserve. Antique furniture and open fires. Magnificent English breakfast.

Bedrooms: 1 double, 1 twin
Bathrooms: 1 public

Bed & breakfast per night:	£min	£max
Single	15.50	25.00
Double	33.00	44.00

Parking for 4

Playden Cottage Guesthouse

HIGHLY COMMENDED

Military Road, Rye TN31 7NY
☎ (01797) 222234

Large character cottage, said to be "Grebe" from E. F. Benson's Mapp and Lucia novels. Personal service in a comfortable family home. Pretty gardens, rural aspect, peaceful.

Bedrooms: 1 double, 2 twin
Bathrooms: 3 en-suite, 1 public

Bed & breakfast per night:	£min	£max
Single	37.50	64.00
Double	50.00	64.00

Half board per person:	£min	£max
Daily	37.00	44.00
Weekly	241.50	285.60

Evening meal 1800 (last orders 2030)
Parking for 7
Cards accepted: Mastercard, Visa

Saint Margarets

COMMENDED

Dumbwomans Lane, Udimore, Rye TN31 6AD
☎ (01797) 222586

Comfortable, friendly chalet bungalow with sea views. Car parking. Shower/WC en-suite. On B2089, 2 miles west of Rye.

Bedrooms: 2 double, 1 twin
Bathrooms: 3 en-suite

Bed & breakfast per night:	£min	£max
Double	30.00	32.00

Parking for 3
Open February–November

Strand House

COMMENDED

Winchelsea TN36 4JT
☎ (01797) 226276
Fax (01797) 224806

The old-world charm of one of Winchelsea's oldest houses, dating from the 15th C, with oak beams and inglenooks. Overlooking National Trust pastureland. Four-poster bedroom. Residents' licence.

Bedrooms: 8 double, 1 twin, 1 triple
Bathrooms: 9 en-suite, 1 private, 1 public

Bed & breakfast per night:	£min	£max
Single	28.00	34.00
Double	45.00	58.00

Evening meal 1800 (last orders 1900)
Parking for 12
Cards accepted: Mastercard, Visa, Switch/Delta

Top o'The Hill at Rye

COMMENDED

Rye Hill, Rye TN31 7NH
☎ (01797) 223284
Fax (01797) 227030

Small, friendly inn offering fine traditional food and cottage-style accommodation. Central for touring Kent and Sussex, Channel Tunnel and ports nearby. Large car park, garden.

Bedrooms: 5 double, 2 twin, 1 triple
Bathrooms: 8 en-suite

Bed & breakfast per night:	£min	£max
Single	24.00	36.00
Double	44.00	50.00

Lunch available
Evening meal 1900 (last orders 2100)
Parking for 32
Cards accepted: Mastercard, Visa

SANDHURST

Kent
Map ref 3B4

Hoads Farm

Listed APPROVED

Crouch Lane, Sandhurst, Cranbrook TN18 5PA
☎ (01580) 850296
Fax (01580) 850296

350-acre mixed farm. 16th C farmhouse, well modernised. On A268 towards Rye left at first turning after village opposite Sandhurst playing fields, farm on right at bottom of hill.

Bedrooms: 3 twin
Bathrooms: 2 public

Bed & breakfast per night:	£min	£max
Single	19.00	
Double	38.00	

Half board per person:	£min	£max
Daily	27.00	30.00
Weekly	170.00	191.00

Parking for 10

For ideas on places to visit refer to the introduction at the beginning of this section.

SARRE

Kent
Map ref 3C3

Attractive Dutch-gabled houses can be seen in this Thanet village. Names of many famous people are inscribed on the walls of the 16th C Crown Inn, noted for the manufacture of cherry brandy.

Crown Inn (The Famous Cherry Brandy House)

COMMENDED

Ramsgate Road, Sarre, Birchington
CT7 OLF
☎ (01843) 847808
Fax (01843) 847914

Ancient traditional inn, convenient for Canterbury. Inglenook fireplaces, gleaming brasses, freshly prepared regional specialities. Excellent locally brewed ales. Half board daily prices are based on a minimum 2-night stay.

Wheelchair access category 3
Bedrooms: 9 double, 2 twin, 1 triple
Bathrooms: 12 en-suite

Bed & breakfast per night:	£min	£max
Single	43.50	
Double	56.50	

Half board per person:	£min	£max
Daily	37.50	40.00

Lunch available
Evening meal 1900 (last orders 2200)
Parking for 40
Cards accepted: Amex, Mastercard, Visa, Switch/Delta

Establishments should be open throughout the year, unless otherwise stated.

Half board prices are given per person, but in some cases these may be based on double/twin occupancy.

SEVENOAKS

Kent
Map ref 2D2

Set in pleasant wooded country, with a distinctive character and charm. Nearby is Knole (National Trust), home of the Sackville family and one of the largest houses in England, set in a vast deer park.
Tourist Information Centre ☎ (01732) 450305

The Bull Hotel

APPROVED

Wrotham, Sevenoaks TN15 7RF
☎ (01732) 885522 & 883092
Fax (01732) 886288

Privately-run 14th C coaching inn, in secluded historic village 15 minutes from Sevenoaks. Just off M20 and M25/26, 30 minutes from Gatwick and London, 1 hour from Dover. Oak beams and inglenook fireplaces. Ideal for local places of interest.

Bedrooms: 1 single, 3 double, 6 twin
Bathrooms: 6 en-suite, 1 public

Bed & breakfast per night:	£min	£max
Single	37.00	42.00
Double	47.00	52.00

Lunch available
Evening meal 1900 (last orders 2200)
Parking for 50
Cards accepted: Amex, Diners, Mastercard, Visa

The Moorings Hotel

APPROVED

97 Hitchen Hatch Lane, Sevenoaks
TN13 3BE
☎ (01732) 452589 & 742323
Fax (01732) 456462
Email: theryans
@mooringshotel.demon.co.uk

Friendly family hotel offering high standard accommodation for tourists and business travellers. 30 minutes from London. Close to BR station.

Bedrooms: 5 single, 5 double, 9 twin, 2 triple
Bathrooms: 21 en-suite, 1 public

Bed & breakfast per night:	£min	£max
Single	34.00	42.00
Double	49.00	59.00

Half board per person:	£min	£max
Daily	44.00	52.00
Weekly	308.00	364.00

Lunch available
Evening meal 1900 (last orders 2100)
Parking for 24
Cards accepted: Amex, Mastercard, Visa, Switch/Delta

SHOREHAM

Kent
Map ref 2D2

Preston Farmhouse

COMMENDED

Preston Farm, Shoreham, Sevenoaks
TN14 7UD
☎ (01959) 522029

210-acre mixed farm. 18th C house in the heart of the Darenth Valley, with the River Darenth running through the farm.

Bedrooms: 2 twin
Bathrooms: 2 public

Bed & breakfast per night:	£min	£max
Single	18.00	20.00
Double	36.00	40.00

SISSINGHURST

Kent
Map ref 3B4

1 Hillview Cottage

Starvenden Lane, Sissinghurst,
Cranbrook TN17 2AN
☎ (01580) 712823 & 0850 909838

Total peace, Kentish countryside. Wonderful views. Tennis court. Riding close by. Minutes from Sissinghurst Castle and close to National Trust properties.

Bedrooms: 1 double, 1 twin
Bathrooms: 1 en-suite, 2 public

Bed & breakfast per night:	£min	£max
Single	20.00	20.00
Double	40.00	40.00

Half board per person:	£min	£max
Daily	32.00	32.00
Weekly	190.00	190.00

Evening meal 1800 (last orders 2000)
Parking for 6

SMARDEN

Kent
Map ref 3B4

Pretty village with a number of old, well-presented buildings. The 14th C St Michael's Church is sometimes known as the "Barn of Kent" because of its 36-ft roof span.

Chequers Inn

COMMENDED

Smarden, Ashford TN27 8QA
☎ (01233) 770217
Fax (01233) 770623
Listed 14th C inn, wealth of oak beams, in heart of the Weald. Ideal for touring and visiting many places of historic interest. 5 golf-courses nearby. Good food always available - fresh fish a speciality.
Bedrooms: 1 single, 2 double, 2 twin
Bathrooms: 3 en-suite, 2 private, 1 public

Bed & breakfast per night:	£min	£max
Single	25.00	35.00
Double	45.00	52.00

Lunch available
Evening meal 1800 (last orders 2200)
Parking for 18
Cards accepted: Mastercard, Visa, Switch/Delta

STELLING MINNIS

Kent
Map ref 3B4

Off the Roman Stone Street, this quiet, picturesque village lies deep in the Lyminge Forest, south of Canterbury.

Great Field Farm

Listed HIGHLY COMMENDED

Misling Lane, Stelling Minnis, Canterbury CT4 6DE
☎ (01227) 709223
Fax (01227) 709223
42-acre mixed farm. Lovely spacious farmhouse with wealth of old pine, fine furnishings, pleasant gardens, paddocks with friendly ponies. Self-contained flat available for B&B or self catering. Quiet location midway Canterbury/Folkestone, adjacent B2068.
Bedrooms: 2 double, 1 twin
Bathrooms: 3 en-suite

Bed & breakfast per night:	£min	£max
Single	18.00	25.00
Double	36.00	40.00

Parking for 6

TENTERDEN

Kent
Map ref 3B4

Most attractive market town with a broad main street full of 16th C houses and shops. The tower of the 15th C parish church is the finest in Kent. Fine antiques centre.

Finchden Manor

HIGHLY COMMENDED

Appledore Road, Tenterden TN30 7DD
☎ (01580) 764719
Early 15th C manor house, Grade II listed, with inglenook fireplaces, panelled rooms and beams. Set in 4 acres of gardens and grounds.*
Bedrooms: 1 single, 2 double
Bathrooms: 1 en-suite, 2 private

Bed & breakfast per night:	£min	£max
Single	26.00	28.00
Double	52.00	56.00

Parking for 3

TUNBRIDGE WELLS

Kent

See under Royal Tunbridge Wells

UCKFIELD

East Sussex
Map ref 2D3

Once a medieval market town and centre of the iron industry, Uckfield is now a busy country town on the edge of the Ashdown Forest.

Old Mill Farm

COMMENDED

High Hurstwood, Uckfield TN22 4AD
☎ (01825) 732279
Fax (01825) 732279
50-acre beef farm. Situated in picturesque valley, off A26. Gatwick, Crowborough, Uckfield and Ashdown Forest nearby. All rooms have private facilities.
Bedrooms: 1 single, 1 twin, 1 triple
Bathrooms: 2 en-suite, 1 private

Bed & breakfast per night:	£min	£max
Single	18.00	20.00
Double	36.00	40.00

Parking for 6

South Paddock

HIGHLY COMMENDED

Maresfield Park, Uckfield TN22 2HA
☎ (01825) 762335
Comfortable quiet country house accommodation set in 3.5 acres of landscaped gardens. Home-made preserves and log fires. Within easy reach of Gatwick, Brighton, Glyndebourne, Hever Castle.
Bedrooms: 1 double, 2 twin
Bathrooms: 1 private, 1 public

Bed & breakfast per night:	£min	£max
Single	34.00	38.00
Double	52.00	56.00

Parking for 6

WADHURST

East Sussex
Map ref 3B4

Village in the Sussex Weald. The village sign depicts an anvil, recalling the iron industry, and also an oasthouse, showing that this is hop country.

Best Beech Inn

COMMENDED

Best Beech, Wadhurst TN5 6JH
☎ (01892) 782046
Fax (01892) 785092

Quiet, rural public house set in pretty Sussex countryside and surrounded by beech trees.
Bedrooms: 1 single, 3 double, 2 twin, 1 family room
Bathrooms: 4 en-suite, 1 private, 1 public

Bed & breakfast per night:	£min	£max
Single	25.00	27.50
Double	35.00	45.00

Half board per person:	£min	£max
Daily	35.00	50.00
Weekly	220.00	270.00

Lunch available
Evening meal 1900 (last orders 2130)
Parking for 30
Cards accepted: Mastercard, Visa

WALTON-ON-THAMES

Surrey
Map ref 2D2

Busy town beside the Thames, retaining a distinctive atmosphere despite being only 12 miles from central London. Close to Hampton Court Palace, Sandown Park racecourse and Claremont Landscape Garden (National Trust), Esher.

Beech Tree Lodge

Listed COMMENDED

7 Rydens Avenue,
Walton-on-Thames KT12 3JB
☎ (01932) 242738 & 886667
Edwardian house in tree-lined avenue near buses, trains, shops, pubs. Handy for London, Hampton Court, Kingston and country theme parks and museums.
Bedrooms: 2 twin, 1 triple
Bathrooms: 2 public

Bed & breakfast per night:	£min	£max
Single	18.00	25.00
Double	36.00	38.00

Parking for 8

The National Grading and Classification Scheme is explained at the back of this guide.

WELCOME HOST

This is a nationally recognised customer care programme which aims to promote the highest standards of service and a warm welcome. Establishments who are taking part in this initiative are indicated by the symbol.

WEST CHILTINGTON

West Sussex
Map ref 2D3

Well-kept village caught in the maze of lanes leading to and from the South Downs.

New House Farm

COMMENDED

Broadford Bridge Road, West Chiltington, Pulborough RH20 2LA
☎ (01798) 812215
Fax (01798) 813209
50-acre mixed farm. 15th C farmhouse with oak beams and inglenook for log fires. 35 minutes' drive from Gatwick. Within easy reach of local inns and golf-course.
Bedrooms: 1 double, 2 twin
Bathrooms: 2 en-suite, 1 private

Bed & breakfast per night:	£min	£max
Single	25.00	35.00
Double	40.00	50.00

Parking for 6

WEST CLANDON

Surrey
Map ref 2D2

Home of Clandon Park (National Trust), the Palladian mansion built in the early 1730s and home of the Queen's Royal Surrey Regiment Museum.

Ways Cottage

Listed COMMENDED

Lime Grove, West Clandon, Guildford GU4 7UT
☎ (01483) 222454
Rural detached house in quiet location, 5 miles from Guildford. Easy reach of A3 and M25. Close to station on Waterloo/Guildford line.
Bedrooms: 2 twin
Bathrooms: 1 en-suite, 1 public

Bed & breakfast per night:	£min	£max
Single	21.50	23.50
Double	37.00	40.00

Half board per person:	£min	£max
Daily	31.50	33.50
Weekly	220.50	234.50

Evening meal 1800 (last orders 2100)
Parking for 2

WEST MALLING

Kent
Map ref 3B3

Became prominent in Norman times when an abbey was established here.

Westfields Farm

COMMENDED

St Vincents Lane, Addington, West Malling ME19 5BW
☎ (01732) 843209
Farmhouse of character, approximately 500 years old, in rural setting. Within easy reach of London, Canterbury, Tunbridge Wells and the coast. Reductions for children. Golf nearby.
Bedrooms: 2 twin, 1 triple
Bathrooms: 2 public

Bed & breakfast per night:	£min	£max
Single	20.00	20.00
Double	40.00	40.00

WINGHAM

Kent
Map ref 3C3

On the A257 halfway between Sandwich and Canterbury. The main street is notable for its many half-timbered buildings.

Dambridge Oast

COMMENDED

Staple Road, Wingham, Canterbury CT3 1LU
☎ (01227) 720082 & (0589) 707828
Fax (01227) 720082

Delightfully converted, Grade II listed oasthouse/granary in peaceful countryside. All rooms en-suite, colour TV. Ideal base for exploring Kent.
Bedrooms: 2 double, 1 twin
Bathrooms: 3 en-suite, 1 public

Bed & breakfast per night:	£min	£max
Single	20.00	35.00
Double	40.00	50.00

Parking for 10

WOKING

Surrey
Map ref 2D2

One of the largest towns in Surrey, which developed with the coming of the railway in the 1830s. Old Woking was a market town in the 17th C and still retains several interesting buildings. Large arts and entertainment centre.

Swallow Barn

COMMENDED

Milford Green, Woking GU24 8AU
☎ (01276) 856030
Fax (01276) 856030

Attractively converted farm buildings on the outskirts of Chobham village. Quiet and secluded. Convenient for Woking railway station, M3, M25, Heathrow, Ascot and famous golf courses.

Bedrooms: 1 double, 1 twin
Bathrooms: 2 private

Bed & breakfast per night:	£min	£max
Single	30.00	
Double	45.00	

Parking for 4

WORTHING

West Sussex
Map ref 2D3

Town in the West Sussex countryside and by the South Coast, with excellent shopping and many pavement cafes and restaurants. Attractions include the award-winning Museum and Art Gallery, beautiful gardens, pier, elegant town houses, Cissbury Ring hill fort and the South Downs.
Tourist Information Centre ☎ (01903) 210022

School House

Listed COMMENDED

11 Ambrose Place, Worthing
BN11 1PZ
☎ (01903) 206823
Fax (01903) 821902

Elegant town centre, 18th C Regency house with gardens. Minutes from sea, shops and 2 theatres. Quiet. Parking. Close to South Downs, Gatwick, Arundel and Chichester.

Bedrooms: 2 twin
Bathrooms: 1 private, 1 public

Bed & breakfast per night:	£min	£max
Single	20.00	28.00
Double	35.00	45.00

Parking for 2
Open March–July, September–November

Tudor Guest House

COMMENDED

5 Windsor Road, Worthing
BN11 2LU
☎ (01903) 210265 & 202042

Ideally situated! 1 minute from seafront, restaurants, pubs, entertainment, etc. Very friendly atmosphere, top class service. Comfortable bedrooms with free trays tea/coffee/chocolate. 3 satellite channels in all rooms. Parking on premises. En-suite rooms available. English or continental breakfast.

Bedrooms: 5 single, 3 double, 1 twin
Bathrooms: 3 en-suite, 1 public, 1 private shower

Bed & breakfast per night:	£min	£max
Single	15.00	17.50
Double	30.00	49.00

Parking for 5

WYE

Kent
Map ref 3B4

Well known for its agricultural and horticultural college. The Olantigh Tower, with its imposing front portico, is used as a setting for part of the Stour Music Festival held annually in June.

New Flying Horse Inn

COMMENDED

Upper Bridge Street, Wye, Ashford
TN25 5AN
☎ (01233) 812297
Fax (01233) 813487

17th C former coaching inn with oak beams and gleaming brasses. Ideal for touring and walking the Kent countryside and coast. Half board daily prices are based on a minimum 2-night stay.

Bedrooms: 1 single, 5 double, 3 twin, 1 triple
Bathrooms: 10 en-suite

Bed & breakfast per night:	£min	£max
Single	38.50	41.00
Double	49.50	52.00

Half board per person:	£min	£max
Daily	37.50	40.00

Lunch available
Evening meal 1830 (last orders 2130)
Parking for 30
Cards accepted: Amex, Mastercard, Visa, Switch/Delta

WELCOME HOST

This is a nationally recognised customer care programme which aims to promote the highest standards of service and a warm welcome. Establishments who are taking part in this initiative are indicated by the symbol.

FARM HOLIDAY GROUPS

This section of the guide lists groups specialising in farm and country-based holidays. Most offer bed and breakfast accommodation (some with evening meal) and self-catering accommodation.

To obtain further details of individual properties please contact the group(s) direct, indicating the time of year when the accommodation is required and the number of people to be accommodated. You may find the Accommodation Coupons towards the back of this guide helpful when making contact. The cost of sending out brochures is high, and the groups would appreciate written enquiries being accompanied by a stamped and addressed envelope (at least 228mm x 127mm). The 'b&b' prices shown are per person per night; the self-catering prices are weekly terms per unit.

The symbol before the name of a group indicates that it is a member of the Farm Holiday Bureau, set up by the Royal Agricultural Society of England in conjunction with the English Tourist Board.

Bed & Breakfast (GB)
Contact: Reservation Service,
96 Bell Street,
Henley-on-Thames,
Oxon RG9 1XS
Tel: Henley (01491) 578803
Fax: (01491) 410806
E-mail:
bookings@bedbreak.demon.co.uk
National reservations service for hundreds of B&B's and farmhouses throughout Britain (London, England, Scotland, Wales and Ireland).
500 properties offering bed and breakfast: £15.50-£49.50 b&b.
Short breaks also available.

Cheshire Farmhouse Accommodation
Contact: Mrs Joyce Percival
Henhull Hall, Welshmans Lane,
Nantwich, Cheshire CW5 6AD
Tel: Crewe (01270) 624158 or
Contact: Mrs Hazel Rush
Golden Cross Farm,
Siddington,
Nr Macclesfield,
Cheshire SK11 9JP
Tel: Congleton (01260) 224358
A group of farms offering first class accommodation, all within easy reach of the motorways and main Cheshire attractions.
23 properties offering bed and breakfast: £15-£24 b&b.
2 self-catering units:
low season (October-March)
£150-£250;
high season (April-September)
£160-£350.
Short breaks also available.

Heart of England
Contact: Rosemary Coleman
Clyffe Farm,
Tincleton, Dorchester,
Dorset DT2 8QR
Tel: Puddletown (01305) 848252
Fax: (01305) 848702
A group of country people offering character cottages in beautiful locations across Dorset. Personally supervised properties with excellent facilities. Ideal for walkers, golfers, cyclists, fishermen, or just viewing the beauty of Dorset and its heritage coastline.
3 properties offering bed and breakfast: £15-£22 b&b.
27 self-catering units:
low season (November-March)
£120-£200;

Continued overleaf

high season (April-October)
£200-£475.
Short breaks also available with some properties.

Let Devon Farms Accommodate You
c/o Court Barton,
Aveton Gifford,
Kingsbridge,
Devon TQ7 4LE
Tel: Kingsbridge (01548) 550055
Fax: (01548) 550312
Small and friendly places. Great hospitality. Self-catering, bed & breakfast or half board in quality assured accommodation on working farms. Many historic houses. Variety of rural locations from sandy beaches to moorland or gently rolling countryside. Free colour brochure, over 100 choices.
70 properties offering bed and breakfast: £13-£25 b&b.
37 self-catering units:
low season (October-March)
£75-£200;
high season (April-September)
£240-£600.
Short breaks also available.

Sherwood Forest
Contact: Fernie Palmer
Norton Grange Farm,
Norton,
Mansfield,
Nottinghamshire NG20 9LP
Tel: Mansfield (01623) 842666
Georgian stone listed farmhouse, set in the heart of Sherwood Forest. Ideally situated for overnight stays or touring the beautiful countryside and the many attractions in Nottinghamshire and Derbyshire.
1 property offering bed and breakfast: £16.50-£17.50 b&b.
Short breaks also available.

Somerset Farm Holiday Group
Contact: Mrs Hilary Millard
Double-Gate Farm,
Godney,
Nr Wells,
Somerset BA5 1RX
Tel: Glastonbury (01458) 832217
Fax: (01458) 835612
Genuine working farms in the heart of beautiful Somerset, all offering exceptional accommodation and a friendliness hard to find anywhere else. Come and try us. You won't be disappointed!
16 properties offering bed and breakfast: from £16 b&b.
18 self-catering units:
low season from £130;
high season from £180.

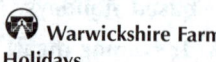

Warwickshire Farm Holidays
The Secretary,
Crandon House,
Avon Dassett, Leamington Spa,
Warwickshire CV33 0AA
Tel: (01295) 770652
Fax: (01295) 770652
A warm welcome at farmhouses offering serviced and self-catering accommodation in comfortable and homely surroundings, situated in historic and picturesque 'Shakespeare country'. Caravan and tent pitches also available.
24 properties offering bed and breakfast: £12-£27 b&b.
25 self-catering units:
low season (October-April)
£70-£350;
high season (May-September)
£80-£450.
Short breaks also available.

CHECK THE MAPS

The colour maps at the back of this guide show all the cities, towns and villages for which you will find accommodation entries.

Refer to the town index to find the page on which it is listed.

GROUP AND YOUTH SECTION

Most of the accommodation establishments listed in this guide are particularly suitable for people looking for relatively low-cost places to stay in England. Some establishments make a special point of providing safe, budget-priced accommodation for young people, for families or for large groups. These places, ranging from Youth Hostels, YMCA and YWCA residences and budget and student hotels to the seasonally available campuses of universities and colleges, are listed individually in the pages which follow.

Information on organisations which specialise in accommodation for young people, families and groups is given below - please contact them direct for further details.

Youth Hostels

The Youth Hostels Association (England and Wales) provides basic accommodation, usually in single-sex bunk-bedded rooms or dormitories, with self-catering facilities. Most hostels also provide low-cost meals or snacks. At the time of going to press, a night's stay at a Youth Hostel will cost between £3.85 and £17.20 (under 18) and between £5.65 and £20.50 (over 18).

In spite of the word 'youth' in the name, there is in fact no upper age limit. Indeed, many Youth Hostels also offer family accommodation, either in self-contained annexes (with kitchen, living room and bathroom) or by letting the smaller, four-to-six bed dormitories as private units. Groups are very welcome at Youth Hostels, whether for educational or leisure pursuits: some hostels offer field study facilities and many more have classrooms. The YHA also offers a wide range of adventure holidays and special interest breaks.

Youth Hostels - from medieval castles to shepherds' huts - can be found all over the country, both in countryside and coastal locations and in towns and cities. You need to be a member of the YHA in order to take advantage of the facilities. Membership entitles you to use not only the 240 hostels in England and Wales but also the thousands of Youth Hostels in other parts of the British Isles and around the world. Membership costs £5.00 (under 18) or £10.00 (over 18). Family membership is available at £10.00 (single-parent family) or £20.00 (two parent family). Prices valid from 1st January 1998.

Further information from:
Youth Hostels Association
Trevelyan House,
8 St Stephen's Hill, St Albans,
Hertfordshire AL1 2DY
Tel: (01727) 855215
Fax: (01727) 844126

YWCA and YMCA

The Young Women's Christian Association, founded in 1855, has grown into the world's largest women's organisation. Among its many activities is the running of over 60 houses in Britain which offer safe, reasonably priced self-catering accommodation, mostly in single rooms, either on a permanent or temporary basis.

Most houses take short-stay visitors only during the summer months. However, some of the houses do accept short-stay visitors all the year round. Although the word 'women' appears in the name of the organisation, many of the residences now take men and boys as well as mothers and girls.

The Young Men's Christian Association (YMCA), founded in 1844, operates on much the same basis as the YWCA, taking people of both sexes at its more than 70 residences around the country either on a permanent or short-stay basis.

Further information from:

YWCA HQ
Clarendon House,
52 Cornmarket Street,
Oxford OX1 3EJ
Tel: (01865) 726110

YMCA
National Council,
640 Forest Road,
Walthamstow,
London E17 3DZ
Tel: (0181) 520 5599

Universities and Colleges

Accommodation in universities and colleges offer excellent value for money with numerous venues spread throughout England, Scotland, Wales and Northern Ireland which provide city centre, seaside and countryside campus locations. This type of accommodation is available for individuals, families and groups and is suitable for leisure trips, conferences and seminars. There are over 100,000 single bedrooms available (with no single supplements) and over 20,000 ensuite rooms with a number of twin and family rooms together with self-catering flats.

Availability is mainly during the academic vacation during the summer from June to September, Easter and some Christmas availability. Some universities provide accommodation throughout the year.

For relaxation, there is a wide choice of recreational facilities, with most venues providing TV rooms, bars and restaurants and a variety of sporting activities, ranging from tennis, squash and swimming to team sports. Activity and special interest holidays are also on offer.

Further information from:

British Universities Accommodation Consortium (BUAC)
Box No 1530, University Park,
Nottingham NG7 2RD
Tel: (0115) 950 4571
Fax: (0115) 942 2505
Email:
carole.formon@nottingham.ac.uk

Connect Venues
The Workstation,
Paternoster Row,
Sheffield S1 2BX
Tel: (0114) 249 3090
Fax: (0114) 249 3091

Other Accommodation

In addition to the above main providers on a countrywide basis of budget accommodation for young people and groups, there are, of course, the many individual student and budget hotels around England and also such places as outdoor and field study centres. Some of these feature in the following pages but for more information on what is available in a particular area, please contact a local Tourist Information Centre.

AT-A-GLANCE SYMBOLS

Symbols at the end of each accommodation entry give useful information about services and facilities. A key to symbols can be found inside the back cover flap.

Keep this open for easy reference.

WHERE TO STAY (GROUP & YOUTH)

Accommodation entries in this section are listed in alphabetical order of place name, and then in alphabetical order of establishment.

Map references refer to the colour location maps at the back of this guide. The first number indicates the map to use; the letter and number which follow refer to the grid reference on the map.

At-a-glance symbols at the end of each accommodation entry give useful information about services and facilities. A key to symbols can be found inside the back cover flap. Keep this open for easy reference.

AIRTON

North Yorkshire
Map ref 4B1

Charming limestone dales village at the head of the River Aire.

Airton Quaker Hostel

The Nook, Airton, Skipton
Contact: Mr & Mrs G Parker, The Nook, Airton, Skipton, North Yorkshire BD23 4AE
☎ (01729) 830263

Converted stable attached to an historic Quaker meeting house built in 1690, in a peaceful village in the Yorkshire Dales.

Bedrooms: 1 double/twin, 1 quadruple, 1 dormitory. Total number of beds: 14
Bathrooms: 1 public

Bed only per person:	£min	£max
Daily	4.75	

WELCOME HOST

This is a nationally recognised customer care programme which aims to promote the highest standards of service and a warm welcome. Establishments who are taking part in this initiative are indicated by the symbol.

AMBLESIDE

Cumbria
Map ref 5A3

Market town situated at the head of Lake Windermere and surrounded by fells. The historic town centre is now a conservation area and the country around Ambleside is rich in historic and literary associations. Good centre for touring, walking and climbing.
Tourist Information Centre ☎ (015394) 32582

YHA Ambleside

Waterhead, Ambleside LA22 0EU
☎ (015394) 32304
Fax (015394) 34408
Contact: Mr Simon Ainley

Situated on the shores of Windermere, with own waterfront and jetty. Panoramic views of Lakeland fells. Family rooms, friendly atmosphere, dining room overlooking lake.

Minimum age 5
Bedrooms: 7 double/twin, 17 triple, 7 quadruple, 21 dormitories. Total number of beds: 227
Bathrooms: 20 public

Bed only per person:	£min	£max
Daily	7.20	10.60

Bed & breakfast per person:	£min	£max
Daily	10.15	13.55

Full board per person:	£min	£max
Weekly	71.05	94.85

Lunch available
Evening meal 1730 (last orders 1930)
Parking for 40
Cards accepted: Mastercard, Visa, Switch/Delta

ARNSIDE

Cumbria
Map ref 5A3

Small coastal village in an Area of Outstanding Natural Beauty, with spectacular views across the Kent Estuary of the Lakeland hills. Excellent base for bird-watching. The incoming tide creates an impressive tidal bore.

YHA Arnside

Oakfield Lodge, Redhills Road, Arnside, Carnforth, Lancashire LA5 0AT
☎ (01524) 761781
Fax (01524) 762589
Contact: Mr John Gibbs

A mellow Tudor-style Edwardian house built for a wealthy doctor. Transformed in 1978 to a hostel and field study centre.

Minimum age 5
Bedrooms: 2 double/twin, 8 quadruple, 5 dormitories. Total number of beds: 72
Bathrooms: 6 public

Bed only per person:	£min	£max
Daily	5.95	8.85

Bed & breakfast per person:	£min	£max
Daily	8.90	11.80

Full board per person:	£min	£max
Weekly	109.00	130.00

Continued ▶

ARNSIDE

Continued

Lunch available
Evening meal 1900 (last orders 1900)
Parking for 10
Cards accepted: Mastercard, Visa, Switch/Delta

ARUNDEL

West Sussex
Map ref 2D3

Picturesque, historic town on the River Arun, dominated by Arundel Castle, home of the Dukes of Norfolk. There are many 18th C houses, the Toy and Military Museum, Wildfowl and Wetlands Centre and Museum and Heritage Centre.
Tourist Information Centre ☎ (01903) 882268

YHA Arundel

Warningcamp, Arundel BN18 9QY
☎ (01903) 882204
Fax (01903) 882776
Contact: The Warden
Georgian building outside ancient town dominated by castle and close to Sussex Downs.
Minimum age 5
Bedrooms: Total number of beds: 60
Bathrooms: 5 public

Bed only per person:	£min	£max
Daily	5.95	8.85

Bed & breakfast per person:	£min	£max
Daily	8.90	11.80

Full board per person:	£min	£max
Weekly	116.90	137.20

Evening meal 1900 (last orders 1800)
Parking for 14
Open April–October
Cards accepted: Mastercard, Visa, Switch/Delta

Information on accommodation listed in this guide has been supplied by the proprietors. As changes may occur you are advised to check details at the time of booking.

BARDON MILL

Northumberland
Map ref 5B2

Small hamlet midway between Haydon Bridge and Haltwhistle, within walking distance of Vindolanda, an excavated Roman settlement, and near the best stretches of Hadrian's Wall.

YHA Once Brewed

Once Brewed, Military Road, Bardon Mill, Hexham NE47 7AN
☎ (01434) 344360
Fax (01434) 344045
Contact: Mr & Mrs Keen
Purpose-built hostel. Central heating, full meal service, dormitories or family rooms.
Bedrooms: 1 double/twin, 2 triple, 13 quadruple, 5 dormitories. Total number of beds: 87
Bathrooms: 6 public

Bed only per person:	£min	£max
Daily	5.90	8.75

Bed & breakfast per person:	£min	£max
Daily	8.85	11.70

Full board per person:	£min	£max
Weekly	61.95	81.90

Evening meal 1800 (last orders 1900)
Parking for 80
Open February–November
Cards accepted: Mastercard, Visa, Switch/Delta

BASSENTHWAITE

Cumbria
Map ref 5A2

Standing in an idyllic setting, nestled at the foot of Skiddaw and Ullock Pike, this village is just a mile from Bassenthwaite Lake, the one true "lake" in the Lake District. The area is visited by many varieties of migrating birds.

Bassenthwaite Parish Rooms

Bassenthwaite, Keswick
Contact: Mrs Alison Trafford, Booking Secretary, Bassenthwaite Parish Rooms, Management Committee, Bassenthwaite Hall Farm, Bassenthwaite, Keswick, Cumbria CA12 4QP
☎ (017687) 76393
Village hall. School Road off A591. Minimum booking is for 12 people, 3 nights.
For groups only
Bedrooms: Total number of beds: 50
Bathrooms: 1 en-suite, 3 public

Bed only per person:	£min	£max
Daily	2.00	2.00

Parking for 10

BATH

Bath & North East Somerset
Map ref 2B2

Georgian spa city beside the River Avon. Important Roman site with impressive reconstructed baths, uncovered in 19th C. Bath Abbey built on site of monastery where first king of England was crowned (AD 973). Fine architecture in mellow local stone. Pump Room and museums.
Tourist Information Centre ☎ (01225) 477101

The City of Bath YMCA

International House, Broad Street Place, Bath BA1 5LH
☎ (01225) 460471
Fax (01225) 462065
Email: info@ymca.u-net.com.
Contact: Mr A Teasdale
Open to both sexes and all ages. Centrally located and only minutes away from Bath's major attractions. A convenient base for city and West Country tours. Half board weekly rates available for individuals and groups.
Minimum age 17
Bedrooms: 38 single, 36 double/twin, 8 triple, 3 dormitories. Total number of beds: 190
Bathrooms: 30 public

Bed & breakfast per person:	£min	£max
Daily	10.00	14.50

Lunch available
Evening meal 1700 (last orders 1900)
Cards accepted: Mastercard, Visa, Switch/Delta

A key to symbols can be found inside the back cover flap.

For further information on accommodation establishments use the coupons at the back of this guide.

BEER

Devon
Map ref 1D2

Formerly noted for lace-making and smuggling, this picturesque fishing village lies close to some of Devon's most striking cliff scenery at Beer Head. Smugglers' caves. Quarries to west of village were worked in Roman times.

YHA Beer

Bovey Combe, Townsend, Beer, Seaton EX12 3LL
☎ (01297) 20296
Fax (01297) 23690
Large house standing in landscaped grounds, on hillside to the west of a picturesque fishing village.
Minimum age 7
Bedrooms: 5 quadruple, 3 dormitories. Total number of beds: 40
Bathrooms: 4 public

Bed only per person:	£min	£max
Daily	5.95	8.85

Bed & breakfast per person:	£min	£max
Daily	8.90	11.80

Full board per person:	£min	£max
Weekly	116.70	137.20

Lunch available
Evening meal 1900 (last orders 1815)
Parking for 15
Open April–October
Cards accepted: Mastercard, Visa
50

BELFORD

Northumberland
Map ref 5B1

Small market town on the old coaching road, close to the coast, the Scottish border and the north-east flank of the Cheviots. Built mostly in stone and very peaceful now that the A1 has by-passed the town, Belford makes an ideal centre for excursions to the moors and coast.

The Outdoor Trust

Windy Gyle, Belford
Contact: Mr P A Clark, The Outdoor Trust, Windy Gyle, Belford, Northumberland NE70 7QE
☎ (01668) 213289
Fax (01668) 213289
Email: outdoor@demon.co.uk
Outdoor activity courses for individuals, families and groups. Expert instruction, excellent equipment and locations. Quality accommodation and food. Approved by RYA, BCU and AHOEC.
Bedrooms: 1 double/twin, 1 triple, 5 dormitories. Total number of beds: 45
Bathrooms: 8 public

Bed & breakfast per person:	£min	£max
Daily	10.50	

Lunch available
Evening meal from 1830
Parking for 5
42

BLAXHALL

Suffolk
Map ref 3C2

Unspoilt village featured in the writings on country lore of George Ewart Evans. Sheep used to graze on the former common lands beside the River Alde and smuggling was popular.

YHA Blaxhall

Heath Walk, Blaxhall, Woodbridge IP12 2EA
☎ (01728) 688206
Fax (01728) 689191
Old school near Suffolk heritage coast and heathland. Home of author George Ewart Evans whose wife was headmistress of the school.
Bedrooms: 7 dormitories. Total number of beds: 40
Bathrooms: 2 public

Bed only per person:	£min	£max
Daily	5.95	8.85

Bed & breakfast per person:	£min	£max
Daily	8.90	11.80

Full board per person:	£min	£max
Weekly	116.90	137.20

Evening meal 1900 (last orders 1800)
Open March–November
Cards accepted: Mastercard, Visa
25

The symbols in each entry give information about services and facilities. A key to these symbols appears at the back of this guide.

BOSCASTLE

Cornwall
Map ref 1B2

Small, unspoilt village in Valency Valley. Active as a port until onset of railway era, its natural harbour affords rare shelter on this wild coast. Attractions include spectacular blow-hole, Celtic field strips, part-Norman church. Nearby St Juliot Church was restored by Thomas Hardy.

YHA Boscastle Harbour

Palace Stables, Boscastle PL35 0HD
☎ (01840) 250287
Fax (01840) 250615
In superb position on harbour edge where Valency River enters National Trust preserved fishing harbour.
Minimum age 5
Bedrooms: 4 dormitories. Total number of beds: 25
Bathrooms: 3 public

Bed only per person:	£min	£max
Daily	5.35	8.00

Bed & breakfast per person:	£min	£max
Daily	8.30	10.95

Full board per person:	£min	£max
Weekly	112.70	131.25

Evening meal 1900 (last orders 1800)
Open March–October
Cards accepted: Mastercard, Visa

BRADFORD

West Yorkshire
Map ref 4B1

City founded on wool, with fine Victorian and modern buildings. Attractions include the cathedral, city hall, Cartwright Hall, Lister Park, Moorside Mills Industrial Museum and National Museum of Photography, Film and Television.
Tourist Information Centre ☎ (01274) 753678

University of Bradford

Bradford
Contact: Ms A Milton & Ms E Fazakerley, Conference Officer, University of Bradford, Bradford, West Yorkshire BD7 1DP
☎ (01274) 384887
Fax (01274) 385505
Email: conference-office@bradford.ac.uk
Attractive, compact campus in a

Continued ▶

BRADFORD

Continued

convenient location for touring the peaks, dales and Bronte country. Sports facilities including swimming pool, sauna and solarium.
Minimum age 10
Bedrooms: 1300 single. Total number of beds: 1300
Bathrooms: 135 en-suite, 200 public

Bed only per person:	£min	£max
Daily	12.92	30.73

Bed & breakfast per person:	£min	£max
Daily	17.57	36.00

Lunch available
Evening meal from 1800
Parking for 1000
Open January, March–April, June–September, December
13 950

BRIGHTON & HOVE

East Sussex
Map ref 2D3

Brighton's attractions include the Royal Pavilion, Volks Electric Railway, Sea Life Centre and Marina Village, Conference Centre and "The Lanes" and several theatres. Neighbouring Hove is a resort in its own right.
Tourist Information Centre ☎ (01273) 323755; for Hove (01273) 778087

University of Brighton

Moulsecoomb Place, Lewes Road, Brighton, East Sussex
Contact: Mrs Evelyn Mohan, University of Brighton, Conference Office, Moulsecoomb Place, Lewes Road, Brighton, East Sussex BN2 46A
☎ (01273) 643167 & 643168
Fax (01273) 642610
The university has a variety of residential accommodation in Brighton and Eastbourne available to groups, conference organisers and self-catering visitors in July, August and September.
For groups only
Bedrooms: 1000 single
Bathrooms: 750 en-suite

Bed only per person:	£min	£max
Daily	10.00	15.00

Bed & breakfast per person:	£min	£max
Daily	17.50	19.75

Lunch available
Evening meal 1800 (last orders 1900)
Parking for 300
Open July–September
Cards accepted: Amex, Mastercard, Visa
250

BRISTOL

Map ref 2A2

Famous for maritime links, historic harbour, Georgian terraces and Brunel's Clifton suspension bridge. Many attractions including SS Great Britain, Bristol Zoo, museums and art galleries and top name entertainments. Events include Balloon Fiesta and Regatta.
Tourist Information Centre ☎ (0117) 926 0767

University of Bristol

Senate House, Tyndall Avenue, Bristol
Contact: Ms Jenny Bowden, University of Bristol, Conference Office, The Hawthorns, Woodland Road,, Bristol BS8 1UQ
☎ (0117) 9238028
Fax (0117) 9238265
Email: conference-office@bris.ac.uk
We have 10 residences in city, suburban or rural locations, including acres of historic gardens.
For groups only
Minimum age 12
Bedrooms: 1200 single, 25 double/twin. Total number of beds: 1250
Bathrooms: 210 en-suite, 425 public

Bed & breakfast per person:	£min	£max
Daily	17.65	37.60

Lunch available
Parking for 60
Open March–April, June–September
1000

BURLEY

Hampshire
Map ref 2B3

Attractive centre from which to explore the south-west part of the New Forest. There is an ancient earthwork on Castle Hill nearby, which also offers good views.

YHA Burley

Cottesmore House, Cott Lane, Burley, Ringwood BH24 4BB
☎ (01425) 403233
Fax (01425) 403233
Contact: The Manager
A comfortable and friendly hostel in spacious grounds where the forest comes up to the gate.
Minimum age 5
Bedrooms: 1 quadruple, 4 dormitories. Total number of beds: 36
Bathrooms: 3 public

Bed only per person:	£min	£max
Daily	5.95	8.85

Bed & breakfast per person:	£min	£max
Daily	8.90	11.80

Full board per person:	£min	£max
Weekly	116.90	137.20

Lunch available
Evening meal from 1900
Parking for 10
Open February–December
Cards accepted: Mastercard, Visa

CAMBRIDGE

Cambridgeshire
Map ref 2D1

A most important and beautiful city on the River Cam with 31 colleges forming one of the oldest universities in the world. Numerous museums, good shopping centre, restaurants, theatres, cinema and fine bookshops.
Tourist Information Centre ☎ (01223) 322640

Clare College

Box CL/C92, Memorial Court, Queens Road, Cambridge CB3 9AJ
☎ (01223) 333203
Fax (01223) 357664
Email: aw215@cam.ac.uk
Contact: Ms Ann Waldman

Second oldest of the Cambridge colleges and peacefully located close to the city centre. Accommodation is for groups and conferences only - regrettably no individual reservations.
For groups only
Minimum age 18
Bedrooms: 125 single, 5 double/twin. Total number of beds: 150
Bathrooms: 51 public

Bed & breakfast per person:	£min	£max
Daily	27.50	35.00

Lunch available

Evening meal 1830 (last orders 2000)
Parking for 20
Open April, July–September
S TV 80 SP

CANTERBURY

Kent
Map ref 3B3

Place of pilgrimage since the martyrdom of Becket in 1170 and the site of Canterbury Cathedral. Visit St Augustine's Abbey, St Martin's (the oldest church in England), Royal Museum and Art Gallery and the Canterbury Tales. Nearby is Howletts Wild Animal Park. Good shopping centre.
Tourist Information Centre ☎ (01227) 451026

UKC Hospitality

Tanglewood, The University,
Canterbury CT2 7LX
☎ (01227) 828000
Fax (01227) 828019
Email: conferencecanterbury
@ukc.ac.uk
Contact: Mr Russell Bodycomb

Flexible and comfortable accommodation facilities in one of 4 colleges in attractively situated parkland campus overlooking the cathedral. Value-for-money self-catering in 5/6-bedded houses is also available - ideal for families. Sports facilities.
Minimum age 10
Bedrooms: 1490 single,
31 double/twin. Total number of beds: 1552
Bathrooms: 268 en-suite, 160 public

Bed & breakfast per person:	£min	£max
Daily	15.90	24.40

Lunch available
Evening meal 1800 (last orders 1900)
Parking for 1200
Open March–April, July–September
Cards accepted: Mastercard, Visa
10 S TV 392
OAP SP T

Please mention this guide when making your booking.

CHALFONT ST GILES

Buckinghamshire
Map ref 2D2

Pretty, old village in wooded Chiltern Hills yet only 20 miles from London and a good base for visiting the city. Excellent base for Windsor, Henley, the Thames Valley, Oxford and the Cotswolds.

Buckinghamshire College

Newland Park, Gorelands Lane,
Chalfont St Giles HP8 4AD
☎ (01494) 603064
Fax (01494) 603078
Email: julie.wainwright
@buckscol.ac.uk
Contact: Ms Julie Wainwright
15 minutes from M25, in 300 acres of parkland, at the centre of which is an 18th C manor house. Especially suitable for groups. Extensive catering and conference facilities.
For groups only
Bedrooms: 1050 single,
7 double/twin. Total number of beds: 1064
Bathrooms: 133 en-suite, 200 public

Bed only per person:	£min	£max
Daily	12.00	35.00

Bed & breakfast per person:	£min	£max
Daily	14.00	35.00

Full board per person:	£min	£max
Weekly	150.00	300.00

Lunch available
Evening meal 1700 (last orders 2000)
Parking for 800
Open June–September
Cards accepted: Mastercard, Visa
S TV 242
OAP SP

CHEDDAR

Somerset
Map ref 1D1

Large village at foot of Mendips just south of the spectacular Cheddar Gorge. Close by are Roman and Saxon sites and famous show caves. Traditional Cheddar cheese is still made here.

YHA Cheddar

Hillfield, Cheddar BS27 3HN
☎ (01934) 742494
Fax (01934) 744724
Contact: Mr Martin Allen
Modernised Victorian house in Mendip village, close to famous Gorge and caves. A special welcome given to families.
Minimum age 5
Bedrooms: 3 double/twin,
5 quadruple, 4 dormitories
Bathrooms: 4 public

Bed only per person:	£min	£max
Daily	5.95	8.85

Bed & breakfast per person:	£min	£max
Daily	8.90	11.80

Full board per person:	£min	£max
Weekly	116.90	137.20

Evening meal from 1830
Parking for 12
Open February–December
Cards accepted: Mastercard, Visa, Switch/Delta
UL S TV
SP T

CHORLEY

Lancashire
Map ref 4A1

Set between the Pennine moors and the Lancashire Plain, Chorley has been an important town since medieval times, with its "Flat-Iron" and covered markets. The rich heritage includes Astley Hall and Park, Hoghton Tower, Rivington Country Park and the Leeds-Liverpool Canal.

Lancashire College

Southport Road, Chorley PR7 1NB
☎ (01257) 276719
Fax (01257) 241370
Contact: Mrs A Bithell
Purpose-built adult residential college. Lounge/bar, well designed and equipped teaching suite and conference accommmodation.
For groups only
Minimum age 18
Bedrooms: 45 single. Total number of beds: 48
Bathrooms: 9 en-suite, 12 public

Bed & breakfast per person:	£min	£max
Daily	27.14	34.19

Lunch available
Evening meal from 1830
Parking for 100
Cards accepted: Mastercard, Visa, Switch/Delta
S 100 SP

The symbol after an establishment name indicates that it is a Regional Tourist Board member.

COVERACK

Cornwall
Map ref 1B3

Fishing village with thatched cottages on the Lizard Peninsula. Inland, Goonhilly Downs is an area of botanical importance. Three miles offshore are the notorious Manacles rocks, scene of numerous shipwrecks.

YHA Coverack

Parc Behan, School Hill, Coverack, Helston TR12 6SA
☎ (01326) 280687
Fax (01326) 280119
Large country house, the most southerly hostel in England. An interesting area for field studies. RYA windsurfing activities holidays.
Minimum age 5
Bedrooms: 2 quadruple, 4 dormitories. Total number of beds: 38
Bathrooms: 4 public

Bed only per person:	£min	£max
Daily	5.95	8.85

Bed & breakfast per person:	£min	£max
Daily	8.90	11.80

Full board per person:	£min	£max
Weekly	116.90	137.20

Evening meal 1900 (last orders 1900)
Parking for 12
Open March–October
Cards accepted: Mastercard, Visa
5

DURHAM

Durham
Map ref 5C2

Ancient city with its Norman castle and cathedral, now a World Heritage site, set on a bluff high over the Wear. A market and university town and regional centre, spreading beyond the market-place on both banks of the river.
Tourist Information Centre ☎ (0191) 384 3720

St Aidans College

University of Durham, Windmill Hill, Durham DH1 3LJ
☎ (0191) 374 3269
Fax (0191) 374 4749
Contact: Lt Cdr J C Bull
Modern college in beautiful landscaped gardens overlooking the cathedral. Comfortable standard and en-suite single and twin-bedded rooms, bar, TV lounge, free tennis. Adjacent golf-course.
Bedrooms: 293 single, 66 double/twin. Total number of beds: 425
Bathrooms: 94 en-suite, 48 public

Bed & breakfast per person:	£min	£max
Daily	14.00	28.00

Full board per person:	£min	£max
Weekly	160.00	230.00

Lunch available
Evening meal 1830 (last orders 1900)
Parking for 80
Open January, March–April, July–September, December
Cards accepted: Visa
250

Van Mildert College

University of Durham, Mill Hill Lane, Durham
Contact: Mr J Hirst, Van Mildert College, University of Durham, Durham DH1 3LH
☎ (0191) 374 3900
Fax (0191) 374 3974
College and conference centre in beautiful lakeside surroundings, adjacent to golf course, opposite Botanical Gardens. Half a mile from Durham Cathedral and Castle World Heritage Site. Families and groups welcome.
Minimum age 17
Bedrooms: 380 single, 21 double/twin. Total number of beds: 422
Bathrooms: 30 en-suite, 68 public

Bed only per person:	£min	£max
Daily	14.00	26.00

Bed & breakfast per person:	£min	£max
Daily	15.50	27.50

Full board per person:	£min	£max
Weekly	186.00	280.00

Lunch available
Evening meal from 1800
Parking for 100
Open March–April, July–September, December
400

For further information on accommodation establishments use the coupons at the back of this guide.

EARNLEY

West Sussex
Map ref 2C3

Village with a tiny church on a triangular green, and a butterfly and garden centre.

The Earnley Concourse

Earnley, Chichester PO20 7JL
☎ (01243) 670392
Fax (01243) 670832
Email: earnley@interalpha.co.uk
Contact: The Bookings Secretary
Well equipped residential centre for adults. Weekend and midweek courses in many subjects, as well as conference facilities.
Minimum age 16
Bedrooms: 20 single, 34 double/twin. Total number of beds: 88
Bathrooms: 54 en-suite, 3 public

Full board per person:	£min	£max
Weekly	288.00	410.00

Lunch available
Evening meal from 1900
Parking for 50
Cards accepted: Mastercard, Visa, Switch/Delta
80

EXFORD

Somerset
Map ref 1D1

Sheltered village on the River Exe close to Exmoor. Attractive old houses, shops and inns face the village green and the Methodist chapel has 2 windows by Burne-Jones. A footpath north-eastward leads to Dunkery Beacon, Exmoor's highest point.

YHA Exford

Exe Mead, Exford, Minehead TA24 7PU
☎ (01643) 831288
Fax (01643) 831650
Situated in the centre of Exmoor, with the River Exe flowing through the hostel grounds.
Minimum age 5
Bedrooms: 2 double/twin, 6 quadruple, 4 dormitories. Total number of beds: 51
Bathrooms: 3 en-suite, 3 public

Bed only per person:	£min	£max
Daily	5.95	8.85

Bed & breakfast per person:	£min	£max
Daily	8.90	11.80

Full board per person:	£min	£max
Weekly	116.90	137.20

Evening meal from 1900
Parking for 12
Open March–October
Cards accepted: Mastercard, Visa

FALMOUTH

Cornwall
Map ref 1B3

Busy port and fishing harbour, popular resort on the balmy Cornish Riviera. Henry VIII's Pendennis Castle faces St Mawes Castle across the broad natural harbour and yacht basin Carrick Roads, which receives 7 rivers.
Tourist Information Centre ☎ (01326) 312300

YHA Pendennis Castle

Pendennis Castle, Falmouth
TR11 4LP
☎ (01326) 311435
Fax (01326) 315473
Contact: Mr Francis Lawson
Hostel in Victorian barracks in grounds of Tudor castle. Rooms mostly 4 and 6 beds. Night storage heaters, TV and shower. Either self-catering or meals provided. Washing machine and tumble dryer.
Bedrooms: 4 double/twin, 11 quadruple, 4 dormitories. Total number of beds: 90
Bathrooms: 8 public

Bed only per person:	£min	£max
Daily	5.95	8.85

Bed & breakfast per person:	£min	£max
Daily	8.90	11.80

Full board per person:	£min	£max
Weekly	116.90	137.20

Lunch available
Evening meal from 1900
Parking for 50
Open February–November
Cards accepted: Mastercard, Visa, Switch/Delta

ACCESSIBILITY

Look for the symbols which indicate accessibility for wheelchair users. These are described in detail at the front of this guide.

GALMPTON

Devon
Map ref 1D2

YHA Maypool

Maypool, Brixham TQ5 0ET
☎ (01803) 842444
Fax (01803) 845939
Contact: Mr David Rowe
Built in 1883 for owner of local boatyard. Views of Kingswear and Dartmouth down through the Dart Valley.
Minimum age 5
Bedrooms: 1 triple, 2 quadruple, 10 dormitories. Total number of beds: 93
Bathrooms: 5 public

Bed only per person:	£min	£max
Daily	5.35	8.00

Bed & breakfast per person:	£min	£max
Daily	8.30	10.95

Full board per person:	£min	£max
Weekly	112.70	131.25

Evening meal from 1900
Parking for 40
Open March–October
Cards accepted: Mastercard, Visa, Switch/Delta

GIGGLESWICK

North Yorkshire
Map ref 5B3

Picturesque Pennine village of period stone cottages with ancient market cross, stocks and tithe barn. Parish church is dedicated to St Alkeda, an Anglo-Saxon saint. During restoration work the tomb of a 15th C knight with his horse was discovered.

Yorkshire Dales Field Centre

Holme Beck, Raines Road, Giggleswick, Settle BD24 OAQ
☎ (01729) 824180
Fax (01729) 824180
Contact: Mrs A Barbour

Comfortable dales barn in quiet corner of renowned village, Three Peaks area of Yorkshire Dales. Any group of 12 people-plus. Good food provided or self-catering basis.
For groups only
Bedrooms: 2 single, 2 quadruple, 4 dormitories. Total number of beds: 30
Bathrooms: 4 public

Bed only per person:	£min	£max
Daily	9.00	9.00

Bed & breakfast per person:	£min	£max
Daily	14.00	14.00

Full board per person:	£min	£max
Weekly	120.00	180.00

Evening meal 1730 (last orders 1930)
Parking for 8

GUESTLING

East Sussex
Map ref 3B4

Probably the meeting place of the governing body of the Cinque Ports, known as "Court Guestling". Three miles from Hastings.

YHA Hastings Guestling Hall

Rye Road, Guestling, Hastings
TN35 4LP
☎ (01424) 812373
Fax (01424) 814273
Contact: The Manager
Large house in countryside with views across the Channel. Three miles north east of historic Cinque Port and popular seaside resort of Hastings.
Bedrooms: 2 quadruple, 5 dormitories. Total number of beds: 50
Bathrooms: 3 public

Bed only per person:	£min	£max
Daily	5.95	8.85

Bed & breakfast per person:	£min	£max
Daily	8.90	11.80

Full board per person:	£min	£max
Weekly	116.90	137.20

Evening meal 1900 (last orders 1800)
Parking for 20
Open February–December
Cards accepted: Mastercard, Visa

HARROGATE

North Yorkshire
Map ref 4B1

A major conference, exhibition and shopping centre, renowned for its spa heritage and award winning floral displays, spacious parks and gardens. Famous for antiques, toffee, fine shopping and excellent tea shops, also its Royal Pump Rooms and Baths.
Tourist Information Centre ☎ (01423) 537300

West End Outdoor Centre

West End, Summerbridge, Harrogate
Contact: Mrs M Verity, West End Outdoor Centre, Whitmoor Farm, West End, Summerbridge, Harrogate, North Yorkshire HG3 4BA
☎ (01943) 880207
Fax (01943) 880207
Self-catering bunkhouse with panoramic views over Thruscross reservoir. Well-appointed facilities, 12 miles from Harrogate and Skipton, 30 miles from York. Tourist Board inspected.
Bedrooms: 4 double/twin, 4 quadruple, 1 dormitory. Total number of beds: 30
Bathrooms: 1 en-suite, 4 public

Bed only per person:	£min	£max
Daily	5.00	7.00

Parking for 15
30

HASSOCKS

West Sussex
Map ref 2D3

Small residential town with views to the South Downs.

Stafford House

91 Keymer Road, Hassocks BN6 8QJ
☎ (01273) 845530
Contact: Mrs Barbara Lees
Residential and day course centre, group bookings only. Minimum 15-45 guests for residential, 10-25 for self-catering.
For groups only
Bedrooms: 31 single, 4 double/twin, 2 triple. Total number of beds: 45
Bathrooms: 7 public

Bed only per person:	£min	£max
Daily		10.70

Bed & breakfast per person:	£min	£max
Daily		13.80

Full board per person:	£min	£max
Weekly		264.00

Lunch available
Evening meal (last orders 1830)
Parking for 48
60

HATFIELD

Hertfordshire
Map ref 2D1

The old town is dominated by the great Jacobean Hatfield House, built for Robert Cecil and still in the Cecil family. It has many interesting exhibits and extensive gardens open to the public.

University of Hertfordshire

College Lane, Hatfield
Contact: Mrs Tracey Thrower, University of Hertfordshire, College Lane, Hatfield, Hertfordshire AL10 9AB
☎ (01707) 284007
Fax (01707) 284057
Campus holiday accommodation in 3-and 5-person flats and 7-bedroom houses. All are self-contained units with fully-equipped kitchen and private bathroom. Hatfield is only 22 miles from London. Please note: prices below are for self-catering only per week.
Minimum age 18
Bedrooms: 800 single, 40 double/twin. Total number of beds: 880
Bathrooms: 90 en-suite, 2 public

	£min	£max
Weekly	190.00	360.00

Lunch available
Evening meal 1800 (last orders 2030)
Parking for 970
Open July–September
Cards accepted: Mastercard, Visa, Switch/Delta
420

Establishments should be open throughout the year, unless otherwise stated.

The symbol after an establishment name indicates that it is a Regional Tourist Board member.

HUNSTANTON

Norfolk
Map ref 3B1

Seaside resort which faces the Wash. The shingle and sand beach is backed by striped cliffs and many unusual fossils can be found here. The town is predominantly Victorian. The Oasis family leisure centre has indoor and outdoor pools.
Tourist Information Centre ☎ (01485) 532610

YHA Hunstanton

15 Avenue Road, Hunstanton PE36 5BW
☎ (01485) 532061
Fax (01485) 532632
Detached Victorian house in seaside resort on the Wash.
Bedrooms: 2 triple, 3 quadruple, 4 dormitories. Total number of beds: 46
Bathrooms: 4 public

Bed only per person:	£min	£max
Daily	5.95	8.85

Bed & breakfast per person:	£min	£max
Daily	8.90	11.80

Full board per person:	£min	£max
Weekly	116.90	137.20

Lunch available
Evening meal 1900 (last orders 1830)
Open March–December
Cards accepted: Mastercard, Visa
40

IRONBRIDGE

Shropshire
Map ref 4A3

Small town on the Severn where the Industrial Revolution began. It has the world's first iron bridge built in 1779. The Ironbridge Gorge Museum, of exceptional interest, comprises a rebuilt turn-of-the-century town and sites spread over 6 square miles.
Tourist Information Centre ☎ (01952) 432166

YHA Ironbridge Gorge

John Rose Building, High Street, Coalport, Telford TF8 7HT
☎ (01952) 433281
Fax (01952) 433166
Contact: Mr & Mrs A Dyde
Two sites in the Gorge offer budget accommodation for groups, families

and individuals. Meeting rooms available with full catering service.
Minimum age 5
Bedrooms: 21 dormitories. Total number of beds: 97
Bathrooms: 10 public

Bed only per person:	£min	£max
Daily	6.50	9.70

Bed & breakfast per person:	£min	£max
Daily	9.45	12.65

Full board per person:	£min	£max
Weekly	66.15	88.55

Lunch available
Evening meal from 1900
Parking for 6
Open February–November
Cards accepted: Mastercard, Visa, Switch/Delta
60

KEMSING

Kent
Map ref 2D2

YHA Kemsing

Cleves, Church Lane, Kemsing, Sevenoaks TN15 6LU
☎ (01732) 761341
Fax (01732) 763044
Contact: The Manager
19th C vicarage close to Kemsing church, in very attractive and extensive grounds.
Minimum age 5
Bedrooms: 8 dormitories. Total number of beds: 50
Bathrooms: 4 public

Bed only per person:	£min	£max
Daily	5.95	8.85

Bed & breakfast per person:	£min	£max
Daily	8.90	11.80

Full board per person:	£min	£max
Weekly	116.90	137.20

Evening meal 1900 (last orders 1900)
Parking for 10
Open February–December
Cards accepted: Mastercard, Visa
5 30

For further information on accommodation establishments use the coupons at the back of this guide.

KESWICK

Cumbria
Map ref 5A3

Beautifully positioned town beside Derwentwater and below the mountains of Skiddaw and Blencathra. Excellent base for walking, climbing, watersports and touring. Motor-launches operate on Derwentwater and motor boats, rowing boats and canoes can be hired.
Tourist Information Centre
☎ (017687) 72645

Calvert Trust, Keswick

Little Crosthwaite, Underskiddaw, Keswick CA12 4QD
☎ (017687) 72254
Fax (017687) 73941
Contact: Mr J Crosbie
A converted farmstead specially adapted for people with disabilities. Wide range of outdoor activities. Accessible self-catering cottages also available.
Minimum age 8
Bedrooms: 4 single, 8 double/twin, 4 triple, 2 quadruple, 2 dormitories. Total number of beds: 41
Bathrooms: 4 en-suite, 10 public

Full board per person:	£min	£max
Weekly	140.00	225.00

Lunch available
Evening meal from 1800
Parking for 20
8 170

KIELDER FOREST

Northumberland
Map ref 5B1

City of Newcastle Outdoor Education Service

"Kielder Log Cabins', Little Whickhope, Kielder Forest, Northumberland
Contact: Mr G Little, City of Newcastle Outdoor, Education Centre, 121 Trewhitt Road, Heaton, Newcastle upon Tyne, NE6 5DY NE6 5DY
☎ (0191) 265 1311
Fax (0191) 276 586
2 x 16 berth Scandinavian log chalets, full double glazing, tumble dryer in each chalet. Separate male and female toilet facilities and showers. Chalets are on private site overlooking the reservoir.
For groups only
Bedrooms: 2 double/twin, 4 quadruple, 2 dormitories. Total number of beds: 32
Bathrooms: 4 public

Bed only per person:	£min	£max
Daily	6.20	7.70

Parking for 10
8

LINCOLN

Lincolnshire
Map ref 4C2

Ancient city dominated by the magnificent 11th C cathedral with its triple towers. A Roman gateway is still used and there are medieval houses lining narrow, cobbled streets. Other attractions include the Norman castle, several museums and the Usher Gallery.
Tourist Information Centre ☎ (01522) 529828

YHA Lincoln

77 South Park, Lincoln LN5 8ES
☎ (01522) 522076
Fax (01522) 567424
Contact: Mr H Yardley
Good home cooking is the hallmark of this Victorian villa on the outskirts of Lincoln. Families, individuals and groups are all welcome.
Bedrooms: 2 double/twin, 1 triple, 1 quadruple, 5 dormitories. Total number of beds: 50
Bathrooms: 4 public

Bed only per person:	£min	£max
Daily	5.95	8.85

Bed & breakfast per person:	£min	£max
Daily	8.90	11.80

Full board per person:	£min	£max
Weekly	110.95	137.20

Evening meal 1900 (last orders 1800)
Parking for 8
Open February–December
Cards accepted: Mastercard, Visa, Switch/Delta
40

WELCOME HOST

This is a nationally recognised customer care programme which aims to promote the highest standards of service and a warm welcome. Establishments who are taking part in this initiative are indicated by the symbol.

LONDON

Colour maps 6 & 7 at the back of the guide show place names and London Postal Area Codes and will help you locate accommodation in your chosen area of London

Aedis Accommodation

86 Balham Park Road, London
SW12 8EA
☎ (0181) 672 7656
Contact: Mr K F Munn
Furnished bed sitting rooms with own kitchenettes. Quiet street with no parking restrictions. 5 minutes' walk to shops, 10 minutes to central London by public transport.
Minimum age 5
Bedrooms: 4 single, 2 double/twin.
Total number of beds: 8
Bathrooms: 1 public

Bed only per person:	£min	£max
Daily	5.00	25.00

8

Binnie Court

40 Greenwich High Road,
Greenwich, London
Contact: Mr Paul Turton, Beaver Housing Society, Beaver House, Kivas Hall Mews, London SE13 5JQ
☎ (0181) 297 7030
Fax (0181) 297 7012
Self-catering student accommodation, recently refurbished, close to Greenwich centre and only 5 miles from central London.
Bedrooms: 80 single, 38 double/twin

Bed only per person:	£min	£max
Daily	10.00	12.00

Parking for 23
Open July–September

Campbell House

Taviton Street, London WC1H 0BX
☎ (0171) 391 1479
Fax (0171) 388 0060
Contact: Mr. R L Sparvell
Specially reconstructed Georgian housing providing self-catering accommodation in a peaceful, central London location.
Minimum age 10
Bedrooms: 60 single, 40 double/twin.
Total number of beds: 140
Bathrooms: 25 public

Bed only per person:	£min	£max
Daily	14.50	16.50

Open June–September
25

City of London YHA

36 Carter Lane, London EC4V 5AD
☎ (0171) 236 4965
Fax (0171) 236 7681
Contact: Mr L Parsons
In the centre of the City of London, in an area of narrow, winding streets. Former school for choirboys of St Paul's Cathedral. Other hostels available throughout London - call central reservations for details (0171) 248 6547.
Bedrooms: 2 single, 5 double/twin, 7 triple, 10 quadruple, 16 dormitories. Total number of beds: 191
Bathrooms: 2 en-suite, 10 public

Bed & breakfast per person:	£min	£max
Daily	17.90	

Full board per person:	£min	£max
Weekly	173.95	

Lunch available
Evening meal 1700 (last orders 2000)
Cards accepted: Mastercard, Visa, Switch/Delta
30

Curzon House Hotel

58 Courtfield Gardens, London
SW5 0NF
☎ (0171) 581 2116
Fax (0171) 835 1319
Contact: Mr. C A Otter
Budget accommodation with free use of kitchen, dining room and TV lounge. Homely and friendly atmosphere guaranteed. Weekly rates apply 1 November to 31 June.
Bedrooms: 2 single, 4 double/twin, 2 triple, 11 dormitories. Total number of beds: 62
Bathrooms: 1 en-suite, 5 public

Bed & breakfast per person:	£min	£max
Daily	14.00	23.00

Full board per person:	£min	£max
Weekly	65.00	150.00

Cards accepted: Mastercard, Visa, Switch/Delta

Information on accommodation listed in this guide has been supplied by the proprietors. As changes may occur you are advised to check details at the time of booking.

Driscoll House Hotel

172 New Kent Road, London
SE1 4YT
☎ (0171) 703 4175
Fax (0171) 703 8013
Contact: Mr. T Driscoll
Long or short term accommodation offered to teachers, students and tourists. Weekly full-board price below excludes weekend lunch. During the past 80 years we have accommodated more than 50,000 people from 200 different countries.
Bedrooms: 200 single, 26 double/twin. Total number of beds: 200
Bathrooms: 14 public

Bed & breakfast per person:	£min	£max
Daily	25.00	25.00

Full board per person:	£min	£max
Weekly	150.00	150.00

Lunch available
Evening meal 1730 (last orders 1900)
Parking for 10
5

Earl's Court YHA

38 Bolton Gardens, London
SW5 0AQ
☎ (0171) 373 7083
Fax (0171) 835 2034
Contact: Mr Nick Christian
Victorian town house in a residential area. Close to shops, restaurants, nightlife and all major tourist attractions. Comfortable dormitory accommodation.
For individuals only
Bedrooms: 2 triple, 4 quadruple, 15 dormitories. Total number of beds: 155
Bathrooms: 22 public

Bed & breakfast per person:	£min	£max
Daily	16.45	

Full board per person:	£min	£max
Weekly	163.80	

Evening meal 1700 (last orders 2000)
Cards accepted: Mastercard, Visa, Switch/Delta
5

COLOUR MAPS

Colour maps at the back of this guide pinpoint all places in which you will find accommodation listed.

Ifor Evans Hall/Max Rayne House

109 Camden Road, London
NW1 9HA
☎ (0171) 485 9377
Fax (0171) 284 3328
Contact: Ms. C Marshall
Modern purpose-built hall of residence for the University of London. All rooms are singles or small twins.
Bedrooms: 278 single,
50 double/twin. Total number of beds: 378
Bathrooms: 60 public

Bed only per person:	£min	£max
Daily	13.50	13.50

Bed & breakfast per person:	£min	£max
Daily	18.00	21.50

Evening meal 1730 (last orders 1900)
Parking for 50
Open January, April,
June–September, December

International House Woolwich

109 Brookhill Road, London
SE18 6RZ
☎ (0181) 854 1418
Fax (0181) 855 9257
Contact: Mr B Siderman
Purpose-built student hostel. Self-contained flats for married couples and children. Full en-suite facilities also available. Short-term visitor accommodation available July-September.
Bedrooms: 85 single, 21 double/twin.
Total number of beds: 127
Bathrooms: 21 en-suite, 18 public

Bed & breakfast per person:	£min	£max
Daily	11.93	13.66

Parking for 21
Open April, July–September, December

International Students Hostel Frognal House

99 Frognal, Hampstead, London
NW3 6XR
☎ (0171) 794 6893 & 794 8095
Fax (0171) 435 0724
Contact: Sr. P S Taylor
Historic, listed building in attractive grounds. Family atmosphere. Five minutes Hampstead Heath and underground, 15 minutes central London. Budget rates for long-term students.
For females only
Minimum age 16
Bedrooms: 17 single, 2 double/twin, 4 dormitories. Total number of beds: 40
Bathrooms: 15 public

Bed only per person:	£min	£max
Daily	11.00	16.00

Bed & breakfast per person:	£min	£max
Daily	12.00	17.00

Evening meal from 1845

International Students House

229 Great Portland Street, London
W1N 5HD
☎ (0171) 631 8300 & 631 8304
Fax (0171) 631 8315
Contact: Ms Martina Downes
Comfortable student-style accommodation, centrally located in West End. Easy access to all London's attractions. Close to underground and other public transport. Restaurant, bar and fitness centre on premises.
Minimum age 17
Bedrooms: 169 single,
74 double/twin, 6 triple,
37 quadruple, 5 dormitories. Total number of beds: 531
Bathrooms: 7 en-suite, 95 public

Bed only per person:	£min	£max
Daily	9.99	

Bed & breakfast per person:	£min	£max
Daily	16.00	27.00

Lunch available
Evening meal 1730 (last orders 1930)
Parking for 10
Cards accepted: Mastercard, Visa, Switch/Delta

John Adams Hall (Institute of Education)

15-23 Endsleigh Street, London
WC1H ODP
☎ (0171) 387 4086
Fax (0171) 383 0164
Email: jah@ioe.ac.uk
Contact: Mr M Lam-Hing
An assembly of Georgian houses, the hall retains its old glory. Close to Euston, King's Cross and St Pancras stations.
Bedrooms: 127 single,
22 double/twin. Total number of beds: 171
Bathrooms: 2 en-suite, 26 public

Bed & breakfast per person:	£min	£max
Daily	20.00	22.00

Evening meal 1730 (last orders 1830)
Open January, March–April,
July–September, December
Cards accepted: Mastercard, Visa

Kent House

325 Green Lanes, London N4 2ES
☎ (0181) 802 0800 & 802 5100
Fax (0181) 802 9070
Special off-season and weekly rates for young tourists. Facilities for self-catering. Adjacent to Manor House underground station and 10 minutes from central London.
Minimum age 16
Bedrooms: 3 single, 13 double/twin, 3 dormitories. Total number of beds: 34
Bathrooms: 6 public

Bed only per person:	£min	£max
Daily	14.00	16.00

Bed & breakfast per person:	£min	£max
Daily	22.00	25.00

Parking for 4

Kirness House

29 Belgrave Road, Victoria, London
SW1V 1RB
☎ (0171) 834 0030
Contact: Mrs M Walker
Small hostel very close to Victoria station. Many European languages spoken.
For individuals only
Bedrooms: 6 single. Total number of beds: 10
Bathrooms: 3 public

Bed only per person:	£min	£max
Daily		25.00

Bed & breakfast per person:	£min	£max
Daily		30.00

Cards accepted: Amex

WELCOME HOST

This is a nationally recognised customer care programme which aims to promote the highest standards of service and a warm welcome. Establishments who are taking part in this initiative are indicated by the symbol.

LONDON

Continued

Lancaster Hall Hotel (Youth Annexe)

35 Craven Terrace, Lancaster Gate, London W2 3EL
☎ (0171) 723 9276
Fax (0171) 706 2870
Contact: Mr U Maynard
Within easy walking distance of Hyde Park, Kensington Gardens and Marble Arch. Close to public transport.
Bedrooms: 3 single, 7 double/twin, 4 triple, 3 quadruple. Total number of beds: 41
Bathrooms: 4 public

Bed & breakfast per person:	£min	£max
Daily	20.00	22.00

Evening meal 1800 (last orders 2100)
Parking for 13
Cards accepted: Mastercard, Visa, Switch/Delta
150

Lee Abbey International Students Club

57-67 Lexham Gardens, Kensington, London W8 6JJ
☎ (0171) 373 7242
Fax (0171) 244 8702
Contact: Accommodation Officer
Hostel, run by Christian Community, providing long-term accommodation for students of all faiths and short-term accommodation for anyone. Fees include half-board weekdays, full-board weekends, and bank holidays. Earl's Court underground nearby.
Minimum age 18
Bedrooms: 60 single, 28 double/twin, 10 triple. Total number of beds: 146
Bathrooms: 19 en-suite, 28 public

Bed & breakfast per person:	£min	£max
Daily	17.00	30.00

Lunch available
Evening meal 1800 (last orders 1900)
60

You are advised to confirm your booking in writing.

Map references apply to the colour maps at the back of this guide.

Museum Inn

27 Montague Street, London
Contact: The Manager, 45 Queensborough Terrace, London W2
☎ (0171) 229 7866
Fax (0171) 636 7948
Budget accommodation in the heart of London opposite the British Museum, at affordable prices for young travellers and backpackers. Well placed for theatres, bars and restaurants.
Minimum age 16
Bedrooms: 2 double/twin, 1 triple, 4 quadruple, 6 dormitories. Total number of beds: 60
Bathrooms: 7 public

Bed & breakfast per person:	£min	£max
Daily	12.00	16.00

Cards accepted: Mastercard, Visa

Passfield Hall

1 Endsleigh Place, London WC1H 0PW
☎ (0171) 387 7743 & 387 3584
Fax (0171) 387 0419
University hall of residence with washbasin in all rooms, suitable for individuals and families. Central for Oxford Street and the West End.
Bedrooms: 100 single, 34 double/twin, 10 triple. Total number of beds: 198
Bathrooms: 36 public

Bed & breakfast per person:	£min	£max
Daily	20.50	25.00

Open March–April, July–September
Cards accepted: Mastercard, Visa, Switch/Delta

"Peace Haven"

London Friendship Centre, 3 Creswick Road, London W3 9HE
☎ (0181) 752 0055
Fax (0181) 752 0066
Comfortable residence suitable for groups and school parties, open throughout the year. Individuals and families also welcome. Parking facilities available.
Minimum age 10
Bedrooms: 1 single, 15 double/twin, 3 quadruple, 2 dormitories. Total number of beds: 53
Bathrooms: 6 en-suite, 9 public

Bed & breakfast per person:	£min	£max
Daily	11.50	25.00

Lunch available
Evening meal 1700 (last orders 1900)
Parking for 10
45

Queen Alexandra's House

Bremner Road, Kensington Gore, London SW7 2QT
☎ (0171) 589 3635
Fax (0171) 589 3177
Email: 106635.43 @compuserve.com.
Contact: Mrs C J Raymond
Fine example of Victorian architecture and a long established hostel for women students of all ages in South Kensington. Weekly full board by arrangement.
For females only
Minimum age 17
Bedrooms: 75 single, 2 double/twin. Total number of beds: 81
Bathrooms: 20 public

Bed & breakfast per person:	£min	£max
Daily	25.00	

Open May–August

Quest Hotel

45 Queensborough Terrace, London W2 3SY
☎ (0171) 229 7866
Fax (0171) 727 8106
Email: astorhostels@msn.com
Budget accommodation opposite Hyde Park, walking distance to Portobello market, Queensway for restaurants, bars and cinemas. Affordable prices for young travellers and backpackers.
Minimum age 16
Bedrooms: 1 double/twin, 7 quadruple, 8 dormitories. Total number of beds: 80
Bathrooms: 11 en-suite, 4 public

Bed & breakfast per person:	£min	£max
Daily	12.00	14.00

Cards accepted: Mastercard, Visa

Regency Court Hotel

14 Penywern Road, London SW5 9ST
☎ (0171) 244 6615
Fax (0171) 357 8279
Contact: Mr Rajiv Awasti
All rooms modern and en-suite. A good value well-established hotel, centrally located. Close to Earl's Court and Olympia with direct underground link to Heathrow and London's West End.
Bedrooms: 5 single, 8 double/twin, 1 triple, 1 quadruple. Total number of beds: 27
Bathrooms: 1 en-suite, 5 public

Bed & breakfast per person:	£min	£max
Daily	17.50	30.00

Cards accepted: Amex, Mastercard, Visa

Rotherhithe YHA and Conference Centre

Salter Road, London SE16 1PP
☎ (0171) 232 2114
Fax (0171) 237 2919
Contact: Mr R E Stackhouse
Ultra-modern building with every facility for families and individuals. All rooms have en-suite facilities, there is a restaurant and ample street parking. Special prices for family rooms. Only 1 mile from Tower Bridge. Families, individuals and groups welcome.
Minimum age 5
Bedrooms: 22 double/twin, 16 quadruple, 32 dormitories. Total number of beds: 320
Bathrooms: 70 en-suite

Bed & breakfast per person:	£min	£max
Daily	17.90	

Full board per person:	£min	£max
Weekly	173.95	

Lunch available
Evening meal 1730 (last orders 2030)
Cards accepted: Mastercard, Visa, Switch/Delta
S R TV 75 SP T

Hotel Saint Simeon

38 Harrington Gardens, London SW7 4LT
☎ (0171) 373 0505 & 370 4708
Fax (0171) 589 6412
Contact: Mr. J Gojkovic
Rooms for 1 to 4 people in central London. Nearest underground station is Gloucester Road.
Bedrooms: 6 single, 10 double/twin, 5 dormitories. Total number of beds: 41
Bathrooms: 4 en-suite, 6 public

Bed & breakfast per person:	£min	£max
Daily	9.00	25.00

Cards accepted: Amex, Mastercard, Visa
UL TV OAP SP T

South Bank University

103 Borough Road, London SE1 0AA
☎ (0171) 815 7003
Fax (0171) 815 7099
Email: kays@vax.sbu.ac.uk
Contact: Mr S Kay
Centrally located bed and breakfast and self-catering accommodation for those on a budget
Bedrooms: 600 single. Total number of beds: 600
Bathrooms: 600 en-suite

Bed only per person:	£min	£max
Daily	17.63	21.73

Bed & breakfast per person:	£min	£max
Daily	19.39	23.50

Open July–September
Cards accepted: Mastercard, Visa
12 R TV

Stamford Street Apartments

127 Stamford Street, Waterloo, London
Contact: King's Campus Vacation Bureau, 127 Stamford Street, London SE1 9NQ
☎ (0171) 928 3777
Fax (0171) 928 5777
Brand new residence on the south bank of the Thames close to Waterloo station and Eurostar. The apartments have single bedrooms arranged in units of 4-9 rooms. All rooms en-suite with shower. Other halls of residence in Chelsea, Westminster, Wandsworth, Denmark Hill, Hampstead and Kensington (groups only).
Bedrooms: 558 single
Bathrooms: 558 en-suite

Bed only per person:	£min	£max
Daily	31.00	

Lunch available
Evening meal 1800 (last orders 1900)
Open July–September
Cards accepted: Mastercard, Visa
UL S 200 T

Tent City - Acton

Old Oak Common Lane, East Acton, London W3 7DP
☎ (0181) 743 5708
Fax (0181) 749 9074
Email: tentcity@btinternet.com
Contact: Ms Maxine Lambert
"Tented" hostel and campsite close to East Acton tube. On-site snackbar, free baggage and valuables store. Young and fun!
Bedrooms: 14 dormitories. Total number of beds: 448
Bathrooms: 24 public

Bed only per person:	£min	£max
Daily	5.40	6.00

Lunch available
Parking for 30
Open June–September
UL S R TV OAP SP

A key to symbols can be found inside the back cover flap.

Urban Learning Foundation

56 East India Dock Road, London E14 6JE
☎ (0171) 536 0100
Fax (0171) 536 0107
Contact: Ms Anne Clark
Purpose-built residential training centre, close to central London. Single study bedrooms arranged in 4-7 bedded apartments.
Minimum age 12
Bedrooms: 47 single. Total number of beds: 47
Bathrooms: 1 en-suite, 18 public

Bed only per person:	£min	£max
Daily	20.00	24.00

Lunch available
Cards accepted: Amex, Mastercard, Visa
12 S 80 OAP SP

Victoria Hostel

71 Belgrave Road, London
Contact: 45 Queensborough Terrace, London W2
☎ (0171) 229 7866
Fax (0171) 727 8106
Budget accommodation close to Victoria train and coach stations, Tate Gallery, Big Ben, Buckingham Palace and River Thames. Affordable prices for backpackers and students.
Minimum age 16
Bedrooms: 1 double/twin, 11 dormitories. Total number of beds: 60
Bathrooms: 5 public

Bed & breakfast per person:	£min	£max
Daily	12.50	15.00

Cards accepted: Mastercard, Visa
UL R TV T

Wimbledon YMCA

200 The Broadway, Wimbledon, London SW19 1RY
☎ (0181) 542 9055
Fax (0181) 542 1086
Contact: Mrs Kate Kimpton
Modern, purpose-built residence with sports hall, fitness studio, saunas, dance studio, coffee bar, restaurant and laundry.
Minimum age 12
Bedrooms: 106 single, 34 double/twin. Total number of beds: 170
Bathrooms: 1 en-suite, 20 public

Bed & breakfast per person:	£min	£max
Daily	21.00	

Full board per person:	£min	£max
Weekly	105.00	

Continued ▶

LONDON

Continued

Lunch available
Evening meal 1700 (last orders 1850)
Parking for 30
Cards accepted: Mastercard, Visa
UL S TV 50 SP

Y.M.C.A.

Rush Green Road, Romford
RM7 0PH
☎ (01708) 766211
Fax (01708) 754211
Contact: Mr Dave Ball
8 minutes' walk from Romford rail station, 25 minutes from Liverpool Street station. Easy access to M25 and south coast. Easy travel into London by underground (Elm Park). International hostel with many sports facilities.
Minimum age 18
Bedrooms: 148 single, 2 double/twin.
Total number of beds: 150
Bathrooms: 4 en-suite, 24 public

Bed & breakfast per person:	£min	£max
Daily	16.50	

Full board per person:	£min	£max
Weekly	69.12	129.94

Lunch available
Evening meal 1730 (last orders 1845)
Parking for 120
Cards accepted: Mastercard, Visa
UL S TV 80

LYNTON

Devon
Map ref 1C1

Hilltop resort on Exmoor coast linked to its seaside twin, Lynmouth, by a water-operated cliff railway which descends from the town hall. Spectacular surroundings of moorland cliffs with steep chasms of conifer and rocks through which rivers cascade.
Tourist Information Centre ☎ (01598) 752225

YHA Lynton

Lynbridge, Lynton EX35 6AZ
☎ (01598) 753237
Fax (01598) 753305
Contact: Miss Sue Hunter
Homely Victorian family house on steep wooded gorge of West Lyn River. Home cooking and friendly atmosphere.
Bedrooms: 7 dormitories. Total number of beds: 34
Bathrooms: 4 public

Bed only per person:	£min	£max
Daily	5.95	8.85

Bed & breakfast per person:	£min	£max
Daily	8.90	11.80

Full board per person:	£min	£max
Weekly	116.90	137.20

Evening meal 1900 (last orders 1800)
Parking for 9
Cards accepted: Mastercard, Visa
UL S SP

MALVERN

Hereford and Worcester
Map ref 2B1

Spa town in Victorian times, its water is today bottled and sold worldwide. 6 resorts, set on the slopes of the Hills, form part of Malvern. Great Malvern Priory has splendid 15th C windows. It is an excellent walking centre.
Tourist Information Centre ☎ (01684) 892289 or 862345

YHA Malvern Hills

18 Peachfield Road, Malvern Wells, Malvern, Worcestershire WR14 4AP
☎ (01684) 569131
Fax (01684) 565205
Contact: The Warden
Large house in own grounds next to common. Spectacular views of the hills and Severn Valley.
Bedrooms: 2 double/twin, 4 quadruple, 4 dormitories. Total number of beds: 59
Bathrooms: 3 public

Bed only per person:	£min	£max
Daily	5.35	8.00

Bed & breakfast per person:	£min	£max
Daily	8.30	10.95

Full board per person:	£min	£max
Weekly	112.70	131.25

Lunch available
Evening meal 1900 (last orders 1800)
Parking for 12
Open February–December
Cards accepted: Mastercard, Visa
UL S 25 SP T

Establishments should be open throughout the year, unless otherwise stated.

MANCHESTER

Greater Manchester
Map ref 4B1

The Gateway to the North, offering one of Britain's largest selections of arts venues and theatre productions, a wide range of chain stores and specialist shops, a legendary, lively nightlife, spectacular architecture and a plethora of eating and drinking places.
Tourist Information Centre ☎ (0161) 234 3157 or 234 3158 or 436 3344

The Manchester Conference Centre and Hotel

PO Box 88, Sackville Street, Manchester M60 1QD
☎ (0161) 200 4076
Fax (0161) 200 4090
Contact: Mr R S Handscombe
Modern year-round conference centre and hotel, in Manchester city centre. Standard and en-suite rooms. Conferences and groups a speciality. Restaurant and bar. Campus accommodation during vacations.
Bedrooms: 2226 single, 74 double/twin. Total number of beds: 2374
Bathrooms: 700 en-suite, 300 public

Bed only per person:	£min	£max
Daily	17.00	64.00

Bed & breakfast per person:	£min	£max
Daily	23.75	71.95

Full board per person:	£min	£max
Weekly	225.00	635.00

Lunch available
Evening meal 1830 (last orders 2100)
Parking for 700
Cards accepted: Amex, Diners, Mastercard, Visa, Switch/Delta
S TV 500 SP T

WELCOME HOST

This is a nationally recognised customer care programme which aims to promote the highest standards of service and a warm welcome. Establishments who are taking part in this initiative are indicated by the symbol.

Student Village

Lower Chatham Street, Manchester
Contact: Miss L Jones, Housing Projects, Student Village Limited, 1st Floor, Lancaster House, 80 Princess Street, Manchester M1 6NF
☎ (0161) 236 1776 & 236 2824
Fax (0161) 236 0449
Email: lindsay@oxton.co.uk

First class budget accommodation for students. 24-hour security, telephone in every bedroom. Ideal city centre accommodation. Summer schools also available.

Bedrooms: 1039 single. Total number of beds: 1039
Bathrooms: 282 public

Bed only per person:	£min	£max
Daily		17.00

Bed & breakfast per person:	£min	£max
Daily		20.00

Full board per person:	£min	£max
Weekly	90.00	

Lunch available
Parking for 140
Cards accepted: Amex, Mastercard, Visa

YHA Manchester

Potato Wharf, Castlefield, Manchester M3 4NB
☎ (0161) 839 9960
Fax (0161) 835 2054
Contact: Mr D Green

Purpose built youth hostel sleeping up to 150 people in four bedded rooms all with en-suite facilities. Centrally located for all major attractions in the city. Families, individuals and groups welcome.

Wheelchair access category 3
Bedrooms: 4 double/twin, 30 quadruple, 4 dormitories. Total number of beds: 150
Bathrooms: 37 en-suite

Bed only per person:	£min	£max
Daily	9.00	13.00

Bed & breakfast per person:	£min	£max
Daily	11.95	15.95

Full board per person:	£min	£max
Weekly	132.30	166.25

Evening meal 1730 (last orders 1945)
Parking for 25
Cards accepted: Mastercard, Visa, Switch/Delta

MIDDLESBROUGH

Tees Valley
Map ref 5C3

Boom-town of the mid 19th C, today's Teesside industrial and conference town has a modern shopping complex and predominantly modern buildings. An engineering miracle of the early 20th C is the Transporter Bridge which replaced an old ferry.
Tourist Information Centre ☎ (01642) 243425 or 264330

T A D Centre

Ormesby Road, Middlesbrough, Cleveland TS3 7SF
☎ (01642) 203000
Fax (01642) 244006
Email: info@tad-centre.co.uk
Contact: Mrs K MacNaught

Modern purpose-built training and conference centre. Spacious accommodation furnished to a comfortable standard, with bar and restaurant facilities for delegates.

Minimum age 18
Bedrooms: 40 single. Total number of beds: 40
Bathrooms: 40 en-suite

Bed only per person:	£min	£max
Daily	42.88	45.88

Bed & breakfast per person:	£min	£max
Daily	49.93	51.70

Full board per person:	£min	£max
Weekly	350.00	380.00

Lunch available
Evening meal 1800 (last orders 2130)
Parking for 112
Cards accepted: Amex, Mastercard, Visa, Switch/Delta

The symbols in each entry give information about services and facilities. A key to these symbols appears at the back of this guide.

MINEHEAD

Somerset
Map ref 1D1

Victorian resort with spreading sands developed around old fishing port on the coast below Exmoor. Former fishermen's cottages stand beside the 17th C harbour; cobbled streets climb the hill in steps to the church. Boat trips, steam railway. Hobby Horse festival 1 May.
Tourist Information Centre ☎ (01643) 702624

YHA Minehead

Alcombe Combe, Minehead TA24 6EW
☎ (01643) 702595
Fax (01643) 703016
Contact: Mr Richard Moss

In a secluded position in a wooded combe. Often used by groups for educational visits, also ideal for family holidays. Open for self-catering groups only Nov-Mar.

Minimum age 5
Bedrooms: 2 quadruple, 4 dormitories. Total number of beds: 36
Bathrooms: 4 public

Bed only per person:	£min	£max
Daily	5.95	8.85

Bed & breakfast per person:	£min	£max
Daily	8.90	11.80

Full board per person:	£min	£max
Weekly	116.90	137.20

Evening meal from 1900
Parking for 10
Cards accepted: Mastercard, Visa

The symbol after an establishment name indicates that it is a Regional Tourist Board member.

ACCESSIBILITY

Look for the symbols which indicate accessibility for wheelchair users. These are described in detail at the front of this guide.

NANTWICH

Cheshire
Map ref 4A2

Old market town on the River Weaver made prosperous in Roman times by salt springs. Fire destroyed the town in 1583 and many buildings were rebuilt in Elizabethan style. Churche's Mansion (open to the public) survived the fire.
Tourist Information Centre ☎ (01270) 610983

Regents Theological College

London Road, Nantwich CW5 6LW
☎ (01270) 610800
Contact: Rev G T Richardson
A multi-purpose complex consisting of theological college, English language school, conference/holiday centre and sports facilities. Weekly half-board terms available.
Bedrooms: 8 single, 8 double/twin, 6 triple, 1 quadruple. Total number of beds: 46
Bathrooms: 4 public

Bed & breakfast per person:	£min	£max
Daily	14.00	22.00

Lunch available
Evening meal 1700 (last orders 1800)
Parking for 30
100

NEWCASTLE UPON TYNE

Tyne and Wear
Map ref 5C2

Commercial and cultural centre of the North East, with a large indoor shopping centre, Quayside market, museums and theatres which offer an annual 6 week season by the Royal Shakespeare Company. Norman castle keep, medieval alleys, old Guildhall.
Tourist Information Centre ☎ (0191) 261 0610 or 230 0030 or 261 0691

Leazes Terrace Student Houses

10 Leazes Terrace, Newcastle upon Tyne
Contact: Miss J Handcock, University of Newcastle, Leazes Terrace Student Houses, 10 Leazes Terrace, Newcastle upon Tyne NE1 4LY
☎ (0191) 222 8150
Fax (0191) 222 8150
Good value university accommodation in late Georgian terrace in the city centre, with easy access to shops, transport and leisure facilities.
Minimum age 18
Bedrooms: 72 single, 32 double/twin, 2 triple. Total number of beds: 142
Bathrooms: 17 public

Bed only per person:	£min	£max
Daily	14.00	23.00

Bed & breakfast per person:	£min	£max
Daily	16.50	28.00

Open July–September
12

University of Northumbria Newcastle

Coach Lane Campus Halls of Residence, Coach Lane, Newcastle upon Tyne, Tyne & Wear
Contact: Mrs S Cowell, University of Northumbria, Newcastle, Ellison Place, Newcastle upon Tyne, Tyne & Wear NE1 8ST
☎ (0191) 227 4024
Fax (0191) 227 3197
Accommodation in modern halls of residence, set in pleasant grounds, 3 miles from the city centre. Bed and breakfast with or without evening meal for groups or parties.
Minimum age 16
Bedrooms: 186 single, 50 double/twin. Total number of beds: 286
Bathrooms: 44 public

Bed & breakfast per person:	£min	£max
Daily	15.25	17.75

Full board per person:	£min	£max
Weekly	185.50	360.00

Lunch available
Evening meal 1730 (last orders 1930)
Parking for 100
Open April, July–September
250

NORWICH

Norfolk
Map ref 3C1

Beautiful cathedral city and county town on the River Wensum with many fine museums and medieval churches. Norman castle, Guildhall and interesting medieval streets. Good shopping centre and market.
Tourist Information Centre ☎ (01603) 666071

City College Norwich

Southwell Lodge, Ipswich Road, Norwich NR2 2LL
☎ (01603) 618327 & 773093
Fax (01603) 773301
Contact: Mr John Wheeler
College halls of residence set in a rural tree-screened setting within 10 minutes' walk of Norwich city centre. Lunch and supper available. Weekly room-only rates from £60.00.
Bedrooms: 270 single, 16 double/twin. Total number of beds: 302
Bathrooms: 16 en-suite, 45 public

Bed only per person:	£min	£max
Daily	14.00	18.00

Bed & breakfast per person:	£min	£max
Daily	17.00	21.00

Full board per person:	£min	£max
Weekly	150.00	

Lunch available
Evening meal 1730 (last orders 1900)
Parking for 500
Cards accepted: Mastercard, Visa, Switch/Delta
350

University of East Anglia

Norwich NR4 7TJ
☎ (01603) 593277
Fax (01603) 250585
Email: j.court@uea.ac.uk
Contact: Ms J Court
Modern university in parkland, 2 miles from the centre of Norwich. Comfortable, convenient and compact. En-suite and family accommodation available.
Minimum age 14
Bedrooms: 1300 single, 50 double/twin. Total number of beds: 1300
Bathrooms: 600 en-suite, 70 public

Bed only per person:	£min	£max
Daily	15.40	23.00

Bed & breakfast per person:	£min	£max
Daily	15.40	23.00

Full board per person:	£min	£max
Weekly	172.90	226.10

Lunch available
Evening meal 1700 (last orders 1915)
Parking for 700
Open March–April, June–September
Cards accepted: Diners, Mastercard, Visa, Switch/Delta
500

For further information on accommodation establishments use the coupons at the back of this guide.

NOTTINGHAM

Nottinghamshire
Map ref 4C2

Attractive modern city with a rich history. Outside its castle, now a museum, is Robin Hood's statue. Attractions include "The Tales of Robin Hood"; the Lace Hall; Wollaton Hall; museums and excellent facilities for shopping, sports and entertainment.
Tourist Information Centre ☎ (0115) 947 0661

The Igloo Tourist Hostel

110 Mansfield Road, Nottingham NG1 3HL
☎ (0115) 947 5250
Contact: Mr Steve Maxwell
Dormitory accommodation for backpackers and activity groups, with use of hot showers, TV lounge and kitchen. Open all day, all year. No chores.
Minimum age 8
Bedrooms: 4 dormitories. Total number of beds: 34
Bathrooms: 4 public

Bed only per person:	£min	£max
Daily	8.50	

Bed & breakfast per person:	£min	£max
Daily	10.50	

8 20

OTTERBURN

Northumberland
Map ref 5B1

Small village set at the meeting of the River Rede with Otter Burn, the site of the Battle of Otterburn in 1388. A peaceful tradition continues in the sale of Otterburn tweeds in this beautiful region, which is ideal for exploring the Border country and the Cheviots.

Otterburn Hall

Otterburn NE19 1HE
☎ 0800 591527 & (0191) 385 2822
Fax (0191) 385 2267
Contact: Mrs V Connell
Family holiday hotel, conference venue and training establishment in 100 acres. School, college and corporate visitors welcome. Offering special interest holidays.
Minimum age 8
Bedrooms: 7 single, 50 double/twin, 3 triple, 5 quadruple. Total number of beds: 132
Bathrooms: 60 en-suite

Bed only per person:	£min	£max
Daily	20.00	30.00

Bed & breakfast per person:	£min	£max
Daily	25.00	35.00

Full board per person:	£min	£max
Weekly	175.00	200.00

Lunch available
Evening meal 1900 (last orders 1900)
Parking for 100
Cards accepted: Amex, Mastercard, Visa
140

OXFORD

Oxfordshire
Map ref 2C1

Beautiful university town with many ancient colleges, some dating from the 13th C, and numerous buildings of historic and architectural interest. The Ashmolean Museum has outstanding collections. Lovely gardens and meadows with punting on the Cherwell.
Tourist Information Centre ☎ (01865) 726871

Oxford Backpackers Hostel

9a Hythe Bridge Street, Oxford OX1 2EW
☎ (01865) 721761 & 721987
Fax (01865) 721761
Contact: Mr Brent Smith
Centrally located in the heart of historic Oxford, 2 minutes' walk from bus, coach and train stations. Fully serviced, premium hostel.
Minimum age 12
Bedrooms: 1 single, 2 double/twin, 12 dormitories. Total number of beds: 90
Bathrooms: 6 public

Bed only per person:	£min	£max
Daily	9.00	15.00

Cards accepted: Diners, Mastercard, Visa, Switch/Delta
12

Information on accommodation listed in this guide has been supplied by the proprietors. As changes may occur you are advised to check details at the time of booking.

PORTSMOUTH & SOUTHSEA

Hampshire
Map ref 2C3

The first dock was built in 1194. HMS Victory, Nelson's flagship, is here and Charles Dickens' former home is open to the public. Neighbouring Southsea has a promenade with magnificent views of Spithead.
Tourist Information Centre ☎ (01705) 838382 or 826722

University of Portsmouth Central Reservations

Nuffield Centre, St Michaels Road, Portsmouth, Hampshire PO1 2ED
☎ (01705) 843178 & (0410) 909172
Fax (01705) 843423
Email: liz.jackson@port.ac.uk
Contact: Ms Elizabeth Jackson
Conference and holiday venue in self-catering flats or serviced accommodation, with sport and lecture facilities.
Bedrooms: 1522 single, 124 double/twin. Total number of beds: 1794
Bathrooms: 774 en-suite, 164 public

Bed only per person:	£min	£max
Daily	13.50	20.25

Bed & breakfast per person:	£min	£max
Daily	16.75	23.40

Full board per person:	£min	£max
Weekly	163.65	200.75

Lunch available
Evening meal 1800 (last orders 2130)
Open June–September
Cards accepted: Mastercard, Visa
200

The symbol after an establishment name indicates that it is a Regional Tourist Board member.

The symbols in each entry give information about services and facilities. A key to these symbols appears at the back of this guide.

POSTBRIDGE

Devon
Map ref 1C2

Tiny village in the centre of Dartmoor National Park, famous for its stone clapper bridge, probably medieval, over the East Dart River. Broadun Ring and Broadun Pound are 2 sets of prehistoric remains nearby.

YHA Bellever

Bellever, Postbridge, Yelverton PL20 6TU
☎ (01822) 880227
Fax (01822) 880302
Hostel in the heart of Dartmoor, a good base for walking, moorland studies and adventure training.
Minimum age 5
Bedrooms: 5 quadruple, 2 dormitories. Total number of beds: 36
Bathrooms: 3 public

Bed only per person:	£min	£max
Daily	5.95	8.85

Bed & breakfast per person:	£min	£max
Daily	8.90	11.80

Full board per person:	£min	£max
Weekly	116.90	137.20

Evening meal 1900 (last orders 1800)
Parking for 6
Open April–October
Cards accepted: Mastercard, Visa

ROCHESTER

Kent
Map ref 3B3

Ancient cathedral city on the River Medway. Has many places of interest connected with Charles Dickens (who lived nearby) including the fascinating Dickens Centre. Also massive castle overlooking the river and Guildhall Museum.
Tourist Information Centre ☎ (01634) 843666

YHA Rochester

Capstone Road, Gillingham ME7 3JE
☎ (01634) 400788
Fax (01634) 400794
Contact: The Manager
This brand new hostel is formed from a restored oast house and farm buildings, and has excellent facilities for families and individuals.
Minimum age 5
Bedrooms: 4 double/twin, 7 quadruple, 1 dormitory. Total number of beds: 41
Bathrooms: 6 public

Bed only per person:	£min	£max
Daily	5.95	8.85

Bed & breakfast per person:	£min	£max
Daily	8.90	11.80

Full board per person:	£min	£max
Weekly	116.90	137.20

Evening meal from 1900
Parking for 20
Open February–November
Cards accepted: Mastercard, Visa, Switch/Delta

SAFFRON WALDEN

Essex
Map ref 2D1

Takes its name from the saffron crocus once grown around the town. The church of St Mary has superb carvings, magnificent roofs and brasses. A town maze can be seen on the common. Two miles south-west is Audley End, a magnificent Jacobean mansion owned by English Heritage.
Tourist Information Centre ☎ (01799) 510444

YHA Saffron Walden

1 Myddylton Place, Saffron Walden CB10 1BB
☎ (01799) 523117
Fine 14th C building in market town. Oak panelled room and staircase.
Bedrooms: 5 dormitories. Total number of beds: 38
Bathrooms: 3 public

Bed only per person:	£min	£max
Daily	5.35	8.00

Bed & breakfast per person:	£min	£max
Daily	8.30	10.95

Full board per person:	£min	£max
Weekly	112.70	131.25

Evening meal 1900 (last orders 1800)
Open March–December
Cards accepted: Mastercard, Visa, Switch/Delta

Map references apply to the colour maps at the back of this guide.

ST JOHN'S CHAPEL

Durham
Map ref 5B2

Peaceful village in Upper Weardale. Pubs, village shops and cottages are set around a small market square. Nearby Harthope Burn has an attractive waterfall.

Weardale House

Ireshopeburn, Bishop Auckland, County Durham
Contact: Mr Karen Hutchinson, YMCA Residential Office, Herrington Burn, Houghton-le-Spring, Tyne and Wear DH4 4JW
☎ (0191) 385 2822 & 385 3085
Fax (0191) 385 2267
Multi-activity outdoor centre. Prices quoted below are for full board Monday-Friday. Three-day (Monday-Wednesday or Wednesday-Friday) available at £88; three-day weekend (Friday-Sunday) available at £58. All rates include catering, accommodation and multi-activity course.
For groups only
Minimum age 7
Bedrooms: 3 single, 8 dormitories. Total number of beds: 60
Bathrooms: 12 public

Full board per person:	£min	£max
Weekly	141.00	153.00

Lunch available
Parking for 10

ST JUST-IN-PENWITH

Cornwall
Map ref 1A3

Coastal parish of craggy moorland scattered with engine houses and chimney stacks of disused mines. The old mining town of St Just has handsome 19th C granite buildings. North of the town are the dramatic ruined tin mines at Botallack.

YHA Lands End

Letcha Vean, Cot Valley, St Just-in-Penwith TR19 7NT
☎ (01736) 788437
Fax (01736) 787337
Contact: Miss Katie Harris
House in large grounds in secluded Cot Valley, with views out to sea and footpath to beach and Cornwall coastal path.
Minimum age 5
Bedrooms: 4 dormitories. Total number of beds: 44
Bathrooms: 4 public

Bed only per person:	£min	£max
Daily	5.95	8.85

Bed & breakfast per person:	£min	£max
Daily	8.90	11.80

Full board per person:	£min	£max
Weekly	116.90	137.20

Evening meal 1800 (last orders 1930)
Parking for 10
Open February–November and Christmas
Cards accepted: Mastercard, Visa, Switch/Delta

SALCOMBE

Devon
Map ref 1C3

Sheltered yachting resort of whitewashed houses and narrow streets in a balmy setting on the Salcombe Estuary. Palm, myrtle and other Mediterranean plants flourish. There are sandy bays and creeks for boating.
Tourist Information Centre ☎ (01548) 843927

YHA Salcombe

Overbecks, Sharpitor, Salcombe TQ8 8LW
☎ (01548) 842856
Fax (01548) 842856
Contact: Miss Maggie Copping
Large house in National Trust semi-tropical gardens on cliff just below Sharpitor Rocks, overlooking sea and estuary in an Area of Outstanding Natural Beauty.
Bedrooms: 1 double/twin, 5 quadruple. Total number of beds: 51
Bathrooms: 3 public

Bed only per person:	£min	£max
Daily	5.35	8.00

Bed & breakfast per person:	£min	£max
Daily	8.30	10.95

Full board per person:	£min	£max
Weekly	112.70	131.25

Evening meal 1900 (last orders 1800)
Parking for 10
Open April–October
Cards accepted: Mastercard, Visa
36

SANDOWN

Isle of Wight
Map ref 2C3

The 6-mile sweep of Sandown Bay is one of the island's finest stretches, with excellent sands. The pier has a pavilion and sun terrace; the esplanade has amusements, bars, eating-places and gardens.
Tourist Information Centre ☎ (01983) 403886

YHA Sandown

The Firs, Fitzroy Street, Sandown PO36 8JH
☎ (01983) 402651
Fax (01983) 403565
Contact: Ms Giovanna Maccariello
Large house in popular seaside resort on east side of island, close to sandy beaches.
Bedrooms: 1 double/twin, 1 triple, 1 quadruple, 4 dormitories. Total number of beds: 53
Bathrooms: 4 public

Bed only per person:	£min	£max
Daily	5.95	8.85

Bed & breakfast per person:	£min	£max
Daily	8.90	11.80

Full board per person:	£min	£max
Weekly	116.90	137.20

Evening meal 1900 (last orders 1800)
Parking for 6
Open February–November
Cards accepted: Mastercard, Visa

SCARBOROUGH

North Yorkshire
Map ref 5D3

Large, popular East Coast seaside resort, formerly a spa town. Beautiful gardens and two splendid sandy beaches. Castle ruins date from 1100; fine Georgian and Victorian houses. Scarborough Millennium depicts 1,000 years of town's history. Sea Life Centre.
Tourist Information Centre ☎ (01723) 373333

University College Scarborough

Filey Road, Scarborough YO11 3AZ
☎ (01723) 362392
Fax (01723) 370815
Contact: Mrs E McAdam
Small, friendly college which provides you with the very best facilities to cater for your needs.
Bedrooms: 259 single, 4 double/twin. Total number of beds: 269
Bathrooms: 214 en-suite, 37 public

Bed only per person:	£min	£max
Daily		15.00

Bed & breakfast per person:	£min	£max
Daily		25.56

Full board per person:	£min	£max
Weekly		310.50

Lunch available
Evening meal 1800 (last orders 2000)
Parking for 97
Open January, March–April, July–September, December
200

SHEFFIELD

South Yorkshire
Map ref 4B2

Local iron ore and coal gave Sheffield its prosperous steel and cutlery industries. The modern city centre has many interesting buildings - cathedral, Cutlers' Hall, Crucible Theatre, Graves and Mappin Art Galleries - and Meadowhall Shopping Centre nearby.
Tourist Information Centre ☎ (0114) 273 4671 or 273 4672

Sheffield YMCA

20 Victoria Road, Sheffield S10 2DL
☎ (0114) 268 4807
Fax (0114) 268 3472
Contact: Mr Chris Litherland
A large sports, social and residential centre with facilities for weddings, functions and conferences.
Minimum age 16
Bedrooms: 90 single. Total number of beds: 90
Bathrooms: 12 public

Bed & breakfast per person:	£min	£max
Daily	15.00	

Evening meal 1700 (last orders 1800)
Parking for 30

ACCESSIBILITY

Look for the symbols which indicate accessibility for wheelchair users. These are described in detail at the front of this guide.

SHEFFIELD

Continued

University of Sheffield

Halifax Hall of Residence, Endcliffe Vale Road, Sheffield S10 3ER
☎ (0114) 222 8811 & 222 8813
Fax (0114) 266 3898
Email: n.taylor@sheffield.ac.uk.
Contact: Ms Norma Taylor

Six comfortable halls of residence in a quiet suburb near the city centre and close to the Peak District National Park.

Wheelchair access category 1
Bedrooms: 1886 single, 106 double/twin. Total number of beds: 2311
Bathrooms: 300 public

Bed & breakfast per person:	£min	£max
Daily	20.50	33.10

Full board per person:	£min	£max
Weekly	132.30	220.50

Lunch available
Evening meal 1730 (last orders 1830)
Parking for 600
Open January, March–April, June–August, December
500

SHOREHAM-BY-SEA

West Sussex
Map ref 2D3

Popular seaside resort and an ancient town. The harbour provides a safe yacht anchorage and the River Adur some excellent fishing. The Marlipins Museum contains a wide variety of local history exhibits. Shoreham Aircraft Museum at the airport.

YHA Truleigh Hill

Tottington Barn, Truleigh Hill, Shoreham-by-Sea BN43 5FB
☎ (01903) 813419
Fax (01903) 812016
Contact: Miss Christine Lavin

Ideal base for family or group holidays in a well appointed modern building on old barn site, high up on the South Downs with superb views across farmland to the coast 5 miles away.

Minimum age 5
Bedrooms: 4 double/twin, 3 quadruple, 6 dormitories. Total number of beds: 56
Bathrooms: 4 public

Bed only per person:	£min	£max
Daily	5.95	8.85

Bed & breakfast per person:	£min	£max
Daily	8.90	11.80

Full board per person:	£min	£max
Weekly	116.90	137.20

Evening meal 1900 (last orders 1800)
Parking for 20
Open February–October
Cards accepted: Mastercard, Visa
3 30

SOWERBY BRIDGE

West Yorkshire
Map ref 4B1

Busy little town in the Calder Valley near the Calder Hebble Canal.

Mill Bank Centre

AMIT (Personnel and Training Services), Mill Bank, Sowerby Bridge HX6 3DY
☎ (01422) 824388 & 824189
Contact: Mr J Haymer

Well-equipped residential centre with conference facilities, in a converted chapel overlooking a Pennine conservation village. Centrally heated, with carpets and Continental quilts. Prices vary according to number in group - please ask for details.

For groups only
Minimum age 10
Bedrooms: 1 single, 3 double/twin, 3 dormitories. Total number of beds: 22
Bathrooms: 6 public

Bed only per person:	£min	£max
Daily	18.00	25.00

Lunch available
Parking for 10
20

For further information on accommodation establishments use the coupons at the back of this guide.

Information on accommodation listed in this guide has been supplied by the proprietors. As changes may occur you are advised to check details at the time of booking.

STOW-ON-THE-WOLD

Gloucestershire
Map ref 2B1

Attractive Cotswold wool town with a large market-place and some fine houses, especially the old grammar school. There is an interesting church dating from Norman times. Stow-on-the-Wold is surrounded by lovely countryside and Cotswold villages.
Tourist Information Centre ☎ (01451) 831082

YHA Stow-on-the-Wold

The Square, Stow-on-the-Wold, Cheltenham GL54 1AF
☎ (01451) 830497
Fax (01451) 870102
Contact: The Manager

16th C building in historic market square.

Minimum age 5
Bedrooms: 1 single, 2 quadruple, 5 dormitories. Total number of beds: 50
Bathrooms: 8 public

Bed only per person:	£min	£max
Daily	5.35	8.00

Bed & breakfast per person:	£min	£max
Daily	8.30	10.95

Full board per person:	£min	£max
Weekly	112.70	131.25

Evening meal 1830 (last orders 2000)
Parking for 3
Open February–December
Cards accepted: Mastercard, Visa
5 40

STREATLEY

Berkshire
Map ref 2C2

Pretty village on the River Thames, linked to Goring by an attractive bridge. It has Georgian houses and cottages and beautiful views over the countryside and the Goring Gap.

YHA Streatley

Hill House, Reading Road, Streatley, Reading RG8 9JJ
☎ (01491) 872278
Fax (01491) 873056
Contact: The. Warden

Victorian family house in beautiful village.

Minimum age 5

Bedrooms: 1 triple, 1 quadruple, 9 dormitories. Total number of beds: 51
Bathrooms: 4 public

Bed only per person:	£min	£max
Daily	6.55	9.80

Bed & breakfast per person:	£min	£max
Daily	9.50	12.75

Full board per person:	£min	£max
Weekly	121.10	143.85

Lunch available
Evening meal 1900 (last orders 1800)
Parking for 6
Open February–December
Cards accepted: Mastercard, Visa, Switch/Delta

TORQUAY

Devon
Map ref 1D2

Devon's grandest resort, developed from a fishing village. Smart apartments and terraces rise from the seafront and Marine Drive along the headland gives views of beaches and colourful cliffs.
Tourist Information Centre ☎ (01803) 297428

Torquay Backpackers International Travellers Hostel

119 Abbey Road, Torquay TQ2 5NP
☎ (01803) 299924
Fax (01803) 299924
Contact: Mr Kevin Langan
Independant youth hostel, very central and close to beach. No curfews. Self catering, dormitory style accommodation and twin rooms available.
Minimum age 13
Bedrooms: 2 double/twin, 3 quadruple, 4 dormitories. Total number of beds: 40
Bathrooms: 2 en-suite, 4 public

Bed only per person:	£min	£max
Daily	5.50	7.50

Parking for 4

The symbol after an establishment name indicates that it is a Regional Tourist Board member.

TOTLAND BAY

Isle of Wight
Map ref 2C3

On the Freshwater Peninsula. It is possible to walk from here around to Alum Bay.

YHA Totland Bay

Hurst Hill, Totland Bay PO39 0HD
☎ (01983) 752165
Fax (01983) 756443
Contact: The Manager
Former private home and hotel, on west side of island, near cliff top walks and beaches.
Minimum age 5
Bedrooms: 10 dormitories. Total number of beds: 78
Bathrooms: 4 public

Bed only per person:	£min	£max
Daily	6.55	9.80

Bed & breakfast per person:	£min	£max
Daily	9.50	12.75

Full board per person:	£min	£max
Weekly	121.10	143.85

Lunch available
Evening meal 1830 (last orders 1800)
Parking for 7
Open March–November
Cards accepted: Mastercard, Visa, Switch/Delta

TREYARNON BAY

Cornwall
Map ref 1B2

YHA Treyarnon Bay

Tregonnan, Treyarnon Bay, Padstow PL28 8JR
☎ (01841) 520322
Fax (01841) 520322
Contact: Mr Adrian Richards
House overlooking sandy cove. A super centre for academic and recreational activities.
Minimum age 5
Bedrooms: 1 quadruple, 4 dormitories. Total number of beds: 42
Bathrooms: 1 en-suite, 3 public

Bed only per person:	£min	£max
Daily	5.95	8.85

Bed & breakfast per person:	£min	£max
Daily	8.90	11.80

Full board per person:	£min	£max
Weekly	116.90	137.20

Evening meal from 1900
Parking for 10
Open April–October and Christmas
Cards accepted: Mastercard, Visa

WANTAGE

Oxfordshire
Map ref 2C2

Market town in the Vale of the White Horse where King Alfred was born. His statue stands in the town square.
Tourist Information Centre ☎ (01235) 760176

YHA The Ridgeway

Court Hill, Wantage OX12 9NE
☎ (01235) 760253
Fax (01235) 768865
Contact: Mr S Bunyard
Modern hostel with 4 barns, close to Ridgeway Path. Panoramic views across woodland.
Bedrooms: 7 quadruple, 2 dormitories. Total number of beds: 59
Bathrooms: 5 public

Bed only per person:	£min	£max
Daily	5.35	8.00

Bed & breakfast per person:	£min	£max
Daily	8.30	10.95

Full board per person:	£min	£max
Weekly	112.70	131.25

Lunch available
Evening meal 1900 (last orders 1800)
Parking for 20
Open February–December
Cards accepted: Mastercard, Visa, Switch/Delta

A key to symbols can be found inside the back cover flap.

ACCESSIBILITY

Look for the symbols which indicate accessibility for wheelchair users. These are described in detail at the front of this guide.

WELWYN GARDEN CITY

Hertfordshire
Map ref 2D1

A "garden city" planned by Sir Ebenezer Howard. There are Roman remains nearby and Shaw's Corner, the home of George Bernard Shaw, is 2 miles away at Ayot St Lawrence.

Welwyn Garden City YMCA Residential Club

Peartree Lane, Welwyn Garden City AL7 3UL
☎ (01707) 327930
Fax (01707) 377993
Contact: Mr Michael Fairbeard
Purpose-built residential club set in its own grounds and garden. Ten minutes' walk from the railway station and bus terminal, 30 minutes from London by rail.
Minimum age 18
Bedrooms: 118 single. Total number of beds: 140
Bathrooms: 43 en-suite, 20 public

Bed only per person:	£min	£max
Daily	16.50	20.00

Bed & breakfast per person:	£min	£max
Daily	16.50	20.00

Full board per person:	£min	£max
Weekly	75.00	85.00

Evening meal 1730 (last orders 1830)
Parking for 45
Cards accepted: Mastercard, Visa, Switch/Delta
50

WEST LULWORTH

Dorset
Map ref 2B3

Well-known for Lulworth Cove, the almost landlocked circular bay of chalk and limestone cliffs.

YHA Lulworth Cove

School Lane, West Lulworth, Wareham BH20 5SA
☎ (01929) 400564
Fax (01929) 400640
Contact: The Manager
Purpose-built hostel of cedarwood, with comfortable facilities.
Minimum age 5
Bedrooms: 7 dormitories. Total number of beds: 34
Bathrooms: 2 public

Bed only per person:	£min	£max
Daily	5.95	8.85

Bed & breakfast per person:	£min	£max
Daily	8.90	11.80

Full board per person:	£min	£max
Weekly	116.90	137.20

Evening meal 1900 (last orders 1800)
Parking for 9
Open February–November
Cards accepted: Mastercard, Visa

WINCHESTER

Hampshire
Map ref 2C3

King Alfred the Great made Winchester the capital of Saxon England. A magnificent Norman cathedral, with one of the longest naves in Europe, dominates the city. Home of Winchester College founded in 1382.
Tourist Information Centre ☎ (01962) 840500

King Alfred's University College

Sparkford Road, Winchester SO22 4NR
☎ (01962) 827322
Fax (01962) 827264
Email: ecrshuds@wkac.ac.uk
Contact: Mrs Sarah Hudson
Over 1000 bedrooms in beautiful, historic Winchester. Excellent conference and recreational facilities. Individually tailored packages to suit all groups. Ideal base for exploring the South Coast.
Bedrooms: 996 single, 10 double/twin. Total number of beds: 1026
Bathrooms: 207 en-suite, 170 public

Bed only per person:	£min	£max
Daily	18.00	20.00

Bed & breakfast per person:	£min	£max
Daily	20.00	26.00

Full board per person:	£min	£max
Weekly	265.00	310.00

Lunch available
Evening meal 1800 (last orders 2030)
Parking for 200
Open March–April, July–September
300

Please check prices and other details at the time of booking.

YHA Winchester

The City Mill, 1 Water Lane, Winchester SO23 0EJ
☎ (01962) 853723
Fax (01962) 855524
Contact: The Manager
Charming 18th C watermill (National Trust), straddling the River Itchen.
Bedrooms: 4 dormitories. Total number of beds: 30
Bathrooms: 3 public

Bed only per person:	£min	£max
Daily	5.95	8.85

Bed & breakfast per person:	£min	£max
Daily	8.90	11.80

Full board per person:	£min	£max
Weekly	116.90	137.20

Evening meal 1900 (last orders 1800)
Open March–October
Cards accepted: Mastercard, Visa

YORK

North Yorkshire
Map ref 4C1

Ancient walled city nearly 2000 years old containing many well-preserved medieval buildings. Its Minster has over 100 stained glass windows. Attractions include Castle Museum, National Railway Museum, Jorvik Viking Centre and York Dungeon.
Tourist Information Centre ☎ (01904) 621756 or 621757 or 620557

Fairfax House

99 Heslington Road, York YO1 5BJ
☎ (01904) 432095
Contact: Mrs. A E Glover
Standing in its own grounds, within walking distance of city centre. Reduced rates for children and senior citizens.
Bedrooms: 85 single. Total number of beds: 85
Bathrooms: 14 public

Bed & breakfast per person:	£min	£max
Daily	17.00	19.00

Open March–April, July–September

For further information on accommodation establishments use the coupons at the back of this guide.

York Youth Hotel

11-13 Bishophill Senior, York
YO1 1EF
(01904) 625904 & 630613
Fax (01904) 612494
Contact: Ms Maureen Sellers

Dormitory-style accommodation in the city centre. Private rooms, TV lounge, snack shop, evening meals, packed lunches, games room, residential licence. Families welcome.

Bedrooms: 7 single, 14 double/twin, 1 triple, 4 quadruple, 5 dormitories.
Total number of beds: 120
Bathrooms: 8 public

Bed only per person:	£min	£max
Daily	9.00	12.00

Bed & breakfast per person:	£min	£max
Daily	10.50	14.50

Full board per person:	£min	£max
Weekly	148.05	164.50

Lunch available
Evening meal 1700 (last orders 1900)
Cards accepted: Mastercard, Visa, Switch/Delta

CHECK THE MAPS

The colour maps at the back of this guide show all the cities, towns and villages for which you will find accommodation entries.

Refer to the town index to find the page on which it is listed.

ENQUIRY COUPONS

To help you obtain further information about advertisers and accommodation featured in this guide you will find enquiry coupons at the back. Send these directly to the establishments in which you are interested. Remember to complete both sides of the coupon.

USE YOUR *i*'s

There are more than 550 Tourist Information Centres throughout England offering friendly help with accommodation and holiday ideas as well as suggestions of places to visit and things to do. There may well be a centre in your home town which can help you before you set out. You'll find addresses in the local Phone Book or simply call Freepages 0800 192 192.

COUNTRY CODE

Always follow the Country Code

- Enjoy the countryside and respect its life and work
- Guard against all risk of fire
- Fasten all gates
- Keep your dogs under close control
- Keep to public paths across farmland
- Use gates and stiles to cross fences, hedges and walls
- Leave livestock, crops and machinery alone
- Take your litter home
- Help to keep all water clean
- Protect wildlife, plants and trees
- Take special care on country roads
- Make no unnecessary noise

*i*NFORMATION PAGES

NATIONAL GRADING AND CLASSIFICATION SCHEME

Sure Signs

The Tourist Boards in Britain operate a National Quality Grading and Classification Scheme for all types of accommodation. The purpose of the scheme is to identify and promote those establishments that the public can use with confidence. The system of facility classification and quality grading also acknowledges those that provide a wider range of facilities and services and higher quality standards. Over 30,000 places to stay are inspected under the scheme and offer the reassurance of a national grading and classification.

For 'serviced' accommodation (which includes hotels, motels, guesthouses, inns, B&Bs and farmhouses) there are six classification bands, starting with LISTED and then from ONE to FIVE CROWN. For the new generation of 'lodges', offering budget accommodation along major roads and motorways, there are three classification bands, from ONE to THREE MOON.

Quite simply, the more Crowns or Moons, the wider the range of facilities and services offered.

Quality Grading

To help you find accommodation that offers even higher standards than those required for a Crown or Moon rating, there are four levels of quality grading, using the terms DE LUXE, HIGHLY COMMENDED, COMMENDED and APPROVED. Wherever you see a national grading and classification sign, you can be sure that a Tourist Board inspector has been there before you, checking the place on your behalf - and will be there again, because every place with a national rating is inspected annually.

Establishments are subject to a detailed inspection that assesses the quality standard of the facilities and services provided. The initial inspection invariably involves the Tourist Board inspector staying overnight, as a normal guest, until the bill is paid the following morning. This quality assessment includes such aspects as warmth of welcome and efficiency of service, as well as the standard of furnishing, fittings and decor. The standard of meals and their presentation is also taken into account.

Everything that impinges on the experience of a guest is included in the assessment. Tourist Board inspectors receive careful training to enable them to apply the quality standards consistently and fairly. Only those facilities and services provided are assessed, and due consideration is given to the style and nature of the establishment. B&Bs, farmhouses and guesthouses are not expected to operate in the style of large city centre hotels, and vice versa. This means that all types of establishment, whatever their Crown or Moon classification, can achieve a high quality grade if the facilities and services they provide, however limited in range, are to a high quality standard.

The quality grade that is awarded to an establishment is a reflection of the overall standard, taking everything into account. It is a balanced view of what is provided and, as such, cannot acknowledge individual areas of excellence. Quality grades are not intended to indicate value for money. A high quality product can be over-priced; a product of modest quality, if offered at a low price, can represent good value. The information provided by the combination of the classification and quality grade will enable you to determine for yourself what represents good value for money.

All Inspected

All establishments listed in this guide have been inspected or are awaiting inspection under the National Grading and Classification Scheme. The ratings that appear in the accommodation entries were correct at the time of going to press but are subject to change. If no rating appears in that entry it means that the inspection had not been carried out by the time of going to press. An information leaflet giving full details of the National Grading and Classification Scheme - which also covers self-catering holiday homes and caravan, chalet and camping parks - is available from any Tourist Information Centre.

General Advice and Information

Making a Booking

When enquiring about accommodation, make sure you check prices and other important details. You will also need to state your requirements, clearly and precisely - for example:

- **Arrival and departure dates**, with acceptable alternatives if appropriate.
- **The type of accommodation** you need; for example, room with twin beds, private bathroom.
- **The terms** you want; for example, room only, bed and breakfast, half board, full board.
- **If you have children** with you; their ages, whether you want them to share your room or be next door, any other special requirements, such as a cot.
- **Particular requirements** you may have, such as a special diet.

Booking by letter

Misunderstandings can easily happen over the telephone, so we strongly advise you to confirm your booking in writing if there is time.

If you decide to enquire in writing in the first place, you might find it helpful to use the Accommodation Coupons on pages 395-402, which can be cut out and posted to the places of your choice.

Remember to include your name and address, and a stamped self-addressed envelope, or an international reply coupon if you are writing from outside Britain.

Please note that the English Tourist Board does not make reservations - you should write direct to the accommodation.

Deposits

If you make your reservation weeks or months in advance, you will probably be asked for a deposit. The amount will vary according to the time of year, the number of people in your party and how long you plan to stay. The deposit will then be deducted from the final bill when you leave.

Payment on Arrival

Some establishments, especially large hotels in big towns, ask you to pay for your room on arrival if you have not booked it in advance. This is especially likely to happen if you arrive late and have little or no luggage.

If you are asked to pay on arrival, it is a good idea to see your room first, to make sure it meets your requirements.

Cancellations

Legal contract

When you accept accommodation that is offered to you, by telephone or in writing, you enter a legally binding contract with the proprietor.

This means that if you cancel your booking, fail to take up the accommodation or leave early, the proprietor may be entitled to compensation if he cannot re-let for all or a good part of the booked period. You will probably forfeit any deposit you have paid, and may well be asked for an additional payment.

The proprietor cannot make a claim until after the booked period, however, and during that time every effort should be made by the proprietor to re-let the accommodation.

If there is a dispute it is sensible for both sides to seek legal advice on the matter.

If you do have to change your travel plans, it is in your own interests to let the proprietors know in writing as soon as possible, to give them a chance to re-let your accommodation.

And remember, if you book by telephone and are asked for your credit card number, you should check whether the proprietor intends charging your credit card account should you later cancel your reservation.
A proprietor should not be able to charge your credit card account with a cancellation unless he or she has made this clear at the time of your booking and you have agreed. However, to avoid later disputes, we suggest you check with the proprietor whether he or she intends to charge you credit card account if you cancel.

Insurance
A travel or holiday insurance policy will safeguard you if you have to cancel or change your holiday plans. You can arrange a policy quite cheaply through your insurance company or travel agent. Some hotels also offer their own insurance schemes.

Arriving Late

If you know you will be arriving late in the evening, it is a good idea to say so when you book. If you are delayed on your way, a telephone call to say that you will be late will help prevent any problems when you arrive.

Service Charges and Tipping

These days many places levy service charges automatically. If they do, they must clearly say so in their offer of accommodation, at the time of booking. Then the service charge becomes part of the legal contract when you accept the offer of accommodation.

If a service charge is levied automatically, there is no need to tip the staff, unless they provide some exceptional service. The usual tip for meals is ten per cent of the total bill.

Telephone Charges

Hotels can set their own charges for telephone calls made through their switchboard or from direct-dial telephones in bedrooms. These charges are often much higher than telephone companies' standard charges (to defray the cost of providing the service).

Comparing costs
It is a condition of the National Grading and Classification Scheme, that a hotel's unit charges are on display, by the telephones or with the room information. But in practice it is not always easy to compare these charges with standard telephone rates. Before using a hotel telephone for long-distance calls, you may decide to ask how the charges compare.

Security of Valuables

You can deposit your valuables with the proprietor or manager during your stay, and we recommend you do this as a sensible precaution. Make sure you obtain a receipt for them.

Some places do not accept articles for safe custody, and in that case it is wisest to keep your valuables with you.

Disclaimer
Some proprietors put up a notice which disclaims liability for property brought on to their premises by a guest. In fact, they can only restrict their liability to a minimum laid down by law (The Hotel Proprietors Act 1956).

Under that Act, a proprietor is liable for the value of the loss or damage to any property (except a motor car or its contents) of a guest who has engaged overnight accommodation, but if the proprietor has the notice on display as prescribed under that Act, liability is limited to £50 for one article and a total of £100 for any one guest. The notice must be prominently displayed in the reception area or main entrance. These limits do not apply to valuables you have deposited with the proprietor for safe-keeping, or to property lost through the default, neglect of wilful act of the proprietor or his staff.

Code of Conduct

All the places featured in this guide have agreed to observe the following Codes of Conduct:

1 To ensure high standards of courtesy and cleanliness, catering and service appropriate to the type of establishment.

2 To describe fairly to all visitors and prospective visitors the amenities, facilities and services provided by the establishment, whether by advertisement, brochure, word of mouth or any other means. To allow visitors to see accommodation, if requested, before booking.

3 To make clear to visitors exactly what is included in all prices quoted for accommodation, meals and refreshments, including service charges, taxes and other surcharges. Details of charges, if any, for heating or additional service of facilities should also be made clear.

4 To adhere to, and not to exceed, prices current at time of occupation for accommodation or other services.

5 To advise visitors at the time of booking, and subsequently of any change, if the accommodation offered is in an unconnected annexe, or similar, or by boarding out; and to indicate the location of such accommodation and any difference in comfort or amenities from accommodation in the main establishment.

6 To give each visitor, on request, details of payments due and a receipt if required.

7 To deal promptly and courteously with all enquiries, requests, reservations, correspondence and complaints from visitors.

8 To allow an English Tourist Board representative reasonable access to the establishment, on request, to confirm that the Code of Conduct is being observed.

Comments and Complaints

Hotels and the law

Places that offer accommodation have legal and statutory responsibilities to their customers, such as providing information about prices, providing adequate fire precautions and safeguarding valuables. Like other businesses, they must also abide by the Trades Description Acts 1968 and 1972 when they describe their accommodation and facilities.

All the places featured in this guide have declared that they do fulfil all applicable statutory obligations.

Information

The proprietors themselves supply the descriptions of their establishments and other information for the listings, and they pay to have their entries included in the guide. All the places featured in the guide have also been inspected or have applied for inspection under the National Grading and Classification Scheme.

The English Tourist Board cannot guarantee accuracy of information in this guide, and accepts no responsibility for any error or misrepresentation. All liability for loss, disappointment, negligence or other damage caused by reliance on the information contained in this guide, or in the event of bankruptcy or liquidation or cessation of trade of any company, individual or firm mentioned, is hereby excluded.

We strongly recommend that you carefully check prices and other details when you book your accommodation.

Problems

Of course, we hope you will not have cause for complaint, but problems do occur from time to time.

If you are dissatisfied with anything, make your complaint to the management immediately. Then the management can take action at once to investigate the matter and put things right. The longer you leave a complaint, the harder it is to deal with it effectively.

In certain circumstances, the English Tourist Board may look into complaints. However, the Board has no statutory control over establishments or their methods of operating. The Board cannot become involved in legal or contractual matters.

Feedback Questionnaire

We find it very helpful to receive your comments about the places featured in *Where to Stay* and your suggestions on how to improve the guide. Please send us your views using the Customer Feedback Questionnaire on pages 415-416 - we would like to hear from you.

Return it to:
Department AS,
English Tourist Board,
Thames Tower,
Black's Road,
Hammersmith,
London W6 9EL.

ENQUIRY COUPONS

To help you obtain further information about advertisers and accommodation featured in this guide you will find enquiry coupons at the back. Send these directly to the establishments in which you are interested.

Remember to complete both sides of the coupon.

ABOUT THE GUIDE ENTRIES

Locations

Places to stay are listed under the town, city or village where they are located. If a place is out in the countryside, you will find it listed under the nearest village or town.

Town names are listed alphabetically within each regional section of the guide, along with the name of the county they fall under, and their map reference.

Map references

These refer to the colour location maps at the back of the guide. The first figure shown is the map number, the following letter and figure indicate the grid reference on the map.

Some entries were included just before the guide went to press, so they do not appear on the maps.

Addresses

County names, which appear in the town headings, are not repeated in the entries. When you are writing, you should of course make sure you use the full address and postcode.

Telephone numbers

Telephone numbers are listed below the accommodation address for each entry. Area codes are shown in brackets, and the exchange name is also included (before the code) if it differs from that of the town under which a place is listed.

Price

The prices shown in *Where to Stay 1998* are only a general guide; they were supplied to us by proprietors in summer 1997. Remember, changes may occur after the guide goes to press, so we strongly advise you to check prices when you book your accommodation.

Prices are shown in pounds sterling and include VAT where applicable. Some places also include a service charge in their standard tariff so check this when you book.

Standardised method

There are many different ways of quoting prices for accommodation. We use a standardised method in the guide to allow you to compare prices. For example when we show:

Bed and breakfast, the prices shown are for overnight accommodation with breakfast, for single and double rooms.

The double-room price is for two people. If a double room is occupied by one person there is sometimes a reduction in price.

Halfboard, the prices shown are for room, breakfast and evening meal, per person per day and per person per week.

Some places provide only a continental breakfast in the set price, and you may have to pay extra if you want a full English breakfast.

Checking prices

According to the law, hotels with at least four bedrooms or eight beds must display their overnight accommodation charges in the reception area or entrance. In your own interests, do make sure you check prices and what they include.

Children's rates

You will find that many places charge a reduced rate for children especially if they share a room with their parents. Some places charge the full rate, however, when a child occupies a room which might otherwise have been let to an adult.

The upper age limit for reductions for children varies from one hotel to another, so check this when you book.

Seasonal packages

Prices often vary through the year, and may be significantly lower outside peak holiday weeks. Many places offer special package rates - fully inclusive weekend breaks, for example - in the autumn, winter and spring.

You can get details of bargain packages from the establishment themselves, the Regional Tourist Boards or your local Tourist Information Centre (TIC). Your local travel agent may also have information, and can help you make bookings.

Bathrooms

Each accommodation entry shows you the number of en-suite and private bathrooms available, the number of private showers and the number of public bathrooms.

'En-suite bathroom' means the bath or shower and WC are contained behind the main door of the bedroom. 'Private bathroom' means a bath or shower and WC solely for the occupants of one bedroom, on the same floor, reasonably close and with a key provided. 'Private shower' means a shower en-suite with the bedroom but no WC.

Public bathrooms normally have a bath, sometimes with a shower attachment. If the availability of a bath is important to you, remember to check when you book.

Meals

If an establishment serves evening meals, you will find the starting time and the last order times shown in the listing; some smaller places may ask you at breakfast or at midday whether you want an evening meal.

The prices shown in each entry are for bed and breakfast or half board, but many places also offer lunch, as you will see indicated on the listing.

Opening Period

All places are open all year, except where a specific opening period is indicated.

Symbols

The at-a-glance symbols included at the end of each entry show many of the services and facilities available at each place.
You will find the key to these symbols on the back cover flap. Open out the flap and you can check the meanings of the symbols as you go.

Alcoholic Drinks

All the places listed in the guide are licensed to serve alcohol, unless the symbol UL appears. The license may be restricted - to diners only, for example - so you may want to check this when you book.

Smoking

Many places provide non-smoking areas - from no-smoking bedrooms and lounges to no-smoking sections of the restaurant. Some places prefer not to accommodate smokers, and in such cases the listing information makes this clear.

Pets

Many places accept guests with pets, but we do advise you to check this when you book, and ask about any extra charges or any rules about exactly where your pet is allowed.

Some establishments do not accept dogs at all, and these places are marked with the symbol ✖.

Visitors from overseas must not bring pets of any kind into Britain, unless they are prepared for the animals to go into lengthy quarantine. Because of the continuing threat of rabies, the penalties for ignoring these regulations are extremely severe.

Credit and Charge Cards

The credit and charge cards accepted by a place are listed immediately above the line of symbols at the end of each entry. The abbreviations used are:
Amex - American Express
Diners - Diners
Mastercard - Mastercard/ Eurocard
Visa - Visa/Barclaycard
Switch/Delta - Direct debit cards

If you do plan to pay by card, check that the establishment will take your card before you book.

Some proprietors will charge you a higher rate if you pay by credit card rather than cash or cheque. The difference is to cover the percentage paid by the proprietor to the credit card company.

If you are planning to pay by credit card, you may want to ask whether it would, in fact, be cheaper to pay by cheque or cash. When you book by telephone, you may be asked for your credit card number as 'confirmation'. But remember, the proprietor may then charge your credit card account if you cancel your booking. See under Cancellations on page 383.

Conferences and Groups

Places which cater for conferences and meetings are marked with the symbol 𝐓 (the number that follows the symbol shows the capacity). Rates are often negotiable, depending on the time of year, numbers of people involved and any special requirements you may have.

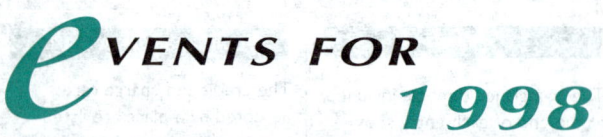

Events for 1998

This is a selection of the many cultural, sporting and other events that will be taking place throughout England during 1998. Dates marked with an asterisk* were provisional at the time of going to press.

January 1998

1-6 January
(began 4 December 1997)
Christmas Tree
Trafalgar Square, London WC2
Contact: (0171) 211 6393

6 January
Old Custom: Haxey Hood Game
The Village, Haxey,
North Lincolnshire
Contact: (01427) 752845

9-18 January
44th London International Boat Show
Earls Court Exhibition Centre,
Warwick Road, London SW5
Contact: (01784) 473377

*23-25 January**
Weekend Book Festival
Dove Cottage and Wordsworth Museum, Town End, Grasmere, Cumbria
Contact: (015394) 35544

February 1998

1 February
Chinese New Year Celebrations 1998: Year Of The Tiger
Centered on Gerrard Street and Leicester Square, London WC2
Contact: (0171) 734 5161

8-13 February
The Wordsworth Winter School
Dove Cottage and Wordsworth Museum, Town End, Grasmere, Cumbria
Contact: (015394) 35544

11-15 February
Tomorrow's World Exhibition
National Exhibition Centre,
Birmingham, West Midlands
Contact: (0181) 948 1666

14-22 February
National Boat, Caravan and Leisure Show
National Exhibition Centre,
Birmingham, West Midlands
Contact: (0121) 7804141

March 1998

5-8 March
Crufts Dog Show
National Exhibition Centre,
Birmingham, West Midlands
Contact: (0171) 493 7838

14-15 March
Ambleside Daffodil and Spring Flower Show
The Old Junior School,
Compston Road, Ambleside,
Cumbria
Contact: (015394) 32252

*17-19 March**
Cheltenham Gold Cup National Hunt Racing Festival
Cheltenham Racecourse,
Prestbury Park, Cheltenham,
Gloucestershire
Contact: (01242) 513014

19 March-13 April
Ideal Home Exhibition
Earls Court Exhibition Centre,
Warwick Road, London SW5
Contact: (0121) 767 4114

28 March
Oxford and Cambridge Boat Race
River Thames, London

April 1998

2-4 April
Grand National Meeting
Aintree Racecourse, Ormskirk Road, Aintree, Merseyside
Contact: (0151) 523 2600

10 April
Grand Steam Rally
Wetheriggs Country Pottery, Clifton Dykes, Penrith, Cumbria
Contact: (01768) 892733

11-12 April
Gateshead Spring Flower Show
Gateshead Central Nurseries, Whickham Highway, Lobley Hill, Gateshead, Tyne and Wear
Contact: (0191) 477 1011

13 April
Old Custom: World Coal Carrying Championship
Start: Royal Oak Public House, Owl Lane, Ossett, West Yorkshire

17-19 April
Morpeth Northumbrian Gathering
Morpeth Town Hall, Town Hall, Market Place, Morpeth, Northumberland
Contact: (01670) 519466

26 April
London Marathon 1998
Greenwich Park, London SE10
Contact: (0171) 620 4117

May 1998

1-31 May
Daventry and District Arts Festival 98
Various venues, Daventry, Northamptonshire
Contact: (01327) 302418

2-3 May
Wallingford Regatta
River Thames Wallingford, Oxfordshire
Contact: (01491) 836517

*2-4 May**
Rochester Sweeps Festival
Various venues, Rochester, Kent
Contact: (01634) 843666

2-4 May
Spalding Flower Festival and Springfields Country Fair
Springfields Show Gardens, Camelgate, Spalding, Lincolnshire
Contact: (01775) 724843

2-24 May
Brighton International Festival
Various venues, Brighton, East Sussex
Contact: (01273) 709709

7-10 May
The Badminton Horse Trials
Badminton House, Badminton, South Gloucestershire
Contact: (01454) 218375

*8-17 May**
Lewis Carroll Centenary Celebration
Various venues, Guildford, Surrey
Contact: (01483) 444333

9-10 May
Fighter Meet 98
North Weald Airfield, Epping, Essex
Contact: (0181) 866 9993

9-23 May
International Newbury Spring Festival
Various venues, Newbury, Berkshire
Contact: (01635) 522733

13-17 May
Royal Windsor Horse Show
Windsor Home Park, Datchet Road, Windsor, Berkshire
Contact: (0171) 341 9341

15-31 May
Bath International Music Festival
Various venues in and around Bath and North East Somerset
Contact: (01225) 463362

16 May
Football: F.A. Challenge Cup Final
Wembley Stadium, London
Contact: (0171) 402 7151

19-22 May
Chelsea Flower Show
Royal Hospital Chelsea, Royal Hospital Road, London SW3

22 May-6 June
English Riviera Dance Festival
Victoria Hotel Ballroom and Town Hall, Torquay, Devon
Contact: (01895) 632143

23-24 May
Air Fete 98
RAF Mildenhall, Suffolk

25 May
Northumberland County Show
Tynedale Park, Corbridge, Northumberland
Contact: (01434) 344443

25 May
Surrey County Show
Stoke Park, Guildford, Surrey
Contact: (01483) 414651

27-28 May
Suffolk Show
Suffolk Showground, Bucklesham Road, Ipswich, Suffolk
Contact: (01473) 726847

June 1998

1 June-29 August
Stamford Shakespeare Company: 1998 Open Air Season
Rutland Open Air Theatre, Tolethorpe Hall, Little Casterton, Leicestershire
Contact: (01780) 756133

12-28 June
51st Aldeburgh Foundation of Music and the Arts
Snape Maltings Concert Hall, Snape, Suffolk
Contact: (01728) 453543

13 June
Trooping the Colour - The Queen's Birthday Parade
Horse Guards Parade, London SW1
Contact: (0171) 414 2479

13-14 June
Northamptonshire Motorshow
Wicksteed Park, Kettering, Northamptonshire
Contact: (01536) 81111

13-20 June
International Ladies Tennis Tournament
Devonshire Park, College Road, Eastbourne, East Sussex
Contact: (01323) 412000

19-27 June
Newcastle Hoppings
Town Moor, Grandstand Road, Newcastle upon Tyne, Tyne and Wear
Contact: (0191) 454 6239

20-27 June
Broadstairs Dickens Festival
Various venues, Broadstairs, Kent
Contact: (01843) 861045

20 June-5 July
Ludlow Festival
Ludlow Castle (ruin), Castle Square, Ludlow, Shropshire
Contact: (01584) 872150

22 June-5 July
Wimbledon Lawn Tennis Championships
All England Lawn Tennis and Croquet Club, Church Road, London SW19
Contact: (0181) 946 2244

23-24 June
Cheshire Show
The Showground, Tabley, Cheshire
Contact: (01829) 760020

27-28 June
Meols Hall Annual Vintage Vehicle Rally
Meols Hall, Churchtown, Southport, Merseyside
Contact: (01704) 28326

*28 June-13 July**
Chichester Festivities
Various venues, Chichester, West Sussex
Contact: (01243) 780192

July 1998

1-4 July
Wisbech Rose Fair
Saint Peters Parish Church, Church Terrace, Wisbech, Cambridgeshire
Contact: (01945) 583086

1-5 July
Henley Royal Regatta
Henley Reach, Henley-on-Thames, Oxfordshire
Contact: (01491) 572153/4

*1-31 July**
Hull International Festival
Various venues, Hull, Kingston upon Hull
Contact: (01482) 223559

*4-5 July**
International Kite Festival
Northern Area Playing Fields, District 12, Washington, Tyne and Wear
Contact: (0191) 514 1235

*4-5 July**
Preston Maritime Festival
Preston Dock Marina, Riversway, Ashton-on-Ribble, Lancashire
Contact: (01772) 558111

4-5 July
Southampton Balloon and Flower Festival
Southampton Common, The Avenue, Southampton, Hampshire
Contact: (01703) 832755

8-11 July
Henley Festival
Henley-on-Thames, Oxfordshire
Contact: (01491) 411353

9-12 July
British Grand Prix 98
Silverstone, Northamptonshire
Contact: (01327) 857273

10-26 July
Buxton Festival
Various venues, Buxton, Derbyshire
Contact: (01298) 72190

12 July
Whalley Abbey Open Day
Whalley Abbey, Whalley, Lancashire
Contact: (01254) 822268

13 July
Yeovilton International Air Day
RNAS Yeovilton, Ilchester, Somerset
Contact: (01935) 456752

14-16 July
Great Yorkshire Show
Great Yorkshire Showground, Wetherby Road, Harrogate, North Yorkshire
Contact: (01423) 561536

*16-18 July**
Reading Real Ale and Jazz Festival
Christchurch Meadow, George Street, Caversham, Reading, Berkshire
Contact: (0118) 956 6226

17-19 July
Weeting Steam Engine Rally
Fengate Farm, Weeting, Brandon, Suffolk
Contact: (01842) 810317

18 July
Cumberland County Show
Rickerby Park, Carlisle, Cumbria
Contact: (01228) 560364

19 July
Cutty Sark Tall Ships' Race
The Harbour, Falmouth, Cornwall
Contact: (01872) 223527

21 July-2 August
Royal Tournament
Earls Court Exhibition Centre, Warwick Road, London SW5
Contact: (0171) 370 8202

23 July
Horse Racing: Glorious Goodwood
Goodwood Racecourse, Goodwood, West Sussex
Contact: (01243) 779922

25-26 July
Family Fun Weekend
The Lawn, Union Road, Lincoln, Lincolnshire
Contact: (01522) 511411

25-26 July
Gateshead Summer Flower Show
Gateshead Central Nurseries, Whickham Highway, Gateshead, Tyne and Wear
Contact: (0191) 477 1011

25 26 July
'Heart Link' Steam and Vintage Festival
Hillside Farm, Rempstone Road, Wymeswold, Leicestershire
Contact: (01509) 880803

26-28 July
Royal Lancashire Show 98
Astley Hall, Astley Park, Chorley, Lancashire
Contact: (01254) 813769

28-30 July
New Forest and Hampshire County Show
New Park, Brockenhurst, Hampshire
Contact: (01590) 622400

29 July
Sandringham Flower Show
Sandringham Park, Sandringham, Norfolk
Contact: (01485) 540860

31 July-7 August
Sidmouth International Festival of Folk Arts
Various venues, Sidmouth, Devon
Contact: (01296) 393293

August 1998

1-2 August
Wigan Pier Cross Country Boat and Steam Rally
Wigan Pier, Greater Manchester
Contact: (01942) 323666

2-3 August
Woodvale International Rally
RAF Woodvale, Southport, Merseyside
Contact: (01704) 578816

5-6 August
168th Bakewell Show
The Showground, Coombs Road, Bakewell, Derbyshire
Contact: (01629) 812736

*5-9 August**
Jazz on the Waterfront - Hull Jazz Festival
Various venues, Hull, Kingston upon Hull
Contact: (01482) 223559

7-9 August
Ambleside Great Summer Flower Show and Craft Fair
Ambleside Rugby Field, Borrans Road, Ambleside, Cumbria
Contact: (015394) 32252

7-9 August
Bristol International Balloon Fiesta
Ashton Court Estate, Long Ashton, Bristol
Contact: (0117) 953 5884

7-9 August
Lowther Horse Driving Trials and Country Fair
Lowther Castle, Lowther, Cumbria
Contact: (01931) 712378

7-9 August
Portsmouth and Southsea Show
Southsea Common, Portsmouth, Hampshire
Contact: (01705) 824355

13-16 August
Guild of Sussex Craftsmen in Action
Michelham Priory, Upper Dicker, East Sussex
Contact: (01273) 890088

14-16 August
Northampton Hot-Air Balloon Festival
Northampton Racecourse, St George's Avenue, Northampton, Northamptonshire
Contact: (01604) 238791

15-16 August
Morecambe Festival of Light and Water
Morecambe Bay, Morecambe, Lancashire
Contact: (01254) 582828

16 August
Lincolnshire Steam and Vintage Rally
Lincolnshire Showground, Grange-de-Lings, Lincoln, Lincolnshire
Contact: (01507) 605937

20-23 August
Southport Flower Show
Victoria Park, Southport, Merseyside
Contact: (01704) 547147

*21 August**
Southwood Pro-Am Tournament
Southwood Golf Club, Ively Road, Farnborough, Hampshire
Contact: (01252) 548700

26 August-1 September
International Beatles Week
Cavern Club, 8-10 Mathew Street, City Centre, Liverpool, Merseyside
Contact: (0151) 236 9091

27-29 August
Port of Dartmouth Royal Regatta
Various venues, Dartmouth, Devon
Contact: (01803) 832435

28-31 August
34th Towersey Village Festival
Towersey Village, Towersey, Oxfordshire
Contact: (01296) 394411

29-30 August
Southport Airshow
Southport Beach, Merseyside
Contact: (01704) 533333

29-31 August
The Diamond Fuchsia Festival
Harlow Carr Botanical Gardens, Crag Lane, Harrogate, North Yorkshire
Contact: (01423) 565418

30-31 August
Notting Hill Carnival
Streets around Ladbroke Grove, London W11
Contact: (0181) 964 0544

31 August
Silloth Carnival
Silloth, Cumbria
Contact: (016973) 31257

September 1998

2-6 September
Great Dorset Steam Fair
South Down, Tarrant Hinton, Dorset
Contact: (01258) 860361

3 September
Buckinghamshire County Show
Weedon Park, Weedon, Aylesbury, Buckinghamshire
Contact: (01296) 83734

4 September-8 November
Blackpool Illuminations
Blackpool Promenade, Blackpool, Lancashire
Contact: (01253) 25212

*5-6 September**
Berwick Military Tattoo
Berwick Barracks, Berwick-upon-Tweed, Northumberland
Contact: (01289) 307113

5-6 September
Chatsworth Country Fair
Chatsworth House and Garden, Bakewell, Derbyshire
Contact: (01263) 711736

5-6 September
Kirkby Lonsdale Victorian Fair
Kirkby Lonsdale, Cumbria
Contact: (015242) 71237

8 September
Widecombe Fair
Old Field, Widecombe-in-the-Moor, Devon

*10-13 September**
International Sea Shanty Festival
Hull Marina and various venues, Hull, Kingston upon Hull
Contact: (01482) 223559

12 September
Romsey Show
Broadlands Park, Romsey, Hampshire
Contact: (01794) 517521

12-13 September
Essex Steam Rally and Country Fair
Barleylands Farm Museum and Visitor Centre, Barleylands Road, Billericay, Essex
Contact: (01268) 532253

12-13 September
Farnborough International Airshow
Farnborough Airfield, Farnborough, Hampshire
Contact: (0171) 227 100

17 September
Thame Agricultural Show
The Showground, Kingsey Road, Thame, Oxfordshire
Contact: (01844) 212737

19-26 September
Scarborough Angling Festival
Scarborough
Contact: (01723) 859480

October 1998

*9-17 October**
Hull Fair
Walton Street Fairground, Hull, Kingston-upon-Hull
Contact: (01482) 223559

9-18 October
Cheltenham Festival of Literature
Town Hall, Imperial Square, Cheltenham, Gloucestershire
Contact: (01242) 22979

11 October
World Conker Championships
The Village Green, Ashton, Northamptonshire

19-20 October
Northampton St Crispin Street Fair
Main Streets of Northampton, Northamptonshire
Contact: (01604) 233500

*19-23 October**
Windermere Powerboat Record Attempts
Low Wood Watersports Centre, Low Wood, Windermere, Cumbria
Contact: (015394) 42595

20 October-1 November
British International Motor Show
National Exhibition Centre, Birmingham, West Midlands
Contact: (0121) 7804141

*31 October**
Grand Firework Spectacular
Leeds Castle, Leeds, Kent
Contact: (01622) 880008

November 1998

5 November
Bridgwater Guy Fawkes Carnival
Town Centre, Bridgwater, Somerset
Contact: (01278) 429288

14 November
Lord Mayor's Show
City of London, London

19 November
Biggest Liar in the World Competition
Bridge Inn, Wasdale, Santon Bridge, Cumbria
Contact: (01946) 67575

28-29 November
National Classic Motor Show
National Exhibition Centre, Birmingham, West Midlands
Contact: (0121) 767 2770

December 1998

*4-9 December**
BBC Clothes Show Live
National Exhibition Centre, Birmingham, West Midlands
Contact: (0121) 780 4133

5-6 December
Festive Food and Drink Fayre
South of England Showground, Ardingly, West Sussex
Contact: (01444) 892048

31 December
Allendale Baal Festival
Market Square, Allendale, Northumberland
Contact: (01434) 683763

USE YOUR i'S

Tourist Information

When it comes to your next England break, the first stage of your journey could be closer than you think. You've probably got a Tourist Information Centre nearby which is there to serve the local community - as well as visitors.

So make us your first stop. We'll be happy to help you, wherever you're heading.

Many Tourist Information Centres can provide you with maps and guides, helping you plan well in advance. And sometimes it's even possible for us to book your accommodation, too.

A visit to your nearest Tourist Information Centre can pay off in other ways as well. We can point you in the right direction when it comes to finding out about all the special events which are happening in the local region.

In fact, we can give you details of places to visit within easy reach... and perhaps tempt you to plan a day trip or weekend away.

Across the country, there are more than 550 Tourist Information Centres so you're never far away. You'll find the address of your nearest Tourist Information Centre in your local Phone Book or call Freepages on 0800 192 192.

IS IT ACCESSIBLE?

If you are a wheelchair user or someone who has difficulty walking, look for the national 'Accessible' symbol when choosing where to stay.

All the places that display a symbol have been checked by a Tourist Board inspector against standard criteria that reflect the practical needs of wheelchair users.

There are three categories of accessibility:

Category 1 Accessible to all wheelchair users including those travelling independently

Category 2 Accessible to a wheelchair user with assistance

Category 3 Accessible to a wheelchair user able to walk short distances and up at least three steps

Establishments in this guide which have a wheelchair access category are listed on pages 10 and 11.

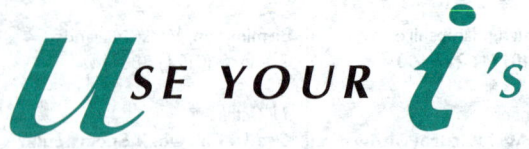

ACCOMMODATION COUPONS

► ***Complete this coupon and mail it direct to the establishment in which you are interested. Do not send it to the English Tourist Board. Remember to enclose a stamped addressed envelope (or international reply coupon).***

► ***Tick as appropriate and complete the reverse side if you are interested in making a booking.***

❏ *Please send me a brochure or further information, and details of prices charged.*
❏ *Please advise me, as soon as possible, if accommodation is available as detailed overleaf.*

Name: *(BLOCK CAPITALS)*

Address:

Postcode:

Telephone number: *Date:*

Where to Stay 1998
Bed & Breakfast, Farmhouses, Inns & Hostels

ENGLISH TOURIST BOARD

► ***Complete this coupon and mail it direct to the establishment in which you are interested. Do not send it to the English Tourist Board. Remember to enclose a stamped addressed envelope (or international reply coupon).***

► ***Tick as appropriate and complete the reverse side if you are interested in making a booking.***

❏ *Please send me a brochure or further information, and details of prices charged.*
❏ *Please advise me, as soon as possible, if accommodation is available as detailed overleaf.*

Name: *(BLOCK CAPITALS)*

Address:

Postcode:

Telephone number: *Date:*

Where to Stay 1998
Bed & Breakfast, Farmhouses, Inns & Hostels

ENGLISH TOURIST BOARD

ACCOMMODATION COUPONS

► **Complete this side if you are interested in making a booking.**

► **Please read the information on pages 383-387 before confirming any booking.**

Please advise me if accommodation is available as detailed below.

From (date of arrival): *To (date of departure):*

or alternatively from: *To:*

Adults *Children* *(ages* *)*

Please give the number of people and ages of children

Accommodation required:

Meals required:

Other/special requirements:

► **Please enclose a stamped addressed envelope (or international reply coupon).**

► **Complete this side if you are interested in making a booking.**

► **Please read the information on pages 383-387 before confirming any booking.**

Please advise me if accommodation is available as detailed below.

From (date of arrival): *To (date of departure):*

or alternatively from: *To:*

Adults *Children* *(ages* *)*

Please give the number of people and ages of children

Accommodation required:

Meals required:

Other/special requirements:

► **Please enclose a stamped addressed envelope (or international reply coupon).**

ACCOMMODATION COUPONS

▶ **Complete this coupon and mail it direct to the establishment in which you are interested. Do not send it to the English Tourist Board. Remember to enclose a stamped addressed envelope (or international reply coupon).**

▶ **Tick as appropriate and complete the reverse side if you are interested in making a booking.**

❑ *Please send me a brochure or further information, and details of prices charged.*
❑ *Please advise me, as soon as possible, if accommodation is available as detailed overleaf.*

Name: *(BLOCK CAPITALS)*

Address:

Postcode:

Telephone number: *Date:*

Where to Stay 1998
Bed & Breakfast, Farmhouses, Inns & Hostels

ENGLISH
TOURIST BOARD

▶ **Complete this coupon and mail it direct to the establishment in which you are interested. Do not send it to the English Tourist Board. Remember to enclose a stamped addressed envelope (or international reply coupon).**

▶ **Tick as appropriate and complete the reverse side if you are interested in making a booking.**

❑ *Please send me a brochure or further information, and details of prices charged.*
❑ *Please advise me, as soon as possible, if accommodation is available as detailed overleaf.*

Name: *(BLOCK CAPITALS)*

Address:

Postcode:

Telephone number: *Date:*

Where to Stay 1998
Bed & Breakfast, Farmhouses, Inns & Hostels

ENGLISH
TOURIST BOARD

ACCOMMODATION COUPONS

▶ **Complete this side if you are interested in making a booking.**

▶ **Please read the information on pages 383-387 before confirming any booking.**

Please advise me if accommodation is available as detailed below.

From (date of arrival): *To (date of departure):*

or alternatively from: *To:*

Adults *Children* *(ages)*

Please give the number of people and ages of children

Accommodation required:

Meals required:

Other/special requirements:

▶ **Please enclose a stamped addressed envelope (or international reply coupon).**

▶ **Complete this side if you are interested in making a booking.**

▶ **Please read the information on pages 383-387 before confirming any booking.**

Please advise me if accommodation is available as detailed below.

From (date of arrival): *To (date of departure):*

or alternatively from: *To:*

Adults *Children* *(ages)*

Please give the number of people and ages of children

Accommodation required:

Meals required:

Other/special requirements:

▶ **Please enclose a stamped addressed envelope (or international reply coupon).**

ACCOMMODATION COUPONS

► **_Complete this coupon and mail it direct to the establishment in which you are interested. Do not send it to the English Tourist Board. Remember to enclose a stamped addressed envelope (or international reply coupon)._**

► **_Tick as appropriate and complete the reverse side if you are interested in making a booking._**

❑ *Please send me a brochure or further information, and details of prices charged.*
❑ *Please advise me, as soon as possible, if accommodation is available as detailed overleaf.*

Name: *(BLOCK CAPITALS)*

Address:

Postcode:

Telephone number: *Date:*

Where to Stay 1998
Bed & Breakfast, Farmhouses, Inns & Hostels

ENGLISH TOURIST BOARD

► **_Complete this coupon and mail it direct to the establishment in which you are interested. Do not send it to the English Tourist Board. Remember to enclose a stamped addressed envelope (or international reply coupon)._**

► **_Tick as appropriate and complete the reverse side if you are interested in making a booking._**

❑ *Please send me a brochure or further information, and details of prices charged.*
❑ *Please advise me, as soon as possible, if accommodation is available as detailed overleaf.*

Name: *(BLOCK CAPITALS)*

Address:

Postcode:

Telephone number: *Date:*

Where to Stay 1998
Bed & Breakfast, Farmhouses, Inns & Hostels

ENGLISH TOURIST BOARD

ACCOMMODATION COUPONS

▶ ***Complete this side if you are interested in making a booking.***

▶ ***Please read the information on pages 383-387 before confirming any booking.***

Please advise me if accommodation is available as detailed below.

From (date of arrival): *To (date of departure):*

or alternatively from: *To:*

Adults *Children* *(ages)*

Please give the number of people and ages of children

Accommodation required:

Meals required:

Other/special requirements:

▶ ***Please enclose a stamped addressed envelope (or international reply coupon).***

▶ ***Complete this side if you are interested in making a booking.***

▶ ***Please read the information on pages 383-387 before confirming any booking.***

Please advise me if accommodation is available as detailed below.

From (date of arrival): *To (date of departure):*

or alternatively from: *To:*

Adults *Children* *(ages)*

Please give the number of people and ages of children

Accommodation required:

Meals required:

Other/special requirements:

▶ ***Please enclose a stamped addressed envelope (or international reply coupon).***

ACCOMMODATION COUPONS

▶ ***Complete this coupon and mail it direct to the establishment in which you are interested. Do not send it to the English Tourist Board. Remember to enclose a stamped addressed envelope (or international reply coupon).***

▶ ***Tick as appropriate and complete the reverse side if you are interested in making a booking.***

❑ *Please send me a brochure or further information, and details of prices charged.*
❑ *Please advise me, as soon as possible, if accommodation is available as detailed overleaf.*

Name: *(BLOCK CAPITALS)*

Address:

Postcode:

Telephone number: *Date:*

Where to Stay 1998
Bed & Breakfast, Farmhouses, Inns & Hostels

ENGLISH TOURIST BOARD

▶ ***Complete this coupon and mail it direct to the establishment in which you are interested. Do not send it to the English Tourist Board. Remember to enclose a stamped addressed envelope (or international reply coupon).***

▶ ***Tick as appropriate and complete the reverse side if you are interested in making a booking.***

❑ *Please send me a brochure or further information, and details of prices charged.*
❑ *Please advise me, as soon as possible, if accommodation is available as detailed overleaf.*

Name: *(BLOCK CAPITALS)*

Address:

Postcode:

Telephone number: *Date:*

Where to Stay 1998
Bed & Breakfast, Farmhouses, Inns & Hostels

ENGLISH TOURIST BOARD

ACCOMMODATION COUPONS

▶ ***Complete this side if you are interested in making a booking.***

▶ ***Please read the information on pages 383-387 before confirming any booking.***

Please advise me if accommodation is available as detailed below.

From (date of arrival): *To (date of departure):*

or alternatively from: *To:*

Adults *Children* *(ages)*

Please give the number of people and ages of children

Accommodation required:

Meals required:

Other/special requirements:

▶ ***Please enclose a stamped addressed envelope (or international reply coupon).***

▶ ***Complete this side if you are interested in making a booking.***

▶ ***Please read the information on pages 383-387 before confirming any booking.***

Please advise me if accommodation is available as detailed below.

From (date of arrival): *To (date of departure):*

or alternatively from: *To:*

Adults *Children* *(ages)*

Please give the number of people and ages of children

Accommodation required:

Meals required:

Other/special requirements:

▶ ***Please enclose a stamped addressed envelope (or international reply coupon).***

ADVERTISEMENT COUPONS

▶ ***Complete this coupon and mail it direct to the advertiser from whom you would like to receive further information. Do not send it to the English Tourist Board.***

To (advertiser's name): ________________________________

Please send me a brochure or further information on the following, as advertised by you in the English Tourist Board's Where to Stay 1998 *Guide:*

____

____

My name and address are on the reverse.

▶ ***Complete this coupon and mail it direct to the advertiser from whom you would like to receive further information. Do not send it to the English Tourist Board.***

To (advertiser's name): ________________________________

Please send me a brochure or further information on the following, as advertised by you in the English Tourist Board's Where to Stay 1998 *Guide:*

____

____

My name and address are on the reverse.

▶ ***Complete this coupon and mail it direct to the advertiser from whom you would like to receive further information. Do not send it to the English Tourist Board.***

To (advertiser's name): ________________________________

Please send me a brochure or further information on the following, as advertised by you in the English Tourist Board's Where to Stay 1998 *Guide:*

____

____

My name and address are on the reverse.

ADVERTISEMENT COUPONS

Name: (BLOCK CAPITALS)

Address:

Postcode:

Telephone Number: Date:

Where to Stay 1998

Bed & Breakfast, Farmhouses, Inns & Hostels

ENGLISH TOURIST BOARD

Name: (BLOCK CAPITALS)

Address:

Postcode:

Telephone Number: Date:

Where to Stay 1998

Bed & Breakfast, Farmhouses, Inns & Hostels

ENGLISH TOURIST BOARD

Name: (BLOCK CAPITALS)

Address:

Postcode:

Telephone Number: Date:

Where to Stay 1998

Bed & Breakfast, Farmhouses, Inns & Hostels

ENGLISH TOURIST BOARD

ADVERTISEMENT COUPONS

► *Complete this coupon and mail it direct to the advertiser from whom you would like to receive further information. Do not send it to the English Tourist Board.*

To (advertiser's name): ______________________________

Please send me a brochure or further information on the following, as advertised by you in the English Tourist Board's Where to Stay 1998 *Guide:*

____

____

My name and address are on the reverse.

► *Complete this coupon and mail it direct to the advertiser from whom you would like to receive further information. Do not send it to the English Tourist Board.*

To (advertiser's name): ______________________________

Please send me a brochure or further information on the following, as advertised by you in the English Tourist Board's Where to Stay 1998 *Guide:*

____

____

My name and address are on the reverse.

► *Complete this coupon and mail it direct to the advertiser from whom you would like to receive further information. Do not send it to the English Tourist Board.*

To (advertiser's name): ______________________________

Please send me a brochure or further information on the following, as advertised by you in the English Tourist Board's Where to Stay 1998 *Guide:*

____

____

My name and address are on the reverse.

ADVERTISEMENT COUPONS

Name: (BLOCK CAPITALS)

Address:

Postcode:

Telephone Number: Date:

Where to Stay 1998

Bed & Breakfast, Farmhouses, Inns & Hostels

ENGLISH TOURIST BOARD

Name: (BLOCK CAPITALS)

Address:

Postcode:

Telephone Number: Date:

Where to Stay 1998

Bed & Breakfast, Farmhouses, Inns & Hostels

ENGLISH TOURIST BOARD

Name: (BLOCK CAPITALS)

Address:

Postcode:

Telephone Number: Date:

Where to Stay 1998

Bed & Breakfast, Farmhouses, Inns & Hostels

ENGLISH TOURIST BOARD

TOWN INDEX

The following cities, towns and villages all have accommodation listed in this guide.

If the place where you wish to stay is not shown, the location maps (starting on page 417) will help you to find somewhere suitable in the same area.

AT-A-GLANCE SYMBOLS

Symbols at the end of each accommodation entry give useful information about services and facilities. A key to symbols can be found inside the back cover flap.

Keep this open for easy reference.

COUNTRY CODE

Always follow the Country Code · Enjoy the countryside and respect its life and work · Guard against all risk of fire · Fasten all gates · Keep your dogs under close control · Keep to public paths across farmland · Use gates and stiles to cross fences, hedges and walls · Leave livestock, crops and machinery alone · Take your litter home · Help to keep all water clean · Protect wildlife, plants and trees · Take special care on country roads · Make no unnecessary noise

CHECK THE MAPS

The colour maps at the back of this guide show all the cities, towns and villages for which you will find accommodation entries.

Refer to the town index to find the page on which it is listed.

S — page no

T — page no

INDEX TO ADVERTISERS

You can obtain further information from any display advertiser in this guide by completing an advertisement enquiry coupon. You will find these coupons on pages 403-406.

Mileage Chart

The distances between towns on the mileage chart are given to the nearest mile, and are measured along routes based on the quickest travelling time, making maximum use of motorways or dual-carriageway roads. The chart is based upon information supplied by the Automobile Association.

	Aberdeen	Aberystwyth	Barnstaple	Birmingham	Brighton	Bristol	Cambridge	Cardiff	Carlisle	Carmarthen	Colchester	Dorchester	Dover	Edinburgh	Exeter	Fort William	Glasgow	Gloucester	Guildford	Holyhead	Hull	Inverness	Kendal	Leeds	Lincoln	Liverpool	Maidstone	Manchester	Middlesbrough	Newcastle	Norwich	Nottingham	Oxford	Penzance	Perth	Plymouth	Sheffield	Southampton	Stranraer	Taunton	York
Aberystwyth	466																																								
Barnstaple	604	211																																							
Birmingham	431	124	177																																						
Brighton	607	285	208	170																																					
Bristol	515	127	99	90	169																																				
Cambridge	463	215	266	97	120	170																																			
Cardiff	532	109	127	107	201	43	202																																		
Carlisle	232	233	371	199	373	281	257	299																																	
Carmarthen	514	47	190	170	264	106	265	67	281																																
Colchester	516	290	291	171	111	195	48	227	310	290																															
Dorchester	596	203	93	172	119	62	179	119	364	182	206																														
Dover	587	326	272	208	82	205	124	237	381	300	115	200																													
Edinburgh	125	332	470	297	472	380	334	398	98	380	387	462	458																												
Exeter	588	195	55	164	175	83	250	111	356	174	275	54	244	455																											
Fort William	155	443	580	408	583	491	466	509	209	491	520	573	610	132	564																										
Glasgow	147	330	468	295	470	378	354	396	96	378	407	460	497	47	452	102																									
Gloucester	480	111	125	55	155	35	150	61	247	124	170	117	191	346	109	457	344																								
Guildford	565	221	179	128	44	105	90	137	332	200	103	97	96	431	151	542	429	99																							
Holyhead	459	104	339	167	341	249	258	204	227	151	332	331	368	326	323	437	324	215	299																						
Hull	360	224	320	134	259	230	139	248	170	311	192	312	263	230	304	379	267	195	238	219																					
Inverness	105	491	629	457	631	539	515	557	257	539	568	621	658	157	613	65	173	505	589	486	428																				
Kendal	279	187	325	152	327	235	244	253	46	235	318	317	354	145	309	256	143	200	285	181	163	304																			
Leeds	328	170	301	116	263	212	147	230	122	218	200	293	271	198	285	331	219	177	220	165	60	380	71																		
Lincoln	388	216	275	98	216	185	95	203	181	266	148	244	219	258	259	391	279	151	173	204	45	440	175	71																	
Liverpool	357	107	273	101	275	183	192	201	125	162	266	265	302	224	257	335	222	149	233	102	127	383	79	74	139																
Maidstone	545	284	232	165	50	166	82	198	339	260	73	160	41	416	204	549	436	151	56	328	221	597	313	229	177	261															
Manchester	352	131	260	88	263	171	160	189	120	179	213	252	290	219	244	329	217	136	220	125	97	378	74	43	84	34	251														
Middlesbrough	275	240	357	171	318	267	298	285	94	288	251	349	322	146	341	280	191	232	276	235	88	307	84	66	122	144	283	113													
Newcastle	235	271	388	202	349	298	229	316	60	319	282	380	353	105	372	239	254	263	307	266	141	266	102	97	153	175	314	144	38												
Norwich	488	277	328	159	168	232	63	264	282	327	59	241	172	359	312	491	379	212	160	321	148	540	276	171	103	240	133	185	223	254											
Nottingham	394	161	234	53	195	144	86	162	188	225	139	226	218	265	218	398	285	109	152	173	92	446	148	73	37	106	179	70	129	160	118										
Oxford	504	159	169	68	109	73	80	105	272	168	124	113	145	371	153	481	369	47	66	240	189	530	226	170	129	174	106	161	226	257	143	103									
Penzance	698	305	108	273	287	193	360	221	466	283	385	166	356	564	109	675	563	219	263	434	414	724	420	396	370	368	317	355	452	482	422	328	263								
Perth	86	379	517	345	519	427	379	446	145	427	432	509	503	41	501	102	61	393	477	374	276	113	193	247	303	271	464	266	192	150	403	309	417	611							
Plymouth	629	236	62	204	218	124	291	152	396	214	316	97	287	495	44	606	494	150	194	365	345	655	350	327	300	299	248	286	383	413	353	259	194	77	543						
Sheffield	364	163	271	75	233	182	122	200	171	263	175	263	246	235	255	380	268	147	190	158	65	429	125	35	47	78	207	38	99	130	147	43	140	365	281	296					
Southampton	571	221	141	134	66	77	131	137	338	200	158	53	151	437	108	548	435	99	48	307	255	596	292	236	196	240	112	227	292	323	193	169	65	220	484	151	207				
Stranraer	232	339	477	305	479	387	363	406	105	387	416	469	507	132	461	188	85	353	437	334	276	258	153	231	288	231	468	226	200	163	388	294	377	571	146	502	277	443			
Taunton	556	162	49	131	159	51	218	78	323	141	243	45	223	422	33	533	420	77	130	292	272	581	277	253	227	225	184	213	309	340	280	186	121	143	470	74	224	93	430		
York	322	198	314	129	275	224	155	243	116	246	209	306	280	193	298	326	213	190	233	192	38	374	91	23	80	101	241	71	49	88	180	86	183	408	239	339	56	250	222	266	
London	546	238	215	120	59	119	60	151	314	214	61	128	77	412	199	523	411	102	30	282	187	572	268	198	143	216	38	203	254	285	115	130	56	309	460	240	168	80	420	167	211

CUSTOMER FEEDBACK QUESTIONNAIRE

We hope you have found this guide useful in selecting accommodation in England which suits your needs.

It is very helpful to the English Tourist Board to receive comments about establishments in *Where to Stay* and suggestions on how to improve the guide, and also on the National Grading and Classification Schemes.

We would like to hear from you. If you wish to do so, you can send us your views using this questionnaire. You need not name the establishment concerned.

Q1 Did you use the *Where to Stay* guide to find:

- Holiday accommodation ☐
- Business accommodation ☐
- Both ☐

Q2 Did you use the establishment's Quality Grading/Crown or Key Classification to help you in making your choice?

- Yes ☐
- No ☐

Q3 If you did, was it the Quality Grading (Approved, Commended, Highly Commended or De Luxe) or the number of Crowns or Keys for facilities that influenced you most?

- The Quality Grading ☐
- The number of Crowns/Keys ☐
- Both ☐

Q4 What was the Quality Grading and Crown or Key Classification of the establishment you chose?

....

Q5 Do you find the National Grades and Classifications:

- Very easy to understand ☐
- Fairly easy to understand ☐
- Difficult to understand ☐

If you found them difficult to understand, please specify why:

....

....

Q6 Was the accommodation you used:

- Hotel ☐
- Guesthouse ☐
- Farmhouse ☐
- Bed & Breakfast ☐
- Self-Catering Holiday Home ☐

Q7 Did the establishment chosen:

- Exceed your expectations ☐
- Meet your expectations ☐
- Fail to meet your expectations ☐

If it failed to meet your expectations, please specify how:

....

....

Q8 Would you say the establishment offered good value for money?

- Yes ☐
- No ☐

Q9 Was there any feature of your stay that you would particularly praise or criticise (please specify):

....

....

....

Q10 Have you bought a *Where to Stay* guide before?

Yes ☐

No ☐

If yes, how long ago:

Last year ☐

2 years ago ☐

More than 2 years ago ☐

Q11 Did you find the *Where to Stay* guide:

Very easy to use ☐

Fairly easy to use ☐

Difficult to use ☐

Q12 Are there any aspects of the *Where to Stay* guide that you would particularly praise or criticise (please specify):

....

....

....

Q13 Is there any additional information not already featured in this guide that you would find helpful (please specify):

....

....

....

Please would you give us a few details about yourself:

Q14 Are you:

Married ☐

Single ☐

Q15 Do you have dependent children?

Yes ☐

No ☐

If yes, how many ☐

Q16 Into which age group do you fall?

17-24 ☐

25-34 ☐

35-44 ☐

45-54 ☐

55+ ☐

Q17 Are you an overseas visitor (i.e. from outside the UK visiting this country)?

Yes ☐

No ☐

Q18 Did you travel alone or with a party?

Alone ☐

Party of people ☐

of which .... were adults

and .... children

Q19 How long did you stay in the establishment?

.... nights

Q20 Do you plan to use the guide to book any further stays this year?

Yes ☐

No ☐

If yes, how many ☐

Q21 What other sources of information did you use in selecting your accommodation (please specify):

....

....

Q22 Did you obtain your copy of *Where to Stay* from

Bookshop ☐

Tourist Information Centre ☐

Other (please specify) ☐

Thank you for giving us your views. Please return this questionnaire to: Department AS, English Tourist Board, Thames Tower, Black's Road, Hammersmith, London W6 9EL.

LOCATION MAPS

Every place name featured in the accommodation listings pages of this Where to Stay *guide has a map reference to help you locate it on the maps which follow. For example, to find Colchester, Essex, which has 'Map ref 3B2', turn to Map 3 and refer to grid square B2.*

All place names in the listings pages are shown in black type on the maps. This enables you to find other places in your chosen area which may have suitable accommodation - the Town Index (preceding pages) gives page numbers.

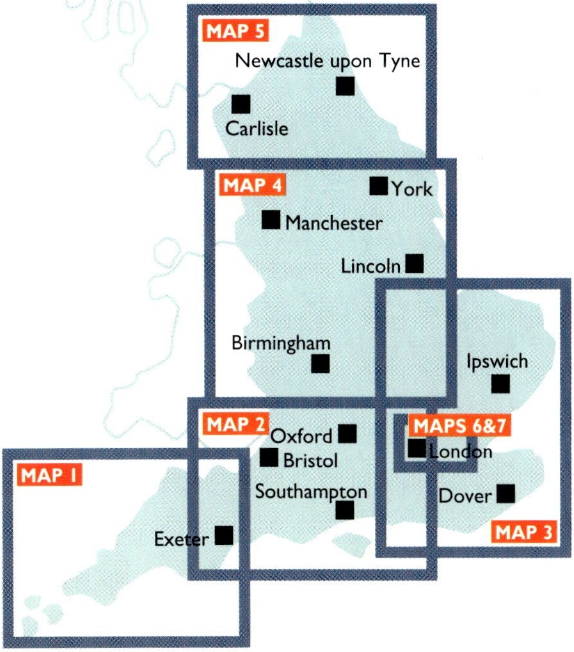

MAP 1

A
B
1
2
3
Boscastle
Tintagel
Padstow
St Kew
A39
Treyarnon Bay
A30
St Mawgan
Bodmin
Newquay
St Wenn
Newquay
Tregaswith
A392
A30
A391
A390
Goonhavern
St Austell
A39
Truro
Grampound
A390
Mevagissey
Gorran Haven
St Ives
A30
Carbis Bay
A39
Mylor Bridge
St Just-in-Penwith
A394
Falmouth
Perranuthnoe
Penzance
Sennen Cove
Helston
Coverack
Mullion
Isles of Scilly
Isles of Scilly (St. Mary's)

Produced by COLIN EARL Cartography

MAP 2

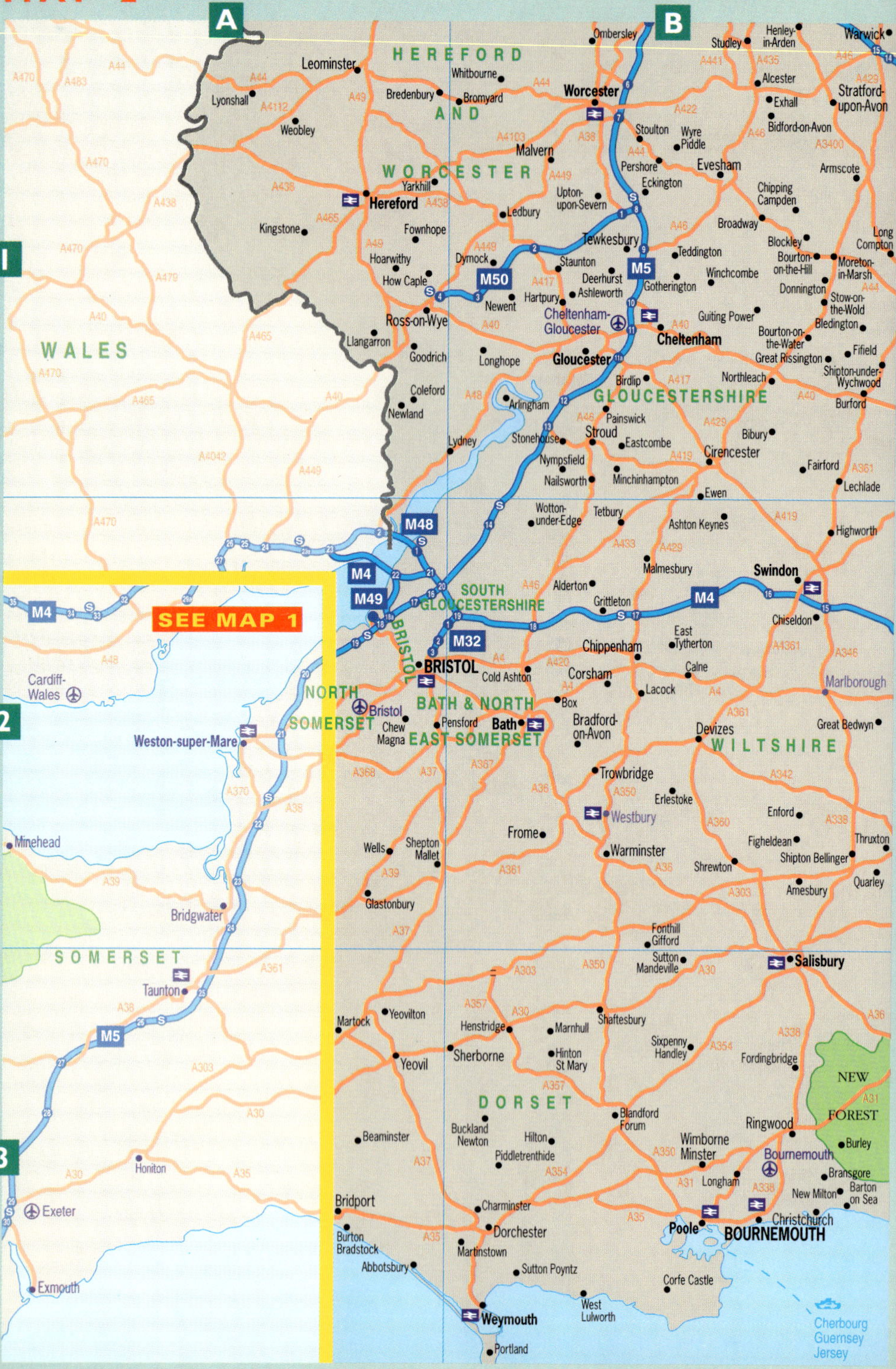

A
B
I
2
3
HEREFORD
AND
WORCESTER
WALES
GLOUCESTERSHIRE
SOUTH GLOUCESTERSHIRE
NORTH SOMERSET
BATH & NORTH EAST SOMERSET
WILTSHIRE
SOMERSET
DORSET
NEW FOREST
SEE MAP 1
Leominster
Lyonshall
Weobley
Whitbourne
Bredenbury
Bromyard
Ombersley
Worcester
Studley
Henley-in-Arden
Warwick
Alcester
Exhall
Stratford-upon-Avon
Bidford-on-Avon
Stoulton
Wyre Piddle
Pershore
Evesham
Malvern
Yarkhill
Hereford
Kingstone
Fownhope
Ledbury
Upton-upon-Severn
Eckington
Armscote
Chipping Campden
Broadway
Long Compton
Blockley
Bourton-on-the-Hill
Moreton-in-Marsh
Tewkesbury
Teddington
Hoarwithy
Dymock
Staunton
How Caple
Deerhurst
Ashleworth
Winchcombe
Gotherington
Donnington
Stow-on-the-Wold
Newent
Hartpury
Cheltenham-Gloucester
Cheltenham
Guiting Power
Bledington
Ross-on-Wye
Llangarron
Goodrich
Longhope
Gloucester
Bourton-on-the-Water
Great Rissington
Fifield
Shipton-under-Wychwood
Birdlip
Northleach
Burford
Coleford
Newland
Arlingham
Painswick
Stroud
Bibury
Lydney
Stonehouse
Eastcombe
Cirencester
Nympsfield
Nailsworth
Minchinhampton
Fairford
Lechlade
Ewen
Wotton-under-Edge
Tetbury
Ashton Keynes
Highworth
Malmesbury
Swindon
Alderton
Grittleton
Chiseldon
East Tytherton
Chippenham
Cold Ashton
Corsham
Calne
BRISTOL
Bristol
Lacock
Marlborough
Box
Chew Magna
Pensford
Bath
Bradford-on-Avon
Devizes
Great Bedwyn
Trowbridge
Erlestoke
Westbury
Enford
Frome
Figheldean
Thruxton
Wells
Shepton Mallet
Warminster
Shrewton
Shipton Bellinger
Amesbury
Quarley
Glastonbury
Fonthill Gifford
Sutton Mandeville
Salisbury
Martock
Yeovilton
Henstridge
Marnhull
Shaftesbury
Sixpenny Handley
Fordingbridge
Yeovil
Sherborne
Hinton St Mary
Blandford Forum
Beaminster
Buckland Newton
Hilton
Piddletrenthide
Wimborne Minster
Ringwood
Bournemouth
Burley
Bransgore
Barton on Sea
New Milton
Longham
Bridport
Charminster
Christchurch
Poole
BOURNEMOUTH
Burton Bradstock
Dorchester
Martinstown
Abbotsbury
Sutton Poyntz
Corfe Castle
West Lulworth
Weymouth
Portland
Cherbourg
Guernsey
Jersey
Cardiff-Wales
Weston-super-Mare
Minehead
Bridgwater
Taunton
Honiton
Exeter
Exmouth
M4
M5
M32
M48
M49
M50
A44
A470
A483
A4112
A49
A438
A465
A479
A40
A4042
A449
A48
A417
A419
A429
A46
A435
A441
A422
A4103
A38
A433
A420
A4361
A346
A342
A338
A360
A350
A36
A361
A37
A368
A367
A39
A303
A357
A30
A354
A35
A31
A348
A370

Produced by COLIN EARL Cartography

MAP 3

1
2
A
B
C
LINCOLNSHIRE
RUTLAND
CAMBRIDGESHIRE
NORFOLK
SUFFOLK
BEDFORDSHIRE
SEE MAP 2
THE BROADS
Grantham
Sleaford
Boston
Spalding
Skillington
South Witham
Swayfield
Corby Glen
Stamford
Rutland Water
Peterborough
Wadenhoe
Stoke Doyle
Kettering
Huntingdon
St Ives
Chatteris
Wisbech
Upwell
Ely
King's Lynn
Hunstanton
Thornham
Choseley
Burnham Overy Staithe
Great Bircham
Sandringham
Hillington
Little Walsingham
Thursford
Fakenham
Blakeney
Sheringham
Cromer
Mundesley
North Walsham
Aylsham
Hevingham
Beetley
Dereham
Swaffham
Wroxham
Rackheath
Norwich
NORWICH
Potter Heigham
Great Yarmouth
Reedham
Stoke Holy Cross
Hethersett
Wymondham
Attleborough
Lowestoft
Beccles
Bungay
Southwold
Blythburgh
Thetford
Garboldisham
Diss
Fressingfield
Saxstead
Framlingham
Saxmundham
Aldringham
Aldeburgh
Blaxhall
Eyke
Woodbridge
Felixstowe
Harwich
Ipswich
Haughley
Woolpit
Beyton
Bury St. Edmunds
Newmarket
Lawshall
Hartest
Lavenham
Kersey
Hadleigh
Capel St Mary
East Bergholt
Dedham
Bradfield
Wix
Colchester
Nayland
Stoke-by-Nayland
Sudbury
Great Yeldham
Earls Colne
Braintree
Thaxted
Great Dunmow
Esbjerg
Gothenburg
Hamburg
Hook of Holland
Cambridge
London Stansted
Stevenage
Luton
Bedford
A1(M)
M11
M1

Produced by COLIN EARL Cartography

MAP 4

A
B
1
2
3
Douglas
Belfast
Douglas
YORKSHIRE DALES
NATIONAL PARK
Airton
Hellifield
Knaresborough
A1(M)
Harrogate
Goldsborough
LANCASHIRE
NORTH YORKSHIRE
Garstang
St Michael's on Wyre
Great Eccleston
Singleton
BLACKPOOL
M6
M55
PRESTON
Lytham St. Anne's
Clitheroe
Colne
Burnley
M65
Blackburn
Ilkley
Otley
Keighley
Oakworth
Haworth
Leeds-Bradford
Horsforth
LEEDS
Garforth
BRADFORD
WEST YORKSHIRE
Hebden Bridge
Lydgate
Bacup
Todmorden
Walsden
Sowerby Bridge
Halifax
HUDDERSFIELD
Wakefield
M62
M1
Southport
Chorley
M61
M66
Rochdale
Bury
Bolton
Wigan
Holmfirth
Oldham
M58
GREATER MANCHESTER
MANCHESTER
Salford
M67
MERSEYSIDE
M57
LIVERPOOL
Birkenhead
M63
Hyde
Stockport
Altrincham
Warrington
Runcorn
Liverpool
Ashley
Manchester
Styal
Wilmslow
PEAK DISTRICT
NATIONAL PARK
SHEFFIELD
SOUTH
Bamford
Hathersage
Castleton
Whaley Bridge
Eyam
Froggatt
Calver
Tideswell
Litton
Cressbrook
Buxton
Holmesfield
Ashford in the Water
Bakewell
Chesterfield
M56
M53
Acton Bridge
Northwich
Knutsford
Macclesfield
Chester
CHESHIRE
Tarporley
Sandbach
Crewe
Rushton Spencer
Leek
Two Dales
Matlock
Ashover
Wessington
Aldwark
Butterton
Waterhouses
Wirksworth
Crich
Endon
WALES
Malpas
Nantwich
Newcastle-under-Lyme
STOKE-ON-TRENT
Madeley
Onneley
Oakamoor
Alton
Cheadle
DERBYSHIRE
Belper
Ashbourne
Barlaston
STAFFORDSHIRE
Market Drayton
Stone
DERBY
Oswestry
Wem
Ruyton-XI-Towns
Stafford
Abbots Bromley
Burton upon Trent
Newport
Rugeley
Yoxall
Shrewsbury
Telford
M54
Lichfield
Minsterley
Pontesbury
Stiperstones
Ironbridge
Much Wenlock
Church Stretton
WOLVERHAMPTON
WALSALL
Wentnor
Bridgnorth
M6
Lea Marston
Hinckley
Nuneaton
Bishop's Castle
SHROPSHIRE
Chelmarsh
WEST MIDLANDS
Fillongley
BIRMINGHAM
Birmingham
Clun
Clunbury
Craven Arms
Stourbridge
M42
Hampton in Arden
Meriden
Berkswell
COVENTRY
M5
Solihull
Balsall Common
Clungunford
Cleobury Mortimer
Kidderminster
WARWICKSHIRE
Bucknell
Ludlow
Tenbury Wells
Rock
Bromsgrove
M40
Kenilworth
Leamington Spa

Produced by COLIN EARL Cartography

MAP 5

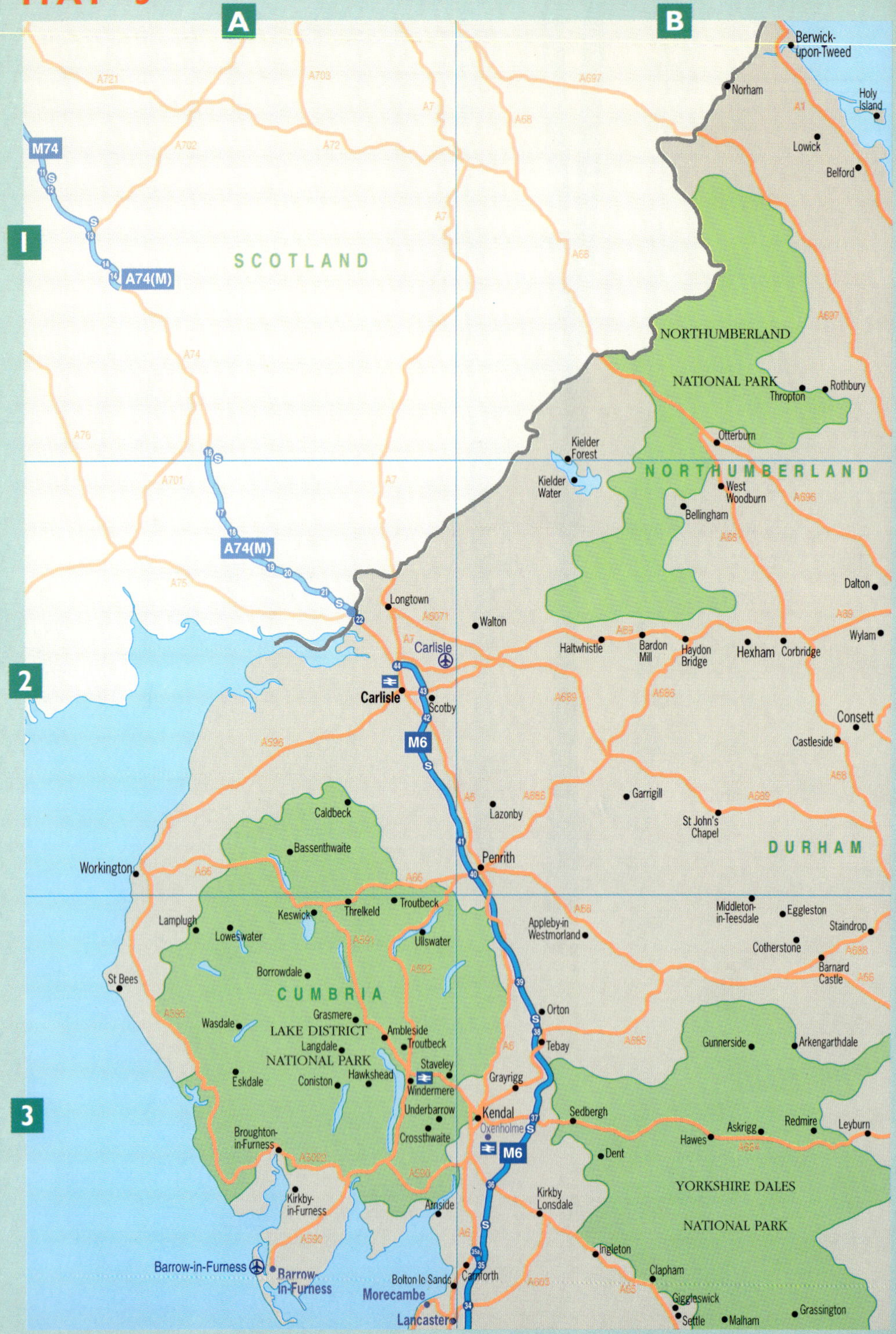

A
B
1
2
3
M74
A74(M)
A74(M)
M6
M6
SCOTLAND
NORTHUMBERLAND
NATIONAL PARK
NORTHUMBERLAND
DURHAM
CUMBRIA
LAKE DISTRICT
NATIONAL PARK
YORKSHIRE DALES
NATIONAL PARK
Berwick-upon-Tweed
Norham
Holy Island
Lowick
Belford
Rothbury
Thropton
Otterburn
Kielder Forest
Kielder Water
West Woodburn
Bellingham
Dalton
Longtown
Walton
Carlisle
Carlisle
Scotby
Haltwhistle
Bardon Mill
Haydon Bridge
Hexham
Corbridge
Wylam
Consett
Castleside
Garrigill
St John's Chapel
Lazonby
Caldbeck
Bassenthwaite
Workington
Penrith
Troutbeck
Threlkeld
Keswick
Lamplugh
Loweswater
Ullswater
Appleby-in Westmorland
Middleton-in-Teesdale
Eggleston
Staindrop
Cotherstone
Barnard Castle
Borrowdale
St Bees
Orton
Tebay
Grasmere
Wasdale
Ambleside
Troutbeck
Langdale
Staveley
Gunnerside
Arkengarthdale
Eskdale
Coniston
Hawkshead
Windermere
Grayrigg
Underbarrow
Kendal
Oxenholme
Sedbergh
Askrigg
Redmire
Leyburn
Hawes
Dent
Crossthwaite
Broughton-in-Furness
Kirkby-in-Furness
Arnside
Kirkby Lonsdale
Ingleton
Clapham
Barrow-in-Furness
Barrow-in-Furness
Bolton le Sands
Carnforth
Morecambe
Lancaster
Giggleswick
Settle
Malham
Grassington
A721
A703
A697
A7
A68
A1
A702
A72
A7
A68
A74
A697
A76
A701
A7
A696
A68
A75
A6071
A7
A69
A69
A686
A689
A596
A6
A686
A689
A68
A66
A66
A591
A592
A66
A688
A66
A595
A6
A685
A5092
A590
A684
A590
A6
A683
A65

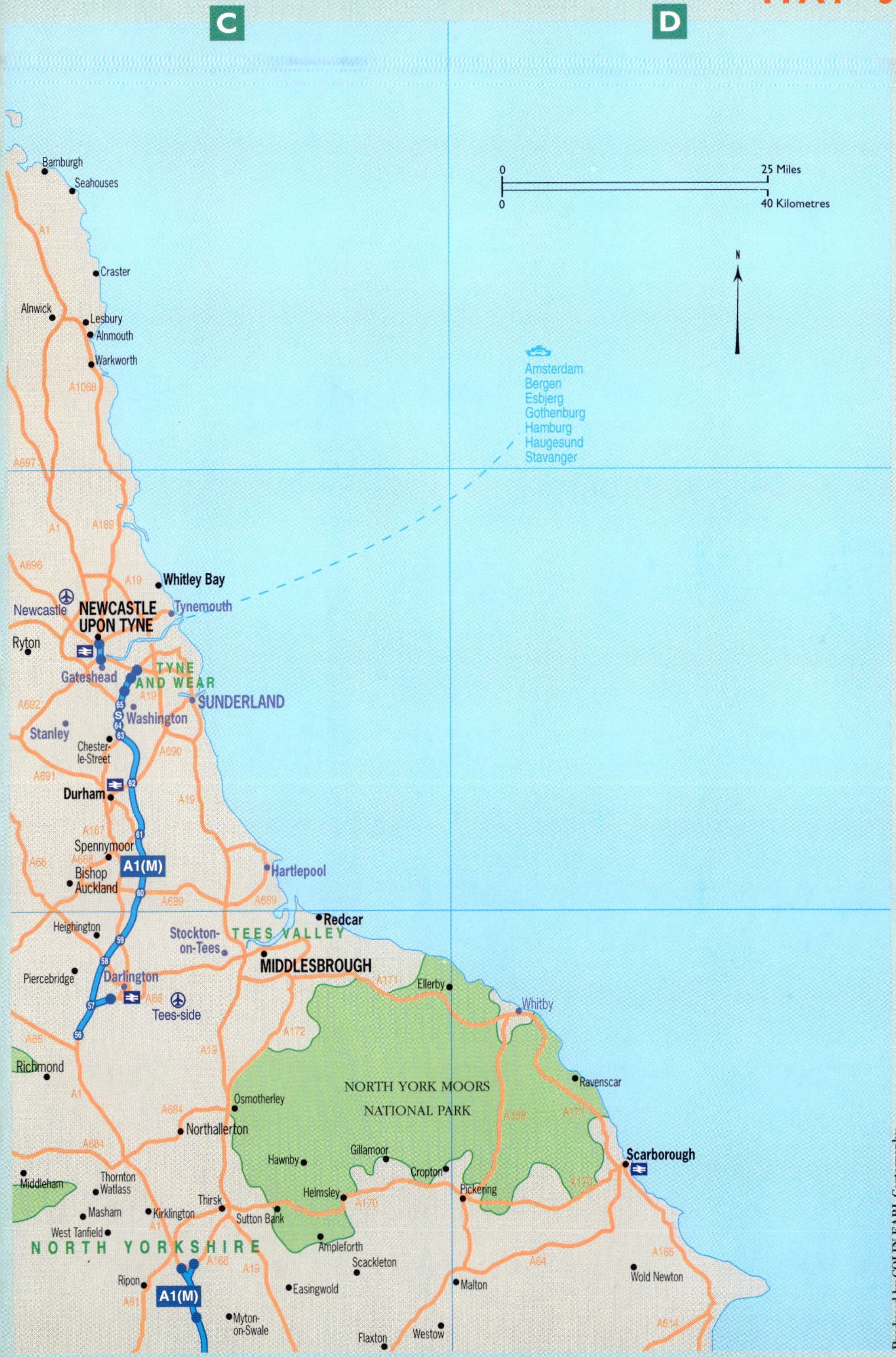
C
D
0
25 Miles
0
40 Kilometres
N
Amsterdam
Bergen
Esbjerg
Gothenburg
Hamburg
Haugesund
Stavanger
Bamburgh
Seahouses
A1
Craster
Alnwick
Lesbury
Alnmouth
Warkworth
A1068
A697
A1
A189
A696
A19
Whitley Bay
Newcastle
NEWCASTLE
UPON TYNE
Tynemouth
Ryton
Gateshead
TYNE
AND WEAR
A19
SUNDERLAND
A692
Washington
Stanley
Chester-
le-Street
A690
A691
Durham
A19
A167
Spennymoor
A688
A68
A1(M)
Bishop
Auckland
A689
A689
Hartlepool
Redcar
Heighington
Stockton-
on-Tees
TEES VALLEY
MIDDLESBROUGH
Piercebridge
Darlington
A66
Tees-side
A171
Ellerby
Whitby
A66
A172
A19
Richmond
A1
Ravenscar
NORTH YORK MOORS
NATIONAL PARK
Osmotherley
A684
Northallerton
A169
A171
A684
Gillamoor
Hawnby
Cropton
Scarborough
Middleham
Thornton
Watlass
Helmsley
Pickering
A170
A170
Masham
Kirklington
Thirsk
Sutton Bank
A1
West Tanfield
NORTH YORKSHIRE
Ampleforth
A168
A19
Scackleton
A165
A64
Ripon
A1(M)
Easingwold
Malton
Wold Newton
A61
Myton-
on-Swale
A614
Flaxton
Westow

Produced by COLIN EARL Cartography

MAP 6

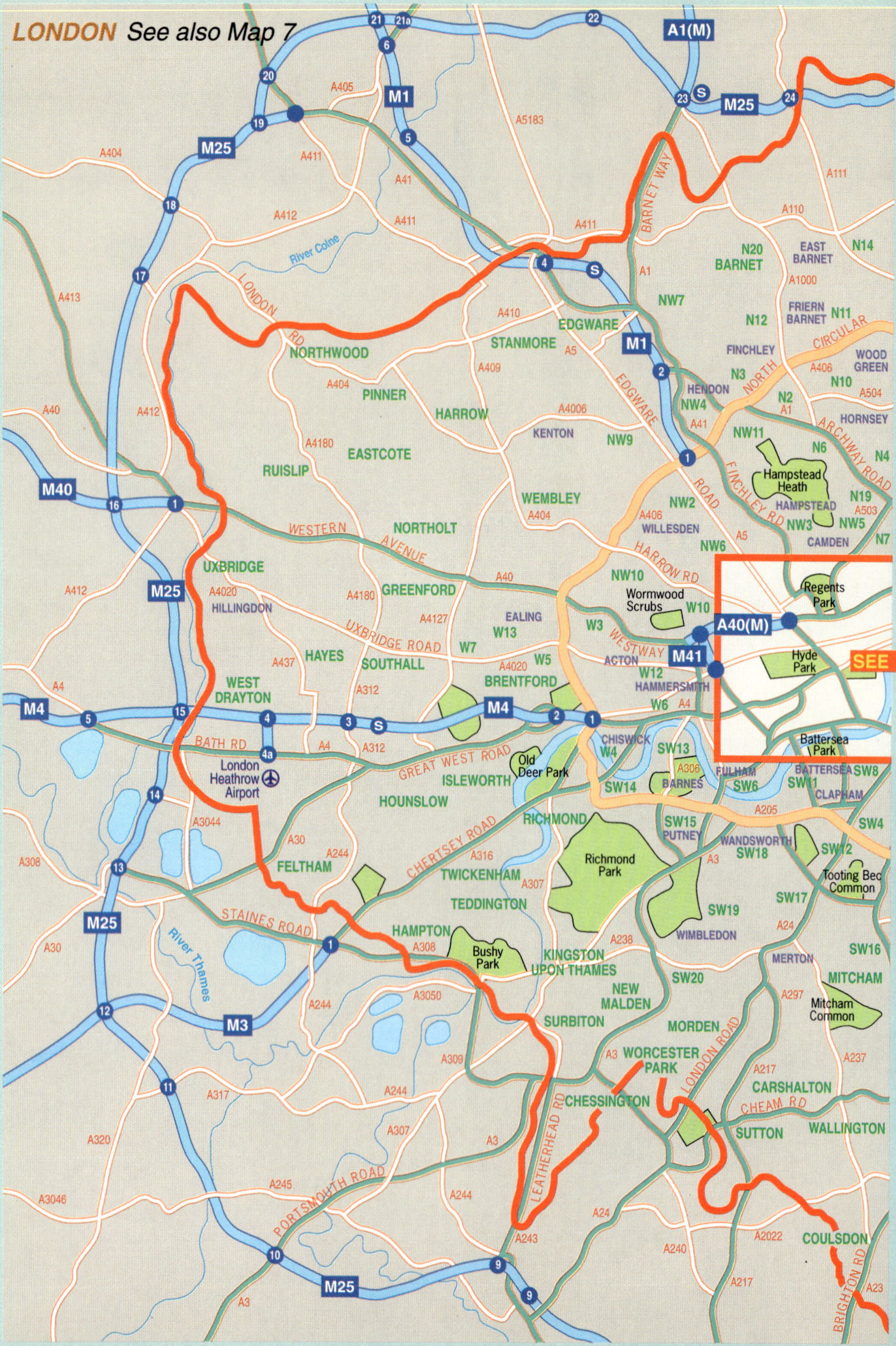
LONDON See also Map 7
M25
M1
A1(M)
M40
M4
M3
A40(M)
M41
A405
A5183
A404
A411
A41
A412
A413
A411
A111
A110
A1000
River Colne
LONDON RD
NORTHWOOD
PINNER
HARROW
STANMORE
EDGWARE
BARNET WAY
A410
A409
A5
EDGWARE RD
KENTON
A4006
NW9
NW7
A1
N20
BARNET
EAST BARNET
N14
N12
FRIERN BARNET
N11
FINCHLEY
NORTH CIRCULAR
WOOD GREEN
N3
HENDON
N10
A406
A504
N2
A1
NW4
A41
HORNSEY
ARCHWAY ROAD
NW11
N6
N4
Hampstead Heath
HAMPSTEAD
N19
A503
FINCHLEY RD
NW3
NW5
CAMDEN
N7
NW2
A406
WILLESDEN
A5
NW6
HARROW RD
NW10
Wormwood Scrubs
W10
Regents Park
Hyde Park
SEE
Battersea Park
A40
A4180
RUISLIP
EASTCOTE
WEMBLEY
A404
WESTERN AVENUE
NORTHOLT
UXBRIDGE
A4020
HILLINGDON
A4180
GREENFORD
A4127
EALING
W13
W3
WESTWAY
ACTON
W12
HAMMERSMITH
W6
A4
UXBRIDGE ROAD
W7
A437
HAYES
SOUTHALL
A4020
W5
BRENTFORD
WEST DRAYTON
A312
A4
BATH RD
A4
A312
London Heathrow Airport
GREAT WEST ROAD
ISLEWORTH
HOUNSLOW
Old Deer Park
CHISWICK
W4
SW13
A306
BARNES
FULHAM
SW6
BATTERSEA
SW8
SW11
CLAPHAM
SW14
RICHMOND
A205
SW4
SW15
PUTNEY
WANDSWORTH
SW18
SW12
A3
Tooting Bec Common
Richmond Park
CHERTSEY ROAD
A316
TWICKENHAM
A307
TEDDINGTON
SW19
WIMBLEDON
SW17
A24
SW16
MERTON
A3044
A30
A244
FELTHAM
A308
STAINES ROAD
A30
River Thames
HAMPTON
A308
Bushy Park
KINGSTON UPON THAMES
A238
NEW MALDEN
SW20
MITCHAM
A297
Mitcham Common
A3050
A244
SURBITON
MORDEN
A309
A3
WORCESTER PARK
LONDON ROAD
A237
A217
CARSHALTON
CHESSINGTON
CHEAM RD
SUTTON
WALLINGTON
A317
A244
A307
A3
LEATHERHEAD RD
A320
A245
PORTSMOUTH ROAD
A244
A3046
A24
A243
A240
A2022
COULSDON
A217
BRIGHTON RD
A23
A3

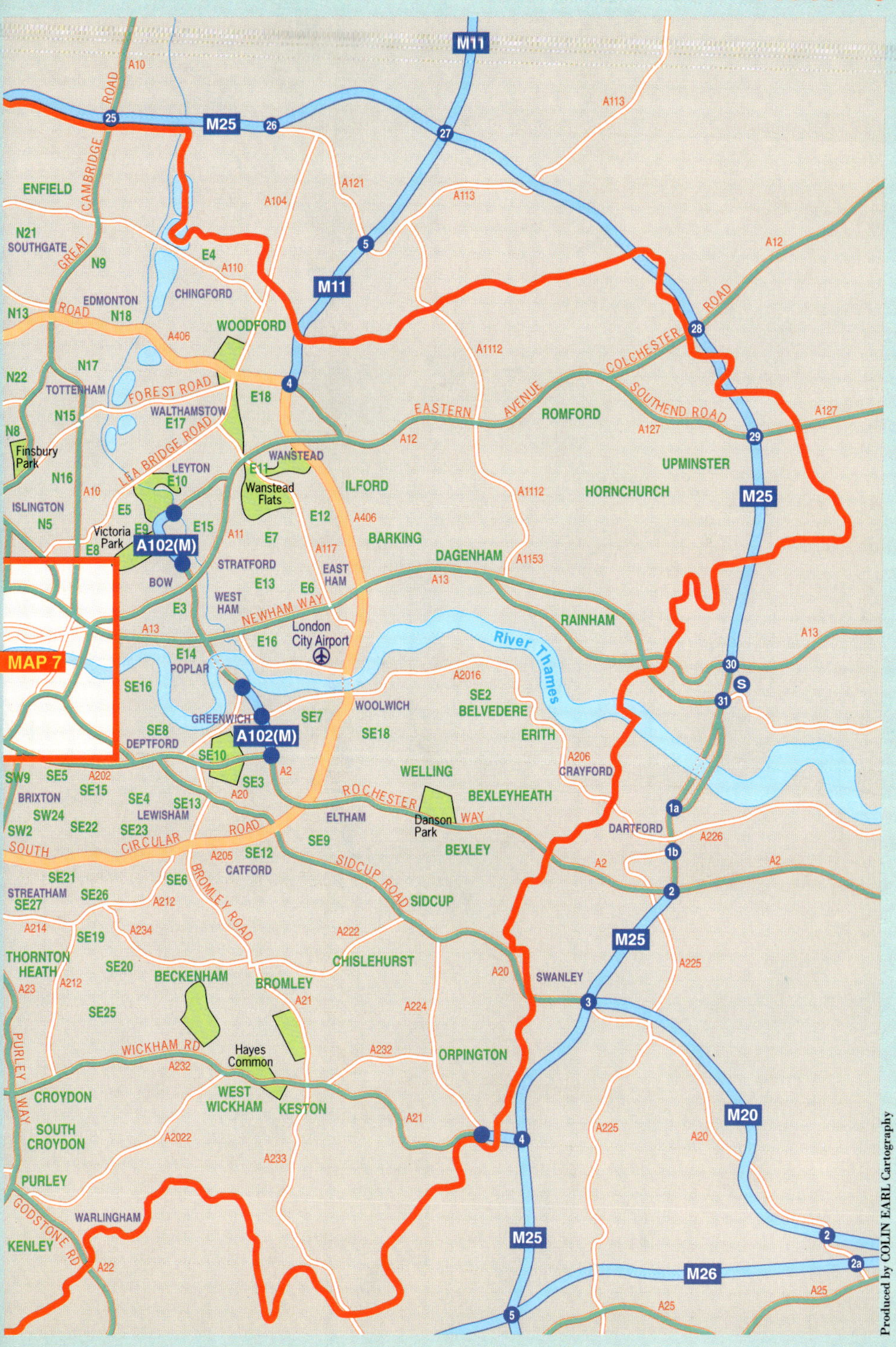

Produced by COLIN EARL Cartography

MAP 7

LONDON See also Map 6

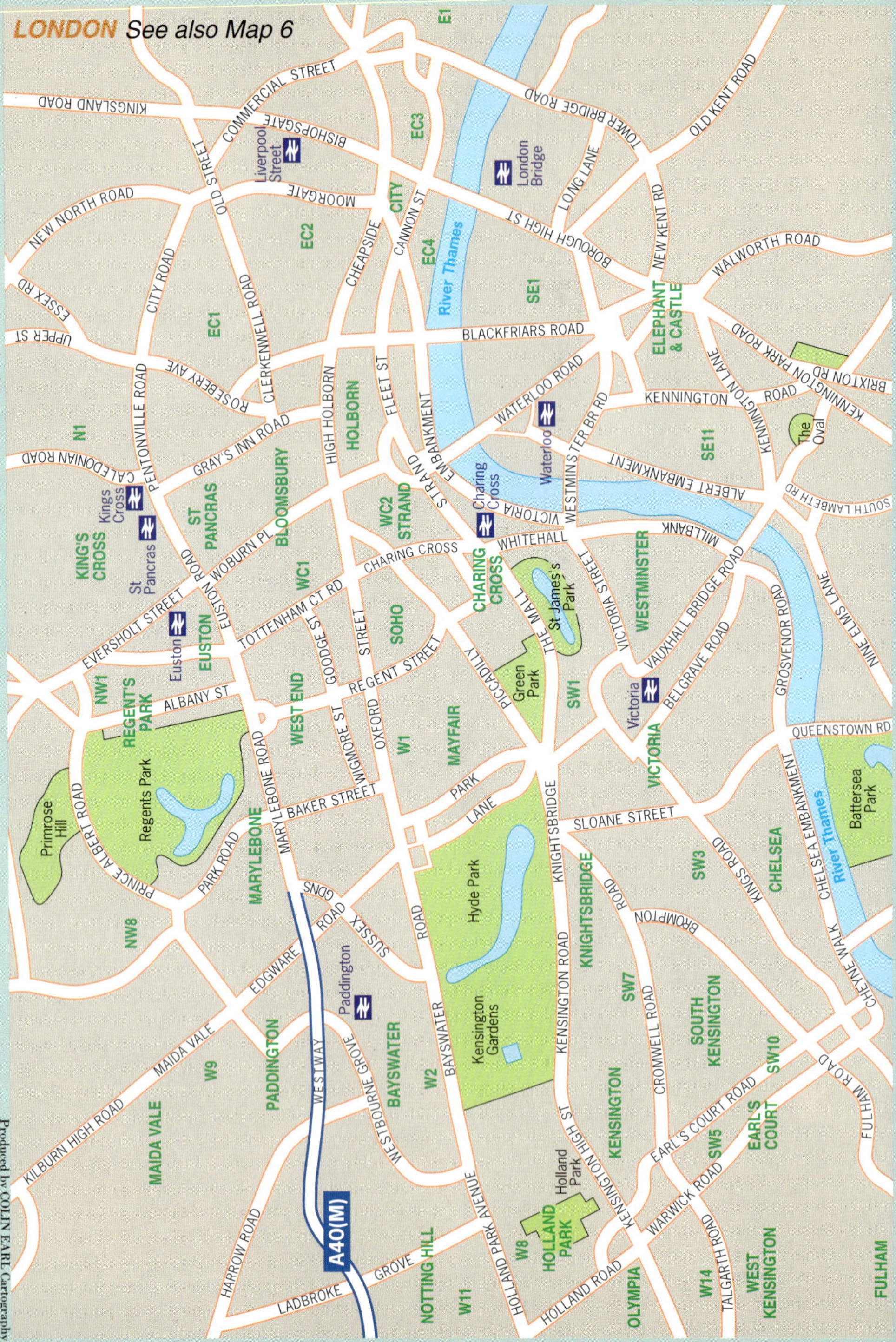

Produced by COLIN EARL Cartography

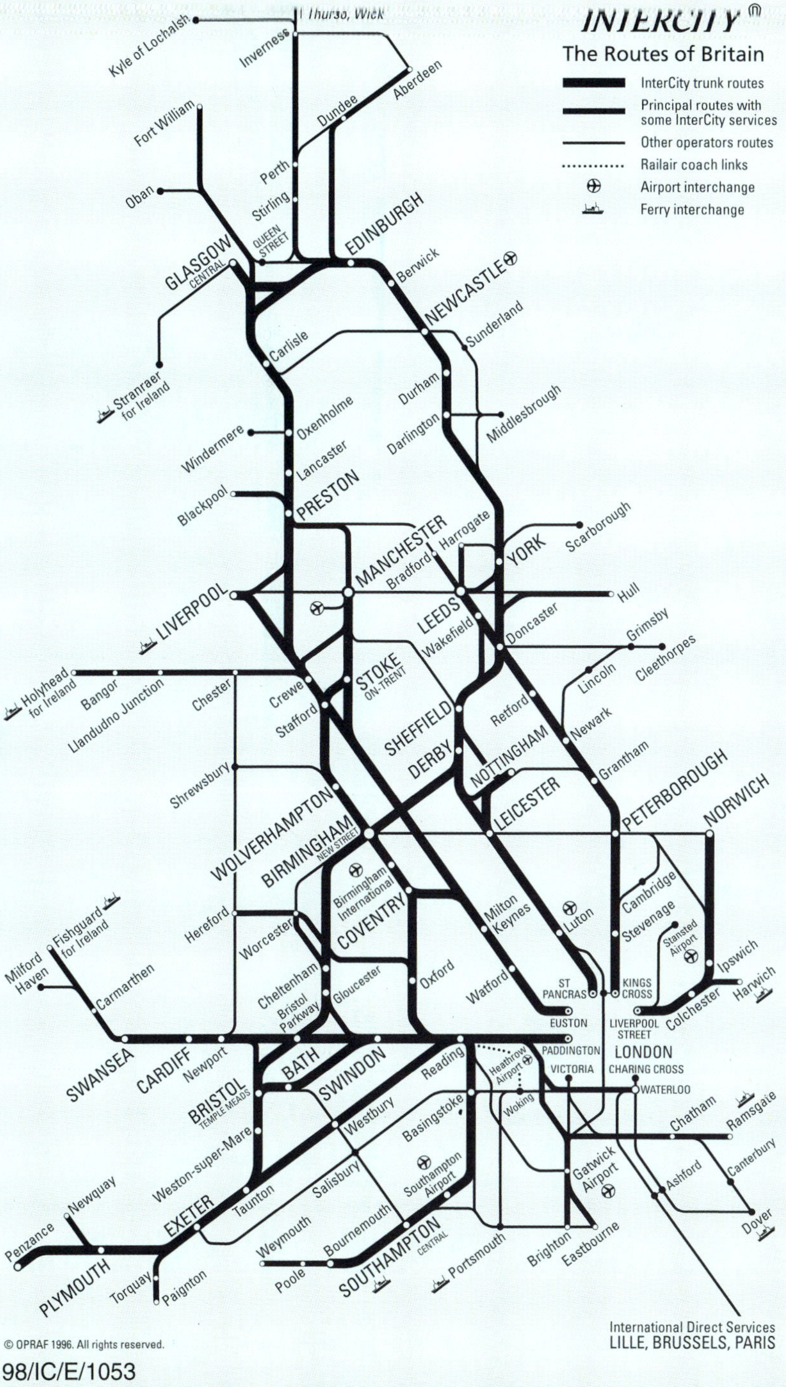
INTERCITY
The Routes of Britain
InterCity trunk routes
Principal routes with some InterCity services
Other operators routes
Railair coach links
Airport interchange
Ferry interchange
Thurso, Wick
Kyle of Lochalsh
Inverness
Aberdeen
Dundee
Fort William
Perth
Oban
Stirling
QUEEN STREET
EDINBURGH
GLASGOW
CENTRAL
Berwick
NEWCASTLE
Sunderland
Carlisle
Stranraer for Ireland
Durham
Darlington
Middlesbrough
Oxenholme
Windermere
Lancaster
PRESTON
Blackpool
MANCHESTER
Harrogate
Bradford
YORK
Scarborough
LIVERPOOL
LEEDS
Hull
Wakefield
Doncaster
Grimsby
Cleethorpes
Holyhead for Ireland
Bangor
Llandudno Junction
Chester
Crewe
Stafford
STOKE
ON-TRENT
Lincoln
SHEFFIELD
Retford
Newark
DERBY
NOTTINGHAM
Grantham
Shrewsbury
WOLVERHAMPTON
LEICESTER
PETERBOROUGH
NORWICH
BIRMINGHAM
NEW STREET
Birmingham International
COVENTRY
Milton Keynes
Luton
Cambridge
Stevenage
Stansted Airport
Hereford
Worcester
Cheltenham
Gloucester
Bristol Parkway
Oxford
Watford
ST PANCRAS
KINGS CROSS
Ipswich
Harwich
Colchester
Fishguard for Ireland
Milford Haven
Carmarthen
EUSTON
LIVERPOOL STREET
SWANSEA
CARDIFF
Newport
BATH
SWINDON
Reading
Heathrow Airport
PADDINGTON
LONDON
VICTORIA
CHARING CROSS
WATERLOO
BRISTOL
TEMPLE MEADS
Westbury
Basingstoke
Woking
Chatham
Ramsgate
Weston-super-Mare
Southampton Airport
Gatwick Airport
Ashford
Canterbury
Salisbury
Newquay
Taunton
EXETER
Dover
Penzance
Weymouth
Bournemouth
SOUTHAMPTON
CENTRAL
Portsmouth
Brighton
Eastbourne
PLYMOUTH
Torquay
Paignton
Poole
International Direct Services
LILLE, BRUSSELS, PARIS

98/IC/E/1053

*Y*OUR QUICK GUIDE

***Where to Stay** makes it quick and easy to find a place to stay that offers the standard of quality and facilities you're looking for.*

The TOWN INDEX (starting on page 407) and the LOCATION MAPS (starting on page 417) show all cities, towns and villages with accommodation listings in this guide.

1 Town Index

If the place you plan to visit is included in the town index, turn to the page number given to find accommodation available there. Also check that location on the colour maps to find other places nearby which also have accommodation listings in this guide.

1

Batley *West Yorkshire*	158
Battlesbridge *Essex*	317
Beadnell *Northumberland*	100
Bedale *North Yorkshire*	158
Bedford *Bedfordshire*	317
Belford *Northumberland*	100
Bellingham *Northumberland*	100
Belper *Derbyshire*	285
Belton *Leicestershire*	286
Berkhamsted *Hertfordshire*	318
Berrynarbor *Devon*	372
Berwick-upon-Tweed *Northumberland*	100
Bexhill-on-Sea *East Sussex*	509
Bexleyheath *Greater London*	43
Bibury *Gloucestershire*	217

2

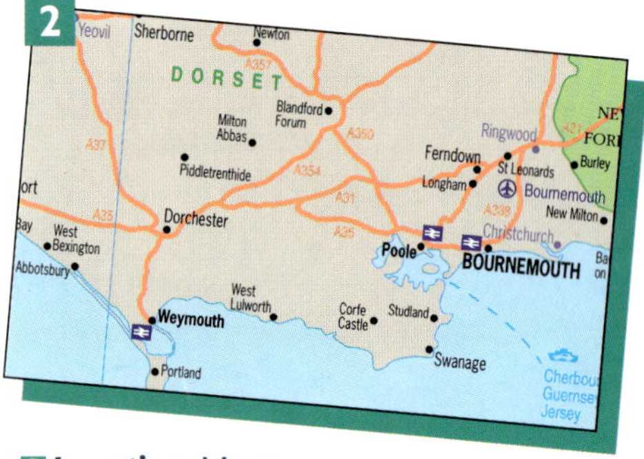

2 Location Maps

If the place you want is not in the town index - or you only have a general idea of the area in which you wish to stay - use the colour location maps to find places in the area which have accommodation listings in this guide.

When you have found suitable accommodation, check its availability with the establishment and also confirm any other information in the published entry which may be important to you (price, whether bath and/or shower available, children/dogs/credit cards welcome, months open, etc).

If you are happy with everything, make your booking and, if time permits, confirm it in writing.